A· REPERTORY;

OR,

SYSTEMATIC ARRANGEMENT AND ANALYSIS

OF THE

Homœopathic Materia Medica.

VOL. I.

HAHNEMANN PUBLISHING SOCIETY.

LIVERPOOL:

THE HON. SECRETARY, 117, GROVE STREET, E.

LONDON:

H. TURNER, 170, FLEET STREET, E.C.

NEW YORK:

BOERICKE AND TAFEL, 145, GRAND STREET.

1878.

PRINTED BY J. E. ADLARD, BARTHOLOMEW CLOSE.

EXPLANATORY REMARKS

CHAPTERS I, II, AND III.

———————

THE volume of symptoms of the Disposition, Mind, and Head, called the 'Pathogenetic Cyclopædia,' has hitherto figured as the first portion of the Repertory, but its plan is so different from that of the other parts, its form so bulky, and the number of medicines that have been added to the Materia Medica since its publication is so considerable,* that it was thought desirable to have the symptoms belonging to these chapters arranged in a similar repertorial fashion to those of the other chapters.

The task was assigned to me, and I have expended no little time and trouble in arranging the vast amount of material proper to these three chapters on the plan of the other parts, with modifications necessitated by the peculiarities of the organs and functions they refer to.

Dr. A. Stokes was originally associated with me in this work, and he arranged the symptoms in Chapter III from "Coldness" down to "Movements." I was unfortunately unable to avail myself of his labours, as the plan I adopted differed considerably from that on which he had worked. I wish, however, to express my thanks to Dr. Stokes for his co-operation and my high opinion of the excellence of his work.

Most of the alterations I have introduced in the original plan will be obvious at a glance, but I may describe here some of the most important. Any departures I have made from the original plan have been made with the view of lessening the labour of the

---

* The *Path. Cycl.* contained 323 medicines, the present work 505.

A

practitioner who consults the work, and they are none of them of such a serious character as to destroy or, in fact, affect the uniformity of the whole work.

The list of medicines given at p. 1 *et seq.* is not a complete list of all the medicines employed in homœopathic treatment, but only of those with symptoms referring to the subjects of these chapters. I have availed myself of the first six volumes of Dr. Allen's great 'Encyclopædia,' these being the only ones published when I went to press, and from their pages I have been able to add many symptoms and several new medicines not to be found elsewhere. I have also received several unpublished symptoms from Dr. Berridge, whose immense industry in collecting the materials for his valuable 'Pathogenetic Record' has enabled him to render me this service. I am also indebted to him for some of the symptoms in Chapter III, Section IV, more particularly those at p. 268.

Under the heading of a character-symptom (such as all the symptoms indicated by old English and Roman letters), when a small letter above the line follows the name of a medicine, it implies that the symptom contains also the variety of that character indicated by the small letter. Thus, p. 14, under " $\mathfrak{h}^b$. Disinclination for bodily labour," we have " hy-x^i.," which means that this symptom also includes " $\mathfrak{h}^i$. Disinclination for intellectual labour," and so under the heading " $\mathfrak{h}^i$.," we find " hy-x^b." The symptom, as recorded in the proving, is " Disinclination for mental or bodily exertion." So also at p. 128, under " d^a. Throbbing of blood-vessels," we find " T.glo^b.," implying that this symptom also includes " d^b. Distension of blood-vessels," under which heading it will again be found as " T.glo^a." The actual symptom of the proving is " Throbbing in the temples and rush of blood to the head, increasing until the temporal arteries were seen and felt to the touch to be throbbing violently."

In the last-mentioned symptom the anatomical seat of the symptoms is indicated by the prefixed capital T., and this plan of indicating the anatomical seat is followed in most places where the character-symptom has varieties two or more of which may be associated in one symptom. But in other parts, and notably among pains of the head, their concomitants and conditions, the small letter above the line after the medicine's name indicates the anatomical seat of the symptom or pain. In the case of the large regional divisions of the head-pains, such as FOREHEAD, TEMPLES, CROWN, &c., the small letter indicates the particular spot in the region where the pain occurs; thus, p. **163**, under "II^1. **Burning**," we find "men^g.," which means that the pain is seated over the left eye, and, accordingly, we shall find the symptom repeated in the anatomical subdivision of the "Forehead," at p. 174, under the rubric "F^g. **Above the left eye**," where we shall find it as "men.II^1."

In Sections V and VI of Chapter III a different arrangement has been followed. Throughout these sections the small letters above the line after the medicine's name always refer to the anatomical seat of the symptom, and among the character-symptoms, if there are several varieties of that character to be recorded in the same symptom, the letter indicating the character is repeated with its small letters, showing the varieties. Thus, p. 269, under "k^d. **Boils**," we find "led^f.k^1.," which means that the seat of the symptom is "f.," *i. e.* the forehead; and that, besides boils, there are also "k^1. **Pimples**," which precisely reproduces the symptom of the proving, "Pimples and boils on the forehead."

A small letter above the line following the figure indicative of a pain indicates the course, quality, or direction of the pain. In other chapters of this Repertory it was the custom to indicate these characteristics by adding the Roman numeral I, but I have adopted the plan described which increases the clearness and conciseness of the symptoms. These qualities, &c., of pains are chiefly confined to Sections II and III of Chapter III, but they are occasionally met with in other parts, and are always indicated by the small letter above the line following the figure denoting the pain. Symptoms with these characteristics will be found collected together and arranged in Section IV. It would have needlessly increased the size of the work to have inserted in this section all pains showing such characteristics, so I have made a selection of the most important of them for this section, but wherever in other sections the pain occurs the letter denoting its course, &c., will be found along with it.

I have reversed the order observed in other parts of the Repertory of the *concomitants* and *conditions*, placing the former before the latter, as I conceive that to be the most natural sequence, the concomitants being generally an integral part of the symptom, and subject to the same conditions as the character-symptom or pain.

In Sections II and III of Chapter III, where the pain alluded to is undefined, I have not put the Roman numeral I, as that would have been superfluous.

There are some other peculiarities which I hope may be found useful; these are the classification of "complex pains" in connection with each anatomical region, the collection of the same pains in various parts, and of different pains in various parts.

In Section V, the "ANATOMICAL REGIONS" contain all the localized symptoms of that section, whereby much space is saved.

As our Materia Medica is constantly being increased by the addition of new medicines and new provings, I would advise each practitioner who possesses this part to have his copy interleaved for the purpose of gradually adding, as they are published, the new symptoms belonging to these chapters.

In the list of medicines three whose head-symptoms have been here registered have inadvertently been omitted from the list of medicines—they are Aconitine, acn.; Aconitum ferox, ac-f.; and Derris pinnata, der.

R. E. DUDGEON.

LONDON; *October*, 1878.

MEDICINES AND THEIR ABBREVIATIONS

IN

CHAPTERS I, II, AND III.

Abies canadensis ....ab-c.
Abies nigra ....abi.
Absinthium ....abs.
Acetic acid......................ac-x.
Aconitum cammarum ....ac-c.
Aconitum lycotonum ....ac-l.
Aconitum napellus ....aco.
Actæa spicata ....ac-s.
Æthusa cynapium..............æth.
Æsculus hippocastanum ......æsc.
Æsculus glabra.................æs-g.
Agaricus muscarius ....aga.
Agaricus pantherinus ....ag-p.
Agrostemma githago ....ags.
Agnus castus....................agn.
Agave americana ....agv.
Ailanthus glandulosus ....ail.
Alcohol sulphuris..............al-s.
Allium sativum..................all.
Aloe socotrina ....alo.
Alumen ....aln.
Alumina ....alm.
Ambra grisea....................amb.
Ammoniaci gummi ....am-g.
Ammonium causticum.........amm.
Ammonium bromidum.........am-b.
Ammonium carbonicum ......am-c.
Ammonium muriaticum ......am-m.
Amphisbæna......................amp.
Amygdala amara ....amy.
Amyl nitrite ....aml.
Anacardium orientale ....ana.
Anagallis arvensis..............an-a.
Angustura........................ang.

Angustura spuria...............an-s.
Anisum stellatum...............ani.
Anthemis nobilis ....anh.
Anthrakokali ....ank.
Antimonium crudum ....ant.
Apis mellifica ....aps.
Apocynum androsæmifolium..ap-a.
Apocynum cannabinum ......apo.
Aranea diadema ....ara.
Aranea scinencia ....a-sc.
Argentum ....arg.
Argentum muriaticum.........ag-m.
Argentum nitricum ....ag-n.
Aristolochia milhomens ......ari.
Arnica montana.................arn.
Arsenicum album...............ars.
Arsenicum citrinum............ar-c.
Arsenicum hydrogenisatum...ar-h.
Arsenicum iodatum ....ar-i.
Arsenicum metallicum.........ar-m.
Artemesia abrotanum ....at-a.
Arum italicum ....am-i.
Arum triphyllum ....aru.
Arundo mauritanica............ard.
Asafœtida ....asa.
Asarum europæum ....asr.
Asclepias syriaca ....as-s.
Asclepias tuberosa ....as-t.
Asimina triloba.................asi.
Asparagus ....asp.
Asterias rubens ....ast.
Athamanta ....ath.
Atropinum ....atr.
Aurum ....aur.

B

Aurum muriaticum	au-m.	Cassada	css.
Aurum mur. natron	au-n.	Castor equi	cs-e.
Aurum sulphuratum	au-s.	Castoreum	cas.
Badiaga	bad.	Caulophyllum thalictroides	cph.
Baptisia tinctoria	bap.	Causticum	cau.
Baryta acetica	ba-a.	Cedron	ced.
Baryta carbonica	ba-c.	Centaurea togana	cnt.
Baryta muriática	ba-m.	Cepa	cep.
Belladonna	bel.	Cereus bonplandii	ce-b.
Benzoic acid	bz-x.	Cereus serpentinus	ce-s.
Berberis vulgaris	ber.	Cervus brasilicus	cr-b.
Bismuthum oxidum	bis.	Chamomilla	cha.
Bismuthum subnitricum	bs-n.	Chelidonium majus	chd.
Blatta americana	bla.	Chenopodii glauci aphis	chp.
Boletus laricis	b-la.	China officinalis	chi.
Borax	bor.	Chininum arsenicosum	ch-a.
Bothrops lanceolatus	bth.	Chininum sulphuricum	ch-s.
Bovista	bov.	Chloral hydrate	cl-h.
Branca ursina	bra.	Chlorine	clo.
Bromium	bro.	Chloroform	clf.
Bryonia alba	bry.	Chromic acid	ch-x.
Bufo (rana)	buf.	Chromium oxidatum	crm.
Bufo sahytiensis	bu-s.	Cicuta virosa	cic.
Cactus grandiflorus	cac.	Cimex lectularius	cim.
Cadmium sulphuratum	cad.	Cimicifuga racemosa	cmf.
Cainca	cai.	Cina	cin.
Cajeput oil	caj.	Cinchoninum sulphuricum	cn-s.
Caladium seguinum	cld.	Cinnabar	cnb.
Calcarea acetica	ca-a.	Cistus canadensis	cis.
Calcarea carbonica	ca-c.	Citrus vulgaris	cit.
Calcarea caustica	c-cs.	Clematis erecta	cle.
Calcarea phosphorica	c-ph.	Cobalt	cob.
Calcarea sulphurica	ca-s.	Coca	cca.
Calendula officinalis	cln.	Coccinella septempunctata	ccn.
Caltha palustris	clt.	Cocculus indicus	coc.
Camphora	cam.	Coccus cacti	ccs.
Cancer fluviatilis	cnc.	Cochlearia armoracia	coh.
Canchalagua	cnu.	Codeine	cod.
Canna glauca	cna.	Coffea cruda	cof.
Cannabis indica	cn-i.	Coffea tosta	cf-t.
Cannabis sativa	can.	Coffeine	cfn.
Cantharis	cth.	Colchicum	cch.
Capsicum annuum	cap.	Collinsonia	csn.
Carbo animalis	cb-a.	Colocynthis	col.
Carbo vegetabilis	cb-v.	Colocynthinum	cly.
Carbolic acid	ca-x.	Comocladia dentata	com.
Carboneum hydrogenisatum	cr-h.	Coniinum	cnm.
Carboneum sulphuratum	cr-s.	Conium maculatum	con.
Carduus benedictus	crd.	Convolvulus duartinus	cvl.
Carlsbad	car.	Copaiba	cop.
Cascarilla	csc.	Corallium rubrum	cor.

Cornus circinata	crn.	Franzensbad	frz.
Cotyledon	cot.	Fucus visiculosus	fuc.
Crocus sativus	cro.	Gallic acid	ga-x.
Crotalus horridus	crt.	Galvanism	glv.
Croton tiglium	ctn.	Gambogia	gam.
Cubeba	cub.	Gastein	gas.
Cundurango	cun.	Gelsemium sempervirens	gel.
Cuprum	cup.	Genista tinctoria	gen.
Cuprum aceticum	cu-a.	Gentiana cruciata	gn-c.
Cuprum arsenicosum	c-ar.	Gentiana lutea	gn-l.
Cuprum sulphuricum	c-su.	Ginseng	gin.
Cyclamen europæum	cyc.	Glonoine	glo.
Daphne indica	dph.	Gnaphalium polycephalum	gna.
Digitalis purpurea	dig.	Gossypium	gos.
Digitaline	dgn.	Granatum	grn.
Dioscorea villosa	dio.	Graphites	grp.
Dirca palustris	dir.	Gratiola officinalis	grt.
Doryphora decemlineata	dor.	Guaiacum	gui.
Drosera rotundifolia	dro.	Guano	gua.
Dulcamara	dul.	Guarana	gun.
Elaps corallinus	elp.	Guarea trichilioides	gur.
Elaterium	elt.	Gymnocladus canadensis	gym.
Electricitas	elc.	Hæmatoxylon campechianum	hæm.
Eleis guineensis	ele.	Hamamelis virginica	ham.
Equisetum	equ.	Hedeoma puligioides	hed.
Erecthiles hieracifolius	ech.	Heliotropium	hlt.
Erigeron canadense	eri.	Helleborus fœtidus	hl-f.
Eryngium aquaticum	er-a.	Helleborus niger	hel.
Eryngium maritimum	er-m.	Helonias dioica	hln.
Ether	eth.	Hepar sulphuris	hep.
Eucalyptus globulus	euc.	Hippomanes	hpm.
Eugenia jambos	eug.	Hura brasiliensis	hur.
Eupatorium perfoliatum	ept.	Hydrastis canadensis	hdr.
Eupatorium purpureum	ep-p.	Hydrocotyle asiatica	hyd.
Euphorbia amygdaloides	eu-a.	Hydrocyanic acid	hy-x.
Euphorbia corollata	eu-c.	Hydrophobine	hfb.
Euphorbium	eub.	Hyoscyamine	hyn.
Euphrasia officinalis	eup.	Hyoscyamus niger	hyo.
Eupion	epn.	Hypericum perforatum	hyp.
Evonymus europæus	evo.	Iberis amara	ibe.
Fagopyrum esculentum	fag.	Ignatia amara	ign.
Fagus sylvatica	fgs.	Indigo	ind.
Fel tauri	fel.	Indium	idm.
Ferrum	fer.	Inula helenium	inu.
Ferrum iodatum	f-io.	Iodine	iod.
Ferrum magneticum	f-mg.	Iodoform	iof.
Ferrum muriaticum	f-mu.	Ipecacuanha	ipc.
Ferrum phosphoricum	f-ph.	Iris fœtidissima	ir-f.
Filix mas	fil.	Iris versicolor	irs.
Fluoric acid	fl-x.	Itu	itu.
Formica rufa	for.	Jaborandi	jab.

Jacaranda caroba	jac.
Jalapa	jal.
Janipha manihot	jan.
Jatropha curcas	jat.
Juglans cinerea	jug.
Juglans versicolor	jg-v.
Juncus effusus	jun.
Kali bichromicum	k-bi.
Kali bromatum	k-br.
Kali carbonicum	k-ca.
Kali chloratum	k-cl.
Kali cyanatum	k-cy.
Kali ferrocyanatum	k-fc.
Kali hydriodicum	k-hy.
Kalmia latifolia	klm.
Kissingen	kis.
Kreosote	kre.
Laburnum	lab.
Lachesis	lah.
Lachnanthes	lch.
Lactic acid	la-x.
Lactuca sativa	la-s.
Lactuca virosa	la-v.
Lamium album	lam.
Lapathum	lap.
Laurocerasus	lau.
Ledum palustre	led.
Lepidium bonariense	lep.
Leptandra virginica	lpt.
Lilium tigrinum	lil.
Linaria vulgaris	lna.
Linum catharticum	lin.
Lippspringe	lip.
Lithium	lth.
Lobelia cardinalis	lo-c.
Lobelia inflata	lo-i.
Lobelia syphilitica	lo-s.
Lolium temulentum	lol.
Lupulus	lup.
Lycopersicum esculentum	lyp.
Lycopodium clavatum	lyc.
Lycopus virginica	lcp.
Macrotin	mac.
Magnesia carbonica	mag.
Magnesia muriatica	mg-m.
Magnesia sulphurica	mg-s.
Magnet	mgt.
Magnet, north pole	mt-n.
Magnet, south pole	mt-s.
Mancinella	mnc.
Mandragora	mad.
Manganum	man.
Manganum muriaticum	mn-m.
Manganum oxydum	mn-o.
Melastoma	mel.
Melilotus officinalis	mel.
Menispermum canadense	mns.
Mentha piperita	m-pi.
Mentha pulegium	m-pu.
Menyanthes	men.
Mephitis	mep.
Mercurialis	mrl.
Mercurius	mer.
Mercurius aceticus	mr-a.
Mercurius corrosivus	mr-c.
Mercurius cyanatus	m-cy.
Mercurius iodatus flavus	mr-f.
Mercurius iodatus ruber	mr-i.
Mercurius sulphuricus	mr-s.
Mezereum	mez.
Millefolium	mil.
Mimosa humilis	mim.
Mitchellia repens	mit.
Momordica	mom.
Morphia	mor.
Morphia acetica	mo-a.
Morphia muriatica	mo-m.
Morphia sulphurica	mo-s.
Moschus	msc.
Murex purpurea	mur.
Muriatic acid	mu-x.
Murure leite	mrr.
Myrica cerifera	myr.
Myristica sebifera	my-s.
Nabulus serpentaria	nab.
Naja tripudians	naj.
Narcotine	nar.
Narcotine, acetate of	nr-a.
Narcotine, muriate of	nr-m.
Natrum arsenicatum	na-a.
Natrum carbonicum	nat.
Natrum muriaticum	na-m.
Natrum nitricum	na-n.
Natrum phosphoricum	na-p.
Natrum sulphuricum	na-s.
Niccolum	nic.
Nitric acid	ni-x.
Nitrum	nit.
Nuphar lutea	nup.
Nux juglans	nx-j.
Nux moschata	nx-m.
Nux vomica	nx-v.

Nymphæa odorata	nym.	Rumex crispus	rum.
Œnanthe crocata	œna.	Ruta graveolens	rut.
Oleander	oln.	Sabadilla	sbd.
Oleum animale	ol-a.	Sabina	sab.
Oleum morrhuæ	ol-m.	Sambucus	sam.
Oniscus asellus	oni.	Sanguinaria canadensis	san.
Opium	opi.	Santonine	snt.
Origanum vulgare	ori.	Sarracenea purpurea	src.
Osmium	osm.	Sarsaparilla	sar.
Pæonia	pæo.	Scrophularia nodosa	scr.
Paris quadrifolia	par.	Scutellaria laterifolia	scu.
Paullinia pinnata	pau.	Secale cornutum	sec.
Pediculus capitis	ped.	Sedinha	sed.
Petiveria tetrandra	ptv.	Selenium	sel.
Petroleum	pet.	Senecio aureus	snc.
Phillandrium aquaticum	phl.	Senega	sng.
Phosphoric acid	ph-x.	Senna	snn.
Phosphorus	pho.	Sepia	sep.
Physostigma	phs.	Serpentaria	ser.
Phytolacca decandra	phy.	Silica	sil.
Pimpinella saxifraga	pim.	Sinapis nigra	sin.
Piper methysticum	pi-m.	Solanum arrebenta	so-a.
Plantago	plg.	Solanum lycopersicum	so-l.
Platina	pla.	Solanum mammosum	so-m.
Platina chlorica	pl-c.	Solanum nigrum	so-n.
Plectranthus	plc.	Solanum oleraceum	so-o.
Plumbago littoralis	plm.	Solanum tuberosum ægrotans	so-t.
Plumbum	plb.	Spigelia anthelmia	spi.
Plumbum aceticum	pb-a.	Spiggurus spinosa	spg.
Podophyllum peltatum	pod.	Spiranthes	spr.
Polygonum punctatum	pgn.	Spongia tosta	spo.
Polyporus officinalis	pol.	Squilla maritima	squ.
Pothos fœtida	pot.	Stannum	stn.
Prunus spinosa	pru.	Staphisagria	stp.
Psorine	pso.	Sticta pulmonaria	sti.
Ptelea	ptl.	Stillingia sylvatica	stl.
Pulsatilla nigricans	pul.	Stramonium	str.
Pulsatilla nuttalliana	pl-n.	Strontian	sto.
Ranunculus acris	rn-a.	Strychnine	sty.
Ranunculus bulbosus	rn-b.	Sulphur	sul.
Ranunculus repens	rn-r.	Sulphur iodatum	su-i.
Ranunculus sceleratus	rn-s.	Sulphuric acid	su-x.
Raphanus sativus	rap.	Sumbul	sum.
Ratanhia	rat.	Tabacum	tab.
Rheum palmatum	rhe.	Tanacetum vulgare	tan.
Rhododendron chrysanthum	rho.	Tarantula	trn.
Rhus glabrum	rs-g.	Taraxicum	trx.
Rhus radicans	rs-r.	Tartar emetic	tar.
Rhus toxicodendron	rhs.	Taxus baccata	tax.
Rhus venenata	r-vn.	Teplitz	tep.
Rhus vernix	rs-v.	Terebinth	ter.

Thea sinensis	tea.	Veratrinum	vrn.
Teucrium marum verum	ten.	Verbascum thapsus	vrb.
Theridion curassivicum	thr.	Vinca minor	vin.
Thuja occidentalis	thu.	Viola odorata	vi-o.
Tilia europæa	til.	Viola tricolor	vi-t.
Tongo	ton.	Vipera redi	vp-r.
Trifolium pratense	trf.	Vipera torva	vp-t.
Triosteum perfoliatum	tri.	Wisbaden	wis.
Tradescantia diuretica	tra.	Xanthoxylum fraxinium	xan.
Uranium nitricum	ur-n.	Xyphosura americana	xyp.
Urtica urens	urt.	Zincum	zin.
Valeriana officinalis	val.	Zincum oxydatum	zn-o.
Veratrum album	ver.	Zizia aurea	ziz.
Veratrum viride	ve-v.		

INDEX TO CHAPTER I.

PART I.—a. MORAL SYMPTOMS.

CHAPTER I.

PART I.—α. MORAL SYMPTOMS.

a. **Apathy, listlessness, indifference, phlegm, dryness of manner.**—ab-c.u^b—ac-c.—aga.u.; $\flat^o$.—alo.φ.—alm.u.a$^1\flat$.—ag-n.ƙ.ω$^{2\cdot8}$.—ars.—asr.βℯ^a.—bel.ƀ$^{b\cdot i}$.—ber.—bov.ƙ. 121 (122).—buf.—bu-s.—ca-a.ƀ^s.—c-ph.—cb-v.—cer.a$^1\flat^b$.—ce-s.—cle.—cca.—cod.—con.ƙ.8.31.; ƙ.rv.4.—crn.φ.—crt.ƙ.; ƙ.u^{ee}.γ.μ^2. ρ.ω^2.—cup.—cu-s.—dig.; a$^1\flat^s$.5.—fer.u.—gel.a$^1\flat^s$.γ.er.—gur.—gym. ham.u^{tt}.—hel.—hur.—hyd.—hfb. —ign.—ind.—iod.—ipc.—k-br.u. —k-bi.u.—k-ca.ƀ^e.—k-cl.ƙ.m.χ^1.5. —lab.—lah.a$^1\flat^o$; ƀ^o.—lna.u.γ.— lyc.—mgt.ƀ.φ.—mrl.—mez.a$^1\flat^{b\cdot s}$. —mim.—mo-s.—nat.—na-m.ɡ.; ƙ. —ni-x.ƙ.—nx-m.—opi.a$^1\flat$.—pau. —ph-x.ƀ^s.ζ.; q.—pla.—ptl.—rs-r.φ. —rut.—sab.—sep.—str.—sul.ƙ. —trn.—til.ƀ^s.φ.—ver.—vrb.—vi-t. ƀ^c.ƙ.—xyp.β.ℯ.—zin.

—— *as if he had not slept enough.* —dig.

—— *followed by increased sensitiveness.*—cb-a.

—— *followed by sensitive, peevish humour.*—bėl.

—— *followed by restlessness and scolding.*—msc,

—— *followed by cheerfulness.*— mrl.ƙ.u.

—— *alternating with anxiety and restlessness.*—na-m.

—— *alternating with irritability.* —asa.

—— *alternating with thoughtfulness.*—ag-n^v.

—— *following weeping and hypochondriacal humour.*—pho.

—— *following tendency to laugh at everything.*—sbd.

a^a. **Indifference to everything.**— ac-c.—aga.—ail.—ana$^{c\cdot d}$.—arn.— bel.ƀ$^{b\cdot i}$.—can.u^{cc}.—cap.—cb-v.— cro.—dig.—hyd.—ign.—lep.— mrl.—mez.ƀ^c.ƙ.—nx-m.—pho.— sec.—sep.—stp.ƙ.m.—vp-r.—ziz. ƙ.u^b.

—— *except eating and sleeping.*— jug.

a^b. **Indifference to external things.** —agn.—ca-a.ɡ$^{d\cdot e}$.ℝ^t.a^{1}a^b.—cn-i.— cha.—chi.ƀ^c.—cic.—lyc.; u^b.— mrl.u.—opi.; a$^1\flat^s$.—rs-g.—rum. a$^1\flat$.ω^2.—stn·u.a$^1\flat^s$.ℵc^b.—stp.ƀ$^{c\cdot t}$.— trn.a$^1\flat^b$.—ver.ℝ^a.ɧ.ɳρ,aa.rp.— vp-r^b.—trn.a$^1\flat$.

a^c. **Indifference to agreeable things.** —amb^d.ƙ.—ana.; $^{a\cdot d}$.—cin^d.—crn. —opi^d.—rho^d.—stp.—str, a^d. **Indifference to disagreeable, or irritating things.**—amb^c.k.—ana$^{a.c}$.—ard—bor.—cin^c.—ccs.—cof.—opi^c.—rho^c.

a^x. **Indifference to dictates of conscience.**—cn-i.

a^e. **Indifference to important things.**—ca-a.u.—fl-x.—my-s.

a^f. **Indifference to those usually dearest to him.**—pho.—pla.

a^g. **Indifference to society.**—na-m^p.—rhs.

a^h. **Indifference to all he hears.**—cb-v.—vp-r^b.

a^i. **Indifference to music.**—cb-v.

a^j. **Indifference to the future.**—ail.—hur.k^b.I.

a^k. **Indifference to life.**—abs.—ars.—phy.b^o.3-99.

a^l. **Indifference to threats of death.**—bel.

a^m. **Contempt for life.**—ni-x.u^{dd}.

a^n. **Contempt for others.**—cic.ε.u^{ee}.—par.—pla. ; κ^1.

a^o. **Contempt for everything.**—alm.—chi.

a^p. **Want of sympathy.**—na-m^g.—pla.a^{1}b.8.122.—sep.—spi.—squ.b^c.

a^q. **Carelessness.**—aga.—idm.—nx-m.x.

a^r. **Everything seems dead to him, as if he had no life in him.**—aco.u^a.—mez.k.

a^s. **Notices nothing.**—mrl.

a^t. **Nothing makes an impression.**—rhe.b^c.

a^u. **Lukewarmness in business.**—aga.—my-s.

a^v. **Frivolity.**

—— *alternating with thoughtfulness.*—ag-n.

CONCOMITANTS.

a^{1}a. *Increased thoughtfulness.*—ca-a^b.g$^{d.e}$.x^t.

a^{1}b. *Absence of mind.*—alm.u^a.—pla^p.8.122.—rum^b.ω^x.—trn^b.

a^{1}b^o. *Forgetfulness.*—lah.

a^{1}b^s. *Cloudiness of mind.*—dig.5.—gel.γ.εr.

a^{1}b^s. *Stupidity.*—opi^b.

a^{1}v. *Stupefaction.*—opi.

βe. *Confusion of head.*—xyp.

βe^a. *Stupid feeling.*—asr.

γ. *Headache.*—gel.a^{1}b^s.εr.—lna.u.

ε. *Pain in ear.*—gel.a^{1}b^s.γ.

ζ. *Bores in his nose.*—ph-x.b^c.

ηp,aa. *Heat and redness of face.*—ver^b.h.x^a.r^1.

ηc^b. *Pale face and dark rings round eyes.*—stn.

κ^1. *Hunger.*—pla^n.

r^{1}p. *Heat of hands.*—ver^b.h.x^a.η.

rv. *Paralysis of limbs.*—con.k.4.

φ. *Sleepiness.*—alo.—crn.—mgn.b.—rs-r.—til.b^c.

χ^1. *Chilliness.*—k-cl.k.m.5.

ω^2. *Debility.*—ag-n.k.ω^8—rum^b.a^1.

ω^8. *Trembling.*—ag-n^2.k.ω^2.

CONDITIONS.

3-99. *On awaking in morning.*—phy^k.b^o.

4. *In the afternoon.*—con.k.rv.

5. *In the evening.*—dig.a^{1}b^s.—k-cl.k.m.χ^1.

8. *In the open air.*—con.k.31.—pla^p.a^{1}b.122.

31. *By walking.*—con.k.8.

121. *By solitude.*—bov.(122).

122. *When in society.*—bov.121.—pla^p.a^{1}b.8.

b. **Laziness, indolence, inactivity.**—aga.δ.κ^4.66.; k.a^{1}b^y.ω^2.—alo.3. ; βv.γ.ω^2.—arn.—ars^m.—bla.—bu-s.k.—cth^o.a.—ca-x.—cep.3.—cca.φ.—crn.—dir.a^{1}b^s.—er-a.—f-mg.gui.—hur.—lyc.u.—iod.s.u.—k-bi.ω^2.—lah$^{i.o}$.—lau^o.—mgt.a.φ.—mt-n.—mim.a.—na-m^o.—nx-v.ω^2.—opi.βv.—ph-x^i.a^{1}b.—plb^o.u.5.—rn-s^i.3.—rhe^c.—sar^o.a^{1}b^n.—so-t^o.—spo^c.u.—spr.ε.—squ^i.3.—sul.—tan.u^b.—trn^c.k.γq.θ^δ.κ.φ.ω^2.—teu$^{b.i}$.—vrb.φ.8.30.—ziz.x^b.

—— *following desire to sing and gaiety.*—spo.a^{1}b.

—— *followed by gaiety.*—trn.ω^2.3.

b^a. **Disinclination for amusement.**—ba-c.—cun.—lil.—oln^o.—pet^o.s.—sul$^{e.c.m.o}$.f.5.

b^b. **Disinclination for bodily labour.**
—aco^i.—bel^i.a^a.—c-ph.u.—ch-s.—col$^{f.i}$.—crn^i.φ.—dro^i.k.a^{1}b^y.—fer^i.u.—frz^i.λ.—hy-x^i.—hyp^i.—k-bi^i.—rs-r^i.5.—rum.k.—sul$^{i.m.o}$.—teu^i.

b^c. **Disinclination for conversation and speaking.**—aco.—aga.; °u.; k.5.122.—am-m.u.a^{1}a^b.—ant.; ε.—arn^i.8.31.—ars.a^{1}b^a.; g.—at-a.—aru.—asi.—aur.u.—ba-c.k.—bel.; ε.—bis.1.(5).—bro.—bry°.—bu-s.k.—cac.k.l.—ca-a.u^a.γ.7.(8).—c-ph.u.—cn-i.; 66.—cb-a.a.ε.—cr-h.—car.u.—cas.u.83.—cha.—chd.—chi.a^b.u.—cle^g.u.; (5).—cof.u.—col.—crt.—cyc.; a.u.—dig.—dio.ε.k.5.—dir.—er-m.—fag. 4.—fer^f.ε.; °.—gel.a^{1}b^a.—grt$^{e.m}$.—ham.u.—hln.—hep.u^a.3.30.—hpm. 3.—hdr.k.—ign^{ey}.π^1.—ipc.; t.u.—jab.—jat.u.—k-bi.—klm°.a^{b}b^b.—lil.—lyc.; u.—mt-s.—mag.ђ.u.—mg-m.ε.—mg-s.u.4.—mnc.—men.ε.—mer.k.u.—mez.a^a.k.—mur.—na-a.—nat.—na-m.—na-s.u.3.—nic.u.—ni-x.—nx-j.—opi.—ox-x.; s.η^i.—pet^a.ε.—ph-x.a.ζ.; u.—plm.—plb.66.—rhe.a^t.—rs-r.; a^{1}b^a.—sab.u.; 3.31.—spi.—spo.u^{dd}; u.—squ°.a°.—stn.; f^a.—stpt.a^b.a^{1}b.—sto.u.a^{1}a^b.—str.—sul.u.; $^{a.e.m.o}$f. 5.; rvkk.—su-x.—tab.—trn.o^j.; k.γq.θ^3.κ.φ.ω^2.—trx^c.k.3.—thu.u. γq.—til.a.φ.—ton°.u.—ver.o^2. vi-o.k.a^{1}b^p.—vi-t.u.; a^{1}b.4.5.—wis. u.—zin.u.

———— *in fits of two or more hours.*—cyc.

———— *sat all day with head leaning on hand.*—iod.

b^d. **Disinclination for driving.**—pso.

b^e. **Disinclination for everything.**—am-g.—am-c.—ber.—bov.66.—ca-c.u.—coc.—ccs.ω^2.—crt.k.—cup.—dul.u.—grt$^{e.m}$.—iod.—k-bi.—kis.φ.—mnc.—rut°.f.—sul.k.5.; $^{a.c.m.o}$f.5.—thr°.—xyp.

b^{ey}. **Disinclination for opening eyes.**—ign^c.

b^f. **Disinclination for seeing friends.**—abs.—bel.ε.p.—col$^{b.i}$.—fer^c.ε.—sel°.

b^g. **Disinclination for going out.**—cle^c.u.

b^i. **Disinclination for intellctual labour.**—ac-x.—aco.—alo.; a^{1}a.—alm.—anh.a^{1}a^b.—au-m.—bel^b.a^a.—bu-s.—c-ph.—ca-x.—cn-i.k.—car^r.—chi.φ.; °.—ch-s.—cnb.—cob°.—cca.—cch.u^b.—col$^{b.f}$.—crn^b.φ.—crt.—dro^b.k.a^{1}b^y.—fag.—fer^b.u.—frz^b.λ.—gas.—gel.—grt.—ham.ε.—hpm.—hdr.—hy-x^b.; u^b.—hyo°; 4.—hyp^b.—jug.a.—k-br.—klm.g.—lah°.—lo-i.—lyc.—mg-m.k.—mep.a^{1}a^d.—mu-x.—na-a.—na-m.—na-n.—ni-x.a^{1}b^a.—nit.u^{dd}.;—nx-j.—nx-v.γd.—ol-a.æ^w.a^{1}b.ηp^3.—ph-x.a^{1}b^a.—pho.—phy.—pla.—ptl°.ω^2.; κ^5.ω^3.—rs-r^b.5.; °a^{1}b^b.—ser.u.—so-n.φ.—squ.3.—stp.u.—sul$^{b.m.o}$.—sum.—tea^b.—vi-t.

———— *following increased mental activity.*—cle^i.u.χ^2.

b^l. **Disinclination for literary labour.**—ipc.a^{1}b^a.—lil.—rhs.βε.

b^m. **Disinclination for movement.**—alo.—ars.—bu-s.—dio.—ept.—grt$^{c.i}$.—ham.k.—klm.—lah.—mt-n.19.—pho.γp.—phy.—sul$^{b.i.o}$.; $^{a.c.m.o}$f.5.

b^o. **Disinclination for occupation or work**—ac-l.—aga^c.u.; a.—agn.—alo.g^e.ђ^q.; k.βε.4(5).; βε.—alm.ε.3.—am-c.—ana.u^{cc}.—arn.f^b.—asa.u.—ast.5.—ba-a.u.—bor.; q.4.—bov.ђ.u.—bro.—bry^c.—bu-s.4.—cad.v.—ca-a.a^e.u.l^l.—ca-c.u^b.v^{1}q.—c-ph.—cth.a.; k°.—cap^t.—ca-x.—cau.—chi^i.—ch-s.—cn-s.—cle.3. 99.—cob^i.—coc.; δ.—cof.—cch.—con.—cop.—ctn.k.—cup.—cyc.g. k.u.—evo.—fer^c.—fl-x.—gn-l.k.l.—gam.—grn.γq.—grp.—ham.q. u^{dd}.—hur.—hdr.—hy-x.k.—hyo^i.—idm.—iod.; βε.—k-ca.—kis.—lah.a.k.ω^2.—lah^i.—la-v.q.—lam.—lau.—lil.—mt-n.5.—mt-s.u.—mg-m.u.—mg-s.φ.ω^2.—mnc.—men.—mer.—mez.a.k.—mil.—naj.γ.—nat.—na-m.; φ.4.; aa.; k^j.—ni-x.—nit.—nx-j.—nx-v.—oln.—oni.ξ^1.—pau.—ph-x.—pho.k.—phy.a^k.3.

99.—plb.u.5.—ptl^i.ω^2.—pul.ѕ.ѕ.
π^1.; u.—rn-s.ḳ.φ.5.; u.—rho.—
rhs.—r-vn.ḳ.—rut^e.f.—sbd.—sel^t.
—sep.a^{1}ḃ^b.—ser.a^{1}ḃ^a.βє.—so-t.—
spg.5.—squ^c.a^p.—stn.a^{1}ḃ^a.—stp.
—str.—sul.; $^{b \cdot i \cdot m}$; $^{a \cdot c \cdot e \cdot m}$f.5.—tar.
q.—trx.ḃ.—tep.u.20.35.—thr^e.—
til.—ton^c.u.—tri.ḳ.φ.—vrb.—vi-t.
—zin.f.ḳ.ѡ.66.

  —— *in fits of two or more hours.*—
    cyc.
  —— *as after drinking coffee.*—
    sul.ѕ.
  —— *followed by liking for work.*
    —cyc.

b^r. Disinclination for reading.—
aco.—caj.—car^i.—wis^{wa}.

b^t. Disinclination for thinking.—
aga.a^{1}ḃ^a.γd.ηp.—cap^o.—csc.—cle.
u^a.—lyc.4.—nit.γp.ηp.ω^2.3.—pet.
a^{1}ḃ^o.—ptl.ω^4.—rhs^c.ω^2.—rum.3.—
squ.ḳ.; wr.—tep.γ.20.35.

b^{wa}. Disinclination for walking.—
alo.—wis^r.

b^{wr}. Disinclination for writing.—
squ^t.

CONCOMITANTS.

a^{1}a. *Increased power of thought.*—
    alo^o.—na-m^o.

a^{1}a^b. *Thoughtfulness.*—sto^c.u.

a^{1}a^b. *Buried in thought.*—am-m^c.u.
    —anh^i.

a^{1}a^d. *Increased flow of ideas.*—mep^i.

a^{1}ḃ^b. *Distraction of thoughts.*—ol-a^1.
    ҳ^w.

a^{1}ḃ^b. *Inability to fix attention.*—
    rs-r$^{i \cdot o}$.—sep^o.

a^{1}ḃ^n. *Awkwardness.*—sar^o.

a^{1}ḃ^o. *Forgetfulness.*—pet^t.

a^{1}ḃ^p. *Weakness of memory.*—vi-o^c.ḳ.

a^{1}ḃ^s. *Disturbance of thinking power.*
    —aga^t.γd.ηp.—stp$^{c \cdot t}$.a^b.

a^{1}ḃ^s. *Difficulty of thinking.*—ser^o.βє.
    —stn^o.

a^{1}ḃ^s. *Weakness of mind.*—ars^c.—
    ipc^l.—ni-x^1.—vi-t^c.4.5.

a^{1}ḃ^s. *Stupidity.*—gel^c.—ph-x^1.—rs-r^c.

a^{1}ḃ^y. *Obtuseness of senses.*—aga.ḳ.
    ω^2.—dro$^{b \cdot i}$.ḳ.

βѡ. *Intoxication.*—opi.

βє. *Confusion of head.*—alo^o.ḳ.4
    (5).—iod^o.—rhs^1.—ser^{o}a^{1}ḃ^a.

γd. *Congestion of head.*—aga^t.a^{1}ḃ.
    ηp.—nx-v^i.3.

γp. *Hot forehead.*—nit^{t}ηp.ω^c.3.—
    pho^m.γ.99.

γq. *Weight of head.*—grn^o.—trn^c.
    ḳ.θ^3.κ.φ.ω^2.—thu^c.u.

γ. *Headache.*—ant^c.є.—ca-a^c.u^a.7.
    (8).—crt.ḳ.u^{ee}.u^2.ρ.ω^2.—naj^o.
    —pho^m.γp.99.—tep^t.20.35.

δ. *Pain in eyes.*—aga.κ^4.66.

δP^1. *Contracted pupils.*—coc^o.

ζ. *Bores in his nose.*—ph-x^c.a.

η^{ia}. *Fulness of face.*—ox-x^c.ѕ.

ηp. *Heat of face.*—aga^t.a^{1}ḃ.γd.—
    nit^t.γp.ω^2.3.

θ^3. *Furred tongue.*—trn^c.ḳ.γq.κ.φ.
    ω^2.

κ. *Bad taste.*—trn^c.ḳ.γq.θ^3.φ.ω^2.

κ^4. *Pain in stomach.*—aga.δ.66.

ᴧ^5. *Nausea.*—ptl^i.ω^3.

λ. *Distended abdomen.*—frz$^{b \cdot i}$.

μ^2. *Diarrhœa.*—crt.ḳ.u^{ee}.γ.ρ.ω^2.

ξ^1. *Erections.*—oni^o.

o^2. *Weak voice.*—ver^c.

π. *Pain under short ribs.*—zin^o.f.
    ḳ.66.

π^1. *Panting respiration.*—pul^o.ѕ.ḃ.

ρ. *Heartache.*—crt.ḳ.u^{ee}.γ.μ^2.ω^2.

rѵkk. *Trembling of limbs.*—sul^c.

ѵ^{1}q. *Heaviness of feet.*—ca-c^o.u^b.

φ. *Sleepiness.* —— chi^i. —— cca.——
    crn$^{b \cdot i}$.—kis^e.—mgt.a.—mg-s^o.
    ω^2.——na-m^o.4.——rn-s^o.ḳ.5.—
    so-n^i.—trn^c.ḳ.γq.θ^3.ω^2.—til^c.a.
    —tri^o.ḳ.—vrb.3.80.

χ^2. *Heat.*—cle^i.u.

ω^2. *Debility, weariness.*—aga.ḳ.a^1
    ḃ^y.—alo.—ccs^e.—crt.ḳ.u^{ee}.γ.
    μ^2.ρ.—k-bi.—lah.a.ḳ.—mg-s^o.
    φ.—nit^t.γηp.3.—nx-v.—ptl$^{i \cdot o}$.
    —rhs$^{c \cdot t}$.—trn^c.ḳ.γq.θ^3.κ.φ.

ω^3. *Faintness.*—ptl^i.κ^5.

ω^4. *Malaise.*—ptl^t.

CONDITIONS.

1. *By day.*—bis^c.(5).
3. *In the morning.*—alo.—alm^o.є.

—cep.—cle°.99.—hpm^c.—hep^c.u^a.30.—na-s^c.u.—nit^t.γ np.ю².—nx-v^i.γd.—phy°.a^k.99.—rn-s^i.—rs-r^{b.i}.—rum^t. sab^c.31.—squ^i.—tar.—trx^{c.o}. k.—vrb.φ.30.

4. *In the afternoon.*—alo°.k.βt.(5). —bor°.q.—buf°.—fag^c.—hyo^i. —lyc^t.—mg-s^c.u.—na-m°.φ. —vi-t^c.a^lb.5.

5. *In the evening.*—aga^c.k.122.— alo°.k.βt.4.—ast°.—bis^c.1.— cle^c.—dio^c.t.k.—mt-n°.— plb°.u.—rn-s°.k.φ.—spg°.— sul^e.k.; ^{c.e.a.m.o}.f.—vi-t^c.a^lb.4.

7. *In the warm room.*—ca-c^c..u^a.γ. (8).

8. *In the open air.*—arn^c.31.— ca-c^c.u^a.γ.7.

19. *When sitting.*—mt-n^m.

20. *When at rest.*—tep^t.γ.35.

30. *On rising.*—hep^c.u^a.3.—vrb.φ.3.

31. *By walking.*—arn^c.8.—sab^c.3.

35. *When moving.*—tep^t.γ.20.

66. *After dinner.*—aga.δ.κ^4.—bov^e. cn-i.—plb^c.—zin°.f.k.π.

83. *During menses.*—cas^c.u.

99. *On waking.*—cle°.3.—pho^m.γ.γp. phy°.a^k.3.

122. *In society.*—aga^c.k.5.

ε. **Ennui, the time seems long.**—alm. b°.3.—amp.—ba-c.u.—cam.—con. u.—dir.—elp.—ele.121.—hur.a^j. k^b.I.—lah.ω^s.—lyc.—mg-m.g.h.5. —mnc.—nat.h.f^c.k^b.; a^lb.3.—nit. k.I.—nx-v.—pau.—pet.b^{a.o}.—plm. a^a.—plb.b^e.; b^c.a^lb.4.—spr.b.— trn.a.u.—zin.п.h.

—— *insuperable.*—alm.

—— *and crowds of unrememorable events.*—cam.

CONCOMITANTS.

a^lb. *Abstracted.*—nat.—plb.b^c.4.
ω^s. *Trembling.*—lah.

CONDITIONS.

3. *In the morning.*—alm.b°.—nat. a^lb.

4. *In the afternoon.*—plb.b^b.a^lb.

---

5. *In the evening.*—mg-m.g.h.

121. *When alone.*—ele.

δ. **Dislike to solitude.**—bel.h^{j.k}.— bis.—cad.b°.—ca-c.ηb.r^lv^lb.—cle. u^{ee}.—con.t^a.—der.g.—dro.g.— ele.h.—k-ca.h.—lil.—lyc.h.—mez. q.—rn-b.h^j.5.—sep.—str.

—— *to be alone in the dark.*— str.

CONCOMITANTS.

ηb. *Coldness of face.*—ca-c.r^lv^lb.
r^lb. *Coldness of hands.*—ca-c.ηb.v^lb.
v^l. *Coldness of feet.*—ca-c.ηb.r^lb.

CONDITION.

5. *In the evening.*—rn-b.h^j.

ζ. **Love of solitude.**—aco.—alm.k.3. —anh.k^c.I.—ant.b^c.βп.γ.—aur.k. —au-s.—bel.b°; b^f.p.—bu-s.k.— cac.—c-ph.—ca-s.ж^w.—cb-a.b^c.k. —chi.k.—cic.a^n.u^{ee}.; h^n.t.a^la^b.— cle.; b^c.п.m.u^{ee}.—cca.—con.h^{c.d}.aa^b. —cup.h^{ag}.k.—cyc.a^la^b.—dig. dio.—elp.; k.—eug.—fer.b^{c.f}.—gos. g.I^c.—grp.u.—grt.k.—ham.b^l.— bln.—hep.u^b.—k-ca.h.—lah.a^la^b.— led.m.u.—lyc.—mt-s.—mg-m.b^c.— men.b^c.—nat.h^{d.a}.—na-m.—nic.h. ω^s.—nx-v.k.q.o^j.p.—pan.—pho.a. b°.u^c.—ptl.—rs-r.—rhs.k.—sep. δb.—tan.k.—tep.b°q.u^{ee}.

—— *prefers to walk alone.*—caj.

—— *alternating with bursts of pleasantry and sarcasm.*— rs-r.

CONCOMITANTS.

a^la^b. *Thoughtfulness.*—— cic.h^n.t.— con.h^{c.d}.—cyc.—lah.
βп. *Intoxication.*—ant.b^c.γ.
γ. *Headache.*—ant.b^c.βп.
δb. *Closed eyes.*—sep.
ω^s. *Trembling.*—nic.h.

CONDITION.

3. *In the morning.*—alm.k.

η. **Discomfort.**—glv.—grt.b^{c.m.o}.— msc.βa.——na-m^b.u.—ni-x.u.3-30.

—opi.—rut.ḃ°·º.—ser.γ.3.—sul.
ḫᵃ·ᶜ·ᵉ·ᵐ·º.5.—val.k̇.κ¹.

fᵃ. **Bodily discomfort.**—stn.ḃᶜ.

fᵇ. **Uneasiness.**—alm.gʰ.—am-g.—
ank.γq.ω².—ccs.g.—dro.i̇.k̇.—lol.g.
—merⁱ.q.a¹ςᵃ.—na-m.u.—pet.
ph-x.gᵇ.—pho.g.γp,hh.105.—trn.
q.r¹e.52.—vrn.g.ω.—vp-r.k̇ᶠ.γ.δaᵇ.
ηcᵈ,aa.θ³.κ³.μ¹.ν¹.ρ.σ¹.φ.ψp.ω³.

fᶜ. **Bodily uneasiness.**—arnᵉ.ḃº.—
ph-x.g.—pho.3.

fᵈ. **Internal uneasiness.**—aco.g.πiᵃ,q.
π¹.ρ¹.—cld.γ.δ.65.—la-v.g.—lo-i.
lyc.—mag.r¹kk.—mg-m.k̇.—nat.
—nx-v.k̇.—par.γ.φ¹.2.—ph-x.ḃº.—
pho.g.—rhs.q.—sep.rᵈ.—str.a¹ḃᵖ.

fᵉ. **Mental uneasiness.**—am-c.q.—
aps.ξ³.—arnᶜ.ḃº.—am-i.—chi.—
dro.g.i̇.—k-ca.—mer.g.k̇.—pla.
ḫᵃᵍ.k̇.m.q.—rhs.g.ij.; g.ḫ.ρ.π¹.—
ver.g.k̇.

fᶠ. **Uneasiness, as if something were
preying on him.**—manᶜ·ᵉ.—mer.

fᵍ. **Uneasiness, as if some calamity
were about to happen.**—alm.5.—
man.—mer.ḃᶜ.—tab.gᵍ.5.

fʰ. **Uneasiness, as if he had not
performed his duty.**—pul.

fⁱ. **Uneasiness, as if he had com-
mitted a crime.**—merᵇ.q.a¹ςᵃ.

CONCOMITANTS.

a¹ḃᵖ. *Loss of memory.*—strᵈ.

a¹ςᵃ. *As if going mad.*—merᵇ·ⁱ.q.

βa. *Giddiness.*—msc.

γq. *Weight in the head.*—ank.ω².

γp,hh. *Heat and perspiration in head.*
—phoᵇ.g.

γ. *Headache.*—cldᵈ.δ.65.—parᵈ.
φ¹.2.—ser.3.—vp-r.ḃ.k̇ᶠ.δaᵇ.ηcᵈ,
aa.θ².κ³.μ¹.ν¹.ρ.σ¹.φ.ψp.ω³.

δaᵇ. *Glistening eyes.*—vp-r.ḃ.k̇ᶠ.γ.
ηcᵈ,aa.θ³.κ³.μ¹.ν¹.ρ.σ¹.φ.ψp.ω³.

δ. *Pain in eyes.*—cldᵈ.γ.65.

ηcᵈ,aa. *Yellow complexion with red
cheeks.*—vp-r.ḃ.k̇ᶠ.γ.δaᵇ.θ³.κ³.
μ¹.ν¹.ρ.σ¹.φ.ψp.ω³.

θ³. *Tongue white with red borders.*
—vp-r.ḃ.k̇ᶠ.γ.δaᵇ.ηcᵈ,aa.κ³.μ¹.
ν¹.ρ.σ¹.φ.ψp.ω³.

cj. *Dryness of throat.*—rhsᵉ.g.

κ¹. *Loss of appetite.*—val.k̇.

κ³. *Thirst.*—vp-r.ḃ.k̇ᶠ.γ.δaᵇ.ηcᵈ,aa.
θ³.μ¹.ν¹.ρ.σ¹.φ.ψp.ω³.

μ¹. *Constipation.*—vp-r.ḃ.k̇ᶠ.γ.δaᵇ.
ηcᵈ,aa.θ³.κ³.ν¹.ρ.σ¹.φ.ψp.ω³.

ν¹. *Diuresis.*—vp-r.ḃ.k̇ᶠ.γ.δaᵇ.ηcᵈ,
aa.θ³.κ³.μ¹.ρ.σ¹.φ.ψp.ω³.

ξ³. *Metrorrhagia.*—apsᵉ.

πiᵃ,q. *Heaviness, fulness of chest.*—
acoᵈ.g.π¹.ρ¹.

π¹. *Difficulty of breathing.*—acoᵈ.
g.π.ρ¹.—rhsᵉ.g.ḫ.ρ.

ρ. *Scraping at heart.*—rhsᵉ.g.ḫ.
π¹.

ρ. *Weak pulse.*—vp-r.ḃ.k̇ᶠ.γ.δaᵇ.
ηcᵈ,aa.θ³.κ³.μ¹.ν¹.σ¹.φ.ψp.ω³.

ρ¹. *Palpitation.*—acoᵈ.g.π.π¹.

σ¹. *Pain in loins.*—vp-r.ḃ.k̇ᶠ.γ.δaᵇ.
ηcᵈ,aa.θ³.κ³.μ¹.ν¹.ρ.φ.ψp.ω³.

r¹kk. *Trembling of hands.*—magᵈ.

r¹e. *Contraction of fingers.*—trnᵇ.
q.52.

φ. *Sleepiness.*—vp-r.ḃ.k̇ᵗ.γ.δaᵇ.ηcᵈ,
aa.θ³.κ³.μ¹.ν¹.ρ.σ¹.ψp.ω³.

φ¹. *Sleeplessness.*—parᵈ.γ.2.

ψp. *Heat of skin.*—vp-r.ḃ.k̇ᶠ.γ.δaᵇ.
ηcᵈ,aa.θ³.κ³.μ¹.ν¹.ρ.σ¹.φ.ω³.

ω. *Burning prickling all over, like
electrical emanations.*—vrnᵇ.
g.

ω². *Weariness, debility.*—ank.γq.

ω³. *Disposition to faint.*—vp-rᵇ.
k̇ᶠ.γ.δaᵇ.ηcᵈ,aa.θ³.κ³.μ¹.ν¹.ρ.σ¹.
φ.ψp.

CONDITIONS.

2. *At night.*—parᵈ.γ.φ¹.

3. *In the forenoon.*—phoᶜ.—ser.γ.

3-30. *In the morning on rising.*—
ni-x.u.

5. *In the evening.*—almᵍ.—sul.
ḫᵃ·ᶜ·ᵉ·ᵐ·º.—tabᵍ.gᵍ.

52. *By music.*—trnᵇ.q.r¹.

65. *When smoking.*—cldᵈ.γ.δ.

105. *During thunder.*—phoᵇ.

g. **Anxiety.**—ac-x.—aco.u.—alm.k̇.;
u.—ana.—aps.—arn.k̇.—ars.—
asp.u.—aur.—au-s.k̇.—ba-m.—
bel.—bis.ḫ.—bor.—cac.k̇.—ca-c.

c

k.; u.—cam.—cth.—cap.—c-ba.k.
—cb-v.k.—cau.—ced.—cep.—
cha.—chi.—ch-s.—clo.—coc.—
cof.—cf-t.—col.—con.u.—cu-a.—
c-ar.—cu-s.—dig.—dgn.—dro.k.
—fer.—grp.k.—hel.—byo.—ign.
—iod.—la-v.k.—lyc.—mg-m.ḥ.—
mer.ḥ.—mr-c.—mo-a.—msc.—
mu-x.—nat.—na-m.—ni-x.k.—
nx-v.—opi.—pho.—pul.—rhs.ḥ.
—rut.ḥ.—sec.—sng.—sep.ḥ.; u.
—squ.—stn.k.—sul.k.—tab.ḥ.—
tar.—ver. &c.

—— *frightful.*—cth.—hyo.—mer.
—plb.—sec.—sng.
—— *deathly.*—ars.—coc^m.—eu-c.
—hel.κ⁵.
—— *rising from under ribs.*—dro.
—— *rising from abdomen.*—str.
—— *as if shut up in a cellar.*—
na-m.3-99.(111).
—— *with inclination to run away.*
—glo.
—— *urging him to walk up and
down.*—plg.
—— *as if enveloped in a black
vapour.*—bov.
—— *as if in hot air.*—pul.
—— *as if he lived in a harassing
process.*—ni-x.
—— *with need to lie down.*—ph-x.
4.
—— *followed by red miliary rash
and sweat.*—str.a¹ᵩ.
—— *followed by head- and bellyache.*—æth.q.
—— *followed by perspiration.*—
bel.
—— *following cheerfulness* —cau.
βε.γ.ᵣ.υ.φ.ω⁸.3-99.—tarᵉ.u.5.
—— *alternating with indifference.*
—na-m.q.

gᵃ. **Anxiety about trifles.**—anaᵃ·ᵏ·ⁿ.
—ba-a.—ca-c.I.—chi.—con.fᵇ.I.ω.
82.lau.φ¹.—silⁱ.

gᵇ. **Anxiety about himself.**—alm.u.
—nat.
—— *as if he would go mad.*—na-m.;
5-16.

gᵇᵃ. **Anxiety about his health.**—

cld.—coc.3.—cop.—grt.—k-ca.ḥ.
—ph-x.k.; fᵇ.—pul.—sep.u.ω².

gᵇᵇ. **Anxiety as if a fit were coming on.**—alm.3.—arg.—plaᵇᵈ.ρ¹.
π¹.ω⁸.—pul.εᵥ.rll.χ¹.5-16.
—— *as if about to have an attack
of epilepsy.*—alm.
—— *as if about to have an attack
of apoplexy.*—arg.

gᵇᶜ. **Anxiety as if he were poisoned.**
—eub.

gᵇᵈ. **Anxiety as if about to die.**—
aco.—mg-s.ηcᵇ.—msc.—na-m.—
plaᵇᵇ.ρ¹.π¹.ω⁸.—pul.ω⁸.—rhs.ᵣ.υ.;
ω².2.—rut.q.π¹χ².4.—sep.—sul.

gᶜ. **Anxiety about his eternal salvation.**—hur.

gᵈ. **Anxiety about the present.**—
agaᵉ.fᵇ.—antᵉ.1.—ca-aᵉ.aᵇ.a¹aᵇ.—
iod.k.

gᵉ. **Anxiety about the future.**—
agaᵈ.fᵇ.—anaᵃ·ᵏ·ⁿ.—antᵈ.1.—bry.
—ca-aᵈ.aᵇ.a¹aᵇ.—cic.k.—dro.k.—
gin.—hpm.5.—iod.—man.—na-m.
—na-p.—ph-x.k.—pso.q.ᵣ¹kk.—
rs-r.ḥ.k.—spi.ḥ.; u.—stp.ḥᵈ.—
tar.u.5.—thu.bᵉ.

gᶠ. **Anxiety as if something important were about to happen.**—
cth.3.

gᵍ. **Anxiety as if something bad
were about to happen.**—aco.—aml.
—ana.a¹ᵣ.—ars.—ast.I.4.—bel.
cauʰ.ḅᵒ.fᵇ.—ch-s.—cle.fᵇ.u.81.—cyc.
—dir.—dro.—χ.¹².—glo.—hel.—hep.
k.n.5.—hfb.u.—klm.—lip.—merⁱ.
q.; k.—msc.—nx-v.3-99.5.—pul.—
rhs.k.6.(8-31).—sab.—spo.—sul.
—tab.fᵇ.5.

gʰ. **Anxiety as if something bad had
happened.**—alm.fᵇ.βε.; χ².ω⁴.—
cauᵍ.—fer.; φ¹.2.—grp.ηp.ᵣ¹ᵥ¹b.5.
—tabᵏ.ḥ.k.Iᶜ.q.ᵣ.4.(50.72).

gⁱ. **Anxiety as if guilty of a crime.**
—alm.ḥ.—am-c.4.(5).—ars.—atr.
ρ¹.φ¹.—cac.—chd.q.—cinᵐ.ḥ.8-31.
—coc.—cyc.k.—digⁿ.—fer.—grp.
ᵣ.—ign.—mg-s.3-99.—mer.; fᵇ.ḥ.;
ᵍ.q.;a¹bᵍ.—na-m.χ²·³.2.—nx-v.ḥ.—
rhe.γ.29.35.—rut.ḥ.—silᵃ.—sto.ḥ.
—zin.—zn-o.

Anxiety as if about to do something awful.—hfb.

g^j. **Anxiety about others' health.**—coc.k.

g^k. **Anxiety causing him to move about.**.—aco.q.—ana$^{a \cdot e \cdot n}$.—sbd.—sil.—stp^n.—tab^h.ḥ.k.l^c.q.π.4.(50.72).—zin.3.

g^l. **Anxiety causing him to crouch together.**—ba-m^n.

g^m. **Anxiety, precordial.**—alo.e.—ars.ω^3.—bel.; γ.ηaa.κ.—c-ph.—cnc.ḥ.—cin^i.ḥ^i.8-31.—coc.—con.—cup.—lah.κ^5.ρ^1.—lyc.—mr-c.—na-m.—opi.q.—pho.κ^7.ρ^1.ω^8.—pla.ḥ.u.—pul.n.κ^5.—rhs.ḥ.φ^1.χ^3.4.—str.π^1.—trn.ḥ^a.k.(34).—xan.

—— *hypogastric.*—na-m.ι^2.2.

g^n. **Anxiety, internal.**-aco.—ana$^{a \cdot e \cdot k}$.—ars.—ba-m^l.—cth.k.—cb-a.k.2.5.(3).—dig^l.—lyc.5.—pæo.ḥ.5.—stp^k.—vi-t.r.ω^2.

g^o. **Anxiety, hysterical.**—con.

g^p. **Anxiety about his work.**—mgt.ω^2.—pul.3.

CONCOMITANTS.

a^1a^b. *Thoughtfulness.*—ca-a$^{d \cdot e}$.a^b.—nit.

a^1a^h. *Exalted ideas.*—la-v.k.l.γ.o.5.

a^1b. *Want of clear consciousness.*—alm.3-99.—mer^i.ḥ.

a^1b^s. *Absence of thought.*—mer^i.

a^1c^m. *Delusions.*—ana.; ḥ.πd.χ^2.-ber.ḥ.—pul.ḥ.3-99.

a^1v. *Stupefaction.*—ni-x.—str.

βa. *Vertigo.*-aco.δo$^{d \cdot e}$.8.—grp.u.γ.—nx-m.βv.—nx-v.q.κ$^{5 \cdot 6}$.—sng.—ver.—vrn.κ$^{1 \cdot 5}$.

βb. *Staggering.*—fl-x^8.γ.ν.

βc. *Falling forwards.*—ni-x.a^{1}c.ρ.χ^1.

βv. *Intoxication.*—nx-m.βa.

βe. *Confusion.*—aco.γ.ηp.π^{1}ω^2.—alm.γ.; ^{h}f^b.—cau.γ.r.υ.φ.ω^8.3-99.—con.u.3.66.

βe^a. *Stupid feeling.*—cau.

γp. *Heat of head.*—cac.k.η.—lau.(8).—mag.67.—pho.r^{1}p,aa.(18).—sul.a^{1}b^o.υb.

γhh. *Sweat on the forehead.*—aco.π^1.—nx-v.; χ^2.

γd. *Rushing into head.*—aco.βe.ηp.π^{1}ω^2.

γ. *Headache.*—aco.π.ρ^1.—bel^m.ηaa.κ.—bz-x.—bov.δ.f^b.5.115.—cam.l.q.ρ.—can.—cau.βe.r.υ.φ.ω^8.3-99.—fl-x^8.βb.ν.—glo.—grp.u.βa.—rn-b.ω^2.63.—rhe^i.29.35.

γ. *Frontal headache.*—alm.βe.—la-v.k.l.a^{1}a^d.o.5.

δ. *Pain in eyes.*—bov.f^b.γ.5.115.

δo$^{d \cdot e}$. *Sight dazzled, vision indistinct.*—aco.a^{1}a.8.—lyc.5.

e. *Earache.*—alo^m.

ev. *Noises in ears like music.*—pul^{bb}.r^{1}ll.χ^1.5-16.

ζ^3. *Coryza.*—na-m.κ.ω^2.8.82.

ηb. *Cold cheeks.*—na-m.χ^2.ω^2.83.

ηc^b. *Pale face.*—phy.—pul.ḥ^j.r^{1}b.χ^2.ω^8.5.

ηc^b. *Earthy complexion.*—mg-s^{bd}.

ηp. *Heat of face.*—aco.βe.γ.π^1.ω^2.—cac.k.γ.—cb-v.5.—cha.ν.r^{1}hh.—grp.r^{1}υ^{1}b.5.—mer.ḥ.r^{1}hh.

ηaa. *Redness of face.*—bel^m.γ.κ.—sep.χ.5.

ηhh. *Sweat on face.*—nat.

ηhh. *Cold sweat on face.*—ars.ω^8.—mu-x.

ij. *Dryness of throat.*—rhs.f^d.

κ. *Bitter taste.*—bel^m.γ.ηaa.

κ. *Sweet taste and blood-spitting.*—na-m.ζ^3.ω^2.3.82.

κ^1. *Anorexia.*—dro.k.—vrn.βa.κ^5.

κ^{4}hh. *Sweat on scrobiculus cordis.*—nit.4.

κ^4. *Oppression of stomach.*—ba-m.κ^5.—grp.—phy.

κ^4. *Burning in stomach.*—jat.χ^1.

κ^4. *Beating in epigastrium.*—con.q.π.—fer.

κ^4. *Jerks in scrobiculus.*—ca-c.

κ^5. *Nausea.*—ars.χ^2.2.—ba-m.κ^4.—ca-c.χ^3.—grp.q.χ^3.—hel.—lah^m.ρ^1.—nx-v.κ^6.o^{1}π^1.; q.βa.κ^6.—pul^m.n.—vrn.βa.κ^1.

κ^6. *Vomiting.*—aco.—nx-v.κ^5.o^1.π^1.; q.βa.κ^5.—vp-t.

κ^7. *Bitter eructation.*—pho^n.ρ^1.ω^8.

λf^b. *Cramp in abdomen.*—aur.n.

λp. *Heat in abdomen.*—cai.

—— *alternating with chilliness.*—bov.q.

λ. *Pulsation in abdomen.*—alm.π.ρ^1.

λ. *Pain in abdomen.*—ars.ω^8.——c-ph.—cep.q.—cot.—frz.

λ^2. *Rumbling in bowels.*—bor.—elc.q.

λ^2. *Flatulent distension.*—cot.

μ^8. *Urging to stool.*—cha.

ν. *Pain in bladder.*—fl-x.^{s}.βb.γ.

ν^2. *Urging to urinate.*—na-m^m.2.

ξ^3. *Retarded menses.*—na-m.κ.3.82.

ξ^3. *Profuse menses.*—na-m.χ^2.2.

oe. *Contraction of glottis.*—la-v.k.l.a^{l}a^h.γ.5.

o^1. *Cough.*—nx-v.$\kappa^{5\cdot6}$.π^1.

o^2. *Speechlessness.*—ign.

πd. *The blood seems to boil in chest.*—ana.h.a^{l}c^m.χ^2.

πi^a,q. *Heaviness and fulness of chest.*—aco.f^d.π^1.ρ^1.—rhs.π^1.ρ.(94).

πp. *Heat of chest.*—ol-a.

π. *Pulsation in chest.*—alm.λ.ρ^1.—con.q.κ^4.

π. *Darting pain in chest.*—aco.ρ^1.γ.

π. *Oppression of chest.*—iod.—jat.ϕ^1.2.—tab$^{h\cdot k}$.h.k.l^c.q.4.(50.72).

π^1. *Sense of suffocation.*—aco.—ni-x.ρ.

π^1. *Oppressed breathing.*—aco.; f^d.π.ρ^1.; γhh.; βe.γ.ηp.ω^2.—ars.—bor.128.—pla$^{bb\cdot bd}$.$\rho^1\omega^8$.—rhs.f^d.h.ρ.; π.ρ.(94).——rut^{bd}.q.χ^2.4.—str^m.

π^1. *Rapid breathing.*—nx-v.$\kappa^{5\cdot6}$.o^1.plg.ω^2.41.—sng.

ρ. *Pain at heart.*—spo.l.m.χ^2.

ρ. *Pressure at heart.*—rhs.σ^1.

ρ. *Heart feels pressed down.*—cha.l^a.χ^3.

ρ. *Scraping at the heart.*—rhs.f^d.h.π^1.

ρ. *Stitches above heart.*—ni-x.a^{l}c.βc^a.χ^1.

ρ. *Full, irritable pulse.*—cam.l.q.γ.

ρ. *Pulse alternately slow and quick.*—rhs.π^1.(94).

ρ^1. *Palpitation.*—aco.γ.π.; f^d.π.π^1.; ηp.γ.βe.ω^2.π^1.--alm.λ.π.—asp.u.—atr^i.ϕ^1.—bor.$\omega^{2\cdot8}$.—c-ph.--cha.ω^8.--lah^m.κ^5.--mgt.2.—mez.3.65^a.; l.χ^1.ω^2.5.—na-m.5.—-ni-x.ω^8.83.; π^1.—nx-v.n.2.—pho^n.κ.$^7\omega^8$.—-pla.31.; ρ^1.86.122.; $^{bb\cdot bd}$.π^1.ω^8.—pso.—pul.

σr. *Rigor over back.*—na-m.γhh.χ^1.

σhh. *Perspiration on back.*—rhs.f^b.$\omega^{2\cdot8}$.3.

σ^1. *Tearing in loins.*—rhs.ρ.

τ. *Pains in arms.*--cau.βe.γ.ν.ϕ.ω^8.3-99.

τ^1b. *Cold hands.*—grp^h.ηp.ν^1b.5.—pul.h^j.ηc^b.χ^2.ω^8.5.

τ^1p. *Hot hands.*—pho.γp.τ^1aa.(18).

τ^1aa. *Red hands.*—pho.γp.τ^1p.(18).—pul.τ^1kk.4.

τ^1hh. *Sweat on hands.*—mer.h.ηp.

τ^1hh. *Cold sweat on palms.*--cha.b.ηp.

τ^1kk. *Trembling of hands.*—pla.χ^2.—pso^a.q.—pul.τ^1aa.4.

τ^1ll. *Twitching in hand.*—pul^{bb}.ϵd.χ^1.5-16.

τ.v. *Bruised and drawing pains in limbs.*—rhs^{bd}.

τ.v. *Feeling as if limbs were drawn asunder.*—nat.q.

ν. *Pains in legs.*—cau.βe.γ.τ.ϕ.ω^8.3-99.

ν^1b. *Cold feet.*—grp^h.ηp.τ^1b.5.—sul.a^{1}b^o.γp.

ϕ. *Sleepiness.*—bor.—cau.βe.γ.τ.v.ω^8.3-99.

ϕ^1. *Sleeplessness.*—ars.χ^2.—atr^i.ρ^1.—ch-s.2.—fer.2.—jat.π.2.—k-hy.—lau^o.—nat.5.118.—rhs^m.χ^3.4.—sul.5-16.

χ^1. *Shivering.*—aco.—dro^g.χ^2.

χ^1. *Chilliness.*——na-m.γhh.σ.——ni-x.a^{l}c.βc^a.ρ.

χ^1. *Coldness.*—jat.κ^4.——mez.l.ρ^1.ω^2.5.—nit.

χ^2. *Heat.*——alm^h.f^b.——ana.h.a^{l}c^m.πd.—ang.u.χ^3.——ars.ϕ^i; κ^5.2.—crt.—dro^g.χ^1.——grt.ω^2.(8).—na-m^i.χ^3.2.; ηb.ω^8.83.; ξ^3.2.

—nx-v.γhh.—pla.r^{1}kk.—pul.
ḫ^j.ηc^b.r^{1}b.ω^8.5.—rut^{bd}.π^1.4.—
sep.η^1aa.5.—spo.l.m.ρ.

χ^3. *Sweat.*—ang.u.χ^2.—ca-c.κ^5.—
cau.—cha.l^a.ρ.—fl-x—grp.q.
κ^5.—kis.—mag.35.—na-m^1.χ^2.
2.—nic.35.—nit.—nx-v.—
rhs^m.ϕ^1.4.
—— *cold.*—ars.

ω. *Burning, pricking, as from electrical aura.*—vrn.f^b.
ω. *Shooting pain in the body.*—
mag.ω^2.30.
ω. *Ebullition of blood.*—alo.—
mer.2.
ω. *Oppression of every limb.*—
con^a.f^b.l.82.
ω^2. *Weariness, fatigue, debility.*—
aco.γ.ηp.$\beta\varepsilon$.π^1.——bor.ω^8.ρ^1.—
cle.k.—grt.χ^2.(8).—iod.—
mag.ω.30.—mez.l.ρ^1.χ^1.5.—
na-m.ηb.χ^2.83.; κ.ζ^3.8.82.—
plg.π^1.41.—rn-b.γ.63.—rhs.
f^b.σhh.ω^8.3.; ^{bd}.2.—sep^{ba}.u.—
vi-t^n.r.

ω^3. *Fainting.*—ars^m.
ω^4. *General ill feeling.*—tab.
ω^8. *Trembling.*——amb.—ars.k^g.—
bor.ρ.ω^2.—cau.$\beta\varepsilon$.γ.r.v.ϕ.3-99.
—cha.ρ^1.—cof.—cro.—grp.
—lam.q.——mez.5.—nat.—
pho^n.$\kappa^4\rho^1$.——pla$^{bb.bd}$.ρ^1.π^1.—
pul.ḫ^j.ηc^b.r^{1}b.χ^2.5.; ^{bd}.—rhs.
ḫ.; f^b.σhh.ω^2.3.—sar.

CONDITIONS.

1. *By day.*—ant$^{d.e}$.—bel.q.
2. *At night.*——aln.—ars.κ^5.χ^2.—
cb-a^n.k.5.(3).—ch-s.ϕ^1.—fer.ϕ^1.
—jat.π.ϕ^1.—mgt.ρ^1.—mt-n^{ba}.
b^c.k.—mer.ω.—mr-c.—na-m^i.
$\chi^{2.3}$.; $^m\nu^2$.; χ^2.—nx-v.n.ρ^1.; b.
q.βa.$\kappa^{5.6}$.—rhs^{bd}.ω^2.—ver.
2-99. *At night, on waking.*—ars.5-16.
3. *In the morning.*—alm^{bb}.—cth^f.
cb-a^n.k.2.5.— coc^{ba}.—con.u.
$\beta\varepsilon$.66.—mg-m.6.(8).—mez.ρ^1.
65^a.— na-m.κ.ζ^3.ω^2.82.—ni-x.
q.—pul^p.——rhs.f^b.σhh.$\omega^{2.8}$.—
ver.—zin^k.
3-99. *In the morning, on waking.*—

alm.a^{1}ḃ^a.—cau.$\beta\varepsilon$.γ.r.v.ϕ.ω^8.—
chd.—mg-s^i.—na-m.(111).—
nx-v^g.5.—pul.ḫ.a$^1\varepsilon^m$.

4. *In the afternoon.*—am-c^1.(5).—
ast^g.l.—ca-c.(γl.κ^5.3).—nit.;
κ^4hh.—ph-x.—pul.r^{1}aa,kk.—
rhs^m.ϕ^1.χ^3.—rut^{bd}.q.π^1.χ^2.—
tab.ḫ.(50).; $^{h.k}$.ḫ.k.l^c.q.π.(50.
72).
5. *In the evening.*—amb.—am-c^1.4.
—bov.f^b.γ.δ.115.—cb-a^n.k.2.
(3).—cb-v.ηp.—grp^h.ηp.r^{1}v^{1}b.
—hep^g.k.n.—hpm^e.—k-ca.
la-v.k.l.a$^1\gamma$.o.—lyc.δ.o.—mg-
m.ε.ḫ.—mez.ω^8.; l.ρ^1.χ^1.ω^2.—
nat.ϕ^1.118.—ni-x.k.82.—nx-
v^g.3-99.—pæo^n.ḫ.—pho.; ^{bd}.
—pul.ḫ^j.ηc^b.r^{1}b.χ^2.ω^8.——rn-b.
ḫ^q.o.u^{gg}.—rhs.ḫ.n.—sep.ηaa.
χ^2.—tab^g.f^b.—tar^{e}u.—ver.66.
5-16. *On lying down in the evening.*
—ars.2-99.—na-m^b.—nx-v.
pul^{bb}.eD.r^{1}ll.χ^1.—sul.ϕ^1.
5. *In the forenoon.*—lyc^n.—na-m.ρ^1.
6. *In a room.*—car.ḫ.(8).—mg-m.
3.(8).—rhs^g.k.(8-31).—val.k.
8. *In the open air.*—aco.a^{1}a.δo.—
ard.——car.ḫ.6.—grt.χ^2.ω^2.—
lau.γp.—mg-m.3.6.
8-31. *By walking in open air.*—
cin$^{i.m}$.ḫ.—rhs^g.k.6.
18. *By standing.*—pho.γp.r^{1}p,aa.
20. *When at rest.*—aco.ρ^1.35.
29. *When stooping.*—rhe^i.γ.35.
30. *By rising from bed.*—mag.ω.ω^2.
31. *By walking.*——cle^g.f^b.u.—pla.
ρ^1.—tab.k^a.
34. *By exercise.*—trn^m.ḫ^a.k.
35. *During motion.*——aco.ρ^1.20.—
bor.—mag.χ^3.—nic.χ^3.—rhe^i.
γ.29.
41. *By mental exertion.*—plg.π^1.ω^2.
50. *By weeping.*—dig.ḫ^d.k.—tab$^{h.k}$.
ḫ.k.l^c.q.π.4.(72).; ḫ.4.
51. *By noise.*—aga.—sil.p.
63. *When eating.*—rn-b.γ.ω^2.
65^a. *Before eating.*—mez.ρ^1.3.
66. *After food.*—con.u.$\beta\varepsilon$.3.—lah.
—ver.5.
67. *By hot food.*—meg.γp.
72. *Before vomiting.*—san.

72. *By vomiting.*—arn.β*a,ε.*—*hl-f.*—*tab*ʰ·ᵏ.ḣ.k̇.Iᶜ.q.π.4.(50).
73. *Before stool.*—cad.122.
82. *Before menses.*—conᵃ.fᵇ.I.ω.—na-m.; κ.ζ³.ω.3.—ni-x.k̇.5.—stn.k̇.(83).
83. *During menses.*—mer.—na-m. ηb.χ².—ni-x.ρ¹.ω⁸.—*stn.*k̇.82.—zin.
86. *By speaking.*—pla.ρ¹.122.
94. *By deep breathing.*—rhs.π¹.ρ.
99. *On awaking.*—so-t.
105. *From thunder.*—ni-x.
111. *By the light.*—na-m.3-99.
115. *By candlelight.*—bov.fᵇ.γ.δ.5.
118. *After a foot-bath.*—nat.φ¹.5.
121. *By solitude.*—pho.u.
122. *In society.*—cad.73.—pet.—pla.ρ¹.86.
128. *By driving.*—bor.π¹.—pso.

ħ. **Fear** (*Peculiar*).

ars. From fear he jumps out of bed and creeps into his wardrobe, whence he can with difficulty be persuaded to come out.
bor. The infant at the breast starts when any one clears his throat or sneezes.
ca-c. She fears those about her perceive her distraction of mind.
cn-i. All around appears a great mystery and is terrifying.
cic. Great fearfulness whenever the door is opened, and at every word, though not loudly spoken, she feels, from fright, shoots in the left side of the head.
cro. Disagreeable feeling, as if he longed for something, without knowing what, with a kind of apprehension, whereby he is always of a cheerful humour.
cup. A kind of fearfulness; he felt as though he must tread lightly in order to avoid doing harm or disturbing those in the room with him.
hur. A door suddenly opened makes her tremble.

ign. He fears every trifle, especially objects approaching him.
ipc. Cautious, fearful; he regards trifles as important.
irs. Afraid he is going to be ill, and afterwards laughs at his fears, which soon return, followed by blindness and activity.
k-ca. She starts with a loud cry at an imaginary occurrence (*e. g.* as if a bird flew towards the window).
lyc. In the evening when dark great fright when a door he tries to open is stiff.
mer. At a slight surprise, excessive fright; she trembles all over as if paralyzed, a monstrous glow comes into right cheek, which immediately swelled and became bluish-red, and remained so for two hours; she was so affected she could not compose herself; all her limbs feel as if bruised; violent febrile rigor and giving way of the knees compelled her to lie down from time to time.
spo. She is very fearful, and is especially and incessantly tortured by a frightful picture of a long-passed sad incident.
sul. Great fright on being called by his name.
trn. Whilst walking, a disagreeable feeling like what occurs after fear or terror, lasts half an hour, and is followed by languor.

ħ. **Fear, timidity, apprehensiveness.**—aco.g.—ac-c.—alo.g.—alm.—am-c.—am-m.u.—aps.g.—arn.—ars.—ar-c.g.—aur.—ba-c.—ba-m.—bel.g.—bis.g.—bov.u.—ca-c.u.—cam.—cnc.gᵐ.—cth.u.—cap.g.—cb-a.—cau.—cha.—cic.—cof.—crt.g.—cup.—dph.—dig.k̇.—ele.—glo.—grp.—hep.k̇.—hyo.—iod.—k-ca.k̇.—kis.—lab.—led.—lip.k̇.

—lyc.u.—mt-n.g.—mag.—mg-m.
g.—men.g.—mer.g.—nic.k.—ni-x.
—nit.u.—nx-v.—opi.—pet.—phl.
—pho.k.; g.—plb.—pul.—rhs.g.
—rut.g.—sec.k.—sep.u.—sil.—
spi.k.—stn.—str.—sul.g.—su-x.
k.u.—tab.—ver.—xan.—zin., &c.

Fear as if from epigastrum.—dig.—
mez.

—— *apparently proceeding from
abdomen.*—asa.u.

—— *from the heart.*—aur.q.—lyc.
40.—menª.—mr-cª.—mez.
—pho.

—— *following hurry.*—bz-x.

—— *on thinking of anything disagreeable.*—pho.

—— *unendurable.*—cf-t.

—— *from having been brave becomes timid.*—k-br.

ђª. **Fear of something bad happen-
ing.**—aco.—aga.k.—alm.fᵇ.k.l.—
ana.g.aˡₑᵐ,; ᵈk.—ast.l.—atr.fᵇ.—
aur.lˢ·ʰ.—au-m.k.—cld.131.—ca-a.
g.; k.—ca-c.fᵇ.; ʳ.—ca-s.k.—cic.gₑ.
uᵇ.—cle.k.—cch.k.—dig.k.52.—
dir.—elt.—gin.—glo.π.—grpᵃˢ.—
hy-x.—iod.—k-hy.kʲ.—lab.8-128.
—lil.—mac.—mag.g.ω⁸.(5-16).—
mg-s.kʲ.3.—men.—mr-c.—mez.—
nab.3.—na-mᵗ.ω²·⁸.5.—na-p.—nic.
k.—pso.g.q.rˡ.—rhsª.97.—str.—tab.
k.4; k.κ⁵.π.(50).—val.5.—vin.k.

ђᵃᵃ. **Fear lest he should fall.**—aco.
—str.

ђᵃᵇ. **Fear lest he should hurt himself.**—cld.—cn-i.

ђᵃᶜ. **Fear lest he should kill himself.**—rhs.g.5.

ђᵃᵈ. **Fear of being bitten.**—hyo.

ђᵃᵉ. **Fear lest he should be run
over.**—anh.5.8.—pho.

ђᵃᵉ. **Fear of disease.**—ars.—bor.—
ca-cª.kᶠ.—ca-x.5-16.—eth.k.—irs.
—jan.—k-ca.g.—lil.kʲ.—mac.—
na-m.k.m.—pho.—podᵃˢ.

—— *that his brain is softening.*—
at-a.

ђᵃˡ. **Fear of catching cold.**—sul.

ђᵃ². **Fear of having a fit.**—aga.—
arg.—cn-i.; aˡₑᶜ.γq.—nx-m.

ђᵃ³. **Fear of ulceration of stomach.**
—ign.

ђᵃ⁴. **Fear of typhus.**—trn.

ђᵃ⁵. **Fear of consumption.**—ca-cᵈ.
—pau.—sepᵃˢ.

ђᵃ⁶. **Fear of losing senses.**—alm.;
βₑ.—ca-c.—cn-i.—cb-a.aˡᵲ.βₑᶜ.—
clo.k.aˡᵇᵖ.—gur.—str.

ђᵃ⁷. **Fear lest he should not get
well.**—all.—ca-c.—cit.l.—k-ca.—
tar.gª.u.5.

ђᵃᶠ. **Fear of being poisoned.**—all.—
glo.—hyo.—rhs.

ђᵃᵍ. **Fear of dying.**—aco.—agn.k.—
aps.; πˡ.—ars.kᶠ.l.ω².—aur.ω².—
bel.—cac.—cn-i.—cthʳ.—cau.fᵇ.
—cf-t.ω⁸.—cop.m.—cupⁿ.ₑ.k.—
dig.—eu-c.—glo.—grpª.—hyo.—
ign.—irs.—lo-i.πˡ.—mg-s.ηcᵇ.—
msc.; ηcᵇ.ω⁸.—ni-x.—nitʳ.—nx-m.
—nx-v.—pho.—plaᵘ.—podᵃ.—
phy.—rap.—sepᵃ⁵.—squ.g.—
tabᑫ·ʳ.κ⁵·⁶.66.(72).—tri.

ђᵃʰ. **Fear of being drowned.**—cn-i.

ђᵃⁱ. **Fear of being suffocated.**—str.

ђᵇ. **Fear of what he previously
hoped for.**—bel.g.

ђᶜ. **Fear of the present.**—arnᵈ.g.—
conᵈ.ₑ.aˡₐᵇ.

ђᵈ. **Fear of the future.**—arn.; ᶜ.—
ba-c.k.5.—bry.g.—ca-cᵃ⁵.—conᶜ.ₑ.
aˡₐᵇ.—dig.g.k.4.(50).—k-ca.k.—
nat.ₑ.—rs-r.g.k.—stp.g.—str.—
sul.

—— *that he is eternally lost.*—
cn-i.

ђᵉ. **Fear of rain.**—elp.

—— *of stormy weather (thunder).*
—na-m.χ³.2.

—— *of water.*—fgs.—hyo.—str.

ђᶠ. **Fear for others.**—ba-a.—ca-cª.
—cauᵗ.g.ω⁸.51.—hep.8-31.—sul.g.

ђᵍ. **Fear of doing harm.**—cup.

ђᵍˡ. **Fear lest he should let things
fall.**—cca.3.

ђʰ. **Fear of committing murder.**—
ars.g.ω⁸.—der.—sul.

ђⁱ. **Fear as if conscience-stricken.**
—chdᵘ.51.—cin.gᵐ.8-31.—nx-v.g.
—sto.g.

ђʲ. **Fear of ghosts and visions.**—bel.

ɒ.—bro.5.121.—cn-i.—lyc.5.—pho.5.——pul.ɡ.ηcᵇ.ʳ¹b.χ².ω⁸.5.—rn-b.5.—zinᵏ.

—— *of being alone in dark.*—cam.

ħᵏ. **Fear of thieves.**—bel.ɒ.—con.—ign.2.—so-ɩᵏ.2.—zinʲ.

ħˡ. **Fear that some one is behind him.**—ana.18.31.

ħᵐ. **Fear that he is surrounded by enemies.**—ana.ɡ.πd.χ².

ħⁿ. **Fear of persons (anthropo-phobia.**—aco.—aur.ɡ.—ba-a.—ba-c.ₖ.—cb-v.ηaa.ρ.—cic.ℓ.ɩ.a¹aᵇ.—con.ɒ.—crt.a.ₖ.γ.μ².ρ.ω².—cupᵃᵍ.ℓ.ₖ.—nat.—sep.—stn.

ħᵒ. **Bashfulness.**—aur.—ba-a.ɡ.ɩ.χ³.8-31.

ħᵖ. **Cautiousness.**—ipc.—mt-nʳ.ɡ.

ħᑫ. **Pusillanimity.**—aga.——ang.—aur.——ba-c.ɡ.——cb-vˢ.—car.ɡ.—con.ₖʲ.——k-caʳ.——lyc.ₖ.a¹aᵈ.—mu-xʳ.u.——ni-x.ₖ.a¹aᵇ.——pho.ₖ.—rn-b.ɡ.ₖ.o.uᵍ·ᵈᵈ.5.——sul.ₖ.m.—tabᵃᵍ·ʳ.κ⁵·⁶.66.(72).—thu.

ħʳ. **Cowardice.**——aur.ₖᶠ.——ba-c.—cthᵃᵍ.——cau.——chi.——cup.—hy-x.—iod.ₖ.——k-caᑫ.——lyc.ɡ.——mt-nᵖ.ɡ.—mt-s.——mu-xᑫ.u.——na-m.ₖ.ρ¹.—nitᵃᵍ.—opi.—plb.—pul.φ².3-99;κ.40.——sil.—tabᵃᵍ·ᑫ.κ⁵·⁶.66.(72).

ħˢ. **Easily startled.**—alo.ɡ.——ang.—ant.—arnᵗ.—ars.—bel.;ɡ.ɩ⁸.δoᵇ.ρ¹.ʳ¹w.χ¹·².2.—ber.ɡ.—bor.——bry.u.—cam.—can.51.—cb-vᑫ.——crd.ɡ.χ³.51.—cha.—coc.——con.—cu-a.—glo.—hpm.γ.51.——hur.ω⁸.51.—hyo.ω⁵·⁸.—hyp.——iod.—k-ca.; 11.—k-hy.—lycᵗ.—mgt.51.——mt-s.11.—mer.5.—mez.ρ.——msc.ω⁸.51.—mu-x.—nr-m.51.—nat.51.—na-p.ρ¹.2.—ni-x.——nx-vᵗ.β.a,ɒ.—pho.—rhsᵃ.97.—sbdᵗ.51.—sam.—spoᵗ.υq.——str.uᵇ.——su-x.u.—sum.—tab.ɒ.ω⁸.2.51.—tar.

ħᵗ. **Fright.**—arnˢ.——aur.——cb-v.ₖᶠ·ⁱ.—cauᶠ.ɡ.ω⁸.51.—cic.γ.—eth.a¹ℓᵇ.—ign.—iod.u.—irs.ω⁸.—lyc.u.; ˢ.—na-m.—opi.—pho.—sbdˢ.51.—sep.ₖ.—spoˢ.υq.—str.—sul.—ver.—xan.—zin.uᵇ.

ħᵘ. **Terror.**—aloᵃˢ·ᵗ.ɡ.q.—chdⁱ.51.—

cam.—cn-i.114.—cl-h.——glo.—grp.—mor.—mur.ɡ.—pho.—plaᵃᵍ.—str.u.

ħᵛ. **Superstitious thoughts.**—con.

ħʷ. **Horrible fancies.**—rho.

CONCOMITANTS.

a¹aᵇ. *Thoughtfulness.*——cicⁿ.ℓ.ɩ.—conᶜ·ᵈ.ℓ.—ni-xᑫ.ₖ.

a¹aᵈ. *Fanciful.*—lycᑫ.ₖ.

a¹bᵖ. *Loss of memory.*—cloᵃᵍ.ₖ.

a¹ℓᶜ. *Wandering mind.*—cn-iᵃᵍ.γq.

a¹ℓᵐ. *Delusions.*—anaᵃ.ɡ.

a¹ɒ. *Stupefaction.*—cb-aᵃᵍ.βℓ.

βa. *Giddiness.*—ccs.—nx-vˢ.βɒ.

βℓ. *Confusion of head.*—almᵃᵍ.—bov.u.—cb-aᵃᵍa¹ɒ.

βℓᵇ. *Empty feeling of head.*—kis.—na-m.

βɒ. *Intoxication.*—nx-v.5-31; ˢβa.

γq. *Heaviness of head.*——cn-iᵃᵍ.a¹ℓᶜ.

γhh. *Sweat on forehead.*—sep.ω⁸.

γ. *Sensitiveness of brain.*—lah.5.

γ. *Pain in head.*—cicᵗ.—crtⁿ.a.ₖ.μ².ρ.ω².—hpmˢ.51.—-mag.u.4 (5).

δoᵇ. *Blindness.*——belˢ.ɡ.ɩ⁸.ρ¹.ʳ¹w.χ¹·².2.

ηcᵇ. *Pale face.*—mscᵃᵍ.ω³.—pulʲ.ɡ.ʳ¹b.χ².ω⁸.5.—ver.ɩ⁸.q.

ηcᵇ. *Earthy complexion.*—mg-sᵃᵍ.

ηp. *Hot face.*—ver.a.ηaa.ʳ¹p.

ηaa. *Red face.*—cb-vⁿ.ρ.86.—elc.ρ¹.—ver.a.ηp.ʳ¹p.

ɩp. *Heat in throat.*—hyp.

ɩiⁱᵈ. *Feeling of swelling in throat.*—+glo.

κᴬ. *Deranged stomach.*—lah.

κ⁵. *Nausea.*— alm.5.6.8-31.86.—tabᵃᵍ·ᑫ·ʳ.κ⁶.66.(72).;ᵃₖ.π.(50).

κ⁶. *Vomiting.*—tabᵃᵍ·ᑫ·ʳ.κ⁵.66.(72).

κ⁷. *Eructation.*—ver.

μ². *Diarrhœa.*—crtⁿ.a.ₖ.γ.ρ.ω².

π. *Chest symptoms.*—gloˢ.

πd. *Blood boils in chest.*—anaᵐ.ɡ.χ².

πe. *Chest feels contracted.*—alm.—glo.—phl.66.—ph-x.χ².

π. *Oppression of chest.*—tabˢ.ₖ.κ⁵.(50).

π^1. *Difficulty of breathing.*—aps^{as}.
—lo-i^{as}.—rhs $\mathfrak{l}^{b}$.$\mathfrak{g}$.ρ.

ρ. *Heartache.*—crt^{n}.a.$\mathfrak{k}$.γ.μ^2.ω^2.

ρ. *Scraping at heart.*—rhs.$\mathfrak{l}^{b}$.$\mathfrak{g}$.π^1.

ρ. *All the pulses beat.*—cb-v^{n}.ηaa.
86.

ρ^1. *Palpitation of heart.*—aur.ω^2.
ϕ^1.--bel^{s}.$\mathfrak{g}$.$\mathfrak{l}^{s}$.δo^{b}.r^1.$\chi^{1\cdot2}$.2.—
cca.--elc.ηaa.--mez^{s}.--na-m^{r}.
$\mathfrak{k}$.--na-p^{s}.2.--nx-m.

σ^2ii^{d}. *Neck feels swollen.*—glo.

r^1b. *Cold hands.*--pul^{j}.$\mathfrak{g}$.ηc^{b}.χ^2.ω^8.5.

r^1p. *Hot hands.*—ver.a.ηp,aa.

r^1w. *Motions of hands.*--bel^{s}.$\mathfrak{g}$.$\mathfrak{l}^{s}$.δ
o^{b}.r^1.$\chi^{1\cdot2}$.2.

r^1kk. *Trembling of hands.*—pso^{s}.$\mathfrak{g}$.

v. *Weight in legs.*—spo$^{s\cdot t}$.

ϕ^1. *Sleeplessness.*—aur.ρ^1.ω^2.--rhs.
$\mathfrak{g}^{m}$.

ϕ^2. *Anxious dream.*—pul^{r}.$\mathfrak{g}$.3-99.

ϕ^2. *Sad dreams.*—lep.99.

χ^1. *Chilliness.* — bel^{s}.$\mathfrak{g}$.$\mathfrak{l}^{s}$.δo^{b}.ρ^1.r^1
w.χ^2.2.

χ^2. *Heat.*—ana^{m}.$\mathfrak{g}$.πd.--bel^{s}.$\mathfrak{g}$.$\mathfrak{l}^{s}$.
δo^{b}.ρ^1.r^1w.χ^{1}.2.--opi.q.ω^2.--
ph-x.πe.--pul^{j}.$\mathfrak{g}$.ηc^{b}.r^1b.ω^8.5.

χ^3. *Cold sweat.*--crd^{s}.$\mathfrak{g}$.51.—
na-m^{e}.2.

ω^2. *Weakness.*-- am-c.4.(5).-ag-n.
u.$\omega^{2\cdot8}$.8-30.-ars^{ag}.$\mathfrak{k}^{f}$.$\mathfrak{l}$.-aur^{ag}.;
ρ^1.ϕ^1.-crt^{n}.a.$\mathfrak{k}$.γ.μ^2.ρ.-na-m$^{a\cdot t}$.
ω^8.5.-opi.q.χ^2.

ω^3. *Fainting.*—msc^{ag}.ηc^{b}.

ω^5. *Convulsions.*—hyo^{s}.ω^8.

ω^8. *Trembling.*—ag-n.u.ω^2.8-30.—
ars^{h}.$\mathfrak{g}$.--aur.$\mathfrak{g}^{n}$.--ba-a.--cb-a.
$\mathfrak{l}$.5.--cau$^{f\cdot t}$.$\mathfrak{g}$.51.--cha.—
cf-t^{ag}.— hur.51.—hyo^{s}.ω.^{5}.—
irs^{t}.--mag^{a}.$\mathfrak{g}$.(5-16).--msc^{s}.
51.--na-m$^{a\cdot t}$.ω^2.5.--nic.$\mathfrak{c}$.—
pul^{j}.$\mathfrak{g}$.ηc^{b}.r^1b.χ^2.5.--rhs.$\mathfrak{g}$.--
sep.γhh.--sul^{s}.4.--tab^{s}.$\mathfrak{v}$.
2-51.

CONDITIONS.

2. *At night.*--alo.51.81.--bel^{s}.$\mathfrak{g}$.
$\mathfrak{l}^{s}$.δo^{b}.ρ^1.r^1w.$\chi^{1\cdot2}$.--cau.
ign^{k}.--k-ca.16.--na-m^{e}.χ^3.—
na-p^{s}.ρ^1.--so-t^{k}.--tab^{s}.$\mathfrak{v}$.ω^8.51.

3. *In the morning.*—cca^{gl}.--mg-s^{s}.
$\mathfrak{k}^{j}$.--nab^{a}.

3-30. *On rising in morning.*—ag-n.u.
$\omega^{2\cdot8}$.

3-99. *On awaking in the morning.*—
pul^{r}.$\mathfrak{g}$.ϕ^2.

4. *In the afternoon.*—am-c.ω^2.
(5).—dig^{d}.$\mathfrak{g}$.$\mathfrak{k}$.(50).—mag.u.
γ.(5).—nat.5.—sul^{s}.ω^8.—tab.
$\mathfrak{g}$.(50).; $^{a}\mathfrak{k}$.—tar^{d}.$\mathfrak{g}$.u.

5. *In the evening.*—alm.κ^5.6.
8-31.86.--am-c.ω^3.4.--anh^{ae}.8.
-ba-c^{d}.-bro^{j}.121.--cld.--cb-a.
$\mathfrak{l}$.ω^8.—cau.--lah.γ.--lyc^{j}.$\mathfrak{l}$.
mgt^{s}.--*mag*.u.γ.4.--mg.m.c.$\mathfrak{g}$.
--mer^{s}.--nat.4.--na-m$^{a\cdot t}$.$\omega^{2\cdot8}$.
--pæo.$\mathfrak{g}^{n}$.--pho^{j}.--pul^{j}.$\mathfrak{g}$.ηc^{b}.
r^1b.χ^2.ω^8.--rn-b^{q}.$\mathfrak{g}$.$\mathfrak{k}$.o.u$^{g\cdot dd}$.;^{j}.
--rhs^{ac}.$\mathfrak{g}$.--tab.--val^{s}.—
zin.$\mathfrak{l}$; u^{b}.3.

5-16. *In the evening, in bed.*—ca-x^{a}.
—mag^{a}.$\mathfrak{g}$.ω^8.

5-31. *In the evening, when walking.*
—nx-v.$\beta\mathfrak{v}$.

5. *In the forearm.*—nic.$\mathfrak{l}$.

6. *In the room.*—alm.κ^5.5.8-31.86.
—car.$\mathfrak{g}$.(8).

8. *In the open air.*—anh^{ae}.5.—
car.$\mathfrak{g}$.6.

8-31. *By walking in open air.*—alm
κ^5.5.6.86.—ba-a^{o}.$\mathfrak{g}$.$\mathfrak{i}$.χ^3.—cin^{l}.
$\mathfrak{g}^{m}$.—hep^{r}.

8-128. *When driving in open air.*—
lah^{a}.

11. *When touched.*—k-ca^{s}.--mt-s^{s}.

16. *When lying in bed.*—k-ca.2.

18. *By standing.*—ana^{l}.31.

19. *By sitting.*—iod.

31. *By walking.*—ana^{l}.18.

40. *By disagreeable intelligence.*—
pul^{r}.$\mathfrak{k}$.

40. *By vexation.*—lyc.

50. *By weeping.*—dig^{d}.$\mathfrak{g}$.$\mathfrak{k}$.4.—grp.
—tab.$\mathfrak{g}$.4.; $^{s}\mathfrak{k}$.κ^5.π.

51. *By noise.*—alo.2.81.—alm.—
can^{s}.--crd^{s}.$\mathfrak{g}$.χ^3.--cau$^{f\cdot t}$.$\mathfrak{g}$.ω^8.
—chd$^{l\cdot u}$.--hpm^{s}.γ.--hur.ω^8.
--msc^{s}.ω^8.--nr-m^{s}.--nat^{s}.—
sbd.$^{s\cdot t}$.--tab^{s}.$\mathfrak{v}$.ω^8.2.

52. *By music.*—dig^{a}.$\mathfrak{k}$.

66. *After food.*—cth.$\mathfrak{k}$.—mg-m.$\mathfrak{l}$.
—phl.π.—tab$^{ag\cdot q\cdot r}$.$\kappa^{5\cdot6}$.(72).

72. *By vomiting.*—tab$^{ag\cdot q\cdot r}$.$\kappa^{5\cdot6}$.66.

D

81. *After pollution.*—alo.2.51.
82. *Before menses.*—ca-c.u.—sul. f^d.

81. *After pollution.*—alo.2.51.
82. *Before menses.*—ca-c.u.—sul. f^d.
86. *By speaking.*—alm.κ^5.5.6.8-31.
  —cb-v^n.ŋaa.ρ.
97. *On going to sleep.*—rhs$^{a.s}$.
98. *During sleep.*—aln.
99. *On awaking.*—lep.ϕ^3.
107. *By draught of air.*—cn-i.
114. *In the dark.*—cn-i^u.
115. *At sight of bright objects.*—cn-i.
121. *By solitude.*—ars$^{∞}$.—bro^j.5.
128. *By driving in a carriage.*—lip.
131. *When shaving.*—cld^a.

i. Suspicion, mistrust.—ana.ħ^l.18. 31.—cn-i.—cic.; *t.*ħ^n.a^{1}a^b.—cca. u^l.ƀ.—dro.f^e.g.; f^b.ƙ.—lah.; u^c.—lyc.u.—mer.u$^{b.l}$.; u^o.—opi.—rut.u. —su-x.ħ.
  —— *fearful.*—bel.
  —— *that people are talking about her, and judging ill of her.* —ba-a.g.ħ^o.χ^3.8-31.

i^a. Doubting humour.—lah.4.

CONCOMITANTS.

a^{1}a^b. *Thoughtfulness.*—cic.*t.*ħ^n.
χ^3. *Perspiration.*—ba-a.g.ħ^o.8-31.

CONDITIONS.

4. *In the afternoon.*—lah^a.
8-31. *When walking in the open air.* —ba a.g.ħ^o.χ^3.
18. *When standing.*—ana.ħ^l.31.
31. *When walking.*—ana.ħ^l.18.

j. Jealousy.—cam.—hyo.
  —— *maniacal.*—lah.5.
j^a. Envy.—lil.—pul.$\kappa^{a.b}$.

CONDITION.

5. *In the evening.*—lah.

k. Depression of the disposition (*Peculiar*).

aur. He imagines he has lost the affections of others; this makes him sad even to tears.
dro. He is dejected about the hos-tility of others on all sides, and, at the same time, discouraged and anxious about the future.
fer. Surroundings seem large, attaches importance to trifles, earnest mood.
hel. On seeing a happy person he becomes melancholy, and then he first feels truly unhappy.
lam. Excessive sadness, he thought he was suffering undeserved adversity, but not without desire for work.
mt-s. He dislikes cheerful faces.
pla. When the spirits are cheerful the body is suffering, and *vice versa*, when the spirits are affected the body is well.
sul. A number of generally disagreeable, angering, vexatious ideas (but also funny things and melodies), chiefly out of times long past, occur to her; they force themselves upon her, one after another, so that she cannot get rid of them, by day, when doing nothing, but worst in the evening in bed, when they prevent sleep.
val. Anxious hypochondriacal feeling, as if surrounding objects were strange to him and he were isolated from them; the room appears deserted and uncomfortable, which compels him to leave it.
ver. When employed cheerful; when doing nothing gloomy, cannot think properly, is silent and reserved.
vi-t. Sadness about his domestic re-tions.

k. Depressed, low spirits, heaviness of spirits, dull or dismal humour, dejection, gloominess, sadness, cheerlessness, unhappiness, grief, melancholy, hypochondriasis.—ab-n.—aco.—æsc.—aga.—alm.—amb.—am-c.—am-m. —ana.— ang.u.—ant.—ag-n.—

ars.—at-a^f.—asr.u.—as-t.—aur.—au-s.g.—bap.—ba-a.u.—ba-c.—bel.u—ber.—bov.—bry.u.—cac.—ca-c.—ca-s.; ħ^a.—cam.—cn-i.—can.—cb.a.—car.u.—cr-s.—ca-x.I.φ.—css.—cas.—cau.u.—ced.—chi.—ch-s.—cic.—cmf.—cnb.—cle.—coc.—cof.—cch.—col.—con.—crn.u.—cot.—cro.g.—crt.—cup.—dig.ħ.—dio.—dro.g.—ele.—fag.—glv.u.—gel.—grp.g.; u.—hel.—hep.ħ.—hyo.—ign.—idm.—iod.—irs.—k-bi.—k-ca.—lah.—lau.—lil.—lol.—lyc.—mac.u^b.—mag.ħ.—mg-m.u.—man.u.—mer.g.—mit.—mu-x.—myr.—nat.—na-m.—ni-x.u.—nx-v.u.—opi.—pet.—phl.—ph-x.—pho.—pla.—pso.—pul.u.—rn-b.—rs-r.—rhs.—sar.—sep.—spi.ħ.; u.—stn.—stp.u.—sul.—su-x.u.—tab.—trn.—tar.g.—thu.—vi-t.u.—zin.u.—zn-o., &c.

—— *long-lasting.*—bth.

—— *alternating with over-excitement.*—agn^u.m.—ast.

—— *alternating with sexual excitement.*—lil.

—— *followed by obtuseness and indifference.*—pho^x.(50).

—— *followed by cheerfulness.*—bry.—grp.l.5.—men^x.—mrl.a.u.ω^2.—ori.—pla.u.—sec.—zin.ħ.—ziz.

—— *following cheerfulness.*—cle.—cof.—cyc^n.u.—hln.—k-cl.—opi.—pet.—pla.l.3.5.—sec.

k^a. Gloomy, sad, melancholy thoughts.—alm^y.—amb-ρ.—bry.—ca-c.u.—cb-a^e.I.—chd^e.l.q.—cle^e.—cor.; ^{v}.—ccs.—hur.; ^{e}.—hyd.—lyc.—nat.ħ.—na-s^j.—ni-x.—ol-a—ori.—phl.ħ^a.l.—rhs.g.ħ.ω^2.—rut.4.5.—sul^j.g u a^{1}a^b.8-31.

k^b. Thoughts of death.—aco.—agn.—am-c.l.—cam.—cn-i.—cb-a.—cau.f^b.g.—chd.—con.—crt.—cup.ε.ħ^n.—grp.—jug.—opi.—str.l.5.16.—trn.3.—zin.ω^2.4.

k^c. Thoughts of disease.—alm.—ars.121.—chd.—lep.—mur.—

na-m.m.—na-p.—ph-x.—pho.—sep^e.—sul.

k^d. Despair of life.—ars.; I.χ^{1}ω^2.—ba-c^f.ħ^q.—ca-c.l.χ^2.—cn-i.aħ^d.—cha^o.—der.—hel.—hur^h.—k-br.—k-ca.l.—k-fc^j.—kre.5.—na-s^f.m.—thr^r.

k^e. Thoughts of coming evil, sad forebodings.—am-c.χ^1.5.—ana^f.i.—anh.ε.l—cb-a^a.l.—cas.4.—cau.82.—chd^a.l.q.—cle^a.—cch.—cyc^j.—hel.—hur^a.; ^{i}.—mg-s^j.3.—mer.g.—mu-x^o.b^c.a^{1}a^b.—na-m.l^h.—pso^h.—rum.—sep^c.—so-t.—trn.l.q.—vi-t$^{o·s}$.

—— *to his relatives.*—ars.g.

k^f. Hopelessness, despondency, despair.—amb.—ana.b.ω^2.; ^{e}.i.—arn.—ars.—at-a.—ast.l—aur.—ba-c^d.ħ^q.—bel.—b-la.—cn-i.—cb-a.—cb-v^j.ħ.—cas^j.(5).; ^{p}.—chi.q.—ch-s^j.—coc.—dph.—dig.u^b.—eri.*rv*.—gel.—grp.—hln.—hur^h.—hyo.u.—irs.—lpt.—lil.2.—lyc^j.; l.; ^{g}.—na-m.ω^2.—na-p.5.—na-s^d.m.—opi.u.—ori.—plg.—pol.u^b.—pso.n.—rhs.u.—snc.5.—spi.n.χ^1.—str.—tar.π.φ.χ^1.5.—ver.—vrb.ħ.—vp-r.f.γ.δa^b. ηc^d, aa. θ^3, κ^3, μ^1, ν^1, ρ, σ^1. χ^2.ω^3.φ.—vp-t.q.γ.—wis.u^{ff}.b.—xan.

—— *thinks he is going to be sick.*—irs.

—— *about his eternal salvation.*—str.

k^g. Inconsolableness.—chi.—lyc^f.—mt-n^t.g.ħ.—nat.u^{dd}.—pho.l.l^a.3.—spo.g.l.m.ρ.

k^h. Forsaken feeling.—ba-c.ħ^d.5.—cam.—cb-a.—hur^f.; ^{d}.—lam^j.l—mg-ın^q.l.—nat.ε.ħ.—pla.—pso^e.—pul.b^c.—rhs.g^g.6(8).

k^i. Feels unfortunate.—hur^e.—lyc.l^j.—mac.

k^j. Lachrymose humour.—am-c.5.aps.—ars.—au-m.—bel.s.—bry.u.—en-i.—cth.—cb-a.ħ^q.—cb-v^f.ħ.; o.—ced.—cha.φ^1.r.v.—chi.40.—ch-s^f.—con.l.; g^a.q.ω^2.82.—cot.ı.—crt.—cyc^e.—dig.—gin.—hur.

—hyp.—iod.—ipc.𝔟^{c}.u.—k-ca.8. 34.—k-br.—k-fc^{d}.—lil.𝔥^{æ1}.—lam^{h}.𝔩.—lyc^{f}.; χ^{1}.; 𝔟^{c}.u.—mt-n.χ^{1}.—mt-s.u.8.—mg-s^{e}.3.—man.—men.—mrl.—msc.u.—nat.; 𝔩^{c}.$\omega^{2 \cdot 8}$.—na-m.𝔟^{o}.; 5.—na-s^{a}.—nic. 𝔥.—ni-x.—opi.—ph-x^{q}.—pla.5.; u.(50).; 6.(8).—pso.u.—pul.𝔤.u.—rhs.—rut^{s}.—sar.4.—sep.; u^{b}.—sil.—stp.; u.—sul.; 𝔥.; u.3.5.; ^{a}.𝔤.u.α^{1}a^{b}.8-31.—su-x.𝔤.𝔥.—trn.ω^{9}.3.; κ^{4}.; ^{v}.5.—til.—vin.—zin.𝔥.(5).; χ.83.

𝔨^{k}. **Religious melancholy.**—ars^{o}.—aur.𝔩$^{g \cdot h}$.—rs-r.

𝔨^{l}. **Sentimentality.**—mnc.—pso.

𝔨^{m}. **Languishing.**—amp.—col.—hy-x.η.ω^{2}.—lau.ω^{2}.η.

𝔨^{n}. **Gravity, solemnity, quietude.**—æth.𝔣^{c}.u.γp.(5).—am-c.—am-m.—ars.—bel.u.—bor.—ch-s.𝔟.ω^{2}.—cca.(5).—eub.𝔟^{c}.122.—grt^{o}.—ign^{x}.—led.—nx-v.𝔟^{c}.—ph-x.8-31.(6).—pul.—rum.—snc^{y}.α^{1}a^{b}.5.—stn^{o}.𝔤^{e}.—stp^{o}.𝔟^{c}.—sul.—thu.—til.—val.α^{1}a^{b}.—ziz.ω.

—— *alternating with cheerfulness.*—cyc.u.

𝔨^{o}. **Reservedness.**—an-s.—ag.n.—ars^{k}.—bis.—bra.—cth.𝔟^{o}.—cap.—cb-a.𝔱.—car.—cha^{d}.—eub.æ^{t}.—eup.𝔟^{c}.—grt^{n}.—hel.—hyo.𝔟^{c}.—ind.—man.α^{1}a^{b}.4.—mu-x.83.; ^{e}.𝔟^{c}.α^{1}a^{b}.—na-m.—ni-x.𝔟^{c}.—nx-v.𝔤.; 𝔟^{c}.α^{1}𝔟^{c}.—ol-a.𝔟^{c}.—opi.𝔟^{c}.—phl.α^{1}a^{b}.—pho.α^{1}a^{b}.—sbd.—sar.—stn^{n}.𝔤^{e}; 𝔟^{c}.𝔣^{a}.—stp^{a}.𝔟^{c}.—vi-t$^{e \cdot s}$.

𝔨^{p}. **Longing.**—cas^{f}.—ipc.

𝔨^{q}. **Home-sickness.**—cb-a.—hel.—hpm.5.—lip.—mg-m^{h}.𝔩.—mer.—ni-x.—ph-x^{j}.—snc.—sil.

𝔨^{r}. **Want of self-reliance.**—ana.—ang.—ag-n.—ba-a.—kis.—lyc.—na-m.—nx-v.—oln.—rs-r.—thr^{d}.

𝔨^{s}. **Discontented with himself.**—aur.𝔥^{r}.—bry.u^{dd}.—cau.—hep.—k-ca.—mt-s.—man.𝔟^{c}.𝔤^{e}.u.α^{1}𝔟^{f}.—men.𝔥.q.u.—mer.u.—ni-x.(50).—pan^{x}.—ph-x^{t}.—rut^{j}.—sul.u^{dd}.—vi-t$^{e \cdot o}$.

𝔨^{t}. **Self-reproach.**—ars.u$^{x \cdot dd}$.—hur.—hyo^{w}.—mt-n^{g}.𝔤.𝔥.—ph-x^{s}.

𝔨^{u}. **Self-contempt.**—agn.𝔪.—cob.

𝔨^{v}. **As if a misfortune had happened.**—am-m.—coc^{a}.—hur.—mt-s.—pho.—sep.—trn^{j}.5.

𝔨^{w}. **As if oppressed by crime.**—cob.—con.a.ω^{2}.4.—hyo^{t}.—sbd.

𝔨^{x}. **Everything is disagreeable, pleasure in nothing.**—ars.—car. 4.—con.—eup.𝔟.—hep.—ign^{n}.κ.κ^{1}.—ipe.—mg-m.a.𝔟^{c}.3.—men.—mer.—mez.𝔟^{o}.—mu-x.ω^{2}.4.8.—na-m^{y}.—nx-v.𝔟^{c}.—ol-a.—pan^{s}.—pet.u^{b}.—pho.(50).—pru.—pul.—rho.—rhs.𝔟^{f}.—sam.u.—sar.5.—spo.u.γ.κ^{1}.ϕ.ω^{2}.—stn.—stp.𝔩.—thu.𝔤^{e}.

𝔨^{y}. **Disagreeable thoughts and recollections.**—alm^{a}.—am-c.—coc.𝔟^{e}.—hep.—kis.—lab.ρ.—man.—mez.u.—na-m^{x}.; ω^{2}.—na-p.—snc^{n}.α^{1}a^{b}.5.—sep.; π^{1}.ρ.—sul.𝔷.

𝔨^{z}. **Sorry for himself.**—aga.

CONCOMITANTS.

α^{1}a. *Inclined for mental work.*—cau.𝔤.u.—mns.

α^{1}a^{b}. *Thoughtfulness.*—man^{o}.𝔣^{a}.u.4.—mu-x$^{e \cdot o}$.𝔟^{c}.—ni-x.𝔥^{q}.—phl^{o}.—pho^{o}.—snc$^{n \cdot y}$.5.—spr.—sul$^{a \cdot j}$.𝔤.u.8-31.—val^{n}.

α^{1}𝔟. *Confusion of ideas.*—mns.—mur.𝔟^{a}.5.

α^{1}𝔟^{f}. *Mistakes in speaking.*—man^{s}.𝔤^{e}.u.

α^{1}𝔟^{p}. *Weakness of memory.*—ber.α^{1}𝔟^{s}.—vi-o.𝔟^{c}.

α^{1}𝔟^{s}. *Difficulty of thinking.*—ber.α^{1}𝔟^{p}.—nx-v^{o}.𝔟^{c}.—opi.

α^{1}𝔟^{s}. *Absence of thoughts.*—agn.a^{b}.𝔟^{o}.—arn.

α^{1}𝔟^{t}. *Folly.*—ars.

α^{1}𝔟^{y}. *Obtuseness of senses.*—aga.𝔟.ω^{2}.

α^{1}𝔠^{m}. *Delusions.*—k-br.

α^{1}𝔡. *Stupefaction.*—plb.ϕ.

β𝔢. *Confusion of head.*—alo.𝔟^{o}.u^{dd}.5.(5).—bov.u^{b}.—mep.κ^{5}.

γ. *Inclined to hang head.*—ver.𝔩.𝔡𝔢.

γp. *Heat of head.*—æth^n.b^c.u.(5).
—ant.

γq. *Heaviness of head.*——aru.ϕ^1.
ω^2.

γq. *Heaviness in back of head.*—
tar.g.

γ. *Headache.*——ag-n.ηc^d.θj.κ.ω^2.5.
——ars.66.——c-ph.a^{1}b.e$\mathfrak{d}$.ϕ.χ.ω^2.
——cod.——crt.a.$\mathfrak{h}^n$.μ^2.ρ.ω^2.——irs.
——ptv.I.——spo^x.u.κ^1.ϕ.ω^2.——thr.
5.31.——vp-r^f.f^b.δa^b.ηc^d,aa.θ^3.
κ^3.μ^1.ν^1.ρ.σ^1.χ^2.ω^3.——vp-t^f.q.

δa^b. *Glistening eyes.*——vp-r^f.f^b.γ.ηc^d,
aa.θ^3.κ^3.μ^1.ν^1.ρ.σ^1.χ^2.ω^3.

δe. *Watering of eyes.*—nx-m^j.δ.—
ver.I.γ.

δ. *Burning of eyes.*—nx-m^j.δe.

δ. *Sore eyes.*—mt-n.I.5.

δo. *Sight affected as in fever.*—
dig.ω^4.

δo. *Dimness of vision.*—pet.b^c.3.

e$\mathfrak{d}$. *Singing in ears.*——c-ph.a^{1}b.γ.
ϕ.χ^3.ω^2.

η. *Smiling countenance.*—hy-x^m.
ω^2.—lau^m.ω^2.

ηc^b. *Pale face.*—cn-i.

ηc^d. *Yellow complexion.*—ag-n.γ.θ.
κ.ω^2.5.——vp-r^f.f^b.γ.δa^b.ηaa.θ^3.
κ^3.μ^1.ν^1.ρ.σ^1.ϕ.χ^2.ω^3.

ηp. *Hot face.*—cop.I.$\tau\nu$b.4.

ηaa. *Red cheeks.*—vp-r^f.f^b.γ.δa^b.ηc^d.
θ^3.κ^3.μ^1.ν^1.ρ.σ^1.ϕ.χ^2.ω^3.

θj. *Dry lips.*—ag-n.γ.ηc^d.κ.ω^2.5.

θ^3. *Moist white tongue with red
borders.*—vp-r^f.f^b.χ.δa^b.ηc^d,aa.
κ^3.μ^1.ν^1.ρ.σ^1.ϕ.χ^2.ω^3.

ι. *Choking in throat.*—cot^j.—
iod.o.

κ. *Insipid taste of food.*—ign$^{n\cdot x}$.
κ^1.

κ. *Bitter taste.*—am-m.κ^4.—ag-n.
γ.ηc^d.θ.ω^2.5.

κ^1. *Anorexia.*—dro.g.—ign$^{n\cdot x}$.κ.—
spo^x.u.γ.ϕ.ω^2.—val.f.

κ^3. *Thirst.*—vp-r^f.f^b.γ.δa^b.ηc^d,aa.θ^3.
μ^1.ν^1.ρ.σ^1.ϕ.χ^2.ω^3.

κ^4. *Weakness of stomach.*—trn^j.

κ^5. *Nausea.*—cod.ϕ.——mep.βe.—
pet.ρ.—trn.ω^2.—ver.χ^1.

κ^7. *Sour eructations.*—pl-n.

κ^7. *Bitter eructations.*—am-m.κ.

λ. *Aching under short ribs.*—zin.
b^o.f^a.66.

λ^2. *Flatulence.*—nx-m.

μ^1. *Constipation.*——vp-r^f.f^b.γ.δa^b.
ηc^d,aa.θ^3.κ^3.ν^1.ρ.σ^1.ϕ.χ^2.ω^3.

μ^2. *Diarrhœa.*——crt.a.$\mathfrak{h}^n$.γ.ρ.ω^2.—
fer.

ν. *Diuresis of clear urine.*—vp-r^f.
f^b.γ. δa^b.ηc^d, aa.θ^3.κ^3.μ^1. ρ.σ^1.ϕ.
χ^2.ω^2.

ξ. *Increased sexual desire.*—naj.

o^2. *Speaks in a low voice.*—ol-a.66.

π. *Pain in chest.*—tar^f.ϕ.χ^1.5.

π^1. *Oppressed breathing.*—aln.g.3.
——ant.I.u^b.5.51.——sep^y.ρ.

π^1. *Short breathing.*—lah.b.χ^1.

ρ. *Sinking at heart.*—amb^a.—pet.
κ^5.

ρ. *Pain in heart.*—crt.a.$\mathfrak{h}^n$.γ.μ^2.
ω^2.—spo^g.g.I.m.

ρ. *Ebullition of blood.*—lah^y.

ρ. *Feeble, small pulse.*—vp^f.f^b.γ.
δa^b.ηc^d,aa.θ^3.κ^3.μ^1.ν^1.ϕ.χ^2.ω^3.

ρ. *Quick pulse.*—sep^y.π^1.

ρ^1. *Palpitation.*—na-m.$\mathfrak{h}^r$.

σ^1. *Pain in loins.*—cop.s.83.——
vp-r^f.f^b.γ.δa^b.ηc^d,aa.θ^3.κ^3.μ^1.ν^1.
ρ.ϕ.χ^2.ω^3.

$\tau\nu$b. *Cold extremities.*—cop.I.ηp.4.

$\tau\nu$. *Bruised pain in limbs.*—cha^j.
ϕ^1.

$\tau\nu$. *Aching in all the joints.*—eri^f.

ν. *Pain in ankles.*—aco$^{b\cdot f}$.

νq. *Weight of legs.*—grp.

ϕ. *Sleepy.*—c-ph.a^{1}b.χ.e$\mathfrak{d}$.χ^3.ω^2.—
cle.—cod.κ^5.——pau.——pla.e.I.
u.86.——plb.a^1$\mathfrak{d}$.——rn-s.b^o.5.
——rs-r.u^{dd}.——spo^x.u.γ.κ^1.ω^2.—
tar^f.π.χ^1.5.——vp-r^f.f^b.γ.δa^b.ηc^d,
aa.θ^3.κ^3.μ^1.ν^1.ρ.σ^1.χ^2.ω^3.

ϕ^1. *Sleeplessness.*——aru.γq.ω^2.——
cb-a.g^n.5.2.(3).——cha^j.$\tau\nu$.

χ. *Fever.*—pet.—zin^j.83.

χ^1. *Chilliness.*—am-c^e.5.—ars^d.ω^2.
—cam.b.—k-cl.a.m.5.—lah.b.
π^1.—lyc^j.—mt-n^j.—pul.u.—
spi^f.n.—tar^f.π.ϕ.5.—ver.κ^5.

χ^2. *Heat.*—vp-r^f.f^b.γ.δa^b.ηc^d,aa.θ^3.
κ^3.μ^1.ν^1.ρ.σ^1.ϕ.ω^3.

—— *as if warm water were thrown
over her.*—ca-c^d.I.

χ^3. *Sweat.*—c-ph.α^1b.$\gamma.\epsilon$b.$\phi.\omega^2$.
ω. *Suffering.*—ziz^n.
ω^2. *Weariness, weakness.*—aga.b. α^1b^y.—amp.3.(31).—ana^f.b.5. an-s.b.—ag-n.$\gamma.\eta^1.\theta.\kappa$.5.—ars^a. χ^1.—bov.5.—c-ph.α^1b.$\gamma.\epsilon$b.ϕ. χ^3.—ca-s.u.5.—cam.ω^8.—cau. —ch-s^n.b.—cca.5.—con^j.g^a.q. 82.; ^{w}.a.4.—crt.a.h^n.$\gamma.\rho.\mu^2$.—dgn.—eri.—hy-x^m.η.—lah.3. —lau.; ^{m}.η.—lo-i.—lyc.—mag.—mrl.a.u.—mu-x^x.5.8. —nat^j.l^c.ω^8.—na-m^y.; ^{f}.—ph-x.u^b.—rhs^a.g.h.—sab.—sec.ω^4.—sep.—spo^x.u.$\gamma.\kappa^1.\phi$. —trn.κ^5.—zin^b.4.
ω^3. *Fainting.*—vp-r^f.f^b.$\gamma.\delta$a^b.ηc^d,aa. $\theta^3.\kappa^3.\mu^1.\nu^1.\rho.\sigma^1.\phi.\chi^2$.
ω^4. *Ill-feeling.*—dig.bo.—sec.ω^2.
ω^8. *Trembling.*—nat^j.l^c.ω^2.
ω^9. *Yawning.*—cam.ω^2.—trn^j.3.

CONDITIONS.

2. *At night.*—lil^f.—trn.(66).
3. *In the morning.*—aln.g.π.—amp.ω^2.(31).—*cb-a*.g^n.ϕ^1.5.2. —lah.ω^3.—mg-m^x.a.b^c.—mg-s$^{e.j}$.—ptv.l.—pet.b^c.δo.—pho^g.l.l^a.—sep.; 83.—sul^j.u. 5.—su-x.—trn^j.ω^9.; ^{b}.—trx. b$^{c.o}$.
3-30. *On rising in morning.*—cer.—hep.b^c.(16).
3-99. *On awaking in the morning.*—an-s.—cb-a.g.—cop.(31).—k-ca.5-97.—ni-x.—pet.u^c.—pho.l.l^i.100.
4. *In the afternoon.*—*aga*.5.—alm.ι.—ca-s.5.—car^x.—cas^f. —coc.—con^w.a.ω^2.—cop.l.ηp. $\tau\nu$b.—hy-x.—ign.—man^o.f^b.u. α^1a^b.—mu-x^x.ω^2.8.—pla.5.—rut^a.5.—sul.8.—zin^b.ω^2.
5. *In the evening.*—aga.b^c.122.—*alo*.b^o.u^{dd}.5.—am-c^j.—ant. —ba-c^h.h^d.—bov.ω^2.—ca-s.4.; u.ω^2.—*can*.5.—cb-a.g^n.ϕ^1.2. (3).—*cb-v*.$^{f.j}$.—*cca*^{n}.—cyc.—dig.g.h^d.(50).—grp.l.—hpm^q. —ign.—k-ca.l.—k-cl.a.m.χ^1. —kre^d.—lyc.—mt-n.l.δ.—mag.u.a^w.1.—mur.b^a.α^1b.—na-m^j.—na-p^f.—ni-x.g.82.—pho.113.—pla^j.; 4.—rn-s.; b^o.ϕ.—rut^a.4.—snc^f.; $^{n.y}$.α^1a^b. —sep.—str^b.l.—sul.b^e.; ^{j}.u.3. —tar^f.$\pi.\phi.\chi^1$.—thr.γ.31.—*zin*^{j}.h.
5-97. *On going to sleep in the evening.* —k-ca.3-99.
5. *In the forenoon.*—aga.(4).—alo.b^o.u^{dd}.$\beta\iota$.(5).—am-c^e.χ^1. —ana^f.b.ω^2.—ant.l.u^b.π^1.51. —aps.m.—ag-n.$\gamma.\eta$c^d.$\theta.\kappa.\omega^2$. —can.(5).—sar^x.
5. *At noon.*—*æth*^{n}.b^c.u.γp.
6. *In a room.*—ph-x^n.8-31.—pla^j.(8).—rhs^h.g^g.(8).—trn. (8).
8. *In the open air.*—k-ca^j.34.—mt-s^j.u.—mu-x^x.ω^2.4.—*pla*^{j}. 6.—*rhs*^{h}.g^g.6.—sul.4.—*trn*.6.
8-31. *On walking in the open air.*—con.—ph-x^n.(6).—sep.—sul$^{a.j}$.g.u.α^1a^b.
16. *By lying down.*—hep.b^c.3-30. —str^b.l.5.
31. *When walking.*—aco.b^e.u.—*cop*.3-99.—*amp*.ω^2.3.—thr.γ. 5.—thu.f^b.
34. *By exercise.*—k-ca^j.8.
40. *By vexation.*—chi^j.—k-bi.—pul.h^r.
43. *By reading.*—cro.
50. *By weeping.*—*dig*.g.h^d.5.—*ni-x*^{s}.—*pho*^{x}.—*pla*^{j}.u.
51. *By noise.*—ant.l.u^b.π^1.5.—pho.
52. *By music.*—dig.h^d.—lyc.
55. *By bleeding of nose.*—k-cl.
66. *After food.*—ars.γ.—*cle*.—nx-v.—ol-a.o^2.—*trn*.2.—zin. b^o.f^a.λ.
81. *By pollution.*—ham.—na-p.
82. *Before menses.*—cau^e.—con^j. g^a.q.ω^2.—fer.—lyc.u.—ni-x. g.5.—stn.g.(83).
83. *During menses.*—am-c.—cop. s.σ^1.—fer.s.—mu-x^o.—na-m. —sep.3.—sil.g^m.n^a.—*stn*.g. 82.—zin^j.χ.

84. *After menses.*—alm.—fer.
99. *On awaking.*—lep. ; ♄.
100. *By dreams.*—pho.l.l^i.3-99.
113. *In twilight.*—pho.5.
121. *By solitude.*——ars^c.——bov.a. (122).
122. *In society.*—aga.b^c.5.——*bov* a. 121.—eub^n.b^c.

I. **Expressions of emotion** (*Peculiar*).

aur. He imagines he has lost the affections of others, and this makes him sad even to tears.

cam. The boy creeps into a corner and howls and weeps ; everything said to him he takes in bad part, as if he were being ordered ; he imagines he is injured and abused.

cn-i. He shouts, leaps about, and claps his hands with joy.
He sings and extemporises both words and music.

cau. Extravagantly sympathising, on listening to the adventures of others and hearing the cruel trials they have undergone, she is quite overcome with weeping and sobbing, and cannot be made happy again.

lyc. He weeps and howls at first over the past, then over future ills.

na-m. He thought others pitied him and wept.

pla. Silence and involuntary weeping soon after the most friendly discourse, so that she is annoyed at it herself.

stp. She will not listen to anything any one says, hides her face, and weeps without cause.

I. **Weeping.**—aco$^{e.j.k}$.♄^{q}.k^f.——all.98.—alm.f^b.♄^{a}.k^a. ; ^{h}.k^e.—amy.k.—anh.k^e.c.—ant.k.u^b.x^1.5.51.—aps.—arg.—arn.—ars^h.b^c. ; ^{b} ; u.—ast.k^f. ; 51.—au-m.k.—bel^b. ; ^{a} ^{h}.♄. ; u.99.—bry.—ca-c. ; 5.u^b.—cam.q. ; f^d.q —-cn-i.—cth.u^b ; o.—-cb-a. ; ♄^{u}.ω^8.5.—cb-v.g.ω^8.4.8.—css.θ^1.—

cau^b.—cha^h.—cin^j.—cit.♄^{æ7}.—cle.♄^{r}.5.—coc.—cop.k.ηp.rvb.4.—crt.—dig.g.♄^{d}.4.(50).—dul.u^{ff}.a^{1}c^m.3.—elc.♄.q.—grp.k.5.(3). ; k. ; 51. ; 5. ; u. ; ♄.—hep.k.—hur.c. ; u^{ff}.—hfb.γ.—ign.40.—k-br.—k-ca.k.—k-hy.u. ; o.—kis.—kre.ρ.52. ; u.3.—lyc. ; k^f. ; a^{1}c^c.82.83. —mt-n.k.δ.5.—mt-s.—mg-m.♄.k^q.—mer.—mez.—msc.u.—nat^c.k.ω$^{3.8}$.—na-m^h.k^e. ; 121. ; b^o.—na-s.52.—ni-x. ; k^a. (50).—nx-v$^{d.j.k}$.k^g.b^c.ηp.aa. ; 40. ; ^{b} ; ♄.u^g.—opi^a.—ptv.k.3.—pet.♄.k.—phl.k^a.♄^{a}.—pho^a.k^g.3. ; k.3-99. **100.** ; x^{ii}.—pla.g^{bd}. ; b^c.k.u.86. ; u. (50).—pul.u^{dd}.—rhs.k. ; λ^2.—rut.k^a.—sab.u.—sep.k.—sil.86.—spo.g.k^g.m.ρ.χ^2.—stp.86. ; u.—sul. ; o. ; q.2.89.——tab.g.♄.(50).——trn.k^v.ρ.v. ; γ.ρ.2. ; 40.—tep.—ver.k.γ.δc.

—— *following cheerfulness.*—pla.k.3.5.

—— *at laughable things.*—pla.k.3.5.

—— *about a pain.*—opi.

—— *on being looked at.*—kis.—na-m.

—— *on being reproved.*—ca-c.—pla.

—— *on thinking of long past evils.*—na-m.

—— *when disturbed at work.*—pul.u.

I^a. **Whimpering, whining, moaning.**—aco.ω.—alm.κ^8.84.—ars.—bel^b.l.♄.—cha.g.ρ.χ^3.—cic^h.—k-br.—kis^i.q.—lch.γ.—nx-v$^{j.k}$.—opi.l.—pho.l.k^g.3.—squ.—zin.u.γ.

—— *hoarse.*—chi^g.

I^b. **Sobbing.**—ars.—cau.l.—lo-i.—nx-v.l.—spr^j.

I^c. **Sighing.**—ail.—alm^d.—am-c.—ag-n.g^m.ω^4.66.—bry.—ca-x.k.φ.—cha^d.k.—cmf.k.—cch.g.—cot.—dig^d.—gos.f.g.—hur.—mac.a$^{lb^a}$.—nat.l.k.ω$^{2.8}$.—sul.k.o^2.—tab.q.

I^d. **Groaning.**—alm^c.—ars.—bel.3. ; f.91. ; f.98.—cha.ηp.—c.k.—cca.x^1.5.44.—dig^c.—hel^f.—hpm^g.q.2.81.—hy-x.—mr-c.—nx-v$^{j.k}$.l.k^g.b^c.

ηp,aa.—pul^f.11.73.—sar.k.—sil.γ. a^{1}ɒ^a.—str.—trn.k^f.o^1.ω^9.—ver.s.

—— *as in hydrocephalus.*—so-n.
—— *alternating with hopping and dancing.*—bel.

I^e. **Wailing.**—aco$^{j.k}$.I.ђ^q.k^f.

I^f. **Grunting.**—bel^d.91.; ^{d}.98.—hel^d. —pul^d.11.73.

I^g. **Crying, screaming.**—æth.—ars^j. ω^3.—aur^h.k^d.—bad.—bel.ω^8.; ^{h}.δP$^{1.2}$. —buf^i.—cth.a^{1}ɒ^a.—cr-h.—cha.ω^5. —chi^a.; q.—ch-s.2.—cin.11.— c-ar.q.—elp.—hpm^d.q.2.81.—ign^h. u^c.—ipc^h.ηc^b.—nx-v.—plb.ω^5.— snn.q.φ^1.—str.—ver.g.q.; ђ.q.ηc^b.

—— *like barking.*—cth.

I^h. **Howling.**—aco$^{j.k}$.g.—alm.l.k^e. ars.I.b^c.—bel.I.; ^{a}.I.ђ.; ^{g}.δP$^{1.2}$.— cld.a^{1}a^o.40.—cha.I.; 40.—cic^a.— cof.k^a.(8).—ipc^g.ηc^b.χ^1.—mor. na-m.I.k^e.—nx-v.I.u^g.

I^i. **Lamentations.**—buf^g.—coc.k^n.— ign.51.—kis^a.q.—sul^j.κ$^{1.3}$.r^1.

—— *as in hydrophobia.*—so-n.

I^j. **Complaints.**—aco$^{h.k}$.g.; $^{e.k}$.I.ђ^q.k^f. —ac-s.—ars^g.ω^3.; g.λ.ω^6.π^1.—cin.I. —nx-v$^{a.k}$.; I$^{d.k}$.k^g.ɒ^e.ηp,aa.—spr^b. —sul^i.κ$^{1.3}$.r^1.

I^k. **Reproaches.**—aco$^{e.j}$.I.ђ^q.k^f.—hyo. u^v.—mez.—nx-v$^{a.j}$.; I$^{d.j}$.k^g.ɒ^e.ηp, aa.—rs-r.3.5.

—— *about trifles.*—aco$^{j.h}$.g.

I^l. **Grumbling.**—pho.o.

I^m. **Tearing off the clothes.**—chd.g.

CONCOMITANTS.

a^{1}a^o. *Talkativeness.*—cld^h.40.

a^{1}c^c. *Raving.*—lyc.I.82.83.

a^{1}c^m. *Hallucinations.*—dul.I.u^{tt}.3.

a^{1}ɒ^a. *Loss of consciousness.*—cth^g. —sil^d.γ.

γ. *Inclination to hang the head.* —ver.I.k.δε.

γ. *Headache.*—hfb.—lch^a.—sil^d. a^{1}ɒ^a.—trn.I.ρ.2.—zin.u.

δε. *Watering eyes.*—ver.I.k.γ.

δP$^{1.2}$. *Easily dilating and contracting pupils.*—bel$^{g.h}$.

δ. *Pain in eyes.*—mt-n.I.k.5.

ηc^b. *Pale face.*—ipe$^{g.h}$.χ^1.—ver^g. ђ.q.

ηp. *Heat of face.*—cha^d.—cop.I. k.rɒb.4.

ηp,aa^1. *Hot, red cheeks.*—nx-v.I$^{d.j.k}$. k^g.ɒ^e.

θ^1. *Grinding of teeth.*—css.

κ^1. *Anorexia.*—sul$^{i.j}$.κ^3.r^1.

κ^3. *Thirst.*—sul$^{i.j}$.κ^1.r^1.

κ^8. *Hiccough.*—alm^a.84.

λ. *Pain in abdomen.*—ars^j.g.π^1. ω^6.

λ^3. *Rumbling in bowels.*—rhs.I.

o^1. *Cough.*—trn^d.k^f.ω^9.

o^2. *Low speech.*—sul^c.k.

π^1. *Laboured and short breathing.* —ant.I.k.u^b.5.51.—cca^d.5.44.

π^1. *Loss of breath.*—ars^j.g.λ.ω^6.

ρ. *Lightness at heart.*—kre.I.52.

ρ. *Pain in heart.*—spo.I.g.k^g.m. χ^2.—trn.I.k^v.v.; I.γ.2.

ρ. *Heart feels pressed down.*— cha^a.χ^3.

τ^1. *Wringing of hands.*—sul$^{i.j}$.κ$^{1.3}$.

ɒb. *Cold legs.*—trn.I.k^v.ρ.

τɒb. *Cold extremities.*—cop.I.k.ηp. 4.

φ^1. *Sleeplessness.*—snn^g.q.

χ^1. *Chilliness.*—ipc$^{g.h}$.ηc^b.

χ^2. *Heat.*—spo.I.g.k^g.m.ρ.

χ^3. *Perspiration.*—cha^a.ρ.

ω. *Sensitive to touch.*—aco^a.

ω^2. *Weakness.*—nat^c.I.k.ω^8.

ω^3. *Fainting.*—ars$^{g.j}$.

ω^4. *Ill-feeling.*—ag-n^c.g^m.66.

ω^5. *Convulsions.*—cha^g.—plb^g.

ω^6. *Restlessness.*—ars^j.g.λ.π^1.

ω^8. *Trembling.*—bel^g.—cb-a.I.ђ^u. 5.—cb-v.I.g.4.8.—nat^c.I.k.ω^2.

ω^9. *Yawning.*—trn^d.k^f.o^1.

CONDITIONS.

2. *At night.*—cb-s^g.—hpm$^{d.g}$.q. 81.—sul.I.q.89.—trn.I.γ.ρ.

3. *In the morning.*—bel^d.—dul.I. u^{tt}.a^{1}c^m.—grp.I.k.5.—kre.I.u. —ptv.k.—pho.I.I^a.k^g.—pla.I. k.5.—rs-r^k.5.

3-99. *On waking in morning.*—pho. I.k.100.

4. *In the afternoon.*—cb-v.I.g.ω^8.

8.—cop.l.k.ηp.rʋb.—dig.l.g.
ƅᵈ.(50).
5. *In the evening.*—cb-a.l.ƅᵘ.ω⁸.
—cle.l.ƅʳ.—ccaᵈ.π.44.—grp.l.
k.(3).—mt-n.l.k.δ.—pla.l.k.
4.—rs-rᵏ.3.
5. *In the forenoon.*—ant.l.k.uᵇ.π¹.
51.
8. *In the open air.*—cb-v.l.g.ω⁸.
4.—cofᵉ.kᵃ.
11. *When touched.*—cinᵉ.—pulᵈˑᶠ.
73.
40. *By vexation.*—cldᵇ.a¹aᵒ.—chaᵇ.
—ign.l.—nx-v.l.—trn.l.
44. *When writing.*—ccaᵈ.π¹.5.
50. *By weeping.*—dig.l.g.ƅᵈ.4.—
ni-x.l.kᵃ.—pla.l.u.—tab.l.g.ƅ.
51. *By noise.*—ast.l.—igni.
51. *By the sound of bells.*—ant.l.
k.uᵇ.5.
52. *By music.*—cop.l.—grp.l.
kre.l.ρ.—na-s.l.
66. *After food.*—ag-nᶜ.gᵐ.ω⁴.
73. *Before stool.*—pulᵈˑᶠ.11.
81. *By pollution.*—hpmᵈˑᵍ.q.2.
82. *Before menses.*—lyc.l.a¹cᶜ.83.
83. *During menses.*—lyc.l.a¹cᶜ.82.
84. *After menses.*—almᵃ.
86. *When talked to.*—pla.l.bᶜ.ᵉ.k.
u.—sil.l.—stp.
89. *By coughing.*—sul.l.q.2.
91. *By breathing.*—belᵈˑᶠ.
98. *When asleep.*—all.l.—belᵈˑᶠ.
99. *On awaking.*—bel.l.u.
100. *By dreams.*—pho.l.k.3-99.
121. *By solitude.*—na-m.l.

m. **Weariness of life, desire for
death.**—ac-s.k.—agn.kᵘ.ᵴ.—aps.
kᵃ.5.—aur.—au-s.—bel.g.; nᵃ.g.
kʲ.8-31.— ber.g.u.; u.λ.83.—cb-v.
k.—cau.g.ƅ.— chd.—chi.k.—
cop.ƅᵃᵍ.—der.n.—eu-c.—grt.gᵇᵃ.
uᵇˑᶜ.—k-br.ᴀ.u.—k-bi.ƅⁿ.k.—k-cl.
a.k.χ¹.5.—kis.u.ω².—kre.k.—led.
ᴇ.u.—mer.; ᴀ.—mez.ƅᶜ.—nat.
3-99.—na-m.k.—na-s.kᵈˑᶠ.—ni-x.;
ƅᵃᵍ.; uᵈᵈ.—nx-v.g.q.—ori.—pho.
—phy.κ⁸.; 3-99.—pla.ᶠ.ƅᵃᵍ.k.q.—
plb.u.—rhs.—rut.kᵃ.4.5.—sep.n.
sil.—spo.g.kᵍ.l.ρ.χ².—stp.aᵃ.k.—

sul.k.; ƅq.k.—su-x.k.—thu.—ziz.
k.

CONCOMITANTS.

κ⁸. *Vomiting of blood.*—phy.
λ. *Pain in abdomen.*—ber.u.83.
ρ. *Pain in heart.*—spo.g.kᵍ.l.χ².
χ¹. *Chilliness.*—k-cl.a.k.5.
χ². *Heat.*—spo.g.kᵍ.l.ρ.
ω². *Weariness.*—kis.u.

CONDITIONS.

3-99. *On waking in the morning.*—
nat.—phy.
4. *In the afternoon.*—rut.kᵃ.5.
5. *In the evening.*—k-cl.a.k.χ¹.
rut.kᵃ.4.
5. *In the forenoon.*—aps.kᵃ.
8-31. *When walking in open air.*—
bel.nᵃ.g.kʲ.
83. *During menses.*—ber.u.λ.

n. **Inclination to suicide** (*Collective*).—alm.—antᶜ.2.—aur.g.λ.—
au-m.—bel.; ᵃ.m.g.kʲ.8-31.; ᵇ.; ᵈ.
cb-vᶜ.—cle.k.κ⁵.r¹.ʋl.ω⁴.—crtᵈ.
der.m.—droᵃ.g.5.—grt.g.—hep.g.
ƅᵃ.k.—hpm.k.—hyoᵃ.kᶠ.—mor.k.—
nx-v.g.ρ¹.2.; g.; ᵈ.—pso.k.; kᶠ.—
pul.gᵐ.κ⁵.—rhs.g.ƅ.113.—sep.m.
—silᵃ.gᵐ.k.83.—spi.kᶠ.χ¹.—str.—
tar.a¹cᶜ.

—— *with dread of an open window
or knife.*—chi.g.χ².2.5.
—— *at sight of blood or of a knife.*
—alm.
—— *from pain.*—nx-v.

nᵃ. **Inclination to drown himself.**
—bel.m.g.kʲ.8-31.—dro.g.5.—hyo.
kᶠ.—sil.gᵐ.k.83.
nᵇ. **Inclination to hang himself.**—
bel.
nᶜ. **Inclination to shoot himself.**—
ant.2.—cb-v.
nᵈ. **Inclination to throw himself
from a height or the window.**—
bel.—crt.—nx-v.—ori.—str.
nᵍ. **Inclination to poison himself.**—
lil.

E

CONCOMITANTS.

$\alpha^1 c^c$. *Raving.*—tar.

κ^5. *Nausea.*—-cle.ꞵ.r^1.v^1.ω^4.——pul. $\mathfrak{g}^m$.

λ. *Cramp-like contraction in abdomen.*—aur.$\mathfrak{g}$.

ρ^1. *Palpitation.*—nx-v.$\mathfrak{g}$.2.

r^1. *Shooting in palms.*—cle.ꞵ.v^1.ω^4.

v^1. *Shooting in soles.*—cle.ꞵ.r^1.ω^4.

χ^1. *Chilliness.*—spi.ꞵ^f.

χ^2. *Heat.*—chi.$\mathfrak{g}$.2.5.

ω^4. *Ill-feeling.*—cle.ꞵ.r^1.v^1.

CONDITIONS.

2. *At night.*—ant^e.—chi.$\mathfrak{g}$.χ^2.5.—nx-v.$\mathfrak{g}$.ρ^1.

5. *In the evening.*—chi.$\mathfrak{g}$.χ^2.2.—dro^a.$\mathfrak{g}$.

8-31. *When walking in open air.*—bel^a.m.$\mathfrak{g}$.ꞵ^j.

83. *During menses.*—sil^a.$\mathfrak{g}^m$.ꞵ.

113. *In the twilight.*—rhs.$\mathfrak{g}$.ħ.

o. **Oversensitiveness** (*Peculiar*).

lah. Very sensitive disposition; she weeps at receiving thanks.

sep. Very sensitive from a slight cause; a fit of desperately furious grimaces with hiccough; she throws herself on the bed and remains lying there all day; just before the catamenia.

o. **Oversensitiveness** (*Collective*).—aco^j.p.; ^{k}ꞵ.—all^d.—arn$^{b.c}$.—ars$^{h.j}$.p.u^{dd}.; ^{f}.$\mathfrak{g}$.ꞵ^j.—-ast.Ɩ.—cb-v.u^b.—cic^o.$\mathfrak{g}$.—cle^a.$\mathfrak{g}$.ꞵ.ꞩ.—coc.—cch$^{j.n.p.q}$.—col.—con^b.p.γ.—crt^i.Ɩ.—dig^d.ꞵ^f.u^b.—grn.ꞩ.——ign.—iod.u^b.; ^{a}.—k-ca.u^b.—k-hy.Ɩ.—lah^i.Ɩ.χ^2.—lyc.Ɩ.—mer^i.γ.(19).—mez.u.—nat.$\omega^{3.8}$.—na-s^k.ꞵ.Ɩ.—nit.ħ.q.u.—nup^l.—nx-v.; $^{j.n}$.; $^{h.k}$.p.; ^{k}.Ɩ.; ^{r}.p^b.—pho.; ^{n}.p.; ^{s}.χ^2.; ^{m}.ꞵ.; σ^1.—pla.; ꞵ^j.—pso.u^b.; ^{d}.ω^8.—pl-n^e.ꞵ^j.—sbd.ꞩ.α^1b^a.—sep.κ^8.82.—sul^c.Ɩ.—tab.ħ.—ver.α^1a.—zin^s.ω^8.; ^{h}.u^{ff}.

o^a. **Oversensitiveness to external impressions.**—cle.$\mathfrak{g}$.ꞵ.ꞩ.—iod.

o^b. **Oversensitiveness to agreeable impressions.**—arn^c.

o^c. **Oversensitiveness to disagreeable impressions.**—arn^b.—sul.I.

o^d. **Oversensitiveness to moral impressions.**—all.—dig.ꞵ^f.u^b.—pso.ω^8.

—— tender conscience.—ign.

o^e. **Oversensitiveness to irritating impressions, injuries.**—pl-n.ꞵ^j.

o^f. **Oversensitiveness to anxious impressions.**—ars.$\mathfrak{g}$.ꞵ^j.

o^g. **Oversensitiveness to mental impressions.**—pho.χ^2.—zin.ω^8.

o^h. **Oversensitiveness to conversation.**—ars^j.p.u^{dd}.—con.p.γ.—nx-v^k.p.—zin.u^{ff}.

o^i. **Oversensitiveness to reading.**—crt.Ɩ.—lah.Ɩ.χ^2.—mer.γ.5.(19).

o^j. **Oversensitiveness to bright light.**—aco.p.—ars^h.p.u^{dd}.—cch$^{n.p.q}$.—nx-v^n.

o^k. **Oversensitiveness to music.**—aco.ꞵ.—na-s.ꞵ.Ɩ.—nx-v^h.p.

o^l. **Oversensitiveness to the sufferings of animals.**—nup.

o^m. **Oversensitiveness to the crying of a child.**—pho.ꞵ.

o^n. **Oversensitiveness to odours.**—cch$^{j.p.q}$.—nx-v^j.—pho.p.

o^o. **Oversensitiveness to sad stories.**—cic.$\mathfrak{g}$.

o^p. **Oversensitiveness to touch.**—cch$^{j.n.q}$.

o^q. **Oversensitiveness to rudeness.**—cch$^{j.n.p}$.

o^r. **Oversensitiveness to the shaking of the floor.**—nx-v.p^b.

CONCOMITANTS.

α^1a. *Increased mental powers.*—ver.

α^1b^a. *Difficulty of comprehension.*—sbd.ꞩ.

γ. *Headache.*—con^h.p.—mer^i.5. (19).

κ^8. *Hiccough.*—sep.82.

σ^1. *Weak feeling in loins.*—pho.

χ. *Heat.*—lah^i.Ɩ.

—— *as if deluged by hot water.*—pho^s.

ω^3. *Faintness.*—nat.ω^3.

ω^8. *Trembling.*—nat.ω^3.—pso^d.—zin^s.

CONDITIONS.

5. *In the evening.*—mer^i.γ.(19).
19. *By sitting and laying down head.* mer^i.γ.5.
82. *Before menses.*—sep.κ^8.

p. Intolerance of noises (*Collective*). —aco^a.; ^{g}.k.; o^j.—amb^g.γd.—am-c. —ars.—ca-c. ; b^a.3.—coc.—con.o^h. γ.—ign.δP^2.—iod.—ipc.u^c.—mnc^d. —nat^h.g^m.ω$^{2\cdot8}$.(16).—ni-x$^{b\cdot e}$.γ.— nx-v$^{f\cdot h\cdot i}$.; ^{b}.—ph-x.γ.35.—pho^h.γ. —ptl.u.—sep. ; ^{h}.—sil.g. ; ^{f}.—tan. —thr.; βa.θ^1.κ^5.—zin^f.k.u^b.

—— *noise hurts.*—lyc.
—— *noise goes through every limb.* —aco^g.k.—coc.—mnc^c.— sab^g.γ.χ^{3}ω^2.(8-31).

p^a. Intolerance of the slightest noise.—aco.—cnb.
p^b. Intolerance of the noise of footsteps.—ni-x^e.γ.—nx-v.
p^c. Intolerance of the noise of a hammer.—mnc.
p^d. Intolerance of the noise of sawing wood.—mnc.
p^e. Intolerance of water splashing. —ni-x^b.γ.
p^f. Intolerance of the sound of the voice.—nx-v.$^{h\cdot i}$—sil.—zin.k.u^b.
p^g. Intolerance of music.—aco.k.— amb.γd.—cha.—sab.γ.χ^3.ω^2.(8-31).
p^h. Intolerance of instrumental music.—nat.g^m.ω$^{2\cdot8}$.(16).—nx-v$^{f\cdot i}$. —pho.β.a^a.—sep.
p^i. Intolerance of vocal music.— nx-v$^{f\cdot h}$.

CONCOMITANTS.

βa. *Vertigo.*—thr.θ^1.κ^5.
γ. *Weakness of head.*—pho^h.
γd. *Blood to head.*—amb^g.
γ. *Weight and clawing in forehead.* —con.o^h.
γ. *Headache.*—ni-x$^{b\cdot e}$.——ph-x.35. —sab^g.χ^3.ω^2.(8-31).
δP^2. *Dilated pupils.*—ign.
θ^1. *Pain in teeth.*—thr.βa.κ^5.
κ^5. *Nausea.*—thr.βa.θ^1.
χ^3. *Sweat.*—sab^g.γ.ω^2.(8-31).

ω^2. *Weakness.*—nat^h.g^m.ω^8.(16).— sab^g.γ.χ^3.(8-31).
ω^8. *Trembling.*—nat^h.g^m.ω^2.(16).

CONDITIONS.

3. *In the morning.*—ca-c.b^a.
16. *By lying down.*—nat^h.g^m.ω$^{2\cdot8}$.
8.31. *By walking in open air.*—sab^g. γ.χ^3.ω^3.
32. *By shock.*—ph-x.γ.

q. Restlessness (*Peculiar*).
cha. The child can only be kept quiet by carrying it about in the arms.
cle. About 5 p.m. involuntary running about in the streets with great ease and rapidity, as if he floated along. He cannot find a place of rest either in the room or the open air. After this had lasted two hours, he felt as if destitute of all sensation, power of will, or of thought. At 9 p.m. he was quite prostrated with painful uneasiness all through the body, and a shooting, throbbing headache from within outwards as if the head would burst, and the feet feel as if fastened to the floor with leaden weights.
hel. He could neither sit, stand, nor lie, and pointed always to his heart.

q. Restlessness (*Collective*).—æth. g.; g.γ.λ.—aga$^{a\cdot b}$.—ail.—all.k.121. —alo.s. ; ^{e}.s. ; η.—aln.s.—alm.b. 17.19.—amb.1. ; π.; s.— -ana k.γ. χ^1.—ant.—arn$^{a\cdot b}$.b^{wo}.—ars^a.g. ; γ.λ.v. ; u.; g.k.—aur.r$^{d\cdot e}$.; ^{c}.—bap. f^b.φ^2.—bel. ; g. ; a^{1}c^m.—ber.g.— bov.g.λ.χ^1.—bry.g.—cld.b^e.a^{1}b^o.— ca-c.g. ; ^{b}.g.βε. ; ρ.; 5.; u.—c-ph.— clt.g.—cth.16.19.—cap.r^h.—cb-a.r. —cb-v.5.; 1.; g^i.l.ω^8.4.8.122.; l. ced.; a^{1}b.—chd.; g^i.—cin.—coc.r^h. —cro.g.k.—crt.ω^2.; g.b.—dro^b.43.— dul.—elc.g.λ^3.—gn-c.γ.19.—grp. k^x.(8.31).—ham.b^o.u^{dd}.—hel.g^s.— hfb.g.ω^2.—hyo.; r.æ^w.—iod^a.—jat.

βa.ρ.χ¹.—k-bi.ʂ.ʀ.—k-caᵇ.—k-hy.γ.
—klm.bⁱ.—kre.uᵇ.82.—lah.ʀ.γ.κ⁶.; ᵇ.
—lamᵃˑᵇ.—ledᵇ.u.—mgt.ʀ.ηp,hh.ω².
—mer.2.—mr-c.—mo-a. ; γ.λ.
mscᵇ.ω².—naj.4.—nat. ; g.ʀ.ʀ. ; ᵇ.5.
43. ; ˢ.u.—ni-x.ʂ.u.—nit.ꝑ.o.u.—
nx-v.δP².; ε.o.—opi.gᵐ.—pb-x.a.
pho.—phy.—plb.—pso.g.ꝑᵃ.ω⁸.⊥
rut.γ.χ².5.—sbd.g.—sil.uff.—stp.u.
—str.—sul.; ᵃ.Ⅰ.o¹.2.; ᵇ.—su-x.—
trn.f.ε.γw. ; uᶜ.v¹w.—tar.ꝑ. ; ᵇᵒ.—
vp-r.ω³.—vp-t.ʂᶠ.γ.—zin.g.3.

—— *dislike to sit still.*—idm.—
   iod.—lah.ʀᶜ.
—— *incessant change of posture.*
   —aco.—alm.16.19.—bis.u.
   —cth.—cqm.—mer.ʂʷ.—
   rhs.fᵈ.
—— *tossing about in bed.*—aco.
   uff.—ars.ʂ.κ³.—bel.—cam.Ⅰ.
   —cha.g.γ.α¹bʸ.λ.—cup.
   lah.2.—lch.—mr-c.ꝑ.
—— *getting out of bed and lying*
   down again.—mer.2.
—— *cannot remain long at one*
   occupation.—aco.—aps.βε.
   —asa.χ¹.(8).—bis.—ca-c.
   g.—nat.—so-m.—stn.—
   thr.ʂˣ.—ver.
—— *going from one place to*
   another.—agaᶜ.—alo.g.ꝑᵃᵍˑu.
   —alm.—am-c.—ana.ʂ.γ.χ¹.
   —aps. ; Ⅰ.—ars.—asa.χ¹.
   (8). ; gᵐ.π¹.ω⁴.—aur.ꝑ. ; ᵇᵒ.
   —bel.—bry.g.—cth.γp.—
   cb-v.g.ω⁸.—crt.—grp.g.ʀ.
   —hpm.—hyo.—lam.g.ω⁸.
   —mer.—na-m.—scu.—
   sep.g.ʂ.—spi.ꝑ.—stn.—
   tab.Ⅰᵉ.—val.ʀʳ.ω⁸.
—— *running about.*—c-ar.Ⅰˢ.—
   iod.φ¹.—msc.—pru.
—— *after apathy.*—msc.uᵍ.
—— *wants to walk about continu-*
   ally.—ori.
—— *runs about the house.*—aco.ʀ.
   —cth.
—— *desire to run out of the house.*
   —all.—elp.
—— *driving him into open air.*—
   lah.ʀ.—pho.

—— *alternating with indifference.*
   —na-m.
qᵃ. **Restlessness of body.**—agaᵇ.—
   arnᵇ.ᵇᵒ.——ars.g.—iod.—lamᵇ.—
   sul.Ⅰ.o¹.2.
qᵇ. **Restlessness of mind, incon-**
   stancy.—agaᵃ.—am-c.fᵉ.—arnᵃ.ᵇᵒ.
   —ca-c.g.βε.—dro.43.—ign.—k-ca.
   —lah.—lamᵃ.—led.u.—lyc.ʂ.α¹bᵃ.
   —msc.ω².—nat.5.43.—stn.—sul.
qᶜ. **Inward restlessness.**—aga.—alo.
   ʂ.—aur.

CONCOMITANTS.

α¹bᵒ. *Forgetful.*—cld.ꝑᵉ.
α¹bᵃ. *Diminished intellectual powers.*
   —lycᵇ.ʂ.
αbʸ. *Obtuseness of senses.*—cha.g.
   γ.λ.
βa. *Vertigo.*—jat.ρ.χ¹.
βε. *Confusion of head.*—aps.—
   ca-cᵇ.g.
γp. *Heat of head.*—cth.
γw. *Movement of head.*—trn.ε.f.
 γ. *Headache.*—æth.g.λ.—ana.ʂ.
   χ¹.—ars.λ.v.— cha.g.α¹bʸ.—
   gn-c.19.—k-hy.—lah.ʀ.κ⁶.—
   mo-a.λ.—rut.χ².5.—vp-t.ʂᶠ.
δP². *Dilated pupils.*—nx-v.
ηp,hh. *Heat and sweat of face.*—
   mgt.ʀ.ω².
 η. *Unsteady, anxious look.*—alo.
κ³. *Thirst.*—ars.ʂ.
κ⁶. *Vomiting.*—lah.ʀ.γ.
 λ. *Bellyache.*—æth.g.γ.—ars.γ.v.
   —bov.g.χ¹.—cha.g.α¹bʸ.—
   mo-a.γ.
λ². *Rumbling in bowels.*—elc.g.
o¹. *Cough.*—sul.Ⅰ.2.
 π. *Constriction of chest.*—amb.
 π. *Pain in chest.*—k-bi.ʂ.
π¹. *Difficulty of breathing.*—asa.
   gᵐ.ω⁴.
 ρ. *Pain in heart.*—hfb.g.ω².
 ρ. *Ebullition in blood.*—ca-c.
 ρ. *Weak pulse.*—jat.βa.χ¹.
 ʀ. *Arms feel drawn asunder.*—
   nat.g.ʀ.
v¹w. *Movements of feet.*—trn.uᶜ.
 v. *Pains in knees.*—ars.γ.λ.
φ¹. *Sleeplessness.*—iod.

ϕ^2. *Frightful dreams.*—bap.f^b.

χ^1. *Chilliness.*——ana.k.γ.——asa. (8).—bov.g.λ.—jat.βa.ρ.

χ^2. *Heat.*—rut.γ.5.

ω^2. *Weakness.*—hfb.g.ρ.—mgt.r. ηp,hh.—msc^b.

ω^3. *Fainting.*—vp-r.

ω^4. *Ill-feeling.*—asa.g^m.π^1.

ω^8. *Trembling.*—cb-v.g. ; g^i.l.4.8. 122.—lam.—pso.g.b^a.—val. k^r.

CONDITIONS.

1. *By day.*—amb.—cb-v.
2. *At night.*—lah.—mer.—sul.l.o^1.
3. *In the morning.*—zin.g.
4. *In the afternoon.*—cb-v.g^i.l.ω^8. 8.122.—naj.
5. *In the evening.*—ca-c.—cb-v. —nat^b.43.—rut.γ.χ^2.
5. *In forenoon.*—hfb.
8. *In the open air.*—asa.—cb-v. g^i.l.ω^8.4.122.
8-31. *By walking in open air.*—grp. k^x.
16. *When lying.*—alm.19.—cth.19.
19. *When sitting.*—alm.16.—cth. 16.—gn-c.γ.
43. *When reading.*—dro^b.—nat^b.5.
82. *Before menses.*—kre.u^b.
121. *When alone.*—all.k.
122. *In society.*—cb-v.g^i.l.ω^8.4.8.

r. **Hurry** (*Collective*).—aco$^{a \cdot d}$.q.; ^{r}.— amb^e.—bz-x.b.—cam^d.—cn-i^a.—cap^b. q.—cb-a.q.—coc^h.q.—con.—grp.g.q. hyo.q.k^w. ; ^{h}.——ign$^{e \cdot f}$.g.α^1b$^{f \cdot h}$.41. ; α^1b^y.ηd.——k-ca$^{d \cdot e}$.—lah^c.q. ; q.γ.κ^8. —lau.—lil.—mgt.q.ηp,hh.ω^2.; r.; v. —mt-n. ; $\frac{x}{2}^c$.—mer^f.—nat.g.q.r. na-m.; g.—opi$^{d \cdot e}$.——ph-x^f.——pul. —sep^d.f^d.—str.—sul^b. ; q.1.— su-x^d.ω^2.—vi-t^d.g^n.ω^2.

r^a. **In movements.**—aco^d.q.—cn-i.

r^b. **In pace.**—str.—sul.

r^c. **In eating.**—lah.q.—pi-m.

r^d. **In occupation or work.**—aco. q.—aur^e.q.—cam.—k-ca^e.—opi^e. —pul.—sep.f^d.—su-x.ω^2.—vi-t.g^n. ω^2.

r^e. **In mental occupations.**—amb. —aur^d.q.—ign^f.g.α^1b$^{f \cdot h}$.41.—k-ca^d. —opi^d.

r^f. **In speech.**—aco.—ign^e.g.α^1b$^{f \cdot h}$. 41.—mer.—ph-x.

r^g. **In writing.**—ptl.α^1b^o.γ.

r^h. **Officiousness.**—cap.q.—coc.q.— hyo.

CONCOMITANTS.

α^1b$^{f \cdot h}$. *Mistakes in speaking and writing.*—ign$^{e \cdot f}$.g.41.

α^1b^o. *Forgetfulness.*—ptl^g.γ.

α^1b^y. *Obtuseness of senses.*—ign.ηd.

γ. *Headache.*—lah.g.κ^6.——ptl^g. α^1b^o.

ηd. *Blood mounts to face.*—ign. α^1b^y.

ηp,hh. *Heat and sweat of face.*— mgt.q.ω^2.

κ^8. *Vomiting.*—lah.g.γ.

r. *Pain in arm.*—mgt.—nat.g.q.

ω^2. *Weakness.*——mgt.q.ηp,hh.— su-x^d.—vi-t^d.g^n.

CONDITIONS.

1. *By day.*—sul.q.
41. *After mental exertion.*—ign$^{e \cdot f}$. α^1b$^{f \cdot h}$.

s. **Excitement.**—ac-x.——aco.k^w.— alo.q.; 2.; 3-99.——aln.q.—alm. k^a.u^{dd}.—amb.q.; g.γ.ϕ^1.χ^8.2.—am-c. —am-m.86.— ag-n.γi^a,p.—ars. bel.l.— c-ph.— cam.k^w.— cn-i.4.— cth.—cr-s.2.—ch-s.—cle.b^i.—cca. k^w.5.—cch.b^i.—cfn.αb^b.—fer.k.83. —for.—gas.—grn.o.—grp.r^{1}p.86. —gun.5.—hyo.ηa^h.—ind.k^t.—iod. b.u.; 4.—k-hy.—kis.k^w.—kre.u.p. —lab.——lil.l.α^1c^m.—lin.5.—lyc.q^b. α^1b^a.—mep.γp.—mrl.—m-cy.2.— mo-a.—nr-a.γ.—str.—trn.52.

—— *furious.*—eth.

—— *violent.*—eth.

—— *wild.*—clf.

—— *dances about, laughs, talks nonsense.*—cn-i.

—— *as from intoxication.*—cod. γv.—msc.ρ.

—— *as after drinking tea.*—hyp.

—— *as if hurried.*—cb-v.

—— *as from unpleasant news.*—aln.

—— *as precedes delirium.*—bap.

—— *excited fantasies.*—cfn.

—— *alternating with depression.*—agn.—ast.—pet.æ^w.ω^8.

—— *followed by stupefaction.*—eth.

—— *followed by perspiration.*—trn.52.

—— *by good news.*—alo.5.

—— *agreeable.*—cl-h.—gas.

CONCOMITANTS.

a^{1}b^a. *Diminished intellect.*—lyc.q^h.

γi^a. *Fulness of head.*—ag-n.γp.

γp. *Heat of head.*—ag-n.γi^a.—mep.

γ^v. *Itching of head.*—cod.

γ. *Headache.*——amb.g.φ^1.χ^3.2.—nr-a.

ηa^h. *Wild look.*—hyo.

ρ. *Quick pulse.*—msc.

r^{1}p. *Hot hands.*—grp.86.

φ^1. *Sleeplessness.*—amb.g.γ.χ^3.2.

χ^3. *Sweat.*—amb.g.γ.φ^1.2.

ω^8. *Trembling.*—pet.æ^w.

CONDITIONS.

2. *At night.*——alo.——amb.g.γ.φ^1.χ^3.—cr-s.—m-cy.

4. *In afternoon.*—cn-i.—iod.

3-99. *On rising in morning.*—alo.

5. *In the evening.*—alo.—cca.æ^w.—gun.—lin.

52. *By music.*——trn.

83. *During menses.*—fer.k.

86. *By talking.*—am-m.—grp.r^{1}p.

t. **Variable humour** (*Collective*).—aco^a. ; ^{c}.; ^{d}.; ^{j}.—alo^p.66.; ^{w}. ; ^{x}.—alm. ; ^{k}.—amb^b.—ana^f.—ag-n^v.—ars^o. ; ^{f}.; ^{t}.—asa^o.—asr^a.—ast^b.—aur^c.5.; ^{q}.—bel^a. ; ^{y}.—bor^c.—bov.—ca-c^x.;^{f}.—can.—cap^c.—cb-a^a.—car.—cau^q. ; ^{a}.—chi.^{a}.b^t.—cle^a.—cca.—cro^u.ω^7.5. ; ^{q}. ; ^{a}. ; ^{t}. ; ^{r}.5.—cup^1.—cyc^q.; ^{aa}.—der^d.a^{1}a^d.—fer^a.—fl-x^a.—for^a.—gel^a.—hyo^a.—ign^a.; ^{1}.—iod^a.—irs$^{ff.gg}$.—k-br^d.—

k-ca$^{a.i}$.—lap^a.—lyc^c.; ^{a}.; ^{bb}.—mt-n^a. ; ^{h}.—mr-c^x.—mr-f^a. ; ^{ii}—nat^a.—na-m^1.rv.—na-s^q.—ni-x^a.—nx-m.; ^{a}.; ^{c}.; ^{cc}.—nx-v$^{c.g}$.—opi^x.—ori^{hh}.—pho^o.—pso^a. ; $^{a.m}$.—sar.—snc^b.—sep^a. ; ^{c}.—spi^a.—spo^q.—stp^{dd}.—str^c.—sul^c.—trn^a.; ^{f}.π.ω^9.; ^{q}.—tar^q.—zin^a.; ^{n}.—ziz^a.; ^{c}.

t^a. **Alternately gay and sad.**—aco.—asr.—ca-s.—cb-a.—cau.—chi.b^t.—cle.—cro.—fer.—fl-x.—for.—gel.—ign.—iod.—lap.—lyc.—mt-n.—mr-f.—nat.—ni-x.—nx-m.—pso.; ^{m}.—sep.—spi.—trn.—zin.—ziz.

t^b. **Alternately excited and sad.**—amb.—ast.—snc.

t^c. **Alternately weeping and laughing.**—aco.—aur.5.—bor.—cap.—lyc.—nx-m.—nx-v^g.—sep.—str.—sul.—ziz.

t^d. **Alternately weeping and singing.**—aco.—der.a^{1}a^d.—k-br.

t^e. **Alternately groaning and dancing.**—bel.

t^f. **Alternately cheerful and anxious.**—ana.—ars.—ca-c.

t^g. **Alternately anxious and indifferent.**—nx-v^c.

t^h. **Alternately good-humoured and cowardly.**—mt-n.

t^i. **Alternately fearful and hopeful.**—k-ca^a.

t^j. **Alternately despairing and hopeful.**—aco.

t^k. **Alternately confident and irresolute.**—alm.

t^l. **Alternately good- and bad-humoured.**—cup.—hfb.—ign.—na-m.rv.—pso.—trn.π.ω^9.

t^m. **Alternately depressed and irritable.**—pso^a.

t^n. **Alternately irritable and timid.**—zin.

t^o. **Alternately irritable and indifferent.**—ars.—asa.—pho.

t^p. **Alternately unsympathetic and jocular.**—alo.66.

t^q. **Alternately happy and peevish.**—aur.—cau.—cro.—cyc.—na-s.—spo.—trn.—tar.

t[r]. **Alternately passionate and repentant.**—cro.5.

t[s]. **Alternately composed and passionate.**—hyo.—k-ca[i].

t[t]. **Alternately friendly and ill-humoured.**—ars.—cro.

t[u]. **Alternately tender, extravagant, and angry.**—cro.ω[7].5.

t[v]. **Alternately thoughtful and frivolous.**—ag-n.

t[w]. **Alternately prostrated and mentally active.**—alo.

t[x]. **Alternately apathetic and good-humoured.**—alo.—opi.

t[y]. **Alternately weeping and cross.**—bel.

t[z]. **Alternately cross and humourous.**—ca-c.—hyo.—mr-c.

t[aa]. **Alternately inclined and disinclined for work.**—cyc.

t[bb]. **Alternately anxious, laughing, and weeping.**—lyc.

t[cc]. **Alternately grave and jocular.**—nx-m.

t[dd]. **Alternately cheerful, anxious, and contented.**—stp.

t[ee]. **Alternately gay and angry.**—cr-s.

t[ff]. **Alternately desponding and laughing.**—irs.

t[gg]. **Alternately displeased and lively.**—irs.

t[hh]. **Morose and weak one day, lively the next.**—ori.

t[ii]. **Cheerful in open air, depressed in room.**—mr-f.

CONCOMITANTS.

π. *Stitches in false ribs.*—trn[l].ω[9].

$\tau\upsilon$. *Lightness of limbs.*—na-m[l].

ω[7]. *Spasms.*—cro[u].5.

ω[9]. *Yawning.*—trn[l].π.

CONDITIONS.

5. *In the evening.*—aur[c].—cro[u].ω[7].; [r].

66. *After dinner.*—alo[p].

u. Ill-humour (*Peculiar*).

cin. He rejects everything offered him, even such things as he used to be fondest of. Will not be quieted by any persuasion; deaf to endearments.

con. The propinquity and conversation of passers-by is very disagreeable to him, he is disposed to assault and maltreat them.

cro. Reproaches uttered against her make her very cross; she wishes to justify herself, but the word dies on her lips; she is vexed at remaining silent and tries again to speak, but her tongue refuses its office.

fl-x. Tendency when alone to imagine all sorts of things that might happen, such as repulsion to persons he is intimately connected with, as all servants must be dismissed, children turned out of doors, betrothal broken off, marriage dissolved, &c.

Feels hatred towards persons when they are absent, which goes off when they are present.

lah. Impetuous, he demands definite answers, when it is not at all suitable.

man. Ill-humoured, the gayest music does not cheer him, but he is revived by the saddest.

pla. At variance with all the world, everything seems too narrow for her, with lachrymose disposition.

sar. Excessively cross, the flies on the wall annoy her.

ver. He searches for faults in others and taunts them with them. He cannot bear to be spoken to.

u. Ill-humour, peevishness, crossness, fretfulness —aco.&.—alo.—alm.—am-c.—am-m.♭.—ana.&.—ant.—arn.&.—ars.—as-t.—asp.g.—aur.—ba-a.&.—bel.—bor.—bov.—bry.♭.—ca-c.&.—c-ph.♭[o].—cb-v.—cau.—cha.—chd.—chi.—ch-s.—cof.—cch.—col.—con.—crn.&.—dio.—ele.—evo.—fl-x.—

grp.—hpm.—hyo.k.—ipc.—k-ca.
—lah.—lyc.k.—mt-s.—mag.—
mg-m.k.—man.—mer.—msc.—
mu-x.—nat.—na-m.—ni-x.k.—
nit.k.—nx-v.—ol-m.—pet.—ph-x.
—pho.—pla.ḫ.—pul.—rn-b.—rho.
—rum.—rut.—sar.—sep.g. ; ḫ.—
sin.—spi.k.—stn.—stp.—sul.—
su-x.k.—tab.—ver.—vi-t.—zin.
&c.

—— *with her children.*—irs.
—— *as if had not slept enough.*—
    mg-m.
—— *as if had no life.*—aco.
—— *after good humour.*—na-s.
—— *after gaiety.*—cau.b^c.k^o.—
    cle$^{b \cdot y}$.b^o.g.k.ψ.χ^3.—lyc^{ff}.
    opi.—ol-a.—tar.g^e.5.
—— *followed by apathy.*—pho$^{b \cdot e \cdot g}$.
—— *followed by gaiety.*—mrl.a.k.
    ω^2.—pla.k.
—— *followed by liveliness and*
    jocularity.—coc^y.

u^a. **Sulkiness, surliness, unaccom-**
modating, sternness.—æsc$^{b \cdot c}$.—
aga$^{b \cdot c}$.—alm.—am-c.g.—atr.$^{c \cdot cc}$.—
aur.k^o.—bry.—cnb.4.—cle. ; ^{d}.99. ;
b^t.—fer.b$^{i \cdot o}$.—lah$^{c \cdot e}$.g.q.π.ω.—man^t.
—mns.—men.—mr-f.—mu-x.b^o.
5.—plc.b$^{c \cdot o}$.α^1b.—sin.—su-x^{ff}.—
tea^{cc}.b^c.

u^b. **Irritability.**—ab-c.a.—ac-x.ω^8.—
æsc$^{a \cdot c}$.—aga. ; ^{c}.—aloe^{ee}.—amb.ω^8.
86.—am-m.5.(66).—ag-n.ḫ.$\omega^{2 \cdot 8}$.
3-99.—arn^{cc}.—ars^w.tu.—at-a^e.—
aru.—aur.—ba-a.—bel.θj.—b-la.
—bov.k.βe. ; ^{w}.—bry.ḫ.—buf.k. ; ^{ff}.
—cac.—cad.—ca-c.I.o. ; g. ; k.ω^2.
3.34. ; ^{c}.3.73.—c-ph.o. ; ^{e}.b^c.—ca-s.
4.—cth^c.5. ; ḫ.k^j.ϕ.—cb-v. ; α^1b^s. ;
o. ; βe. ; ^{e}.5. ; ^{c}.—cr-s.k.—car^c.χ^2.
—cas.b^c.83.—cau.v.40.—cer.—
cha.—chd.k^j.—clo^c.—cl-h.—cic.
g^e.—cnb.—cle^y.b^o.g.k.χ^3.ψv.—
cca.—coc^y.—ccs.—cch.—crt.—
c-ar.χ.—dph.ω^8.—dig.k.—dgn.k.
—dor.—elp^c.—equ.ω^2.—epn.—
eup.—fag.—fel.—gel^{ff}.—grp^e.3.k.
4. ; q.—grt^c.g^{ba}.m.—hln.—hep^{cc}.e.
—hur.—hy-x.b^i.—hfb.γ.—irs.

k-bi.—k-ca.—k-hy.—klm.3.5.—
kre.q.82.—lau.b^i.—lpt.k.—lil.3-99.
—lin.—lip.—lyc.ḫ. ; k. ; ^{e}. ; a^b. ; 5.
—mt-n.—mg-m.82.—mg-s^{dd}.o.—
mns.—mer^c. ; $_i$ ^{1}.í.—mu-x$^{c \cdot y}$.—nab.
5.—nat.—na-a.—na-m.r.v. ; ^{c}.k.—
na-p.—nx-m.—nx-v. ; $^{e \cdot i}$.—opi.—
ped^c.—ph-x.k.ω^2.—pho$^{e \cdot g}$. ; ḫ^r. ; ω^8.
—phy.k.—pl-n.—plg.5.—pol.k^t.—
ptl.—rs-r.—rum.—sil.g^w.—sin.—
so-a^{ff}.—so-o^{ff}.—so-t^y.—spi.—spg^g.
—stn.ηp.—str.ḫ. ; γ.—sul. ; b^c. ;
^{c}.k^o.—su-x.k.—trn^y. ; $^{c \cdot x}$.—tep.I. ;
^{d}.86. ; ḫ^o.—teu.γ.66.86.—tri.—
vi-t.ḫ^c.—xan.—zin.ḫ. ; k.p.86. ; ḫ.3.
(5).—ziz.a^a.k.

—— *after indifference.*—pho.
—— *after sleep.*—ch-s.
—— *about trifles.*—dgn.
—— *towards his children.*—k-hy.
—— *cannot bear to be spoken to.*—
    na-s.3.
—— *desire to run away.*—mez.

u^c. **Irascibility, anger, quarrel-**
someness.—aco. ; α^1c^e.—æsc$^{a \cdot b}$.—
aga^b.—alm.k^j.4.—amb.k^j.—am-c. ;
g.5.—ana^q.—ang^y.—aps$^{e \cdot w \cdot cc}$.—
arn.—ars.—atr$^{a \cdot cc}$.—aur. ; ^{d} ; ^{e} ; g.
—ba-c.—bel. ; g^w.—ber.41.—bry. ;
k^j.—buf.—ca-c^b.3.73. ; ^{z}.—ca-s.—
cam.p^a.—can.—cth^i. ; ^{cc}.k^j. ; ^{b}.5.—
cap. ; g$^{f \cdot w}$.—cb-a^i.—car.3.99. ; ^{b}.χ^2.
—cau.o.χ^1. ; 100. ; $^{o \cdot p}$; p.—ce-s.—
cha^p. ; ^{x} ; δP^3.86.99. ; ^{1}.83.—chd.—
chi^i. ; ^{e} ; ^{y}.I^k. ; ^{p} ; ^{dd}.o.—cnb.—clo^b.
—cch.—con.—cop.γd,p.ω^8.—cyc^w.
—dig.k.—dul.—elp^b.—epn.—
f-mg.—for.—gam.3.99.—grn.—
grp.—grt^b.g^{ba}.m.—hel.—hpm. ; ^{cc}.
4. ; χ^2.5. ; ω^2.—hur^{ff}.α^1b^s.—hyo.—
ign.—idm.—iod.—ipe. ; k.—k-ca.
—k-hy.—lah. ; $^{a \cdot e}$.g.q.π.ω.—la-v.—
led.—lep^{dd}.k.—lyc^o.tu.p.—mgt.γ.
—mt-s.8-31.—mg-s.—mrl. ; g.—
mer^b.—mez.—msc$^{e \cdot i}$.—mu-x$^{b \cdot y}$.—
nat. ; g^w. ; $^{e \cdot l}$.—na-m^b.k. ; 5.a.b^c.5. ;
^{i} ; ^{y}.—nic$^{e \cdot i}$.5. ; $^{l \cdot ff}$.(5).—ni-x.ω^8. ;
^{e} ; ^{k}.—nx-v.—ped^b.—pet.3. ; k.3-
99. ; k^j. ; χ^2.—phl.—ph-x^y. ; χ^2.—
pho. ; g.ḫ.k^j. ; g.—pla^e. ; $^{y \cdot ee}$.b^c.—

pot.—pul.—rn-b^g.; 5$^{w.dd}$.g.b^q.5.—
rat.—rut.—sbd.k.—sng.k.; x^w.;
sep.; x^w.; ^{bb}g.ρ^l.χ^8.—sil 5.—so-m.
—so-t^l.; $^{e.f}$.—stn^y.b^c.; ^{d}.; ^{e}.—stp.
x^w.—str.x^w.—sto.; ^{e}.—sul.; $^{w.y}$.
^{b}.k^o.—su-x.b^c.—trn$^{b.x}$.—tep.x^w.
—thu.—til.—ver^y.—vin.—vi-t.

—— *soon followed by repentance.*
—vin.

u^d. **Furious rage.**—ars.; 66.—aur^c.
g; ω^8.—ba-a^e.—cld.—ce-s.—chd^y.;
g.—cle^a.99.—cch.11.40.54.111.—
cro.—dro.—fl-x.—hep^e.—hfb.—
hyo^e.; $^{e.g}$.—lah.—lyc^x.—mt-s^e.ω^8.
—mez.—msc.ηc^b.—nat.—ni-x^h.k^f.
—nx-v.—oln.—opi.—pho^i.—sbd.
—sep.γd.δo.—so-n.—stn^c.—str.—
trn.α^{1}b^s.

—— *in thought.*—fl-x.
—— *paroxysms of convulsive rage.*
—bel.
—— *alternating with convulsions.*
—str.

u^e. **Violence, disposed to fight,
thrash, or kill some one, or
smash things.**—œsc.—aps$^{c.w.cc}$.—
at-a^b.—aur^c.—bel.—ba-a^d.—bor^w.;
g.h.—c-ph^c.b^c.—cb-v^b.5.—cr-s.—
chd.ω^8.—chic.—cof.—com^k.—der^g.
—elp.—fer^q.—grp^b.3.k.4.—hep^d.
—hpm.—hur^{ff}.—hdr^i.—bfb.—
hyo.; ^{d}; $^{d.g}$.—k-ca.—lah$^{a.c}$.g.q.π.ω.
—lil.—lyc^b.—mt-s^d.ω^8.; ^{k}.ηf^c.—
mr-f.—msc$^{c.i}$.—nat$^{c.1}$.—ni-x^c.—
nx-v$^{b.i}$.—pho$^{b.g}$.—pla^c.—so-t$^{c.f}$.—
stn^c.—sto^c.—sul.

u^f. **Disposed to injure himself.**—
nat^{dd}.g^e.—so-t$^{c.e}$.—str.

u^g. **Scolding, abuse.**—alo^x.4.—am-c^c.
5.—aur^c.; ^{d}.—bor$^{e.h}$.—cth.—cap^v.
I^k.—cor^b.—der^e.—ele.—hfb.—
hyo.; $^{d.e}$.—klm^b.—msc.δc^d.ηc^b.θj.
ω^8.—nx-v.; I.; ^{w}.—pho$^{b.e}$.—sng.a.
—sep.—spg^b.—str.—ver.

u^h. **Oaths, curses.**—bel.—bor$^{e.g}$.—
ce-s.—cor^g.—lil.5.—ni-x^d.k^f.

u^i. **Spite, malice.**—ars^j.—cth^c.—
cb-a^c.—chic.—ele.—hdr^c.; ^{i}.—
k-hy^c.—msc$^{c.e}$.—na-m^c.—nic$^{c.e}$.5.
—nx-v$^{b.e}$.—par^k.—pet.—pho^d.

u^j. **Scoffing, sarcastic.**—ars^i.—cn-i.

u^k. **Scorn, contemptuous laughter.**
—alm.—cic^{ee}.c.—com.x^g.; ^{e}.—
gui.—ipe.; b^c.—mt-s^e.ηf^c.—ni-x^c.
—par^i.

u^l. **Intolerance of contradiction,
captiousness, fault-finding.**—arn.
—ars.c$^{h.j}$.p.—c-ph.—cn-i.—cha^c.
83.—cop.—grn.—hln.—hdr.—
ign.I^k.—irs^b.—k-cy.—lyc^y.—mer^b.
i.—nat$^{c.e}$.—nic$^{c.ff}$.(5).—nup.—
nx-v.—oln.—so-t^c.—str.—ver.

—— *intolerant of small children.*
—k-ca.

u^m. **Haughtiness.**—ard.—dro.
u^n. **Imperiousness, rudeness.**—au-s.
u^o. **Blustering, insolence.**—arn.; ^{p}.—
cau$^{c.p}$.—eug.x^g.—lyc^c.w.p.—mer.i.
u^p. **Grumbling.**—alm.—arn^o.—bis.
I^i.—bry.—ca-a.a^e.—c-cs.ω^2.—cln.
f^b.χ^1.—cth.—cau.5.; $^{c.o}$.—cha^{cc}.; ^{c}.
—chic.

u^q. **Disputatiousness.**—ana^c.—fer^e.
—lyc.

u^r. **Wildness.**—opi^s.—pet.
u^s. **Cruelty.**—at-a.—opi^r.
u^t. **Resentment.**—ber.z.—man^a.—
ni-x.

u^u. **Revenge.**—lah.100.
u^v. **Easily offended, disposed to
imagine insults.**—ana.—aur^y.—
cth.—cap.; ^{g}.I^k.—cha.—chi^{dd}.—
coc.o.—fer.—hfb.—hyo.I^k.—k-fc^b.
—sar.—sul.

u^w. **Takes jokes, &c., in bad part.**—
aco.—am-c.—ang^{dd}.k.—aps$^{c.e.cc}$.
—ars^b.w.—bor^e.—bov^b.—cb-a.—
coc^y.—cyc^c.—na-m.—nx-v^g.—
pul.; b^c.5.—sab.—sil.I^l.—spi.k$^{n.o}$.
—sul$^{c.y}$.—thu.

u^x. **Angry with himself.**—alo^g.4.—
ars^{dd}.—bel.—c-ph.—cau.g.k.—
cha^c.—cnb.—coc.—lyc^d.—ni-x.k.
—pul.—sul.—trn$^{b.c}$.

u^y. **Easily vexed.**—aco.—ang^c.; g.
χ$^{s.s}$.—arn.—ars.; ^{d}.—aur^v.—au-s.
—bel.I.—cha^c.—chd^d.—chic.I^k.—
cle^b.b^o.g.k.χ^8.ψv.—coc^w.; I.δP^1.
κ^1.; ^{b}.—con.—fl-x.—grp.—hep.—
ipe.—irs.—k-ca.; p.3.5.—k-fc.—
lau.—lyc^l.—mag.(5).—mu-x$^{b.c}$.—

na-m^c.—na-p.—nit.—opi.—phl.η.
—ph-x^c.—pla$^{c\cdot ee}$.b^c.—rhs^{ff}.—sep.
—sil.—so-t^b.—spi.—spg.—spr.
stn^c.b^c.—stp.b^c. ; l.86.—tan.—tea.
ω^2.—ver^c.—zin.

u^x. **Vexatious thoughts.**——am-m.
a^{1}b^s.3.—ca-c^c.—cof.k^a.l^h.(8).—con.
—ign.—k-ca.3.99.—mez.—pho.

u^{aa}. **Disposed to seek for vexatious things.**—pho.

u^{bb}.—**Raking up old grievances.**—
cha.—cop.—for.—glo.—lyc.2.99.
—na-m.k^x.—sep^c.g.ρ^1.χ^3.

u^{cc}. **Displeased with everything.**—
am-c.—aps$^{c\cdot e\cdot w}$.—arn^b.—atr$^{a\cdot c}$.—
bis.q.—can.a^a.—cha^p.—cof.b^c.—
cch.—eug.—eu-a.(66).—grt.
hep^b.ℓ.—hpm.; ^{c}.4.—ign^{dd}.5.—iod.
—nat.—pul.—sam.—sep.—spo.
—sul.—tea^a.b^c.

u^{dd}. **Discontent.**——alo.f^b.$\beta\ell$. ; b^o.k.
$\beta\ell$.4.(5).—alm.k^f.—ang^w.k.—ars^x.
—aur.—bry.k^s.—chi^c. ; ^{v}.—con.—
fer.a^{1}b^b.—fl-x.λ.—ham.—hpm.3.
—ign^{cc}.5.—led^{ee}.—lep^c.k.—men.
b.k^s.q.—mer.k^s.—nat^f.g^e.—ni-x.a^m.
—nit.b^i.—nx-j.5.—pho.—pla.—
plb.3.99.—pul.l 3.99.—rs-r.k ϕ.—
rut.k^j.—sep.—sil.—spo.b^c.—stn.
—thu.

u^{ee}. **Unfriendliness, aversion to persons, misanthropy.**——aco.—alo^b.
—aur.—ca-c.—cick.ℓ. ; a^n.—cop.
—crt.a.k.γ.μ^2.ρ.ω^2.—fl-x.—hyd.—
led^{dd}.—lyc. ; g^m.—nat.—na-m.—
pho.—pla$^{c\cdot y}$.b^c.—sel.b^o.—stn.
sul.b^c.tu.—tep.b^o.ℓ.q.

u^{ff}. **Impatience.**—all.—amb.—amp.
—ars.g.—buf^b.—ca-c.k^f.—cb-v.;
k^f.u^c.—col.—dul.l.a^1ℓ.3.—gel^b.—
gin.—ham.a.—hep.—hur.s.5.; ^{c}.
a^{1}b^s. ; ^{e}.—hfb.γ.—hyo.—ipc.—
k-cy.—lil^b.—lyc. ; 3-99.—nic$^{c\cdot l}$.
(5).—ni-x.4.—plg.q.$\beta\ell^a$.—rs-r.k.
—rhs^y.—sil.q.—so-a^b.—so-o^b.—
spi.g^e.—sul.—su-x^a.—trn.b^o.—
wis.k^f.b.—zin. ; 86. ; γ.

u^{gg}. **Effects of vexation.**—rhs.ξ^3.

u^{hh}. **Deceitful.**—cl-h.a^{1}b.

CONCOMITANTS.

a^{1}a^b. *Sunk in thought.*—am-m.b^c.5.
—man.f^a.—stp.—sto.b^c.

a^{1}b. *Absence of mind.*—alm.a.

a^{1}b^b. *Distraction.*—plc^a.b$^{c\cdot o}$.

a^{1}b^f. *Mistakes in speaking.*—man.b^c.
g^c.k^s.

a^{1}b^o. *Forgetfulness.*—mag.

a^{1}b^p. *Weak memory.*—so-l.

a^{1}b^s. *Slow thinking power.*—hur$^{c\cdot ff}$.

a^{1}b^s. *Weakness of intellect.*—bry.—
cb-v^b.—chi.—stn.a^b.ηc^b.

a^{1}b^s. *Absence of ideas.*—trn^d.

a^{1}b^s. *Stupidity.*—am-m^x.3.—chi.

a^{1}b^y. *Obtuseness of senses.*—oln.b^e.

a^1ℓ^c. *Raving.*—aco^c.

a^1ℓ^m. *Hallucinations.*—dul^{ff}.l.

βa. *Giddiness.*—ca-c.ϕ^1.5.—hpm.γ.

$\beta\ell$. *Confusion of head.*—alo^{dd}.f^b. ;
b^o.k.4.(5).—bov^b.k. ; $\natural$.
cb-v^b.—con.g.3.66.—cyc.κ.
99.—sar.5.

$\beta\ell^a$. *Stupid feeling.*——na-s.3-99.
(66).—plg^{ff}.q.

γd. *Congestion of head.*—cop^c.γp.ω^8.

γd. *Feeling as if would have a fit
of apoplexy.*—sep^d.δo.

γp. *Heat of head.*——æth.b^c.k^n.(4).
—cop^c.γd.ω^8.

γq. *Heaviness of head.*—k-hy.66.
—sar.3.

γ. *Headache.*——am-c.5. ; κ^4l.—
bel.l^a.— bov.4.—bry.—ca-a.
b^c.6.(8).—cha.l^a.μ^1.—crt^{ee}.a.
k.μ^2.ρ.ω^2.— hln^b.—hpm.βa.—
hfb^b.; ^{ff}.—ign.—mgt^c.—mnc^{ff}.
—spo.k^x.κ^1.ϕ.ω^2.—str^b.—teu^b.
66.86.—zin.l^a. ; ^{ff}.

$\delta\ell^d$. *Fixed eyes.*—msc^g.ηc^b.θj.ω^8.

δP^1. *Contracted pupils.*—coc^y.l.κ^1.

δP^3. *Insensible pupils.*—cha^c.86.99.

δo. *Blackness before eyes.*——sep^d.
γd.

η. *Wrinkled forehead.*——man^c.3.
86.

ηc^b. *Pale face.*—mez.—stn.a^b.a^{1}b^s.

ηc^b. *Pale face, blue lips.*—msc^g.$\delta\ell^d$.
θj.ω^8.

ηf^c. *Distorted features.*—mt-s$^{e\cdot k}$.

η. *Cross face.*—phl^y.

ηp. *Hot face.*—pho.$\kappa^{1\cdot4\cdot5}$; $\rho^{l}.r^{l}$b. —sar.ḃ°.—stn^b.

ηaa. *Red face.*—spi.ḳ.

θ. *Puts hands in mouth.*—trn.ɛ. $\kappa^{3\cdot4}.\pi.v.$

θj. *Dry mouth.*—bel^b.—msc^g.δc^d. ηc^b.ω^3.

θ^l. *Toothache.*—mr-i.

θ^2. *Spitting.*—ca-c.

κ. *Bad taste.*—cyc.βɛ.99.—mr-i. 3-99.

κ^l. *Anorexia.*—coc^y.I.δ.P^l.—pho. ηp.$\kappa^{4\cdot5}$.—spo.ḳ^x.γ.φ.ω^2.

κ^2. *Hunger.*—lyc.5.

κ^3. *Thirst.*—trn.ɛ.θ.κ^4.π.v.

κ^4. *Pain in stomach.*—am-c.γ.1.— pho.ηp.$\kappa^{1\cdot5}$.—trn.ɛ.θ.κ^3.π.v.

κ^5. *Nausea.*—pho.ηp.$\kappa^{1\cdot4}$.

κ^8. *Hiccough.*—agn.

λ. *Discomfort in abdomen.*—fl-x^{dd}.

λ. *Pain in abdomen.*—-alo.ḣ^n.— ber.m.83.—frz.

λ. *Bearing down in hypogastrium.* —pla.ξ^3.

λi. *Flatulent distension.*—alo.

μ^l. *Constipation.*—cha.I^a.γ.

μ^2. *Diarrhœa.*—crt^{ee}.a.ḳ.γ.ρ.ω^2.

ξ^2. *Hysterical.*—trn.

ξ^3. *Profuse menses.*—pla.λ.

ξ^3. *Clots of blood passed.*—rhs^{gg}.

π. *Pressure on chest.*-lah$^{a\cdot c\cdot e}$.g.q.ω.

π. *Tightness of chest.*—cha.

π. *Pain in chest.*—trn.ɛ.θ.$\kappa^{3\cdot4}$.v.

π^l. *Quick breathing.*—ver.g.ρ^l.

ρ. *Heartache.*—crt^{ee}.a.ḳ.γ.μ^2.ω^2.

ρ^l. *Palpitation.*— asp.g.—pho.ηp. r^{l}b.—sep$^{c\cdot bb}$.g.χ^3.—ver.g.π^l.

σ. *Backache.*—alo.5.

τ. *Stretching arms.*—sel.b.

τv. *Torpidity of limbs.*—na-m^b.

τ^lb. *Cold hands.*—pho.ηp.ρ^l.

v. *Desire to move legs.*—trn.ɛ.θ. $\kappa^{\cdot3\cdot4}.\pi.$

v. *Weakness of knees.*—cau^b.40.

φ. *Sleepiness.*— ca-c.βa.5.—cln.— cth^b.ḃ.ṡ^j.—lch.o.—rs-r^{dd}.ḳ.— spo.ḳ^x.γ.κ^l.ω^2.

χ. *Feverish.*—c-ar^b.

χ^l. *Chilliness.*—cln^p.f^b.—cau^c.o.

χ^2. *Heat.*—ang^y.g.χ^3.—-car$^{b\cdot c}$.— hpm^c.5.—pet^c.—ph-x^c.

χ^8. *Sweat.*—ang^y.g.χ^2.—-c-ph^c.— cle$^{b\cdot y}$.ḃ°.ψv.—mag.—sep$^{c\cdot bb}$.g. ρ^l.

ψv. *Itching of skin.*—cle$^{b\cdot y}$.ḃ°.χ^8.

ω. *Ebullition.*—lah$^{a\cdot c\cdot e}$.g.q.π.

ω. *Obtuseness of whole body.*— gn-l.

ω. *Feels as if taking cold.*—sab.

ω^2. *Weakness.*— aps.—ag-n^b.ḣ.ω^8. 3-99.—ca-c^b.ḳ.3.34.—c-cs^p.— cau.83.—crt. ; ^{ee}.a.ḳ.γ.μ^2.ρ.— equ^b.—grt.4.—hpm^c.—kis. m.—mt-n.— mrl.a.ḳ.—ph-x^b. ḳ.— pho.—spo.ḳ^x.γ.κ^l.φ.

ω^3. *Fainting.*—msc^g.δc^d.ηc^{b}θj.

ω^8. *Trembling.*— amb^b.86.—ag-n^b. ḣ.ω^2.3-99.—aur^d.—chd^e.— cop^c.γd,p.—dph^b.—mt-s$^{d\cdot e}$.— ni-x^c.—pho^b.—sep^c.

CONDITIONS.

1. *All day.*—am-c.γ.κ^4.

2-99. *On waking at night.*—lyc^{bb}.

3. *In the morning.*—am-c.— am-m^x.3.—ars.—ca-c^b.ḳ.ω^2. 34. ; $^{b\cdot c}$.73.—clo.—cca.111.— cou.g βɛ.66.— grp$^{b\cdot e}$.ḳ.4.— hpm. ; ^{dd}.—k-ca^y.p.5.—klm^b. 5.—kre.I.—lyc.—man^c.η.86. —mr-i.—na-s$^{b\cdot c}$.(4). ; ḃ^c.— pet^c. ; sar.γq.—sep.—stp.— zin^b.ḣ.(5). ; ḳ.

3-99. *On rising or waking in morn-ing.*—-ag-n^b.ḣ.ω$^{2\cdot8}$.—bov.— cb-a.—car$^{b\cdot e}$.—gam^c.—irs^b. —k-ca^x.—lil^b.—lyc^{ff}.—mg-m. -— mr-i.κ.—na-s.βɛ^a.(66).— ni-x.f.—pet^c.ḳ.—plb^{dd}.—pul^{dd}. I.—sul.—su-x.

4. *In the afternoon.*—æth. ; æth. ḃ^c.ḳ^n.γp.—alo$^{g\cdot x}$. ; ^{dd}.ḃ°.ḳ.βɛ. (5).— alm^c.ḳ^j.—bor.I^k.—bov. γ.—ca-s^b.—can.—cnb^a.—grt. ω^2.—hpm$^{c\cdot cc}$.—hy-x.—*mag.*— 5.83.—mg-s.ḃ^c.—mr-c.— na-s$^{b\cdot c}$.3.—pho.—plb.ḃ°.— sar.βɛ.5.—zin.

5. *In the forenoon.*—am-c.γ.— am-m^b.(66).—cb-v$^{b\cdot e}$.—cau^p.— hur^{ff}.ṡ.—mag.83.(4).—na-p. —rn-b$^{c\cdot w\cdot dd}$.g.ḣ4.5.—sar.4.βɛ.

5. *In the evening.*—sesc.—alo^{dd}. b^o.k.4.; alo.σ.—am-c^{c·g}.; *am-c.* (66).—am-m.b^c.a¹a^b.—*bis*.b^c. —ca-c.—cth^{b·c}.—for.b.ḥ.— hpm^c.χ².—ign^{cc·dd}.—k-ca^y.p. 3.—klm^b.3.—lil^h.—lyc.κ². —mt-s.100.—*mag*^y.; mag.; b^e. —mg-m.k.—mu-x^a.b^o.—nab^b. —na-m^c.a.b^c.5.—nic^{c·e·i}; *nic*^c. ^{l·ff}.—nx-j^{dd}.—plg^b.—pul^w.b^c. —rn-b^c.5.^{w·dd}.g.ḅq.—sil^c.— tar.g^e.—*vrb.*—*vi-t.*—*zin*^b.ḥ. 3.; x^v.

6. *In the room.*—ca-a.b^c.γ. (8).

8. *In the open air.*—*ca-a.*b^c.γ.6. —*cof*^x.k^a.l^h.—mt-s.k^j.—*stn.*

8-31. *By walking in open air.*— mt-s^c.

11. *When touched.*—cch^d.40.54. 111.

31. *When walking.*—aco.b^e.k.

34. *By exertion.*—ca-c^b.k ω².3.

40. *By rudeness.*—cch^d.11.54.111.

41. *By mental labour.*—ber^c.— bor.

54. *By strong odours.*—cch^d.11. 40.111.

66. *By eating.*—am-c.(5).—am-m^b. 5.—ars^d.— cha.—con.g.βε.3. —*eu-a*^{cc}.—k-hy.γq.—*na-s.* βε^a.3-99.—teu^b.γ.86.

73. *Before stool.*—ca-c^{b·c}.3.

82. *Before menses.*—kre^b.q.—lyc. k.—mg-m^b.

83. *During menses.*—ber.m.λ.— cas^b.b^c.—cau.ω².—cha^{c·l}.— mag.; 5(4).

84. *After menses.*—fer.

86. *By speaking.*—amb^b.ω⁸.—cha^c. δP³.99.—man^c.η.3.— na-m.— stp^y.l.—tep^{b·d}.—teu^b.γ.66.— zin^b.k.p. ; ^{ff}.

98. *In sleep.*—lah^u.

99. *On awaking.*—css.—cha^c.δP³. 86.—cle^{a·d}.; f^b.g^g.—cyc.βε.κ. —jan.

100. *After a siesta.*—cau^c.—mt-s.5.

100. *In dreams.*—lah^u.

102. *By cold.*—alo^{dd}.110.

110. *By rain or bad weather.*— alo^{dd}.102.—am-c.

111. *By bright light.*—cca.3.— cch^d.11.40.54.

b. **Irresolution, slow resolution.**— alm.a¹b.—ars^d.—ba-a^c. ; f.—bry. ḥ.—bu-s^c.— cac.—canⁱ.a¹a^d.—cth^g. —cha.g.u^{cc}.ηp.r¹hh. ; J.—chi.— cca.í.uⁱ.—coh.—cof^g.g.—cup.u^{dd}. —dph.q.—f-mg^c.—grp.a¹b^p. ; f. a¹b^p.—grt^h.—gun.— hel.—hfb.— ign^g.u^{c·ff}.—iod.a¹b.—k-ca.—kis. —lyc^a.a.—mgt^e.r.—mt-s^{b·c}.— mg-m.—mez.—nat^{a·d}. ; ^d.3-99.— na-m^f.b^o.; ^b.—nx-m.—nx-v.g. ; b^o.; ^e.—opi^g.—pet. ; ^k.—pho.k.—plaⁱ. —pul. ; b^o.k^f.π¹.—rs-r^c.—rut.u.— sil^g.a¹b.—spg.tø.—sul.b. ; ^b.k.βa.ε. —trx.b^o.—thu^g.a¹b^b.—wis.k^f.u^{ff}. —zin^g.q.

b^a. **Irresolution in acts.**—lyc.a.— nat^d.—nx-m.

b^b. **Irresolution in ideas.**—mt-s^c.— na-m.—sul.k.βa,ε.

b^c. **Irresolution in projects.**—ba-a. —bu-s.—f-mg.—mt-s^b.—rs-r.

b^d. **Irresolution in wishes.**—ars.— nat^a. ; 3-99.

b^e. **Hesitation.**—bry.ḥ.—mgt.r.— nx-v.

b^f. **Hesitation in making up his mind.**—ba-a.—grp.; a¹b^p.—na-m.b^o.

b^g. **Inconstancy.**—cth.—cof.g.— ign.u^{c·ff}.—opi.—sil.a¹b.—spg.tø.— thu.a¹b.—zin.q.

b^h. **Inconstancy at work.**—grt.

bⁱ. **Fickleness.**—can.a¹a^d.—pla.

b^j. **Conscientious scruples.**—cha.

b^k. **Without a will of his own.**— pet.

CONCOMITANTS.

a¹a^d. *Liveliness of fancy.*—canⁱ.

a¹b^b. *Distraction.*—thu^g.

a¹b^p. *Weak memory.*—grp. ; ^f.

a¹b^s. *Difficulty in reflecting.*—iod.

βa. *Vertigo.*—sül^b.k.βε.

βε. *Cloudiness of head.*—sul^b.k. βa.

ηp. *Heat of face.*—cha.g.u^{cc}.r¹hh.

π¹. *Panting respiration.*—pul.b^o. k^f.

r¹hh. *Sweat on palms.*—cha.g.u^{cc}.ηp.

CONDITION.

3-99. *In the morning on waking.*—nat^d.

w. **Capriciousness.**—alm.u.—am-c.—ars.u^b.—bry.—cb-a.u^{cc}.—cha.k^j.q.—glv.u^e.—hep.u.—ign.u$^{cc.dd}$.5.—k-ca.u^l.—kre.s.u.—lyc.u.; u$^{c.o}$.p.—ph-x.—pul.; x^v.—sec.—sil.; y^c.spg.b^g.—spo.a^{l}a^d.—sul.b^c.u^{ee}.

CONCOMITANT.

a^{l}a^d. *Witty humour.*—spo.

CONDITION.

5. *In the evening.*—ign.u$^{cc.dd}$.

x^a. **Covetousness.**—bry.—cin.—col.pul.u^{dd}.; ^{b}.j^a.—rhe.l.

x^b. **Greed.**—pul^a.j^a.

y. **Obstinacy.**—aco.—alo.u^c.—alm^c.—ana.u^c.—arn.; $^{d.u^{cc}}$.—aur^c.—au-m.—ca-c.u.; ^{c}; $^{c.u}$; $^{c.k}$.—cam^a.u^c.—cth^c.u^o.4.—cap.k^n.u.; $^{c.l^h}$.cau^c.; u^c.—cr-s.k.—chi^b.—dig^b.dro.—ele^b.—gui.—hep^c.b^f.—hur^c.—k-ca^c.u^{dd}.—kre.s.u.—lyc.u$^{c.o}$.; ^{b}.—mns.u.—nx-v^c.—pho.—rut^d.—sep^c.u^b.l.ηp.—sil$^{b.c}$.w.—spo^c.—sul.u.—vi-t^b.

y^a. **Positiveness.**—cam.u^c.

y^b. **Disobedience.**—chi.—dig.—ele.—lyc.—sil^c.w.—vi-t.

y^c. **Contrariety.**—alm.—aur.—ca-c.; u.; k.—cth.u^o.4.—cap.l^h.—hep.b^f.—hur.—k-ca.u^{dd}.—nx-v.—sep.l.u^l.ηp.—sil^b.w.—spo.

y^d. **Contradictoriness.**—arn.u^{cc}.—rut.

CONCOMITANT.

ηp. *Heat of face.*—sep^c.l.u^l.

CONDITION.

4. *In the afternoon.*—cth^c.u^o.

z. **Resolution.**—aco.—ch-s.b^b.—nat$^{a.c}$.—opi^a.—sul.u^x.—su-x.

z^a. **Courageousness.**—ber.u^c.—bov.x^w.—nat^c.—opi.x$^{t.w}$.—squ.

z^b. **No fear of death.**—opi.

z^c. **Boldness.**—can.—ign.—mt-n.r.msc.—nat^a.—opi.
—— *as after drinking wine.*—mt-n.

x. **Exaltation of the disposition.**

x^a. **Freedom from care.**—aga^w.—cap^d.—mt-n^b.—na-m^b.—pho$^{q.v}$.r^{l}p,aa.χ^2.—ver.a^a.b.ηp,aa.r^{l}p.

x^b. **Placid humour, tranquillity, calmness.**—æsc^w.—aga$^{c.t}$.—alo$^{f.t.w}$.; 5.—amb.—arn^w.—ars.—ard.—as-s.—au-m$^{f.w}$.—cer.—chd^w.—clo$^{f.w}$.—cof.—cnm.a^{l}b^v.—cyc.—dig^x.—dro^w.; $^{g.w}$.—eth.—lah.—lau^e.—led^w.; $^{f.s.w}$.—mgt.k^n.3.—mt-n^a.—mnc.5.—men^g.mo-a.—msc.—mu-x^w.—na-m^a.—nic$^{v.w}$.—opi.; ^{g}.—ox-x^w.—spi$^{f.w}$.
—— *as if going into a beautiful dream.*—abs.
—— *as if brain were rounded and symmetrical.*—abs.
—— *as if in heaven.*—opi.; φ^l.
—— *after the opposite state.*—mez.

x^c. **Composure.**—aga$^{b.t}$.—hfb.stn^v.—su-x.—trn^w.χ^3.ω.52.—vi-t^d.
—— *unpleasant impressions did not affect him.*—fel.

x^d. **Equable humour.**—cap^a.—k-cy.—vi-t^c.

x^e. **Comfort.**—aga^w.—aur^w.—clo^w.ccs.—gam$^{s.w.bb}$.—lah.81.—lau^b.—plb.δp.4.8-31.—trn$^{w.ii}$.52.—ton.

x^f. **Contentedness.**—alo$^{b.t.w}$.; ^{w}.5.—aur$^{w.x}$.—au-m$^{b.w}$.—cap.—cr-h.cau$^{x.w.bb}$.—clo$^{b.w}$.—coc$^{w.kk}$.; ^{w}.cyc^w.—fl-x.—hdr^p.—led$^{b.s.w}$.mag^{bb}.—mg-s.—na-m$^{j.p}$.—opi$^{a.w}$.—spi$^{o.w.r}$.ρ^l.; $^{b.w}$.—trx$^{p.w}$.—wis.
—— *but easily angered.*—cap$^{cc.kk}$.

x^g. **Self-complacency.**—aur$^{v.bb}$.—car$^{v.bb}$.—com.—dro$^{b.w}$.—f-mg^h.mg-s.—men^b.—opi^b.; $^{s.w}$.

x^h. **Pride.**—f-mg^g.—ham.—hfb.—pla.

x^i. **Self-reliance.**—ang^w.—tea.

x^j. **Mildness.**—k-cy^w.—na-m$^{f.p}$.

x^k. **Benevolence.**—lah^w.ω.

x^l. **Willing disposition.**—hel^w.—par.

æ[m]. **Loving disposition.**—hur.— ox-x.—pho.—pla[w·ii].8.

æ[n]. **Sympathy.**—lah[bb]—lau[w].4.

æ[o]. **Trusting disposition.**—hyd.— spi[f·w].π.ρ[1].

æ[p]. **Hope.**—hdr[f].—hyd.—na-m[f·j].— trx[f·w].—wis[s].

æ[q]. **Things look brighter.**—cn-i.— eug.78.—fl-x.—pho[a·v].r[1]p,aa.χ[2].— pla[w·ii]

æ[r]. **Pleasant anticipations.**—ang.f[b]. a[1]a.—aur.ω[8].—pso.

æ[s]. **Agility.**—bel.—chi.—ccs[w].— cof[w].—con[w].—cot[w].—elc[w].—fl-x[w]. —gas.a[1]a.—gam[e·w·bb].—hyo. iod[w].—lau[t].—led[b·f·w].—ol-a[w].— opi[f·w].; [g·w].—ox-x[w].a[1]a.—phl[w].χ[2]. —pi-m.—ver.—wis[p].

—— *as if borne on wings.*—thu[w].

æ[t]. **Inclined for work.**—aga[b·c].— alo[b·f·w].; 4.; κ[1].3.; γ.—ars[w].—bel. —bor[w].5.—bro.—bry.—ce-b.— ca-a.a[1]a.—cf-t.—dig.—fel.—ind. s.—iod.a[1]b[v].—lah[w·bb·aa].—lau[s].— lip.—lcp.—mns.k̄.—m-pi.—mrl[w]. q.—na-a.—opi[w].ʒ[a].—plb.a[1]a[b].4.— pho.a[1]b[b].3.—pso[v·w].3.—sar.4.— ver.

—— *following disinclination for work.*—xyp.

æ[u]. **Inclined for play.**—alo[w·bb·ii].— cmf[w].a[1]a.ω[8].—elp.—lah[w·ii].—ox-x[w]. —trn[w].

æ[v]. **Good-humour.**—ang[w].8-31.— ars[bb].—at-a.—aur[g·bb].—ca-s.4.— cn-i.—carg[bb].—cau[bb].5.—hdr. mnc.—mrl[w·kk].—mez[bb].βʊ.—msc. u[c].—naj.—na-m[w].—na-s[w].; [w].4.— nic[b·w].—opi[w].—ph-x[w].—pho.4.; [a·q]. r[1]p,aa.χ[2].—plb[w].(4).—pso[t·w].3.— rut.—sar[w·kk].—stn[c].—stp[w·x].; [w·bb]. —trn.; [w].8.(6).—thu.—zin[w].; [bb].

—— *hilarious.*—ca-s.κ.κ[7].

—— *after peevishness.*—inu[w].

æ[w]. **Cheerfulness, liveliness, gaiety, high spirits, joyousness, happy humour.**—aco.; [cc·ee].—æsc[b].— aga.; [s].; [e].; 5.4.; b[c].; a[1]a.— alo[b·f·t].; [b].; [f].5.; [u·bb·ii].; a[1]a.κ[1]. 3-99.—alm.δ𝑟[d].8-31.—am-c.—ana. 4.—ang[v].8-31.; [i].; a[1]a.—anh.—

arg[bb].—arn[bb].; [b].—ars[t].; a[1]a.—at-a[bb]. s.—as-t.5.—asp.—ast.5.—aur[f·x].; [e].—au-m.; [b·f]—ba-c.—bel[cc·dd].; 66. —bor[t].5.—bov.ʒ[a].—bro.—bu-s.5.; [bb].—ca-a[x·bb].—ca-s.e.; 4.—cam.s. —cn-i[bb].; [ii].—can.4.—cth[bb].; δ𝑟[c]. —cb-a.—ca-x.5.—cr-s.—cph.— cau[f·x·bb].—chd.; [b].—chi.δ𝑟[d].— ch-s.; 5.—clo[e].; [b·f].—cl-h[ii·kk]. cmf[u].a[1]a.ω[8].—cnb.πi[a].3.; 8-31.— cle.; 3-99.—cob.—cca.s.5.; a[1]a. —ccs.; [s].; a[1]a.—coc[f·kk].; [f].—cod. —cof[s].—cf-t.φ[1].—cch.—con[bb].; [s]. —cot[s].; [cc].—cro.; [bb·kk].—cyc[f].; [z].5.—dig.ω[2].—dro[b].; [b·g].—elc[s].— ele[ii].121.—er-m[cc].3-99.—epn.— fag.—fer.5.—fl-x.; [s].—for.a[1]a.— glv.a[1]a.—gas.—gel.—glo[bb·kk].a[1]a[d].— grn[s].—grt[bb].—gam[e·s·bb].—hel[l].— hdr.—hyd.; [p].—hfb.—ind.—iod[s]. —iof.—ipc[bb·kk].—k-bi[ii].—k-cy[j]. kis.s.—lah.3.; [k·ω].; [u·ii], [t·aa·bb].— lau[n].4.—led[b·f·s].—lep[ii].—lyc.; βa.—mnc[cc].—men.—mrl.; u[c].; [t].q.; [bb].βa.; [v·kk].—mr-f[bb].—mr-i. 5.—mit.3-99.— mu-x[f].—nat[x]. na-m[v].; [cc·ee].; [kk].—na-s[v].; [v].4.; 75.—nic[b·v].—nx-m[gg·ii].; [bb]. ol-a[s].—opi.; 2.; [f·s].; [g·s].; [v].—ox-x[b].; [s].a[1]a.; a[1]a.4.; [u].—par[bb].—ped.; 5.; [ii·mm].—ptv[cc].—phl.5.; [s].χ[2].— ph-x[v].—pho.; [cc].—phy.—pla[ee].— plb.; [v].(4).—pru.—pso[t·v].3.—sbd. —src.—sar.; [v·kk].—sec.φ[1].; [kk]. snc.—sng[t].—spi[f·o].π.ρ[1].; [b·f].: a[1]a. —squ.—stn.—stp[v·x].; [v·bb].—str. —sul.—su-x.—sum.a[1]a.—tab.; [ee·ii].—tan.—trn[kk].; [ii].; [v].8.(6).; ω[8].122.; [u].; [c].χ[8].ω.52.; [e·ii].52.; [ii].— trx[f·p].—tep.u[c].—teu[bb].χ[2].5.—tea. —thr[cc].βι.γp,q.—thu.; [s].—ton. tri.—val.; 5.; a[1]a.—ver[ll].; a[1]a. wis.—zin.; 5.; [v].

—— *as from intoxication.*—can. —cod.—for.πb.92.—mg-s. —ox-x.s.ρ.—tab[bb].—ziz.

—— *as from coffee-drinking.*— val.

—— *as if had got good news.*— hfb.

—— *as if born anew.*—cth.δ𝑟[c].

—— *bordering on madness.*—cro. γ.δo.ηc[b].

—— *extravagant.*—am-c.—bel[ll]. u[c].—ch-s.—iod[bb].—nat[bb]. —ph-x.—str.—vrb[ii].

—— *stupid hilarity.*—ard.

—— *but weeps at trifles.*—arg.

—— *following ill-humour.*—inu[v]. —vi-t[bb].5.

—— *following low spirits.*—-bry. —cas.5.—cyc.ω^8.—mr-f.— pla[m·ii].8.

—— *following low spirits and laziness.*—zin.

—— *followed by low spirits.*—gel. —grp.—pet.$s.\omega^8$.—pla[q·ii]. —ziz.

—— *followed by crossness.*—-cle. a[1]a.—hyo[kk].—na-s.—ol-a. —opi[cc·ii].—sng.—tar.

—— *followed by prostration and disinclination for mental work.*—cle.a[1]a.—spo[cc].

—— *followed by sleepiness.*—bel. —cca.

—— *followed by exhaustion.*—- pho.

—— *alternating with melancholy.* —asr.

—— *alternating with bodily suffering.*—pla.

x^x. **Sociableness.**—aur[f·w].—-ca-a[w·bb]. —cau[f·w·bb].—chd[bb].—cot.s.—dig[b]. —hyd.—nat[w].—stn[bb].—stp[v·w].

x^y. **Time seems short.**—thr.

x^z. **Flow of delightful fancies.**— cn-i.—cod.—cyc[w].5.—opi.; ϕ^1.

x^{aa}. **Ecstasy.**—aga.a[1]a.—cup.a[1]a.— jat.μ^2.—lah.[t·w·bb].—opi.—trn[ee].52.

· —— *sublime.*—crt.

x^{bb}. **Loquacity.**—-agn.s.——alo[u·w·ii]. —-amb.$g.s.\gamma.\phi^1.\chi^3.\omega^2$.2-16.—arg[w]. —arn[w].—ars[v].—ar-h.s.—at-a[w·cc]. s.——aur[s·v].——bel.; ξ.; δf^e. bu-s^w.—ca-a[w·x].—-cn-i[w].—cth[w]. car[s·v].—-cau[f·w·x].; [v].5.—chd[x].— cmf.—ccs.—cf-t.—con[w].—cot[w]. cro[w·kk].—eth.—gas.—glo[w·kk].a[1]a[d]. —grt[w].—gam[e·s·w].—hpm.u.—hyd. —hyo.—iod[w].—ipc[w·kk].—k-hy[kk].

—— *lah*[t·w·aa].; 5.; [n].—mag[f].—mrl[w]. βa.—mez[v].βv.—mr-f[w].—nat[w].— nx-m[w].—par[w].—sel.—stn[x]. stp[v·w].—str.83.; [ii].—tab[w].—trx.— · teu[w].χ^2.5.—thr.a[1]a.ϕ^1.—thu.—ver. —zin.; [v].

—— *as if drunk.*—mep.

—— *after ill-humour.*—vi-t[w].5.

—— *followed by dumbness.*—bel.

x^{cc}. **Inclination to sing.**—aco[w·ee].— bel.; [w·dd].; [ii].—cn-i.—cap[f·kk]. cr-s.—cro.; 98.; [ii].—er-m[w].3-99. —hfb.—hdr.—lo-c.—lyc[dd].— mnc[w].—mr-f[w·dd].—nat.—na-m[w·ee].; u.γ.—opi[w·ii].—ptv[w].; [w·ii].—pho[w].-- pla[dd].—spo[w].—tab.—teu.—thr[w]. $\beta e.\gamma$p,q.—ver.2.

—— *to shout.*—at-a[w·bb].

x^{dd}. **Inclination to whistle.**—bel[w·cc]. —cn-i.—cb-a.—lyc[cc].—mr-f[w·cc]. —pla[cc].

x^{ee}. **Inclination to dance.**—aco[w·cc]. —aps[ff·ii].—cl-h.—grt[w·ff].—na-m[w]. [cc].—pla[w].—tab[w·ii].—trn[aa].52.

—— *alternating with groaning.*— bel.

x^{ff}. **Inclination to leap.**—aps[ee·ii].; 100.—grt[w·ee].

x^{gg}. **Flow of humourous ideas.**— cn-i.—nx-m[w·ii].

x^{hh}. **Involuntary smiling.**—aur.86. —bel.—lyc.

x^{ii}. **Laughter at trifles or without cause.**—ac-l.——aga.χ^1.5-16.—- alo[u·w·bb].—alm.5-16.—am-c.— aps[ee·ff].—arn.—ard.——bel.; [cc].— cn-i[w].—cb-v.o.s.rnn.—cs-e.—cl-h[w]. [kk].—cro[kk].$\omega^2.\delta$P[2].; [cc].—cup.5.—ele[w]. 121.—hyo.; 82.—k-bi[w].—k-cy.— lah[u·w].—lep[w].—nx-m[w·gg].—opi[w·cc]. —ped[w·mm].—pho.s.—-ptv[kk].; [w·cc]. —pla[m·w].8.; [q·w].—str[bb].—tab[w·ee]. —trn[w].; [e·w].52.; [w].—trx.—ver·ηaa. —vrb[w].—zin.—zn-s.ψv.

—— *spasmodic.*——cup.—eth.—- pho.l.

—— *to tears.*—na-m.

—— *without liveliness.*—na-m.— pho.

—— *foolish.*—eth.—hyo.
—— *at serious things.*—lyc.
—— *at misfortunes.*—aps.
—— *but easily angered.*—arn.
—— *till the face becomes purple and loins ache.*—cn-i.
—— *following crossness.*—str.
—— *followed by indifference.*—sbd.$b^t.\gamma$.
—— *followed by sadness.*—pla$^{q.w}$.
—— *alternating with moaning.*—ver.

$\mathfrak{x}^{ij}$. **Laughter to death.**—cro.
$\mathfrak{x}^{kk}$. **Jocularity.**—bel.——cac.—cn-i.—cap. ; $^{f.cc}$.—cl-h$^{w.ii}$.—coc$^{f.w}$.cro$^{ii}.\omega^2.\delta P^2$. ; $^{w.bb}$.—glow$^{bb}.a^1 a^d$.—hyo^w.—ign.—ipc$^{w.bb}$.—k-cy^w.—k-hy^{bb}.—lah.—mrl$^{v.w}$.—na-m^w.—nx-m.χ^1.—ptv^{ii}.—pla.—rs-r.ϵ.—sar$^{v.w}$.—sec^w.—su-x.—trn^w.

—— *foolish.*—nx-m.
—— *after indifference.*—men.
—— *after gravity.*—pla.

$\mathfrak{x}^{ll}$. **Wantonness.**—bel^w.u^c.—cn-i.val.ρ.—ver^w.
$\mathfrak{x}^{mm}$. **Mocking humour.**—ped$^{w.ii}$.
$\mathfrak{x}^{nn}$. **Disposition to make grimaces.**—bel.
$\mathfrak{x}^{oo}$. **Heavenly raptures.**——cn-i.—crt.

CONCOMITANTS.

$a^1 a$. *Increased mental activity.*—aga^{aa}.—alo$^w.\kappa^1$.3-99.—ang^w.; $^{r}.f^b$.—ars^w.—cle^w.—cmf$^{u.w}$.ω^8.——cca^w.—ccs^w.—cup^{aa}.—glv^w.—gas^s.—ox-x$^{s.w}$.; ^{w}.4.—spi$^{b.f.w}$.——sum^w.—thr$^{bb}.\phi^1$.—val^w.—ver^w.
$a^1 a^b$. *Thoughtfulness.*—plb^t.4.
$a^1 a^d$. *Lively fancy.*—glo$^{w.bb.kk}$.
$a^1 b^b$. *Inability to fix thoughts.*—pho^t.3.
$a^1 b^v$. *Slow thought.*—cnm^b.—iod^t.
βa. *Giddiness.*—lyc^w.—mrl$^{w.bb}$.
$\beta \epsilon$. *Confusion of head.*—thr$^{w.cc}$.γp,q.
βv. *Intoxication.*—mer$^{v.bb}$.
γp. *Head hot.*—thr$^{w.cc}$.$\beta\epsilon.\gamma$q.

γq. *Head heavy.*—thr$^{w.cc}.\beta\epsilon.\gamma$p.
γ. *Headache.*—alo^t.—amb^{bb}.$\mathfrak{g}$.$\mathfrak{s}.\phi^1.\chi^3.\omega^2$.2-16.—cro$^w.\delta$o.$\eta$c^b.—na-m^{cc}.$\mathfrak{u}$.—sbd$^{ii}.\mathfrak{b}^t$.
δc^d. *Staring eyes.*—alm^w.8-31.—chi^w.
δf^s. *Squinting.*—bel^{bb}.
δP^2. *Dilated pupils.*—cro$^{ii.kk}.\omega^2$.
δp. *Diminished myopia.*—plb^s.4.8-31.
δo. *Obscuration of sight.*—cro^w.$\gamma.\eta$c^b.
δr^c. *Objects seem brighter.*—cth^w.
ηaa. *Red face.*—ver^{ii}.
ηp,aa. *Red, hot face.*—ver$^a.a^a.\mathfrak{b}.r^1$p,aa.
ηc^b. *Pale face.*—cro^w.$\gamma.\delta$o.
κ. *Sour taste.*—ca-s$^v.\kappa^7$.
κ^1. *Good appetite.*—alo$^w.a^1 a$.3-99.; ^{t}.3.
κ^7. *Eructations.*—ca-s$^v.\kappa$.
μ^2. *Diarrhœa.*—jat^{aa}.
ξ. *Lasciviousness.*—bel^{bb}.
πb.92. *Cold feeling in chest when inspiring.*—for^w.
πi^a. *Fulness of chest.*—cnb^w.
π. *Oppression of chest.*—spi$^{f.o.w}$.ρ^1.
ρ^1. *Palpitation.*—spi$^{f.o.w}.\pi$.
ρ. *Vascular excitement and quick pulse.*—ox-x$^w.\mathfrak{s}$.—val^{ll}.
τ. *Weakness of arms.*—cb-v^{ii}.o.$\mathfrak{s}$.
τ^1p,aa. *Hands hot and red.*—pho$^{a.q.v}$.χ^2.—ver$^a.a^a.\mathfrak{b}.\eta$p,aa.
ϕ^1. *Sleeplessness.*——amb^{bb}.$\mathfrak{g}$.$\mathfrak{s}.\gamma$.$\chi^3.\omega^2$.2-16.—cf-t^w.—opi^b.; ^{z}.—sec^w.—thr$^{bb}.a^1 a$.
χ^1. *Chilliness.*—nx-m^{kk}.
χ^1. *Rigor.*—aga^{ii}.5-16.
χ^2. *Heat.*—phl$^{s.w}$.—pho$^{a.q.v}.r^1$p,aa.—teu$^{w.bb}$.5.
χ^3. *Perspiration.*——amb^{bb}.$\mathfrak{g}$.$\mathfrak{s}.\gamma$.$\phi^1.\omega^2$.2-16.—trn$^{c.w}.\omega$.52.
ψ. *Tickling all over body.*—zn-s^{ii}.
ω. *Feeling of fulness.*—lah$^{k.w}$.
ω. *Bruised feeling.*—trn$^{c.w}.\chi^3$.52.
ω^2. *Weakness.*—amb^{bb}.$\mathfrak{g}$.$\mathfrak{s}.\gamma.\phi^1.\chi^3$.2-16.—cro$^{ii.kk}.\delta P^2$.—dig^w.
ω^3. *Trembling.*—aur^r.—cmf$^{u.w}.a^1 a$.—cyc^w.—pet$^w.\mathfrak{s}$.—trn^w.122.

CONDITIONS.

2. *At night.*—opi^w.—ver^{cc}.

2-16. *At night in bed.*—amb^{bb}.g.s. $\gamma.\phi^1.\chi^3.\omega^2$.

3. *In the morning.*—alo$^t.\kappa^1$.—lah^w.—mgt.$\mathfrak{k}^n$.—phot.$_a$l$\mathfrak{h}^b$.—pso$^{t.v.w}$.

3-99. *In the morning on waking.*—alo$^w.a$l$a.\kappa^1$.—cle^w.—er-m$^{w.cc}$.—hdr^w.—mit^w.

4. *In the afternoon.*—aga^w.5.—alo^t.—ana.—ca-s^v.; ^{v}.—can^w.—lau$^{n.w}$.—na-s$^{v.w}$.—ox-x^w.$_a$la.—pho^v.—*plb$^{v.w}$.*; plb$^e.\delta p$. 8-31.; $^t.a$la^b.—sar^t.

5. *In the evening.*—aga$^{ii}.\chi^1$.—alo$^{f.w}$.—as-c^w.—ast^w.—bu-s^w.—ca-x^w.—ch-s$^{w.z}$.—cas^w.—cca^w.s.—cup^{ii}.—cyc^w.—fer^w.—lah^{bb}.—mnc^b.—mr-i^w.—ped^w.—pbl^w.—teu$^{w.bb}.\chi^2$.—val^w.—vi-t$^{w.bb}$.—zin^w.

5-16. *In the evening in bed.*—aga^{ii}.χ^1.—alm^{ii}.

5. *In the forenoon.*—aga^w.4.—alo^b.—bor$^{t.w}$.—cau$^{v.bb}$.

6. *In the room.*—trn$^{v.w}$.8.

8. *In open air.*—trn$^{v.w}$.(6).

8-31. *By walking in open air.*—alm^w.δc^d.—ang$^{v.w}$.—cnb^w.—plb^e.δp.4.

52. *By music.*—trn$^{c.w}$.$\chi^3.\omega$.; $^{aa.cc}$.; $^{e.w.ii}$.

66. *After food.*—bel^w.

75. *After loose stools.*—na-s^w.

78. *After urinating.*—eug^q.

81. *By pollution.*—lah^e.

82. *Before menses.*—hyo^{ii}.

83. *During menses.*—str^{bb}.

86. *When speaking.*—aur^{hh}.

98. *During sleep.*—cro^{cc}.

100. *In dream.*—aps^{ff}.

121. *When alone.*—ele$^{w.ii}$.

122. *In society.*—trn^w.ω^8.

PART II.—a¹. MENTAL SYMPTOMS.

PART II.—a¹. MENTAL SYMPTOMS.

a. Increased intellectual powers (*Peculiar*).

nx-v. Clear perception of his existence; fine, strong, right feeling for what is right and wrong.

a. **Increased activity of mind, increased understanding, increased capacity for intellectual operations, increased power of thought, freedom of mind.**—aco.; ^{j}.; ^{a}.; ^{d}.; ^{b}.; ^{c}.—aga$^{d.i.j}$.aα^{aa}.—alm.—amb^f.—ana^a.; ^{d}.; ^{d}.5.; γ.—an-a.—ang$^{a.e}$.χ^2.4.; ^{e}.af^b,α^r.4.—anh.—arn.—ars^n.; aα^w.—aur^a.; $\chi^{1.3}$.$\omega^{2.8}$.—bad.—bel^b.aq. 2.; ^{n}.ao,t,u^b.; ^{a}.; $^{a.d}$.—bov^b.—bro.—bu-s.—ca-a^b.aα^h,g$^{d.e}$,α^t.—c-ph.—cam^g.aα.—cn-i.—can^c.b^b.; ^{d}.b^i.—cap^n.—cb-v.—cr-s.—chi. aα^t.; ^{e}.; $^{d.e}$.; ^{e}.5.—cmf.—cob.—cca^d.c^b.; $\alpha\alpha^w$.—ccs.aα^w.—coc^b.—cod.—cof$^{d.e.g}$.; ^{d}.; $^{a.c}$.—cf-t.—cub. —cup^h.aα^{aa}.—cyc^d.aα^w.5.—dig.aα^t.; ^{d}.; $\beta\ell$.—eth.—fag.3.—fl-x^a.—for.; aα^w.—glv.aα^w.—gas^d.; aα^s.—glo^d. a$\alpha^{w.kk}$.—grt^b.—hpm^d.5.—hy-x^n.—hfb.—hyo^a.—lah^d.aα^{bb}.; ^{c}.; $^{d.e}$.; ^{c}.aα^t.ϕ^1.5.—ibe.—la-x.—lau^n.—lip.—lcp.—lyc.—mgt.a$\frac{1}{2}$,α^s.—mt-s^d.—mnc.aα^t.—mep^d.ab^o.—mr-s.5.—mrr^d.—na-a.—na-p.5.—nx-m.—nx-v^c.3-99.—opi^d.aα^w.; aα^t.; ^{b}.ϕ^1.2.; $^{a.d}$.ϕ^1.2.; aα^t.$\beta\upsilon$.—ox-x.; ^{j}.; a$\alpha^{s.w}$.; ^{m}.aα^w.—ped.—pho.r^{1}p,aa.χ^2.; ^{d}.ω^8.5.; ^{c}.; ^{c}.43.—phs.ω^2.—pi-m.—pla.a$\alpha^{c.s}$.—plb. aα^t.—pul^c.; 5.—rhs.; π^1.—src.—

sng^a.—sil^k.—sin.—so-t^d.; $^{a.d}$.—spi^a.—sty.—sul^h.—sum.aα^w.—tan.—ter.—thu.—val.aα^w.; $^{a.c}$.; 5.—ver.ao.; ^{n}.aα^w.—vrb^f.—vi-o.; b^p.γ.—zin^d.—ziz^d.

—— *following diminished intellectual powers.*—ox-x.
—— *following heat of body.*—cle.
—— *followed by difficulty of thinking.*—vi-o.
—— *followed by perspiration and prostration.*—cle.
—— *alternating with absence of mind.*—alm.

a^a. **Increased memory.**—aco.—ana.—ang^e.χ^2.4.—aur.—bel.; ^{d}.—cof^c.—cf-t.—fl-x.—hyo.—la-x.—opi^d.ϕ^1.2.—spi.—val^c.
—— *for things that happened long ago.*—cn-i.—ibe.
—— *for places.*—sng.
—— *for words.*—hfb.
—— *for music.*—lyc.

a^b. **Thoughtfulness, buried in thought.**—aco.—bel.aq.2.—bov.—ca-a.aα^b,g$^{d.e}$,α^t.—cn-i.—coc.—grt.—ham.k.—msc.
—— *alternating with frivolity.*—ag-n.

a^c. **Rapid change of thought.**—aco.—cn-i.—cob.—cof^a.—cch.2.—lab.; aα^t.ϕ^1.5.—mor.—nx-v.3-99.—pho.; 43.—pul.—val^a.

a^d. **Increased imagination, great flow of ideas, lively fancy.**—aco.—aga$^{i.j}$.aα^{aa}.—ana.; 5.—

bel^a.——bu-s.——cn-i.——chi^e.——cca. r^m.——cof$^{e·g}$.——cf-t.——cch.ϕ^1.2.—— cyc.aæ^w.5.——der.at^c.——dig.——gas.—— glo.aæ$^{w·kk}$.——lah.aæ^{bb}.; ^{e}.——mt-s. ——mep.ab^o.——mor.——mrr.——opi. aæ^w.; ^{a}.ϕ^1.2.——pho.ω^8.5.——so-t.; ^{a}. ——zin.

—— *flow of theoretical ideas.*—— cn-i.——so-t.
—— *dreamy imagination.*——ziz.
——, *flow of ridiculous speculative ideas.*——cn-i.

a^e. **Increased inventive faculty, scheming tendency.**—ang^a.χ^2.4.; b^b.af^b,æ^r.4.——chi.; ^{d}.; 5.——cof$^{d·g}$.—— lah^d.

a^f. **Voluptuous ideas.**——amb.——bel. ——vrb.

a^g. **Increased appreciation of the beautiful.**——cam.aæ.——cn-i.—— cof$^{d·e}$.

a^h. **Elevated contemplations and aspirations.**—cup.aæ^{aa}.——ham.b^c. ——hyo.r^b.——opi.ϕ^1.2.

—— *religious enthusiasm.*——sul.

a^i. **Making verses.**——aga$^{d·j}$.aæ^{aa}.
a^j. **Prophesying, lucid vision.**——aco. ——aga$^{d·i}$.aæ^{aa}.——cn-i.

—— *sees his own circulation.*—— cn-i.
—— *can read the titles of books at twelve feet distance in the dark.*——cn-i.(78).

a^k. **Increased power of expression.** ——sil.
a^l. **Increased presence of mind.**—— ox-x.
a^m. **Increased power of concentra- tion.**——cf-t.——ox-x.aæ^w.
a^n. **Increased activity of the senses.** ars.——bel.ao,t,u^b.—— cap.——hy-x. la-x.—lau.——ver.aæ^w.
a^o. **Increased perception of the ludicrous.**——cn-i.——ham.
a^p. **As if two trains of thought in mind.**——hfb.

CONCOMITANTS.

aa^b. *Indifference to external things.* ca-a^b.ag$^{d·e}$,æ^t.

ab^o. *Disinclination for work.*—— mep^d.
af^h. *Uneasiness.*——ang^e.b^b.aæ^r.4.
ag^d. *Anxiety about the present.*—— ca-a^b.aa^b,g^e,æ^t.
ag^e. *Anxiety about the future.*—— ca-a^b.aa^b,g^d,æ^t.
ao. *Sensitiveness.*—— bel^n.at,u^b.—— ver.
aq. *Restlessness.*——bel^b.2.
as. *Excitement.*
—— *as from intoxication.*—— cam^g.
at. *Variable humour.*——bel^n.ao,u^b. ——der^d.
au^b. *Irritability.*——bel^n.ao,t.
aʒ. *Resolution.*——mgt.aæ^s.
aæ^c. *Composure.*——pla.aæ^s.
aæ^r. *Pleasant anticipations.*——ang^e. b^b.af^b.4.
aæ^s. *Agility.*——mgt.aʒ.——ox-x.aæ^w. ——pla.aæ^c.
aæ^t. *Inclined for work.*——ca-a^b.aa^b, g$^{d·e}$.——chi.——dig.——lah^c.ϕ^1.5. ——mnc.——opi.; βv.——plb.
aæ^w. *Cheerfulness.*——cca.——ccs.—— cyc^d.5.——glv.——glo^d.aæ^{kk}.—— opi^d.——ox-x.aæ^s.; ^{m}.——sum.—— val.——ver.
aæ^{aa}. *Ecstasy.*——aga$^{d·i·j}$.——cup^h.
aæ^{bb}. *Loquacity.*——lah^d.
aæ^{kk}. *Buffoonery.*——glo^d.aæ^w.
β. *Confusion of head.*
—— *as from intoxication.*—— dig.
βv. *Intoxication.*——opi.aæ^t.
γ. *Headache.*——ana.——vi-o.b^p.
r^1. *Slow breathing.*——rhs.
r^{1}p. *Heat of hands.*——pho.r^{1}aa.χ^2.
r^{1}aa. *Redness of hands.*——pho.r^{1}p. χ^2.
ϕ^1. *Sleeplessness.*——cch^d.2.——lah^c. aæ^t.5.——opi^h.2.; $^{a·d}$.2.
χ^1. *Cold.*——aur.χ^3.$\omega^{2·8}$.
χ^2. *Heat.*——ang$^{n·e}$.4.——pho.r^{1}p,aa.
χ^3. *Perspiration.*——aur.χ^1.$\omega^{2·8}$.
ω^2. *Weakness.*——aur.$\chi^{1·3}$.ω^8.——phs.
ω^8. *Trembling.*—— aur.$\chi^{1·3}$.ω^2.—— pho^d.5.

CONDITIONS.

2. *At night.*—bel[b].aq.—cch[c].; [d].
φ[1].—opi[h].φ[1].; [a.d].φ[1].

3-99. *In the morning, on awaking.*—fag.—nx-v[c].

4. *In the afternoon.*—ang[a.e].χ[2].;
[e].af[b],ӕ[r].|

5. *In the evening.*—ana[d].—chi[e].
—cyc[d].aӕ[w].—lah[c].aӕ[t].φ[1].—mr-s.—na-p.—pho[d].ω[8].—pul.—val.

5. *In the forenoon.*—hpm[d].

43. *By reading.*
—— *a silly story.*—pho[c].

78. *After urinating.*—cn-i[j].

b. Diminished intellectual powers (*Peculiar*).

agn. Imbecile state, during which he smiles in a silly manner on people, even when engaged in serious conversation, conducts himself in a shy and foolish manner and talks nonsense; on lying down in order to relieve his head, fanciful figures, grimacing faces hover before him, during the day while his eyes are shut.

cf-t. Loss of mental energy.

fl-x. Difficult comprehension while reading philosophical works, whereas all facts are easily and clearly comprehended.

hel. Diminished power over the mind and body; when he does not pay attention the muscles refuse their office, the gait is unsteady, the bread falls out of his hand; if talked to when drinking, the glass slips from the grasp.

oln. When reading, he does not understand when he thinks about understanding it, but if he does not think about this he understands what he reads well enough.

sbd. The mind seems too excited, as if on the stretch, the disposition, on the contrary, is little sensitive, cold; but after a few days the mind declines remarkably, he can now only comprehend things with difficulty; thinks slowly; on the other hand, the disposition is more excitable; everything affects him profoundly.

stp. Loss of the thinking faculty when he speaks or thinks about a subject and any one interrupts him; or if his attention is directed to other thoughts, he immediately forgets the first and cannot recal them.

str. In the intervals of half-consciousness he knows what occurred in the waking dreamy state, but cannot remember what he did or said in the previous lucid intervals.

He talks with some one whom he did not recognise, and replies to him as if he were sensible, but cannot remember the conversation when he again comes to himself.

trn. Complete loss of memory, does not understand questions put to him, does not remember persons of his intimate acquaintance, nor the prayers he is in the habit of saying. Afterwards a moment of gaiety, followed by profound sadness, with tendency to weep and complain, palpitation of heart, oppression of chest, headache, heat and sweat.

thr. Thinking is difficult for him when it is comparative, but not creative, *e.g.* he can easily work out things, but with difficulty choose remedies; he easily writes essays, but it is difficult for him to ascertain the species of a plant.

vi-o. Morbid affection of the imagination; pictures present themselves to his fancy; he makes an effort to observe them, but before he can do so they are gone.

Incomplete ideas only present themselves, which seem to be familiar; he tries to arrange them but cannot retain them. On attempting to complete them, the imperfect idea is expelled by another equally incomplete; his judgment remains unimpaired; he has an air of thoughtfulness and dejection.

b. Confusion of mind, of thoughts, bewilderment, absence of mind.
——ac-x.——aco.43.44.——ac-c.—— agn°.—-alm.ab.——am-c.; 86.—— ang^b.—arn^b.—ars.—at-a.—ast.ω^2. —bel.δt^m.; φ.—bth.—ca-c.γq.δh^n.83. —ca-s.ax.5.——cn-i.——cau^p.4.5.—— ca-x.ω^3.—cr-b.—cas.—cau.—cnt. —cl-h.—ch-x.—cmf.—cca.—cch. —con.—crn.—c-ar.—dig.—dir^h. —fag.—gel.—glo.ω^2.; δo.—grn.— gur.—hdr.—hyo.—irs.—jab.— jug.—k-br.—k-bi.—lyc.—mns.ak. —mr-c.—mil.5.70.—mur.ab^a.k.— na-m.——nx-m.43.——ptv.—plb.— pol^p.—pot^b.——ptl.—snt.—spr.— sti.—sul^{o-s}.ab^c.—tan.—thu^c.—trf. —vi-o^b.—xan.

—— *familiar things appear strange to him.*—glo.
—— *as if in a reverie.*—mrl.
—— *as if catarrh were coming on.* —ana.
—— *he knows not what he is about.*—bel.—bry.16.
—— *forgets what he is about.*— jug.
—— *he knows not what he would say.*—kis.
—— *alternating with activity of mind.*—alm.δ^1.e^1.

b^a. Unobservant.——asr.——mac.I.— mt-s^b.af^b,g,b^c.—sul.—thu.

—— *of the lapse of time.*—elp.

b^b. Inability to fix thoughts or attention, distraction.——aco.——

ac-l.—-agn.43.—ail.—all.—alm.43. —am-c.—ana^p.—ang.; a^e.χ^2.4.; a^e. af^b,x^r.4.—anh.ab^i.——as-c.γ.—arn. —ars^c.—ba-c.—bel°.—bov.—cam°. a^c.; βb.; ω.; $^{p \cdot y}$.βa,b.e.π^1.—cn-i.— can$^{f \cdot h \cdot s}$.——cth$^{f \cdot s}$.——cb-a^h.—ca-x.; 43.—cr-s.—car^q.; ^{f}.—cau.—ce-b. aa.——cha.—chd°.——ch-s^p.; 44.— cl-h.—cmf.—cnb.(8).—coc.—cof. 43.; ^{p}.—cfn.as.—cch°.; 19.—col. —crn.; ^{s}.2.—cro$^{o \cdot r}$.—cu-a.—dgn. dir.—elp.—er-a^s.—fag^p.—fer.u^{dd}. —fl-x.—gel^s.—glo.43.44.—grp.— ham.ag,u.—hel.—hur.; 41.—hdr. —hy-x^s.—hfb.—hyo^c.—ibe.—ign. —idm.—iod.aa.—irs.—k-br.— k-ca.—klm.ab$^{c \cdot o}$.—lah.ax^{bb}.φ.ω^2. 5.; βe.; 43.—lam^p.βe.—lau.—lil.au. —lol.—lyp.14.—lyc^f.5.; βe.γ.— lcp.—mac.—mgt.; 43.—mt-s^a.af^b, g,b^e.—mag.af^c.ω^3.44.——mrc.— man.—mer^c.—mez^c.; 43.—mit.— mo-a.—msc.—myr.φ.—my-s^c.— nat.; 3.—na-a.—na-m.; 5.—nx-j. —nx-m.—nx-v.—oln.43.; ^{c}.43.— ol-a.ab^i,x^w.—opi.—ori.—ph-x.— pho.ax^t.3.—phs.—pla^s.aa^q.8.122.; ^{p}.; ^{o}.—plg.ω^2.—ple.ω^7.—pot.—pul. —rn-s.—rho^s.—rs-r.ab^i.—rbs^s.— rs-v.—src.—sar.—scu.—snc.— sep.ab^o.; ^{f}.—sil.γ.κ^4.5.—so-t^c.— spi.—stn.aq,b^h.—stp.; ^{c}.—sti.— str.—sul^n.; ^{l}.—su-x^f.—tab^s.; ^{c}.βe. γq.66.(72).——tan.—tep^p.φ.—ter. —thu.—vrb^c.—vi-o^c.ab^c.—zin.; ^{s}.

—— *thoughts seem to chase each other through brain.*—ptl.
—— *in working.*—lyc.

b^c. Persistence of certain thoughts. —æth.—ars^b.——cth^s.3.—cb-v^v.γ. —hyo.; ^{b}.—iod.—kis.—lam.t^s.— mer^b.—mez^b.—mu-x.—my-s^b.— nx-m.βb.—oln^b.43.—osm.—pet. —ph-x.—pso.—pul.—sep$^{f \cdot m}$.af.— so-t^b.—stp^b.—tab^b.βe.γq.66.(72). —thu.—vrb^b.—vi-o^b.

—— *of disagreeable thoughts.*— rhs.
—— *of humourous thoughts.*— nx-m.

b^d. **Want of volition.**—aps.βe^a.—ign$^{f \cdot h \cdot s}$.5.41.

—— *with feeling of power.*—ca-a.

b^e. **Loss of presence of mind.**—bor. βa.; $^s.ab^i.\gamma.v$.3.(8-31).—k-ca.—na-m.

b^f. **Mistakes in speaking.**—ac-x.—alm.—am-c.—ag-n$^{s \cdot y}.o^2$.; $^s.ak.\beta e$.γd,q.σ^2.—ca-c.—can.o^2.; $^{b \cdot h \cdot s}$.—cth$^{b \cdot s}$.—car^b.; ^{s}.; $^{b \cdot h}$.—cau.—cr-s.—ce-s.—chi^h.—ch-s$^{m \cdot q}$.—cca.—con^p.—cot^o.—crt^s.ab; $\rho.\chi^1$.—cu-s.—cyc^o.—dio.—grp^h.—hæm$^s.\beta e.\gamma$q.—ham.—hep^h.—hyo.—ign$^{d \cdot h \cdot s}$.5.41.—ir-f^h.—k-br.—k-ca.—k-cy.—kis.—lil.—lyc.; ^{b}.5.—mgt^o.a$\dot{t}$.—man^s.ab^c,g^e,k^s,u.—mer$^s.\beta a.\epsilon a$.; ^{g}.$\beta e.\phi$.; ^{p}.—mor.—mur^p.—na-m^p.; ^{s}.—nx-m.—nx-v$^{i \cdot s}$.; ^{h}.—osm.—ph-x.—rs-r.a$\dot{a}$.—sec^s.—sep^b.; $^{c \cdot m}$.af.—sil.; βa.—str.—sul.—su-x^b.—thu.

—— *amnesic aphasia.*—k-br.—k-cy.

—— *but speaks rationally of exalted subjects.*—lyc.

—— *as if delirious.*—cha^s.

b^g. **Mistakes in reading.**—cha^h.; o^2.—byo.—lyc^p.—mer$^f.\beta e.\phi$.—sil$^{h \cdot s}$.4.(5.66).—stn$^s.\beta a$.

b^h. **Mistakes in writing.**—am-c^i.—bz-x.—bov.—c-ph.—cn-i.—can.; $^{b \cdot f \cdot s}$.—cb-a^b.—car$^{b \cdot f}$.—ce-s.—cha^g.—chi^f.—ch-s.—ch-x.—cch.—cro^p.—crt.—dio.—dir.—fl-x^j.—grp^f.—hep^f.—hdr.—ign$^{d \cdot f \cdot s}$.5.41.—ir-f^f.—k-br.—lah.—la-x.—lo-s.$\beta e.\gamma$.—lyc.—mt-n.—na-m.—nx-m.—nx-v^f.—ptl^o.a$\dot{t}$.—pul.—rho$^{o \cdot s}$.—rhs.—sep.—sil$^{g \cdot s}$.4.(5.66).—so-m^s.—sum.

—— *confounding right and left.*—fl-x.

—— *foreign languages.*—cep.

b^i. **Mistakes in calculating.**—ail.—am-c^h.—mer^s.—nx-v$^{f \cdot s}$.—sum.

b^j. **Mistakes respecting time.**—ana.—cic.—cro^k.—elc.3.4.—fl-x^h.—hur.—lah.

b^k. **Mistakes respecting objects.**—cro^j.

b^l. **Mistakes respecting localities.** hur.—sul^b.

b^m. **Mistakes in work.**—bel^o.—cep^o.4.70.—ch-s$^{f \cdot q}$.—mgt.—mo-m.—nat^n.—nx-v.—rut^s.—sel.

b^n. **Awkwardness.**—nat^m.

—— *in work.*—sul^b.

—— *knocks against things.*—ipc.—na-m.—nx-v.—opi$^o.\beta b$.

—— *puts on his clothes awkwardly.*—hel.

—— *lets things drop.*—bov.—bry.—hel.—na-m.—nx-v.

b^o. **Forgetfulness.**—aga.; ^{s}.—agn.—alm.—am-c.γ.—ars^p.—ba-a.—ba-c.—bel.γ.; ^{m}.; ^{b}.—bro.—bry^s.—bu-s.—cld.—ca-a.γ.43.—ca-c.; βa.—c-ph.—cam.ω^5.—cn-i^s.—can^v.a$\dot{k}$.; 44.—cth.—cr-s.—cep^m.4.70.—chd^b.—cch^b.—cot^f.—cro.; $^{b \cdot r}$.—ctn.—cyc^f.—fl-x.—gin.—glo.—grp.—gym.—hpm.5.43.—hdr.u.—hyo.—ibe.—lah.a$\dot{a}$.—lyp.—mac^b.—mgt^f.a$\dot{t}$.—mag.a$\dot{u}$.—mit.—msc.—naj.—nat.—na-a.—na-m.—na-p.—nit$^s.\beta e$.—nx-m.; ^{s}.—opi$^n.\beta b$.—pet.ab^t.—ph-x.43.—pho.βa.—pla^b.—pso.—ptl.a$\dot{t}^g.\gamma$.; ^{h}.a$\dot{t}$.—rn-s.—rho$^{h \cdot s}$.; 86.—rhs^p.—sec^t.—sil^p.; βa.3.—spi^p.; ^{v}.—stp^p.—sto.—sul.; ^{s}.ab^c.; βe.—zin.

—— *but recollection returns when half asleep.*—sel.

—— *of what he was about to write.*—cn-i.—na-m.

—— *of what he was going to say.*—cn-i.

—— *in a reverie.*—hyo.

—— *forgets to wind up watch.*—fl-x.

—— *of what he is going to do.*—c-ph.—chd^s.—hdr.u.—kre.

b^p. **Loss of memory, weakness of memory.**—aco.—ac-c.—ag-p.—æth.—ail.—alm.—amb^s.—aml.—ana.; ^{b}.; (4).; ^{v}.4.—arg.βa.19.42.—ag-n$^s.\gamma$.; $^s.o^2$.—ars.; ^{o}.—aru.—as-t.—au-m.—ba-c.—bel.—ber^s.a$\dot{k}$.—bor.—bov.—bry.—bu-s.; ^{s}.(5).—ca-c^s.—c-ph.—cam.; $^{b \cdot y}$.

βa,𝔟.e𝔡.π1.—cn-i.—can.4.5.—cb-v.—ca-x.—cr-s.—cau.—ch-s^{b}.—clo.a𝔟^{a6},𝔨.—cl-h^{s}.au.—cic$^{s\cdot y}$.—cle.—coc^{b}.—coa.—cof^{b}.—con.; 99.; ^{f}.—cop.a𝔨.—cro^{h}.—crt.—cup^{s}.—cyc.—dph.—der.—dig.; ^{s}.γp.; βa.—elc^{y}.a𝔟^{s}.—epn.—fag^{b}.—fer.—glo.—grp.—gui.—ham.—hel^{s}.γq.—hep.au.—hdr.—hy-x.—hyo.—hyp.—ibe.—ign.—irs.—jug.—k-br.—k-ca^{s}.β𝔟^{h}.—k-cy.—kis.—kre.—lah.—la-x.—la-v.—lam^{b}.β𝔢.—lau.; 4.—lil.—lyp.au.—lyc.; ^{g}.—mt-n.a𝔵^{w}.—man.—mrl.—mer.—mez.; ^{s}.γ.—mo-m.—msc.; γ.—mur^{f}.—nat.—na-m^{f}.; 𝔢^{a}.—na-p.—ni-x.; ω^{3}.—nx-m.44.—œna.—ol-a.—opi.; $^{s\cdot y}$.—ptv.—pla^{b}.—plb.—pol.—pso.—ptl.—rs-g.—rs-r.—rhs^{o}.; ^{s}.βa.γ.44.—rut^{v}.; ^{s}.—sab.—src.—sep.; ^{s}.a𝔵^{t}.—sil^{o}.—so-l^{s}.14.—spi.; ^{o}.—stn.3-99.—stp^{o}.—str.; a𝔣^{b}.; βa.δo.3-30.; a𝔣.—trn.a𝔟^{i}.; a𝔩,𝔩^{c},𝔱,𝔟,𝔵^{w}.; ^{s}.—tep.βa.; ^{b}.φ.; γ.26.—thu.—til^{y}.—trf.—ver.—vrb.—vi-o.; a𝔟^{c},𝔨.; a.γ.

—— *sudden.*—ca-s.66.
—— *absolute.*—k-br.
—— *as if half asleep.*—cup.
—— *as if in a dream.*—bel.—hyo.—na-m.
—— *in reverie.*—grt.
—— *for dates.*—aco.
—— *for words.*—arn.—bap.—cb-a.—cca.—cch.—nx-m.—sul.—ver.
—— *for places.*—nx-m.—pso.
—— *thinks his mother is dead.*—na-m.
—— *followed by liveliness of memory.*—cyc.
—— *followed by headache.*—vi-o. a.
—— *as if in occiput.*—k-ca.86. (47).
—— *after an attack of catalepsy.*—cam.
—— *periodical.*—cb-v.

𝔟^{q}. **Loss of memory for names.**—ana.3.—car^{b}.—.ch-s$^{f\cdot m}$.—clo^{r}.—gui.—lth.—lyc.—mer.—na-a.—oln.—ptl.—rhs.—xyp.

—— *for his own names.*—k-br.—sul.

𝔟^{r}. **Loss of memory for persons.**—clo^{q}.—cro$^{b\cdot p}$.—mer.

𝔟^{s}. **Weakness of head, of intellectual power, of thinking power, difficulty of comprehension, incapacity for mental work, obtuseness of mind, stupidity.**—abi.—ac-x.—aco.—alm.—amb.—am-g.—am-c.—ana.—ant.—aps.—ag-n.—arn.—ars.—ard.—at-a.—am-i.—ard.—asa.—as-t.—bap.—ba-m.—bel.—ber.—bov.—bry.—ca-c.—c-cs.—c-ph.—cam.—cn-i.—can.—cb-v.—cr-h.—cr-s.—cha.—chd.—chi.—cn-s.—cnb.—cle.—cof.—cfn.—col.—cod.—con.—cop.—cot.—cro.—cup.—dig.—dio.—dir.—elp.—evo.—fag.—for.—glo.—gel.—grp.—ham.—hel.—hln.—hep.—hpm.—hyo.—ibe.—ign.—iod.—irs.—k-br.—k-cy.—k-ca.—lah.—la-s.—la-v.—lep.—lil.—lol.—lyc.—lcp.—mt-n.—mns.—mer.—mr-c.—mr-s.—mez.—mit.—mo-a.—msc.—nat.—na-m.—ni-x.—nx-m.—nx-v.—oln.—opi.—ox-x.—ph-x.—phs.—plb.—pul.—rs-r.—rhs.—rut.—sec.—sep.—sil.—so-n.—spi.—stn.—str.—sul.—su-x.—tab.—tan.—trn.—thu.—ver.—vi-o.—zin., &c.

—— *periodical.*—chi.
—— *as if drunk.*—dig.
—— *as if the reason stood still.*—mt-n.γ.ω^{3}.
—— *almost without consciousness.*—ni-x.—stn^{g}.βa.
—— *as if going mad.*—chd.
—— *as if deaf.*—cha.—ni-x.
—— *as if about to faint.*—bry.ηp. 18.
—— *as when going to sleep.*—asr.
—— *in a reverie.*—arn.—chi.—grt^{p}.—gui.3.19.—ign.—

mez.—ol-a.—rhs.—spi.δc^d. sul.86.

—— *as if in a dream.*—cha.— mgt.—ol-a.—squ.—zin.

—— *as if all objects were absent.* —rhs.βa.

—— *as after a fever.*—sar.b.

—— *in scientific matters.*—nx-v.

—— *for transcendental considerations.*—cof.

—— *only fitted for mechanical operations.*—iod.

—— *preventing all work.*—stp.

—— *but continuing to work.*—ol-a.

—— *followed by indifference.*—sbd^z.ax^{ii}.

—— *followed by increased mental powers.*—ox-x.

—— *following increased mental power.*—cle.$v^1q.\omega^2$.—vi-o.

—— *following ecstasy.*—lah.ω^2.

b^t. Imbecility.—ant.—ag-n.$c^{c.m}$.— ars.—ba-m.—bry^s.—can.—hyo^y. —mer.—nx-m.—opi^s.—plb.—sec.; ^{o}.—so-n.—str.

b^u. Idiocy.—abs.—aga^y.; $^s.\beta$.—aps. —bel.—cr-s.—cnt.—cl-h.—hyo. —plb.

b^v. Weakness of imagination, slow flow of ideas.—acn.—ana^p.4.— bry.—caj.—ca-c$^s.\beta e$.—can$^o.ak$.; δ. —cb-v$^c.\gamma$.—cau.—chi.; ab^m.—cod. —cnm.ax^b.—iod.ax^t.—ipc.—mt-n. —nx-m.; $^x.ab^c$.—ox-x^s.3.—ph-x.ab^i. —pho.—rhs.—rut^p.—sep.—spi^o.

—— *with undiminished faculty of judging of facts and events.* —bry.

b^w. Incoherence of thought.—gel. —hyo.as.

b^x. Slow speech.—ars.—bel.—hyo. δo.—nx-m^v.ab^c.—thu.

b^y. Obtuseness of senses.—aga^u.— ana.ag.—ag-n.ab^o.; $^{t.s}.v^2$.—asa—. cam$^{b.p}.\beta a,b.es.\varpi^1$.—ced.—cha^s.; φ. —cic$^{p.s}$.—cca.—con.—cup.; ^{s}.— cu-s.—dro.$ab^{b.i}.k$.—elc$^p.ab^s$.—hel. —hy-x.—hyo.ab.; ^{t}.—lau.—lil.4. —lol.—msc^p.—na-m^s.ak^f.—nx-m.

—opi$^{p.s}$.—plb.ω^5.—rn-b.—rho.— rhs.26.—sec.—str.—tan.—til^p.

—— *of taste, smell, and feeling.* —opi.χ^1.

—— *loss of reason.*—str.

—— *as if intoxicated.*—nx-m^s.

—— *as if he had got a blow on the forehead.*—nat.

—— *felt as if could not rise again, when he stooped.*—rhs.

b^z. Sufferings from mental work. —pul.

—— *left brain fatigued.*—at-a.

—— *unconsciousness.*—nx-m.

—— *crossness.*—ber.

—— *giddiness.*—ph-x^s.

—— *headache.*—am-i.—ca-x.— mo-a.—pho.—sbd^s.ax^{ii}.

—— *head affected.*—coc.

—— *heat of face.*—xyp.ηp.5.

—— *nausea.*—aur.

—— *nervous irritation of bowels.* nx-m.

—— *fatigue.*—car.

—— *exhaustion.*—aur.—cha.— sel.

—— *especially reading and writing.*—cch.

CONCOMITANTS.

aa. Apathy.—ce-b^b.—rs-r^f.

aā. Indifference.—dig^s.5.—lah^o.

aa^b. Indifferent to everything.— bel^s.ω^2.

aa^b. Indifference to external things. —opi^s.—stn^s.au.ηc^b.

aa^q. Unsympathizing.—pla$^{b.s}$.8.122.

ab. Laziness.—cb-v^s.—crt$^{f.s}$.— hyo^y.

ab^a. Disinclination for amusement. —mur.ak.

ab^b. Disinclination for bodily exertion.—dro^y.ab^i,k.

ab^c. Disinclination for conversation. —gel^s.—man$^{f.s}.ax^e$,k^s,u.— nx-m$^{v.x}$.—rs-r^s.—rhs.ω^2.— sul$^{o.s}$.—vi-o$^{b.c}$.; ^{p}.ak.—vi-t^s.

ab^i. Disinclination for mental work. —alm^s.—bor$^{e.s}.\gamma.v$.3.(8-31).

—dro^y.ab^b.k.)—ni-x^s.—ol-a^b. aæ^w.—ph-x^v.—rs-r^b.—trn^p.

ab^m. *Disinclination for movement.*—chi^v.

ab^o. *Disinclination for occupation.*—ag-n^y.—cyc^s.—sep^b.—ser^s. βε.—stn^s.

ab^t. *Disinclination for thinking.*—bap^s.—pet^o.

af. *Discomfort.*—sep$^{c.f.m}$.

af^b. *Uneasiness.*—ang^b.a^e.aæ^r.4.—ast^s.βε^b.γ.ρ.2-99.—mt-s$^{a.b}$a.g, b^e.—str^p.

af^c. *Inward uneasiness.*—mag^b.ω^8. 44.

ag. *Anxiety.*—alm^s.ηp.ω^2.—ana^y. —mt-s$^{a.b}$.af^b,b^e.

ag^e. *Anxiety about the future.*—man$^{f.s}$.ab^c,k^s,u.

ab^{æ6}. *Fear of going mad.*—clo^p.ak.

ab^s. *Starting.*—elc$^{p.y}$.

ak. *Low spirits.*—ag-n$^{f.s}$.βε.γd.σ^2. —arn^s.—ber$^{p.s}$.—can$^{o.v}$.—clo^p.ab^{æ6}.—cop^p.—dro^y.ab$^{b.i}$. —mns.—mur.ab^a.—opi^s.ω^2.—vi-o^p.ab^c.

ak^a. *Gloomy thoughts.*—sul^s.8-31.

ak^f. *Despondency.*—na-m$^{s.y}$.

ak^s. *Discontented with himself.*—man$^{f.s}$.ab^c,g^e,u.

al. *Tears.*—trn^p.al^c,t,b,æ^w.

al^c. *Sighing.*—trn^p.al,t,b,æ^w.

aq. *Restlessness.*—ced.—hfb^s.2.—stn^b.ab^h.

at. *Haste.*—mgt$^{f.o}$.—ptl$^{h.o}$.

ar^s. *Hurry in writing.*—ptl^o.χ.

at. *Variable humour.*—trn^p.al,l^c,b, æ^w.

at^a. *Alternately gay and sad.*—chi^s.

au. *Crossness.*—ars^s.βa^b.—ber^z.—evo^s.—hep^p.—hyo^s.φ.4.—lil^b. —mag^o.—man$^{f.s}$.αb^c,g^e,k^s.—stn^s.aa^b.ηc^b.

au^d. *Furious rage.*—trn^s.

ab. *Irresolution.*—alm.—iod^s.—trn^p.al,l^c,t,æ^w.

ab^e. *Hesitation.*—mt-s$^{a.b}$.af^b,g.

ab^h. *Inconstancy at work.*—stn^b.aq.

aæ^r. *Pleasant anticipations.*—ang^b. a^e.af^b.4.

aæ^t. *Inclined for work.*—pho^b.3.—sep$^{p.s}$.

aæ^w. *Cheerfulness.*—ca-s.5.—ol-a^b. ab^i.—trn^p.al,l^c,t,b.

aæ^{bb}. *Loquacity.*—lah^b.φ.ω^2.5.

βa. *Vertigo.*—amb.—arg^p.19.42. —ars^s.—bor^e.—bry^s.γw.—ca-c^o.—cam$^{b.p.y}$.βb.εb.π^1.—cth^s.—dig^p.—gel^s.γq.δo.—hæm^s.—mer$^{f.s}$.εa.—nat^s.—ph-x$^{s.z}$.—pho^o.—rhs^s.; p^s.γ.44. —sil^o.3. ; ^{f}.—stn^s.—str$^{p.s}$.δo. 3-30.—sul^s.—tep^p. ; ^{s}.χ^3.

βb. *Staggering.*—cam^b.; $^{b.p.y}$.βa.εb. π^1.—nx-m^c.—opi$^{n.o}$.

βε. *Confusion of head.*—ana^s.3-99. —ag-n$^{f.s}$.ak.γd.σ^2.—bov^s.—ca-c$^{s.v}$.; ^{s}.—con^s.43.—cop^s.—dig^s.—fer^s.—hæm$^{f.s}$.γq.—iod^s. —lah^b.—lam$^{b.p}$.—lo-s^h.γ.—lyc^b.γ.—men^s.6.(8).—mer$^{f.s}$. φ.—ni-x^s.—nit^s.—opi^s.—ph-x^s.—ser^s.ab^o.—sul^o.—tab$^{b.c}$.γq.66.(72).—thu^s.

βε. *Brain feels paralysed.*—aga$^{s.u}$. —ca-c$^{s.v}$.

βε^a. *Stupid in head.*—aps^d.—plg^s.

βε^b. *Empty head.*—ars^s.au.—ast^s. af^b.γ.ρ.2-99.—cop^s.—lyc^s.41.

βb. *Whirring in head.*—k-ca$^{p.s}$.

γc. *Horripilation in head.*—amb^s.

γd. *Congestion of head.*—ag-n$^{f.s}$.ak. βε.γ.σ^2.

γi^a. *Fulness of head.*—ag-n$^{p.s}$.γp.; ^{s}.γp,q.ηp. ; $^{f.s}$.ak.βε.γd.σ^2.—bor$^{e.s}$.ab^i.v.3.(8-31).—idm^s. 43.

γp. *Heat of head.*—aga^s.δ.—ag-n. $^{p.s}$.γi^a.; ^{s}.γq.ηp.—dig$^{p.s}$.

γq. *Heaviness of head.*—ag-n^s.γp. ηp.—ca-c.δh^n.83.—gel^s.βa.δo. —hæm$^{f.s}$.βε.—hel$^{p.s}$.—tab$^{b.c}$. βε.66.(72).

γw. *Movements in brain.*—bry^s.βa.

γw. *As if something fell from one side of the head to the other.* —tep^p.26.

γ. *Head affected.*—coe^s.

γ. *Headache.*—am-c^o.—a-sc^b.—ars^s.κ^4.—bel^o.—ca-a^o.43.—cn-i^s.—can^s.δc^d.—cb-v$^{c.v}$.

cup^s.——lo-s^h.βe.——lyc^b.βe.—
lep^s.——mt-n^s.ω^3.——mez$^{p.s}$.——
mo-a$^{b.z}$.——msc^p.——pho^z.——ptl^s.;
^{o}.ar^g.——rhs$^{p.s}$.βa.44.——scu^s.3.
——str.——vi-o^p.a.

γ. *Head as if compressed.*—aps^s.
γ. *Electric shocks through head.*
  —ast^s.af^b.βe^b.ρ.2-99.
γ. *Troublesome sensation in head.*
  —aps^s.
γ. *Uneasiness in head.*—sil^b.κ^4.5.
$\delta \zeta^d$. *Staring.*—can^s.γ.; ^{v}.—spi^s.
δh^n. *Eyes gummed up.*—ca-c.γq.83.
δe. *Eyes weak and watery.*—opi^s.
  π^1.
δ. *Pain in eye.*—aga^s.γp.
δo. *Failure of sight.*—aco^s.—alm.
  ea.—gel^s.βa.γq.--glo.—hyo^x.
  —str$^{p.s}$.βa.3-30.
δt^m. *Flickering before eyes.*—bel.
ϵa. *Failure of hearing.*—alm.δo.—
  mer$^{f.s}$.βa.
$\epsilon \upsilon$. *Noises in ears.*—cam$^{b.p.y}$.βa,b.
  π^1.
ηp. *Heat of face.*—alm^s.a$\mathfrak{g}$.ω^2.—
  ag-n^s.γp,q.——bry^s.18.——xyp^z.
  5.
ηc^b. *Pale face, dark round eyes.*—
  stn^s.aa^b.u.
κ^4. *Uneasiness in scrobiculus.*—sil^b.
  γ.5.
κ^4. *Sinking in scrobiculus.*—ars^s.γ.
κ^5. *Nausea.*—aur^z.
o^2. *Stuttering speech.*——agn$^{f.s.y}$.;
  $^{p.s}$.—cha^g.
o^2. *Loss of voice.*—can^f.
π^1. *Short anxious breathing.*—opi^s.
  δe.
π^1. *Suffocation.*—cam$^{b.p.y}$.βa,b.$\epsilon \upsilon$.
ρ. *Quick pulse.*—ast^s.af^b.βe^b.γ.2-
  99.—crt^f.χ^1.
σ^2. *Throbbing in neck.*—ag-n$^{f.s}$.a$\mathfrak{k}$.
  βe.γd.
τ^1. *Shooting in finger-joints.*--msc^s.
υ. *Weakness of legs.*—bor$^{e.s}$.ab^i.
  γi^a.3.(8-31).
υ^1q. *Heaviness of feet.*—cle^s.ω^2.
ϕ. *Sleepiness.*——ang^s.43.—bel.—
  cha^y.——hyo^s.; ^{s}.au.—kis^s.—
  lah^b.a$\mathfrak{æ}^{bb}$.ω^2.5.——mer$^{f.s}$.βe.——
  mr-s^s.——myr^b.——na-m^s.4.—

nx-m^s.43.——opi^s.——stn^s.——
sum^s.—tep$^{b.p}$.
χ^1. *Coldness.*——crt^f.ρ.——mrs^s.——
  opi^y.
χ^2. *Heat.*—ang^b.a^e.4.
χ^3. *Perspiration.*—c-ph^s.40.
  —— *cold.*—tep^s.βa.
ω. *Weight and stiffness of body.*—
  cam^b.
ω^2. *Prostration, weakness.*——alm^s.
  a$\mathfrak{g}$.np.——ast.——aur^z.——bel^s.aa^b.
  ——car^z.——cha^z.——cle^s.υ^1q.——
  cch^s.——glo.—lah^b.a$\mathfrak{æ}^{bb}$.ϕ.5.; ^{s}.
  ——mns^s.——ni-x.——opi^s.a$\mathfrak{k}$.—
  plg^b.——rn-b^s.--rhs^s.ab^c.——sel^z.
  ——spo^s.——xyp^s.
ω^2. *Desire to lean against some-*
  thing.—gym^s.
ω^3. *Threatened syncope.*—mt-n^s.γ.
ω^5. *Convulsions.*—lol^s.—plb^y.
ω^5. *Subsultus tendinum.*—cam^o.
ω^7. *Cramp.*—ple^b.
ω^8. *Trembling.*—ca-x^a.
ω^8. *Trembling of hands.*—-mag^b.
  af^c.44.

CONDITIONS.

2. *At night.*—crn$^{b.s}$.--for^s.—hfb^s.
  q.
2-99. *On waking at night.*—ast^s.af^b.
  βe^b.γ.ρ.
3. *In the morning.*—ana^q.—bor$^{e.s}$.
  ab^i.γi^a.v.(8-31).--cth$^{c.s}$.—elc^j.
  4.—gui^s.19.——nat^b.—ox-x$^{s.v}$.
  ——ph-x^s.121.——pho^b.a$\mathfrak{æ}^t$.——
  scu^s.γ.—sil^o.βa.—sul^s.41.
3-30. *On rising in morning.*—str$^{p.s}$.
  βa.δo.
3-99. *In the morning on waking.*—
  ana^s.βe.—stn^p.
4. *In the afternoon.*—ana^p.; ana.
  $^{p.v}$.—ang^b.a^e.χ^2.; ^{b}.a^e.af^b,$\mathfrak{æ}^r$.—
  can^p.5.——cep$^{m.o}$.70.——elc^j.3.
  ——fag^s.(66).--hyo^s.au.ϕ.—
  lau^p.—lil^y.——na-m^s.ϕ.——rs-r^s.
  —sep^s.——sil$^{g.h.s}$.(5.66).
5. *In the evening.*—ana^s.a^d.——
  bu-s$^{p.s}$.——ca-s.a$\mathfrak{æ}$.—can^p.4.—
  dig^s.a$\mathfrak{a}$.—hpm^o.43.—ign$^{d.f.h.s}$.
  41.—lah^b.a$\mathfrak{æ}^{bb}$.ϕ.ω^2.—lyc$^{b.f}$.——

mil.70.—na-in.—rs-r^s.—*sil*^g.
h·s.4.(66).—xyp^z.*η*p.

5. *In the forenoon.*—ars^s.—cot^s.
—sil^b.γ.κ⁴.

6. *In a room.*—men^s.*βe*.(8).

8. *In the open air.*—cnb^b.—men^s.
βe.6.—pla^{b·s}.*αa*^q.122.

8-31. *By walking in open air.*—bor^{e·s}.
abⁱ.γi^a.*v*.3.—sul^s.*a*k^a.

14. *By leaning head against any-thing.*—lyp^b.—so-l^{p·s}.

16. *When lying.*—bry.—zin^s.72.(47).

18. *When standing.*—bry^s.*η*p.

19. *When sitting.*—arg^p.42.—cch^b.
—gui^s.3.

26. *By moving head.*—tep^p.γw.
26. *By turning head.*—rhs.

27. *On crossing or raising arms.*—spr^s.

31. *When walking.*—rhs^s.66.

40. *By disagreeable news.*—c-ph^s.χ³.

41. *By mental exertion.*—hep^s.—hur^b.—ign^{d·f·h·s}.5.—lyc^s.*βe*^b.—rn-b^s.—sul^s.3.

42. *When thinking.*—arg^p.19.—ni-x^s.

43. *By reading.*—aco.44.—agn^b.—alm^b.—ang^s.*φ*.—ca-a^o.γ.—ca-x^b.—cof^b.—con^s.*βe*.—glo^b.44.—hpm^o.5.—idm^s.γi^a.—lah^b.—mgt^b.—mez^b.—nx-m^s.; *φ*.—oln^b.; ^{b·c}.—ph-x^o.

44. *By writing.*—aco.43.—can^o.—ch-s^b.—glo^b.43.—mag^b.*αf*^c.*ω*^s.—nx-m^p.—rhs^{p·s}.*βa*.γ.

47. *On shutting eyes.*—k-ca^p.86.—zin^s.72.(16).

66. *After food.*—ca-s^p.—fag^s.—grp^s.—rhs^s.31.—sil^{g·h·s}.4.(5).—tab^{b·c}.*βe*.γq.(72).

70. *By drinking wine.*—cep^{m·o}.4.—mil.5.

72. *By vomiting.*—asr.—tab^{b·c}.*βe*.γq.66.—zin^s.(16.47).

83. *During menses.*—ca-c.γq.*δh*ⁿ.—lcp^s.

86. *When speaking.*—am-c.—k-ca^p.(47).—mez^s.—rho^o.—sul^s.

97. *After sleep.*—gym^s.

99. *On awaking.*—æsc.—con^p.
121. *When alone.*—ph-x^s.3.
122. *In society.*—pla^{b·s}.*αa*^q.8.

ɩ. **Delirium, delusions** (*peculiar*).

aco. He cannot think or reflect on anything; knows nothing and has no conception of anything with his head as formerly; but feels that all these operations of his mind take place in the pit of his stomach; after two hours he is twice attacked with vertigo, and his thinking faculty returns to his head as usual.

alm. Such confusion of head as if his consciousness were without his body; when he speaks it seems to him as if another had said it, and when he sees any-thing, as if another saw it, or as if he must first be changed into another person before he can see it.

ant. Madness, imbecility; she did not leave the bed, never spoke when not addressed, asked neither for food nor drink, she ate readily when it was offered her, when hungry, and refused when not hungry; at the same time she always plucked at her neckerchief, or folded and un-folded a cloth, or pulled out threads from the bedclothes and laid them together; she was so insensible that she lay on the motions that escaped from her, without being aware of it, and never complained of pain.

bel. Madness; running about the streets naked, making grimaces, dancing, laughing loud, and doing nonsensical acts.

Makes hideous faces, sticks out the tongue, makes a noise with the tongue, chokes, vomits.

At one time hastily catches

hold of those about him, and then draws back frightened.

Along with burning heat of body, with open, staring, and motionless eyes, such furious madness that she must be held fast to prevent her injuring others, and when thus held she spat on those about her.

Delirium, with alternate laughing and crying, ridiculous grimaces, singing, shouting, agitation of the whole body, and jerking gesticulation with fingers.

Phantasies, in which everything appears beautiful, artistic, and glittering, and during which a greater knowledge of mechanics is displayed than was formerly observed.

cam. Desire to leap out of bed, lightness of all movements, lifts legs high over things in the way, without actual increase or diminution of strength.

Imagines he is dead, that he is alone in the world, that he is forsaken of God, that he is a demon, that he is in hell, with a certain power of reasoning. The heavens and earth appear lifeless. The sense of feeling is lost; the eyes protrude. He desires to weep, but the eyes are dry. He thought of throwing himself out of window, but some remains of sense withheld him. He is horribly frightened and would flee he knows not whither. His whole body feels quite cold, he seems to have no vital heat. Hot tea seems quite cold to him when he drinks it.

can. Gay ecstasy, with dancing, singing, appetite, lasciviousness, desire to murder.

cic. Madness; after unusual sleep, heat of the body; she sprang out of bed, danced, laughed, and did all sorts of foolish things; drank a great deal of wine, hopped about, clapped her hands, and her face was very red all night.

crt. She cries several times "He is in the lions' den, but they won't bite him."

At 6 p.m. attacks of mania; zoo-magnetic state, in which she does not reply to questions, but fancies she hears a voice on her left side and behind her; she follows it and knocks against the shut doors, which she scratches with her nails. These attacks are sometimes interrupted with bursts of laughter, and always end in a flood of tears.

eug. Forgetful of all decorum, he crept into a corner and said he must sleep.

glo. Coming up the street, things look strange to him; had to look every little while to see if he was in the right street; the houses looked out of their places.

The walk home seemed three times as long as it was.

hyo. Laughable solemn deeds in improper clothing, mingled with fury. (In a priest's frock, over his shirt, he wishes to go to church to preach and perform divine service, and falls furiously on those who seek to prevent him.)

Along with constant burning heat and cries, he breathes with difficulty, and makes powerful motions with his hands.

Excessively furious and naked, he passes day and night sleeplessly with cries.

Ecstasia, lucid vision, with peculiar expression of tranquility, cheerfulness, and contentment; calm, thoughtful, bright eyes, with dilated pupils;

small, slow, rare pulse ; quick, powerful rising up ; endeavours with much eloquence, in elegant language and well selected expressions, with animated gestures and friendly smiling, to prove that he was quite well and at home, and also that he wished to go out, at the same time complete sleeplessness.

mg-m. Deception of the fancy, when she was reading a book, as if some one read after her and compelled her to read quicker, with buzzing and humming all around her ; on rising up she imagined she saw about her great clouds and rocks, that gradually disappeared again ; thereafter anxiety, fearfulness, uneasiness, so that she knew not how to calm herself ; on looking round about her all disappeared, but recurred twice while reading again.

mer. Madness; she uncovers herself at night, pulls the straw about and scolds ; by day she leaps up high (like a wanton woman) both out of doors and in the room ; she talks and scolds much to herself, knows not her nearest relations ; spreads out the spittle she ejects with her foot, and licks it up again ; she also licks cow-dung and the dirt out of puddles ; she often takes small stones in her mouth without swallowing them, and complains of a cutting pain in bowels ; much coagulated blood escapes at stool; she does no harm to any one, but defends herself violently when any one touches her ; she will not do anything she is told, will not sit down to dinner, though she has most days taken an inordinate quantity of food and drink ; she looks very pale and sunken,

and appears to be much weaker than before.

msc. He sits buried in thought, speaks aloud but incomprehensibly to himself, throws about his arms, crosses them over one another, and makes so many grimaces, that one fears for his intellect ; or he walks about but sits down again immediately, puts his hands above his head, and complains of violent pains without saying where they are.

sec. Confusion of the reason and deliria, bordering on mania ; he was furious and could only be restrained with difficulty ; after a few hours violent vomiting, followed by long, deep sleep ; there remained vertigo as if drunk, with prostration.

str. He thinks he is dying and will not live over the night ; he rejoices that he is going to die, and gives directions about his funeral.

He converses with absent persons as though they were present, and addresses inanimate objects (as chessmen) by the names of such persons, but observes none of those standing about him.

He walks about the room absorbed in himself, with fixed sparkling eyes surrounded by blue circles, but takes no notice of surrounding objects, and is entirely occupied with the objects of his fancy.

She leapt up with great force and anxiety, and held fast by her mother as if in despair, crying out that she would fall, and kept her hold as firmly as though she were on the edge of an abyss ; then she became quiet, whistled, pointed with her finger to muscæ volitantes, which she pursued with eyes and hands and at which she snatched, and when she found she got nothing, looked sulky.

vp-t. The eyes look as if he were raving mad, with staggering and stumbling forwards, he talks about going home, tumbles against a bureau, rises and falls again, finally remains lying with red face, heavy head, tongue between his teeth, rattling and death, with turgescence of vessels of dura mater and surface of the brain.

c^a. **Feeling as if going mad, losing senses, consciousness.**—aco.γ.; γ. 8-31.—aga.γ.——bov.βa.——brv.—cn-i.——cot.rl.3-99.——hpm.$\beta \iota^c$.—lam.b^c.—lil.5.—mag.γ.5.2.——mg-s. βe^a.——mrl.βa.33.——mer^m.ab^{ag}.—msc.γ.——na-m.——sep.βa.29.66.—sul.βe^a.

—— *if she did not hold tightly on to herself.*—lil.

c^b. **Delirium.**—aco.—ag-p.—ant.—ars. ; ω^5.—au-m.γd.—bel^c.; (66).; 2.(1).; δi,aa,P^2.ηc^a.$\iota.\rho.\sigma^2$d.——bis.—cac.2.98.(99).——cam.——cnc.—cth. ; ω^5.——ca-x.; au^d.χ^3.——chi.—ch-s.—cmf.——cod.2.——cfn.——cch. 5. ; 2.——cnm.——con.; ^{d}.——cop.—crt.; 2.; ω^5.——cup.——cu-a.—dig.—dor.——dul.2.——eth.——glo.$\mathfrak{d}^a$.—hy-x.—hyo.a^h.; αq.—hyn^p—iod.—jat.$\mathfrak{d}^a$.—k-br.—k-ca.——lil.—lol.—lyc.2.—mr-c.—mr-s.—mez.—mor.—nit.—nx-m.; b^a.; $\beta a.\phi.\omega$.—nx-v. $^{d.l.m}$.—opi. ; ^{m}.; $^{c.m}$.—pho.ab^{ag}.5.—phy.—plb.δii.ηx^i.$\theta.\lambda.\sigma^1$.2.—rho.—sam^m.—str.; ^{d}.; b^p.—ver.—vrt.—vp-r.κ^6.

—— *transient.*—ac-x.
—— *in paroxysms.*—bel.—con.
—— *bland.*—sec.
—— *quiet.*—tab^c.
—— *muttering.*—dor.—hyo.—mer.
—— *talkative.*—dor.—str.
—— *mirthful.*—con.
—— *fearful.*—str.

Delirium, *suspicious.*—str.
—— *silly.*—aco^e.$u u^c$,$\mathbf{x}^w$.—æth^m.
—— *wild.*—ga-x^c.2.—hy-x.δP^1.ρ. —str^f.—ver$^{c.d.m}$.χ^1.
—— *very violent.*—ars.αq.2.
—— *wants to fight.*—hyo.
—— *furious.*—cic.—dig.2.—mer. —plb.—str.
—— *first merry, then furious.*—bel.
—— *tremens.*—bel.—cmf.—cf-t. mer.—nx-m.
—— *busy.*—bel.
—— *mussitans.*—tar^c.
—— *erotic.*—pho.—str.
—— *visionary love for an ideal woman.*—ant.8-31.
—— *like intoxication.*—ca-x.
—— *alternating with sense.*—bel.
—— *loss of consciousness and personality.*—cam.
—— *as if in a dream.*—bel^m.
—— *dreamy wandering about.*—cam.
—— *as in acute fever.*—hyo.
—— *as if possessed by the devil.*—hyo.
—— *buffoonery.*—aco.—bel.
—— *piercing cries.*—bel.—eth.—pho.ω^5.—str.
—— *makes speeches about himself.*—dor.δi.ηaa,ii.ρ.
—— *jumps out of bed.*—aco$^{c.m}$.
—— *followed by vertigo.*—col.

c^c. **Raving, talking nonsense, shouting.**—aco$^{b.m}$.——æth.——ag-p.—ag-n^m.47.; ^{m}.b^t.—ars^m.—bel^b.; 2.(1).; 5.; δc^d.; $^{l.n}$.$\mathfrak{d}^a$.$\alpha \mathbf{x}^w$.—cam. ; ^{d}.—cn-i.—$ab^{æ2}$.γq.—cth.—chd.βa.κ^5.—chi.χ^2. —cl-h.—clf.—cmf^m.βb^c.δ.P^2.—cin. —cch^d.$\beta \mathfrak{d}$.δab^b.ϕ^1.ω^6.—cup.; ^{d}.δs,c^h ρ.χ^3.—dig.ω^6.2.; αq.2.—dul.—eth. —ga-x^b.2.—glo.γ.—hel.—hyo^m.; $\mathfrak{d}^e$.; ^{d}.; 83.—hyp.ab.γp.δf,aa,P^2.χ^2. 2.—jat.$\mathfrak{d}^e$.βa.—lo-i.ηu.ρ.5.99.—mer.—m-cy.ϕ^1.2.—nx-m$^{j.o}$.βa.ϕ^1. ω^6.—opi$^{b.m}$.; ^{d}.ag.$\beta \mathfrak{d}$.χ^2.—par.—plb.—rhe.—so-n.—str.; ^{d}.al.; ^{d}. ω^5.; ^{l}.au.; al.2.—sul.—tab.$\mathfrak{d}^a$.δc^d. —tar^h.; ^{b}.

Raving *in a high screeching voice.*— str.

—— *about business.*—ars.—-bry. —dor.δi̇.ηaa,ii.ρ.—str.

—— *about religious things.*—ver. b·d·m.χ¹.

—— *about wolves.*—bel.

—— *about dogs.*—bel.ηrii.

—— *bites and barks like a dog.*— bel.

—— *consisting of nonsensical questions.*—aur.ηaa.2.

—— *childish nonsense.*—aco^b.αu^c. æ^w.

—— *gives foolish answers.*—ars.

—— *stupid stuff.*—hyo.—par.

—— *as in sleep.*—bel.

—— *alternation of laughing, weeping, and singing.*—str.

—— *singing.*—bel.γhh.ηc^b.δo^c.εa. —cn-i.—byp.—str.—vir.

—— —— *comic songs.*—clf.

—— *giving the word of command.* —bel.

—— *talks to himself.*—hyo.— mgt.—mt-n.

—— *murmurs to himself.*—clf.— dor.—hyo^m.—tab^b.

—— *disconnected talk.*—hy-x.

—— *improper language.*—nx-m.

—— *in imagination.*—aur.

—— *blaspheming.*—cn-i.

—— *accents last syllable in every word and laughs immoderately.*—cn-i.

—— *obscene.*—clf.

c^d. **Mania,** *madness.*—aco.83.—ac-l. —æth.--ail.--ant.--ars$^{h·m}$.αg,l.γ.εv. ω⁸.; αk.—bel.—cam.θ.—cn-i.γq.ω². --cth.--ch-s.—cof.—cch^c.βv.δa^b. φ¹.ω⁶.—con^b.—crt.v.—cup^m.; ^{c}.δs, t^b.ρ.χ³.—hel.—hyo.; μ².—ind.ω⁵. —led.—lo-i.ω⁵.—lol.—lyc^c.αj,u$^{g·n}$. —mer.; αk^j.—mr-c.—nx-m.; βv. œna.ω⁵.—-opi.; αæ^s.δa^{b}ηaa.; v.— plb.—rho.—sec.—str^b.; ^{m}.; αɪ^a,æ^{ii}. —trn$^{g·m}$.γ.δi̇.λ.ω⁸.; $^{e·g}$.αb^c.—ter.— ver.αɪ.

—— *half mad.*—k-hy.2.

—— *acute.*—ba-m.

Mania, *speechless.*—hyo.δc^b,P².ηaa.

—— *fearless.*—aga.αu^n.βv.

—— *noisy.*—ver.

—— *quarrelsome.*—cup.—hyo.— lyc.

—— *furious.*—ac-l.—cth.—opi.θ.

—— *as if drunk.*—œna.

—— *gay.*—bel.—str.—trn.αæ^{ii}.

—— *timid.*—aga.

—— *despairs of salvation.*—str.

—— *ecstatic.*—str.

—— *amiable.*—cro.

—— *religious.*—str.

—— *sometimes gay, sometimes grave.*—can.

—— *like drunkenness.*—hyo.

—— *like delirium tremens.*—bel. —tab.

—— *a kind of life without himself, as in fever.*—lyc.

—— *with agreeable visions.*—can.

—— *furor uterinus.*—grt.o.ω⁵.

—— *kleptomania.*—abs.

—— *singing.*—bel.—cn-i.—coc. —cup.—hyo.—str.αæ^{ii}.— ver.

—— *sings loose songs.*—hyo.

—— *singing, shouting, spitting, biting.*—bel.

—— *claps her hands above her head and sings.*—ver.o¹.

—— *laughs violently.*—bel.

—— *praying.*—ceb.—ce-s.—str. —ver$^{b·c·m}$.χ¹.

—— *says his prayers to the tail of a mule.*—eub.

—— *says improper things.*—nx-m. —str.

—— *alternation of laughing, crying out, singing, whistling, leaping, catching at flies, floccillation.*—str.

—— *scolding.*—str.

—— *swearing.*—ga-x.—ver.γ.θ².2.

—— *utters horrible cries.*—str^e.

—— *barks like a dog.*—str.

—— *gesticulating.*—hyo.—str. αæ^{ii}.

—— *absurd buffoonery.*—bel.

—— *silly gesticulations.*—nx-m. αæ^{ii}.8.

Mania, *acts as if measuring with a rule.*—ars.

—— *kisses every one.*—ver.82.

—— *spits at those about him.*—can.—cup.a$\varkappa^{ii}$.—hyo.

—— *biting.*—bel.2.; au.100.—buf.—cr-s.—hyo.; γw.—sec^e.ω^7.—str.; ^{e}.ω^5.

—— *tearing, biting, spitting.*—bel.

—— *performs violent actions.*—sec.—str.

—— *scratches with his hands.*—str.$\alpha\varkappa^{ii}$.; ^{c}.al.

—— *strikes about her.*—bel^n.a$\varkappa^{ii}$. γp.δc^d.ηaa.$\theta^{1\cdot3}$.λii.ρ.--hyo.—lyc.—str.; ^{e}.ω^5.

—— *seizes hold of those around.*—opi^c.a$\mathfrak{g}$.βu.χ^2.—str^e.

—— *tries to bite.*—hyo.γw.

—— *wishes to take those he meets by the nose.*—mer.31.

—— *pelts others with stones.*—bel.

—— *throws a hot-water bottle at an imaginary figure.*—cl-h.

—— *tries to kill people.*—sec^e.ω^7.—str.

—— *stamps his feet.*—ver.κ^1.

—— *wanders about.*—cl-h.

—— *runs away.*—bel.—cup.—dig. ab^c.$\mathfrak{p}^b$.—nx-v$^{b\cdot l\cdot m}$.—ver.

—— *running about.*—bel.—hel.—str^m.; $^{l\cdot m}$.; ^{m}.—sul.—ver.

—— *runs about and knocks head against a wall.*—con.

—— *running at objects.*—hyo.δc^h.

—— *runs about howling and crying.*—ver.

—— *crying out and running about.*—ver.ηc^a.

—— *runs about naked.*—bel.—hyo.

—— *strips naked.*—bel.—hyo.; ^{c}.—pho.

—— *rolls on the ground.*—opi^l.au. $\gamma\eta$ii.δí.

—— *creeps about in bed.*—str. a$\varkappa^{ii}$.

—— *jumps out of bed.*—ga-x.

Mania, *jumping up.*—str^c.ω^5.

—— *jumps on the table.*—bel.

—— *dancing.*—bel.—cn-i.—eth.—hyo.—ph-x.—str.a$\varkappa^{ii}$.

—— *dances in a churchyard.*—str.2.

—— *gropes about him.*—hyo.—str^o.; ^{l}.; ^{c}.al.

—— *cuts open the pillows.*—bel.

—— *tears his clothes.*—bel.—sul^m.—ver^e.ab^c.

—— *bites his shoes to pieces and swallows the fragments.*—ver.

—— *eats his own excrement.*—ver.

—— *feels his head, face, and nose.*—hyo.ɒ^e.

—— *does senseless things.*—cam^c. str.

—— *foolish acts.*—bel.—hyo.—mer.—opi.—str.

—— *childish tricks.*—cro.

—— *acts like a monkey.*—hyo.

—— *embraces the stove and climbs up it.*—hyo.

—— *afraid that his body will putrefy.*—bel.

—— *hydrophobia.*—ac-x.—bel.; ω^5.70.—grt.o.ω^5.

—— *with semilateral paralysis.*—hyo.

—— *alternating with consciousness.*—str.

c^e. **Fury.**—ac-l.—ac-s.—æth.—aga.—ars.—bel.; ^{l}.; θ^1.ω^5.—cth.; 11.; ω^5.—hyo.a$\varkappa^{ii}$.ω^5.—lyc^d.a$\int^a$,u$^{g\cdot n}$.—mel.—mer.—opi.—plb.—sec^d.ω^7.—str$^{c\cdot m}$.a$\varkappa^{ii}$.; ^{d}.; ^{d}.ω^5.; ^{l}.au.—ver.χ^2.; ^{d}.ab^c.

—— *with great display of strength.*—hyo.

—— *fearless, threatening.*—aga^g.

—— *seizes those around by the hair.*—bel.

—— *bites at those around him.*—cup.

—— *at sight of water.*—cth.

c^f. **Desire to kill.**—can.—sec^d.—str^b.

c^g. **Injuring himself.**—aga^e.—bel.—trn$^{d\cdot m}$.γ.δí.λ.ω^8.; $^{d\cdot e}$.ab^c.

Injuring himself *and others.*—bel.
—str.
—— *beats his face with his fists.*
—bel.
—— *beats his head against the wall.*—aps.
—— *scratches himself.*—bel.

c^h. **Suicidal mania.**—ars$^{d \cdot m}$.$\alpha \underline{g}$,$l.\gamma$. e$\eth.\omega^8$.—hyo.—naj.—str.—tar^c.
—— *inclination to stab himself through the heart.*—ars.2.
—— *inclination to throw himself out at window.*—cam.
—— *wishes to drown himself.*—hyo.

c^i. **Stupid insanity.**—ant. (see *Peculiar*).

c^j. **Folly.**—ars.$\alpha \underline{k}$.—hyo.—nx-m$^{c \cdot o}$.$\beta a.\phi^1.\omega^6$.—sec.—str.

c^k. **Amentia.**—bel.
—— *for some weeks.*—bel.

c^l. **Does not know his friends.**—bel$^{c \cdot n}$.$\underline{\mathfrak{v}}^a.\alpha \underline{x}^w$.; ^{e}.——hyo.; $\delta o.\epsilon a$.—nx-v$^{b \cdot d \cdot m}$.—opi.; $^d.\alpha u.\gamma \eta ii.\delta i$.—str. 99.; $^d.\delta c^d$.; $^{d \cdot m}$.; $^e.\alpha u$.—tab.—str. ver.

c^m. **Delusions, hallucinations, fixed ideas.**—ars.— bel.—cca.—cn-i.—cha.—con.3.——dgn.—dul.—ign.; 86.— iod.—k-hy.——mor.—nar.—sec.—stp.—str.; ^{d}.
—— *deceptions of the senses.*—bel.—cth.
—— *familiar objects seem strange.*—cn-i.
—— *sees all sorts of imaginary things.*——bel.121.(86).——str.$\alpha \underline{b}$.
—— *fantastic visions.*—ars.—hyo.—opi.
—— *waking visions.*—aco.2.—arn.—cfn.—col.
—— *beautiful visions.*—bel.—cca.
—— *ugly faces appear pleasing.*—cn-i.
—— *that he sees God and his angels.*—eth.
—— *horrible visions.*—bel.—mer.2.—opi.—str.
—— *frightful.*—abs.—cca.—str.

Delusions, *obscene.*—str^c.ξ.
—— *that he is a locomotive.*—cn-i.
—— *that he is a pump.*—cn-i.
—— *that he is an inkstand.*—cn-i.
—— *that he is a saw.*—cn-i.
—— *that he is a bottle of soda-water.*—cn-i.
—— *that he is a hippopotamus.*—cn-i.
—— *that he is a giraffe.*—cn-i.
—— *that he is a fern.*—cn-i.
—— *that her head is too large, and she cannot see past it.*—zin.29.
—— *that his eyes and body are larger.*—opi.
—— *that his eyelashes are infinitely long.*—cn-i.
—— *that his abdomen is fallen in, his stomach devoured, his scrotum swollen.*—sbd.
—— *that his voice is strange.*—cn-i.
—— *that he is getting thin.*—sul.
—— *that he is no weight.*—cn-i.
—— *that he is deaf and dumb and has a cancer.*—ver.
—— *that he is transparent.*—cn-i.
—— *that the nose is transparent.*—bel.
—— *that a part of the head is transparent and spotted brown.*—bel.
—— *that his head is dilated.*—cn-i.
—— *that his feet are in his brain.*—amp.γ.
—— *that she has a goitre.*—ind.
—— *that his fingers and toes are being cut off.*—msc^c.
—— *that he is walking on knees, the legs being off.*—ba-m.$\alpha \underline{g}$.
—— *that he cannot walk.*—ign.
—— *that one leg is enormously long.*—cn-i.
—— *that his leg is floating in the air.*—sti.
—— *that his leg is a tin case filled with stair-rods.*—cn-i.

Delusions, *that he is on horseback.*— cn-i.
—— *that the disease is going to break out of his head.*—str.
—— *that he is being beaten.*—elp.
—— *that he does not exist.*—cn-i.
—— *that he is seasick.*—der.
—— *that he is dying.*—cn-i.—nx-v.—rhs.—str.
—— *that he will soon die and be dissected.*—cn-i.
—— *that he is dead.*—cam.
—— *that he hears his own funeral bell.*—eth.
—— *that he is killed, roasted, and being eaten.*—str.
—— *that he is a child.*—cic.—eth.
—— *that he is two persons.*—cn-i.—lil.al,s.2.
—— *that he is a goose.*—con.
—— *that he is a hunter.*—ver.
—— *that he is a prince.*—ver.
—— *that he is Christ.*—cn-i.
—— *that he is the Creator.*—cn-i.
—— *that she is a great personage.*—pho.
—— *that he is a demon.*—cam.—cn-i.
—— *that he is a commanding officer.*—cup^d.
—— *that he is captain of a vessel.* cn-i.
—— *that she has a large business.*—pho.
—— *that he is rich.*—bel.—cn-i.
—— *that he has a great deal of money sewn up in his clothes.*—k-br.
—— *that she has fine clothes.*—sul.
—— *that he is clad in rags.*—cn-i.
—— *that he is a criminal.*—hyo.
—— *fear of the gallows.*—bel.
—— *that he is going to be married.*—hyo^c.
—— *that she is pregnant.*—ver.
—— *that she is in labour.*—ver.
—— *that she is about to be confined.*—ver.

Delusions, *that he is cracking nuts.*—hyo.
—— *that he has green vegetables for sale.*—cup^d.
—— *that he has chairs to mend.*—cup^d.
—— *that she is washing.*—bel^o.
—— *that she is counting money.*—bel^o.
—— *that she is drinking.*—bel^o.
—— *that he is spinning.*—hyo.—str.$^{c\cdot e}.\alpha\mathbf{x}^{ii}$.
—— *that he is driving sheep.*—aco$^{b\cdot c}$.
—— *that he is driving away peacocks.*—hyo.
—— *that he can fly.*—cn-i.
—— *that he is flying.*—cam$^n.\alpha\mathbf{x}^s.\beta\mathfrak{b}.\kappa^3$.—opi.
—— *that he is going a journey.*—cn-i.—hyo^c.
—— *that he is not resting in his bed.*—sti.
—— *that he is in another room.*—cn-i.
—— *that he is far from home.*—aco.2.16.--cl-h.--ver$^{b\cdot c\cdot d}.\chi^1$.
—— *that he is at home when he is not.*—cn-i.—hyo.
—— *that she is on a distant island.*—pho.
—— *that he is on a mountain ridge.*—cn-i.
—— *that he is in a vast arena surrounded by high walls.*—cn-i.
—— *that he is in another sphere.*—cn-i.
—— *that he is all alone.*—str$^{d\cdot l}$.; $\alpha\mathfrak{b}$.
—— *that he is alone in the world.*—cam.
—— *that he is deserted by all friends.*—k-br.
—— *that he is God-forsaken.*—cam.
—— *that he is the subject of God's vengeance.*—k-br.
—— *that he is in hell.*—cam.
—— *that he is in heaven.*—cn-i.
—— *that he sees cyphers.*—ph-x.γp.$\beta\mathfrak{e}^a$.

Delusions, *that he sees flowing water.*
—mer^a.αþ^{ag}.

—— *that the sun is reeling and clouds dancing.*—cn-i.

—— *that there are clouds and rocks above her.*—mg-m.43.

—— *that he sees a beautiful landscape.*—cn-i.

—— *the room seemed to be a garden.*—ca-c.ʙ^a.

—— *that a hat is a pair of trousers, which he tries to put on.*—str.

—— *objects appear brighter and further asunder.*—cb-a.

—— *things appear strange.*—pla. —stp.αɡ,ʞ^y,m.—str.99. ;
$^{d.l}$

—— *familiar places appear strange.* —rs-r.5.

—— *familiar persons appear grotesque.*—hyo.

—— *persons appear larger.*—cn-i. —cau.βa.8.(6).

—— *objects appear larger.*—cn-i.

—— *things appear small, but he appears large.*—pla.αf,þ,u. βa.(8.112).—str.

—— *objects appear different.*— na-m.

—— *he seems to swell.*—cn-i.

—— *that the sheets are covered with cucumbers.*—bel.

—— *that he sees birds.*—bel.

—— *that he sees beetles and worms.*—ars.—bel.—str.

—— *that he sees rats, mice, and insects.*—-bel.—-cmf.^{c}.βþ^c. δP^2.—str.

—— *that he sees dogs and cats.* —æth^b.—str. ; αþ.

—— *that there is a fierce black dog present.*—bel.

—— *that a dog is biting him.*— str^c. ; αþ.

—— *that he is surrounded by dogs.* —bel.—str.

—— *that he is surrounded by wolves.*—bel.ρ.

—— *that all sorts of animals are dancing on the bed.*—con.

Delusions, *that there is some one present.*—hyo^c.—lyc.5.6.

—— *that some one is behind him.* —crt.—stp.αɡ,þ.

—— *that some one has come in at the door.*—con.2.

—— *that he is surrounded by friends.*—bel.—cn-i.

—— *that the face of a friend is looking out of a brandy bottle.*—bel.

—— *that some one stands menacing at foot of bed.*—cl-h.

—— *that strange persons are looking over his shoulder.*—bro.

—— *that an army is passing.*— cn-i.5.31.

—— *that men are bribed to kill him.*—cn-i.

—— *that she sees strange persons.* —cn-i.—mg-s.35.—nx-v$^{b.d.l}$. —str.

—— *imagines pieces of furniture are persons.*—na-p.2.99.

—— *that he sees old wrinkled women.*—cn-i.

—— *that he sees old men with long beards, distorted faces, and sparks.*—lau.

—— *that he sees dancing satyrs and nodding mandarins.*—cn-i.

—— *that he sees masked figures and fighters.*—opi$^{b.c}$.

—— *that the house is full of rascals.*—ars.χ$^{1.3}$.—cn-i.

—— *that lewd women are in the house.*—k-br.

—— *that he sees demons.*—cn-i.

—— *clutching at phantoms.*—hyo.

—— *that he talks with spirits.*—str.

—— *that she is pursued by evil spirits.*—str^d.

—— *that cowled demons are clutching at him.*—cn-i.

—— *that he is pursued by policemen.*—hyo^c.—k-br.

—— *about persecution and violence.*—k-br.

—— *that his life is threatened by members of his family.*— k-br.

Delusions, *that there is a conspiracy against him.*—k-br.

—— *that a man is in the room who intends to stick a gimlet in his throat.*—mr-f.

—— *that he sees a man hanging.* —ars$^{d.h}$.αg,l.γ.eb.ω^8.

—— *that horrible monsters are about.*—bel.

—— *vision of extraordinary figures.* —cam.—-cic.—trn$^{d.g}$.γ.δί. λ.ω^8.

—— *that he sees a deceased person.* —hep.3-99.—hur.al.

—— *that he sees a corpse on a bier.*—cn-i.

—— *that he or a friend lies on a bier.*—ana.—cn-i.

—— *that a friend lies dead on the sofa.*—ars.αg,b.

—— *that he sees persons who are dead.*—con.

—— *that her child is dead.*— k-br.

—— *that her brother had fallen overboard.*—k-br.

—— *that he sees caricatures, grimaces, satanic faces.*—amb. —ag-n^c.47.—-cn-i.—cau. 47.

—— *that he sees spectres.*—ars. αg,b.— bel.—lah.—opi^b.— str.

—— *sees terrible things on the wall.*—bel.—cn-i.—sam^b.

—— *that he sees the phantom of death.*—crt.

—— *that he sees a splendid meteor.* —cn-i.

—— *that he hears a bell ring.*— cn-i.—ph-x.

—— *that he hears noises.*—hyo.

—— *that he hears voices.*—cn-i. —elp.—lyc.5.6.

—— *that his own voice sounds like thunder.*—cn-i.

—— *hears steps in room.*—cth.

—— *hears knocking under bed.*— cth.

—— *hears persons talking.*—str. 97.

Delusions, *that some one is telling him to kill himself.*—cn-i.

—— *that some one is reading after her.*—mg-m.43.

—— *that he is called by persons far away.*—ana.αg,b^a.— cn-i.

—— *that he hears groans.*—crt.

—— *that he hears music.*—cn-i. —cro.—str.

—— *that he is surrounded by music and perfumes.*—cn-i.

—— *ordinary music appears divine and distant.*—cn-i.

—— *that a draught of water is delicious nectar.*—cn-i.

—— *that he is raised through the air.*—cn-i.

—— *that he is falling.*—str.

—— *that he is tumbling out of bed.*—crt.

—— *that the bed is raised up.*— cth.

—— *that objects are falling.*— hyo.

—— *that the houses in street are nodding.*—cn-i.

—— *that the walls and ceiling are closing in on him.*—cn-i.

—— *that ice-cold hands are squeezing his throat.*—cth.

—— *distances appear increased.* —cn-i.—nx-m.

—— *that space is much expanded.* —cn-i.

—— *time appears earlier.*—sul.

—— *time appears too short.*—coc.

—— *time appears too long.*—cn-i. —nx-m.

—— *that she has too much of everything.*—sul^d.

—— *that he is riding an ox.*—bel.

—— *that his home is on fire.*— bel^b.

—— *that a neighbour's house is on fire.*—hep.3-99.

—— *that men are swine.*—hyo.

—— *alternating with half-confused sleep.*—ars.

c^n. **Jumps out of bed.**—aco$^{b.c.m}$.— bel$^{c.h}$.b^a.αx^w.; ^{d}.αx^{ii}.γp.δc^d.ηaa.θ$^{1.3}$.

λii.ρ.——bry.——cam^m.α℀ˢ.βb.κ³.——
str.; ^m.

ᶜ°. **Makes grimaces.**——bel^m.——hyo.
——nx-m^{c·j}.βa.φ¹.ω⁶.——str^d.

—— *mimicking grimaces.*——bel.

ᶜᵖ. **Carphologia.**——ars.——cch.——hyo.
——hyn^b.——str.

CONCOMITANTS.

αbᶜ. *Silence.*——dig^d.α℣^b.——trn^{d·e·g}.——
ver^{d·e}.

αf. *Discomfort.*——pla^m.αḅ,u.βa.(8.
112).

αg. *Anxiety.*——ana^m.αḅ^a.——ars^m.
αḅ.; ^{d·h·m}.αl.γ·e℣.ω⁸.——ba-m^m.
——stp^m.α℟y,m.; ^m.αḅ.

αḅ. *Fear.*——ars^m.αg.——hyp^c.γp.δf,
aa,P².ρ.χ².2.——stp^m.αg.——str^m.
——pla^m.αf,u.βa.(8.112).

αḅ^a. *Fear of coming evil.*——ana^m.αg.

αḅ^{ag}. *Fear of dying.*——mer^{a·m}.
pho^b.5.

αḅ^{æ2}. *Fear of having a fit.*——cn-i^c.
γq.

αj. *Envy.*——lyc^{d·e}.αu^{g·n}.

α℟. *Sadness.*——ars^j.

α℟y. *Disagreeable recollections.*——
stp^m.αg,m.

αl. *Weeping.*——ars^{d·h·m}.αg.γ.e℣.ω⁸.
——hur^m.——str^{c·d}.; ^c.2.——ver^d.

αlᵃ. *Whining.*——str^d.α℀ⁱⁱ.

αm. *No desire for life.*——stp^m.αg,℟y.

αq. *Restlessness.*——ars^b.2.——hyo^b.

αu. *Crossness.*——bel^d.100.——opi^{d·l}.
γ.ηii.δí.——pla^m.αf,ḅ.βa.(8.112).
——str^{c·l}.

αuᶜ. *Quarrelsomeness.*——aco^{b·c}.α℀^w.

αu^d. *Rage.*——ca-x.χ³.

αu^g. *Scolding.*——lyc^{d·e}.αj,u^n.

αuⁿ. *Imperiousness.*——lyc^{d·e}.αj,u^g.

αu^u. *Revenge.*——aga^d.β℣.

α℣^b. *Disobedience.*——dig^d.αbᶜ.

α℀ˢ. *Agility.*——cam^{m·n}.βb.κ³.——opi^d.
δa^b.ηaa.

α℀^w. *Gaiety.*——aco^{b·c}.αuᶜ.——bel^{c·l·n}.℣ᵃ.

α℀ⁱⁱ. *Laughter.*——bel^{d·n}.γp.δc^d.ηaa.
θ^{1·3}.λii.ρ.——cup^d.——nx-m^d.8.——
str^d.; ^d.αlᵃ.; ^{c·e·m}.——trn^d.

—— *sardonic.*——hyo^e.ω⁵.

βa. *Vertigo.*——bov^a.——cau^m.8.(6).

——chd^c.κ⁵.——jat^c.℣ᵃ.——mrl^a.33.
——nx-m^{c·j·o}.φ¹.ω⁶.; ^b.φ.ω.——
pla^m.αf,ḅ,u.(8.112).——sep^a.29.
66.——tea^a.8-31.

β℀ᶜ. *Lightness of head.*——hpm^a.

βb. *Staggering.*——cam^{m·n}.α℀ˢ.κ³.

β℀ᵃ. *Stupid head.*——mg-sᵃ.——ph-x^m.
γp.——sulᵃ.

β℣. *Intoxication.*——aga^d.αu^u.——
cch^{c·d}.δ.φ¹.ω⁶.——nx-m^d.——opi^{c·d}.
αg.χ².

βḅᶜ. *Roaring in head.*——cmf^{c·m}.δP².

γd. *Congestion of head.*——au-m^b.

γp. *Hot head.*——bel^{d·n}.α℀ⁱⁱ.δc^d.ηaa.
θ^{1·3}.λii.ρ.——hyp^c.δf,aa,P².ρ.χ².
2.——ph-x^m.β℀ᵃ.

γq. *Heavy head.*——cn-i^d.ω³.; ^c.αḅ^{æ2}.

γw. *Turns head from side to side.*
——hyo^d.

γhh. *Sweat on forehead.*——bel^c.δoᶜ.
ea.ηc^b.

γii. *Swollen head.*——opi^{d·l}.αu.ηii.δs.

γ. *Headache.*——aco^a.; ^a.8-31.——
aga^a.——amp^m.——ars^{d·h·m}.αg,l.
e℣.ω⁸.——glo^c.——mag^a.2.5.——
msc^a.——trn^{d·g·m}.δí.λ.ω⁸.——ver^d.
θ².2.

δ. *Eyes swollen and painful.*——
plb^b.η℀ⁱ.θ.λii.σ¹ii.2.

δa^b. *Sparkling eyes.*——cch^{c·d}.β℣.φ¹.
ω⁶.——opi^d.α℀ˢ.ηaa.

δf. *Distorted eyes.*——hyp^c.αḅ.γp.
δaa,P².ρ.χ¹.2.

δs. *Inflamed eyes.*——cup^{c·d}.δc^h.ρ.χ³.
——opi^{d·l}.αu.γηii.

δaa. *Red eyes.*——bel^b.δí,P².ηc^a.ι.ρ.
σ²d.——hyp^c.αḅ.γp.δf,P².ρ.χ¹.2.

δc^d. *Staring eyes.*——bel^c.; ^{d·n}.α℀ⁱⁱ.
γp.ηaa.θ^{1·3}.λii.ρ.——str^{d·l}.
tab^c.℣ᵃ.

δc^h. *Wild look.*——cup^{c·d}.δs.ρ.χ³.——
hyo^d.; ^d.δP².ηaa.

δí. *Projecting eyes.*——bel^b.δaa,P².
ηc^a.ι.ρ.σ²d.——dor^c.ηaa,ii.ρ.——
opi^{d·l}.αu.γηii.——trn^{d·g·m}.γ.λ.
ω⁸.

δoᶜ. *Blindness.*——bel^c.γhh.ea.——
hyo^l.ea.

δP¹. *Contracted pupils.*——hy-x^b.ρ.

δP². *Dilated pupils.*——bel^b.δí,aa.ηc^d.
ι.ρ.σ²d.——cmf^{c·m}.βḅᶜ.——hyo^d.

δ$ɾ^h$.ηaa.--hyp^c.γp.δf,aa.ρ.χ^2.2.----str$^{d.l}$.

εᴅ. *Noise in ears.*—ars$^{d·h·m}$.$α$ǥ,ĺ.γ. ω^8.

εā. *Deafness.*— bel^c.γhh.ηc^b.δo^c.—hyo^l.δᴅ.

.ηæ^i. *Expression astonished.*—plb^b. δii.θ.λii.σ^{1}ii.2.

ηc^a. *Dark blue face.*—bel^b.δí,aa,P^2. ɩ.ρ.σ^{2}d.—ver.

ηc^b. *Pale face.*—bel^c.γhh.δo^c.εā.

.ηaa. *Red face.*—aur^c.2.—bel$^{d·n}$.$α$$æ^{ii}$. γp.δ$ɾ^d$.θ^1.θ^{3}j.λii.ρ.—lo-i^c.ρ^1.5. 99.—opi^d.$αæ^s$.δa^b.

.ηaa. *Dark red complexion and blue lips.*—hyo^d.δ$ɾ^h$,P^2.

ηaa,ii. *Red swollen face.*—dor^c.δí.ρ.

ηii. *Swelling of face.*——bel^c.rii.—opi$^{d·l}$.$α$u.γii.δí.

θ. *Mouth mucous.*——plb^b.δii.ηæ^i. λii.σ^{l}ii.2.

θ. *Foaming at mouth.*—cam^d.

θf^c. *Distortion of mouth.*—opi^d.

θ^1. *Grinding of teeth.*——bel^e.ω^5.; $^{d·n}$.$αæ^{ii}$.γp.δ$ɾ^d$.ηaa.θ^{3}j.λii.ρ.

θ^2. *Flow of saliva.*—ver^d.γ.2.

θ^{3}j. *Dry tongue.*——bel$^{d·n}$.$αæ^{ii}$.γp. δ$ɾ^d$.ηaa.θ^1.λii.ρ.

ɩ. *Loss of power of swallowing.*— bel^b.δí,aa,P^2.ηc^a.ρ.σ^{2}d.

κ^1. *Anorexia.*—ver^d.

κ^3. *Desire for wine.*—cam$^{m·n}$.$αæ^s$. βb.

κ^5. *Nausea.*—chd^c.βa.

κ^6. *Vomiting.*—vp-r^b.

λii. *Swollen abdomen.*—bel$^{d·n}$.$αæ^{ii}$. γp.δ$ɾ^d$.ηaa.θ$^{1·3}$.ρ.

λii. *Abdomen swollen and painful.* —plb^b.δii.ηæ^i.θ.σ^{1}ii.2.

λ. *Pain in abdomen.*—trn$^{d·g·m}$.γ. δí.ω^8.

μ^2. *Diarrhœa.*—hyo^d.

ξ. *Penis erect.*—str$^{c·m}$.

o. *Constriction of glottis.*—grt^d. ω^5.

o^1. *Cough.*—ver^d.

ρ. *Full, rapid, strong pulse.*— cup$^{c·d}$.δs,$ɾ^h$.χ^3.

ρ. *Full pulse.*—bel^m.; ^{b}.δí,aa,P^2. ηc^a.ɩ.σ^{2}d.

ρ. *Quick pulse.*—dor^c.δí.$^{aa·ii}$.—

hyp^c.$α$ꞗ. γp.δf,aa,P^2.χ^2.2.—— hy-x^b.δP^1.

ρ. *Small, quick pulse.*——bel$^{d·n}$. $αæ^{ii}$.γp.δ$ɾ^d$.ηaa.θ^1.θ^{3}j.λii.

ρ^1. *Palpitation.*—lo-i^c.ηaa.5.99.

σ^{1}ii. *Loins swollen and painful.*— plb^b.δii.ηæ^i.θ.λii.2.

σ^{2}d. *Throbbing of carotids.*—bel^b. δí,aa,P^2.ηc^a.ɩ.ρ.

rii. *Swelling of arm.*—bel^c.ηii.

r. *Feeling of trickling of blood down arm.*—cot^a.3-99.

φ. *Sopor.*—nx-m^b.βa.ω.

φ^1. *Sleeplessness.*—cch$^{c·d}$.βꞗ.δa^b.ω^6. —hyo^d.--m-cy^c.2.—nx-m$^{c·j·o}$. βa.ω^6.

χ^1. *Chilliness.*—ars^m.χ^3.--ver$^{b·c·d·m}$.

χ^2. *Heat.*—-chi^c.—hyp^c.$α$ꞗ.γp.δf, aa,P^2.ρ.2.—opi$^{c·d}$.$α$ǥ.βꞗ.— ver^e.

χ^3. *Sweat.*—ars^m.χ^1.—ca-x.$α$u^d.— cup$^{c·d}$.δs,$ɾ^h$.ρ.

ω. *Apoplexy.*—nx-m^b.βa.φ.

ω^2. *As if about to faint.*—cn-i^d. γq.

ω^5. *Convulsions.*—bel^e.θ^1.—cth^e.; ^{b}.—crt^b.—grt^d.o.—hyo^e.$αæ^{ii}$. —lo-i^d.—pho^b.—str$^{d·e}$.; $^{c·d}$. —— *like strychnine.*—ind^d. —— *tetanic.*—ars^b.

ω^6. *Restlessness.*—cch$^{c·d}$.βꞗ.δa^b.φ^1. —dig^c.2.—nx-m$^{c·j·o}$.βa.φ.

ω^7. *Cramps.*—sec$^{d·e}$.

ω^8. *Trembling.*--ars$^{d·h·m}$.$α$ǥ,ĺ.γ.εᴅ. —trn$^{d·g·m}$.γ.δí.λ.

CONDITIONS.

1. *By day.*—bel^c.2.; ^{b}.2.

2. *At night.*—aco.; ^{m}.16.—ars^b.; ^{b}.$α$q.—aur^c.ηaa.—bel^c.(1).; ^{b}. (1).; ^{c}.—cac^b.98.(99).—cod^b. —cch^b.—con^m.—crt^h.—dig^c. ω^6.; ^{b}.; ^{c}.$α$q.—dul^b.—ga-x$^{b·c}$. ——hyp^c.$α$ꞗ.δf,aa,P^2.ρ.χ^3.— k-hy^d.—lyc^b.—mag^a.γ.5.— mer^m.—m-cy^c.φ^1.—na-p^m.99. —plb^b.δii.ηæ^i.θ.λii.σ^1.—str^d.; ^{c}.$α$l.—ver^d.γ.θ^2.

3. *In the morning.*—con^m.

3-99. *In the morning on waking.*— cot^a.rl.—hep^m.

5. *In the evening.*—bel^c.—cn-i^m.
31.—cch^b.—lil^a.—lo-i^c.ŋaa.ρ^1.
99.——lyc^m.6.——mag^a.γ.2.——
pho^b.ab^{ag}.—rs-r^m.

6. *In the room.*——cau^m.βa.8.——
lyc^m.5.

8. *In the open air.*—cau^m.βa.(6).
—nx-m^d.aæ^{ii}.—pla^m.af,b,u.βa.
(112).

8-31. *By walking in open air.*—aco^a.
—ant^b.—tea^a.βa.

11. *When touched.*—cth^e.

16. *On lying down.*—aco^m.2.

29. *On stooping.*——sep^a.βa.66.——
zin^m.

31. *When walking.*——cn-i^m.5.——
mer.

33. *On going down stairs.*—mrl^a.
βa.

35. *When spinning.*—mg-s^m.

43. *When reading.*—mg-m^m.

47. *By shutting eyes.*—ag-n$^{c.m}$.—
cau^m.

66. *By eating.*—bel^b.—sep^a.βa.29.

82. *Before menses.*—ver^d.

83. *During menses.*—aco^d.—hyo^c.

86. *When conversing.*—bel^m.121.—
ign^m.

98. *When asleep.*—cac^b.2.(99).

97. *On going to sleep.*—str^m.

99. *On awaking.*—cac^b.2.98.—lo-i^c.
ŋaa.ρ^1.5.—na-p^m.2.—str^l.; ^{m}.

100. *After sleep.*—bel^d.au.

112. *In the sunshine.*—pla^m.af,b,u.
βa.(8):

121. *When alone.*—bel^m.(86).

ᴅ. Stupefaction, insensibility
(Peculiar).

ars. Absence of the understanding,
and of the external and internal senses; he saw not, spoke
not for several days, heard and
understood nothing; on calling loudly into his ear he
looked at those around him
like a drunken man awakened
out of deep sleep.

ast. Wakes at night with great
uneasiness, feeling as if brain
were shaken by electric shocks;
empty feeling of head, thinking power suspended for several
minutes, followed by hard,
quick pulse, throbbing in temporal arteries.

cam. He rubs his forehead, head,
chest, and other parts, knows
not what ails him; he leans
against things, his senses leave
him, he slips down and falls to
the ground quite stiff, the
shoulders drawn back, the
arms at first somewhat bent,
with hands turned outwards
and fingers stretched out and
slightly flexed, afterwards all
parts extended and stiff, the
head drawn to one side, with
stiff open under jaw, lips
turned inwards and chattering
teeth, closed eyes and constant
twitchings of facial muscles,
general coldness and dyspnœa
for a quarter of an hour.

cle. After running about the streets
with extreme ease and rapidity
he lapses into a state of almost
insensibility, loss of will and
of power of thinking. This is
followed by shooting, throbbing headache from within
outwards, lasting several hours
and rendering him incapable
of reading or writing.

cyc. His mind is in a state of con-
tinual stupefaction, all his
powers slumber; he can neither
rejoice nor be sad, although he
always feels as if after some
recent grief; only when excited
his head becomes somewhat
clearer, and then he behaves
like one just awakened from
sleep, and who only understands half of what has happened.

mer. Unconsciousness and speechlessness; she appeared to sleep
but was pulseless, and looked
like a corpse, though the heat
of the body was normal; in an

ᴋ

hour her reason returned and some tones of the voice; she tried to speak but could not, her speech only returned after twelve hours.

sbd. Thinking is difficult and causes headache; otherwise he has a desire to laugh at everything; afterwards indifference, almost obtuse insensibility.

spi. Vertigo when sitting, standing, and walking, least felt when lying; the head sinks backwards, with nausea in the palate and discomfort in the abdomen and thorax; in the abdomen a pinching pain, with the feeling as if he must go to stool, whereby he loses all consciousness.

str. She recognised no one, did not take any notice of the loudest calling to her, moved her head constantly from side to side; forehead covered with perspiration.

val. Excessively rapid succession of ideas as in intoxication, obscure confused recollections of former thoughts and actions succeed each other with such rapidity that he at last became quite stupefied and destitute of thought and appeared as if in a dream.

ɒ. **Stupefaction, stupor, notices nothing.**—abs.—aco.δb.o².ω⁵.; 65.— æth.βa.γ.κ⁶.χ².—aga.βa.—alm. βbᵃ.—ag-n.ηæᶜ.—arnᵃ.βa.γ.εa.— bel.; ηæᵇ.—bov.—buf.aa.; o².—ca-c. 26.29.; γw.—cn-i.γ.δrᵒ.ω.115.— can.—cb-a.aʰˢᵉ.ʲa.19.; bᵃ.δoᶜ.εa.; 26.31.—ca-x.— cr-h.—chd.3-99. —cnt.—clo.βa.—clf.—cch.16.— dig.—dor.λ².—dul.—eth.—fer.βa. —glo.bᵃ.ω².—grn.—ham.—hy-xᶜ. ρ.—hyo.—ign.—iod.—k-br.— k-cy.— kre.bᵃ.βa,εᵇ.δo.εa.—lab.— lah.εɒ.—la-s.—lau.; βa.—lo-i.— lup.—lyc.γ.εp.5.—mer.— mr-c.—

mil.βa,ɒ.—mor.—mo-a.; δP².λ².— msc.; βaˡ.; βaᵏ.19.—naj.—nar.γ. —nat.3-99.—nit.—nx-m.; rɒb.— nx-v.; (11).—oln.—opi.; βɒ.; δcᵍ.ω².; ᵃ.; bᵃ.—pho.2-99.—pimᵃ. βε.—plb.; ak.; βc.—rho.—rhs. ʀec.; δP².; ω².; βa.—spgᵃ.—str. βa.; δP².; ι.κ³˙⁴.—su-x.—tabᵃ. (72).—tax.—ter.—til.βɒ.; βε.66. —vp-t.λ.—zin.βa.5.; βa.δo.ω².4.5.
—— *periodical.*—cof.
—— *like intoxication.*—nit.— nx-m.—rut.βb.
—— *lethargic.*—cup.
—— *as if he had a board before head.*—opi.βa.ω⁸.
—— *as if after a blow.*—gur.bᵃ.
—— *as if paralysed.*—aga.bʸ.αb, k.γ.ω².—plb.
—— *as if in a dream.*—amb.— cb-a.3.—con.—rhe.—str. aæⁱⁱ.δoᶜ.εa.—val.—ver.
—— *as after a fever.*—sar.
—— *knows not where he is.*—mer. —rn-b.
—— *did not know friends.*—ced.
—— *remains fixed to one spot.*— nx-m.
—— *sits motionless like a statue.* —hyo.—str.
—— *after vertigo.*—æs-g.
—— *after vomiting and diarrhœa.* —ars.
—— *interrupted by screaming.*— bel.
—— *going off when the feet become warm.*—lah.ɒb.

ɒᵃ. **Insensibility, loss of consciousness.**—abs.; ω⁵.—ac-x.—acn.— ac-s.—æth.δcᵈ.ηb.rɒb.—aga.— aln.—amy.o².ω².—ant.—ag-n. bʸ.βa.φ.—arn.βa.γ.εa.—ars.; cᶜ. γhh.δcᵈ.ρ.ω⁸.; o².; βa,εᵃ.; ω⁵.—bel.; γw.θ.; cˡ·ⁿ.aæⁱⁱ; rf.2.; rɒf.—ca-c. cᵐ.; 5.; κ⁴.—cam.δcᵈ.—cn-i.; 52; 115.; βε.γq.—cth.cᶜ.—ca-x.; π¹. cr-h.—cʂʂ.δb.ηcᵇ.θ.μ⁶.π¹.ρ.rɒb.—chd. —ch-s.βa.—cf-t.—cl-h.cᶜ.—clf.κ⁶. —cch.—col.5.70.—cnm.—con.ab. —cro.δo.—crt.δoᶜ.εa.—cup.ω⁵.— der.βa.—dig.—eth.—gel.—glo.cᵃ.;

ω^5.—grt.ab^i.βa.δo.128.(98).—hy-x. ω^2.—hyo.—ign.—jat.ℓ^c.βa.—k-cy. —k-hy.—lah.κ^6.μ^2.—lau.o^3.ω^2.; ω^2. —lo-i.—mel.ζ^2.—mor. ; ηd.$^{m^2}$.π^1. ; θ^2.—mo-a.δP^1.—naj.—nat.βb. na-m.βa.3.30. ; βa.κ^6.—nx-m.βa.ℓ. ω. ; δaa.ν.—nx-v.—oln.—opi.— pæo.γ.κ^5.—ptv^c.16.—pet.—pho. γ. ; aa.—pim.βℓ.—rho. ; βv.—rhs. 26.—sec.—sil.γ.al^d.—so-n.—spg. —stn.γ.χ^1.ϕ.—str. ; δP^2.ηaa.ρ.ω^6. —sty.—tab.(72). ; βa.—trx.γ.κ^5. 19.(8).—tar.—ver.—vp-t.ω.— wis.βa.κ^3.^{8}.ξ^3.$\chi^{1\cdot2}$.$\omega^{2\cdot8}$.128.—xan.

—— *semi-unconsciousness.*—cot. βℓ^c.o^2.2.—eth.

—— *transient.*—bov.βa,ϵ^a.γ.18.— buf.—cn-i.—cth.βa,b.δo. 8-31.—chd.βa.ω^8.—elc.b.γ. ω^2.—glv.—hep.8-31.—hfb. —na-m.βa.—ol-a.4. ; δo^c. ϵa.—rs-r. ; 18.—sil.βa.128.

—— *sudden.*—æna.

—— *by fits, as if going to have an apoplectic attack.*—lah.

—— *as if intoxicated.*—nx-m.b.

—— *like to fall.*—k-ca.

—— *as if he would faint.*—tep. βa.

—— *does not know where he is.*— nx-m.δb.

—— *cannot recognise what she sees.* —æs-c.99.

—— *and yet he answers questions.* —opi.b^y.

—— *falls into the water.*—tep. βa.ϵv.

—— *lies in a corner.*—cup.

—— *to modesty.*—opi.

—— *followed by red miliary eruption and sweat.*—str.a$\mathfrak{g}$.

—— *alternate unconsciousness or delirium.*—cn-i.

v^b. **Coma.**—ag-p.—ag-n.—ags.— ars.—bel.δP^2.ηaa.ρ.τvf.ψ.χ^2.—bth. —cam.—ca-x.—cr-h.—ch-s.— eth.—hy-x. ; ω^5.—hyo.—k-br.— mor.—msc.—naj.—tan.ω^5.

—— *profound.*—mor.

—— *transient.*—mr-c.

—— *during which he hears everything.*—mor.

—— *after vertigo.*—æs-g.

v^c. **Syncope.**—hy-x.ρ.—ign.—mo-a. —msc.ab^{ag}.ηc^b.—ptv^a.16.—tep.βa. τvy.

—— *after piercing cries of pain.* —ars.

CONCOMITANTS.

aa. *Apathy.*—buf.—pho^a.

ab. *Laziness.*—aga.b^y.ak.γ.ω^2.— con^a.

ab^i. *Disinclination for intellectual work.*—grt^a.βa.δo.128.(98).

a$\mathfrak{g}$. *Anxiety.*—str^a.

ab^{æ6}. *Fear of losing senses.*—cb-a. βa.19.

ab^{ag}. *Fear of death.*—msc^c.ηc^b.

ak. *Low spirits.*—aga.b^y.ab.γ.ω^2.— plb.

al^d. *Groaning.*—sil^a.γ.

aæ^{ii}. *Laughter.*—bel^a.$c^{l\cdot n}$.—str.δo^c. ϵa.

βa. *Vertigo.*—æth.γ.κ^6.χ^2.—aga.— ag-n^a.b^y.ϕ.—arn^a.γ.ϵa.—ars^a. βϵ^a.—bov^a.βℓ^a.γ.18.—cth$^{a\cdot c}$. βb.δo.8-31.—cb-a.ab^{æ6}.19. — chd^a.ω^8.—ch-s^a.—clo.—der^a.— fer.—grt^a.ab^i.δo.128.(98).— jat^a.ℓ^c.—kre.b^a.βℓ^b.δo^c.ϵa.—lau. —mil.βv.—na-m^a. ; ^{a}.3.30. ; ^{a}. κ^6.—nx-m^a.βℓ.ω.—opi.ω^8.— sec^a.—sil^a.128.— str.—tab^a. —tep^a.βℓ.ϵv. ; ^{c}.τvy.—wis.$\kappa^{3\cdot8}$. ξ^3.$\chi^{1\cdot2}$.$\omega^{2\cdot8}$.128.—zin.5. ; δo. ω^2.4.5.

βa^k. *Feeling of falling down.*—msc. 19.

βa^l. *Feeling of falling from a height.* —msc.

βb. *Staggering.*—alm.—cth$^{a\cdot c}$.βa. δo.8-31.—nat^a.—rut.

βℓ. *Falling.*—cn-i^a.γq.—nx-m^a.βa. ω.—plb.—tep^a.βa.ϵv.

βv. *Intoxication.*—mil.βa.—opi.— rho^a.—til.

βϵ. *Confusion of head.*—pim^a.— til.66.

$\beta\epsilon^a$. *Stupid head.*—ars^a.βa.—bov^a. βa.γ.18.

$\beta\epsilon^b$. *Vacancy of head.*—-kre.b^a.βa. δo^c.ea.

$\beta\epsilon^c$. *Lightness of head.*—cot^a.o^2.2.

γd. *Boiling in head.*—pæo^a.κ^5.

γp. *Heat of head.*—lyc.ep.5.

γq. *Heaviness of head.*—cn-i^a.$\beta\epsilon$.

γw. *Undulating buzzing in top of head.*—ca-c.

γw. *Shaking of head.*—bel^a.θ.—str. γhh.

γhh. *Cold sweat on forehead.*—ars^a. ϵ^c.$\delta\epsilon^d$.ρ.ω^8.—str.γw.

γ. *Headache.*—æth.βa.κ^6.χ^2.— aga.b^g.ab,k.ω^2.—arn^a.βa.ϵa.— bov^a.βa,ϵ^a.18.—cn-i.δr^o.ω.115. elc^a.b ω^2.—fer.—nar.—pho^a. —sil^a.al^d.—stn^a.γp.ϕ.χ^1.— trx^a.κ^5.19.(8).

δaa. *Red, protruded eyes.*—nx-m^a.vl.

δb. *Eyes half closed.*—css.ηc^b.θ.μ^6. π^1.ρ.rvb.

δb. *Eyes closed.*—aco.o^2.ω^5.— nx-m^a.

$\delta\epsilon^d$. *Fixed eyes.*—æth^a.ηb.rvb.— ars^a.ϵ^c.γhh.ρ.ω^8.—cam^a.

$\delta\epsilon^g$. *Dull eyes.*—opi.ω^2.

δo. *Blackness before eyes.*—cth$^{a \cdot c}$. βa,b.8-31.—cro^a.—grt^a.ab^i.βa. 128.(98).—zin.βa.ω^9.4.5.

δo^c. *Loss of sight.*—ars.ea.—cb-a.b^s. ea.—crt^a.ea.—kre.b^a.βa,ϵ^b.ea. —ol-a^a.ea.—str.ea.a.κ^{ii}.

δr^o. *Objects appear colourless.*— cn-i.γ.ω.115.

δP^1. *Contracted pupils.*—mo-a^a.

δP^2. *Dilated pupils.*—-bel^b.ηaa.rvf. ψ.χ^2.—mo-a.λ^2.—sec.—str. ; ^{a}.ηaa.ρ.ω^5.

ϵp. *Heat of ears.*—lyc.γp.5.

ϵb. *Noise in ears.*—lah.—tep^a.βa,ϵ.

ϵa. *Deafness.*—arn^a.βa.γ.—ars.δo^c. —cb-a.b^a.δo^c.—crt^a.δo^c.—kre. b^a.βa,ϵ^b.δo^c.—ol-a^a.δo^c.—str. δo^c.aκ^{ii}.

ζ^2. *Epistaxis.*—mel^a.

ηb. *Cold face.*—æth^a.$\delta\epsilon^d$.rvb.

ηc^b. *Pale face.*—css.δb.θ.μ^6.π^1.ρ.rvb. —msc^c.ab^{as}.

ηd. *Congested blue face.*-mor^a.π^1.ω^2.

ηaa. *Red face.*—bel^b.δP^2.rvf.ψ.χ^2.— str^a.δP^2.ρ.ω^5.

ηæ^b. *Smiling countenance.*—bel.

ηæ^c. *Suffering expression.*—ag-n.

θ. *Half-open mouth full of saliva.* —css.δb.ηc^b.μ^6.π^1.rvb.

θ. *Foam before mouth.*—bel^a.γw.

θ^2. *Flow of saliva.*—mor^a.

ι. *Burning in throat.*—str.$\kappa^{3 \cdot 4}$.

κ^3. *Thirst.*—str.ι.κ^4.—wis^a.βa.κ^8.ξ^3. $\chi^{1 \cdot 2}$.$\omega^{2 \cdot 8}$.128.

κ^4. *Stomachache.*—ca-c^a.—str.ι.κ^3.

κ^5. *Nausea.*—pæo^a.γ.—trx^a.γ.19. (8).

κ^6. *Vomiting.*—æth.γ.βa.χ^2.—clf^a. —lah^a.μ^2.—na-m^a.βa.

κ^8. *Hiccough*—wis^a.βa.κ^3.ξ^3.$\chi^{1 \cdot 2}$. $\omega^{2 \cdot 8}$.128.

λ. *Cutting in abdomen.*—vp-t.

λ^2. *Rumbling in bowels.*—dor.— mo-a.δP^2.

μ^2. *Purging.*—lah^a.κ^6.

μ^6. *Anus relaxed and wide open.*— css.δb.ηc^b.θ.π^1.rvb.

ξ^3. *Metrorrhagia.*—wis^a.βa.$\kappa^{3 \cdot 8}$. $\chi^{1 \cdot 2}$.$\omega^{2 \cdot 8}$.128.

o^2. *Inability to speak.*—aco.δb.ω^5. amy^a.ω^9.—ars^a.—buf.—cot^a. $\beta\epsilon^c$.2.—lau^a.ω^2.

π^1. *Respiration slow, almost imperceptible.*—css.δb.ηc^b.θ.μ^6. rvb.

π^1. *Snoring, rattling respiration.* —mor^a.ηd.ω^2.

π^1. *Stertorous breathing.*—ca-x^a.

ρ. *Weak pulse.*—hy-x^c.

ρ. *Slow pulse.*—str^a.δP^2.ηaa.ω^6.

ρ. *Pulse small, hard, quick.*— ars^a.ϵ^c.γhh.$\delta\epsilon^d$.ω^8.

rf. *Convulsions of arms.*—bel^a.2.

rvb. *Cold extremities.*—æth^a.$\delta\epsilon^d$.ηb. —css.δb.ηc^b.θ.μ^6.π^1.—nx-m.

rv. *Paralysis of right arm and leg.* —tep^c.βa.

rvf. *Convulsions of limbs.*—bel^a.; ^{b}.δP^2.ηaa.χ^2.ψ.

v. *Immobility of left leg.*—nx-m^a. δaa.

v^1b. *Cold feet.*—lah.

ϕ. *Drowsiness.*—ag-n^a.b^y.βa.— stn^a.γ.γp.χ^1.

χ^1. *Chilliness.*—stn^a.γ.γp.ϕ.—wis^a. βa.$\kappa^{3\cdot8}$.ξ^3.χ^2.$\omega^{2\cdot8}$.128.

χ^3. *Heat.*—æth.γ.βa.κ^6.—bel^b.δP^2. ηaa.τvf.ψ.——wis^a.βa.$\kappa^{3\cdot8}$.ξ^3.χ^1. $\omega^{2\cdot8}$.128.

ψ. *Red spots on skin.*—bel^b.δP^2. ηaa.τvf.χ^3.

ω. *Rigidity.*—nx-m^a.βa,$\mathfrak{c}$.

ω. *Paralysed feeling.*—cn-i.γ.δr^o. 115.

ω. *Swelling.*—vp-t^a.

ω^2. *Weariness.*——aga.b^y.ab,k.γ.—— elc^a·b.γ.—hep^a.——lau^a.—opi. $\delta\mathfrak{c}^g$.—sec.—wis^a.βa.$\kappa^{3\cdot8}$.ξ^3.$\chi^{1\cdot2}$. ω^8.128.—zin.βa.δo.4.5.

ω^2. *Weakness.*—glo.b^s.

ω^2. *Loss of power of movement.*— amy^a.o^2.——lau^a.o^2.—mor^a.ηd. ϖ^1.

ω^5. *Convulsions.*——abs^a.——ars^a.— cup^a.—glo^a.——hy-x^b.—str^a. δP^2,ηaa.ρ.—tan^b.

ω^5. *Convulsions of facial muscles.*— aco.δb.o^2.ω^5.

ω^5. *Trismus.*—aco.δb.o^2.ω^5.

ω^8. *Trembling.*——ars^a.$\mathfrak{c}^c$.γbh.$\delta\mathfrak{c}^d$.ρ. chd^a.βa.——opi.βa.——wis^a.βa. $\kappa^{3\cdot8}$.ξ^3.$\chi^{1\cdot2}$.ω^2.128.

CONDITIONS.

2. *At night.*—bel^a.rf.—cot^a.$\beta\mathfrak{c}^c$.o^2.

2-99. *On awaking at night.*—pho.

3. *In the morning.*——cb-a.—na-m^a. βa.30.

3-99. *On awaking in the morning.*— chd.—nat.

4. *In the afternoon.*—ol-a^a.—zin. βa.δo.ω^3.5.

5. *In the evening.*—ca-c.—col.70. —lyc.$\gamma\epsilon$p.—zin.βa.δo.ω^3.4.

5. *At noon.*—zin.βa.

8. *In the open air.*—trx^a.γ.κ^5.19.

8-31. *By walking in open air.*—cth$^{a\cdot c}$. βa,b.δo.—hep^a.

11. *When touched.*—nx-v.

16. *On lying down.*—cch.—ptv$^{a\cdot c}$.

18. *When standing.*—bov^a.βa,$\mathfrak{c}^a$.γ. —rs-r^a.

19. *When sitting.*—cb-a.ab^{x6}.βa.— msc.βa^1.—trx^a.γ.κ^5.(8).

26. *On moving head.*—ca-c.29.— cb-a.31.—rhs^a.

29. *On stooping.*—ca-c.26.

30. *On sitting up in bed.*—na-m^a. βa.3.

31. *When walking.*—cb-a.26.

52. *By music.*—cn-i^a.

65. *By smoking.*—aco.

66. *After dinner.*—til.$\beta\mathfrak{c}$.

70. *By drinking beer.*—col.5.

72. *By vomiting.*—tab^a.

98. *By sleep.*—grt^a.ab^i.βa.δo.128.

99. *On awaking.*—æsc^a.

115. *By candlelight.*——cn-i^a.; γ. δr^o.ω.

128. *By driving.*—grt^a.ab^i.βa.δo.(98). —sil^a.βa.—wis^a.βa.$\kappa^{3\cdot8}$.ξ^3.$\chi^{1\cdot2}$. $\omega^{2\cdot8}$.

INDEX TO CHAPTER II.

β. SENSORIUM.

CHAPTER II.

β. SENSORIUM.

a. Vertigo, dizziness, giddiness.—abi.—-ac-x.—-acn.—-aga.; b.—:ags.—-æsc.—-alm.—-amb.—-ani.—ant.—aps.—arg.ℓᵃ.—-ag-n.b.—arn.—ars.—-ard.—-asa.—-as-s.—-asp.—atr.—bap.—-ba-c.—-bel.—ber.—bth.—bry.ℓ.—-buf.—clt.—cam.—cn-i.—can.—cth.—cap.bᶜ.; ℓ.—cb-v.ℓ.—-cr-h.—-cr-s.; ℓ.—car.—csc.—css.— cau.ℓ.—-cnt.—cep.—chd.—cl-h.— cic.b.—cmf.—cle.ℓ.—ccs.ℓ.—-cf-t.— cch.ℓ.—col.ℓᵃ.; ℓ.—cly.—com.— cnm.ℓ.—cro.ℓ.—cub.—cup.—c-ar.—cyc.ℓᵃ.—dph.—dig.—dio.—dul.— eu-c.—gas.ℓ.—gel.ℓ.ⅅ.—gn-l.—gin.—grp.—-hur.—hyo.—ign.b.—ind.—jan.—k-br.ℓ.—-la-s.—-la-v.ℓ.—-lau.ℓ.—led.ℓ.ⅅ.—lup.—mel.—mr-c.—mil.—mim.—mor.—mo-m.—msc.—nar.—nr-m.—ni-x.ℓ.—nit.ℓ.—ox-x.—phl.ℓᵃ.— phs.b.—phy.—plg.—plb.ⅅ.—pru.ℓᵃ.—-rho.ℓᵃ.—rhs.ℓᵃ.—sam.ℓ.—sil.ℓ.; b.—sin.—so-n.—squ.ℓ.—tab.b.; ⅅ.—trn.ℓ.—tax.—teu.- -tra.—-vp-t.b.—xan.—ziz. &c.

—— *at frequent intervals.*—aga. 3.; b.ẟo.(41).—alo.—bov.—cam.—cph.—k-bi.—na-m.a¹ⅅᵃ.γ.26.—pla.5.

Vertigo, *as though he would faint.*—dig.aᘝ.18.

—— *as though he would have a fit.*—gas.γd,iᵃ.ρ.ω. —lah.b.a¹ⅅᵃ. 5.—zinˢ.

—— *as if would lose consciousness.*—ni-x.—pho.ℓ.7.—pla.5.—tea.31.

—— *as if half mad.*—nx-m.

—— *knows not what he is about.*—sep.

—— *knows not where he is.*—lyc.—ni-x.2.30.—silᵗ.

—— *as if intoxicated.*—ab-c.—aco.a¹ⅅ.7.— alm.—amp.26.—amy.—ag-n.—ars.b.ℓᵃ. 8-31.—ar-c.8-31.—ar-s.8. 31.--aзr.30.31.--aurˣ.8-31.—bry.γd.—cn-i.— cau.a¹b.— cha.b.3-99.—chd.κ⁵.— coc.ℓᵃ.; 19.—ccs.ab.—dio. b.—erd.—ferˢ.31.—ham.—hyo.—k-ca.b.31.; 18.31. (8).— kre.b.3.8.(6).—lau. --lyc.3.—mt-n.—mt-s.b.—mrl.; ˢ.b.18.19.31.—nit. --nx-m.—ph-x.b 5.18.31.--pi-m.b.33.—pul.; ˢ.κ⁵, 29.—rho.—rhsᵗ·ⁿ.18.—sar. b.—sel.b.ηcᵇ.χ³.ω². —spiᵇ·ᶻ. 31.; ᵖ.—str.b.; a¹bᵖ.ηaʰ.—sto.—sul.—tab.—trx.γw.

8-31.—tep[1].81.(18.19).; [a]b. —til[c].—val[b].29.

Vertigo, *as if after intoxication.*—aco. a[1]b.; γq.3.—aga.3.—bel.κ[5].—bry.—cb-v.5.31.—nit.3.—nx-m.γ.——phl.ε.—phs.ε.ω[2].—spi.ε[b].19.—tep.(31).

—— *as in sea-sickness.*—spr.

—— *as if smoke had got into the brain.*—arg.

—— *as if had not slept enough.*—cb-a.3.

—— *as if from moving head rapidly.*—cb-a.

—— *as if had spun round.*—alm. κ[5].(66).—ana.29.—ang.—bel.κ[5].—pul.κ[5].—squ.κ[5].—thu.

—— *as if held up high.*—rhs.19.

—— *as if sitting on a high chair.*—alo.19.66.— pho.αk.ψ.ω[2].5.

—— *as if head were suspended from a support under skull.*—ce-b.

—— *as when coming from the cold into a warm room.*—nx-v. δa.63.

—— *as if driving in a carriage.*—cyc.γw.14.18.—fer[t].16.47.

—— *as when going down a hill.*—cyc.

—— *as if a gulf behind him, and he would fall into it.*—k-ca. 28.43.

—— *as if all objects stood still.*—dul.δo.5.31.65[a].

—— *like stoppage of blood.*—sng. a[1]b[s].

—— *as if head were too light.*—k-ca.30.

—— *as if there was nothing firm in his head.*—ver.

—— *as if the head would burst.*—con.30.

—— *as if head were compressed.*—dgn.

—— *as from pressure on head.*—vrb.

—— *like a sudden jerk through head.*—mgt.5.16.

Vertigo, *from one part of brain to another.*—nx-v.

—— *in the forehead.*—arn.—asp. γ.—cam.δL.—cca.—cot.—ctn.—glo.—hyn.—idm.γi[a]. 29.—mrl.—nx-m.—pho.γ.—rn-b.γ.—rs-r.

—— *across forehead.*—k-bi.3.29.

—— *in the top of head.*—scr. 18.

—— *in upper part of brain.*—hfb. **5-10.**

—— *in right side of head.*—ctn. δr.

—— *in the occiput.*—-chi.19.—fl-x.5.18.19.28.31.35.—glo.—pet[t].**50.**—rn-b[s].γ.31.—spg.44.—zin[s].18.; [x].31.; μ[s]. 5.19.65.

—— *as if occiput turned round.*—ibe.

—— *coming from the occiput.*—ang.—cb-v.5.31.—snc.

—— *rising from spine to occiput.*—clf.

—— *coming up from back.*—sil[t].

—— *as if eyes lay deep.*—lyc.ε. a[1]b[s].

—— *forcing him to walk to the right.*—cb-a.δo.31.

—— *holds on by bed-post.*—phs.ω[2]. 2.16.

—— *feels as if the bed were drawn from under him.*—str.

—— *compelling him to stoop.*—pet.ηc[b].κ[1·5·7].λ.ρ.φ.18.(16).

—— *must lean on something.*—cb-v.—ni-x.ω[2].3-30.

—— *can scarcely support head.*—sep.

—— *unable to stand.*—cf-t.

—— *loses his balance.*—k-cy.

—— *must lie down.*—ibe.3.—mer.—opi.—pho.ε.; ω[2·5].—sec. str.

—— *would like to dash his head against a wall.*—spr.

—— *when sees a large flat surface.*—sep.

—— *with oscillation, dragging him down from one side, pulling him up from the other by impulses.*—amp.

Vertigo, *lasting four or five weeks.*—sec.

a^1. **Swimming.**—ab-c.—ang.—c-ph.σ^2.8-31.106.—can^d.; ^{b}.—cph.o^l.—ce-b.—cf-t.—eu-c.δo.ω^2.—fer.r^{1}b.—gel.——ham.——hyo.——k-bi.ε.—na-s.—pi-m.ω^2.—ziz.

—— *as from intoxication.*—bel.
—— *as before an emetic operates.*—bap.ε.
—— *as if from catarrh.*—cau.3.
—— *towards left side.*—ox-x.16.
—— *in the top of head.*—rs-r.δo.29.30.
—— *balancing to and fro as if in the water.*—fer.4.
—— *as if brain swam round.*—ham.30.

a^2. **Whirling.**—aco.δb.—am-c.28.—ana.—aps.ω^3.18.; ω^2.—ag-n.γ.3.—arn.a^1b.γ.εa.——asa.——au-m.γ.1.29.35.(8).——ba-m.—bel.κ^5.; λ.δo.30.31.; ε^a.6.(8).——cld.ε.——ca-c.χ^1.γ.3-99.18.31.—c-cs.——can.ε^a.—cb-v.—cau.29.83.(4).; γq.18.19.—ch-s.—cca.—clf.—coc.κ^5.30.—cf-t.ω^2.41.—con.—cro.χ^2.—ctn.ε.γi^a.—cup.—dro.ab^o.—evo.19.—fer^w.κ^5.31.——gn-c.ε.(71).——hyd.ak.a^1b.ω^2.—jun.—kre.a^1b.; ^{s}.28.— lab.——la-v.—lip.—mt-n^d.—mrl.31.—mr-c.γ.εa.5.16.—mu-x.b.8.; δo.6.—my-s^x.3-30.—nat.16.—nx-v.71.——oln.—par.19.—pho.μ^2.$\chi^{1·2·3}$.5.16.—pul.ε^a.φ.; γq.16.29.30.—rn-b.31.; ^{s}.8.—rn-s.19.—rho.16.; 44.(8-35).—rhs.29.31.—sep.; b.γ.εb.5.8.31.—sil^s.γ.3.19.29.30.31.—spi^b.31.—stp.19.(31).—sul$^{d·z}$.5.16.; γ.—trx.γ.—thr.28.—thu.b.19.31.——vin δo.t^k.—vi-o.19.—wis.a^1b^a.$\kappa^{3·8}$.ξ^3.$\chi^{1·2}$.ω.$^{2·8}$.128.

—— *as if head were going round.*—ir-f^x.a^1b.δr^r.4.
—— *like a mill wheel.*—ch-s.
—— *as from intoxication.*—spo.b.
—— *as if would have a fit of apoplexy.*—sep.b.χ^2.19.64.

Whirling, *from right to left.*—my-s.3-99.
—— *so that he knows not what he is about.*—mez.ε^a.
—— *as if brain whirled round.*—bis.—bry.b.3-30.—cn-i.
—— *like a sudden gust of wind.*—bov.
—— *as if all in head were going in slow circles.*—cf-t.εb.
—— *in forehead.*—ctn.γ.ζ.—mer.—msc.29.—nic.κ^5.—stp.ε^a.
—— *in vertex.*—mrl.

a^3. **Swaying.**—ard.30.—ind.γq.
a^4. **Balancing.**—æsc.
—— *in order to keep head erect.*—glo.a^1b.γ.

a^a. **Weakness of head.**—buf.l.—cth.—cau.—hyp.5.—grp.—k-ca.—ph-x.b.3.30.—rhs.a^1b^a.26.29.—zin.λ.

—— *as if something worked round in forehead.*—mer.ε^a.
—— *as after turning round.*—na-m.
—— *could not hold up head.*—at-a.

a^b. **Things seem to go round.**—aco.—agn.—alo.28.33.—alm^s.4.; κ^5.—am-c.3-99.5.—arn.31.; 26.(19.29).—aur.29.(30).—ba-c.κ^5.3-99.; 27.—bel.—bov.; 3-99.—bry^r.18.; 30.(31).; γq.—ca-c.18.31.50^b.—cn-i.—can^1.—cau.δr^m.8.(6).——chd.47.—cic.19.— cca.3.8.35.—cod.47.—con.30.; 16.—cyc^c.; δo.; 8.(6.19).—eub^w.18.—eu-c.—epn.30.—fer.127.—grt.47.(8).—hep.47.—hy-x.—k-bi^s.30.; κ^4.30.—k-cy.—lau.—lyc.κ^5.5.—mag.b.γq.18.; θ^2.κ^5.3-30.; t.—mer.28.—msc^f.—mu-x.8.—na-m.31.; a^1b^a.—na-p^s.3-30.—opi.—ph-x$^{i·t}$.γp.φ.19.31.—pho.b.5.31.; 5.31.(18).——pso.—rhs.18.19.31.(16).—rut.ηp.19.—sbd.30.—sel.$\kappa^{5·6}$.χ^3.—sep.4.16.19.31.—sil.47.65.(46).; ε^a.$\kappa^{5·6}$.3-30.6.(8.128).—so-n.29.—spi^2.31.—stp.26.29.; 2.16.—su-x.19.—tab.; γ.—tep.; ^{s}.; φ.16.—val.29.—ver.—zin.h^a.3-30.

—— *from below upwards.*—gua.3.

—— *horizontally from left to right.*—dgn.κ⁵.o¹.σrb.φ¹.46. 50.(47).
—— *as if the bed went round with him.*—nx-v.5.16.—so-n.16.
—— *things seem to go slowly round.*—hy-x.γ.δc^d,g.—lau. γ.δc^d,g.
—— *as if intoxicated.*—aco^s.b.30. (19.31).
—— *as if something went round in air.*—lau.γ.δc^d,g.ρ.
—— *as if the roof were falling.*—lep^d.3.
—— *objects seem to run together in a confused dance.*—oln. δa^d.8-31.
—— *things seem to go along with him.*—tep.31.
—— *the room seems to go round.* —cod.

a^c. **Things seem to sway backwards and forwards.**—bel.—bry.—cic.; ^p.δa^d.; ^q.—cyc^b.—eug.(49).—glo. b.—hy-x^p.a¹b.δo.—ign.—sum.—tep.—til.—wis.8-31.—zin.19.; ^d. a¹b^a.3-99.
—— *things seem to move.*—hyn. a¹b,b^d.φ.—msc.; γ.—sep.3-30.
—— *things seem to sway up and down.*—msc.26.
—— *things seem to go up and down and sideways.*—ech.
—— *things seem to move near and then far away.*—cic.
—— *things seem in violent agitation.*—ptl.
—— *as in an earthquake.*—fl-x.ε. γ.rx.19.
—— *things seem to sway to left side.*—grt.

a^d. **Feels as if the head moved.**—aml.—ep-p.
—— *from side to side.*—can.
—— *backwards.*—cn-i.—led.
—— *backwards and forwards.*—cb-v.29.; 19.—grt.43.
—— *forwards.*—lep^b.3.—pau.
—— *turned round.*—lau.
—— *as if it would sink in every direction.*—mt-n².
—— *pressing down head.*—na-m. 19.
—— *up and down.*—zin^c.a¹b^a. 3-99.
—— *as if something in head went hither and thither.*—aco.—cyc.14.18.—sil.19.(16).
—— *as if it turned round in brain.* —nx-v.a¹b^a.—stn.a¹b^s,b^a.—sul^{g.s}.5.16.—ver.

a^e. **Feels as if the body swam.**—la-v.16.

a^f. **Feels as if floating in the air.**—msc^h.—nx-j.b^d.5.16.

a^g. **Feels as if raised up.**—ca-c^t.—cn-i.—sil.

a^h. **Feels as if the feet would slip.** —nic.4.8.

a^i. **Feels as if the ground sank.**—k-br.b.—na-m.127.—tep.31.(18. 19).
—— *as if table sank.*—ph-x^{b.t}.γp. φ.19.31.

a^j. **Feels as if the ground were unsteady.**—clf.47.—sul.3.—tep.

a^k. **Feels as if were falling down.** —msc.a¹b.19.

a^l. **Feels as if falling from a height.** —msc.

a^m. **Feels as if thrown over.**—na-m.

a^n. **Feels as if shaken longitudinally.**—mer.16.

a^o. **Feels as if sinking.**—mer².16. (17).

a^p. **Feels as if unsteady.**—ca-a.—cam.—cic^c.δa^d.—cch.—hy-x^c.a¹b. δo.—led.18.31.—mt-n.8-31.—mez. δt^m.—spi.—sul.a¹b^y.8.33.—tab.—trx.ε.8-31.
—— *must lay hold of something.* —cam.
—— *feeling of vacillation.*—phs. ε.31.66.
—— *as if dancing.*—pul^s.50.

a^q. **Feels as swaying to and fro.**—cic^c.—cin.δo^r.ω².30.(16).—k-ca.19. 65^a.—so-n.19.—thu.16.19.

—— *as from strong tobacco.*—rho.

a^r. **Feels as if whirled round.**—bel.
—bry^b.18.—ep-p.—grt.—jat.*ε*.—
msc.—pho.; 47.—til.

—— *from right to left.*—bel.

—— *as if something turned round in body.*—lyc.

—— *feels the air caused by whirling in his face.*—msc.

—— *he knows not what has come over him.*—tep.

a^s. **Feels as if would fall.**—aco^b.฿.30. (19.31).—æth.8.—alo.ag.ſ^β.18.31. —alm.*σ*².19.31.; ^b.4.; (50^c).—am-c. ฿.—ana.—an-s.—ars.5.47.—asr. —ber.*ω*².—ca-c.e฿.*κ*⁵.3-99.; *ω*².; 18.29.31.—car.—cau.19.—cha.31. 66.—cca.—dul.*ω*^{2.8}.3-99.—fer.31. —hæm.—k-bi^b.30.—k-ca.19.— kre².28.—lau.—lil.δ๐.7.(8-31).— mgt.5.16.—mag.29.; a¹฿^a.*κ*⁵.5.19. —mg-m.*γ*q.—mrl.18.19.31.—mer. 6.31.—na-m.*κ*⁵.—na-p^b.3-30.—ni-x. 5.30.—nx-v.δ๐^c.εa.29.30.89.90.— opi.*ε*.19.—ph-x.19.; 3.18.—pho. a¹฿.*γ*.*κ*⁵.3.66.; 3.30.; 5.19.—pul.; ^p.50.; *κ*⁵.29.—rn-b².8.; *γ*.31.—sbd. —sab.; δ฿.*ω*².19.—sel.5.128.—snc. —sep.3.30.—sil.3.29.30.; ².*γ*.3.19. 29.30.31.; *ε*.29.35.; e฿.—spi.18.; 50^a.—stn.฿.8.31.; 19.—str.19.— sul.8.29.31.50^a.66.—su-x.4.30^b.— tep^b.; a¹฿^a.*χ*³.—ter.δ๐.—til.*η*p.*κ*⁵. wis.8-31.; *γ*q.16.—zin.18.; 5.

—— *hither and thither.*—ipc.a¹฿^a. 28.31.—sil.e฿.

—— *as if after drinking.*—la-v. *ε*^b.*γ*.3-99.

—— *as if going to have a fit of apoplexy.*—tep.ag.(8).

—— *as if the bed were tipping over.*—ars.

a^t. **Feels as if would fall forwards.** aln.50^a.—arn.66.—bov.5.—ca-c^g. —cr-s.—cau^v.—chd.; ฿.—clf².— cic.29.—c-ar.*γ*.*ω*.43.(8-31.86).— elp.—fer.33.—grp.; *κ*⁵.29.—grt. *ω*².8.(6).—hel.—lep.—lyc.—lcp^w. —mag^b.—mg-m.3-30.—mg-s.63.

66.—man.18.19.—nit.—pet.50.— phl^{u.v}.6.8.(16).—ph-x.^{b.1}.*γ*p.*φ*.19. 31.—pod.—pul.29.—rn-b.*γ*.—rs-r. 128.—rhs^u.18.; 31.—rut.3-30.— sab.18.— sil.—spi.49.—sul.30.— trx.฿.8-31.

—— *as if the head would fall backwards and forwards.*— ph-x.

—— *as if would be knocked forwards.*—fer.16.47.

—— *as if the head tended forwards.*—ca-a^x.a¹฿.—cup.*ω*². 35.(16).—sar.19.31.

—— *as if drawn forwards.*—iod.

—— *as from intoxication.*—led.*η*. *η*c^b.*χ*².19.29.31.

a^u. **Feels as if would fall backwards.**—aga.—bov.—bro.—bry. b^b.5.—cb-a.a¹b^a.19.—mil^w.31.— nit^w.5.31.—nx-v^v.฿.—pan.5.— phl^{t.v}.6.8.(16).—rhs^t.18.—so-n. 18.—spo.

—— *as if head would fall backwards.*—cn-i.—chi.31.35. (16).; 26.31.—ch-s.29.(16). —rho.ag.16.—str.*φ*.

—— *head sinks backwards.*—spi. a¹฿^a.*κ*⁵.*λ*.*μ*³.*π*.18.19.31.(16).

—— *when going forwards thought he was going backwards.*— sil.

a^v. **Feels as if would fall to one side.**—am-m.31.(8).—bz-x.4.— can.31.—cau^t.—nx-v.; ^u.฿.—pht^{t.u}. 6.8.(16).—pim.3-30.—rhe.18.— squ.3.30.—sul.; *κ*⁵.8.31.

—— *as if head would fall to one side.*—spo.*γ*p.19.

—— *to the side to which he turns.* —phl.*γ*q.

—— *to either side alternately.*— amp.

—— *did not know where he was.* —sil.31.

a^w. **Feels as if would fall to right side.**—ars.31.— ca-a.8-31.—ch-x. 31.—eub^b.18.—itu.—lcp^t.; 5.— mil^u.31.—nit.—rut.8-31.

—— *as if drawn to right side.*—— cca.31.

—— *as if head would hang to right side.*—fer.².κ⁵.31.

—— *as if turned to right side.*—grt.(8).

—— *turns towards right side.*—sil.4.31.

—— *as if would go to the right.*—dio.

aˣ. **Feels as if would fall to left side.** —ana.γ.19.—aur.8-31.—bor.5.31.—cic.31.—dir.81.—dro.81.—ep-p.—eub.8-31.—ir-f.².a¹b.δrʳ.4.—mrl. 3.5.16.18.19.—mez.—my-s².3-30. —nat.—spi.b.31.—sul.b.δo.31.—zin.31.

—— *as if head tended to left side.* —ca-aᵗ.a¹b.—dir.εᶜ.— sil. ηp.γhh.3.63.

aʸ. **Feels as if he stood on his head.** —ph-x.3.16.47.

aᶻ. **Feels as if about to faint.**—ana. γ.19.—sbd.δo.—spiᵇ.31.—sul³⁻ᵈ.5. 16.—tep.a¹bᵃ.—vp-r.72.

CONCOMITANTS.

aȥ. *Apathy.*—pho.γq.(66.70).

abᵒ. *Disinclination for work.*—cup. ω².—dro².—sep.

af. *Discomfort.*—msc.

ag. *Anxiety.*—aco.δtᵐ.8.—alo.; ᵃ. ζ³.18.31.—alm.κ⁵.2.—arn.ε. 72.—bel.b.δoᵈ.κ⁵.ω⁸.—cau.—cofˢ.γq.—dig.ω².; 18.—gam. 30ᵃ.—nx-m.b.—opi.a¹b.—rhoᵘ.16.—tepˢ.(8).—vrn.κ¹·⁵.

agˢ. *As if something bad were about to happen.*—cb-a.δo.

ab. *Fear.*—ccs.—sul.δg.31.49.

abˣˢ. *Fear of dying.*—rhs.16.

ak. *Sadness.*—hydᶜ.a¹b.ω².—pho. φ.ω².

a¹ᵈ. *Groaning.*—lah.2.

aq. *Restlessness.*—fer.a¹b.—jat.χ¹. ρ.—nx-m.

au. *Crossness.*—bor.γiᵃ.3.

au. *Displeased with everything.*—cb-a.

aȥ. *Elation.*—er-a.

a¹b. *Confusion of ideas.*—c-ar.γ.

a¹b. *Confusion of senses.*—ars.—ag-n.κ⁵.—gloᶜ·².γ.—lau.—opi. aȥ.—pho.66.—str.—sulᴾ.8.33.

a¹b. *Absence of mind.*—aco.

a¹bᵇ. *Distraction of thoughts.*—cau. —cha.5.—mrl.33.—opi.—rn-b.

a¹bᵉ. *Loss of presence of mind.*—bor.

a¹bᶠ. *Makes mistakes in speaking.*—sil.

a¹bᵒ. *Forgetfulness.*—arg.19.41.—lip.ε.a¹bˢ.

a¹bᵖ. *Loss of memory.*—c-ph.63.—er-h.κ⁵.—dig.—nx-m.γq.—str.a¹bˢ.δo.3.30.; ηaʰ.—tep.

a¹bˢ. *Dulness of mind.*—fer.aȥ.—gel.γq.δo.—tepˢ.χ³.

a¹bˢ. *Difficulty of comprehension.*—lip.ε.a¹bᵖ.—lyc.ε.

a¹bˢ. *Loss of thought.*—ars.30.—aru.γiᵃ.—bry.γw.—cnm.ε.γ. —for.ε.—ipcˢ.28.31.—kre.εᵇ. a¹b.δoᶜ.εa.—opi.γp.δo.ηaa.κ⁵·⁷. χ³.ω².—ph-x.42.—rn-s.—sng. —stnᵈ.a¹bᵃ.—str.a¹bᵖ.δo.3.30.

a¹bˢ. *Stupidity.*—cb-aᵘ.19.—tar.

a¹bʸ. *Obtuseness of senses.*—ag-n.φ. —dgn.2-99.—bel.—hy-x.ω².

a¹εᵃ. *As if losing senses.*—sep.5.29. 66.

a¹εᵇ. *Delirium.*—nx-m.

a¹εᶜ. *Raving.*—chd.κ⁵.

a¹b. *Stupefaction.*—aco.—æs-g.a¹bᵇ. —æth.γ.κ⁶.χ²·5.—aga.; γ. eb.111.—arn.γ.εa.—ba-c.132. —bov.; ᵃ.3.30.—ca-aᵗ·ˣ.—ca-c.— car.γ.—clo.—cle.γq. 26.28.—dgn.r¹kk.—fgs. gelᵃ.θj.θ³.κ.ρ¹.—grp.5.—hel. —hyd².ak.ω².—hy-xᶜ·ᴾ.δo.—kreˢ.; εᵇ.a¹bˢ.δoᶜ.εa.—lau.—mil.b.—mscᵏ.19.—mu-x.—opi.—phoˢ.γ.κ⁵.3.66.—phy.δo. —sab.—sec.—sil.3.30.—stnˢ. b.8.31.—stp.6.(8).—sul.ω³.3. —zin.5.

a¹b. *As if in a dream.*—ca-c.5.—hynᶜ.a¹bᵈ.φ.

a¹bˢ. *Loss of consciousness.*—cth.δo. ω².8-31.—ch-s.γ.—ctn.—der.

a¹ᵛᵃ. *Transient loss of consciousness.*
——æs-g.b.——bov.γ.18.—cau.
31.ᵃ.19.—chd.ω⁸.——con.33.—
k-cy.ω².—lah.ᵭ.5.——mag.; ˢ.
κ⁵.5.19.—na-m.γ.26. ; ω².3-30.;
κ⁶.; ᵇ.—nx-m.ℓ.ω⁵.—nx-vᵈ.—
rhsᵃ.26.29.——sar.c.κ⁷.π.σ²ii.χ³.
18.——sil.19.128.——spiᵘ.κ⁵.λ.
μ³.π.18.19.31.(16).—stnᵈ.a¹ᵭᵃ.
——tab.——tep.c.eᵭ.; ˢ.—wis².
κ³·⁸.ℓ⁵.χ¹·².ω²·⁸.128.——zincᵈ.3-
99.

a¹ᵛᵇ. *Coma.*—æs-g.

a¹ᵛᵈ. *Picking at bedclothes.*——hynᶜ.
a¹ᵭ.φ.

γd. *Rush of blood to head.*—bel.
δᵭ.eᵭ.—bry.—cac.—c-ph.29.
——eug.30.—gas.γiᵃ.ρ.ω.—k-cl.
85.——lah.76.—msc.(8).——
myr.29.—pul.γ.—sab.γp.—
urt.ℓᵃ.γiᵃ.

γiᵃ. *Fulness of head.*——æs-g.γq.δᵭ.
σ².κ⁵·⁸.——am-m.γq.—aru.aᵭˢ.
bor.au.3. ; 33.—bry.—ch-x.ρ.
2.33.—ctn².ℓ.—fag.30.(19).
—gas.γd.ρ.ω.—gym.ℓᵃ.δᵭ.κ⁵·⁷.
—hln.γ.——idm.29.—la-v.7.
—mer.—pod.—so-n.—til.δᵭ.
—urt.ℓᵃ.γd.

γp. *Heat of head.*—cle.ᵭ.γq,w.ω⁸.
6.—dio.—hy-x.γq.κ⁴p.ρ¹.—
la-x.——mrl.—ni-x.γ.31.—
opi.a¹ᵭᵃ.δᵭ.ηaa.κ⁵·⁷.χ³.ω².—
ph-xᵇ·ⁱ·ᵗ.φ.19.31.—sab.γd.—
spoᵛ.19.

γq. *Heaviness of head.*—aco.κ⁵.29.;
3.—æs-g.γiᵃ.δᵭ.σ⁹.κ⁵·⁶.—am-m.
γiᵃ.—bov.—bryᵇ.; 5.—cb-a.
γw.29.30.—cau².18.19.—cr-b.
3.—cle.ᵭ.γp,w.ω⁸.6.; a¹ᵭ.26.
28.—cofᵇ.aᵹ.—cvl.—con.—
gel.a¹ᵇᵃ.δᵭ.—hep.—hy-x.γp.
κ⁴p.ρ¹.—hyn.ℓa.—k-bi.3-99.
29.(31).—la-v.ᵥq.—lau.—
lip.φ.5.—magᵇ.ᵭ.—mg-mˢ.—
mg-s.99.(30).—naj.ℓ.—nat.
ℓ.34.112.—nic.3.16.(8).—
nx-m.a¹ᵇᵖ.—pæo.ℓ.—phlᵛ.
pho.aa.(66.70).—pru.—pul².
16.29.31.—sec.—tea.31.—
til.γ.δᵭ.—wisᵃ.8.31.

as if had not sleep enough.
—zin.eᵇ.

γv̄. *Itching behind ear.*—ca-c.15.

γw. *Inability to keep up head.*—
æth.a¹ᵭ.γ.κ⁶.χ³.5.—ars.

γw. *Head sways from side to side.*
—cle.ᵭ.γp,q.ω⁸.6.

γw. *Head falls from side to side.*—
trx.8.31.

γw. *Head falls hither and thither.*
—phl.δᵭ.31.

γw. *Movements in head.*—bry.a¹ᵇᵃ.

γw. *As if brain fell forwards.*—
cb-a.γiᵃ.29.30.

γw. *As if brain swayed.*—aco.—
cyc.14.18.

γhh. *Sweat on forehead.*—silˣ.ηp.3.
63.

γiiᵃ. *Head feels swollen.*—mrl.—
rn-b.

γ. *Headache.*—aco.29.—ac-c.δtᵐ.
eᵭ.η.κ⁵.ω³.—æth.a¹ᵭ.κ⁶.χ².5.—
aga.a¹ᵭ.ea.111.—ail.κ⁵.—aln.
5.(16).—anaˣ.19.—aps.5.99.;
90.—ag-n.3.—arn.a¹ᵭ.ea.—
ars.—asr.3.99.—as-s.—asp.
—ath.—au-m³.1.29.35.(8).—
ba-c.29.—bel.12.; ᵭ.—ber.χ¹.
ω².29.—bis.κ⁴·⁷.ρ.χ².5.—bov.
ℓᵃ.a¹ᵭᵃ.18.—bro.ζ².—ca-c.κ⁵.
29.; ².χ¹.3-99.18.31.—c-ph.ᵭ.
83.—cam.δᵴ.—car.a¹ᵭ.—cs-e.
κ⁵3.—cn-s.—cnb.δ.3.30.(66).
—cca.φ.—cnm.ℓ.a¹ᵇᵃ.—cop.
—ctn².ζ.—cun.ζ.—c-ar.aᵭ.—
cyc.5.; σ¹.5.—dig.—ep-p.
—fag.—fl-xᶜ.ℓ.rx.19.—gel.—
gn-c.ℓ.—gloᵃ·ᶜ.a¹ᵭ.—hel.—
hln.γiᵃ.; 29.—hep.26.—hdr.
ω³.5.—hy-x.δℓᵈ.; δℓᵈ.ᵹ.P².ρ.—
hfb.-hyp.κ⁵.3-99.4.-ibe.-ign.
—ind.κ⁵.λiᵃ.λ².(5.8).—irs.—
jat.26.—k-bi.κ⁵.ω².; δᵭ.-k-cl.
5.klm.; κ⁵.r.ᵥ.—lah.κ⁵.—la-vˢ.
ℓᵇ.3-99.-lauᵇ.δℓᵈ.ᵹ,P².ρ.—lo-i.
ω⁸.-lo-c.-lol.-lyc.31.-mnc.
3.66.—mrl².-mer².ᵭ.κ⁵.χ³.4.-
mr-f.—mr-c³.5.16.—m-cy.-
msc.; ℓ.35.; κ⁵.σ.; ˢ.—mu-x.-
nat.41.-na-m.a¹ᵭᵃ.26.—ni-x.
5.; γp.31.—nx-m.—opi.a¹ᵇᵃ.

—pan.—ped.κ^5.—pho.γp.χ^1.; ^{s}.α^1d.κ^5.3.66.; δο.κ^5.o^3.(8).; θ^2. —phs.31.—pgn.—ptl.—pul. γd.—rn-b^s.31.; 5.6.; ^{t}.—sam. 3.26.—san.—sep^2.b.εd.5.8.31. —$sil^{2\cdot s}$.3.19.29.30.31.—so-n. κ^5.λ.μ^3.—spi.26.—str.δο.θ.$\kappa^{3\cdot 4}$. λ^2.—sto.; 5.; 5.—sul.; ^{2}.— tab^b.—tan.κ^5.—trx^2.—tar.ρ^1. —tep.; δο.; ζ^2.; κ^6.—til.γq.δο. —zn-o.

γ. *Like something before forehead he could not see past.*—phl.31.

δg. *Creepy feeling before eyes.*—sul.αb.31.49.

δq. *Weight in eyes.*—lyc.3.

δii^a. *Feeling of swelling of eyes.*—con.

$\delta\varepsilon^d$. *Eyes fixed.*—hy-x^b.γ.δg,P^2.ρ.—lau^b.γ.δg,P^2.ρ.—msc.θ.o^2.

δb. *As if eyes would close.*—aco^2. —sab^s.ω^2.19.

δb. *Eyes close.*—lol.—mg-s.3.

δg. *Eyes too open.*—hy-x.γ.$\delta\varepsilon^d$,P^2. ρ.—lau^b.γ.$\delta\varepsilon^d$,P^2.ρ.

δb. *Difficulty of opening eyes.*—phl.γw.31.

δο. *Obscuration of vision.*—aco.26.—æs-g.γi^a,q.o^2.$\kappa^{5\cdot 6}$.—aga.b.(41). —ana.—arg.—ars.—atr.30. (72).—bel.λ.30.31.; γd.εd.—cth.$\alpha^1 d^a$.ω^2.8-31.—cb-a.; 31.—cph^1.—ced.3-99.—cha.ηp.16.—cin^q.ω^2.30.(16).—cof.29.—col. 5.19.—com.30.—cup.50.—cu-s.ω^2.—cyc^b.—dig.—dgn. 19.; 18.—dul.5.31.65^a.—eu-c^l. ω^2.—epn.—gel.$\alpha^1 b^s$.γq.; b,d.65. —glo.—gun.29.—gym.ε^a.γi^a. $\kappa^{5\cdot 7}$.—hep.63.71.—hy-x.b.—hfb.29.—hyo.; δP^2.—k-bi.66. —la-v.—lil^s.7.(8-31).—lyc. —mer.5.19.; ^{2}.ε^a.7.30.66.(8).—mor.—msc.—mu-x^2.6.—na-m. 29.30.—ni-x.3-30.—nx-v.; 63.; 17.—opi.$\alpha^1 b^s$.γp.ηaa.$\kappa^{5\cdot 7}$. χ^3.ω^2.—par.o^2.43.—pho.; γ.κ^5. o^3.(8).—phy.αb.—pi-m.(47). —rap.—rs-r.29.30.—rhs.31.—sbd^z.—sab.—san.—so-n.30. 35.—str.λ^2.; γ.θ.$\kappa^{3\cdot 4}$.λ^2.; $\alpha b^{p\cdot s}$. 3.30.; ω^3.—sul^x.b.31.—sum.ω. —tep.γ.—ter^s.—til.γi^a.; γ.γq. —vrb^2.

—— *like a veil.*—hy-x.α^1d.—str.λ.

—— *like a watery veil.*—cb-a.αg^s.

—— *like a yellow veil.*—k-bi. γ.

—— *like a dark curtain.*—fer.κ^5.ω^2.100.

—— *all turns black.*—ol-m.

δo^c. *Transient blindness.*—ag-n.—ars.—asa.λ.χ^3.ϕ^1.—hep.ω^2.—kre.ε^b.$\alpha^1 b^s$,d.εa.—mor.—nx-v^s. εa.29.30.89.90.

δo^d. *Dazzling.*—bel.b.αg.κ^5.ω^3.—$cic^{c\cdot p}$.—oln^b.8-31.

δr^g. *Objects appear distant.*—stn.

δr^h. *Diplopia.*—oln.18.50^a.

$\delta r^{j\cdot z}$. *Sees everything green and yellow.*—tep^c.

δr^l. *Objects seem turned upside down.*—eug.19.

δr^m. *Objects appear larger.*—cau^b. 8.(6).

δr^r. *Objects run together.*—ir-$f^{2\cdot x}$. αb.4.

δs. *Photophobia.*—cam.γ.—ch-s. —scu.49.

δt^c. *Vision of sparks.*—cod.53.—tep.

δt^k. *Flames before eyes.*—vrb.

δt^m. *Flickering before eyes.*—aco.8. —ac-c.γ.εb.η.κ^5.ω^2.30.—am-c.3. —mez^p.—str.—tar.30.31.35.

δt^r. *Vision of net.*—hyo.γ.rhb.

δ. *Pain in eye.*—cnb.γ.3-30.(66). —ctn.ε.κ^5.ω^2.8.

δL. *Burning in eyelids.*—cam.

δP^1. *Contracted pupils.*—mez.

δP^2. *Dilated pupils.*—art.ε.$\eta c^{a\cdot b}$.—hy-x.γ.$\delta\varepsilon^d$.; ^{b}.γ.$\delta\varepsilon^d$,g.ρ.—hyo. δs.—lau^b.γ.$\delta\varepsilon^d$.; ^{b}.γ.$\delta\varepsilon^d$,g.ρ.

εa. *Deafness.*—arn^2.α^1d.γ.—kre.ε^b. $\alpha^1 b^s$,d.δo^c.—mar-c.γ.5.16.—nx-v^s.δo^c.29.30.89.90.

εd. *Noise in ears.*—cit.—kf-t^s.—tep.ε.; $\kappa^{5\cdot 7}$.χ^3.ω^2.

εϑ. *Humming in ears.*—sng.

εϑ. *Roaring in ears.*—ac-c.γ.δt^m.η. κ^5.ω^2.—aga.a^{1}ϑ.γ.111.—ag-n. ω$^{2.8}$.—bel.δϑ.—ca-c^s.κ^5.3-99.— cyc.—sep^2.ƀ.γ.5.8.31.—sty.

εϑ. *Ringing in ears.*—ac-c.—eu-c. —m-cy.30.—sil^s.—tep.ɩ.a^{1}ϑ^a.

εϑ. *Singing in ears.*—san.κ^7.o^1.

ζ. *Pain in nose.*—ctn^3.γ.—cun.γ.

ζ^2. *Epistaxis.*—bro.γ.—cam.— sul.3.—tep.γ.

ζ^3. *Coryza.*—alo^s.aᶢ.18.31.—c-ph. ν.31.

ηa^h. *Wild expression.*—str.a^{1}ƀ^p.

ηc^a. *Blue rings round eyes.*—crt.ɩ. δP^2.

ηc^b. *Pale face.*—crt.ɩ.δP^2.—ctn.ɩ. δ.ω^2.8.—led^t.ηp.χ^3.19.29.31.— mag.κ.κ$^{5.7}$.χ^1.5.16.—pet.κ$^{1.5.7}$. λ.φ.18.(16).—sel.ƀ.χ^3.ω^2.

ηp. *Heat of face.*—cha.δϑ.16.— ch-x.ɩ^c.—dul.—led^t.ηc^b.χ^2.19. 29.31.—rut^b.19.—sil^x.γhh.3. 63.—til^s.κ^5.

ηaa. *Red face.*—opi.a^{1}ƀ^s.δϑ.κ$^{5.7}$.χ^3. ω^2.—pho.ɩ.χ^2.26.28.—str.

η. *Pain in face.*—ac-c.γ.δt^m.εϑ.κ^5. ω^2.

θf^d. *Spasm of mouth.*—msc.o^2.

θj. *Dry mouth.*—gel.ᴅ,ɩ^a.θ^3.κ.ρ.

θ. *Clamminess of mouth.*—sng.3.

θ. *Viscid mucus in mouth.*—str.γ. δϑ.κ$^{3.4}$.λ^2.

θ^2. *Flow of saliva.*—mag^b.κ^5.3.30. —pho.γ.

θ^3. *Coated tongue.*—gel.ᴅ,ɩ^a.θj.κ.ρ.

ɩ. *Pain in throat.*—jat.κ^4.φ.

ɩ. *Constriction of larynx.*—lcp.19.

ɩ. *Hawking up mucus.*—ce-s.3.

κ. *Bad taste.*—mag.ηc^b.κ$^{5.7}$.χ^1.5.16.

κ. *Bitter taste.*—gel.ᴅ,ɩ^a.θj.θ^3.ρ.

κ. *Sour taste.*—alm.κ^5.3.(66).

κ^1. *Loss of appetite.*—am-c.κ^5.3.— cyc.κ$^{4.5}$.——pet.ηc^b.κ$^{5.7}$.λ.ρ.φ. 18.(16).—ter.κ^5.—vrn.aᶢ.κ^5.

κ^1. *Desire for black coffee.*—msc. κ^5.

κ^3. *Thirst.*—str.γ.δϑ.κ^4.λ^2.——wis^2. a^{1}ᴅ^a.ɩ^c.ɩ^3.χ$^{1.2}$.ω$^{2.8}$.128.

κ^{4}p. *Heat of stomach.*—hy-x.γp,q.ρ^1.

κ^4. *Weak feeling in stomach.*—aco.

γq.κ^5.29.—aln.5.17.(17.46).— amb.—jug.—k-fc.χ^1.ωx.—tab.

κ^4. *Uneasiness in stomach.*—osm.aq.

κ^4. *Burning in stomach.*—cf-t.

κ^4. *Pain in stomach.*—bel.γ.κ^7.χ^2. 5.31.—cld.κ^5.8.—jat.ɩ.φ.— k-bi^b.30.; κ$^{5.6}$.r^1.—rs-r.4.— str.γ.δϑ.κ^3.λ^2.

κ^{4}i^a. *Fulness of stomach.*—cyc.κ$^{1.5}$.

κ^5. *Nausea.*—aco.γq.κ^4.29.—ac-c. γ.δt^m.εϑ.κ^5.η.ω^2.—ac-l.—æs-g. γi^a.q.δϑ.o^2.κ^6.—ail.κ^6.; γ. alm^b.; κ.3.(66).; aᶢ.2.—aln. ω^2.—am-c.κ^1.3.; 3.(31).—aps. —a-sc.—ag-n.a^{1}ƀ.—ars.16. (30).—ba-c.; ^{b}.3-99.; 29.— bel.; ƀ.aᶢ.δϑ^d.ω^8.—bro.—bry. ω^2.30.—cai.—cld.κ^4.3.—ca-c^s. εϑ.3-99.; γ.29.—c-ph.5.—cam. —cb-a.29.30.—cr-h.a^{1}ƀ.— ce-b.30.—cs-e.γ.3.—chd.a^{1}ɩ^c. —chi.χ^2.—coc^2.30.—col.—crt. —ctn.ɩ.δ.ηc^b.ω^2.8.—cyc.κ$^{1.4}$. —dgn^b.o^1.σr^{1}b.φ.46.50.(47).— ech.—fag.—fer.δϑ.ω^3.; $^{2\text{-}w}$.31. —fl-x.—glo.—grp^t.29.— gym.ɩ^a.γi^a.δϑ.κ^7.—ham.—hep. 5.—hfb.—hyp.γ.3-99.4.— ind.γ.λi^a.λ^2.—idm.λ^1.5.—jug. 3.—jun.31.—k-bi.16.; κ$^{4.6}$.r^1.; γ.ω^2.—k-br.ω^q.—klm.γ.r.ν.— lah.γ.—la-x.3-30.—lep.5.— lo-i.—lol.o^2.—lyc^b.5.—mag^b. θ^2.3-30.; ηc^b.κ.κ^7.χ^1.5.16.; ^{s}. a^{1}ᴅ^a.5.19.—mer^2.ƀ.χ^2.4.; π.8. 31.—mor.—msc.κ^1.;γ.σ.;κ^6.— myr.φ^1.—na-m^s.—nic^2.—ni-x. κ^7.3.—œna.κ^6.ω$^{8.5}$.—opi.a^{1}ƀ^s.δϑ. ηaa.κ^7.χ^3.ω^2.; χ^3.ω^8.65.(70).— ped.γ.—pet.29.; 5.16.; ηc^b.κ$^{1.7}$. λ.ρ.φ.18.(16).——pho^s.a^{1}ᴅ.γ.3. 66.; χ^1.29.—ptl.30.31.—pul.; 29.—san.—sar.3.49.—sel^b.κ^6. χ^3.—sil.; κ^6.; ɩ^b.3-30.; ^{w}.4.31. ^{b}.ɩ^a.κ^6.3.6.30.(8.128).——so-n. γ.λ.μ^3.——spi^u.a^{1}ᴅ^a.λ.μ^3.π.18. 19.31.(16).—squ.—sto.3.— sul.; ^{v}.8.31.—tab.κ$^{6.7}$.6.— tan.γ.—tep.; εϑ.κ^7.χ^3.ω^2.— ter.κ^1.—thr.κ^6.—til^s.ηp.— vrn.aᶢ.κ^1.

Nausea, as from smoking strong tobacco.—zin.2.

κ^6. *Vomiting.*—æs-g.γi^a,q.δo.o^2.κ^5.—ail.κ^5.—der.—k-bi.$\kappa^{4\cdot5}$,r^1.—msc.κ^5.—na-m.a^{1}ɒ^a.—sel^b.κ^5.χ^3.—sil.κ^5.; ^{b}.ℓ^a.κ^5.3.6.30.(8.128).—tab.$\kappa^{5\cdot7}$.6.—tep.γ.—thr.κ^5.; 85.

κ^7. *Eructation.*—bis.γ.κ^4.χ^3.5.31.—gym.ℓ^a.γi^a.δo.κ^5.—mag.ηc^b.κ.κ^7.χ^1.5.16.—ni-x.κ^5.3.—opi.a^{1}ɒ^s.δo.ηaa.κ^5.χ^3.ω^2.—pet.ηc^b.$\kappa^{1\cdot5}$.λ.ρ.φ.18.(16).—san.eɒ.o^1.—sar.ℓ.a^{1}ɒ^a.π.σ^{2}ii.χ^3.18.—tab.$\kappa^{5\cdot6}$.6.—tep.eɒ.κ^5.χ^3.ω^2.

κ^8. *Hiccough.*—wis^2.a^{1}ɒ^a.κ^3.ξ^3.χ$^{1\cdot2}$.ω$^{2\cdot8}$.128.

λi^a. *Fulness of abdomen.*—ind.γ.κ^5.λ^2.(5.8).

λp. *Heat of abdomen.*—hel.

λ. *Weakness in abdomen.*—zin^a.

λ. *Whirling at umbilicus.*—bel.δo.30.31.

λ. *Pain in abdomen.*—asa.δo^c.χ^3.φ^1.—c-ph.γd.σ.ω^2.83.—pet.ηc^b.$\kappa^{1\cdot5\cdot7}$.φ.18.(16).—ptl.—so-n.γ.κ^5.μ^3.—spi^u.a^{1}ɒ^a.κ^5.μ^3.π.18.19.31.(16).—str.δo.

λ^1. *Pain in liver.*—idm.κ^5.5.

λ^2. *Rumbling in bowels.*—dio.—str.γ.δo.$\kappa^{3\cdot4}$.

λ^2. *Discharge of flatus.*—ind.γ.λi^a.κ^5.(5.8.).

μ^3. *Diarrhœa.*—pho^2.χ$^{1\cdot2\cdot3}$.5.16.—str.

μ^3. *Urging to stool.*—so-n.γ.κ^5.λ.—spi^u.a^{1}ɒ^a.κ^5.λ.π.18.19.31.(16).—sul.5.19.—zin.5.19.65.

μ^6. *Pain in anus.*—sul.

ξ^3. *Delayed menses.*—iod.ρ^1.

ξ^3. *Metrorrhagia.*—wis^2.a^{1}ɒ^a.$\kappa^{3\cdot8}$.χ$^{1\cdot2}$.ω$^{2\cdot8}$.128.

o^1. *Tickling cough.*—san.eɒ.κ^7.

o^1. *Short dry cough.*—dgn^b.κ^5.σr^{1}b.φ.46.50.(47).

o^2. *Thickness of speech.*—æs-g.γi^a,q.δo.$\kappa^{5\cdot6}$.

o^2. *Inability to speak.*—lol.κ^5.—msc.θf^d.—par.δo.48.

o^3. *Sneezing.*—pho.γ.δo.κ^5.(8).

πp. *Heat in chest.*—lch.

π. *Discomfort in chest.*—spi^u.a^{1}ɒ^a.κ^5.λ.μ^3.18.19.31.(16).

π. *Like a worm in chest creeping up to throat.*—mer.κ^5.8.31.

π. *Pain in chest.*—sar.ℓ.a^{1}ɒ^a.κ^7.σ^{2}ii.χ^3.18.

ρ. *Slow pulse.*—pet.ηc^b.$\kappa^{1\cdot5\cdot8}$.λ.φ.18.(16).

ρ. *Weak pulse.*—jat.aq.χ^1.

ρ. *Full strong pulse.*—gel.ɒ,ℓ^a.θj.θ^3.κ.

ρ. *Pulse small,weak,rapid.*—hy-x.γ.δc^d,g,P^2.—lau^b.γ.δc^d,g,P^2.

ρ. *Contracted pulse.*—bis.γ.$\kappa^{4\cdot7}$.χ^2.5.31.

ρ. *Suppressed pulse.*—gas.γd,i^a.ω.

ρ. *Rush of blood to heart.*—ars.—sul.5.18.

ρ^1. *Palpitation of heart.*—ch-s.—hy-x.γ.p,q.κ^4p.—iod.ξ^3.—tar.γ.

σ. *Backache.*—c-ph.γd.λ.ω^2.83.

σ. *Pain down spine.*—msc.γ.κ^5.

σb. *Cold back.*—dgn^b.κ^5.o^1.r^{1}b.φ.46.50.(47).

σ^1. *Pain in loins.*—cyc.γ.5.

σ^{2}ff. *Stiffness of nape.*—alm^s.19.31.

σ^{2}ii. *Swollen neck.*—sar.ℓ.a^{1}ɒ^a.κ^7.π.χ^3.18.

σ^2. *Pain in nape.*—c-ph^1.8-31.106.; b,ℓ.31.—chd.χ^2.

rx. *Numbness in arm.*—fl-x^c.ℓ.γ.19.

rhh. *Perspiration on arms.*—hyo.δt^r.r.

r. *Prickling in arms.*—hyo.δt^r.rhh.

r^{1}b. *Cold hands.*—fer^1.—dgn^b.κ^5.o^1.σb.φ.46.50.(47).—mer.ℓ.χ^1.

r^{1}kk. *Trembling of hands.*—bel.—dgn.a^{1}ɒ.—k-bi.$\kappa^{4\cdot5\cdot6}$.

υq. *Weight in legs.*—la-v.γq.

υ. *Pain in lower extremities.*—c-ph.ζ^3.31.

rυ. *Pains in limbs.*—bel.—klm.κ^5.

rυ. *Weakness of legs.*—con.

r^{1}υ^{1}b. *Cold hands and feet.*—sep.

r^{1}υ^1. *Weakness of hands and feet.*—nat.ℓ.6.31.

φ. *Yawning.*—dgn^b.κ^5.o^1.σr^{1}b.46.50.(47).—pet.ηc^b.$\kappa^{1\cdot5\cdot7}$.λ.18.(16).

φ. *Sleepiness.*—æth.30.—ag-n.a^{1}b^y.

—bel.γ.—cle 99.—crt.—hyn. e^{a}.γq.; ^{c}.a^{1}b,d^{a}.—jat.ι.κ^{4}.—k-br. —lau.—lip.γq.5.—mo-a.—myr.; κ^{5}.—ph-x$^{b.i.t}$.γp.19.31. —pho.ak.ω^{2}.5.—pul^{2}.e^{a}.19.—rho.—str^{u}.—tep^{b}.16.—tri.2. 30.

φ. *Restless sleep.*—asa.δo^{c}.λ.χ^{3}.

φ^{1}. *Sleeplessness.*—la-x.2.

φ^{2}. *Dreaming.*—lo-c.

χ^{1}. *Chilliness.*—ca-c^{2}.γ.3-99.18.31. —jat.aq.ρ.—k-fc.κ^{4}.ωx.—mag.ηc^{b}.κ.κ$^{5\cdot7}$.5.16.—mer.e. τ^{1}b.—nx-m.—pho.γ.γp.; ^{2}.μ^{2}. χ$^{2\cdot3}$.5.16.; κ^{5}.29.

χ^{1}. *Rigor down back.*—bel.γ.ω^{2}.29.

χ^{2}. *Heat.*—æth.a^{1}d.γ.κ^{6}.5.—bis.γ. κ$^{4\cdot7}$.5.31.—chd.σ^{2}.—chi.κ^{5}.—cro^{2}.—glo.—led^{t}.ηc^{b},p.19.29. 31.—mer^{2}.b.κ^{5}.4.—pho.ι.ηaa. 26.28.; ^{2}.μ^{2}.χ$^{1\cdot3}$.5.16.—sep^{2}.b. 19.64.—zn-o.

χ$^{1\cdot2}$. *Alternate chills and heats.*—wis^{2}.a^{1}d^{a}.κ$^{3\cdot8}$.ξ^{3}.ω$^{2\cdot8}$.128.

χ^{3}. *Sweat.*—pho^{2}.μ^{2}.χ$^{1\cdot2}$.5.16.—sar.ι.a^{1}d^{a}.κ^{7}.π.σ^{2}ii.18.—sel.b. ηc^{b}.ω^{2}.; ^{b}.κ$^{5\cdot6}$.—ver.2.82.

χ^{3}. *Cold sweat.*—asa.δo^{c}.λ.φ^{1}.—opi.κ^{5}.ω^{8}.65.(70).—tep.ed.κ$^{5\cdot7}$. ω^{2}.; ^{s}.a^{1}b^{s}.

ψv. *Itching of body.*—bro.

ωd. *Flushing of upper body.*—ur-n. ω^{3}.83.

ωx. *Numbness.*—sum.δo^{c}.

ωx. *Numbness and insensibility.*—gas.γd,i^{a}.ρ.—k-fc.κ^{4}.χ^{1}.

ω^{2}. *Weakness.*—ac-c.γ.δt^{m}.ed.κ.κ^{5}. —aln.κ^{5}.—aps.—ag-n.ed.ω^{8}.—ber^{s}.31.;γ.χ^{1}.29.—bry.—ca-c^{s}. —c-ph.γd.σ.83.—cnm.—ctn.e. δ.κ^{5}.8.—cup^{t}.35.(16).; ab^{o}.—cu-s.δo.—cyc.—dul^{s}.ω^{8}.3-99. —elc.—eth.—fer.δo.κ^{5}.—grt^{t}. 8.(6).—gui.e.—hdr.γ.5.—hyd^{2}.ak.a^{1}d.—hy-x.a^{1}b^{y}.—iod. 3.—k-bi.γ.κ^{5}.—lyc.—ni-x. 3.30.—opi.a^{1}b^{s}.γp.δo.ηaa.κ$^{5\cdot7}$. χ^{3}.—pho.ak.φ.5.; ω^{5}.—phs.2. 16.; e.—sab^{s}.δb.19.—san.—snt.—sel.b.ηc^{b}.χ^{3}.—so-n.34. —sto.5.—sul.a^{1}d.3.; ι.3.30.—tep.ed.κ$^{5\cdot7}$.χ^{3}.—ter.e.—til.—wis^{2}.a^{1}d^{a}.κ$^{3\cdot8}$.ξ^{3}.χ$^{1\cdot2}$.ω^{8}.128.

— *as if paralysed.*—sul.ι. 127.

ω^{3}. *Faint.*—aps.18.—bel.—bry κ^{5}. 30.—cth.; a^{1}d^{a}.δo.8-31.—cha. —cin^{q}.δo.30.(16).—cf-t^{2}.41. —cvl.—cu-a.—dig.ag.—eu-c^{l}. δo.—glv.e.—glo.—hep.δo^{c}.—hyo.—idm.κ^{5}.2-99.26.30.—jug.—k-br.κ^{5}.—k-cy.a^{1}d^{a}.—lil^{s}.δo.7.(8-31).—mez.—msc. —nat.70.—na-m.a^{1}d^{a}.3.30.—nx-v.—pi-m^{l}.—ptl.26.—str. δo.—thr.ι.98.—ur-n.ωd.83.

ω^{3}. *Syncope.*—œna.κ$^{5\cdot6}$.ω^{5}.

ω^{5}. *Apoplectic fit.*—nx-m.

ω^{5}. *Rigidity.*—nx-m.ι.a^{1}d^{a}.

ω^{5}. *Spasmodic movements of knees.* —pho.ω^{2}.

ω^{5}.—*Convulsions.*—œna.κ$^{5\cdot6}$.ω^{3}.

ω^{8}. *Trembling.*—ag-n.ed.ω^{2}.—ars. —bel.b.ag.κ^{5}.—cb-v.5.19.99. —cr-h.8-31.—cle.b.γp,q,w.6. —dig.—dul^{s}.ω^{2}.3-99.—lo-i. γ.—opi.κ^{5}.χ^{3}.65.(70).—wis^{2}. a^{1}d^{a}.κ$^{3\cdot8}$.ξ^{3}.χ$^{1\cdot2}$.ω^{2}.128.

ω^{8}. *Shuddering.*—chd.a^{1}d^{a}.

CONDITIONS.

1. *All day.*—au-m^{2}.γ.29.35.(8). —mer.—pla.ρ.48.

2. *At night.*—alm.ag.κ^{5}.—am-c. 3.—ch-x.γi^{a}.ρ.33.—cro.b.30. —dgn.—ham.—lah.al^{d}.—la-x.φ^{1}.—ni-x.30.—phs.ω^{2}.16. —stp^{b}.16.—sul.2.—trn.—tri.φ.30.—ver.χ^{3}.82.—zin.κ^{5}.

2-99. *On waking at night.*—dgn.a^{1}b. —idm.κ^{5}.ω^{3}.26.30.

3. *In the morning.*—aco.γq.—aga.e^{a}.; ι.112.—alm.κ.κ^{5}.(66). —am-c.2.; δt^{m}.; κ$^{1\cdot5}$.; κ^{5}.(31). —am-m.e.6.(8).—ag-n.; γ.—bis.—bor.16.; au.γi^{a}.—cld.κ$^{4\cdot5}$. —cb-a.—cs-e.γ.κ^{5}.—cau.29. (30).—ce-s.—cr-b.γq.—cha. —cle.b.8-31.—cca^{b}.8.35.; (20. 70).—for.44.—gel.66.—gua^{b}. —hep.—hyp.—iod.ω^{2}.—jug.

κ^5.——k-bi.29. ; (67).——k-ca.
5.65^a.——lah.47. ; 18.(19).——
lep$^{b\cdot d}$.——lyc.; δq.——mg-m.(35).
——mg-s.$\delta\mathfrak{b}$.——mnc.γ.66.——mrl^x.
5.16.18.19.——my-s. ——na-m.
ι.——nic.γq.16.(8).——ni-x.$\kappa^{5\cdot 7}$.
——nit.——ph-x^s.18.——pho. ; ^{s}.
$a^1\mathfrak{d}$.γ.κ^5.66. ; γ.δo.κ^5.o^3.(8).——
pso.——sbd.ι^a.19.——sam.γ.26.
——sar.κ^5.49.——sng.θ.——sil.^{a}
65^a. ; ^{x}.ηp.γhh.63.——sto.κ^5.——
sul.$a^1\mathfrak{d}$.ω^2. ; ^{j}. ; ζ^2.——tep.(31).
——ver.

3-30. *On rising in the morning.*——
ac-f.——ail.$\mathfrak{b}$.——asr.γ.——ba-c^b.κ^5.
——bov^s.$a^1\mathfrak{d}$.; ^{b}.——bry^2.$\mathfrak{b}$.——ca-c^s.
$\epsilon\mathfrak{d}$.κ^5. ; γ.χ^1.18.31.——cha.$\mathfrak{b}$.
cnb.γ.δ.(66).——con.——dul^s.$\omega^{2\cdot 8}$.
——gam.——grn.41.43.——k-bi.
γq.29.(31).——lah.$\mathfrak{b}^d$.——la-x.κ^5.
——la-v^s.ι^b.γ.——lyc.$\mathfrak{b}$.——mag^b.θ^2.
κ^5.——mg-m^t.——my-s. ; $^{2\cdot x}$.——
na-m.(16).; $a^1\mathfrak{d}^a$.ω^2.; (117).——
na-p$^{b\cdot s}$.——nic.$\mathfrak{b}$.——ni-x.δo. ; ω^2.
——ph-x.; ^{a}.$\mathfrak{b}$.——pho. ; ^{s}.——pim^v.
——ptl.$\mathfrak{b}$.——pul.——rhs.——rut^t.
sam.——sep^c.; ^{s}.——sil^s.29.; ι^b.κ^5.;
$a^1\mathfrak{d}$. ; $^{2\cdot s}$.γ.19.29.31. ; ^{b}.ι^a.$\kappa^{5\cdot 6}$.
(8.128).——squ^v.——str.$a^1\mathfrak{b}^{p\cdot s}$.$\delta$o.
——sul.ι.ω^2.——tab.——zin^b.$\mathfrak{b}^a$.

3-99. *On waking in the morning.*——
am-c^b.5.——ars.——cap.——cau.ι.
——ced.δo.——grp.——hyp.γ.κ^5.4.
——ol-a.——pho.——zin$^{c\cdot d}$.$a^1\mathfrak{d}^a$.

4. *In the afternoon.*——æsc.——
alm$^{b\cdot s}$.——amb.5.8.31.——bz-x^v.
——cau^3.29.83.——cod.——ctn.$\beta\iota$.
——cyc.——fer^l.——glo.——ham.29.
——hyp.γ.κ^5.3-99.——ibe.——ir-f.
$^{2\cdot x}$.a^1b.δr^r.——mer^3.$\mathfrak{b}$.κ^5.χ^2.——
nic^h.8.——rs-r.κ^4.——sep^b.16.19.
31.——sil^w.31.——su-x^s.30^b.

5. *In the evening.*——aln κ^4.17.(17.
46). ; γ.(16).——am-c^b.8-99.——
aps.γ.99.——ag-n.——ars^s.47.——bis.
γ.κ^4.7.χ^2.31.——bor.31.——bov^t.
——bro.ι.16.——bry^a.$\mathfrak{b}^b$. ; γq.——
cb-a^b.$\mathfrak{b}$.80.(16.29).——cb-v.31.;
ω^8.19.99.——cha.a^1b.——cnb.$\mathfrak{b}^c$.
66.——col.δo.19.——cyc.; γ.; γ.σ^1.
——dio.γ.——ϵr-a.——grp.$a^1\mathfrak{d}$.——hep.

κ^5.——hdr.γ.ω^2.——hfb.31.——hyp^a.
——*ind*.γ.κ^5.λi^a.λ^3.(8).——idm.κ^5.
λ^1.——k-bi.——k-ca.3.——k-cl.γ.——
lah.$\mathfrak{b}$.$a^1\mathfrak{d}^a$.——la-x.——lep.κ^5.——
lcp.19.——mgt^s.16.——mag.ηc^b.κ.
$\kappa^{5\cdot 7}$.χ^1.16. ; ^{s}.$a^1\mathfrak{d}^a$.κ^5.19.——mrl^x.
3.16.18.19.——mer.δo.19.——
mr-c^3.γ.16.——ni-x.16. ; ^{s}.30. ;
γ.——nit$^{u\cdot w}$.——nx-j^f.16.——nx-v^b.
16.——ori.——pan^u.——pet.κ^5.16.
——ph-x.18.31.——pho.16.; a$\ddot{k}$.ϕ.
ω^2.; ^{3}.μ^2.$\chi^{1\cdot 2\cdot 3}$.16.; ^{b}.31.(18).——
pla.——rn-b.γ.6.——rs-v.——sbd.
——sel^s.128.——sep.a^1c^a.29.66.;
^{2}.$\mathfrak{b}$.γ.$\epsilon\mathfrak{d}$.8.31.——sil.18.19. ; 8.
42.——sto.ω^2.——sul.; $^{2\cdot d\cdot z}$.16.; ρ.
18.——trn.ι.——ur-n.——zin.μ^3.
19.65.

5. *In the forenoon.*——aco.ι.——æth.
$a^1\mathfrak{d}$.γ.κ^6.χ^2.——amb.4.8.31.——
ca-c.a^1b^3.——c-ph.κ^5.——ced.
cop.128.——dul.δo.31.65^a.——
fl-x.18.19.28.31.35.——lip.γq.ϕ.
——lyc^b.κ^5.——pho^b.$\mathfrak{b}$.31. ; ^{s}.19.
28.29.——ptl.——sbd.16.——sto.
——sul.μ^3.19.——zin.$a^1\mathfrak{d}$. ; ^{s}.

6. *In a room.*——aga.8. ; aga.28.——
ars.8-31.——bel.——cau^b.δr^m.8.
——cle.$\mathfrak{b}$.γp,q,w.ω^8.——cyc^b.8.
(19).——*grt*^{t}.ω^2. ; grt.(8).——
irs.31.——*kre*.$\mathfrak{b}$.3.8.——mg-m.29.
31.——mer^s.31.; $\mathfrak{b}$.; ^{b}.8.31.γq.——
msc.$\mathfrak{b}$ 31.——mu-x^2.δo.—— nat.ι.
τ^1v^1.31.——pæo.$\mathfrak{b}$.31.——phlt$^{t\cdot u\cdot v}$.
8.(16).——rn-b.γ.5.——sil^b.ι^a.
$\kappa^{5\cdot 8}$.3-30.(8.128).——stp.$a^1\mathfrak{d}$.(8).
——str.$\mathfrak{b}$.18.19.——su-x.(8).——
tab.$\kappa^{5\cdot 6}$.7.

7. *In a hot room.*——aco.$a^1\mathfrak{d}$.——la-v.
γi^a.——lil^s.δo.(8-31).——lyc.——
mer^2.ι^a.δo.30.66.(8).——pho.ι.

8. *In the open air.*——aco.a$\mathfrak{g}$.δr^m.——
æth^s.; *æth*.——aga.31.41. ; (6).;
aga.——amb.4.5.31.——am-m.ι.
6.; ^{v}.31.——ang.——ars.31.6.——
ar-c.31.——ar-s.31.——aur^x.31.
——*au-m*^{3}.γ.1.29.35.——*bel*.ι^a.6.
——bry.31.(19).——ca-a.31. ; ^{w}.
——ca-c.$\mathfrak{b}$.26.31.——c-ph^l.o^2.31.
106.——cth.$a^1\mathfrak{d}^a$.δo.ω^3.31.——
cr-h.31.——cau^b.δr^m.(6). ; *cau*.

——cle.ƀ.3.81.—cca^b.3.35.——
cnm.—ctn.ℓ.δ.κ^5.ω^2.—cyc^b.(6.
19).—dro.31.—eub^x.31.——
gen.4.30.—glo.ƀ.—grt^b.47.;
^{w}.; 6.; grt^t.ω^2.(6)—ind.γ.κ^5.
λi^a.λ^2.(5).—k-ca.18.31.; k-ca^b.
44.—kre.ƀ.3.(6).—lah.—lau.
30.—lil^b.δo.7.(31).—lcp.19.;
31—mt-n^p.31.——mg-m.ℓ^a.63.
γp.6.—mg-s.ℓ.—mn-m.ƀ.——
mer.κ^5.π.31.; ƀ.31.γq.6.; mer^2.
ℓ^a.δo.7.30.66.——msc.48.; γd.
—mu-x^2.ƀ.; ^{b}.—nic.γq.3.16.;
nic^h.4.—oln^b.δo^d.31.—ol-a.29.
——phl$^{t.u.v}$.6.(16).—pho.γ.δo.
κ^5.o^3.—plb.—pod.18.—pul.
31.(29).——rn-b$^{2.s}$.—rho^2.44.
(35).—rut^w.31.—snc.—sep.
31.; ^{2}.ƀ.γ.eꝺ.5.31.—sil.5.42.;
sil^b.ℓ^a.κ$^{5.6}$.3.6.(128).—spi.26.
31.(49).—stn^s.ƀ.31.—stp.a^{1}ꝺ.
6.—sul^s.29.31.**50^a**.66.; ^{p}.a^{1}ƀ^y.
33.; ^{v}.κ^5.31.—su-x.6.—trx.γw.
31.; ^{t}.ƀ.31.; ^{p}.31.—tep^s.aǥ.—
wis^s.31.; ^{c}.31.

12. *When pressed.*—bel.γ.
14. *By leaning head on something.*
 —vrb.
14. *When leaning against something.*—cyc^d.γw.18.
15. *By scratching.*—ca-c.γv.
16. *When lying.*—aco^b.ƀ.—aln.γ.5.
 —aps.19.47.—ars.κ^5.(30).—
 ath.—bor.3.—bro.ℓ.5.—cb-a^b.
 5.30.(29).—cb-v.99.—cha.δo.
 ηp.; *cha.*19.—chi^u.31.35.—ch-s^u.
 29.35.—ctn^q.δo.ω^2.30.—con^b.—
 cup^t.γ.ω^2.35.—fer^t.47.—grt.
 hfb.5.—k-bi.κ^5.—lab.—la-v^e.
 —mgt^s.5.—mag.ηc^b.κ.κ$^{5.7}$.χ^1.
 5.—mrl^x.3.5.18.19.—mer$^{2.o}$.
 (17).; ^{n}.—mr-c^2.γ.5.—nat^2.
 —na-m.3-30.; na-m.—nic.γq.
 3.(8).—ni-x.5.—nx-j^f.5.—
 nx-v^b.5.—ox-x^1.—pet.ʌ^5.5.;
 pet.ηc^b.κ$^{1.5.7}$.λ.ρ.φ.18.—phl$^{t.u.v}$.
 6.8.—pho.5.; ^{2}.μ^2.χ$^{1.2.3}$.5.—
 phs.ω^2.2.—pi-m.γ.—pul^2.γq.
 29.31.—rho^u.aǥ.; ^{2}.—rhs.
 aƀ^{as}.; rhs^b.18.19.31.—sep^b.
 4.19.31.—sil^d.19.—so-n^b.—

spi^u.a^{1}ꝺ^a.κ^5.λ.μ^3.π.18.19.31.—
spr.19.30.—stp^b.2.—sul$^{2.d.z}$.
5.—sum.ƀ.30.—tep^b.φ.—thu.
19,47.; thu.; ^{q}.19.—wis^s.γq.
15. *By laying down head.*—sbd.ƀ.
17. *By lying on back.*—aln.κ^4.5.
 (17.46.).—nx-v.δo.—sul.2.
17. *When lying on side.*—mer$^{2.o}$.
 16.
 —— *on right side.*—aln.κ^4.5.
 17.(46).
18. *When standing.*—aco.—alo^s.
 aǥ.ζ^3.31.—aps.ω^3.—aur.—
 bry$^{b.r}$.—ca-c^a.29.31.; ^{b}.31.
 50^b.; ^{2}.γ.χ^1.8-99.31.— can.—
 cau^2.γq.19.—cop.—cyc^d.γw.
 14.—dgn.δo.—dig.aǥ.—eth.
 —eub$^{b.w}$.—fl-x.5.19.28.31.35.
 —k-bi.31.— k-ca.31.(8).—
 lah.(19).3.—led^p.31.—lep.—
 man^t.19.—mrl^s.19.31.; ^{x}.3.5.
 16.19.— mer.—nx-v.31.66.—
 oln.δr^h.**50^a**.—pet.ηc^b.κ$^{1.5.7}$.λ.ρ.
 φ.(16).—ph-x.5.31.; ^{s}.3.—pho.
 5.31.—pod.8.—rhe^v.—rhs^b.
 19.31.(16).; $^{t.u}$.—sab^t.—sar.
 ℓ.a^{1}ꝺ^a.κ^7.π.σ^{2}ii.χ^3.—scr.—sil.
 5.19.—so-n^u.—spi^s.; ^{u}.a^{1}ꝺ^a.
 κ^5.λ.μ^3.π.19.31.(16).—str.ƀ.6.
 19.—sul.ρ.5.—tep^i.31.(19).—
 zin.19.(31).; ^{s}.
19 *On sitting.*—aco$^{b.s}$.(29).30.—
 æth.(30).—alo.66.—alm^s.σ^{2}ff.
 31.—ana^x.γ.—aps.16.47.—
 arg.a^{1}ƀ^o.41.—arn.26.(29).—
 bel.—bra.43.—bry.8-31.—
 ca-c.(31).—cb-a^u.a^{1}ƀ^s.—cb-v.
 31.; ω^8.5.99.; ^{d}.—cr-s.—
 cau^s.31.; ^{2}.18.—cau^s.—cha.
 (16).—chi.—cic^b.—cca.30.—
 coc.—cch.ℓ.—col.δo.5.—cop.
 —cyc^b.8.(6).—dgn.δo.—eug.
 δr^l.—evo^2.—fag.γi^a.30.—fl-x^c.
 ℓ.γ.rx.—hfb.ƀ.31.—k-ca.; ^{q}.
 ƀ5^a.; ^{s}.—lah.3.18.; lab.—
 led^t.ηc^b.p.χ^2.29.31.—lcp.8.; ι.;
 5.—mt-s.—mag^s.a^{1}ꝺ^a.κ^5.5.—
 man^t.18.—mep.—mrl^s.18.31.;
 ^{x}.3.5.16.18.—mer.; δo.5.—
 msc^k.a^{1}ꝺ.—na-m^d.—opi^s.ℓ.—
 par^2.—phl.35.—ph-x^s.; $^{b.i.t}$.

γp.φ.31.—pho^s.**5**.—*pul*.8-31.; pul³.ℓ^a.φ.--rn-s².--rho.—rhs^b.18.31.(16).—rut^b.ηp.—sbd.ℓ^a.3.—sab^s.δb.ω².—sar^t.31.—sep^b.4.16.31.—sil^d.(16).; 5.18.; a¹ᴅ^a.128.; ^{2-s}.γ.3.19.29.30.31.—so-n^q.—spi^u.a¹ᴅ^a.κ⁵.λ.μ³.π.18.31.(16).; ℓ^b.—spr.16.30.—sps^v.γp.—stn^s.—stp².(31).—str.ᵬ.6.18.; ^s.κ⁵.—sul.μ³.**5**.; ᵬ.—su-x^b.—*tep*ⁱ.31.(18).—thu.47.(16).; ^q.16.; ᵬ.31.—vi-o².—zin.18.(31).;^c.; μ³.5.65.

20. *When at rest.*—aco^d.31.—bel.31.—ca-c.26.—cca.3.(70).—gam.35.—*na-m.*

26. *By moving head.*—chi^u.31.—cle.(29).—equ.— na-m.a¹ᴅ^a.γ.—pi-m.ℓ.γi^a.—sam.γ.3.

26. *By moving head rapidly.*—cb-v.—gen.—k-bi.—msc^c.—pho.ℓ.ηaa.χ².28.

26. *By shaking head.*—aco.δo.—gen.—glo.—hep.γ.—spi.γ.

26. *On raising up head.*—cb-a^b.ᵬ.5.30.(16.29)—crd.29.—cle.26.; a¹ᴅ.γq.28.—hel.29.(30).jat.γ.—mr-c.—pho.28.

26. *On throwing back head.*—glo.

26. *By pressing head into pillow.*—ang.ℓ^a.

26. *On turning the head.*—aga.—amp.—ca-c.20.; ᵬ.8-31.—cle.26.—cun.--idm.κ⁸.ω³.2-99.30.—k-ca.—nat.—ptl.ω³.—rhs^a.a¹ᴅ^a.29.—spi.8-31.(49).—stp^b.29.

—— *suddenly.*—la-x.i^a.

26. *By carrying a weight on head.*—trn.

27. *On moving or raising the arms.*—ba-c^b.—sep.

28. *When turning.*—aga.6.—alo^b.33.—am-c².—cle.a¹ᴅ.γq.26.—fl-x.5.18.19.31.35.—gen.—glo.—ipc^s.a¹ᵬ^s.31.—k-ca.30.; 43.—kre²·ˢ.—mer^b.—na-m.—pho.26.; ℓ.ηaa.χ².26.; **5**.29.—thr².

When turning in bed.—cb-v.29.**65**^c.—mep.35.

29. *When stooping.*—aco.; γ.; γq.κ⁵.—ail.—alm.—ana.—*arn*.26.(19).—a-sc.—aur^b.(30).—au-m².γ.1.35.(8).—ba-c^b.κ⁵.; γ.—ber.30.; γ.χ¹.ω².—ca-c.γ.κ⁵.; 18.31.; 30.83.—c-ph.γd.—cn-i.31.—cb-a^b.ᵬ.5.30.(16).; cb-a.γq,w.ℓ.30.—cb-v^d.; 28.**65**^c.—crd.26.—cau².83.(4).; 3.(30).—cha.—ch-s^u.35.(16).—cic^t.—*cle*.26.—cof.δo.—cun.grp^t.κ⁵.—gun.δo.—ham.hel.26.(30).—hln.γ.—hf^b.δo.—ibe.—idm.γi^a.—inu.k-bi.3.; γq.3.(31).—klm.**50**^a.—lah.—led^t.ηc^b,p.χ.19.31.—mag^s.—mn-m.ᵬ.—men.30.—mep.—mer.30.—msc².; (30).—myr.γd.—na-m.δo.30.—nic.30.—ni-x.30.—nx-v^s.γo^c.ℓa.30.89.90.—ol-a.8.—opi.—pet.κ⁵.; 30.—ph-x.—pho.κ⁵.χ¹.; **5**.28.—plb.**50**.—pul^s.κ⁵.; ².γq.16.31.; ^t.—rs-r^l.δo.30.—rhs^a.a¹ᴅ^a.26.; ².31.—sep.a¹ℓ^a.5.; ².ᵬ.χ².64.—sil^s.3.30.; ^{2-s}.γ.3.19.30.31.; ^s.ℓ.35.so-n^b.—stp^b.26.—sul.; γq.30.; ^s.8-31.**50**^a.66.—sum.30.35.118.—thr.—val^b.

30. *On rising or sitting up.*—abs.—aco^{b-s}.(19.31).—æth.φ.; *æth*.19.—all.—ars.a¹b^s.; *ars*.κ⁵.16.—ard³.—asr.31.—atr.δo.(72).—*aur*^b.29.—ba-c.bel.δo.λ.31.—ber.29.—bry^b.(31).; κ⁵.ω².—ca-c.29.83.—c-ph.—cn-i.; ℓ.γ.—cb-a^b.ᵬ.5.(16.29).; γi^a,w.29.—*cau*.3.29,—cer.κ⁵.—chd.—cin^q.δo.ω².(16).—cca.19.—coc.².κ⁵.—cch.—com.δo[·].—con^b.—cro.ᵬ.2.—cu-a.ω³.—dig.—eug.γd.—epn^b.—fag.γi^a.(19).—fer.—gna.—grt.—*hel*.26.29.ham.—hf^b.—idm.; κ⁵.ω³.2-99.26.—k-bi^{b-s}.; ^b.κ⁴.—k-ca.; 28.—lab.—lau.8.; ℓ.—lyc.—

mg-s.γq.99.——men.29.—mer.
29.; ².ℓª.δ๐.7.66.(8).——m-cy.
eʋ.——msc.29.——na-m.δ๐.29.;
31.; ˢ.κ⁵.; na-m.——na-s.ℓ.——
nic.29.——ni-x.29.; ˢ.5.; 2.——
nx-vª.δ๐ᶜ.ℓa.29.89.90.——oln.——
pet.29.——pho.; 66.——phy.——
ptl.κ⁵.; 31.——rs-rⁱ.δ๐.29.——
sbdᵇ.——so-n.δ๐.35.——spr.16.
19.——sul.γq.29.; ᵗ.——su-x.ʋ.——
sum.ʋ.16.——tar.δtᵐ.31.35.——
tri.φ.2.

30ª. *By spinning.*—gam.aᶢ.
30ᵇ. *When sewing.*—su-xˢ.4.
31. *When walking.*——acoᵈ.20.;
acoᵇ⁻ˢ.(19).30.——aga.8.41.——
aloˢ.aᶢ.ζ³.18.——almˢ.σ²ff.19.
——amb.4.5.8.——am-c.κ⁵.3.——
am-mᵛ.(8).——arn.; ᵇ.——ars.
8.6.; ʷ.——ar-c.8.——asr.30.——
ast.——aurˣ.8.——ba-a.——bel.δ๐.
λ.30.; 20.——bis.γ.κ¹·⁷.χ².5.——
borˣ.5.——bov.ℓª.aⁱʋª.γ.——bryᵇ.
30.; 8.(19).——caj.——ca-a.8.;
ʷ.——ca-c.19.; ca-cˢ.18.29.; ᵇ.
18.50ᵇ.; ᵇ.8.26.; ².γ.χ².3-99.
18.——c-phⁱ.σ².8.106.; ζ³.υⁱ.;
ʋ.ℓ.σ².——cn-i.29.——canᵛ.
——cth.aⁱʋª.δ๐.ω².8.——cb-a.δ๐.
——cb-v.5.; ʋ.; 19.——cr-h.8.
——cauˢ.19.——chaˢ.66.——chiᵘ.
35.(16).; ᵘ.26.——ch-xᵛ.——cicˣ.
——cle.ʋ.3.8.——ccaʷ.——con.——
ctn.8.——cyc.——dgn.——dirˣ.——
dro.8.; ˣ.——dul.δ๐.5.65ª.——
eubˣ.8.——ferˢ.; ²·ʷ.——fl-x.5.18.
19.28.35.——gen.——grt.——hf b.
5.——hyn.ʋ.——hyo.ʋ.——ipc.; ˢ.
aⁱʋª.28.——irs.6.——jun.κ⁵.——
k-bi.18.; k-bi.γq.29.3-99.——
k-ca.18.(8).; ˢ.——ledᵖ.18.; ᵗ.
ηᶜᵇ,p.χ².19.29.——lpt.——lilª.δ๐.
7.(8).——lip.——lyc.γ.——lcp.8.——
mt-nᵖ.8.——mt-s.ʋ.——mg-m.6.
29.——mrlˢ.; ˢ.18.19.——merˢ.
6.; κ⁵.π.8.——msc.ʋ.6.——nat.ʋ.;
ℓ.rⁱ.υⁱ.6.——na-m.30.; ᵇ.——ni-x.
γ.γp.——nitᵘ·ʷ.5.——nx-v.66.
(18).——olnᵇ.δ๐ᵈ.8.——pæo.ʋ.6.——
pet.——phl.γw.δᵇ.; γ.——ph-x.
5.18.; ᵇ·ⁱ·ᵗ.γp.φ.19.——pho.83.;

ᵇ.ᵇ.5.; ᵇ.5.(18).——phs.; ᵖ.66.;
γ.——ptl.κ⁵.30.——pul.8.(19).;
ᵍ.γq.16.29.——rn-b.; ˢ.γ.——rs-r.
——rhsᵇ.18.19.(16).; ᵗ.; δ๐.;
ᵍ.29.——rutʷ.8.——sarᵗ.19.——
sepᶜ.; ᵇ.50.; 8.; ².ᵇ.γ.eʋ.5.8.;
ᵇ.4.16.19.——silᵛ.; ²·ˢ.3.19.29.
30.; ʷ.κ⁵.4.——spi²·ᵇ.; ᵘ.aⁱʋª.
κ⁵.λ.μ³.π.18.19.(16).; 8.26.
(49).; ˣ.ʋ.——spr.——stnˢ.ʋ.8.——
stp.ʋ.; stp².19.——str.114.——
sul.; ˣ.ʋ.δ๐.; ˢ.8.29.50ª.66.;
aʋ.δg.49.; ᵛ.κ⁵.8.——trx.γw.8.;
ᵗ.ʋ.8.; ᵖ.8.——tar.δtᵐ.30.35.;
ᵇ.——tepⁱ.(18.19).; ᵇ.; tep.——
tea.; γq.——thu.ʋ.19.——wisˢ.8.;
ᶜ.8.——zin.18.19.; ˣ.

33. *On going up stairs.*—aloᵇ.28.
——ar-h.ʋ.(33).——bor.γiª.——cai.
——cca.——dig.ℓ.
33. *On ascending.*—sulᵖ.aⁱᵇγ.8.
33. *On going down stairs.*——ar-h.ʋ.
33.——ch-x.γiª.ρ.2.——con.aⁱʋª.
——ferᵗ.——mn-m.ʋ.——mrl.aⁱʋ.
——pi-m.ʋ.
34. *By slight exertion.*—ibe.
34. *By violent exercise.*—nat.ℓ.γq.
112.——so-n.ω².
34. *By running.*—cld.
35. *By motion.*—au-m².γ.1.29.(8).
——bel.——cb-v.——chiᵘ.31.(16).
——ch-sᵘ.29.(16).——ccaᵇ.3.8.——
cf-t.——cupᵗ.γ.ω².(16).——fl-x.5.
18.19.28.31.——gam.20.——k-cl.
γd.——mg-m.3.——mep.28.——
msc.ℓ.γ.——pæo.——phl.19.——
pho.——pi-m.——pul.ℓ.——rho.
44.(8).——silˢ.ℓ.29.——so-n.δ๐.
30.——sum.29.30.118.——thr.
κ⁶.

35. *By moving upper part of body.*
—la-v.
35. *By lifting a weight.*—tar.δtᵐ.
30.31.
40. *By ill-humour.*—ca-c.
41. *By mental exertion.*—aga.ʋ.δ๐.;
aga.8.31.——arg.aⁱᵇᵒ.19.——cf.t².
ω³.——grn.30.43.——klm.——nat.γ.
42. *By meditating.*——ph-x.aⁱʋª.——
sil.5.8.
42. *By thinking of it.*—pi-m.

43. *When reading.*—bra.19.—cup.—grn.30.41.—grt^d.—ham.—k-ca.28.—ph-x.
—— *aloud.*—par.δo.o^3.

44. *When writing.*—for.3.—k-ca^b.8.—rho^3.(8-85).—spg.

46. *On opening eyes.*—aln.κ^4.5.17.(17).—alm.——dgn^b.κ^5.o^1.σrb.φ.50.(47).—*sil^b*.47.65.

47. *On closing eyes.*——aps.16.19.—ars^a.5.——chd^b.——clf^j.—cod^b.——*dgn^b*.κ^5.o^1.σr^{1}b.φ.46.50.——fer^t.16.——grt^b.(8).——hep^b.—lah.3.——pho^r.—*pi-m.*δo.—sil^b.65.(46).——thu.19.(16).

48. *On moving eyes.*—pla.ρ.1.

48. *On moving eyelids.*—msc.(8).

49. *By looking fixedly.*—all.—cau.—*eug^c.*——sar.κ^5.3.——seu.δo.—spi^t.; *spi*.8.31.——sul.aꜧ.δg.31.

50. *On looking up.*—cb-v.—cau.ɩ.—cup.δo.——dgn^b.κ^5.o^1.σr^{1}b.φ.46.(47).——grp.——pet^t.—plb.29.—pul$^{p.s}$.—sep.ꜧ.31.—sil.

50^a. *On looking down.*——aln^t.——klm.29.——mn-m.ꜧ.——oln.δr^h.18.——spi^s.—sul^a.8.29.31.66.

50^b. *By looking round.*—ca-c^b.18.31.—opi.ɩ.

50^c. *By wiping eyes.*—alm^a.

53. *By blowing nose.*—cod.δt^c.

63. *When eating.*—c-ph.aꜧ.——dio.—for.—hep.δo.71.——mg-m.ɩ^a.(8).γp.6.——mg-s^t.66.——nx-v^2.; δo.—sil^x.γhh.ηp.3.

64. *When drinking.*——lyc.——sep^2.ꜧ.χ^3.29.

65. *By smoking.*—gel.ꜧ.ꝺ.δo.——opi.κ^5.χ^3.ω^8.(70).——sil^b.47.(46).—zin.μ^3.5.19.

65^a. *Before a meal.*——dul.δo.5.31.—k-ca^q.19.——sil.3.

65^c. *By gargling.*—cb-v.28.29.

66. *After food.*—alm.κ.κ^5.3.——arn^t.—bry.—cha.; ^{a}.31.—cnb.ꜧ^c.5.; cnb.γ.δ.3-30.——er-a.—gel.3.—k-bi.δo.——k-ca.——kis.—mg-s^t.63.——mnc.γ.3.——mer^2.ɩ^a.δo.7.30.(8).——na-s^b.ꜧ^a.——

nx-v.; 81.(18).—pet.—pho^a.a^{1}ꝺ.γ.κ^5.3.; 30.; a^{1}ꜧ.; *pho.aꜱ.*γq.(70).—phs^p.31.—sep.a^{1}ɩ^a.5.29.—sul^a.8.29.31.50^a.

67. *By drinking coffee or tea.*—cn-i.—cha.—*k-bi*.3.

70. *By drinking wine.*—cca.3.(20).—nat.ω^3.—*pho.aꜱ.*γq.(66).

70. *By drinking water.*—opi.κ^5.χ^3.ω^8.65.

71. *By eructation.*—gn-c^2.ɩ.—hep.δo.63.—nx-v^2.

72. *By vomiting.*—arn.ɩ.ag.—atr.δo.30.—vp-r^a.

75. *After stool.*—cup.a^{1}ꝺ.—lah.γd.

82. *Before menses.*—ver.χ^3.2.

83. *During menses.*—ca-c.29.30.—c-ph.γd.λ.σ.ω^2.——cau^2.29.(4).——pho.31.——thu.—ur-n.ꙍd.ω^3.

86. *By speaking.*—cha.

89. *By coughing.*—nx-v^s.δo^c.eꙁ.29.30.90.

90. *By sneezing.*——aps.γ.——nx-v^s.δo^c.eꙁ.29.30.89.

98. *During sleep.*—thr.ɩ.

99. *On awaking.*—aps.γ.5.—asr.γ.3.——cna.——cb-v.16.; ω^8.5.19.——cle.φ.——mg-s.γq.(30).——zn-o.ɩ.

100. *After a siesta.*—fer.δo.κ^5.φ.ω^2.

103. *By damp.*—bro.

106. *By wind.*—c-ph^1.σ^2.8-31.

111. *By the light.*—aga.a^{1}ꝺ.γ.eꝺ.

112. *In sunshine.*——aga.ɩ.3.—nat.ɩ.γq.34.

114. *In the dark.*—str.31.

117. *By cold water or bathing.*—na-m.3.30.—so-a.

118. *By using warm water.*—sum.29.30.35.

127. *By passing over a stream.*—ang.—bro.——na-m^i.—sul.ɩ.ω^2.

127. *By seeing flowing water.*—fer^b.

128. *When driving.*—hep.—sel^a.5.; a^{1}ꝺ^a.19.——sil^b.ɩ^a.κ$^{5.6}$.3.30.(8).—wis^2.a^{1}ꝺ^a.κ$^{3.8}$.ξ^3.χ$^{1.2}$.ω$^{2.8}$.

128. *When riding.*—cop.5.—rs-r^t.

132. *On going along a narrow path.*—ba-c.a^{1}ꜧ.

b. Staggering, stumbling, inability to stand steady.—aco.ℓ.—æs-g.a. a¹ᴅª.—aga.ℓ.; 8-31.—ail.—aln.κ⁵.—ag-n.a.—asp.a,ℓ.—bel.a.—ca-c.5.—c-ph.a.8-31.—cam.31.—cn-i.ᴅ. 31.—can.ℓ.—cth.a.—cau.—ch-h. cic.ᴅ.; a.—con.—cup.—der.28.—dio.a.γ.—fgs.ᴅ.—gel.ᴅ.—grt.+ glo.aᶜ.; a.8.—grp.a.a¹bᴾ.χ¹.—hy-x. a.δo.—hfb.31.a.19.—hyo.—hyn. a.30.—lah.γq.ηaa.; a¹ᴅª.—lyc.a.3-30.—mgt.31.; aᶜ.31.—mt-n.a.8-31.—mn-m.a.8-31.29.33.50ª.—mrl.a.31.—mer.a².γ.κ⁵.χ².; a.8-31. γq.6.—mr-c.31.—msc.6-31.—mu-x.a².8.—naj.—nat.a¹ᴅª.; a.31.—nic.a.3-30.—nit.31.; a¹.aɡ.γ.χ³.—nx-v.aᵘˑᵛ.31.; ᴅ.rᴠff.—pæo.a.6-31.—pho.aᵇ.5.31.—pi-m.a.33.—pul.5.31.—rho.2.—rhs.; 31.—rut. sec.—sep.a.31.50.—sep.a².γ.eᴅ.—sil.3-30.; aᵇ.κ⁵ˑ⁶.3-30.6.(8.128).; a.—so-t.—stn.a.8-31.—stp.a.—str.; 6.a.18.19.; 31.—sul.18.a.19.; aᵇʸ. 8-33.—su-x.a.30.(16).—sum.30.a. 16.—tab.a.—trx.a.8-31.—tar.a. 31.—thu.31.a².19.; 29.—til.—ver. ᴅ.—vi-t.a.—wis.8-31.; δrᵘ.(4.70).

—— *swaying hither and thither.*— cin.a.δo.ω².30.(16).

—— *as if from the side.*—pul.

—— *inability to stand.*—aco.a.

—— *as if intoxicated.*—aco.aᵇˑˢ. 30.(19).—aga.8-31.—alm. 31.—am-c.5.19.—arsᶜ.aˢ,ℓª. 8-31.—bel.a.aɡ.a¹ℓᶜ.31.—cam.31.—cr-s.—cha.a.3-30.—dio.a.4.8-31.—gel.—hyo.—ipc.ℓª.5.8-31.—k-ca. a.31.—kre.a.3.8.(6).—opi. a.—ph-x.a.5.18.31.—phs.a.—ptl.a.3-30.—pul.a.γp.ηcᵇ. 5.—sar.a.—sec.—sel. spo.a².; ℓ.31.—str.a.

—— *as when coming off a voyage in a boat.*—glo.a.8.

—— *as if he were going to have a fit of apoplexy.*—lah.a.5.

—— *as if from weakness.*—oln.a².

—— *as if standing on unsteady ground.*—sul.3.

—— *as from concussion of brain from a fall on occiput.*— aco.

bª. Staggering forwards.——chd.a.—lil.31.; ᴅ.4.

bᵇ. Staggering backwards.—aga.—bry.a.5.18.; 31.

bᶜ. Staggering to one side.—ars.aˢ. ℓª.8-31.—bry.31.—cap.a.—val.ℓª. 18.

bᵈ. Staggering to right side.—aco. a.29.—rhs.—sbdᵉ.a.γ.

bᵉ. Staggering to left side.——ir-f. a.5.31.; 3-30.6.31.; 30.—nx-m.5. 8-31.—sbdᵈ.a.γ.—so-n.31.—spi. a.31.—sul.a.δo.31.

CONCOMITANTS.

aɡ. *Anxiety.*——bel.a.a¹ℓᶜ.31.—nit. a¹.γ.χ³.

aᵇᴾ. *Loss of recollection.*—grp.a.χ¹.

a¹ᵇʸ. *Obtuseness of senses.*--sul.8-33.

a¹ℓᶜ. *Talking nonsense.*—bel.a.aɡ.31.

a¹ᴅ. *Stupefaction.*—rut.

a¹ᴅª. *Unconsciousness.*——æs-g.a.—lah.a.5.—nat.

γp. *Heat of head.*——cle.γq.δo.ep. ηp.—pul.a.ηcᵇ.5.

γq. *Heaviness of head.*—cle.γp.δo. ep.ηp.—lah.ηaa.

γ. *Headache.*—mer.a².κ⁵.χ².—nit. a¹.aɡ.χ³.—sbdᵈˑᵉ.a.—sep.aˣ.eᴅ.

δo. *Obscuration of sight.*--cin.a. ω².30.(16).—cle.γp,q.ep.ηp.--hy-x.a.—sulᵉ.a.31.

δrᵘ. *Objects appear to move.*—wis.; (4.70).

ep. *Hot ears.*—cle.γp,q.ηp.

eᴅ. *Humming in ears.*—sep.a².γ.

ηcᵇ. *Pale face.*—pul.a.γp.5.

ηp. *Heat of face.*—cle.γp,q.ep.

ηaa. *Red face.*—lah.γq.

κ⁵. *Nausea.*—aln.—mer.a².γ.χ².—sil.aᵇ.κ⁶.3-30.6.(8-128).

κ⁶. *Vomiting.*——sil.aᵇ.κ⁵.3-30.6. (8-128).

σ². *Pain in nape.*--c-ph.a.8-31.; a,ℓ.σ².31.

rᴠff. *Stiff tension of limbs.*—nx-v.ᴅ.

χ¹. *Rigor.*—grp.a.a¹bᴾ.

χ^2. *Heat.*—mer.a^2.γ.κ^5.
χ^3. *Sweat.*—nit.a^1.aɡ.γ.
ω^2. *Weakness.*—cin.a.δo.30.(16).

CONDITIONS.

2. *At night.*—cro.a.30.—rho.
3. *In the morning.*—bry.—kre.a. 8.(6).—sul.
3-30. *On rising in the morning.*— bry.a^2.—cb-a.a^p.—cha.a.— ir-f^e.6.31.—lyc.a.—nic.a.— ptl.a.—sil.; a^b.κ$^{5\cdot6}$.6.(8.128).
4. *In the afternoon.*—dio.a.8-31. —lil^a.ɒ.—*wis.*δr^u.(70).
5. *In the evening.*—-am-c.19.— bry^b.a.18.—cac.—ca-c.a.8-31. —grp.a^2.31.--ir-f^e.31.—lah.a. —nx-m^e.8-31.—ph-x.a.18.31. —pul.a.γp.ηc^b.; 31.
5. *In the forenoon.*—pho.a^b.31.
6. *In a room.*—cle.a.8.—ir-f^e.3- 30.31.—*kre.*a.3.8.—mer.a. msc.31.— pæo.a.31.—sil.a^b. κ$^{5\cdot6}$.3-30.(8.128).—str.a.18. 19.
8. *In the open air.*—-cle.a.6.— glo.a.—mu-x.a^2.—*sil.*a^b.κ$^{5\cdot6}$. 6.3.30.(128).—sul.a.a^{1}b^y.33.
8-31. *On walking in open air.*—aga. —ars^c.a^s,^{e}^{a}.—ca-c.a.5.—c-ph. a.σ^2.—dio.a.4.—ipc.^{e}^{a}.5.8-31. —mt-n.a.—mn-m.a.29.33. 50^a.—mer.a.γq.6.—nx-m^e.5. —stn.a.—trx.a.—wis.
16. *On lying down.*—cin.a.δo.ω^2. 30.—su-x.a.30.
18. *When standing.*—bry^b.a.5.; ^{c}. —ph-x.a.5.31.—rhs.—sul.a. 19.—val^c.e^a.
19. *When sitting.*—aco.a$^{b\cdot s}$.30.— am-c.5.—cn-i.ɒ.31.
28. *On turning head to right or left.*—der.
29. *On stooping.*—aco^d.a.—mn-m. a.8-31.33.50^a.—thu.
30. *When rising up.*—aco.a$^{b\cdot s}$.(19). —ail.a.35.—c-ph.—cin.a.δo. ω^2.(16).—cro.a.2.—hyn.a.— su-x.a.(16).—sum.a.16. —— *from kneeling.*—ir-f^e.

31. *When walking.*—alm.—bel.a. αɡ.a^{1}c^e.—bry^b.; ^{c}.—cam.— cn-i.ɒ.(19).—cic.—ele.—grp. a^2.5.—hfb.a.19.—hyn.a.— ir-f^e.5.; 3-30.6.—k-ca.a.—lil^a. —mgt.; a^c.—mrl.a.—mr-c. msc.6.—nat.a.—nit.—nx-v. a$^{u\cdot v}$.—pæo.a.6.—ph-x.a.5.18. —pho.a^b.5.—pul.5.—rhs.— sep.a.50.—-so-n^e.—spi^e.a.— spo.e.—str.—sul^e.a.δo.—tar. a.—thu.a^2.19.
33. *On ascending.*—sul.a.a^{1}b^y.8.
33. *On going up stairs.*—ar-h.a.
33. *On going down stairs.*—mn-m. a.8-31.29.50^a.—pi-m.a.
35. *When moving.*—ail.a.30.
50. *On looking up.*—sep.a.31.
50^a. *On looking down.*—mn-m.a. 8-31.29.33.
70. *By drinking wine.*--*wis.*δr^u.(4).
128. *When driving.*—*sil.*a^b.κ$^{5\cdot6}$.3-30. 6.(8).

ɛ. Falling.

nx-m. Giddiness gradually passing into stiffness and insensibility, falling from his chair to the ground, followed by sleep, and on awaking gradually phantasies succeeding each other for some hours, until (after six hours) complete consciousness returns; some headache and stupidity remain till following day.

ɛ. Falling.—aco.b.—aga.b.—cn-i.a. γ.30.—cau.a.; a.50.—cic.—cup.a. 30.—dig.a.33.—gel.a,ɒ.—nx-m. a^{1}ɒ^a.19.—œna.a.—plb.—pso.e.2- 99.—rs-r.—sec.a,e.—sul.a.ω^2.3-30.; a.ω^2.127.—trn.a.—tep.a.δr$^{j\cdot z}$.
—— *as if head were overbalanced.* —cha.a.31.66.
—— *and rolling about on ground.* —cic.
—— *like a fulminating fit of apo- plexy.*—hy-x.γ.
—— *falls senseless.*—-sar.a.κ^7.ᴡ. σ^{2}ii.χ^3.—tep.a.eɒ.—thr.30. a.98.

ϵ^a. **Falling forwards.**——phl$^{b \cdot c}$.a.8. (16).

ϵ^b. **Falling backwards.**——phl$^{a \cdot c}$.a.8. (16).

ϵ^c. **Falling to one side.**——phl$^{a \cdot b}$.a.8. (16).

ϵ^d. **Falling to left side.**——ep-p.

CONCOMITANTS.

γ. *Shock in head.*—hy-x.

$\delta r^{j \cdot z}$. *Objects appear green and yellow.*—tep.a.

ϵv. *Ringing in ears.*—tep.a.

κ^7. *Eructation.*—sar.a.π.σ^2ii.χ^3.

π. *Pain in chest.*—sar.a.κ^7.σ^2.χ^3.

σ^2ii. *Swollen neck.*—sar.a.κ^7.π.χ^3.

χ^3. *Sweat.*—sar.a.κ^7.π.σ^2ii.

ω^2. *Weakness.*—sul.a.3-30.

—— *as if paralysed.*—sul.a. 127.

CONDITIONS.

2-99. *On awaking at night.*—pso.ϵ.

3-30. *On rising in the morning.*—sul.a.ω^2.

8. *In open air.*—phl$^{a \cdot b \cdot c}$.(16).

16. *When lying.*—phl$^{a \cdot b \cdot c}$.8.

30. *On rising.*—cn-i.a.γ.—thr.a.98.

30. *On rising from bed.*—cup.a.

31. *On walking.*—cha.a.66.

33. *On going up stairs.*— dig.a.

50. *On looking up.*—cau.a.

66. *After eating.*—cha.a.31.

127. *On crossing running water.*—sul.a.ω^2.

v. **Intoxication.**—ac-x.γq.——ac-s.—æsc.—aga.——ail.γi^a.——amy.; ω.—aml.—aut.; ab^c,ϵ.γ.—asa.—as-t.δo. 60.—bel.; 66.; ϵ.; δo.v^2.; a,b.ηaa.—ber.—cam.—cn-i.b.31.(19).——cth. ——cap.——ch-s.ϵv.ρ.χ^2.; ϵ,b^c.γq.—cl-b.8-99.——cic.b.; 18.19.31.—cit. γ.—cof.$a^1 v$.—con.—cro.δo.ηp. c-ar.—cyc.ϵ.γq.κ^5.—dig.—erd.—euc.—fgs.b.—fer.—gel.a,b.δo.60.; a,ϵ.—grp.—grt.(8).; 66.—hel.ω^4. —hdr.; γ.—hy-x.—hyo.; r^{1}kk.; 66. —ign.—k-ca.—k-hy.—kis.—la-s. —la-v.—lau.; ω.—led.8-31.—lil. b^a.4.—lip.—lol.a.—mt-n.81.; b^a.—

mag.a^b.γq.18.——mer.ηp,aa,ii.66.—mr-c.—mez.az^w.——mil.—mo-a.—nab.—nx-m.γq.——nx-v.; b.rvff.—opi.; b.; a^1a.——par.—phl.8.(6).—pul.66.—rho.—rs-r.γr.κ^5.σr.—rhs. a^s.30.—sec.——sil.——spi.——spr. str.; ωq.; κ^3.v^1.—tab.γ.; $a^1 v^a$.γ.γq.—ter.—til.; κ^5.—val.a$^{2 \cdot b}$.29.—ver.b.

—— *as if head turned round.*—alm.ϵ.v^4.

—— *as from drinking.*—bel.ϵ.ηaa, ii.—cr-s.b.——gn-l.—ign.δ.—mrl.

—— *does not know what ails him.*—arg.

—— *with inclination to lie down.*—bry.

—— *followed by mental depression and exhaustion.*—euc.

—— *walks, lifting feet high, as if had to step over things lying in his way, like a drunken person.*—bel.

v^a. **Giddy intoxication.**—argh.δb.—ag-n.ab.ω^2.——cau.ab^b.——led.ϵ^b.—nx-m.ag.—pul.χ^2.—tab.$a^1 b^y$.

v^b. **Agreeable intoxication.**—aga.

v^c. **Loquacious intoxication.**—bel. —eug.ab.

v^d. **Excited intoxication.**——mo-m. —nx-j.a^f.5.16.——nx-m.

—— *as after spirituous liquors.*—k-hy.

v^e. **Merry intoxication.**—bel.—clf.

v^f. **Hypochondriacal intoxication.** —aur.γi^a.

v^g. **Stupid intoxication.**——cau.—rho.—ter^h.b.χ^3.(78).—thu.—til.

—— *as after pollutions.*—mez.

v^h. **Sleepy intoxication.**——agn.—aps.—arg^a.δb.—ter^g.b.χ^3.(78).—ton.ϵ.

v^i. **Easy intoxication by spirituous liquors.**—alm.—bel.—col.—con. —k-cl.—ter.

CONCOMITANTS.

ab. *Laziness.*—ag-n^u.ω^2.—eug^c.

ab^c. *Disinclination for speaking.*—ant.$\alpha \epsilon$.γ.

at. *Love of solitude.*—ant.*ab*ᶜ.γ.

ag. *Anxiety.*—nx-m*ᵃ*.

*ax*ʷ. *Gaiety.*—mez.

*a*¹*a.* *Increased mental activity.*—opi.

*a*¹*b*ᵇ. *Distraction.*—cau*ᵃ*.

*a*¹*bᵧ.* *Obscuration of senses.*—tab*ᵃ*.

*a*¹*ᴅ.* *Stupefaction.*—cof.

*a*¹*ᴅ*ᵃ. *Loss of consciousness.*—tab.γ. γq.

γiᵃ. *Head feels full of compressed air.*—aur*ᶠ*.

γiᵃ. *Fulness of head.*—ail.

γq. *Heaviness of head.*—ac-x.—ch-s.*t*,*b*ᶜ.—cic.*t*.κ⁵.—mag.*a*ᵇ. 18.—nx-m.—tab.*a*¹*ᴅ*ᵃ.γ.

γ. *Headache.*—ant.*ab*ᶜ,*t*.—cit.—hdr.—tab. ; *a*¹*ᴅ*ᵃ.γq.

γσr. *Shivering in occiput and spine.*—rs-r.κ⁵.

δb. *Eyes closed.*—arg*ᵃ·ʰ*.

δ. *Burning in eyes.*—ign.

δo. *Obscured vision.*—bel.*o*².—as-t.60.—cro.ηp.—gel.*a*,*b*.60.

εᴅ. *Roaring in ears.*—ch-s.ρ.χ².

ηp. *Heat of face.*—cro.δo.—mer. η*aa*,ii.66.

η*aa*. *Red face.*—bel.*t*.ηii. ; *a*,*b*.—mer.ηp,ii.66.

ηii. *Swelled face.*—bel.*t*.η*aa*.—mer. ηp,*aa*.66.

κ³. *Thirst.*—str.*ᴠ*¹.

κ⁵. *Nausea.*—cyc.*t*.γq.—rs-r.γσr.—til.

*ᴠ*¹. *Flow of burning urine.*—str.κ³.

*ᴠ*⁴. *Pain in kidneys.*—alm.*t*.

*o*². *Difficult speech.*—bel.δo.

ρ. *Quick pulse.*—ch-s.εᴅ.χ².

σr. *Rigor in back.*—rs-r.γr.κ⁵.

r¹kk. *Trembling of hands.*—hyo.

rᴠff. *Stiff tension of limbs.*—nx-v.

χ². *Heat.*—ch-s.εᴅ.ρ.—pul*ᵃ*.

χ³. *Sweat.*—terˢ·ʰ.b.(78).

ω. *Dulness of whole body.*—amy.—lau.

ωq. *Heaviness of body.*—str.

ω². *Weakness.*—ag-n.*ab*.

ω⁴. *General malaise.*—hel.

CONDITIONS.

3-99. *In morning on waking.*—cl-h.

4. *In afternoon.*—lil.b*ᵃ*.

5-16. *In the evening on lying down.*—nx-j.*a*ᶠ.

6. *In a room.*—phl.8.

8. *In the open air.*—grt.—phl. (6).

8-31. *When walking in the open air.*—led.

18. *When standing.*—cic.19.31.—mag.*a*ᵇ.γq.

19. *When sitting.*—cn-i.6.31.—cic.18.31.

29. *On stooping.*—val.*a*²·ᵇ.

30. *On rising from bed.*—rhs.*a*ˢ.

31. *When walking.*—cn-i.b.(19).—cic.18.19.—mt-n.—phy.

60. *After smoking.*—as-t.δo.—gel.*a*,*b*.δo.

66. *After eating.*—bel.—grt.—hyo.—mer.ηp,*aa*,ii.—pul.

78. *After urinating.*—terˢ·ʰ.b.χ³.

t. **Confusion** (*Peculiar*).

nx-m. Heavy and pressive confusion of head, with a sensation as if left half of it and face were swollen slightly ; at same time pricking sensation like the streaming of electricity.

t. **Confusion, cloudiness, muddled feeling, maziness.**—acn.—ac-c.—ac-f.—æsc.—aga.—agn.—alo.—am-c.—aml.—ank.—aps. ; b. ; a.—arg.a.—ag-n.—arn.—ars.—aps.a,b.—atr.—aur.—bis.—bro.—bry.—cld.a².—ca-c.—c-ph.a.—cam.—cnc.—cn-i.a.—can.b.—cap. ; a.—cb-v.—cr-h.—cr-s.—csc.—cep.—chd.—chi.—ch-s.b̵ᶜ.—cn-s.a,f.—ccs. ; a.—cof.a.—cch.—col. ; a.—cnm.a.—con.—cro.a.—crt.—cyc.—dig.—dgn.a.—dio.a.—elc.—eth.—eug.—fag.a.—fgs.—fel.—for.—gas. ; a.—gin.—grn.—grt.—gun.—hy-x.—ignᵃ.—jat.a.—jat*ᵃ*.—k-bi.—k-br.—k-ca.—kis.—lah.—la-v.a.—led.a,ᴅ.—lyc.—mt-n.—mt-s.—mad.—m-pi.—mo-a.—msc.—nar.—na-a.—ni-x.a.—nit.a.—nx-m.—

oln—opi.—phl.—ph-x.—pho. ; a.
—plb.—rhe.—rho.—rs-s.—rhs.—
rut.—sab.—sec. ; b.c.—sng.—sep.
—spi.—spr.—spo^a.—str.—sul.a.
—tep.a$^{c\cdot s}$.—ter.—teu.—til.a.
val.—vrb.—vi-t.—wis.—zin.—
zn-o., &c.

—— by fits.—stp.
—— as if intoxicated.—aco.—asr.
γ.γq.—bel.—car.δ.— dig.
a^{1}a.—ign.a^{1}b^s.γ.—nit.—
lau.δo.—lyc.—nx-v.—phl.
—rhs.3.—spo.b.31.—tep.
—ton.φ.
—— as if after intoxication.—
aco.γ.—aga.43.111.--am-m.
—bel.—cam.—cb-v.—cr-s.
—chi.γ. ; θ.3.—cle.3. ; γ.—
coc.b^c.3. ; γq.—ccs.θ^3.κ^1.—
col.—cor.—cro.—iof.—
k-ca.εt.κ^5.—la-v.a^s.γ.δ.3-30.
--—lam.—msc.—nx-v.—
opi.—phl.a.—ph-x.—phs.
a.ω^2.—pso.2-99.—pul.γ.99.
—rho.—sab.—squ.γ.—val.
—— as from smoking.—bel.—spi.
—— as if smoke rose into brain.—
opi.
—— knows not where he is.—thu.
18.
—— as if would lose senses.—pho.
6.
—— as though his head were not
his own.—na-m.
—— preventing letter-writing.—
ptl.a.
—— as from prolonged mental
work.—na-n.—pho.γ.ηi^a.
(41).
—— as if hypochondriacal.—dig.
—— as if in a room where linen
was hung to dry.—cau.29.
8-31.(6).
—— as if enveloped in mist.—pet.
—rhe.a.
—— as from coryza.—ber.aa.γ.γq.
χ$^{1\cdot2}$.ω^2.3-99.—chp.5.—chi.
—col.γq.—con.—ol-a.εa.η.
—sep.a.—so-t.4.—stp.
—— as in typhus fever.—pul.γ.99.

Confusion, *as if after continued
labour in a cold room.—ant.*
—— *as from opium.*—mgt.
—— *as from dancing.*—chi.
—— *as after a ball night.*—atr.
(8).
—— *as if from want of sleep.*—
fer.—ph-x.—rho.—rut.—
sul.—zin.a.γq.
—— *as from disordered stomach.*
—lyc.
—— *as before an emetic operates.*
—bap.a^1.
—— *as if from too much sexual
intercourse.*—ph-x.
—— *as if dragged by the body.*—
mgt.
—— *as if brain were bound up.*—
æth.
—— *as from a skin stretched over
brain.*—ang.
—— *as if going to have headache.*
—cim.
—— *like drawing through head.*—
agn.
—— *brain pressed upwards.*—fl-x.
—— *as if screwed up.*—bry.—
k-ca.γ.
—— *as if a hoop round head.*—
bro.a.
—— *over inside of skull.*—c-ph.
—— *as if brain did not fill skull.*
—con.
—— *in forehead.*—alm.γ.γq.4.—
aps.(66).—ag-n.31.(66).—
bel.—bro.—bry.—cn-i.γq.
—cnc.; γ.—cr-s.a.—car.δ.
—cnt.--cep.71.—chi.—cle.
a.; γp.—cof.γ.8-31.—cch.8.
(6).; a.—col.; a^{1}b^p.—cly.—
cro.—ctn.γ.--cyc.γp; γv.—
dgn.γ.5.—gn-l.χ^2.—grp.γ.
—hæm.γq.—hur.—hyo.δo.
εa.; a^{1}b^s.; 8.—k-bi.—lau.γ.
—lo-i.—lyc.δ.5.—mez.—
nit.γq.--nx-m.—opi.γ.; ηp,
hh.; au.δaa,t.θ^2.κ.—ph-x.—
pla.; γ.--rat.(8).—rhe.γ.—
rho.γ.3-30.; a.; γ.26.; γ.(14.
8-31).--rut.γ.3-99.5.—sab.
γ. ; ζ.—sep.—so-t.4.—stp.

b.—sul.—sum.——thu.—
til^a.ev.ζ^3.—val.γd.—vin.δ.
δo.29.44.—zn-o.γq.

Confusion, *in forehead and temples.*
—ba-a.—col.au$^{z.}$

—— *in forehead and vertex.*—
cch.—k-bi.—pho.

—— *in forehead and right side of
head.*—lo-i.—xyp.γ.v^1.

—— *in forehead and occiput.*—
man.γq.——mez.—squ.γ.—
sum.γq.

—— *in right side of forehead.*—
aco.a.8-31.—ol-a.4.—opi.γp.

—— *in left side of forehead.*—hyo.

—— *over the eyes.*—agn.

—— *in either frontal protuberance alternately.*—la-v.γ.

—— *in temples.*—ctn.—lth.γ.λ.

—— *in right temple.*—k-bi.ζ.

—— *in left temple.*—cyc.

—— *in left temple, parietal regions, and occiput.*—asr.γ.

—— *in top of head.*—crn.γq.—
lo-i.35.—sul.

—— *in both sides of head.*—arn.δ.

—— *in right side of head.*—ana.
—col.—ctn.a.δ.**50**.κ^5.8.ηc^b.
ω^2.—fl-x.γ.—lau.γ.—spi.

—— *in right side of head and right
temple.*—opi.

—— *in left side of head.*—amy.
—ana.—c-cs.γ.—col.γ.δo.ζ.
θ^1.—cly.—con.—lau.—
rs-r.ev.—sul.

—— *in occiput.*—amb.—cb-v.—
cro^a.—ctn.—dgn.—fl-x.—
k-cl.σ^2.—lo-i.—nat.γ.**5**.—
opi.5.—phl.γ.—pim.a.a^{1}b^a.
43.—spi.5.8-31.—ton.φ.—
zin.γp.

—— *in occiput and side of head.*—
xyp.ζ^3.

—— *in occiput, left parietal region,
and forehead.*—ag-n.

—— *in right side of occiput.*—fl-x.

—— *in left side of occiput.*—sep.

—— *coming up from the back.*—
iod.

—— *difficulty of holding up head.*
—atr.—sbd.γq.

Confusion, *head disposed to fall forwards.*—ba-c.au.γq.φ.ω^2.5.
pho.γq.6.29.(8).

—— *followed by headache.*—elt.

ℓ^a. **Dull, stupid feeling.**—am-c.—
aps.—arg.; a.—as-s.—bad.a.—
bap.—ba-a.—ba-c.—ber.a.—bry.
a.—cn-i.—can.a^2.—cap^b.—cph.—
cha.—ch-s.—cic.—cmf.—coc.—
cch.a.—coh.—con.—cro.—c-ar.—
er-m.—euc.—fer.—hyd.a.—jat.—
k-bi.a^1.—lch.—lam.—led.—men.
—mer.a.—mez.a^2.—mo-a.—msc.
—na-m.—na-s.—ni-x.a^a.—nx-m.
—pet.—phl.a.—ph-x.—pho.—
phy.—pla.—pso.—rhs.a.—rs-v.—
sbd.—src.—sec.—sep.; a^2.—sil.—
so-l.—stp.a^2.—str.—sul.—vrb^b.,
&c.

—— *as after mental exertion.*—
na-n.

—— *as if intoxicated.*—æth.—
cau.η^{1}aa.—mez.—rat.—
rhs.19.a$^{t.u}$.18.—thu.

—— *as if after drinking.*—ang.—
bry.γ.3-99.—cln.—cmf.—
dul.(8).—glo.—mg-m.—
nic.3.—nit.γq.3.—opi.θ.κ^3.
rv.φ.χ^3.ρ.—rhe.—sbd.

—— *as if he had eaten too much.*
—scr^a.γq.

—— *as from opium.*—cn-i.

—— *as if he did not know himself.*
—buf.—cap.99.

—— *imagines has lost reason.*—
sul.33.

—— *like commencing catarrh.*—
na-a.——lyc.γ.θ.κ^3.—mr-i.γ.
(8-31).

—— *as if from excessive work.*—
ars.af^b.

—— *as if had slept too long.*—
nat.

—— *as if had not slept enough.*
—ars.—fer.γq.3-99.—k-ca.
ak.3-30.—nic.—opi.δ.δp.—
pho.

—— *as after turning round.*—
ca-a.

—— *as after pollutions.*—mez.v.

—— *as if head were tightly bound.* —tar˟.

—— *as if head were screwed in.* —cau.η¹aa.——mg-s.χ²⁻³.3-16.26.

—— *as if too much blood in head.* —sil.—sul.

—— *as if head were pressed forwards.*—cth.γq.

—— *in forehead.*—arg.γ.—cth.γq. —cep.—cnb.——cro.a².6. (8).—dir.3.—fer.γq.—fl-x. —glo.(8).—hel.—hep.γq. ——hpm.——mr-c.——mez.γ. 41.——mit.—mu-x.—nx-m. —nx-vᵃ.a¹ᵭᵃ.5.8.—par.γ.5. —pi-m.ä.γiᵃ.—src.aᶄ.γq.— sep.γ.——tea.ä.γq.31.——til. eᵭ.ζo.

—— *as if a board before forehead.* —aco.—pla.

—— *as if something worked round in forehead.*—mer.

—— *in forehead and temples.*— opi.γ.ρ.

—— *in front and sides of head.*— glo.ηp.

—— *in left side of forehead.*— pso.3.

—— *on right side of head.*—hy-x. γ.—su-x.19.

—— *in left side of head.*—tar.

—— *in occiput.*—glo.—mit.—nx-v.

—— *mounting like a vapour from occiput.*—xoth.81.

ε𝘣. **Emptiness, hollowness.**—am-c. —ana.a¹bˢ.3-99.——ars.——asa.γ.a¹bˢ. —ast.a¹bˢ.γ.ρ.2-99.——bel.——ber. bo-lᶜ.γ.ω².—bov.γ.3.——cac.—ca-c. γ.—cam.——capᵃ.——ch-sᵃ.eᵭ.κ³.χ².; 3.——clf.—cle.—cor.——cyc.γS.η. —dulᵃ.5.—eup.3.—glo.—hpm.λ.; γ.γp.—ign.—jab.——kis.aᶂ.—myr. —na-a.—na-m.aᶂ.——na-p.—nx-v. γ.—ox-x.aᵷ.ω².——polᶜ.γ.ω³.——sng. —zng.

—— *as after drinking beer.*—car.

—— *as after intoxication.*—aco.3. —aga.3.—amb.γ.3.—spi.ä. 19.

—— *as from catarrh.*—arsᵃ.au.

—— *the head feels like a lantern.* —arsᵃ.au.—pul.

—— *in forehead.*—cau.γ.——spi. γS.H.

—— *in temples.*—cyc.γ.

—— *on top of head.*—sin.η.

—— *in left side of head.*—mrl.— stn.γq.

—— *in occiput.*—nat.o².—sep.γ. 2.16.(12).

ε𝘤. **Lightness.**—bo-l𝘣.γ.ω².—cn-i.— ch-s.— clf.—ch-x.ηp.—cnb.ä.— crn.; a.26.29.—crt.γ.θ¹.——dir.aˣ. —elc.—equ.γ.—ep-p.; 3.—gel.a. —grt.aℝʷ.—hpmᵈ.γ.——hfb.—ibe. a.—irs.— k-cy.a¹a.—k-ca.a.30.— la-x.—naj.—ox-x.γ.—pho.—pol𝘣. γ.ω³.—snc.—so-n.γp.—str.aᵃ.

—— *as if contents of head had diminished in weight.*— mom.

—— *as if there were air in head.* —bz-x.

—— *as if borne by air.*—opi.

—— *in occiput.*—sec.

ε𝘥. **Mad feeling in head.**—ch-s.b.— hpmᶜ.γ.

CONCOMITANTS.

aä. *Apathy.*—ber.γ.γq.χ¹·².ω².3-99. —rhoᵃ.

ab. *Laziness.*—chi.φ¹.—cca.

ab. *Inactivity.*—nx-v.γd.26.

abᵉ. *Indifference to everything.*— asrᵃ.—xyp.

abⁱ. *Disinclination for mental work.* —rhs.

abᵒ. *Disinclination for work.*—— am-g.——iod.——mur.γq.φ.—— serᵃ.a¹bˢ.

af. *Discomfort.*—petᵃ.—plc.

af𝘣. *Uneasiness.*—arsᵃ.—bov.aᵷ.γq. δb.5.111.

aᵷ. *Anxiety.*—arn.a.72.——bov.af𝘣. γq.δb.5.111.——capᵃ.a.a¹bⁿ.χ¹. —k-biᵃ.κ⁵.——la-xᵃ.——ox-x𝘣. ω².

aᶂ. *Apprehensiveness.*——kis𝘣.——+ na-m.

ab^m. *Fear of losing consciousness.*— alm.

ak. *Sadness.*—k-ca^a.3-30.—mep^a. f.κ^5.—src^a.γq.—sar.$\delta o.\zeta o.\omega^2$. 19.—stp.—sul.a.ab.

ak. *Hypochondriacal humour.*— ag-n.ω.

aq. *Restlessness.*—jat.χ^1.

au. *Crossness.*—ars$^{a.b}$.—hpm^a.a. γp.$\kappa^{1\cdot3}$.λ^2.ϕ.χ^1.(70).— opi.δaa, $\ell.\theta^3.\kappa$.

au^z. *Vexatious thoughts.*—col.

au^{dd}. *Discontent.*—alo.

ab. *Irresolution.*—sul.a.ak.

a$\mathfrak{x}^w$. *Hilarity.*—grt^c.

a$\mathfrak{x}^{cc}$. *Inclination to sing.*—thr.γp,q.

a^{1}a. *Increased mental power.*—dig. —k-cy^c.

a^{1}a^c. *Rapid flow of thoughts.*—ar-c^a.

a^{1}b^h. *Mistakes in writing.*—lo-s.γ.

a^{1}b^n. *Awkwardness.*—cap^a.a.ag.χ^1.

a^{1}b^o. *Forgetfulness.*—bry.—nit.a^{1}b^s. —sul^a.

a^{1}b^p. *Want of recollection.*—col.

a^{1}b^p. *Weakness of memory.*—col.— pul^a.—src^a.

a^{1}b^s. *Difficulty of thinking.*—ast^b.γ. ρ.2-99.—bov.γq.—bry. cb-v.;3-30.(16).—car.—cnm. a.γ.— cyc.a.γp.naa.κ^5.μ^2.ρ.$\chi^{1\,2}$. 5.—dig.—hæm^a.γq.—ign^a.γ. —iod.—lah.ω^2.3.—lyc.— men.(8).—mez.a.—mo-a. nat^a.γ.—ni-x.—nit.a^{1}b^o. opi.ρ.$\chi^{2\cdot2}$.— ph-x.—pim.a.43. —pul^a.—pl-n.—ser^a.ab^o.— thu.

a^{1}b^s. *Difficulty of understanding.*— ana^b.3-99.—asa^b.γ.—ca-c.— coc^a.43.—cot.γ.γq.5.—lau^a.

a^{1}b^s. *Loss of thought.*—for.a.—hyo. —jat.—kre^a.a.δo.ea.

a^{1}b^y. *Obtuseness of senses.*—ana.ω^2. —ctn.γ.—pim.

a^{1}v. *Stupefaction.*—bry.—gel.a.θj. θ^3.κ.ρ.—sab.

a^{1}v^c. *Transient loss of consciousness.* —bov^a.a.γ.—ni-x^a.8.—nx-v^a. 5.8.

γd. *Rush of blood to head.*—bry. —lah.γp.(66).; γ.γq.ζ^2.3.—

—na-m.84.—nx-v.ab.26.— val.

γi^a. *Fulness of head.*—aco.γq.35.— aga.γ.—a-sc^a.γq.—aru^a.— ca-c.—crn.γp.ηp.—ctn.a^2.— for^a.—gym^a.a.δo.$\kappa^{5\cdot7}$.—hyo. γp.—mg-m.5.—mrl.γ.—mit^a. —pho.; ηi^a.(41).—pi-m^a.a.— sul^a.b.γp.33.—su-x^a.5.—thr.

γp. *Heat of head.*—ag-n.γq.2.— bi-n.—csc.—cau.—cle.—cod. —crn.γi^a.ηp.—cyc.; a.a^{1}b^s.naa. κ^5.μ^2.ρ.$\chi^{1\cdot2}$.5.—dgn.γq.—hpm^a. a.au.$\kappa^{1\cdot3}$.λ^2.ϕ.χ^1.(70).—hyo. γi^a.—k-bi.—lah.γd.(66).— la-v.γ.29.—lau^a.—man.γq. (8).—mr-c.γq.—opi.—osm. —pæo.a.γq.—pet.γq.3.—phl^a. —pim.a^c.ζ^2.—sul^a.b.γii^a.33.— thr.a$\mathfrak{x}^{cc}$.γq.

γq. *Heaviness of head.*—aco.γi^a.35. —aga.—alm.γ.4.—ana.3-30. —an-s.ϕ.—apo.γ.ϕ.—ag-n. γp.2.—a-sc^a.γi^a.—asa.γ.ϕ.— aru^a.—asr.γ.—atr.ϕ.—ba-a^a. — ba-c.au.ϕ.ω^2.5.—ber.aa.γ. $\chi^{1\cdot2}$.ω^2.3-99.—bov^a.γ.5.; af^b, g.δ.5.111.—bry.—c-ph.γ. 3-99.—can.γ.δ.—cth.; ^{a}.— cr-s.—cic^a.—cmf.—cle.γ.; ^{a}. 24.26.—coc.—ccs^a.—col.— cnm.a^{1}b^s.γ.—con.99.—crn.— cot.a^{1}b^s.γ.5.— ctn.—dgn.γp. —dro.—equ.—eup.66.—fer^a. γ.— glv.a.δt^p.—gn-l.γ.44.— gin.—glo.a.δt^p.—hæm.—hed. 3.—hel^a.—hep.—hur.ω^2.— hyo.—ign.—ind^a.5.35.; γ. —jat.—k-br.—k-cy.—k-ca.3. —k-hy^a.—lah.γd.ζ^2.3.—la-x^a. γ.—la-v.γ.4.—lau.a.; ^{a}.ϕ.ω^2. —lyp.—lyc.3.—mag^a.γ. mg-m.5.—man.; γp.(8).— mer.6.16.19.; γ.—mr-c.γp. —msc^a.γ.δ.ζ.—mur.ab^o.ϕ.— mu-x.δ.(12).—naj.a.—nat.a.6. 84.—na-a^a.—nit^a.3.—nx-j.5. (66).—nx-m.—pæo^a.a.; a.γp. —pet.γp.3.—pho.6-29.(8).; ω^2. 3.; ^{a}.66.—phy^a.—plb^a.18.— pul^a.—pl-n^a.3.(4).—rho.3-30.

—rs-rᵃ.δq.φ.——sbd.——sabᵃ.γ.
—srcᵃ.ak.—sarᵃ.γ.—scrᵃ.
so-l.—stnᵇ.—stpᵃ.—sul.—
su-x.3.—sum.—tabᵃ.66.(72).;
ɒ.γ.—teaᵃ.a.31.—thr.aæᶜᶜ.γp.
—til.2.; a¹bˢ.r.v.ω².—zin.;
a.—zn-o.

γ. *Trembling feeling in head.*—ca-c.

γw. *Wagging of head.*—sep.σ².

γhh. *Sweat on head.*—opiᵃ.ηp.

γ. *Headache.*—aco.; 5.—aga.γiᵃ.
—alm.γq.4.—amb.; 35.66.;
ᵇ.3.—amm.—ang.; 31.—aps.
—apo.γq.φ.—ara.ω².5.66.(12).
—a-scᵃ.γiᵃ.—argᵃ.—ar-iᵃ.η.3.
—asa.; 4.; γq.φ.; 99.; a¹bˢ.
—asr.; γq.—ath.—aur.3-30.—
bapᵃ.—ba-a.δ.—ber.aa.γq.χ¹·².
ω².3-99.—bo-lᵇ·ᶜ.ω².—bor.el.5.
—bov.29.; ᵇ.3.; ᵃ.γq.5.—
bryᵃ.3-99.; (71).—ca-c.θ³.
3-99.; ᵇ.—c-cs.—c-ph.γp.
3-99.—cn-i.—can.γq.δ.—cth.
3.—cb-a.4.; ᵃ.—cr-s.—crd.—
cauᵇ.—chiᵃ.—ch-sᵃ.—cimᵃ.—
cle; γq.—cobᵃ.5.35.—cca.—
cch.—ccs.—cof.8-31.—col.
δO.ζ.θ¹.; 29.—cot.a¹bᵃ.γq.5.
—cro.a.δ.—crtᶜ.θ¹.—ctn.ε.;
a¹bʸ.—cup.—c-arᵃ.—cyc.; ᵇ.
—dgn.5.—dulᵃ.—elcᵃ.—equᶜ.
—eup.ζ³.5.—ferᵃ.γq.—fl-x.3.
—forᵃ.—gn-c.a.—gn-l.γq.44.
—glo.; ᵃ.—grp.3.; ᵃ.3.—helᵃ.
4.;ζ³.—hpmᵃ.a.γp.au.κ¹·³.φ.χ¹.
(70).; ᶜ·ᵈ.—hyo.8.—hy-x.ɒ.δo.;
ᵃ.—ignᵃ.a¹bᵃ.; δ.; δ.3-99.33.35.
—iod.; ᵃ.κ².—jat.—k-ca.—
klmᵃ.κ⁵.σ².—kre.θ¹.—lab.3.;
γq,d.ζ².3.—la-xᵃ.γq.—la-v.29.
γp.; γq.4.; aˢ.δO.3-30.—lau.
—lth.λ.—lo-i.ηp.5.66.—lo-s.
a¹bʰ.—lycᵃθ.κ³.—magᵃ.γq.—
mg-m.5.99.—mg-sᵃ.5.—mrl.
γiᵃ.—merᵃ·3-30.; γq.—mr-fᵃ.
2-99.—mr-i.(8-31).—mez.41.
—mo-a.—msc.; ᵃ.35.; ᵃ.γq.δ.
ζ.—nat.a¹bˢ.; 5.—na-aᵃ.—
na-m.χ³.; 12.—nit.—nx-j.δ.
—ol-aᵃ.3.(4).—opiᵃ.; ρ.; 66.—

ox-x³.—parᵃ.5.—ped.3-30.—
pet.—phl.; ᵃ.5.—phoᵃ.(66).
—pla.—podᵃ.φ.3.—polᵇ·ᶜ.ω³.
—pot.—pulᵃ.— rn-s.—rap.
3-30.—rhe.δii,P².—rho.;
(8-31.14).—rhs.ε.—rut.3-99.
5.—sbd.a.—sab.; ᵃ.γq.—sarᵃ.
γq.—sec.—sep.; 2.16.(12).
—serᵃ.(5).—spi.—squ.; 3.—
stp.3.—sul.3.; δLj.δo.; εɒ.—
su-x.—sum.—tab.ɒ.γq.—trn.
—tar.; ᵃ.—til.f.—val.5.—
ver.δP¹.18.19.(17.29).—vi-o.
—vi-t.—xyp.ζ³.; v¹.—zn-o.

γS. *Prickling in scalp.*—cyc.; ᵇ.η.

γS. *Scalp tender.*—spi.γH.

γH. *Hair on end.*—spi.γS.

δaᶜ. *Dull eyes.*—glo.δε.ηp.ρ¹.

δgᵇ. *Formication in eyes.*—ctn.

δp. *Heat in eyes.*—opiᵃ.δb.

δq. *Heaviness of eyes.*—rs-s.γq.φ.

δaa. *Redness of eyes.*—opi.au.δε.θ³.κ.

δii. *Swollen eyes.*—rhe.γ.δP².

δb. *Eyes close.*—bov.afᵇ,ɡ.γq.δ.5.
111.—can.γ.γq.—opiᵃ.δp.

δε. *Lachrymation.*—cep.ζ³.—glo.
δaᶜ.ηp.ρ¹.—opi.au.δaa.θ³.κ.

δ. *Pain in eyes.*—asr.19.(31).—
ba-a.γ.—bov.afᵇ,ɡ.δb.5.111.—
car.—cro.a.—ctn.50.a.ηcᵇ.κ⁵.
8.ω².—ign.γⱼ; γ.3-99.33.35.—
lyc.5.—mscᵃ.γ.γq.ζ.—mu-x.
γq.(12).—nx-j.γ.—pulᵃ.—
rho.8.—sng.—sep.8-31.—
vin.δo.29.44.

δo. *Dimness of vision.*—cyc.—
gymᵃ.a.γiᵃ.κ⁵·⁷.—hy-x.ɒ.γ.—
hyo.εa.—lau.—merᵃ.a².6.66.
(8).—sar.ak.ζ³.ω².19.—secᵃ.a.
b.εa.—str.—sul.a.; γ.δLj.
vin.δ.29.44.

δo. *Loss of sight.*—kreᵃ.a.a¹bˢ.εa.

δoᵈ. *Dazzling.*—lilᵃ.3.

γtᵖ. *Lightnings before eyes.*—glo.a.
γq.

δLj. *Dryness of eyelids.*—sul.γ.δo.

δLq. *Heavy lids.*—ferᵃ.γiᵃ.

δO. *Pain in orbit.*—col.γ.ζ.θ¹.; 4.—
la-v.aᵃ.γ.3-30.

δP¹. *Contracted pupils.*—arn.—ver.
γ.18.19.(17.29).

δP^2. *Dilated pupils.*—rhe.γ.δii.

e. *Pain in ear.*—asr^a.—bor.γ.5.—ctn.—rhs.γ.

e. *Pain under ear.*—ctn.γ.

ϵa. *Dulness of hearing.*—ag-n.eυ.—hyo.δo.--k-ca.κ^5.—ol-a.η.—rs-r.—sec^a.a,b.δo.—tab.ζ.

ϵa. *Deafness.*—kre^a.a.ab^s.δo.

eυ. *Noises in ear.*—cle.κ.3-99.—rho.ζo.3-99.—tep^a.

eυ. *Humming in ears.*—ag-n.ϵa.

eυ. *Roaring in ears.*—cyc.—sul.γ.—til^a.ζo.

eυ. *Ringing in ears.*—atr.a.ω^2.5.—ch-s$^{a.b.}$$\kappa^3$.$\chi^2$.

eυ. *Singing in ears.*—cot.ηaa.υ.

ζ. *Pain in nose.*—col.γ.δo.θ^1.—eup.53.—k-bi.—msc^a.γ.γq.δ.—sab.—tab.ϵa.

ζo. *Stuffed nose.*—rho.$\epsilon\upsilon$.3-99.—sar.a$\mathfrak{k}$.δo.ω^2.19.—til^a.$\epsilon\upsilon$.

ζ^2. *Epistaxis.*—lab.γ.γq,d.3.—pim.a^c.

ζ^3. *Coryza.*—cep.$\delta\epsilon$.—eup.γ.5.—hel^a.γ.—pho.ω^2.19.29.(8.34.116).—xyp.γ.

ηc^b. *Pale face.*—ctn.a.δ.50.κ^5.8.ω^2.

ηi^a. *Fulness of face.*—pho.γi^a.(41).

ηp. *Heat of face.*—alm.—ch-x^c.—crn.γi^a,p.—gn-l.—glo.δa^c,ϵ.ρ^1.; ^{a}.—lo-i.γ.5.66.—lupγp.λ.—opi.ηbb.; ^{a}.γhh.—xyp.λ.

ηaa. *Red face.*—cau.—cot.eυ.υ.—cyc.a.a^{1}b^s.γp.κ^5.μ^2.ρ.$\chi^{1.2}$.5.

ηhh. *Sweat on face.*—opi.ηp.

η. *Prickling in face.*—cyc^b.γS.

η. *Pain in face.*—ar-i^a.γ.3.—mr-f^a.—ol-a.ϵa.—sin^b.

θj. *Dry mouth.*—chi.3.—gel^a.θ^3.κ.ϕ.ρ.—lyc^a.γ.κ^3.—opi^a.κ^3.$\tau\upsilon$.ρ.ϕ.χ^3.

θ^1. *Grinding of teeth.*—crt.γ.

θ^1. *Toothache.*—col.γ.δO.ζ.—kre.γ.

θ^2. *Flow of saliva.*—cyc.$\kappa^{4.7}$.66.

θ^3. *White tongue.*—ccs.κ.—gel^a.θj.κ.ϕ.ρ.—opi.au.δaa,ϵ.κ.

θ^3. *Dry, slimy tongue.*—ca-c.γ.3-99.

ιg^b. *Formication in velum palati.*—trn.ξ^1.

ι. *Difficulty of swallowing.*—cup^a.κ.

κ. *Slimy taste.*—ccs.θ^3.—opi.au.δaa,ϵ.θ^3.

κ. *Bitter taste.*—cle.eυ.3-99.—gel^a.θj.θ^3.ϕ.ρ.

κ. *Sweet metallic taste.*—cup^a.ι.

κ^1. *Dislike to tobacco.*—hpm^a.a.au.γp.κ^3.λ^2.ϕ.χ^1.(70).

κ^1. *Loss of appetite.*—coc^a.χ^3.—val^a.μ^3.ν^1.

κ^3. *Hunger.*—iod^a.γ.

κ^3. *Thirst.*—ch-s$^{a.b}$.eυ.χ^2.—hpm^a.a.au.γp.κ^1.λ^2.ϕ.χ^1.(70).—lyc^a.γ.θj.—opi^a.θj.$\tau\upsilon$.ρ.ϕ.χ^3.

κ^4. *Pain in stomach.*—cyc.θ^2.κ^7.66.

κ^4. *Feeling of indigestion in stomach.*—rs-r^a.5.

κ^5. *Nausea.*—ctn.8.a.δ.50.ηc^b.ω^2.—cyc.a.a^{1}b.γp.ηaa.μ^2.ρ.$\chi^{1.2}$.5.—grp.κ^6.3.—gym^a.a.γi^a.δo.κ^7.—inu.5.—iof.—k-bi^a.a$\mathfrak{g}$.—k-ca.ϵa.—klm.γ.5.—mep^a.f.a$\mathfrak{k}$.—na-a^a.γq.—ver^a.

κ^6. *Vomiting.*—ctn.

κ^6. *Sour vomiting.*—grp.κ^5.3.

κ^7. *Eructation.*—cyc.θ^2.κ^4.66.—gym^a.a.γi^a.δo.κ^5.

λ. *Empty feeling in belly.*—hpm^b.

λ. *Pain in belly.*—lth.γ.—lup.γp.ηp.

λ. *Burning in abdomen.*—xyp.ηp.

λ^2. *Flatulence.*—hpm^a.a.au.γp.$\kappa^{1.3}$.ϕ.χ^1.(70).—sar^a.

λ^2. *Rumbling in bowels.*—amm.(75).

μ^1. *Constipation.*—hyo.σ^1.

μ^2. *Diarrhœa.*—cyc.a.a^{1}b^s.γp.ηaa.κ^5.ρ.$\chi^{1.2}$.5.

ν^1. *Bilious urine.*—val.κ^1.

ξ^1. *Erection of penis.*—trn.ιg^b.

o^2. *Weak, hoarse voice.*—nat^b.

o^3. *Sneezing.*—pho.$\tau\upsilon$q.5.

π. *Tightness of chest.*—sep^a.ω^2.—til.a.

π^1. *Difficulty of breathing.*—sep^a.χ^1.

ρ. *Hard, quick pulse.*—ast^b.a^{1}b^s.γ.2-99.

ρ. *Hard, contracted, quick pulse.*—opi.a^{1}b^s.$\chi^{2.3}$.

ρ. *Small, weak, quick pulse.*—opi^a.θj.κ^3.$\tau\upsilon$.ϕ.χ^3.

o

ρ. *Full pulse.*—gel^a.θj.θ^3.κ.φ.

ρ. *Slow, weak pulse.*—opi.γ.

ρ. *Hard, full pulse.*—cyc.a.a^{1}b^s. γp.ηaa.κ^5.μ^2.χ$^{1 \cdot 2}$.5.

ρ^1. *Palpitation.*—glo.δa^c.ε.ηp.

σ. *Pain in back.*—klm.γ.

σ^1. *Weakness in loins.*—mo-a.ω^2.

σ^1. *Pain in loins.*—hyo.μ^1.—lth. 18.

σ^{2}ff. *Stiff neck.*—cic^a.χ^1.—-for^a.— k-cl.—sep.γw.

σ^{2}ii. *Swelling of cervical glands.*— bel.

υ. *Bubbling sensation in left vastus externus.*—cot.ε℧.ηaa.

υ. *Pain in left thigh.*—mg-m^a.

υ^1. *Pain in big toe-joint.*—xyp.γ.

τυq. *Heaviness of limbs.*—pho.o^3.5.

τυ. *Weakness and trembling of limbs.*—opi^a.θj.κ^3.ρ.φ.χ^3.

τυ. *Bruised feeling and trembling of limbs.*—til.a^{1}b^s.γq.ω^2.

φ. *Sleepiness.*—an-s.γq.—apo.γ.γq. —asa.γ.γq.—atr.γq.—bz-x.— con^a.—gel^a.θj.θ^3.κ.ρ.—hpm^a.a. au.κ$^{1 \cdot 3}$.λ^2.χ^1.(**70**).—hyn^a.a.γq. —k-bi.a.—lau^a.γq.ω^2.—lna.— mer^a.—-mur.ab^o.γq.—naj.— na-m.—nit^a.—-nx-v^a.—opi^a.θj. τυ.ρ.χ^3.—pho.ω^2.83.—pod^a.γ. 3.—pul^a.a^2.19.—-rs-s^a.γq.δq. —tar^a.—ton.

φ^1. *Sleeplessness.*—chi.ab.

χ^1. *Chilliness.*—arg.γ.—cap^a.a.aℊ. a^{1}b^n.—-cic^a.σ^{2}ff.—-hpm^a.a.au. γp.κ$^{1 \cdot 3}$.λ^2.φ.(**70**).—jat.aq.

χ^2. *Heat.*—ch-s$^{a \cdot b}$.ε℧.κ^3.—cyc.— gn-l.—hel.29.—-mg-s^a.χ^3.3- 16.26.—na-m.γ.—-opi.ab^s.ρ. χ^3.—zn-o.

χ$^{1 \cdot 2}$. *Chill and heat alternately.*— ber.aa.γ.γq.ω^2.3-99.—-cyc.a. a^{1}b^s.γp.ηaa.κ^5.μ^2.ρ.5.

χ^3. *Sweat.*—-mg-s^a.χ^2.3-16.26.— opi.a^{1}b^s.ρ.χ^2.

χ^3. *Cold sweat.*—coc^a.κ^1.—opi^a.θj. κ^3.τυ.ρ.φ.

ω. *Bruised feeling of body.*—sil.

ω. *Throbbing all over body.*— ag-n.aℊ.

ω^2. *Weariness.*—atr.a.ε℧.5.—ba-c.

au.γp.φ.5.—-ctn.a.δ.**50**.ηc^b.κ^5. 8.—lab.a^{1}b^s.3.—-man^a.19.— mo-a.σ^1.—pho.φ.83.; ζ^3.19.29. (8.34.116).—-sar.aℊ.δo.ζo.19.- sil.86.—-ter.a.—-teu^a.—-til. a^{1}b^s.γq.τυ.

ω^2. *Weakness.*—-ana.a^{1}b^y.—-ara.γ. 5.66.(12).—-ber.aa.γ.γq.χ$^{1 \cdot 2}$. 3-99.—bo-l$^{b \cdot c}$.γ.—-hur.γq.— lau^a.γq.φ.—-ox-x'aℊ.—phs.a. —pho.γq.3.—rn-b^a.**5**.—sep^a. τ.

ω^3. *Faintness.*—gui.a.—pol$^{b \cdot c}$.γ.

ω^3. *Trembling.*—msc.

CONDITIONS.

2. *At night.*—-ag-n^a.γ.γi^a.3-30.; γp,q.—-car^a.γi^a.3-99.(30).— ctn.—sep^b.γ.16.(12).—til.γq.

2-99. *On awaking at night.*—ast^b. a^{1}b^s.γ.ρ.—mr-f^a.γ.—pso.

3. *In the morning.*—aco^b.—aga^b. —alm^a.(30).—alo.—amb.γ. —ar-i^a.γ.η.—bov^a.a.30.; ^{b}.γ. buf^a.66.—cth.γ.—cb-a.—chi. θj.—ch-s^b.—cle.—-cca.(**70**. 116).—coc.♄^{c}.—cch.—dir.— ep-p^c.—eup^b.—-fag.—fer^a.— fl-x.; γ.—grp^a.; γ.; κ$^{5 \cdot 6}$.; ^{a}.γ.— hed.γq.—hyo.—k-ca.γq.— lah.; γ.; a^{1}b^s.ω^2.; γ.γd,q.ζ^2.— lil^a.δo^d.—lyc.γq.—na-p^a.— nic^a.—nit.γq.—ol-a^a.γ.(4).— osm^a.—pet.γp,q.—pho.γq.ω^2. —pod^a.γ.φ.—-pso.—pl-n^a.γq. (4).—rn-s.—rhs.—squ.γ.— stp.γ.—-sul.γ.—su-x.γq.— thu^a.

3-16. *In bed in the morning.*—mg-s^a. χ$^{2 \cdot 3}$.26.

3-30. *On rising in the morning.*— ana.γq.—aur.γ.—-bi-n.—cb-v. a^{1}b^s.(16).—-car^a.γi^a.3-99.—ctn. —eup.(128).—fer^a.γq —ign. —-k-ca^a.aℊ.—la-℧.a^a.γ.δo^d.— mg-m^a.—mer.(8).—ped.γ.— pho^a.—rap.γ.—rho.; γq.— sbd^a.a.19.(31).—sep.—sul.

3-99. *On awaking in the morning.*— aco.—ag-n.—ana.a^{1}b^s.—ars. ba-c.—ber.aa.γ.γq.χ$^{1 \cdot 2}$.ω^2.—

bry³.γ.——ca-c.γ.θ³.——c-ph.γ.
γq.34.(41.102).—cle.; є🝔.κ.—
c-arª.γ.—hyp.—ign.γ.δ.83.35.
—merª.—phoª.(30).—rho.є🝔.
ζo.—rut.γ.5.—sul.—til.—
zn-o.a.

4. *In the afternoon.*—alm.γ.γq.—
asa.γ.—cb-a.—col.δO.—fag.
—helª.γ.——la-v.γ.γq.—lilª.—
mr-iª.—ol-aª.γ.8.—pl-nª.γp.8.
—so-t.

5. *In the evening.*—aco.γ.—ara.γ.
ω².66.(12).——-atr.a.є🝔.ω².—
ba-c.γq.φ.au.ω².——bor.γ.є.—
bovª.γ.γq.; afᵇ,ɡ.γq.δᵬ.111.—
cb-v.31.—chp.—*col.*66.; col.
—cyc.a.—dulª·ᵇ.—eup.γ.ζ³.
—dgn.γ.; γp.—grtª.18.31.(16).
—hpm.——inu.κ⁵.—klmª.γ.κ⁵.
—lo-i.γ.ηp.66.—lyc.δ.—mg-m.
γiª.——nx-vª.aᵗ🝔ª.8.—opi.—
parª.γ.—pho.o³.τυq.—rs-rª.κ⁴.;
16.—rut.γ.3-99.——*sar.*—sel.
—*ser*ª.γ.—spi.8-31.—stnª.—
sul.; **5.**—val.γ.

5-16. *On lying down in the evening.*
—bro.a.—lil.

5. *In forenoon.*——crm.——cobª.γ.
35.——cot.aᵗ🝔ˢ.γ.γq——fag.—
indª.γq.35.—mg-mª.γq.; γ.99.
—mg-sª.γ.—-nat.γ.—nx-j.γq.
(66).—ol-a.—phlª.γ.—rn-bª.
ω².——sarª.aᵬ,u.4.——sul.5.—
su-xª.γiiª.

6. *In a room.*——am-m.a.(8).—
bry.(8).——cau.3-31.29.—cch.
8.——croª.a².(8).——merª.a².δo.
30.66.(8).——mer.γq.16.19.—
nat.a.γq.34.—pho.γq.29.(8).

8. *In open air.*——am-m.a.3.6.
——atr.——ba-c.19.—bry.6.—
cch.(6).——cnm.—croª.a².6.—
ctn.—dulª.—gloª.——hyo.γ.—
nit-n.——mg-mª.a.63.γp.6.—
mg-s.a.—man.γp,q.—men.aᵗᵬˢ.
—merª.a².δo.6.30.66.; 3-30.
ni-x.aᵗ🝔ᶜ.——nx-vª.aᵗ🝔ᶜ.5.; ª.
112.—parª.—pho.γq.6.29.; ζ³.
ω².19.29.(34.116).——*rat.*—
rho.δ.—sul.; *sul.*75.

8-31. *By walking in open air.*—aco.

a.—cau.29.(6).—cof.γ.—*dgn.*
γ.—k-cl.—*mr-i*ª.γ.—na-m.—
*rho.*γ.(14).—sep.δ.—spi.5.—
sul.—trx.a,ᵬ.

12. *By pressure.*—ara.γ.ω².5.66.—
epn.—mu-x.γq.δ.—na-a.γq.—
na-m.γ.—*sep*ᵇ.γ.2.16.

14. *By laying head on table.*—
*rho.*γ.(8-31).

16. *On lying down.*—-cb-v.aᵗᵬˢ.3-30.
—*grt*ª.5.18.31.—hepª.—mer.
γq.6.19.——rs-r.5.——sepᵇ.γ.2.
(12).

17. *By lying on back.*—ver.γ.δP¹.
18.19.(29).

18. *When standing.*——bovª.a.aᵗ🝔ª.
γ.—grtª.5.31.(16).—lth.σ.—
plbª.γq.—stp.a.86.—thu.—val.
aᵘ,ᵬ.—ver.γ.δP¹.19.(17.29).

19. *When sitting.*—-asr.δ.(31).—-
ba-c.(31).—*bry.*31.—-manª.
ω².—mer.γq.6.16.—opi.aˢ.—
pho.ζ³.ω².29.(8.34.116).——
pulª.a².φ.—rhsª.aᵗ˒ᵘ.18.—sbdª.
a.3-30.(31).—-sar.aᵬ.δo.ζo.ω².-
spi.a.——su-x.—thu.31.—val.
—ver.γ.δP¹.18.(17.29).

20. *When at rest.*—arg.a.

24. *On raising head.*—cleª.γq.26.
—nx-vª.γq.25.

26. *On shaking head.*—crnᶜ.a.29.
—glo.

26. *On moving head.*—mg-sª.χ²·³
3-16.

26. *On turning head.*—cleª.γq.24.

29. *When stooping.*—bov.γ.—cau.
3-31.(6).——col.γ.—crnᶜ.a.26.
——elcª.—hel.χ².——pho.γq.6.
(8).; ζ³.ω².19.(8.34.116).——
valª.—*ver* γ.δP¹.18.19.(17).—
vin.δ.δo.44.

30. *On rising up.*—-almª.3.—bovª.a.
3.—k-caᶜ.a.—lauª.a.—merª.
a² δo.6.66.(8).—-na-s.a.—*pho*ª.
3-99.

31. *By walking.*—aga.; *aga.*—ang.
γ.—-ag-n.(66).—*asr.*δ.19.—
athª.—bel.—bry.(19).—cb-v.
5.—grtª.5.18.(16).—na-m.—
*sbd*ª.a.3-30.19.——spo.ᵬ.—*sul.*
—teaª.a.γq.—thu.19.

33. *By going up stairs.*—ign.γ.δ.
3-99.35.—sulᵃ.; ♭.γp,iiᵃ.

34. *By exercise.*——c-ph.γ.γq.3-99.
(41.102).—nat.a.γq.6.——pho.
ζ³.ω².19.29.(8.116).

35. *By motion.*—aco.γp,q.—amb.γ.
66.—bel.——cobᵃ.γ.5.— ign.γ.
δ.3-99.33.——indᵃ.γq.5.—lo-i.
—mscᵃ.γ.—pulᵃ.a.

41. *By mental exertion.*—-c-ph.γ.γq.
3-99.34.(102).— mag.—mez.
γ.—na-m.—pho.γ.ηiᵃ.

43. *By reading.*——aga.111.—cocᵃ.
aᵇbˢ.—lil.44.—parᵃ.49.—pim.
a.aᵇbˢ.

44. *By writing.*——ag-nᵃ.——gn-l.γ.
γq.—lil.43.—vin.δ.δо.29.

49. *By looking fixedly.*—parᵃ.43.

50ᵇ. *On looking around.*—opi.a.

53. *On blowing nose.*—eup.ζ.

55. *By epistaxis.*—psoᵃ.

63. *When eating.*——mg-mᵃ.a.(8).
γp.6.

66. *After eating.*——aga.——amb.γ.
35.—aps.—ara.γ.ω².5.(12).—
ag-n.31.——bufᵃ.3.——cb-v.—
coc.70.—col.(5).— eup.γq.—
cyc.θ².ₓ⁴·⁷.—lah.γd,p.—lo-i.γ.
ηp.5.—merᵃ.aᵃ.δо.6.30.(8).—
mez.—milᵃ.— nat.γ.—ni-x.—
nx-j.γq.5.—opi.γ.—-pho.; ᵃ.
γq.; pho.γ.— tabᵃ.γq.(72).—
tilᵃ.—zin.

70. *By drinking.*—coc.

70. *After drinking coffee.*——-ag-n.
—cca.3.(116).—hpmᵃ.a.au.γp.
κ¹·³.λ².φ.χ¹.

71. *By eructation.*——bry.γ.—-cep.
—gn-c.a².—sanᵃ.

72. *By vomiting.*——arn.a.ag.—tabᵃ.
γp.66.

74. *During stool.*—dio.—tonᵃ.75.

75. *After stool.*——amm.λ².—-tonᵃ.
74.

75. *By expulsion of flatus.*—mr-c.
—sul.(8).

83. *During menses.*—pho.ω².φ.

84. *After menses.*—na-m.γd.

86. *By speaking.*——sil.ω².—stp.a.
18.

89. *By coughing.*—rum.

96. *By yawning.*—bry.

99. *On awaking.*—aga.—-asa.γ.—
cap.—con.γq.— lin.——mg-m.
γ.5.—pul.γ.—sul.

100. *After a siesta.*—ca-c.—cb-vᵃ.

102. *By cold.*——c-ph.γ.γq.3-99.34.
(41).

111. *By the light.*—aga.43.——bov.
afᵇ,g.γq.δb.5.

112. *In sunshine.*—nx-vᵃ.8.

116. *By washing.*——cca.3.(**70**).——
cyc.—pho.ζ³.ω².19.29.(8.84).

128. *By driving.*—bry.—eup.3-30.

130. *By covering head.*—sto.

f. Enlarged feeling (*Peculiar*).

ag-n. If the pain is all over head
the head appears too large; if
it is only semilateral the eye of
the affected side appears too
large.

    Feeling of dilatation of whole
body, especially face and head;
he feels as if the bones of the
skull came asunder, with increased heat.

**f. Enlarged, dilated, distended,
swollen feeling.**—æth.ηr¹iiᵃ.8-31.
(6).—aps.; ι.—ag-n.γ.; ηiiᵃ.χ³.ωiiᵃ.
—bap.ʊ.—bel.γ.—ber.——bov.γ.—
ca-c.γ.——cn-i.——cob.a.ω².74.——
dph.γ.—dig.-—for.γq.——glo.; γiᵃ.
—gui.γ.γd.19.——hyp.—lch.γ.—
la-v.a.——lau.γ.γp,bh.—lth.γ.—
man.γq.—mep.ℓ.aᴋ.κ⁵.—mrl.; a.—
mim.—na-m.— nx-m.γw.—-par.γ.
δ.—phl.γiᵃ,q.—rn-b.; a.——rn-s.—
rs-r.; 16.(30).——til.ℓ.—ton.γ.—
trf.

—— *brain feels larger.*—bel.; γ.
—cn-s.a,ℓ.—dul.ℓ.30.

—— *as if brain pressed against
skull.*—aco.

—— *as if brain were distended in
all directions.*—glo.

—— *head feels too thick.*—-cyc.
[TᵇVl³].

—— *as large as a bushel.*—aps.

—— *as large as a barrel.*—jug.

—— *enormously large.*—ar-i.——cor.

—— *as if had a strange head or something upon it.*—thr.

–—— *in forehead.*—aga.γ.ι.ιj.——la-x.γiª.——mg-s.ε.γ.γiª.——mrl.—nx-m.a.γ.—pi-m.

—— *in temples and occiput.*—ccn. γ.—pi-m.

—— *in right temple.*—ber.γ.11.

—— *in crown.*—cep.γq.—lch.γ.

–—— *on one side.*—hur.

—— *on left side.*—glo.γ.29.—— nx-m.ε.γ.γq.

—— *in occiput.*—bry.γx.—pi-m.

fª. Elongated feeling.—hyp.

CONCOMITANTS.

aк. *Low spirits.*—mep.ε.к⁵.

γd. *Congestion of head.*—gui.γ.19.

γiª. *Fulness of head.*—glo.γ.—la-x. —mg-s.ε.γ.—phl.γq.

γp. *Heat of head.*—lau.γ.γhh.

γq. *Heaviness of head.*—cep.——man.—nx-m.ε.γ.—phl.γiª.

γw. *Drawn upwards.*—lch.

γx. *Numbness of head.*—bry.

γhh. *Sweat on head.*—lau.γ.γp.

γ. *Headache.*— aga.ι.ιj.—ag-n.—bel.—ber.11.—bov.—ca-c.—ccn.—dph.—dul.30.—glo.29.; γiª.—gui.γd.19.—lau.γp,hh.—lth.—mg-s.ε.γiª.—nx-m.ε.γq.; a.—par.δ.—ton.

γ. *As if split open with a wedge.* —lch.

δ. *Eyes as if pressed out.*—par.γ.

ηiiª. *Face feels swollen.*—æth.rˡiiª. 8-31.(6).—ag-n.χ³.ωiiª.

ιj. *Dryness in throat.*—aga.γ.ι.

ι. *Pain in throat.*—aga.γ.ιj.—aps.

к⁵. *Nausea.*—mep.ε.aк.

rˡiiª. *Hands feel swollen.*—æth.ηiiª. 8-31.(6).

χ³. *Heat.*—ag-n.ηωiiª.

ωiiª. *Swollen feeling of body.*—ag-n. ηiiª.χ³.

ω³. *Weakness.*—cob.a.74.

CONDITIONS.

6. *In a room.*—æth.ηrˡiiª.8-31.

8-31. *By walking in open air.*—æth. ηrˡiiª.(6).

11. *By touch.*—ber.γ.

16. *By lying down.*—rs-r.(30).

19. *On sitting.*—gui.γ.γd.

29. *On stooping.*—glo.γ.

30. *On rising up.*—dul.γ.—rs.r.16.

74. *During stool.*—cob.a.ω².

g. Small feeling of head.—aco.γp. —grtª.f.

gª. Small feeling of brain.—glo.—grt.f.

CONCOMITANT.

γp. *Heat of head.*—aco.

ђ. Noises in head (*Peculiar*).

rs-r. Dull pain in occiput and forehead, morning and evening, increased by intellectual labour in the evening, and attended by a rasping sound at occiput when the scalp is moved by occipito-frontalis muscle.

The action of occipital portion of occipito-frontalis muscle is both heard and felt; the sound is like the wind among the leaves of distant trees, the sensation like a cap on occiput.

ђ. Noise.—ars.ε.——cb-v.43.——ch-s. ε,ɒ.γq.—dig.

ђª. Humming.—aco.—gur.—hypᵇ.ε. —k-bi.—kreᶜ.γ.29.83.—lah.γ.—la-v.γeiª.—lyc.γp.—mgt.—mt-n.ɒ. —mu-x.——ni-x.—ph-x.γ.89.——pho.; ᵇ.—pul.—rhs.ε.γ.—stnˣ.—stp.γ.; γ.5.29.31.—tep.ω³.—zin. aᵇ.3-30.

—— *like bees.*—cb-v.

—— *as after intoxication.*——coc. ε.3.

—— *as from dull noises at a distance.*—k-bi.

—— *as when a bell has been struck.* —sar.5.

—— *in forehead.*—aml.—nx-v.4. 5.—sul^b.a.26.31.—ver^b.γ.

—— *in temples.*—amb.

—— *in right temple.*—man.γ.

—— *in vertex.*—aml.—sul.

—— *on the side of head on which he lies.*—mg-m.3-16.

—— *in left side of head.*—thu.γx. єʊ.

♄^b. **Buzzing.**—hyp^a.ɛ.—pho^a.

—— *in forehead.*—sul^a.a.26.31.— ver^a.γ.—vi-t.19.

—— *in top of head.*—ca-c.a¹ʊ.

♄^c. **Roaring, rushing.**—aco.—cn-i^{l·z}. 98.—cmf.a¹ɩ^m.—cnb.a.5.66.—cof^m. γ.єa.—cu-s.γ.—fer.γ.—glv^k.—grp. —hyd.2.—kre^a.γ.29.83.—nat.— ni-x.—nx-v.a².—opi.ɛ.γq.— ph-x. —pho.19.—pul.єʊ.—tep.

—— *like boiling water.*—aco.γp.

—— *as if sitting near a noisy stream.*—aur.

—— *as from rush of blood to head.* —pet.γw.єʊ.

—— *in upper part of head.*—elc.

—— *in right side of head.*—-nic. γ.2.

—— *in occiput.*—pim.γ.

♄^d. **Splashing.**— hep.—hyo.γ.31.— —nx-v^e.31.—rhs.—spi.31.

—— *like water.*—-bel.—cn-i^v.γ.γp. so-t.

—— *in forehead.*—asa^e.

—— *in left side of head.*—-cb-a.31.

♄^e. **Bubbling.**—nx-v^d.31.—-par.af^b. γ.φ¹.2.—pul^w.2.—sar^f.4.

—— *in forehead.*—asa^d.

—— *in temples.*—bry.

—— *from right side of occiput to ear.*—jun.γ.

♄^f. **Gurgling.**—pim^r.—sar^e.4.

—— *in right temple.*—k-ca.

♄^g. **Simmering.**

—— *as from boiling water.*—ba-c.

♄^h. **Whirring.**—k-ca.a¹b^{p·s}.—la-v.γ. 89.

—— *in right side of forehead.*— la-v.3.

♄ⁱ. **Noise like a whirlwind.**—cro.

♄^j. **Crepitation.**—cn-i^o.ωjj.

—— *synchronous with pulse.*—pul. 31.

—— *like bending gold tinsel backwards and forwards, in temples, nose, and forehead.* —aco.

—— *in occiput.*—ca-c.σ²p.**5**.

—— *near ear, synchronous with pulse.*—cof.

♄^k. **Cracking or snapping.**—glv^e.

—— *as if something broke.*—-car. 2-16.—sep.σ².26.

—— *in vertex.*—cof.19.—con.31.

—— *in left half of head.*—cha^v.

♄^l. **Noise like a crash or explosion.** —-cn-i^{c·z}.98.—dig.ab^{s·t}.4.98.—ptv.16.

♄^m. **Hammering.**—cad.—cof^c.γ.єa.

—— *as if a carpenter were at work with hammer and chisel.*—ars.

♄ⁿ. **Chirping.**

—— *like grasshoppers.*—bry.

—— *in left temple.*—ang.

—— *in occiput, as if a cricket were in lumbar vertebræ.*—aga. ζ.16.

♄^o. **Ringing.**—ars.—cad.—cn-i^j.ωjj. —sul.

♄^p. **Noise like striking a loose wire.** —phl.3-99.

♄^q. **Twang like harp string.**—lyc.γ.

♄^r. **Tones like an empty cask.**— pim^f.

♄^s. **Resonance of voice.**—zin.

♄^t. **Creaking.**

—— *in left side of occiput.*—aga.12.

♄^u. **Clicking.**

—— *in occiput.*—cb-v.19.

♄^v. **Rattling.**

—— *in left side of head.*—cha^k.

—— *as of musketry.*—cn-i^d.γ.γp.

♄^w. **Hears pulse.**—pul^e.2.

♄^x. **Rasping.**

—— *in occiput.*—rs-r.γ.21.

♄^y. **Like wind among trees.**

—— *in occiput.*—rs-r.21.

♄^z. **Vibration of external noises.**— cn-i^{c·1}.98.—stn^a.

CONCOMITANTS.

$a f^b$. *Uneasiness.*—par^e.γ.φ^1.2.

$a b^{s \cdot t}$. *Frightened starting.*—-dig^l.4. 98.

$a^l b^p$. *Loss of memory.*—k-ca^h.ab^s.

$a^l b^s$. *Loss of thought.*—k-ca^h.ab^p.

$a^l c^m$. *Delusions.*—cmf^c.

$a^l b$. *Stupefaction.*—ca-c^b.

γi^a. *Fulness of head.*—la-v^a.ei^a.

γp. *Heat of head.*-—aco^c.—cn-i$^{d \cdot v}$. γ.—lyc^a.

γq. *Heaviness of head.*—-ch-s.b,ε. —opi^c.ε.

γw. *Trembling and undulation in^a head.*—pet^c.εb.

γx. *Numbness of head.*—thu^a.εb.

γ. *Headache.*--cn-i$^{d \cdot v}$.γp.—cof$^{c \cdot m}$. εa.--cu-s^c.—fer^c.—hyo^d.31.— jun^e.—-kre$^{a \cdot c}$.29.83.—lah^a.— la-v^h.89.—lyc^q.—man.—nic^c. 2.—-par^e.af^b.φ^1.2.—ph-x^a.89. —-pim^c.—rs-r^x.21.—rhs^a.ε^b. —stp^a. ; ^{a}.5.29.31.—ver$^{a \cdot b}$.

ei^a. *Fulness in ears.*—la-v^a.γi^a.

εa. *Deafness.*—cof$^{c \cdot m}$.γ.

εb. *Roaring in ear.*——pet^c.γw.—- pul^c.

εb. *Humming in ear.*—thu^a.γx.

ζ. *Crackling in nose.*—aga^n.16.

σ^{2}p. *Warmth in nape.*—ca-c^j.5.

σ^2. *Pain in nape.*—sep^k.26.

φ^1. *Sleeplessness.*—par^e.af^b.γ.2.

ωjj. *Vibration through body.*-cn-i$^{j \cdot o}$.

ω^3. *Syncope.*—tep^a.

CONDITIONS.

2. *At night.*—-hyd^c.—-nic^c.γ.— par^e.af^b.γ.φ.—pul$^{e \cdot w}$.

2-16. *When lying at night.*—car^k.

3. *In morning.*—coc^a.ε.—la-v^h.— zin^a.ab.30.

3-16. *In bed in morning.*—mg-m^a.

3-99. *Awakes him in the morning.*— phl^p.

4. *In afternoon.*—dig^l.ab$^{s \cdot t}$.98.— nx-v^a.5.—sar$^{e \cdot f}$.

5. *In evening.*--cnb^c.a.66.—nx-v^a. 4.—stp^a.γ.29.31.

5. *In forenoon.*—ca-c^j.σ^{2}p.—sar^a.

12. *By pressure.*—aga^t.

16. *When lying.*—aga^u.ζ.—ptv^l.

19. *When sitting.*—-cb-v^u.—-cof^k. —pho^c.—vi-t^b.

21. *On moving occipito-frontalis muscle.*—rs-r^x.γ. ; ^{y}.

26. *On shaking head.*—-squ^d.—- sul$^{a \cdot b}$.a.31.

29. *On stooping.*—-kre$^{a \cdot c}$.γ.83.— stp^a.γ.5.31.

30. *On rising from stooping.*—zin^a. a^b.3.

31. *When walking.*—cb-a^d.—con^k. —hyo^d.γ.—-nx-v$^{d \cdot e}$.—pul^j.— spi^d.--stp^a.γ.5.29.--sul$^{a \cdot b}$.a.26.

43. *When reading.*—cb-v.

66. *After eating.*—cnb^c.a.5.

83. *During menses.*—kre$^{a \cdot c}$.γ.29.

89. *By coughing.*—la-v^h.γ.

98. *During sleep.*—cn-i$^{c \cdot l \cdot x}$.—dig^l. ab$^{s \cdot t}$.4.

INDEX TO CHAPTER III.

γ. **HEAD.**

P

Section II.
CONCOMITANTS OF PAINS IN THE HEAD.

SECTION III.
CONDITIONS OF PAINS OF HEAD.

Q

SUB-SECTION II.

CONCOMITANTS OF PAINS IN SCALP.

CHAPTER III.

γ. HEAD.

SECTION I.—CHARACTER.

b. **Coldness.**—F.aco.—O.aga.— aln.*r*¹b.—-C.aru.V⁷.—P.*l*.asr.— bz-x.—-T.ber.—-ca-c.V¹⁰.χ¹.—O. chd.—F.cmf.V⁷.δ.2.—P.con.x.— C.elc.(11).—F.glo.—C.grt.(**130**). —-hur.*rv*.—-F.hy-x.ηb.—-jan.— k-ca.I.θ¹.—-C.k-hy.VII¹.(101).— P.lah.—P.*l*.lo-i.Hb.—-lyc.—-C.man. Hb.—msc.V¹.—C.na-m.II⁵.δb.—- O.nit.I.—-T.*l*.ol-a.V⁶.—-pau.πrb. —F.phl.p.—P.*l*.pho.ε.; P.*l*.IV³.— phy.—T.*r*.pla.gb.—T.rho.—spr.— sul.; C.—C.ver.*v*b.

—— *internal.*—arn.VI³.Hb.—F. bel.

—— *coolness.*—C.aga.VII⁵.—-C. au-m.—F.cmf.—F.cis.

—— *like cool air.*-F.*r*.ag-n.δ.—pet.

—— *like cool air rising from navel.* —C.O.aco.

—— *like cold wind following warmth.*—F.lau.

—— *spreading to back.*—pla.

—— *creeping chills.*—at-a.VI².

—— *icy coldness.*—F.*r*.aga.p.; C. —P.*r*.ba-c.II¹.—ca-c.—F. C.lau.—C.val.4.12.

—— *as if touched with a cold thumb.*—F.arn.

—— *as if touched by a cold hand.* —F.hyp.δ.4.

—— *as if a cold cloth were spread over brain.*—glo.

—— *as if from a wet cloth.*—T.*l*. gam.4.

—-— *as if wetted with iced water.* —F.glo.

—— *like cold water dropping.*—P. can.—P.*l*.cro.—F.C.P.trn.

—— *as if deluged with cold water.* —sbd.

—— *a cold drizzle.*—car.Hb.

—— *like cold water falling from head over body.*—trn.3.6.

—— *as if ice lay there.*—O.c-ph. gb.p.—C.ir-f.——F.C.lau.σ. σ²b.

—— *as if frozen.*—O.nx-v.—pho. 8.

—— *as if the blood forsook it.*— aln.*r*¹b.

—— *sensitive to cold.*—grt.—lyc. —na-m.—pho.

—— *and warmth.*—ver.Hdd.

——*following warmth of forehead.*—sbd.

—— *alternating with heat.*—pho.

——*following headache and sweat.* —phl.

ANATOMICAL SEAT.

F. FOREHEAD.—aco.—ar-c.—cmf. V⁷.δ.2.—hy-x.ηb.—phl.p.

—— *coolness.*—cmf.

—— *as if touched with a cold thumb.*—arn.

—— *as if touched with a cold hand.*—hyp.δ.4.

—— *like cold water dropping.* —C.P.trn.

—— *as if ice water were poured on.*—glo.

—— *as from ice.*--aga.*r*.p.--lau.

—— *like cold wind following warmth.*—lau.

—— *with external heat.*—aga.*r*.

T. TEMPLES.—ber.—gam.*l*.4.—ol-a. *l*.V⁶.—pla.*r*.g^b.—rho.g.

C. CROWN.---elc.(11).—k-hy.VII¹. (101).—man.H*b*.—na-m.II⁵.δ*b*. —sul.—ver.*v*¹*b*.

—— *coolness.*-aga.VII⁵.-au-m.

—— *as if uncovered.*—aru.V⁷.

—— *like cool air from navel.*— O.aco.

—— *like cold water dropping.* —F.P.trn.

—— *icy coldness.*-aga.-val.4.12.

—— *as if a piece of ice lay there.*—ir-f.—lau.

—— *preceded by itching.*—aga.

P. PARIETAL REGIONS.—asr.*l*.—— ba-c.*r*.II¹.—con.x.—lah.—lo-i. *l*.H*b*.—pho.*l*.*e*.; IV³.

—— *like cold water dropping.*— can.—cro.*l*.—F.C.trn.

C. OCCIPUT.—aga.—chd.—nit.I.

—— *like cool air from navel.*— C.aco.

—— *as if frozen.*—nx-v.

COURSE AND PROGRESS.

aco. *Cold air from navel to vertex and occiput.*

—— *First coldness, rigor, and paleness of finger ends, then of fingers; then cramp in soles and calves; lastly, coldness in forehead.*

ag-n. *Cool air from right frontal eminence into right eye.*

chd. *Coldness rising up from nape into occiput.*

lau. *As if ice lay on crown, then on forehead, then on nape, then in small of back, causing headache to go off.*

pla. *Cold in occiput down to back, where it becomes burning pain, then into a hollow tooth.*

CONCOMITANTS.

δ*b*. *Shutting of eyes.*—C.na-m.II⁵.

δ. *Pain in eyes.*—F.ag-n.—F.cmf. V⁷.2.—F.hyp.4.

e. *Pain in ear.*—P.*l*.pho.

η*b*. *Coldness of face.*—F.hy-x.

θ¹. *Toothache.*—k-ca.I.

π*b*. *Coldness of chest.*—pau.r*b*.

σ*b*. *Coldness of back.*—F.C.lau.σ²*b*. —pla.

σ²*b*. *Coldness of nape.*—F.C.lau.σ*b*.

r*b*. *Coldness of arms.*—pau.π*b*.

r¹*b*. *Cold hands.*—aln.

*v*¹*b*. *Cold feet.*—C.ver.

rv. *Coldness of limbs.*—hur.

χ¹. *Shivering.*—ca-c.V¹⁰.

CONDITIONS.

2. *At night.*—F.cmf.V⁷.δ.

3. *In morning.*—trn.6.

4. *In the afternoon.*—T.*l*.gam.— F.hyp.δ.—C.val.12.

6. *In a room.*—trn.3.

8. *In open air.*—pho.

11. *By touch.*—C.elc.

12. *On pressing hat on head.*—C. val.4.

101. *By heat.*—C.k-hy.VII¹.

130. *By covering.*—C.grt.

d. **Congestion; rush of blood.**— ac-x.—aco.*a*g.β*e*.η*p*.π¹.ρ¹.ω².; *a*g. alo.; F.O.δ.—aln.δ*b*.; δ*b*.—alm.β*a*. δ*o*.*e*ᵭ.φ.—amb.—an-s.—aps.; iᵃ.q. V¹.—ag-n.*a*ᵏ.*a*¹*b*^f·s.σ².——asa.η*p*.— ast.iᵃ.p. VII¹.—aur.; 29.(30).— au-m.*a*¹*c*^b.—au-s.—F.bad.; p.I.— bel.q.β*a*.29.; 26.; η¹aa.; F.29.—O. bor^a.—bry.; β*a*,ᵭ.—cac.; β*a*.; I.— ca-c.η*p*.5.; p.; p.83.—cam.; (8).— cn-i.; C.—can.; p.V¹.; p.w.—cth. η*p*,aa.29.—cb-a.β*e*.—cb-v.; p.β*e*.— car.q.*a*ᵏ.*a*¹*b*^s.β*e*.—cau.5.; p.—chd.; O.--chi.—ch-s.5.—cn-s.—clf.—cle. —ccs.V¹.; 7.(8).——cof.η*p*,aa.; 86. —cf-t.—cch.——cop.I.η*p*.; η.66.— cor.η*d*.29 —crn.η*d*.—crt.I.μ¹.; ω⁵. —ctn.—cu-a.—cyc.δ*d*.; I.aq.δ*o*.—

der.κ⁵.—dig.ε¹.—-dgn. ; 4.—dir.iª.
π.σ².—dor.—elp.φ².—elc.VI³.—
ept.VI³.—euc.*aß.*—eug.βa.30.—
ferᵇ.ηp.—F.fl-x.5.31. ; p.I.—for.
πd.—-glv.I.a**g**,**f**.ζ².κ³⋅⁶.π¹.χ².—F.
gas.—glo.iª.; l.; Tᵃᵇ.; Bᵃ.iª.σ².; iª.I.
83. ; πd.—grt.VIII⁴.abⁱ.a¹ᴅª.βa.δ¹.
35.—ham.σ².—hur.—hyd.—hfb.
16.—hy-x.δo.—hyo.—ign.ζ.—ind.
—inu.φ¹.2.—iod.—jat.—k-bi.—
k-ca.q.V¹.18. ; βᴅ.—k-cl.βa.34.—
k-hy.—klm.η*l*p.—kis.Fhh.; πd.ᴠ¹b.-
lah.; βε.; δtᶜ.ωll.; εᴅ.; I.5.; 4.29.;
V¹.θ¹.ζ². ; p.; βa. ; μ⁴.—la-x.δo.5.
30. ; σ².—lau.βεª.—lil.q.ζ².8.—lin.
βa.26.—lup.δd.—lyc.3-99.; O.29.
—mt-n.ηp.—mt-s.—mag.65.; 5.
—F.mg-s.q.3-30.—mad.—man.ηp.
16.18.19.31.—mer.—mr-c.I.—
mil.5-**10**.; 29.(30).—mor.—mo-aᵈ.
—mo-m.ω.—msc.; q.; βa.(8).
—-naj.**5**.—-nat.VIII⁴.**30**.(30). ;
p.5.6.19.(8.16).—na-m.Fhh.; βε.
84.—-ni-x.; δd.ζd.26.53.; q.29.;
p.; a¹bº.δo.—-nit.—nx-v.ab.βε.26.
—O.ol-a.6.—opi.—pæo.χ³.; a¹bʸ.
κ⁵.—pet.VI³.85.; w.εᴅ.ω⁸.—pho.
5.; ηp,aa.19.—pim.p.4.; p.w.βε.
ζ².—plb.V¹.—pul.II⁴.βa.—C.rn-b.
8-31. ; F.4.; βε.SVI².—-rs-r.—
rhs.29.—sab.p.βa.—san.εᴅ.λ.χ².—
sar.—sec.—sng.δd.29.—sep.—sil.
βεª.; VI³.; iª.30.; q.FC.VIII⁴.;
ηp,aa.; Tr.—-so-a.ηaa.— spo.; p.
σ².; F.—str.; σ².—sty.—sul.; 74.
128.; V¹.δ.εa.; χ².; 83.; p.βε.
ηp.35.—tab.p.—tep.— urt.iª.βa,εª.
-—val.βε.; iª.; iª.ηp.—-ver.29.—
F.vi-o.VI².—ziz.iª.ηd.

—— *like a flash of lightning.*-cn-i.
—— *with every pulse.*—hel.V⁶⋅¹⁰.
   (8).
—— *as if intoxicated.*—cau.(8).
—— *as if about to have a fit of*
   apoplexy.—ast.iª.—fl-x.a¹bˢ.
   —tep.
—— *as if blood rushed from heart*
   to head.—nx-m.
—— *as if blood streamed from*
   below upwards, or from
   within outwards.—ox-x.

—— *as if a fluid rushed from right*
   to left.—lil.
——, *as if blood stagnated.*—ba-c.
—— *one half of head, face, and*
   nose feel paralysed.—k-cl.
—— *as if he were hanging head*
   downwards.—glo.
—— *preceded by headache.*—lah.
   4.29.31.; **5**.29.
—— *followed by headache.*—iod.
   —k-ca.p.w.
—— *followed by compression of*
   temples.—bry.
—— *followed by epistaxis.*—grp.
   ηp.5.—lah.4.29.31.
—— *alternating with congestion*
   to heart.—glo.

dª. **Throbbing of blood-vessels.**—
T.aco.—O.ail.—T.aml.—O.asr.ωz.
—bel.ωz.; T.—O.bor. — cau.VIII⁴.
—T.ced.—F.cnt.—T.ch-a.4.—T.
chd.I.—cch.—ch-s.VII³.εᴅ.ηp.; T.
p.εᴅ.5. ; T.aß.5.; F.ηp.4.—T.cnb.iª.
q.--T.crt.—T.cu-a.—cyc.φ¹.2.16.—
dgn.2.—T.ech.κ⁵.χ¹⋅²⋅5.—T.ethᵇ.—
T.fer.iª.q.—T.gloᵇ. ; Baiª.σ².—
F.T.hel.ηp.—mil.ρ.—T.mor.—Tr.
mu-x.16.—T.myr.Iª.a¹ᴅ.—T.naj.
iª.16.—T.na-a.—T.nx-m.—opi.;
iª.—pso.41.—pul.I,—O.rhs.—T.
so-n.I.ηp,aa.σ²d.—sul.

—— *as if bone were raised up.*—
   F.bel.

dᵇ. **Distension of blood-vessels.**—
T.ac-x.p.—bap.βf.; ii.—T.cph.iª.
V¹.— T.ced.—T.ch-s.r¹.5.—cl-h.
σ²d.—T.cu-a.—T.ethª.—fer.ηp.—
T.gloª.; T.ηaa.—opi.—san.—T.
thu.19.

—— *like whipcords.*—T.gloª.

dᶜ. **Phrenitis.**—cad.—cth.ω⁵.—cup.
—eth.—glo.—hyρ.abˢ.
—— *as if brain were inflamed and*
   beat painfully against skull.
   —dph.
—— *fatal.*—cam.

dᵈ. **Apoplexy.**—bel.—hy-x.—mer.
—mo-a.—nx-m.βa; a¹c.βa.φ.—
œna.δP².ηcª,ii.π¹.rᴠ.—nx-m.—str.

ANATOMICAL SEAT.

F. FOREHEAD.—O.alo.δ.—bad.; p.I.
—bel.29.—cnt.q.— ch-sᵃ.ηp.4.
—cnb.—dir.V¹.3.—fag.—fl-x.
5.31.—gas.— T.helᵃ.ηp.—la-x.
δd.ζd.5.19.—ing-s.q.3.30.—
rn-b.4.—spo.—vi-o.VI².
——— *as if bone were raised up.*
—belᵃ.

T. TEMPLES.—ac-xᵇ.p.—acoᵃ.—amlᵃ.
—bel.—cphᵇ.iᵃ.—ced.—chdᵃ.I.
—ch-aᵃ.4.—ch-sᵃ.I.*as.*5.; ᵃ.p.
εᴅ.5.; ᵇ.r¹d.5.—cnb.iᵃ.q.—crtᵃ.
—cu-aᵇ.—ethᵃ·ᵇ.—ech.κ⁵.χ¹·²·5.
—ferᵃ.iᵃ.q.—gloᵃ·ᵇ.; ηaa.—F.helᵃ.
ηp.—morᵃ.—mu-xᵃ.r.16.—myrᵃ.
Iᵃ.a¹ᴅ.—naj.iᵃ.16.—na-aᵃ.—
nx-mᵃ.—sil.r.—so-nᵃ.I.ηp,aa.
σ²d.—thuᵇ.

C. CROWN.—rn-b.8.31.—ur-n.iᵃ.q.
II¹.65.

O. OCCIPUT.—ailᵃ.—F.alo.δ.; ᵃ.c.—
asr.ωz.—borᵃ.—chd.—cnb.p.v.
εp,v.—glo.a¹ςᵃ.—lyc.29.—ol-ὰ.
6.—rhsᵃ.

Ba. BASE OF BRAIN.—gloᵃ.iᵃ.σ².—
pi-m.σ²d.

CONCOMITANTS.

aᵇ. *Inactivity.*—nx-v.βε.26.
abⁱ. *Disinclination for intellectual
   occupation.*—grt.VIII⁴.a¹ᴅᵃ.
   βa.δo.35.
af. *Disquiet.*—glv.I.aℊ.ζ².κ³·⁶.π¹.χ².
aℊ. *Anxiety.*—aco. ; βε.ηp.π¹.ρ¹.ω².—
   cyc.I.δo.—glv.I.af.ζ².κ³·⁶.π¹.χ².
aᴋ. *Low spirits.*—ag-n.a¹bᶠ·ˢ.σ².—
   car.q a¹bˢ.βε.
aᏚ. *Excitement.*—T.ch-s.I.5.
a¹bᶠ. *Mistakes in speaking.*—ag-n.
   aᴋ.a¹bˢ.σ².
a¹bᴾ. *Cannot recollect.*—ni-x.δo.
a¹bˢ. *Diminished intellect.*—ag-n.aᴋ.
   a¹bᶠ.σ².—car.q.aᴋ.βε.—hyoᶜ.
a¹bʸ. *Dulness of senses.*—pᴂo.κ⁵.
aςᵃ. *Feeling of losing reason.*—O.
   glo.
a¹ςᵇ. *Delirium.*—au-m.—nx-mᵃ.βa.φ.
a¹ᴅ. *Stupor.*—T.myrᵃ.Iᵃ.
a¹ᴅᵃ. *Loss of consciousness.*—fl-x.—
   grt.VIII⁴.abⁱ.βa.δo.35.

βa. *Vertigo.*—alm.δo.εᴅ.φ.—bel.q.
   29.— bry.βᴅ.—cac.—eug.30.
   —glo.—grt.VIII⁴.abⁱ.a¹ᴅᵃ.λo.
   35.—k-cl.34.—lin.26.—msc.
   (8).—nx-mᵈ. ; ᵈ.a¹ςᵇ.φ.—pul.
   II⁴.—sab.p.
βᴅ. *Intoxication.*—bry.βa.—k-ca.
βε. *Confusion.*—aco.aℊ.ηp.π¹.ρ¹.ω².
   —cb-a.—cb-v.p.—car.q.aᴋ.
   a¹bˢ.—na-m.84.— nx-v aᵇ.26.
   —pim.p.w.ζ².—rn-b.8.VI².—
   sul.p.
βεᵃ. *Stupid feeling.*—lau.—sil.
βiiᵃ. *Head feels large.*—bapᵇ.
δd. *Congestion of eyes.*—cth.—F.
   la-x.ζd 5.19.—lup.—ni-x.ζd.
   26.53.—sng.29.
δd. *Congestion of optic nerves.*—cyc.
δ. *As if eyes would be pressed out.*
   —F.O.alo.—sul.V¹.εa.
δᴃ. *Closure of eyes.*—aln.
δᏏ. *Difficulty of opening eyes.*—aln.
δo. *Dimness of vision.*—alm.βa.εᴅ.
   φ.—cyc.I.aℊ.—grt.VIII⁴.abⁱ.
   a¹ᴅᵃ βa.35.—hy-x.—la-x.5.
   30.—ni-x.a¹ᴃᵒ.
δo. *Veil before eyes.*—ni-x.a¹bᴾ.
δtᶜ. *Sparks before eyes.*—lah.ωll.
δP². *Dilated pupils.*—œnaᵈ.ηcᵃ,ii.
   π¹.rʋε.
εvp. *Itching and heat of ears.*—O.
   cnb.p.v.
εa. *Deafness.*—sul.V¹.δ.
εᴅ. *Noise in ears.*—alm.βa.δo.φ.—
   ch-sᵃ.VII³.ηp. ; Tᵃ.p.5.—dig.
   —lah.—pet.w.ω⁸.—san.λ.χ².
ζ. *Sensitiveness of nose.*
   ——— *as if epistaxis were
      coming on.*—ign.
ζd. *Congestion of nose.*—ni-x.δd.
   26.53.
   ——— *as if blood would spurt
      out.*—F.la-x.δd.5.19.
ζ². *Epistaxis.*—glv.I.af.ℊ.κ³·⁶.π¹.
   χ².—lah.V¹.θ¹.—lil.q.8.—
   pim.p.w.βε.
ηcᵃ. *Livid face.*—œnaᵈ.δP².ηii.π.rιε.
ηd. *Congestion of face.*—cop.66.—
   cor.29.—crn.—mr-c.—milʳ.
   —ziz.iᵃ.
ηp. *Heat of face.*—aco.aℊ.βε.π¹.o¹.

R

ω^2.—asa.— ca-c.5.—cth.ηaa. 29.—ch-sᵃ.VII³.εᴅ. ; Fᵃ.4.— cof.ηaa.—cop.I.—ferᵃ.—F.T. helᵃ.—klm.—mt-n.—man.16. 18.19.31.—pho.ηaa.19.—sil. ηaa.—T.so-nᵃ.I.ηaa.σ²d.—sul. 35.—val-iᵃ.

ηaa. *Red face.*—bel.—cth.ηp.29.— cof.ηp.—T.gloᵇ.—pho.ηp.19. —sil.ηp.—so-a.—T.so-n.I. ηp.σ²d.

ηii. *Swollen face.*—œnaᵈ.δP².ηcᵃ. π¹.rʋe.

θ^1. *Toothache.*—lah.V¹.ζ².

κ^3. *Thirst.*—glv.I.af,ɡ.ζ².κ⁶.π¹.χ².

κ^5. *Nausea.*—der.—T.ech.χ¹·².5. —glo.πd.—pæo.a¹bʸ.

κ^6. *Vomiting.*

     —— *of grass-green fluid.*— glv.I.af,ɡ.ζ².κ³.π¹.χ².

λ. *Cutting in bowels.*—san.εᴅ.χ².

μ^1. *Constipation.*—crt.I.

μ^4. *Hæmorrhoids.*—lah.

πd. *Determination of blood to chest.* —for.—glo.κ⁵.—kis.ʋ¹b.

πiᵃ. *Fulness of chest.*—dir.iᵃ.σ².

π^1. *Difficulty of breathing.*—aco. aɡ.βε.ρ¹.ω².— glv.I.af.ɡ.ζ².κ³·⁶. χ².—œnaᵈ.δP².ηcᵃ,ii.rʋ.

ρ. *Quick pulse.*—milᵃ.

ρ¹. *Palpitation.*—aco.aɡ.βε.π¹.ω².

σ²d. *Congestion of neck.*—cl-hᵇ.— ham.—la-x.—Ba.pi-m.

σ²d. *Throbbing of cervical vessels.*— ag-n.ak.a¹bᶠ·ˢ.—gloᵃ.Ba.iᵃ.—T. so-nᵃ.I.ηp,aa.—spo.p.—str.

σ²iᵃ. *Fulness of neck.*—dir.iᵃ.π.

σ². *Tight feeling about neck.*—T. gloᵃ.

τ¹d. *Distended veins of hands.*—T. ch-sᵇ.5.

τʋe. *Contracted limbs.*—œnaᶜ.δP². ηcᵃ,ii.π¹.

ʋ¹b. *Cold feet.*—kis.πd.

φ. *Sleepiness.*—alm.βa.δo.εᴅ.— nx-mᵈ.a¹c.βa.

φ¹. *Sleeplessness.*—cycᵃ.2.16.— inu.2.

φ². *Nightmare.*—elp.

χ². *Heat.*— ctn.χ³.—glv.I.af,ɡ.ζ². κ³·⁶.π¹.—san.εᴅ.λ.—sul.

χ¹·². *Flashes of heat across back, followed by coldness there.*— T.ech.κ⁵.5.

χ³. *Sweat.*—ctn.χ².—kis.F.—pæo.

ωd. *Ebullition of blood in body.*— k-ca.p.—mo-m.

ωz. *Pulsation all over body.*—O. asrᵃ.—belᵃ.99.

ωll. *Twitchings.*—lah.δtᶜ.

ω². *Weariness, debility.*—aco.aɡ. βε.π¹.ρ¹.

ω⁵. *Convulsions.*—cthᶜ.—crt.

ω⁸. *Trembling.*—pet.w.εᴅ.

CONDITIONS.

2. *At night.*—cycᵃ.φ¹.16.—dgnᵃ. —inu.φ¹.

3. *In morning.*—F.dir.V¹.—F. mg-s.q.30.

3-99. *On awaking in morning.*—lyc.

4. *In afternoon.*—T.ch-aᵃ.—F. ch-sᵃ.ηp.—dgn.—lah.29.31. —pim.p.—F.rn-b.

5. *In the evening.*—ca-c.ηp.— cau.—ch-s. ; Tᵃ.p.εᴅ.—T.ech. κ⁵.χ¹·².— F.fl-x.31.—nat.p.6. 19.(8.16).—pho.

5-10. *In bed in evening.*—mil.

5. *In forenoon.*—T.ch-sᵃ.aɡ.— lah.29.—la-x,δo.30. ; F.δd.ζd. 19.—mag.—naj.

6. *In a room.*—nat.p.5.19.(8.16). —O.ol-a.

7. *In warm room.*—ccs.(8).

8. *In open air.*—cam.—cau.—ccs. 7.—hel.V⁶·¹⁰.—lil.q.ζ².—msc. βa.—nat.p.5.6.19.(16).—C. rn-b.31.

16. *By lying.*—cycᵃ.φ.2.— hfb.— man.ηp.18.19.31.—T.najᵃ.iᵃ. —nat.p.5.6.19.(8).

     —— *on the part.*—T.r.mu-x.

18. *When standing.*—k-ca.q.V¹.— man.ηp.18.19.31.

19. *When sitting.*—F.la-x.δd.ζd.5. —man.ηp.16.18.31.—nat.p.5.6. (8.16).—pho.ηp,aa.—T.thuᵇ.

26. *On shaking head.*—ni-x.δd.ζd. 53.—nx-v.ab.βε.

26. *On bending head backwards.*— bel.—lin.βa,

29. *On stooping.*—aur.(30).—F.
bel. ; q.βa.—cth.ηp,aa.—cor.
ηd.—lah.4.31.; **5.**; **5.**I.—O.
lyc.— mil.(30).—nat.VIII⁴.
30.(30).——ni-x.q.——rhs. —
sng.δd.—ver.

30. *On rising up.*—aur.29.—eug.
βa.— F.mg-s.q.3.—*mil*.29.—
nat.VIII⁴.29.**30.**—sil.iᵃ.

30. *By lifting.*——nat.VIII⁴.29.
(30).

31. *By walking.*—lah.4.29.—man.
ηp.16.18.19.—C.rn-b.8.
—— *after standing, not after
sitting.*—F.fl-x.5.

34. *By violent exercise.*—k-cl.βa.

35. *By motion.*—grt.VIII⁴.abⁱ.a¹ɒᵃ.
βa.δo.—pet.VI³.—sul.ηp.

41. *By mental exertion.*—psoᵃ.

53. *On blowing nose.*——ni-x.δd.ζd.
26.

65. *When smoking.*—mag.

65. *Before eating.*——C.ur-n.iᵃ.q.
II¹.

66. *After food.*—cop.ηd.

74. *During stool.*—sul.128.

83. *During menses.*—ca-c.p.—glo.
iᵃ.I.—sul.

84. *After menses.*—na-m.βɛ.

86. *By speaking.*—cof.

99. *On awaking.*—belᵃ.ωz.

128. *After driving.*—sul.74.

Course and progress of congestion.

ctn. *Congestion from abdomen to
head, with warm skin and perspiration.*

fl-x. *Like a rush of blood, resembling burning, but with confusion and numbness, first on right
side of forehead, then in right
upper jaw, then in right lower
jaw, then in occiput, then in
bladder and different parts.*

msc. *Rush of blood to head, with
fixed eyes, spasm in mouth, loss
of speech, after 7' return of
speech, rapid and incoherent
talking, followed by deathly*

*paleness and copious perspiration
on face and hair.*

iᵃ **Fulness.**—-aco.; F.q.Iᵃ.—æs-g.q.
V¹.δɒ.κ⁵·⁶.υ².—æsc.V¹.—O.aga.—
ail.ɒ.; II¹.—am-m.q.βa.; p.3-30.
—aml.; F.VII¹-VIII⁴.βɛ.—an-s.
VI³.—F.ang.VIII⁴.—aps.d.q.V¹.
7.—apo.I.—a-sc.q.βɛᵃ.; V¹.βɛᵃ.—
ag-n.; q.; p.VII⁵.(12).; p.aδ2.;
q p.a¹bᵖ.ηp.4.; P.q.V¹.5.—aru.a¹ɒ.
βa.; βɛᵃ.; π.—O.bap.I.—F.ber.—
bla.q.—bor.βa.33.; δ.; σ¹.φ.19.; F.
au βa.3.—bry.βa.—caj.q.—ca-c.; F.
VIII⁴.—c-ph.βɛ.12.—cam.—cn-i.
I.; ηaa.φ.; F.q.V¹.; Or.V⁶.26.—cb-v.
I.—ca-x.; V⁷.; F.I.; V¹.—O.car.q.
7.(8).—cph.dᵇ.V¹.—ch-h.III¹.—
cep.q.—ch-s.—cl-h.—ch-x.2.—
cmf.; p.VII¹-VIII⁴.33.; F.; C.; C.
V¹.—cnb.dᶜ.q.—F.cle.q.——csn.
cob.V².βɛᵃ.3.—crn.(75).; p.βɛ.ηp.
—ctn.βa,ɛ.—c-ar.—dig.I.—dio.—
dir.d.π.σ².; I.3.—euc.—epn.βɛᵃ.—
fag.βa.30.; F.41.; FC.; FO.3.; Fᵒ.
4.31.——for.βɛᵃ.——gel.VIII⁴.—
gn-l.V¹.—glo.d.; F.r.; F.VIII⁴.;
F.I.; T.VIII⁴.; C.; C.VIII⁴.;
CT.VIII⁴.3.; Ba.dᵃ.σ².; VIII⁴.;
ηp.; ηaa.; χ³.——gym.βa,ɛᵃ.δo.;
FC.V¹-VI³.—ham.V⁷; βa.; F.
θ³.; C.abᶜ.a¹aᵍ.—FC.hel.p.q.βɛᵃ.—
hln.I.βa.—irs.—jac.—jug.2.—C.
k-bi.q.—k-cy.ζ∂ffᵃ.—klm.βɛᵃ.3-99.
—kis.δ.—lah.; χ³·—la-x.βa.; q.;
C.—la-v.βa.7.; ɛɒ.; βɛ.4.——lau.;
F.—lil.V¹⁰ˢ.——lin.—T.lth.ɛr.5.—
FO.lo-c.V⁷.26.35.— mg-m.βɛ.3.—
F.mg-s.iiᵈ.βɛ.——mns.V⁷.q.; 2.—
mrl.V¹-VII⁵.29.; V¹-VII⁵.βɛ.——
mer.I.βa.—mr-f.q.— mr-i.—mr-s.
VI³.—mil.100.—F.mit.—F.naj.5.;
dᵃ.16.—na-a.p.5.—na-m.δ.; βa.—
na-p.q.—nic.q.VI⁴.29.; au.5.—
ni-x.—opi.dᵃ.ɛɒ.—CO.osm.V¹.4.
22.—F.ox-x.—pet.p.q.3.29.—phl.
q.iiᵈ.—pho.ɛɛ.; βɛ.; q.βɛ.; ηiᵃ.(41).
——F.phy.ω⁹.——F.pod.βa.—pgn.
VIII⁴.—pso.41.—O.pl-n.p.—ru-s.
q.; F.—C.rs-g.I.—rs-r.; F.; F.I.
—rhs.q.w.29.; q.VI³.ɛɒ.—rs-v.—

rum.*ak*.——F.san.I.4.——src.p.II[5].;
P.—-snc.——sil.d.30.——so-n.βa.—
spr.p.q.——spo.q.29.——sul.q.; p.—
su-x.q.; βe[a].5.——tan.——O.thr.βe.—
til.; q.ω[2].; F.βa.δo.——trf.——C.ur-n.
d.q.II[1].65.——urt.d.βa,e[a].——val.; d.
ηp.; C.d.——xan.——ziz.d.ηd.

—— *apopleptic.*——ail.——ast.d.——
ter.V[1].αI[8].

—— *as from drinking wine.*——cca.
4.

—— *as from charcoal vapour.*——
F.am-c.V[1].

—— *as after taking cold.*——cnb.
V[1].(8).

—— *as if the head would burst.*
——FC.am-c.— F.cn-i.q.V[1].
——dph.—ipc.III[1].——mer.
ni-x.I.——ptv.4.

—— *as if the top of head would
rise off.*——la-x.

—— *as if too full of blood.*——la-x.
3.4.——sul.

—— *as if blood would spurt from
nose.*——la-x.29.

—— *as if skull were stuffed full.*
——glo.—idm.

—— *as if not enough room in skull.*
——dph.

—— *as if brain were confined in
too small a space.*——scu.

—— *as if screwed in.*——til.

—— *as if brain were pressed
against skull.*——c-ph.35.——
c-ar.——k-ca.

—— *as if brain were swollen.*——
epn.——la-x.

—— *as if everything were turning
round in head.*——ind.

—— *like threatened nervous headache.*——T.gna.

—— *as if from a ligature round
neck.*——con.βa.63.

—— *can scarcely turn head.*——
bry.

—— *causing head to hang down.*
——cle.q.——phl.q.

—— *as if would fall backwards.*
——O.kre.q.

—— *followed by confusion.*——cyc.
p.βa.

—— *followed by weakness in legs.*
——bor.ab[1].a[1]b.3.(8-31).

ANATOMICAL SEAT.

F. FOREHEAD.——aco.q.I[8].——aml.
VII[1]–VIII[4].βe.— ang.VIII[4].—
ber.——bor.au.βa.3. – ca-c.VIII[4].
——ca-x.I.; V[1].—cn-i.q.V[1].—cnt.
q.—ch-x.VIII[4].π.v.; C.3-99.—
cnb.V[1].—cle.q.——cl-h.κ[5].——cca.
q.; V[1].5.——dgn.p.q.31.—dir.—
equ.V[7].[S[t].ff[a].]ηp.50.——C.fag.;
41.; O.3.; l.4.31.—gel.—glo.r.;
ii[d].; I.—gym.V[1]–VI[3].—ham.θ[8];
ι.—C.hel.p.q.βe[a].——hln.——hdr.
q.3.7.(8-31).; (12).——ind.p.q.
τv.3.——idm.βa.29.; p.—jug.—
lau.—lil.; q.3-99.——O.lo-c.V[7].
26.35.—mg-s.ii.βe.—mit.—naj.
5.—ox-x.——phy.ω[9].——pi-m.βa,e.
V[1].—pod.βa.——rn-s.——rs-r.; I.
—san.I.—til.βa.δo.

—— *as if stuffed full.*——glo.
VIII[4].

—— *as if brain were packed in
front.* —equ.3.

—— *as if anterior lobes were
too large for skull.*——
ham.

—— *as if head would burst.*——
C.am-c.——cn-i.

—— *as from charcoal vapour.*——
am-c.V[1].

T. TEMPLES.——fag.; VI[3].—-C.glo.
VIII[4].—gna.——lth.er.4.5.

C. CROWN.——P.l.ch-s.44.——F.ch-x.
3-99.——F.fag.——glo.; VIII[4].;
T.VIII[4].; F.λπi[a].——F.gym.V[1].
VI[3].—ham.ab[c].a[1]a[8].——F.hel.p.q.
βe[a].--k-bi.q.--O.osm.V[1].4.22.—
rs-g.I.——ur-n.d.q.II[1].65.--val.d.

—— *as if head would burst.*—
F.am-c.——cph.p.VIII[4].

—— *as if something were pumped
in.*——glo.

—— *as if full of blood.*—la-x.
3.4.

P. PARIETAL REGION.——ag-n.q.V[1].
5.-——C.ch-s.44.——glo.r.43.[T.
d[a].].—lin.5.8.—src.

O. OCCIPUT.——aga.——bap.L—caj.q.

—cn-i.*r*.V^6.26.——car.q.7.(8).—
con.*βe*.——F.fag.3.——glo.; p.
VIII^4.; V^1.; VIII^4.19.——F.
lo-c.V^7.26.35.——C.osm.V^1.4.22.
—pl-n.p.—thr.*βe*.
—— *as if would fall backwards.*
—kre.q.

Ba. BASE OF BRAIN.—glo.d^a.*σ*^{2}d.

CONCOMITANTS.

ab^c. *Disinclination for speaking.*—
C.ham.*a*^{1}*a*^{g}.

ab^i. *Disinclination for intellectual
work.*—bor.*a*^{1}b.3.(8-31).

ab^o. *Disinclination for work.*—klm.
βe^a.3-99.

ak. *Sadness.*—rum.

a[^{g}. *Cries.*—ter.V^1.

ag. *Excitement.*—ag-n.p.2.—gel.

au. *Ill-humour.*—F.bor.*β*a.3.

a^1*a*^{g}. *Increased appreciation of the
sublime.*—C.ham.*ab*^{c}.

a^{1}b. *Absence of mind.*—aru.*β*a.—
bor.*ab*^{i}.3.(8-31).

a^{1}b^p. *Loss of memory.*—ag-n.p.q.*η*p.4.

*β*a. *Vertigo.*—am-m.q.—aru.*a*^{1}b.—
bor.33.; F.au.3.—bry.—con.
63.—ctn.*βe*.—cyc.p.—fag.30.
(19).—gym.*βe*^{a}.*δ*o.—hln.I.—
la-x.—la-v.7.—mer.I.—na-m.
—na-p.q.41.—F.pod.— so-n.
—F.til.*δ*o.—urt.d.*βe*^{a}.

βe. *Confusion.*—F.aml.VII^1–VIII^4.
—O.con.—crn.p.*η*p.—ctn.*β*a.
—la-v.4.—mg-m.3.—F.mg-s.
ii^d.—mrl.V^1–VII^5.—pho.; q.
*η*i^a.(41).—O.thr.

βe^a. *Dulness.*—a-sc.q.; V^1.—aru.
—cob.V^2.3.—epn.—gym.*β*a.
*δ*o.—F.C.hel.p.q.—klm.*ab*^{o}.
3-99.—su-x.5.—urt.d.*β*a.

δ. *As if eyes were held fast.*—bor.

δ. *As if eyes would be pressed out.*
—kis.—na-m.

*δ*q. *Heavy eyes.*—F.cca.*δ*o.

*δ*o. *Dimness of sight.*—æs-g.q.V^1.
κ$^{5·6}$.*o*^{2}.—F.cca.*δ*q.—gym.*β*a,
e^a.—F.til.*β*a.

e. *Pain in right ear.*—T.lth.4.5.

*e*b. *Noise in ears.*—la-v.—opi.d^a.
—rhs.q.VI^3.

ee. *Stopped feeling of ears.*—pho.

*ζ*ff^a. *Tension across nose.*—k-cy.*θ*ff^a.
3.

*η*d. *Rush of blood to face.*—ziz.d.

*η*i^a. *Full feeling of face.*—pho.q.
βe (41).

*η*p. *Heat of face.*—ag-n.p.q.4.—
crn.p.*βe*. — equ.V^7.[S^f.ff^a.]**50**.
—gel.—glo.—val.d.

*η*aa. *Redness of face.*—cn-i.*φ*.—glo.

*θ*ff^a. *Tension of corners of mouth.*—
k-cy.*ζ*ff^a.3.

θ^g. *Prickling in tongue.*——glo.
VIII^4.30.31.

θ^g. *Pain at root of tongue.*—F.
ham.

ι. *Pain in throat.*—F.ham.

κ^5. *Nausea.*—æs-g.q.V^1.*δ*o.*κ*^{6}.*o*^{2}.—
F.cl-h.—glo.p.V^1.

κ^6. *Vomiting.*—æs-g.q.V^1.*δ*o.*κ*^{5}.*o*^{2}.

*λ*i^a. *Fulness in abdomen.*—FC.glo.
*π*i^a.

o^2. *Thickness of speech.*—æs-g.q.
V^1.*δ*o.*κ*$^{5·6}$.

*π*i^a. *Fulness of chest.*—dir.d.*o*^{2}.—
FC.glo.*λ*i^a.

π. *Chest full of mucus.*—aru.

π. *Empty feeling of chest.*——F.
ch-x.VIII^4.*v*.

ρ. *Lightness at heart.*—ch-x.2.*β*a.
33.

σ^1. *Pain in loins.*—bor.*φ*.19.

σ^{2}d. *Throbbing of cervical vessels.*—
Ba.glo.d^a.

σ^2. *Fulness of neck.*—dir.d.*π*.

v^{1}b. *Cold feet.*—F.ch-x.VIII^4.*π*.

*τ*v. *Pain in arms and legs.*—F.ind.
p.q.3.

φ. *Sleepiness.*—bor.*σ*^{1}.19.—cn-i.
*η*aa.

χ^2. *Heat.*—glo.—lah.—na-p.q.4.

ω^2. *Weakness of limbs.*—til.q.

ω^9. *Yawning.*—F.phy.

CONDITIONS.

2. *At night.*—ag-n.p.*ag*.—ch-x.
*β*a.33.*ρ*.—jug.—mns.

3. *In morning.*—am-m.p.30.—
bor.*ab*^{i}.*a*^{1}b.(8-31).; F.au.*β*a.
—cob.*βe*^{a}.V^2.—dir.I.; q.—F.
equ.——FO.fag.——F.hdr.q.7.

(8-31).—F.ind.p.q.*rv*.—k-cy.
ζθff^d.——mg-m.βℯ.——na-a.—
pet.p.q.29.

3-99. *In morning on waking.*—klm.
ab^o.βℯ^a.—F.lil.q.

4. *In afternoon.*—cca.——F^o.fag.
31.——la-v.βℯ.——C.la-x.3.——
T.lth.*er*.5.——na-p.q.χ^2.—CO.
osm.V^1.22.—ptv.—F.san.I.

5. *In evening.*—P.ag-n.q.V^1.—F.
cca.V^1.—P.lin.8.—T.lth.*er*.4.
—F.naj.—na-a.p.—na-p.

5. *In forenoon.*—ch-s.44.——cnb.
—nic.*au*.—su-x.βℯ^a.

7. *In warm room.*—aps.d.q.V^1.—
O.car.q.(8).-——F.hdr.q.3.(8-
31).—la-v.βa.

8. *In open air.*—O.car.q.7.—cnb.
V^1.—P.lin.5.

8-31. *On walking in open air.*—bor.
ab^i.a^{1}b.3.—F.*hdr*.q.3.7.

12. *By pressure.*—aġ-n.p.VII^5.—
F.*hdr*.
——— *of hat.*—c-ph.βℯ.

16. *When lying.*—naj.d^a.

19. *When sitting.*—bor.σ^1.φ.—fag.
βa.30.—O.glo.VIII^4.

22. *By bending head back.*—CO.
osm.V^1.4.

26. *By shaking head.*——FO.lo-c.
V^7.35.

29. *By stooping.*—la-x.—mrl.V^1—
VII^5.——nic.q.VI^4.—pet.p.q.
3.—rhs.q.w.—spo.q.

30. *On rising.*—am-m.p.3.—fag.βa.
(19).—glo.VIII^4.θ^3.31.—sil.d.

31. *When walking.*—F.dgn.p.q.—
F^o.fag.4.—glo.VIII^4.θ^3.30.

33. *On ascending.*—bor.βa.

35. *By motion.*—c-ph.—FO.lo-c.
V^7.26.

41. *By mental exertion.*—F.fag.—
na-p.q.βa.—*pho*.q.βℯ.*η*i^a.—pso.

43. *When reading.*—glo.P^c.[T.d^a].

44. *When writing.*—ch-s.5.

44. *After writing.*—CP.ch-s.

50. *On looking up.*—F.equ.V^7.
[S$^{ff^a}$].*η*p.

63. *While eating.*—con.βa.

65. *Before eating.*-C.ur-n.d.q.II^1.

75. *By stool.*—crn.

90. *By sneezing.*—F.hdr.
100. *After siesta.*—mil.

p. **Heat of head.**—abi.*η*aa.—ac-x.d^b.
—aco.; g.; C.—æsc.δp.; O.; O.ep.
—æth.; *η*p.—aga.; hh.VIII^4.; q.—
alo.; x.—alm.q.3.; 66.w.29.(30).—
amb.V$^{1.u}$.δp.*η*c^b.4.—am-m.i^a.3-30.;
F.V^1.3.; P^c.5.—aml.VIII^4.—ang.
—ant.VI^4.5.—ap-a.σ^2.φ.φ^2.χ^1.ω^2.
—F.ara.δ*η*p.—ag-n.βℯ.2.; i^a.VII^5.
(12).; i^a.as.2.; i^a.q.a^{1}b^p.*η*p.4.—ari.
—arn.—ast.q.VIII^4.*η*aa.—F.au-n.
q.; O.q.—F.bap.—F.bad.d.I.4.—
ba-c.g^b.VI^3.; VI^3.3-30.; q.*r*^{1}*v*^{1}.3-30.
—bel.; aa.—ber.11.; 4.66.hh.29.
30.—bis.βℯ.—bor.θ.*r*^{1}.—bry.*η*p.aa.
—cld.—ca-c.d.; 5.; d.83.; q.3-99.
26.30.; F.q.; P^d.——c-cs.—c-ph.I.
*η*p.ab,u.—F.cln.I.66.—cam.; VI^4.
——cn-i.VI^2.af^b.&.*rv*b,x.; VI^2.ℯ𝐯.
—can.VIII^4.*η*p,aa.κ^5.——cth.*r*^{1}hh.
66.; aġ.; I.*η*p.—cb-a.aġ.2-16.(30).
—cb-v.I.; F.II^1.—ca-x.; F.III^1.; F.
(12).—car.6.; *η*aa.χ^1.——csc.βℯ.—
cau.βℯ.; V^{1}3.; d.— cep.—cr-b.; F.
*η*p.—chd.*r*^{1}d.χ^2.—I.; F.; C.V^1.; C.
I.; P^d.ℯp.—chi.q.VIII^3.48.—cn-s.;
F.*rv*b.χ^2.—cmf.i^a.VIII^4.—cle.; 𝐫.
66.100.; q.w.βa,b.μ$^{3·5}$.ω^8.3.6.(8).;
F.βℯ.; F.i^a.I.——col.ρ^1.——con.—F.
cvl.(117).—F.c-ar.—crn.i^a.βℯ.*η*p.;
*η*p.; C.—cyc.i^a.βa.; V^1.βℯ.—dig.;
κ^5.—dgn.q.βℯ.—dio.3.—dro.—dul.
—elc.—C.ept.I.(12).—eth.—eup.
V^1.; F.I.—fag.q.(22).—F.fl-x.d.I.
—CO.frz.—glv.βa.—gam.bh.; V^1.
χ^2.——gas.5.——gin.—glo.VIII^4.—
grp.w.hh.; 66.—grt.——F.gym.—
hæm.II^1.—hel.βℯ^a.II^1.; q.*r*^{1}b.χ^1.—
C.hep.V^1.; F.—hur.; T.*η*p.—hdr.
a^{1}b^p.βℯ.(12).—hy-x.βa.—hyo.I.; g^b.
—hyp.VIII.4.—ibe.i^a.σ^{2}i^a.—ign.
—O.ind.w.; V$^{1·s}$.—iod.ρ^1.σ^{2}ii.82.—
jat.ζ^3.; q.; βℯ.*η*.σ.; x.κ^5.ω^9.; O.x.; F.ℯ.
—irs.*η*p.—F.k-bi.βℯ.——k-ca.*η*rp.;
5.(16).; II^1.—k-hy.*η*p,aa.; aġ.83.
—klm.3.—kis.*η*p.—F.kre.I.φ.—lab.
—lab.ζ^3.*r*^{1}p.; d.—F.la-v.βℯ.VI^3.; O.
V^1.*r*^{1}b.; II^1.V^1.—lau.βℯ^a.; q.(98).;
ab,u.F.hh.*v*^{1}b.(8).; F.aġ.(8).; F.hh.

ii^d.r^1p.—lep.χ^3.--O.lo-i.V^7.5.—lil.
—lyc.VIII^4.; T.a^{1}ᴅ.ep.5.— mr-i.I.
—mt-n.—mag.; 5.; ηhh.; «ɡ.χ^2.67.;
ηc^b.;ηaa.r^{1}p.; q.I.83.--mg-m.;βa,ɛ^a.
6.63.(8).; w.χ$^{2.3}$.4 5.83.; ηaa.μ^3.χ^1.;
θ.ι.π^1.ζ^3.; F.III^3.VIII^4.12.; F.b.
VI$^{3.4}$.; F^n.—mg-s.q.30.; III^3.ηaa.;
F.II^1.4.; C.V^6.—man.4.; q.βɛ.(8).;
κ^3.—mep.aṣ.—mrl.; βa.; q.VII^5.;
ηaa.T^b.VI$^{3.4}$.—mer.I.——mez.hh.
VII^1.χ^1.3.; S.—mo-a.; q.; σ^2.rvb.
χ^2.—mo-m.ηp.—msc.O.hh.—nat.;
d.5.6.19.(8.16).; q.ηaa.5.; FC.V^1.;
F.VII^5.—na-m.ɛᴅ.; aɡ.κ^5.; ηp.4.;
(117).; F.V^1.—nic.κ^3.; F.q.4.—
ni-x.; d.; I.βa.31.—F.nit.ab^t.ω^2.—
nx-j.rvb.5-16.—nx-m.; C.III^1.V^{10}.
—ol-a.bh.r^1.; F.hh.rhh.—opi βa.;
ηp.; F.I.—ori.; w.—pæo.q.βa,ɛ.—
ped.—-ptv.q.46.; F.I.δ.4.—pet.q.
βɛ.3.; i^a.q.3.29.**30**^{b}.; VI^3.—phl.βa.
I.r^{1}p.;βɛ^a.; Fb.; F^b.V^1.; P^d.ηaa.r^{1}p.;
I.hh.r^{1}hh.—ph-x.βɛ^a.δt.5-19.; r^{1}b.
86.; F.—pho.aɡ.r^{1}p,aa.(18).; χ^2.
66.; w.; II^1.κ^1.—phy.—pim.d.4.—
pla.x.III^3.au^{ff}.χ^2.--plm.rvb.χ^2.; 31.
—plb.ηaa.—C.pod.I.3.--O.pl-n.i^a.
—rat.q.—rhe.q.—rs-r.; I.; VIII^4.;
C.III^2.; O.II^6.—rut.; aɡ.χ.2.--sbd.
χ^1.—sab.d.βa.--snt.—src.i^a.II^5.—
sar.hh.63.—F.snc.—sep.5.;χ^2.; δo.
ɛa.—ser.—sil.; aɡ.—so-t.4.; χ^2.4.
—spi.—spr.i^a.q.; 30.—spo.βa.19.;
F.ρ.; F.d.σ^2.; O.VI^3.35.—-squ.v^{1}b.
—stn.I.3-99.; a^{1}ᴅ^a.VI^3.φ.χ^1.; F.; F.
II^1.δp.ζp.κ^5.—str.δa^b.--sto.VII^1.
«ɡ,ḅ.ηp,aa.φ.4.--sul.3.; v^{1}b.5.; η.
3-99.; ηaa.; 3-99.(30).; φ^1.; V^1.70.;
O.V^1.—tab.; V^1.—trn.ηaa.r^{1}p,hh.;
O.—tar.35.; F.——F.tax.—P^d.thu.
IV^1.—til.ηp.VI^3.—ton.; 3.—ver.
b.Hdd.—vin.VI^2.——F.vi-o.—zin.
ηaa.; CO.VIII^4.5.

—— *though cold to touch.*—hdr.
—— *agreeable.*—cam.κ^4.—can.—
    nic.6.—thu.V$^{1.6}$.
—— *transient.*--aga,a^{1}ḅ^s.δ.--arn.;
    q.—F.cn-i.; q.—F.cln.5.—
    F.elc.—mg-m.—sul.—tab.
    d.—val.29.
—— *flushes.*—æth.ηaa.χ^2.—am-m.

—glo.—-œna.—sep.—sul.
    d.—zn-o.βɛ.
—— *flushes of heat from chest to
    head.*—glo.
—— *hot pain.*—lil.5.(90).; F.5.
—— *from above downwards.*—glo.
—— *internal.*——F.alm.βɛ^a.—cth.
    aq.--F.cau.66.; F.σp.—chd.
    --dig.a^{1}ḅ^s.--F.grp.VI^4.4.—
    led.bh.σbh.—C.lep.I.—lyc.
    βḅ.--mg-s.V^3.4.—mim.—
    nat.δp.κ^3.2.——F.na-m.—
    nx-v.VlI^1.(12).——pul.βb.
    ηc^b.5.—sum.q.III^3.--thr.q.
    βɛ.aæ$^{w.cc}$.
—— *like a warm breath.*—O.fl-x.
    σ^{2}p.
—— *as if surrounding air were
    hot.*—aet.
—— *as if had stood before a hot
    fire.*—cac.aɡ.ηaa.
—— *as if it radiated heat like a
    stove.* — ca-x.ii^d.
—— *radiating from within out-
    wards.*—cle.q.βb,ɛ.δo.ep.3.
—— *as if bathed in warm water.*
    —cep.V^1.—ptv.
—— *like boiling water.*—O.ind.
—— *as if hot water thrown on
    scalp penetrating to brain.*
    —ptv.
—— *as if tied up in a hot cloth.*—
    ptv.x.III.
—— *as from some stimulating ap-
    plication.*—F^g.rs-r.I.2.
—— *as from wine.*—rs-r.--sbd.ηp.
—— *as if coryza were coming on.*
    —ber.ηp.
—— *as if nose would bleed.*—sep.
    3.
—— *as if perspiration would
    break out.*——F.cau.σp.—
    pho.χ^2.66.—T.rn-b.5.44.
—— *as if a hot body fell for-
    wards.*—F.k-ca.29.44.(30).
—— *alternating with rigor in
    back.*—F.spo.
—— *followed by impatience, in-
    quietude, agitation, ill-
    humour, oppression, desire
    to tear hair.*—trn.

—— *followed by headache and vertigo.*——hpm.——rhs.θ.κ³. 6.100.(5-16).

—— *followed by soreness of head.* —aco.5.

—— *followed by sweat of head.*— plc.

—— *followed by pain in eyeballs.* —an-a.hh.

—— *followed by epistaxis.*—pim. w.βℓ.

—— *followed by pinching in belly.* —lup.βe.ηp.

—— *followed by coldness.*—F.lau.

—— *preceded by coldness.*—C.grt. **130.**

—— *after an appopleptic attack.* —lah.hh.

ANATOMICAL SEAT.

F. FOREHEAD.—alm.βℓ*.--am-m.V¹. 3.——ara.δηp.——au-n.q.——bad.d. I 4.——bap.——ca-c.q.--cln.5. ; I. 66.—ca-x.III¹.; (12).—cau.66.; σp.—cr-b.ηp.—chd.——cn-s.rvb. χ².--cle.βe. ; i*.I.—cvl.(117).— c-ar.'—dgn.i*.q.31.--elc.—eup. I.—fl-x.d.I.--glo.d.—grp.VI⁴.4. --gym.--hep.--idm.i*.--jat.ep.-- k-bi.βℓ.--k-ca.29.44.(80).--kre. I.φ.—la-v.βℓ.VI³. ; O.V¹--VII⁵. r¹b.; II¹--V¹.--lau.αg.(8).; hh.ii^d. r¹p.--lil.I.δ.--mg-m.III³.VIII⁴. 12. ; b.VI³·⁴.; r.—mg-s.II¹.4.— mn-o.q.; V¹.—nat.VII⁵.; C.V¹. —na-m.; V¹.--nic.q.—nit.ab^t.ηp. ω²3.—opi.I.—ptv.I.λ.4.—phl.l. V¹.—ph-x.— rn-b.5.44.—rs-r.l. I.2.—snc.—spo.ρ.; d.σ².—stn.; II¹.δζp.ι⁵.—trx.—tax.—vi-o.

—— *as if warm water trickled down inside.*—glo.

—— *alternately in either protuberance.*—la-v.βe.VI³.

—— *alternating with rigor in back.*—spo.4.

T. TEMPLES.——hur.η.—lyc.a¹ɒ.ep.5. —mrl.l.VI³⁴.

C. CROWN.——aco.——chd.I.; V¹.—— crn.—-pt.I.(12).—O.frz.—grt. **130.**—hep.V¹.—lau.III¹.—lep.

I.—mg-s.V⁶.——mr-i.1.—F.nat. V¹.—nx-m.III¹.V¹⁰.—-pod.I.3. —rs-r.III².—O.zin.VIII⁴.5.

P. PARIETAL REGION.—am-m.r.5.— ca-c.l.—phl.l.ηaa.r¹p.

O. OCCIPUT.— æsc. ; ep.—au-n.q.— fl-x.σ²p.—C.frz.—-ind.w.—jat.; x. ; βℓ.—lo-i.V⁷.5.—-pl-n.i*.— rs-r.II⁶.—-spo.VI³.35.—sul.V¹. —trn.—C.zin.r.VIII⁴.5.

CONCOMITANTS.

ab. *Laziness.*—c-ph.ηp.au.--lau.au· Fhh.v¹b.(8).

ab¹. *Indisposed to think.*—F.nit.ηp. ω².3.

af^b. *Uneasiness.*--cn-i.VI².ak.rvb,x.

ag. *Anxiety.*——cac.ηaa.——cth.— k-hy.83.—-F.lau.(8).——mag. χ².67.—na-m.κ⁵.--pho.r¹p,aa. (18).——rut.χ.2.——sil.—sto. VII¹.ab.ηp,aa.φ.4.

ah. *Apprehensiveness.* ——sto.VII¹. ag.ηp,aa.φ.4.

ak. *Melancholy.*-cn-i.VI².af^b.rvb,x.

aq. *Restlessness.*—cth.

as. *Excitement.*—ag-n.i*.2.—mep.

au. *Ill-humour.*——c-ph.I.ηp.ab.—- lau.ab.Fhh.v¹b.(8).

au^tt. *Impatience.*—pla.x.III³.χ².

a¹b^p. *Loss of memory.*—ag-n.i*.q.ηp. 4.—hdr.βℓ.(12).

a¹b^s. *Mental prostration.*—aga.δ.

a¹b^s. *Weakness of intellectual faculties.*—dig.

a¹ɒ. *Stupor.*—T.lyc.ep.5.

a¹ɒ*. *Unconsciousness.*-——stn.VI³.φ. χ¹.

βa. *Vertigo.*——cle.q.w.βb.μ³·⁵.ω⁸.3. 6.(8).——cyc.i*.--—glv.—hy-x. --mg-m.βℓ*.6.63.(8).——mrl. —ni-x.I.31.—opi.—pæo.q.βℓ. —phl.I.r¹p.—phy.κ⁵.—sab.d. —spo.19.

βb. *Staggering.*--cle.q.w.βa.μ³·⁵.ω⁸. 3.6.(8).; q.βℓ*.ℓo.ep.ηp.3.— pul.ηo^p.5.

βℓ. *Confusion.*—ag-n.2.——bis.— csc.—cau.—F.cle.--crn.i*.ηp. —cyc.V¹.—dgn.q.; 5.—hor. a¹b^p.(12).——jat.η.σ.; O.—-F.

k-bi.— k-br.— F.la-v.VI³.—
lup.ηp.λ.— —man.q.(8).—pæo.
q.βa.—pet.q.3.— phl.—zn-o.

βe^a. *Stupid feeling.*—F.alm.—cle.
q.βb.δo.ep.ηp.3.— —hel.II¹.— —
lau.— —mg-m.βa.6.63.(8).— —
mor.—ph-x.δt.5-19.

βe^c. *Lightness of head.*—so-n.

δa^b. *Sparkling eyes.*—str.

δp. *Heat in eyes.*— —æsc.— —amb.
V¹·ᵘ.ηc^b.4.— F.ara.ηp.— —nat.
κ³.2.—F.stn.II¹.δ.ζp.κ⁵.

δ. *Pain in eyes.*—aga.a¹b^a.—lil.I.—
F.ptv.I.4.— F.stn.II¹.δp.ζp.κ⁵.

δo. *Dimness of vision.*— —cle.q.βb,
e^a.ep.ηp.3.—sep.ea.

δt. *Vision of cyphers.*—ph-x.βe^a.
5-19.

ep. *Heat in ears.*— —O.æsc.— —P^d.
chd.— —cle.q.βb,e^a.δo.ηp.3.— —
F.jat.; O.—T.lyc.a¹v.5.

ea. *Hardness of hearing.*—sep.δo.

ev. *Noise in ears.*—cn-i.VI².—na-m.

ζp. *Heat in nose.*—F.stn.II¹.δp.κ⁵.

ζ³. *Coryza.*—jat.—lah.r¹p.—mg-m.
θıp.π¹p.

ηc^b. *Pale face.*— —amb.V¹·ᵘ.δp.— —
pul.βb.5.

ηp. *Heat of face.*— —æth.— F.ara.δp.
— —ag-n.i^a.q.a¹b^p.4.— —ber.— —
bry.ηaa.— —c-pb.I.ab,u.— —can.
VIII⁴.ηaa.κ⁵.— —cth.I.—F.cr-b.
— —cle.q.βb,e^a.δo.ep.3.— —crn.;
i^a.βe.— —glo.— —T.hur.—jat.βe.
or.—irs.— k-ca.r.— —k-hy.ηaa.
— —kis.—lup.βe.λ.— —mo-m.— —
na-m.4.—F.nit.ab^i.ω².3.— opi.
— pho.VIII⁴.rp,aa.(8).— sbd.
— sto.VII¹.ag,b.ηaa.φ.4.— sul.
3-99.(30).— til.VI³.—zin.ηaa.5.

ηaa. *Red face.*—abi.— æth.χ².— ast.
q.VIII⁴.—bry.ηp.—cac.ag.— —
can.VIII⁴.ηp.κ⁵.— —car.χ¹.— —
k-hy.ηp.— mag.ηp.r¹p.— mg-m.
μ³.χ¹.— —mg-s.III³.— —mrl.— —
nat.q.5.—P^d.phl.r¹p.—plb.— —
sto.VII¹.ag,b.ηp.φ.4.— sul.— —
trn.r¹p,hh.—zin.; ηp.5.

η. *Alternate paleness and redness
of face.*—mag.ηp.

ηhh. *Sweat on face.*—mag.

θj. *Dry lips.*—rhs.κ³.6.100.(5-16).

θp. *Heat of mouth.*— —bor.r¹p.— —
mg-m.ζ³.ıπ¹p.

ıp. *Heat of throat.*—mg-m.ζ³.θπ¹p.

κ¹. *Anorexia.*—pho.II¹.

κ³. *Thirst.*— —man.— nat.δp.2.— —
nic.—rhs.θj.6.100.(5-16).

κ⁴p. *Heat in stomach.*—cam.

κ⁵. *Nausea.*— —can.VIII⁴.ηp,aa.— —
dig.— jat.x.ω⁹.— —na-m.ag.— —
phy.βa.—F.stn.II¹.δ.δζp.

λ. *Pinching in belly.*—lup.βe.ηp.

μ³. *Urging to stool.*—cle.q.w.βa,b.
μ⁵.ω⁸.3.6.(8).— —mg-m.ηaa.χ¹.

μ⁵p. *Heat in rectum.*—cle.q.w.βa,b.
μ³.ω⁸.3.6.(8).

πp. *Heat of chest.*—cle.66.100.

π¹p. *Hot breath.*—mg-m.ζ³.θıp.

ρ. *Quick, hard pulse.*—F.spo.

ρ¹. *Palpitation.*—col.— iod.o².82.

σp. *Heat in back.*—F.cau.

σr. *Rigor in back.*—jat.βe.ηp.

σhh. *Sweat on back.*—led.hh.

σ²d. *Throbbing in carotids.*— —mo-a.
rvb.χ².—F.spo.d.

σ²p. *Heat in neck.*—ap-a.φ.φ².χ¹.ω².
— —O.fl-x.

σ²i^a. *Fulness of neck.*—ibe.i^a.

σ². *Tension and swelling of neck.*
— —iod.ρ¹.82.

r¹b. *Cold hands.*— —F.la-v.O.V¹.— —
ph-x.86.

r¹b. *Cold fingers.*—hel.q.χ¹.

r¹d. *Distended veins of hands.*— —
chd.χ².

r¹p. *Heat of hands.*—cth.66.—lah.
ζ³.—F.lau.hh.ii^d.— —mag.ηp,aa.
— —ol-a.hh.— —phl.βa.I.; P^d.
ηaa.— —pho.ag.(18).; VIII⁴.
ηp.(8).

r¹p. *Heat of palms.*—bor.θp.—trn.
ηaa.r¹hh.

r¹aa. *Red hands.*—pho.ag.r¹p.(18).

r¹hh. *Sweat on hands.*—ol-a.Fhh.— —
phl.hh.I.— —trn.η¹aa.r¹p.

v¹b. *Cold feet.*— —lau.ab,u.Fhh.(8).
— —squ.—sul.5.

v¹. *Burning in toes.*—c-pb.

rvb. *Cold extremities.*— —cn-i.VI².
a^b,k.rvx.— F.cn-s.χ².— mo-a.
σ²d.χ².—nx-j.5-16.— plm.χ².

τυx. Numb extremities.—-cn-i.VI^2. af^b,k.rvb.

r^{1}v^{1}b. Cold hands and feet.—-ba-c.q. 3-30.

φ. Sleepiness.— ap-a.σ^{2}p.φ^2.χ^1.ω^2. — F.kre.I.—stn.VI^3.a^{1}ɒ^a.χ^1. —sto.VII^1.aɡ,ƅ.ηp,aa.4.

φ^2. Troublesome dreams.—-ap-a. σ^{2}p.φ.χ^1.ω^2.

χ. Febrile uneasiness.—rut.aɡ.2.

χ^1. Chilliness.—-ap-a.σ^{2}p.φ.φ^2.ω^2. —car.ηaa.—hel.q.r^{1}b.—mg-m. ηaa.μ^3.—mez.hh.VII^1.3.— sbd.—stn.VI^3.a^{1}ɒ^a.φ.

χ^2. Heat.—æth.ηaa.—-chd.r^{1}d.— F.cn-s.rvb.—gam.V^1.—mag. aɡ.67.—mg-m.w.χ^3.4.5.83.— mo-a.σ^{2}d.rvb.— pho.66.—pla. x.III^3.au^{ff}.—sep.—so-t.4.

χ^3. Sweat.—glo.ηp.—-mg-m.w.χ^2. 4.5.83.

χ^3. Cold sweat.—lep.

ω^2. Lassitude.—ap-a.σ^{2}p.φ.φ^2.χ^1.— F.nit.aƅ^i.ηp.3.

ω^8. Trembling.—-cle.q.w.βa,ƅ.μ$^{3·5}$. 3.6.(8).

ω^9. Yawning.—jat.x.κ^5.—F.phy.

CONDITIONS.

1. *All day.*—C.mr-i.
2. *At night.*—-ag-n.βℓ. ; i^a.aℓ.— nat.δp.κ^3.—F^b.rs-r.I.—rut. aɡ.χ.
2-16. *At night in bed.*—cb-a.aɡ.(30).
3. *In morning.*—alm.q.—-F.am-m. V^1.—-cle.q.w.βa,ƅ.μ$^{3·5}$.ω^8.6. (8). ; q.βƅ,ℓ^a.δo.εp.ηp.—-dio. —klm.—-mez.hh.VII^1.χ^1.— F.nit.aƅ^i.ηp.ω^2.—-pet.q.βℓ.—- C.pod.I.—sep.—sul.—ton.
3-30. *On rising in morning.*—am-m. i^a.—-ba-c.VI^3. ; q.r^{1}v^{1}b.—spr. —*sul*.ηp.3-99.
3-99. *On waking in morning.*—-ca-c. q.26.30.—stn.I.—sul.ηp.(30).
4. *In afternoon.*—-ag-n.i^a.q.a^{1}ƅ^p. — F.bad.d.I.—ber.66.hh.29. 30.—F.grp.VI^4.—hyp.VIII^4. — mg-m.w.χ$^{2·3}$.5.88.—-mg-s. V^3.; F.II^1.—man.—na-m.ηp. —F.nic.q.—F.ptv.I.δ.—pim.

d.—so-t. ; χ^2.—-F.spo.—sto. VII^1.aɡ,ƅ.ηp,aa.φ.

5. *In evening.*—-aco.II^5.—-P^c. am-m.—ca-c.—F.cln.—dgn. p.—gas.—k-ca.(16).—F. lil.(90).—O.lo-i.V^7.—-T.lyc. a^{1}ɒ.εp.—mag.—-mg-m.w.χ$^{2·3}$. 4.83.—C.mr-i.—nat.d.6.19. (8.16).—nx-j.rvb.16.—ph-x. βℓ^a.δt.19.—-pul.βƅ.ηc^b.—-F. rn-b.44.—*rhs*.q.I^a.θj.κ^3.6.100. (16).—sep.—sul.v^{1}b.—zin. ηp,aa. ; CO.VIII^4.

5. *In forenoon.*—ant.VI^4.—nat.q. ηaa.

6. *In a room.*—car.—cle.q.w.βa,ƅ. μ$^{3·5}$.ω^8.3.(8).—mg-m.βa,ℓ^a.63. (8).—nat.d.5.19.(8.16).—-nic. —— *from open air.*—ind.— rhs.q.I^a.θj.κ^3.100.(5-16).

8. *In open air.*—cle.q.w.βa,ƅ.μ$^{3·5}$. ω^8.3.6.—-*lau*.ab,u.F.hh.vb.; aɡ. —-mg-m.βa,ℓ^a.6.63.; 66.—*man*.q. βℓ.—nat.d.5.6.19.(16).—-na-a. i^a.—*pho*.VIII^4.ηp.r^{1}p,aa.

11. *When touched.*—ber.
12. *By pressure.*— ag-n.i^a.VII^5.— F.ca-x.—-hdr.a^{1}ƅ^p.βℓ.—-nx-v. VII^1.
16. *On lying down.*—k-ca.5.—nat. d.5.6.19.(8).—-nx-j.rvb.5.— *rhs*.q.I^a.θj.κ^3.6.100.(5).
18. *By standing.*—pho.aɡ.r^{1}p.
19. *When sitting.*—-nat.d.5.6.(8. 16).—ph-x.βℓ^a.δt.5.—spo.βa.
22. *By bending head back.*—*fag*.q.
26. *On moving head.*—ca-c.q.3-99. 30.
29. *When stooping.*—-F.k-ca.44. (30).—pet.i^a.q.3.**30^b**.—val.
30. *On rising.*—-ca-c.q.3-99.26.— cb-a.aɡ.2-16.—F.*k-ca*.29.44. —mg-s.q.
30^b. *When sewing.*—pet.i^a.q.3.29.
31. *By walking.*—-F.dgn.i^a.q.— glo.VIII^4.—ni-x.I.βa.—plm.
35. *By motion.*—*pho*.βℓ^a.—O.spo. VI^3.—trx.
44. *When writing.*—-F.k-ca.29. (30).—F.rn-b.5.
48. *On moving eyes.*—chi.q.VIII^3.

63. *When eating.*——mg-m.βa,ℓ*ª*.6. (8).——sar.hh.
66. *After eating.*—ber.4.hh.29.30. —F.cln.I.——-cth.r¹p.—F.cau. —-cle.πp.100.——mg-m. (8).— pho.χ³.
67. *By hot food.*—mag.ag.χ².
70. *By drinking beer.*—sul.V¹.
82. *Before menses.*—iod.ρ¹.σ².
83. *During menses.*—ca-c.d.—k-hy. ag.—mag.q.I.— mg-m.w.χ²·³. 4.5.
86. *By speaking.*—ph-x.r¹b.
90. *By sneezing.*—lil.5.
98. *During sleep.*—lau.q.
100. *After siesta.*——cle.πp.66.—- rhs.q.Iª.θj.κ³.6.(5-16).
117. *By cold bath.*——-cvl.——eup.—- na-m.
130. *By covering.*—O.grt.

Course and progress of heat.

aco. *Dry sensation first in lips, then in mouth, with heat mounting from chest to head.*
ags. *Sensation of heat and burning rises into vertex from left lower jaw, almost makes her crazy.*
alm. *Heat rising from stomach into head in the forenoon.*
cld. *Heat rises into head from below.*
cyc. *Heat rising up into head, lasting till evening.*
fl-x. *From nape to occiput like a warm breath.*
glo. *Glow of heat rising from chest to head.*
ind. *Flying heat rising from stomach to back of head while sitting.*
mg-m. *Heat in head after dinner, as if coming from stomach, better in open air.*
na-n. *Burning hot feeling over left temple changing into a pressing-in pain there, followed by hot feeling on right side of head and external ear, passing into general heat of face, with pressive pain in left frontal protuberance.*
na-s. *After the vertigo heat rising from body up to head, becoming*

worse till sweat broke out on forehead.
opi. *Warm feeling from head to right forearm.*
pho. *Much heat in head, especially forehead and face, also in hands, sometimes with throbbing in head, sometimes rising from back, at times going off in open air.*
Mounting of heat from chest into head and whole body on taking soup, as if sweat would break out.
plc. *Sudden heat in head, followed immediately by sweat on hairy scalp; on its drying the forehead feels cold to touch.*
plb. *Heat often rises into head as if from abdomen.*

q. **Heaviness.**—ac-x.βυ.—aco.; w.— æsc.—aga.; βℓ.; p.—ag-p.—alm.p. 3.; βℓ.I.4.——amb.V¹.5.——am-g.— am-c.—am-m.iª.βa.—ana.βℓ.3-30. —aps.; V¹.—apo.—ag-n.iª.—ari. —arn.p.—ar-i.iiᵈ.I.--ast.—bap.— ba-m.—ber.—bis.—bla.iª.—bor. —bry.—buf.—cai.——cam.—cb-a. —cb-v.—ca-x.—cr-h.; I.—cr-s.— crd.——cas.I.——cau.V¹.—cep.; iª.— cha.—chd.—chi.—ch-s.—cn-s.— clf.—cnb.—cle.—coc.—col.—con. —cot.—ctn.—cup.—cu-a.—cyc. —dgn.—dul.—epn.—fag.—fer.-- fl-x.V⁷.—for.iiᵈ.—gel.—glo.; I.— gun.—hur.; VIII⁴.—hyd.—hy-x. I.—hyo.; I.—hyp.—ign.—iod.— ipc.—irs.—jac.I.——k-bi.—la-s.— lep.I.—lol.I.——lyc.—mt-s.gᵇ.V³. —mag.I.; II⁷,—mnc.—mad.βℓ.— man.iiᵈ.—-men.——mrl.p.VII⁵.— mer.—mor.p.—mo-a.; VII².; p.— msc.; d.—mrr.——my-s.—nar.— ni-x.V⁷.——nit.; I.—oln.——ol-a. V¹.——oni.—opi.——pan.——pau. I.—ped.—phl.; iª.iiᵈ.—ph-x.; V¹. —pho.—pru.—pul.—rn-b.—rn-s. iª.—rat.p.—rhe.p.--rs-r.—r-vn.— rs-v.—sab.——san.——sec.—sng.— sil.—spi.VII¹.——spr.iª.p.—spo.—- stp.—str.—sul.iª.—sum.p.III.—

trn.—tar.—ve-v.—vrb.I.—wis.— xan., &c.

—— *monstrous.*—-bry.—-dro.— r-vn.

—— *dull.*—oni.

—— *as if too full of blood.*—lil.d. ζ^2.8.

—— *as from carbonic acid.*—ni-x. 3-99.

—— *as if intoxicated.*—asr.βe.V^1. —bel.—nx-m.

—— *as if had been drinking wine or spirits.*—aco.βa.3.—aga.; βe.3.—coc.βa.—dul.V$^{3\cdot s}$.— fer.au.βe^a.—gas.βa.κ^5.— lah.βa.κ^5.—lau.—nit.βe^a.3. —sab.5.—F.so-t.3-99.

—— *as if he had eaten too much.* —scr.βe.

—— *as if he had not slept enough.* —mag.βe.3-30.(35.116).— zin.βa,e.

—— *as if he had slept with head too low.*—pho.a^{1}b^b.βa.I.3-30.

—— *as from prolonged work.*— nat.βa,e.112.

—— *as after a long illness.*—cln.3.

—— *as if coryza were coming on.* —ber.p.V^1.aa.ηp.χ^1.3.—lau.

—— *as during severe catarrh.*— FT.sep.d.

—— *as if a weight lay on head.*— coc.—phl.

—— *like a weight in brain.*—nx-v. —sil.

—— *like a lump in brain.*—chd.

—— *as if a great weight pressed on brain.*—ac-l.—ars.e℧. 3-30.

—— *as if a weight fell forwards.* —nx-v.29.—rhs.ηp.

—— *as if bound in a vice.*—chd.

—— *crushing weight.*—F.glo.

—— *brain feels compressed.*—— hyp.

—— *as if temples were pressed together.*—sar.βe^a.

—— *like pressure forwards.*—grt.

—— *as if brain were pressed forwards.*—-bry.—-F.cth.βe^a. —lau.—thu.

Heaviness, as if integuments were stretched.—dul.g^b.

—— *as if encircled by a tight skin.*—hel.a^{1}b.

—— *weighing head downwards.*— lau.(30).—-mt-n.—-mrl.x. VII^5.—snn.29.

—— *as if head weighed too much.* —lil.

—— *as if head would sink forwards.*—agn.σ^2.—ba-c.au. βe.φ.ω^2.5.—F.ber.δ.29.— equ.3.—C.hpm.31.—-par. —rhs.i^a.29.—sul.βe^a.(31). —su-x.i^a.—tab.

—— *as if brain would fall forwards.*—-F.cb-a.29.βa.30.— lau.29.(30).—rhs.ηp.29.— su-x.

—— *as if head would fall down.* —-C.alm.III^3.18-29.—bel. —ber.

—— *as if head had hung down.*— opi.

—— *can scarcely support head.*— cro.V^1.3-99.—-glo.—man. au.—mez.—oln.βe.κ^5.30. (16).—phl.i^a.—pul.—sbd. βe.—sil.—so-t.—tab.—tar.

—— *as if he could not hold it steady.*—squ.19.

—— *head drawn to one side.*— F.sil.VI$^{3\cdot4}$.

—— *head sinks backwards.*—cam. βa.—chi.19.—O.k-ca.σ^{2}ff. —phl.

—— *drawing head forwards.*—F. itu.x.—oln.—vi-t.30.(29).

—— *as if head would fall to every side.*—bry.V$^{1\cdot a}$.—fl-x.V$^{1\cdot s}$.θ^2.

—— *as if head were drawn backwards.*—F.zin.5.83.

—— *as if he could not raise head.* —sep.

—— *could not lift head from pillow.*—iof.

—— *as if he would fall forwards.* —alm.19.29.—gas.βa.κ^5.— plb.—zin.

—— *as though he could not sit up.*—bap.

Heaviness, as if he could not rise again.—pul.29.
—— *alternating with clearness of mind.*—mur.
—— *followed by headache.*—lah.3.
—— *following headache.*—cca.

ANATOMICAL SEAT.

F. FOREHEAD.—aco.βa.κ⁴·⁵.29.; C.—æth.δb.au.63.—-aga.—all.δb.—am-c.I.4.; VIII⁴.66.—am-m.χ²·³.—amp.; P.—amy.—aml.—ang.3-30.—an-s.βe.φ.—arn.—ars.VIII⁴.5.--aru.βe.3.—asp.—au-m.; V¹.; 19.—au-n.1.; V¹.; 19.; p.—ba-c.r.V¹.—bel.I.δ.3-99.—ber.δ.29.—bis.V¹.5.—bov.a¹b.βe.V¹.; l.V¹.δ.δo.3.35.--bro.I.112.(114).—buf.δLq.--ca-c.43.44.; p.—cam.—cn-i.p.—cth.βeª.—cb-a.29.βa.30.—cb-v.V⁷.—O.ca-x.—css.—cr-b.βa.3.—cnt.iª.—cer.—cis.—cf-t.—con.V⁶.aoʰ,p—col.βeª.---cvl.βa.—ctn.iª.βe.—dgn.V¹.; iª.p.31.—dul.; VI³·⁵.—elp.—fer.βeª.—f-io.—fl-x.V⁷.5.29.; κ⁵.35.—glo.; T.—gam.VIII⁴.5.; V¹.4.(8).—hæm.—C.hel.iª.p.βe.; p.δ.σb.3.31.; ak.βe.V¹.31.—hep.βeª.—hpm.—hur.—hdr.iª.3.7.(8-31).--hyn.—hyo.29.—itu.x.——C.jac.δq.ζ³.3.—jan.—k-bi.δo.31.—k-ca.I.—k-hy.l.3-30.—lah.V¹.—lau.V⁷.29.; δiiᵈ.; 8.--lil.iª.3-99.--lth.1.--mag.18.; C.VI⁴.66.--mg-m.4.—O.man.βe.- --mn-o.p.—C.mr-i.; VIII⁴ⁿ.—mit.—mo-a.—naj.j.—na-a.—na-m.V¹.; l.V¹.—nic.βa.3.16.30.(8).; βa.18.—nit.I.; βe.—O.r.nup.r.V⁷.--opi.—C.ox-x.3.—pau.l.—ptv.p.46.—phy.βe.—plb.3.66.--rho.βe.3-30.—rs-r.βe.δq.φ.—rhs.p.VII².θj.κ³.6.100.(5.16).—src.ak.βe.——T.sep.d.—sil.VI³·⁴.--so-n.--so-t.3-99.--spr.I.—sto.V².VI³.——trn.δe,b.; κ⁴·⁵.2.—T.l.tax.l.89.—tea.βa,e.31.—ton.30.; δb.—zin.5.83.--zn-o.βe.

—— *as if a stone lay there.*—elc.—rut.

Heaviness, as if full of lead.—cle.I.p.—lyc.l.
—— *like a weight pressing forwards in forehead.*—rhs.
—— *pressing down head.*—æth.au.19.
—— *as if something heavy sank down in it.*—nx-v.29.βeª.24.
—— *as if all would come out at forehead.*— aco.iª.—kre.—mg-s.p.(30).
—— *head tends to fall forwards.*--ber.--b.29.--itu.x.--pho.βe.6.29.(8.53).
—— *as if from stomach.*—con.V⁶.aoʰ.p.

T. TEMPLES.—bel.V¹.ea.—bov.—O.cb-a.l.βe.—fer.—F.glo.—k-hy.r.—ni-x.χ¹.--nup.5.—nym.phy.—rhs.V¹·ᵘ.—sar.l.; 3.—F.sep.d.—F.l.tax.l.δe.89.

—— *as if a weight hung at both sides of head.*—aga.11.—rhs.

C. CROWN.—F.aco.—alm.III³.—-O.cb-a.V¹.83.(4).—cas.VI⁴.66.—cep.iiᵈ.—ch-s.5.—dig.—equ.—F.hel.iª.p.βe.—hpm.31.—ir-f.κ⁴.—k-bi.iª.—O.k-hy.I.2.5.—lau.29.(30).; V¹·ᵘ.6-31.29.—-mt-s.—F.mag.VI⁴.66.——F.mr-i.—na-a.βeª.26.29.---F.ox-x.3.—ped.—ptv.δb.—phs.l.—phy.—rhs.31.—ser.—so-t.5.—squ.3-99.

—— *as if a weight lay there.*—ind.4.29.—msc.I.—phl.
—— *as if it would be crushed in.*—aml.βe.
—— *as if head would fall down.*—alm.III³.18-29.—hpm.31.

P. PARIETES.—am-c.l.16.—F.amp.—ag-n.iª.V¹.5.——bov.r.V¹.--ced.r.iiᵈ—elp.VI³.--grt.l.--hdr.r.φ.—k-ca.l.—k-hy.3.--klm.r.3.l.5.—lip.—lyc.l.VI⁴.—pi-m.—sab.l.VI³.—stn.l.V¹.βeᵇ.—su-x.l.—trn.l.

—— *as if head would fall to right side.*—am-c.*r*.

O. OCCIPUT.—æth.VIII[4].—aur.βє. 3-30.—au-n.p.—ba-a.VII[5].— bel.V[1].—bis.V[1].35.—bov.af,ɡ. βє.δ.5.115.—ca-c.V[1].—cb-a.; T. *l*.βє.; C.V[1].83.(4).—F.ca-x.— car.i[a].6.(8).—chd.—clf.βa.— cle.I.βє.—cop.(12).—dul.—fer. 4.—hel.V[1].99.——ind.V[7].5.— k-ca.βє.; σ[2]ff.—C.k-hy.I.5.2.; 5. —kre.βa[u].i[a].—la-v.V[7].—lyc.; I. 35.—mg-m.—F.man.βє.—mez.— mu-x.V[6].VI[3].βa.δ๐.σ[2]ii.4.—myr. ζ.—na-m.V[1].; VIII[4].σ[2]ff.; V[1].ω[2]. 66.—nic.—nit.V[1].—F.*r*.nup.*r*. V[7].—pæo.V[1].3.5.—ph-x.V[10·zz] 29.(22).—plb.; VI[3].; V[1].δb.(18). —ptl.βє[a].—sab.(12).; σq.—sel. w.δ.єᴅ.—sep.3.—stn.V[3].—sul. V[1].σ[2].3-30.—tab.I.—trx.V[1].; 30.(29).—tar.aɡ,k.—thu.35.— til.—tri.I.

—— *as if full of lead.*—k-ca.σ.[2]ff. —lah.βa.3-99.—pet.—spo. 31.

—— *as if head would sink back- wards.*—k-ca.σ[2]ff.—mu-x. —opi.

—— *making it difficult to raise head.*—chd.2-99.

Ba. BASE OF BRAIN.—nup.

CONCOMITANTS.

aᾱ. *Apathy.*—ber.p.V[1].ηp.χ[1].3.

ab. *Laziness.*—gam.σ[1].φ.

ab[c]. *Disinclination to talk.*——thu. aᴜ.

ab[e]. *Disinclination for everything.* —bel.φ.

ab[o]. *Dislike for work.*—grn.ηaa.ρ.ω[2].

af. *Uneasiness.*— ank.ω[2].—O.bov. aɡ.βє.δ.5.115.

aɡ. *Anxiety.*—O.bov.af.βє.δ.5.115. —cof.βa.—O.tar.ak.

ak. *Sadness.*—F.hel.βє.V[1].31.—F. —src.βє.—O.tar.aɡ.

ao[h]. *Oversensitiveness to speaking.* —F.con.V[6].ap.

ap. *Intolerance of noise.*——F.con. V[6].ao[h].

aᴜ. *Ill-humour.*—F.æth.δb.63.; F. 19.—ba-c.βє.φ.ω[2].5.—bov.a[1]b[s]. VIII[4].ζ๐.16.100.—fer.βє[a]. — k-hy.66.—man.—sar.3.--thu. ɑb[c].

aᴞ[w]. *Gaiety.*—thr.p.βє.

a[1]b[b]. *Inability to collect thoughts.*— ca-c.δh[n],є.3.83.—hel.a[1]b[p].— pho.βa.I.3-30.

a[1]b[p]. *Loss of memory.*—ag-n.i[a].p.ηp. 4.—hel.a[1]b[b].—nx-m.βa.

a[1]b[s]. *Diminished intellectual power.* —F.bov.V[1].βє.; VIII[4].au.ζ๐. 16.100.—cot.—gel.βa.δ๐. — ipc.—til.βє.*r*ᴠ.ω[2].

a[1]c[b]. *Wandering mind.*—cn-i.

a[1]ᴅ. *Stupor.*—crt.—tab.I.βᴅ.

a[1]ᴅ[a]. *Loss of consciousness.*——cn-i. βє.

βa. *Vertigo.*—aco.3.; F.κ[4·5].29.— alm.I.4.—am-m.i[a].——F.bel. βᴅ.—bov.; w.18.—bry.; 29. 43.(24).—cam.—cn-i.βє.— cr-b.; F.3.—chi.— cof.aɡ.— F.cvl.—dgn.5.29.30.—gas. κ[5].—gel.a[1]b[s].δ๐.—hep. hy-x.—k-bi.3-30.29.(31).— lah.κ[5].—lau.βє.—mag.βᴅ. 18.; 3-30.(31).—mg-m.— mg-s.3-99.(30).—mer.6.βb. 8-31.—mur.—O.mu-x.V[6]. VI[3].δ๐.σ[2]ii.—naj.βє.—nat.βє. 112.—na-m.βє.3-99.—F.nic. 3.16.30.(8).; F.18.—nx-m. ɑb[p].—nx-v.βᴅ.3.—pæo.βє.— phl.—pho.a[1]b[p].I.3-30.; p.δL. ζ.—phy.πᴠq.5.—plm.— pru. —pul.16.29.31.—sec.—F.tea. βє.31.— til.V[1].δ๐.—ver.—zin. βє.

βb. *Staggering.*—cle.; p.μ[3·4].(8).— lah.ηaa.—mer.6.βa.8-31.— vp-t.ηaa.

βє. *Confusion.*—aga.; 3.—C.aml.— ana.3-30.—an-s.i[a].I.; F.φ.— ars.—aru.; F.3.—asa.V[1].φ.— asr.V[1].—O.aur.3-30.—ba-a. —ba-c.aᴜ.φ.ω[2].5.— F.bov.V[1]. a[1]b[a].; V[2].5.—c-ph.I.3-99.— can.V[1].δb.—cn-i.βa.—cth.— T.*l*.O.cb-a.--cr-s.—car.i[a].δLǁǁ.

28.29.; 66.(8-31).—ced.5.—
ch-s.βυ.ευ.—cmf.—cle.3-30.;
O.I.—coc.—ccs.—con.—dig.
p.—dio.—dro.—equ.5.--eup.
66.—gn-l.V¹.VII⁵.43.—gin.
—FC.hel.iᵃ.p.; F.29.31.; aᵏ.
V¹.31.—hur.ω².—hyo.—hyp.
iᵃ.—ign.—jat.--F.k-ca.3.; O.
—la-v.V¹.VI³.4.—lau.βa.; φ.
--mag.3-30.(35.116).--mg-m.
—FO.man.; p.(8).——mer.6.
16.19.; V⁷.——msc.V¹.δ.ζ.—
mur.—mu-x.δ.(12).——naj.βa.
—nat.βa.112.--na-m.βa.3-99.;
d.84.—ni-x.κ⁵.--F.nit.—nx-j.
5.(66).—oln.κ⁵.30.(16).--opi.
ρ.; ευ.—pæo.βa.—pet.p.3.—
pho.3.; F.6.29.(8.53).; iᵃ.
(41).—F.phy.—rho.; F.3-30.
--F.rs-r.δq.φ.—sbd.—src.;
F.aᵏ.—scr.--stn.5.—stp.—
sul.——su-x.3.---tab.βçᵃ.66.
(72).—tan.——F.tea.βa.31.—
thr.; p.aᵡʷ.—til.aᵇ.rv.ω².; 2.
—zin.βa.—F.zn-o.

βçᵃ. *Head stupid.*--F.cth.—cic.--F.
col.--crt.—dor.—fer.au.; V¹.;
F.—hel.--F.hep.—ind.5.26.
—k-hy.--lau.p.(98).—mg-m.
5.—mez.——mo-a.24.---na-a.
κ⁵.; C.26.29.—nic.iᵃ.V².29.--
nit.3.—F.nx-v.24.29.—opi.d.
ηp,hh.σ².φ.—plb.18.—O.ptl.
—pul.——sar.——so-n.——sul.
(31).—tab.βç.66.(72).

βçᵇ. *Empty feeling.*—P.l.stn.V¹.

βυ. *Intoxication.*—F.bel.βa.—ch-s.
βç.ευ.--lil.ζ².8.—mag.βa.18.—
nx-m.—nx-v.βa.3.—tab.I.a¹υ.

δaᶜ. *Dull eyes.*—irs.I.—cot.δb.λ².

ᵋaᶜ. *Eyes dejected.*—cn-i.

δhⁿ. *Lids gummed together.*——ca-c.
a¹bᵇ.δç.3.83.

δq. *Weight in eyes.*—FC.jac.ζ³.3.
—F.rs-r.βç.φ.

δff. *Stiffness of eyes.*--F.hel.p.δ.σb.
3-31.

δiiᵈ. *Eyes feel too large.*—F.lau.

δ. *Pain in eyes.*——ail.(12).——F.
bel.3-99.——F.ber.29.——F.l.
bov.V¹.δo.3.35.; VI⁴.29.—F.

com.—ctn.βç.--F.hel.p.δff.σb.
3.31.—hur.35.—msc.βç.V¹.ζ.
—mu-x.βç.(12).--nat.66.—
rhs.48.—O.sel.w.ευ.

δ. *As if eyes were drawn backwards.*——O.bov.aᶠ,ɡ.βç.δb.5.
115.

δb. *Closure of lids.*——F.æth.au.63.
—O.bov.aᶠ,ɡ.βç.δb.5.115.—
bry.III³.VI³.—can.V¹.βç. —
cot.δaᶜ.λ².—O.plb.V¹.(18).

δç. *Lachrymation.*——ca-c.a¹bᵇ.δhⁿ.
3.83.--cb-à.δo.3.--F.trn.δb.—
FT.l.tax.89.

δb. *Difficulty of raising eyes.*—F.
ton.

δb. *Difficulty of opening eyes.*—F.
all.—C.ptv.δLq.——F.trn.δç.;
p.κ⁹.3-99.

δo. *Dim vision.*—F.l.bov.V¹.δ.3.35.
—cb-a.δç.3.——cot.—gel.a¹bˢ.
βa.— F.k-bi.5.31.—lau.V¹·ᵘ.
--O.mu-x.V¹.VI³.βa.σ².--pho.
—til.V¹.βa.

—— *figures and letters look
blurred.*—ail.

δoᵈ. *Dazzling of eyes.*—cep.iᵃ.

δᵍ. *Photophobia.*—pul.

δLq. *Heaviness in eyelids.*——F.buf.
—C.ptv.δb.—plm.

δLii. *Swollen lids.*—hyo.

δLll. *Quivering of lids.*—car.iᵃ.βç.28.
29.

δL. *Pain in eyelids.*—pho.p.βa.ζ.

ᵋa. *Deafness.*—T.bel.V¹.

ευ. *Noise in ears.*——ars.6.(8).;
3-30.—ch-s.βç,υ.——ibe.κ⁵. —
mur.—opi.βç.—rhs.iᵃ.VI³.—
O.sel.w.δ.

ζo. *Stuffed nose.*—bov.VIII⁴.au.
a¹bᵃ.16.100.

ζ. *Pain in nose.*—msc.βç.V¹.δ.—
O.myr.—pho.p.βa.δL.

ζ². *Epistaxis.*—hur.30.—lil.υ.8.

ζ³. *Coryza.*—FC.jac.δq.3.

ηcᵇ. *Pale face.*—alm.ω².

ηp. *Heat of face.*——ag-n.iᵃ.p.a¹bᵖ.
4.—ber.p.V¹.aà.χ¹.3.—cof.—
opi.d.βçᵃ.ηhh.σ².φ.—rhs.29.—
trx.ηaa.

ηaa. *Red face.*—ast.p.VIII⁴.—grn.

$ab^\circ.\rho.\omega^2$. —-lah.βb.—trx.ηp.— vp-t.βb.

ηhh. *Sweat on face.*——opi.d.βe^a.ηp. $\sigma^2.\phi$.

θj. *Dry lips.*——F.rhs.p.VII^2.κ^3.6. 100.(5.16).

θ^2. *Ptyalism.*—fl-x.V$^{1.s}$.——pho.π. ωq.5.

θ^2. *Bloody saliva.*—mag.16.100.

θ^3. *Tongue feels burnt.*—phy.

ιj. *Dryness of fauces.*—F.naj.

κ. *Insipid taste.*—nat.V^1.2.99.

κ^3. *Thirst.*——F.rhs.p.VII^2.θj.6. 100.(5.16).

κ^4. *Pain in stomach.*—C.ir-f.

κ^4. *Weak feeling in pit of stomach.* aco.βa.κ^5.29.—F.tru.κ^5.2.

κ^5. *Nausea.*-aco.βa.κ^4.29.-F.fl-x. 35.—gas.βa.—grt.ϕ.66.—ibe. eb.—lah.βa.——mag.ω^9.—na-a. βe^a.5.—ni-x.βe.—oln.βe.30. (16).—trn.κ^4.2.

κ^9. *Pyrosis.*—trn.p.δb.3-99.

λ. *Soreness over bowels.*—mr-i.

λ^2. *Flatulent distension of abdomen.*—cot.δa^c.

μ^3. *Call to stool.*——cle.p.βb.μ^4p. (8).

μ^4p. *Heat in rectum.*——cle.p.βb.μ^3. (8).

πq. *Weight in chest.*——cle.π^1.30.— phy.βa.vq.5.

π. *Tightness of chest.*—pho.θ^2.ωq. 5.128.

π^1. *Deep breathing.*—cle.πq.30.

ρ. *Quick pulse.*—grn.ab°.ηaa.ω^2.

ρ. *Quick weak pulse.*—opi.βe.

σ. *Weariness in back.*—lo-i.

σq. *Weight in back.*—O.sab.

σ. *Pain in back.*—gam.ab.ϕ.

σ^1. *Pain in loins.*—gam.ab.ϕ.

σ^2. *Weakness of muscles of nape.* —fag.V^7.5.—so-l.—vi-o.

σ^2ff. *Stiff neck.*—O.k-ca.—sar.26.

σ^2ff. *Stiffness of nape.*——O.na-m. VIII^4.

σ^2ii. *Swollen and painful gland in nape.*— O.mu-x.V^6.VI^3.βa.δo. 4.

σ^2. *Weakness of cervical muscles.* —lyp.

σ^2. *Pressure on nape.*—-agn.—-O. sul.V^1.3-30.

σ^2. *Feeling of a ligature round neck.*—opi.d.βe^a.ηp,hh.ϕ.

τ. *Pain in shoulder.*—cup.

τ^1b. *Cold fingers.*—hel.p.χ^1.(101).

υ. *Weariness of legs.*—cb-a.2.

υq. *Heaviness of legs.*—phy.βa. πq.5.

$\tau^1\upsilon^1$b. *Cold hands and feet.*—ba-c. 3-99.p.30.

$\tau\upsilon$q. *Heaviness of limbs.*—kis.

$\tau\upsilon$. *Bruised feeling and trembling of limbs.*—til.a^1b^s.βe.ω^2.

ϕ. *Sleepiness.*——F.an-s.βe.— apo. I.—asa.βe.V^1.—ba-c.au.βe.ω^2. 5.—bel.ab^e.——cca.I.3.—gam. ab.σ^1.—grt.κ^5.66.——P^c.hdr.— ipc.—lau.βe.-opi.d.βe^a.ηp,hh. σ^2.—pim.43.—F.rs-r.βe.δq.

χ. *Fever.*—trn.

χ^1. *Coldness.*—bel.p.V^1.aa.ηp.3.— hel.p.τ^1b.(101).

χ^1. *Rigor.*—T.ni-x.

χ^2. *Heat.*—F.am-m.χ^3.—pho.66.

χ^3. *Perspiration.*——F.am-m.χ^2.— pho.V^7.

——— *on the forehead.*—glo.

ω. *Discomfort of the body.*—sto.

ωq. *Heaviness in upper part of body.*—pho.θ^2.π.5.

ω^2. *Weakness.*—alm.ηc^b.—ank.af. —ba-c.au.βe.ϕ.5.——chi.3-99. ——grn.ab°.ηaa.ρ.——hur.βe.— hyp.3.—jat.V^1.—O.na-m.V^1. 66.—til.a^1b^s.βe.$\tau\upsilon$. ; i^a.

ω^9. *Yawning.*—mag.κ^5.

CONDITIONS.

1. *All day.*—F.au-n.—dgn.——F. lth.

2. *At night.*—cb-a.υ.——dir.i^a.—- CO.k-hy.I.5.——lil.——F.trn. $\kappa^{4.5}$.—til.βe.

2-99. *On waking at night.*——O.chd. —nat.V^1.κ.

3. *In the morning.*—aco.βa.—aga. βe.—alm.p.—ars.V^1.— F.aru. βe.——ber.p.V^1.aa.ηp.χ^1.— F.l. bov.V^1.δ.δo.35.--bry.III^3.VI^3. δb.--ca-c.a^1b^b.δh^n,e.83.—cln.

—cb-a.δε,ο.—F.cr-b.βa.—cca.
I.φ.—com.—dir.iᵃ.—-equ.—
epu.βε.— hed.βε.—-F.hel.p.δ.
σb.31.——F.hdr.7.(8-31).--—
hyp.ω².——FC.jac.δq.ζ³.——F.
k-ca.βε.——P.k-hy.; I.(30).
——P.r.klm.l.5.——lah.—
mg-m.— man.I.5.——na-m.—
nit.βεᵃ.—T.nup.—nx-v.; βa,
ɒ.—FC.ox-x.—O.pæo.V¹.5.
——pet.p.βε.; iᵃ.p.29 **30**ᵇ.——
pho.βε.—F.plb.66.—pl-n.(4).
--sar.au.; Tᵇ.—O.sep.--su-x.
βε.

3-30. *In morning on rising.*——am-m.
—ans.βε.—F.ang.—ars.εɒ.—
O.aur.βε.——cas.—cle.βε.——
bpm.—bur.--k-bi.βa.29.(31).
——Fᵇ.k-hy.; *k-hy.*I.——mag.
βa.(31).—*mg-s.*βa.3-99.—*nic.*
3.16; F.nic.3.16.(8).——pho.
a¹bᵇ.βa.——F.rho.βε.—-sep.—
sto.II⁷.VI³·⁴.—O.sul.V.σ².—
ton.99.; VIII⁴.

3-99. *In morning on waking.*--ba-c.p.
r¹v¹b.30.——F.bel.δ.——ca-c.p.
26.30.—c-ph.I.βε.—chi.ω².—
cro.V¹.—ctn.βε.—-fer.——O.
lah.βa.--lil.iᵃ.--mg-s.βa.(3-30).
—na-m.βa,ε.—ni-x.——F.so-t.
--C.squ.--trn.p.ɔ̀ɓ.κ⁹.--ton.30.

4. *In the afternoon.*—alm.βε.I.—
F.am-c.I.——ag-n.iᵃ.p.a¹bᵖ.ηp
——buf.—-Tᵇ.O.cb-a.V¹.83.—
cεp.p.—erd.--O.fer.--F.gam.
V¹.(8).—gel.—hyp.—F.jan.
—F.k-hy.—la-v.βε.V¹.VI³.—
F.mg-m.—nx-j.V¹.66.—*pl-n.*
3.

5. *In the evening.*—amb.V¹.—P.
ag-n.iᵃ.V¹.——F.ars.VIII⁴.—
ba-c.au.βε.φ.ω².——O.bov.af,g.
βε.δb.115.; V².—ced.βε.—C.
ch-s.—dgn.βa.29.30.—crd.—
O.fer.——F.fl-x.V⁷.29.—-CO.
k-hy.I.2.; O.—Pᵈ.klm.r.3.—
man.I.3.--na-a.βεᵃ.κ⁵.--O.pæo.
V¹.3.—pho.θ².π.ωq.--F.rhs.p.
VII².θj.κ³.6.100.(16).—rum.
—sep.I.16.—C.so-t.—stn.20.
35.; βε.—F.zin.83.

5. *In the forenoon.*——ch-s.(102).
—equ.ω².—fag.σ².I.—F.gam.
VIII⁴.——hel.d.V¹.VII⁵·ˢ.(8).
—ind.βεᵃ.20.; O.V⁷.—lah.—
mg-m.βεˢ.——nup.——nx-j.βε.
(66).—phy.βa.πυq.—-sab.—
spg.

6. *In the room.*——ars.εɒ.(8).—O.
car.iᵃ.(8).—C.lau.V¹·ᵘ.29.31.
——mer.βa,b.8-31.; βε.16.19.
——F.pho.βε.29.(8.**53**).——F.
rhs.p.VII².θj.κ³.100.(5.16).

7. *In a warm room.*——F.hdr.3.
(8-31).

8. *In the open air.*——ars.εɒ.6.—O.
car.iᵃ.6.——cle.p.βb.μ³·⁴.——F.
*gam.*V¹.4.—*hel.*d.V¹.VII⁵·ˢ.5.
—F.lau.—lil.d.ζ².—*man.*p.βε.
——F.*nic.*βa.3.16.30.——F.*pho.*
βε.6.29.(**53**).

8-31. *On walking in open air.*—car
βε.66.—F.*hdr.*iᵃ.3.7.

11. *By touch.*—T.aga.

12. *By pressure.*—ail.δ.—O.cop.—
mu-x.βε.δ.——na-a.βεᵃ.——O.sab.

14. *By supporting head.*—stp.

16. *By lying.*——Pᵈ.am-c.——bov.
VIII⁴.au.a¹ɒ.ζo.100.--mag.ƀ².
100.; F.--mer.βε.6.19.--nic.3.
(30).; F.βa.3.30.(8).--nx-m.
—oln.βε.κ⁵.30.—pul.βa.29.31.
-F.*rhs.*p.VII².θj.κ³.6.100.(5).
—sep.I.5.—sul.19.29.35.

17. *By lying on the side.*——men.
V¹.VI³.

18. *By standing.*—C.alm.29.—ars.
19.—-bov.w.βa.—-k-ca.w.V¹.
—mag.βa,ɒ.—F.nic.βa.—plb.
βεᵃ.; O.V¹.δ.

19. *When sitting.*——F.æth.au.——
alm.29.— ars.18.—F.au-n.—
chi.—-cic.—-mer.βɒ.6.16.—-
squ.—sul.16.29.35.

20. *When at rest.*—stn.5.35.

22. *By bending back head.*——*fag.*
p.—O.*ph-x.*V¹⁰·ˣˣ.29.

24. *By raising head.*—bry.βa.29.
43.——dro.(29).——ign.d.VI³.
(29).—mo-a.βεᵃ.— so-t.29.—
spo.

26. *By moving head.*—asr.w.——

T

ca-c.p.3-99.30.—ind.βe^{a}.**5**.–C. na-a.βe^{a}.29.—sar.σ^{2}ff.—spi.I.

28. *By turning.*——car.i^{a}.βa.δLll. 29.

29. *By stooping.*—F.aco.βa.$\kappa^{4\cdot5}$.— alm.19. ; C.18.——F.ber.δ.——bov.VI^{4}.δr.——bry.βa.43.(24). ——ca-a.VIII^{3}.(30).——cam. —F.cb-a.βa.30.—ca-x.—car. i^{a}.βe.δLll.28.——F.com.101.— O.con.(30).—dgn.βa.5.30.— dro.24.—F.fl-x.V^{7}.5.—F.hel. βe.31.——F.hyo.——ign.d.VI^{3}. 24.——C.ind.—k-bi.βa.3-30. (31).—k-hy.—F.lau.V^{7}. ; C. (30). ; (30).; C.V$^{1\cdot u}$.6-31.— C.na-a.βe^{a}.26.——nic.i^{a}.V^{2} βe^{a}. ——F.nx-v.βe^{a}.24.—F.ptv.— pet.i^{a}.p.3.**30**^{b}.--O.ph-x.V$^{10\cdot zz}$. (22).——F.pho.βe.6.(8.**53**).— pul. ; βa.16.31.—rhs.i^{a}. ; ηp. —sun.—so-t.24.——spo.i^{a}.— sul.16.19.35.——tab.——O.trx. 30.—vi-t.30.

30. *By rising.*—ca-a.VIII^{3}.29.—— ca-c.p.3-99.26.— cle.πp.π^{1}.— O.con.29.--dgn.βa.5.29.--hur. ζ^{2}.—-iof.——C.lau.29. ; 29. ; V$^{1\cdot u}$.δo.—oln.βe.κ^{5}.(16).—O. trx.(**29**).—vi-t.(29).

30. *On rising from stooping.*—grt. —F.mg-s.p.—ton. ; F.

30^{b}. *By sewing.*—pet.i^{a}.p.3.29.

31. *By walking.*——bu-s.——F.dgn. i^{a}.p.—F.hel.βe.29. ; F.p.δ.σb. 3. ; F.alk.βe.V^{1}.——C.hpm.—— k-bi.βa.29.3-30. ; F.k-bi.δo.5. ——C.lau.V$^{1\cdot u}$.6.29.——mag.βa. 3-30.—ptv.—pul.βa.16.29.— rhe.VI^{4}.——C.rhs.——O.spo.— sul.βe^{a}.—F.tea.βa,e.

33. *On going up stairs.*—rs-v.ii.

35. *By motion.*—F.bis.V^{1}. ; O.V^{1}. .—F^{b}.bov.V^{1}.γ.δ.δo.3.—cth.V^{1}. —F.fl-x.κ^{5}.—-O.lyc.I.—mag. βe.3-30.(116).—-stn.5.20.—- sul. ; 16.19.29.—O.thu.

41. *By mental exertion.*—pho.i^{a}.βe.

42. *By thinking.*—na-m.86.

43. *By reading.*——bry.βa.29.(24). —F.ca-c.44.—ctn.i^{a}.—pim.ϕ.

44. *By writing.*—F.ca-c.43.—-gn-l. V^{1}.VII^{5}.βe.

46. *By opening eyes.*—F.ptv.p.

48. *By moving eyes.*—chi.p.VIII^{3}. —rhs.δ.

53. *By wrinkling forehead.*——F. pho.βe.6.29.(8).

55. *By epistaxis.*—dig.

63. *When eating.*—F.æth.au.δ.

66. *By eating.*—F.am-c.VIII^{4}.—— car.βe.(8-31).—C.cas.VI^{4}.— eup.βe.— grt.κ^{5}.ϕ.——k-by.au. — FC.mag.VI^{4}.—nat.δ.—O. na-m.V^{1}.ω^{2}.—nx-j.βe.**5**. ; nx-j. V^{1}.(4).—opi.--F.plb.3.—tab. βe,e^{a}.(72).

66. *On taking soup.*—pho.χ^{2}.

72. *By vomiting.*—tab.βe,e^{a}.66.

78. *By copious urination.*—gel.; i^{a}.

83. *During menses.*—all.84.—ca-c. $a^{1}b^{b}$.δh^{n},e.——T^{b}O.cb-a.V^{1}.(4). —mag.p.I.—mg-s.p.—F.zin. 5.

84. *After menses.*——all.(83).—— na-m.d.βe.

86. *By speaking.*—na-m.42.—wis.

89. *By coughing.*—FT^{b}.tax.δ.

98. *By sleep.*—lau.p.βe^{a}.

99. *On awaking.*—O.hel.V^{1}.

100. *After a siesta.*—bov.VIII^{4}.au. $a^{1}b^{b}$.ζo.16.——mag.θ^{2}.16.——F. rhs.p.VII^{2}.θj.κ^{3}.6.(5.16).

101. *By heat.*-—F.com.29.——hel.p. r^{1}b.χ^{1}.

102. *By cold.*—ch-s.**5**.

112. *By exposure to sun.*—F.bro.I. (114).—nat.βa.e.

114. *In the dark.*—F.bro.I.112.

115. *By candlelight.*——O.bov.af,g. βe.δb.5.

116. *By washing.*——mag.βe.3-30. (35).

128. *When riding.*—phy.θ^{3}.

r^{a}. **Rigor, or horripilation.**—aga. —O.alm.III^{2}.29.—am-c.g^{b}.H.$\mathfrak{b}$.6. ——O.ber.βa.F.V^{1}.σr.ω^{2}.29.——P^{d}. ped.H$\mathfrak{b}$.3.

—— *followed by intoxicated feel- ing, nausea, and uneasiness in occiput.*—O.rs-r.

ANATOMICAL SEAT.

P. PARIETAL REGION.—ped.H.ƀ.3.
O. OCCIPUT.—alm.III².29.—ber.βa.
F.V¹.σr.ω³.29.

CONCOMITANTS.

σr. *Rigor in back.*-—O.ber.βa.F.V¹.
ω³.29.
ω³. *Swooning.*—O.ber.βa.F.V¹.σr.29.

CONDITIONS.

3. *In the morning.*—Pᵈ.ped.Hƀ.
6. *In the room.*—am-c.gᵇ.Hƀ.
29. *On stooping.*-—O.alm.III².—O.
ber.βa.F.V¹.σr.ω³.

w. **Movements of head** (*objective*).
wᵃ. **Unsteadiness.**—— cleʰ.p.βb,ᵗᵃ.δo.
εp.ηp.3.—rs-r.
wᵇ. **Shaking, nodding, wagging,
moving, or swaying.**——ars.——
au-m.——au-s.-—bel. ; a¹ᴅᵃ.θ.——
bry.κ⁵.——cn-i.-——cau.44.——epn.
31.——lyc.βa.——nx-m.βf.-—sep.βℓ.
σ²ff.—trn.r¹ᵥ¹w.
—— *feeling of.*—hel.
1.—— *backwards and forwards.*——
aur.—cha.—lam.—lyc.
2.—— *hither and thither.*——ars.-—
opi.—str.κ³.3. ; κ⁸.
3.—— *sideways.*——aur.—-bel.θ².r¹.
—cle.p.q.βa,ƀ.6.(8).—lyc.
4.—— *forwards.*—na-m.
wᶜ. **Convulsive movements.**-——cam.
coc.—-str.rf. ; φ. ; δf.θ¹.——trn.αu.
r¹w.
wᵈ. **Jerking or twitching.**——cic.σ².
rllᵃ.—str.16.
1.—— *forwards.*—sep.3.
2.—— *backwards.*——alm.aƀ.rllᵃ.——
bov.q.βa.18.—eth.
3.—— *to left side.*—k-ca.σff.
wᵉ. **Falling.**
1.—— *hither and thither.*—bel.-—
phl.βa.δƀ.31.
2.—— *forwards.*—elp.— hpm.q.30.
—par.q.—pau.βa.
3.—— *backwards.*—cam.q.βa.-—cch.
—dio.V¹⁰·ᶻ.—k-ca.q.σff.-—
opi.q.—spi.βa.

*Falling backwards, as if anterior
muscles of neck were paralysed.*——dig.19.31.
4.—— *to left side.*—nx-m.φ.
5.—— *to both sides.*——str.aĺᵍ.r.——
trx.βa,ƀ.8-31.
6.—— *to one side.*—eth.
wᶠ. **Raising up.**
—— *from pillow.*—str.
wᵍ. **Alternate raising and sinking.**
—— *as if drunk.*—bel.
wʰ. **Hanging forwards.**--cleᵃ.p.βb,ᵗᵃ.
δo.ep.ηp.3.—cl-h.—ign.
wⁱ. **Drawing.**
1.—— *forwards.*—hy-x.
——, *feeling of.*—san.
2.—— *backwards.*—aco.—cn-i.βa.-—
ced.V¹.VII¹.——cer.—cic.
—cch.—cup.—dgn.--k-cy.
-——lab.—mor.—-mu-x.
ni-x.VI³.3.63.—phl.VI³.—
str.—-ton.VI³.VII⁵.
3.—— *sideways.*—ca-a.*l.*βa.20.35.--
cam.—cup.—sil.q.VI³·⁴.
4.—— *first right then left.*—ang.
wʲ. **Turning sidewards.**
—— *to either side.*—cch.—hpmᵐ.
—mer.—ori.p.—str.
—— *to left side.*—lyc.—trnᵏ.αu.
wᵏ. **Rubbing head against something.**—trnʲ.αu.
wˡ. **Boring head in pillow.**—bel.2.
—str.
wᵐ. **Difficulty of moving head.**—
er-a.—gur.—hpmʲ.2.
wⁿ. **Trembling.**—bel.rᵥkk.—cit.—
mer.—tab.43.
wᵒ. **Inclination to throw head back.**
—glo.
wᵖ. **Inability to hold up head.**—
con.—gel.—glo.q.—str.

CONCOMITANTS.

aƀ. *Fear.*—almᵈ·².rllᵃ.
aˡq. *Cries.*—strᵉ·⁵.r.
αu. *Choler.*—trnᶜ.r¹w. ; ʲ·ᵏ.
a¹ᴅᵃ. *Loss of senses.*—belᵇ.θ.
βa. *Vertigo.*-—bovᵈ·².q.18.—ca-aⁱ·³.
20.35.—camᵉ·³.q.— cn-i¹·².-—
cleᵇ·³.p.q.βƀ.6.(8).-—lycᵇ.——

pau$^{e.2}$. —phl$^{e.1}$.$\delta\mathfrak{h}$.31.—spi$^{e.3}$.
—trx$^{e.5}$.$\beta\mathfrak{d}$.8-31.

$\beta\mathfrak{b}$. *Staggering.*——cle$^{b.3}$.p.q.βa.6.
(8).; $^{a.h.}$p.$\beta\epsilon^{a}$.$\delta\mathfrak{o}$.ϵp.ηp.3.

$\beta\mathfrak{d}$. *Intoxicated.*—trx$^{e.5}$.βa.8-31.

$\beta\epsilon$. *Confusion of head.*—sep^{b}.σ^{3}ff.

$\beta\epsilon^{a}$. *Stupid head.*—cle$^{a.h}$.p.$\beta\mathfrak{b}$.$\delta\mathfrak{o}$.ϵp. ηp.3.

βf. *Head feels large.*—nx-m.

δf. *Convulsive movements of eyes.* —str^{c}.θ^{1}.

$\delta\mathfrak{h}$. *Difficulty of opening eyes.*—— phl$^{e.1}$.βa.31.

$\delta\mathfrak{o}$. *Dimness of vision.*—cle$^{a.h}$.p.βb, ϵ^{a}.ϵp.ηp.3.

ϵp. *Hot ears.*—cle$^{a.h}$.p.βb,ϵ^{a}.$\delta\mathfrak{o}$.ηp. 3.

ηp. *Hot face.*—cle$^{a.h}$.p.βb,ϵ^{a}.$\delta\mathfrak{o}$.ϵp. 3.

θ. *Foam before mouth.*—bel^{b}.$a^{1}\mathfrak{v}^{a}$.

θ^{1}. *Grinding of teeth.*—str^{c}.δf.

θ^{2}. *Viscid saliva hangs down from mouth.*—bel$^{b.3}$.τ^{1}.

κ^{3}. *Thirst.*—str$^{b.2}$.3.

κ^{5}. *Nausea.*—bry^{b}.

κ^{8}. *Hiccough.*—str$^{b.2}$.

υ^{2}. *Inability to pronounce words distinctly.*—cic^{d}.rll^{a}.

σff. *Stiffness of muscles of nape and back.*—k-ca$^{e.3}$.q.; $^{d.3}$.

σ^{2}ff. *Tension of muscles of neck.*—— sep^{b}.$\beta\epsilon$.

τ. *Raising of arms over head.*—— str$^{e.5}$.al^{q}.

τf. *Convulsive movements of arms.* —str^{c}.

τll^{a}. *Jerking of arm.*—alm$^{d.2}$.$a\mathfrak{h}$.— cic^{d}.υ^{2}.

τ^{1}. *Clapping of hands.*—bel$^{b.3}$.θ^{2}.

τ^{1}w. *Movements of hands.*—trn^{c}.au.

$\tau^{1}\upsilon^{1}$w. *Movements of hands and feet.* trn^{b}.

$\tau\upsilon$kk. *Trembling of limbs.*—bel^{æ}.

ϕ. *Snoring.*—str^{c}.

φ. *Sleepiness.*—nx-m$^{e.4}$.

CONDITIONS.

2. *At night.*—bel$^{i.1}$.
3. *In the morning.*—cle$^{a.h}$.p.$\beta\mathfrak{b}$,ϵ^{a}. $\delta\mathfrak{o}$.ϵp.ηp.——ni-x$^{i.2}$.VI^{3}.63.— sep$^{d.1}$.—str$^{b.2}$.κ^{3}.

6. *In a room.*—cle$^{b.3}$.βa,$\mathfrak{b}$.(8).
8. *In open air.*—cle$^{b.3}$.βa,$\mathfrak{b}$.6.
8-31. *When walking in open air.*—— trx$^{e.5}$.βa,$\mathfrak{v}$.
16. *When lying.*—str^{d}.
18. *When standing.*—bov$^{d.2}$.q.βa.
19. *When sitting.*—dig$^{e.3}$.31.
20. *When at rest.*—ca-a$^{i.3}$.βa.35.
30. *On rising up.*—hpm$^{e.2}$.q.
31. *When walking.*——dig$^{e.3}$.19.—— epn^{b}.—phl$^{e.1}$.βa.$\delta\mathfrak{h}$.
35. *When moving.*—ca-a$^{i.3}$.βa.20.
43. *When reading.*—tab^{æ}.
44. *When writing.*—cau^{b}.
63. *When eating.*—ni-x$^{i.3}$.VI^{3}.3.

w. Motion in the brain (*subjective*).

w^{n}. **Looseness.**—aco.35.64.86.--alo^{v}. V^{1}.VIII^{4}.8-31.(66).--am-c.—asr^{v}. q.22.--ba-a.V^{3}.3-30.26.(4).—ba-c^{v}. 26.—cb-a.35.——cau^{v}.8-31.——cic^{v}. 3-99.31.(42).——P.cly$^{w.ee}$.II^{3}.31. 128.—-con.26.—-gen.dd.—-glo.o. II^{5}.26.—grp.—gui.3.31.--F.k-ca^{y}. —C.kal.I.28.—la-v.V^{1}.7.——mg-s. ——mez^{ee}.26.——mu-x.**35**.——F.naj. p.—F^{b}.na-m.VI^{3}.; T.VI^{3}.26.; $^{ee.}$ 4.5.33.—na-s^{bb}.**5**.29.—nic$^{bb.3}$.; F. $^{bb.}$—nit.VI^{3}.—rhs^{ee}.26.—stn^{ee}.26. ——stp^{bb}.III.20.35.——F.su-x$^{bb.1}$.; F$^{a.}$$^{ee.}$I.26.

w^{o}. **Motion.**——FC.bry.a^{1}b^{s}.βa.—glo. 26.—k-ca.26.—lah.26.—mg-s.35. —msc.V^{1}.VII^{5}.—F.phl.—rhe.29. —rhs.31.—sep.26.—so-n.26.

—— *as if something moved from back of neck up to head.*— glo.

—— *as if driving in a coach with eyes shut.*—cyc.14.βa.18.

w^{p}. **Vibration.**--ind.p.6.30.(8).--T^{a}. k-ca^{s}.——lyc.31.——mag.35.; F^{b}. 31.35.—nx-v^{v}.31.—sil.32.—T.sto. 5.—O.sul.I.4.31.—vrb.31.—zin. 86.

—— *as of a steel spring.*—grt.$\delta\mathfrak{o}$. ea.3.19.

w^{q}. **Undulation.**—chi^{ee}.VII^{1}.—glo. 28.—grp.q.χ^{3}.; III.4.—ind^{s}.v.$\delta\mathfrak{o}$.

5.—mg-m.p.$\chi^{2\cdot3}$.4.5.83.; V^1.6.(8). FC.a^1b^b,ʊ.18.35.—F.mer.VIII^4.— mil.29.(30).—par.VIII^4.33.—F. pet.VII^1.(35).; ^{ii}d.eʊ.—sel.q.δ.εʊ. —sul.βε.5.

—— *synchronous with pulse.*—— alm.29.66.(30).

—— *as from throbbing of arteries.* —hyo.V^1.29.

—— *as if there was water in it.*— bel.q.

—— *like beating of waves.*—F.cin. V^1.

—— *wave-like upward motion.*—— glo.

—— *from occiput to sinciput.*—— snc.βa.

w^r. **Splashing.**—F.asa^s.——bel.—P^d. cb-a.31.—hep.——hyo^v.31.—nx-v^s. 31.—rhs.—so-t.—spi.31.; F.^{v}.26. —squ.26.

w^s. **Bubbling or ebullition.**—F.asa^r. .—T.bry.—eu-a.4.——ind^q.v.δo.5.; ^{p}.p.6.30.(8).; O.p.—O^b.jun.V^1.— T^a.k-ca^p.——nx-v^r.31.——par.af^d.ϕ^1. 2-99.——pul.z.2.——O.spi.16.31.35. (19.22).

w^t. **Wavering.**—na-a.28.—nx-v.

w^u. **Quivering.**—can.κ^4.πll^b.—la-v^v. 89.

w^v. **Shaking.**—alo^n.V^1.VIII^4.8-31. (66).—asr^n.q.22.——ba-c^n.26.; 32. —ca-c.VI^4.35.; O^b.26.31.—cic^n. 3-99.31.(42).—coc.26.31.86.—C^b. crt^w.31.33.; χ^1.—O.elc.33.—glo. 26.—hyo^r.31.—k-ca.I.—la-v^u.89.; VIII^4.5.20.——led.32.—lyc.31.—— mt-n.51.—mg-s.31.66.—man.26.; V^1.κ^4.35.——mez.I.4.26.—nup.V^2. 31.—nx-m^{ee}.26.—nx-v^p.31.—pho. V^1.30.99.——sep.32.—F.spir.26.; V^1.δr.3.16.28.74.—tab.3.35.—vi-t. q.V^1.βε.31.

—— *from all sides.*—rho.31.

—— *like an echo in the head.*—— ca-a.31.

w^w. **Swinging about.**—aco.βa.—bel. V^6.VII^3.—F.bry.V^1.64.——O.ca-x. .—P.cly$^{n\cdot ee}$.II^3.31.128.——C^b.crt^v. 31.33.—la-v.βa.δb.26.—lyc.VII^1. 30.31.33.

w^x. **Rolling about.**-c-ar.βa^t.43.(8-31. 86).—eug.II^1.δε.5.72.—F.bur.

w^y. **Turning or twisting about.**— ind.i^a.—F.k-ca^n.— pet$^{aa\cdot hh}$.ab^o.— rhs.8-31.—sil$^{aa\cdot hh}$.

w^z. **Jumping about.**—lep.—so-t.29.

w^{aa}. **Whirling.**— c-ar.41.——pet$^{y\cdot hh}$. ab^o.—C.sbd.V^1.—sil$^{y\cdot hh}$.

w^{bb}. **Falling.**-—F.nic^n.—stp^n.III.20. 35.

1.—— *Hither and thither.*—cro.26. —sil.βa.19.(16).—F.su-x^n.

2.—— *Forwards.*—alm^p.29.66.(30). —F.ber.q.29.—F.cb-a.q.29. βa,c.30.-——F.cha.VI^4.16.28. 30.—cof.V^1.29.—dig.22.— gur.—k-ca.29.— P^d.lau.q.8. 29.(30).—F.mg-s^v.I.29.89. —nx-v.29.——rhs.i^a.q.29.— su-x.q.—O.tar.29.

3.—— *From side to side.*—nic^n.— tep.a^1b^p.26.

—— *to the left temple.*—— na-s^n.5.29.

—— *to the side to which it is moved.*—-am-c.VII. ϕ^1.26.

w^{cc}. **Rising and sinking.**—F.bel.I. 31.(12).—cob.31.

w^{dd}. **Crawling as of a worm.**—alm. V^8.VI^1.

w^{ee}. **As if brain knocked against skull.**— ars.35.——chi^q.VII^1.——P. cly$^{n\cdot w}$.II^3.31.128.——dph.I.——glo. 26.—hy-x.I.29.—lau.I.2.——mez^n. 26.—nx-m^v.26.——rhs^n.26.——stn^n. 26.—-sul.26.; V^1.26.—F^a.su-x^n. I.26.

—— *against forehead.*—-na-m^v.4. 5.33.

—— *like a ball striking against skull.*—pla.χ^2.5.8.31.

w^{ff}. **Surging up.**—O.cn-i.

—— *up from neck.*—cn-i.

w^{gg}. **Oscillation.**—chp.

—— *balancing.*—bel.VIII^1.31.33.

—— *pendulum-like.*—cn-i.

w^{hh}. **As if something alive in head.** —crt.——hyp.v.2.16.——pet$^{y\cdot aa}$.ab^o. —sil.$^{y\cdot aa}$.

w^{ii}. **Trembling.**—ind.i^a.v.31.—pet^q. d.e𝔳.—P.pla.x.VI^3.

w^{jj}. **Like a foreign body moving about.**—pho.p.

w^{kk}. **As if a leaden ball rolled about.** —hfb.

w^{ll}. **Rotary movement in brain.**— c-ar.41.

ANATOMICAL SEAT.

F. FOREHEAD.—asa$^{r.s}$.—bel^{cc}.31. (12).—ber$^{bb.2}$.q.29.—bry^w.V^1. 64.; C.^{o}.a^{1}b^s.βa.—cb-a$^{bb.2}$.29.βa, ℓ.30.—cha$^{bb.2}$.VI^4.16.28.30.— cin^q.V^1.—-hur^x.—k-ca$^{n.y}$.— mag^p.ℓ.31.35.—mg s$^{v.bb.2}$.29.89. C.man^q.a^{1}b^b,𝔳.— mer.VIII^4.— naj^n.p.— na-m^n.ℓ.VI^3.—nic$^{n.bb}$. —pet^q.VII^1.(30).—phl^o.—spir$^{.v}$. 26.—su-x$^{n.bb.1}$.; r.$^{n.ee}$.I.26.

T. TEMPLES.—bry^s.—k-ca$^{p.s}$.r.— na-m^n.VI^3.26.—sto^p.5.

C. CROWN.—F.bry^o.a^{1}b^s.βa.—ca-x^w. —crt$^{v.w}$.ℓ.31.33.—kal^n.I.28.— sbd^{aa}.V^1.

P. PARIETES.—cb-a^r.ℓ.31.—cly$^{n.w.ee}$. II^3.31.128.—lau$^{bb.2}$.ℓ.8.29.(30). —pla^{ii}.x.VI^3.

O. OCCIPUT.—ca-c^v.r.26.31.—cn-i^{ff}. —elc^v.33.—ind^s.p.—jun^s.r.V^1. —spi^s.16.31.35.(19.22).—sul^p. 4.31.—tar$^{bb.2}$.29.

CONCOMITANTS.

a𝔟^o. *Disinclination for work.*— pet$^{y.aa.hh}$.

af^d. *Internal uneasiness.*—par^s.φ^1. 2-99.

a^{1}b^p. *Weak memory.*—tep$^{bb.3}$.26.

a^{1}b^s. *Loss of thought.*—FC.bry^o.βa.

a^{1}𝔳. *Stupefaction.*— FC.man^q.a^{1}b^b, 𝔳.18.35.

βa. *Vertigo.*—aco^w.—FC.bry^o. a^{1}b^s.— F.cb-a$^{bb.2}$.29.βℓ.30.— c-ar^x.43.(8-31.84).—cyc^o.14. 18.—snc^q.

βℓ. *Falling.*—F.cb-a$^{bb.2}$.29.βa.30.

βℓ. *Confusion.*—sul^q.5.—vi-t^v.q.V^1. 31.

δ. *Pain in eyeballs.*—sel^q.q.e𝔳.— spi^v.V^1.3.16.31.74.

δ𝔟. *Closing of eyes.*—la-v^w.26.

δℓ. *Lachrymation.*—eug^x.II^1.5.72.

δ𝔳. *Indistinct vision.*—grt^p.ea.3. 19.—ind$^{q.s}$.v.5.

ea. *Deafness.*—grt^p.δ𝔳.3.19.

e𝔳. *Noise in ears.*—pet^q ^{ii}.d.— sel^q.q.δ.

κ^{4}ll^b. *Quivering in stomach.*—can^u. π ll^b.

κ^4. *Pressure in epigastrium.*— man^v.V^1.35.; v.

π ll^b. *Quivering in chest.*—can^u.κ^{4}ll^b.

v. *Pain in legs.*—ind^{ii}.i^a.31.

φ^1. *Sleeplessness.*—am-c$^{bb.3}$.VI^3. 26.—par^s.af^d.2-99.

χ^1. *Rigor.*—crt^v.

χ^2. *Heat.*—mg-m^q.p.χ^3.4.5.83.— pla^{ee}.5.8.31.

χ^3. *Perspiration.*—grp^q.q.— mg-m^q.p.χ^2.4.5.83.

CONDITIONS.

2. *At night.*—hyp^{hh}.v.16.—pul^s.z.

2-99. *At night on waking.*—par^s.af^d. φ^1.

3. *In the morning.*—grt^p.δ𝔳.ea.19. —gui^n.31.—spi^v.V^1.16.28.74. —tab^v.35.

3-30. *On rising in morning.*—ba-a^n. V^3.26.(4).

3-99. *On waking in morning.*—cic$^{n.v}$. 31.(42).

4. *In the afternoon.*—ba-a^n.V^3. 3-30.26.—grp.III.—mg-m^q. p.χ$^{2.3}$.5.83.—mez^v.I.26.— na-m$^{n.ee}$.5.33.—O.sul^p.31.

5. *In the evening.*—eug^x.II^1.δℓ. 72.—mg-m^q.p.χ$^{2.3}$.4.83.— na-m^{n-ee}.4.33.—pla^{ee}.χ^2.8-31. —T.sto^p.—sul^q.βℓ.

5. *In the forenoon.*—ind$^{q.s}$.v.δ𝔳. —la-v^v.VIII^4.20.—na-s$^{n.bb}$. 29.

6. *In a room.*—ind$^{p.s}$.p.30.(8).— mg-m^q.V^1.(8).

7. *In a warm room.*—la-v^n.V^1.

8. *In the open air.*—ind$^{p.s}$.p.6.30. —P^d.lau$^{bb.2}$.29.(30).—mg-m^q. p.V^1.6.

8-31. *By walking in open air.*—

alo^{n·v}.V¹.VIII⁴.(66).—cau^{n·v}. — c-ar^x.βa^t.43.(86).—pla^{ee}. χ².5.—rhs^y.

12. *By pressure.*—F.*bel*^{cc}.I.31.
14. *When leaning.*—cyc°.βa.18.
16. *When lying.*——F.cha^{bb·2}.VI⁴. 28.30.—hyp^{hh}.v.2.—*sil*^{bb·1}.19. —O.spi^a.31.35.(19.22).; V¹. 3.28.74.
18. *When standing.*——FC.man^q. a¹b^b,ɒ.35.
19. *When sitting.*—grt^p.ɗɒ.ɛa.3.— sil^{bb·1}.(16).—O.*spi*^a.16.31.35. (22).
20. *When at rest.*—la-v^v.VIII⁴.5. —stp^{n·bb}.III.35.
22. *By bending head forwards or backwards.*—asr^{n·v}.q.—dig^{bb·2}. —O.*spi*^a.16.31.35.(19).
26. *By moving head.*——am-c^{bb·3}. VI³.φ¹.—ars^v.V¹.31.—ba-aⁿ. V³.3-30.(4).—ba-c^{n·v}.——O^b. ca-c^v.31.—coc^v.31.86.—conⁿ. —cro^{bb·1}—gloⁿ.o.II⁵.; ^v.; ^{ee}.; °.—k-ca°.—lah°.—la-v^w.ɗb.— mar^v.; ^v.V¹.κ⁴.—mez^v.4.; ^{n·ee}. T.na-mⁿ.VI³.——nx-m^{v·ee}.—— rhs.^{n·ee}.-sep°.-so-n°.-F.spi^{r·v}. —squ^r—stn^{n·ee}.—sul^{ee}.; ^{ee}.V¹ F^a.su-x^{n·ee}.—tep^{bb·3}.a¹b^p.
28. *By turning.*—F.cha^{bb·2}.VI⁴.16. 30.—glo^q.——C.kalⁿ.I.——spi^v. V¹.3.16.74.
28. *By turning head quickly.*—— na-a^t.
29. *By stooping.*—alm^q.66.(30).; ^{bb·2}.p.66.(30).—F.ber^{bb·2}.-F. cb-a^{bb·2}.βa,c.30.—cof^{bb·2}.V¹.— hy-x^{ee}.I.—hyo^q.V¹.-k-ca^{bb·2}.- P^d.lau^{bb·2}.8.(30).; ^{ee}.I.——F. mg-s^{v·bb·2}.89.——mil^q.(30).— na-s^{n·bb}.5.—nx-v^{bb·2}.—rhe°.— rhs^{bb·2}.i^a.q.—so-t^z.—O.tar^{bb·2}.
30. *By rising up.*——alm^q.29.66.; ^{bb·2}.p.29.66.——F.cha^{bb·2}.VI⁴. 16.28.——ind^{p·s}.p.6.(8).——P^d. *lau*^{bb·2}.8.29.-lyc^w.VII¹.31.33. —*mil*^q.29.—pho^v.V¹.99.
31. *By walking.*—F.bel^{cc}.I.(12).; ^{gg}.VIII¹.33.-ca-a^v.; O^{b·v}.26. —P^d.cb-a^r.—cic^{n·v}.3-99.(42).

—cob^{cc}.——coc^v.26.86.——P. cly^{n·w·ee}.II³.128.——C^b.crt^{v·w}. 33.—guiⁿ.3.— hyo^{r·v}.——ind^{ll}. i^a.ʋ.——lyc^v.; ^p.; ^w.VII¹.30. 33.— F^b.mag^p.35.—mg-s^v.66. ——nup^v.V².—nx-v^p.; ^{r·s}.—— rho^v.—rhs°.—spi^r.; O.^a.16.35. (19.22).——O.sul^p.4.—vrb^p. —vi-t^v.q.V¹.βɛ.
32. *By stumbling.*——ba-c^v.——led^v. —sep^v.—sil^p.
33. *By going up stairs.*——bel^{gg}. VIII¹.31.——C^b.crt^{v·w}.31.— O.elc^v.——lyc^w.VII¹.30.31.— na-m^{n·ee}.4.5.—par^q.VIII⁴.
35. *By motion.*——acoⁿ.64.86.—— ars^{ee}.— ca-c^v.VI⁴.—cb-aⁿ.— mag^p.; F^b.^p.31.——mg-s°.— man^v.; ^v.V¹.κ⁴.; FC.q.a¹b^b,ɒ. 18.——F.pet^q.VII¹.——O.spi^s. 16.31.(19.22).——stp^{n·bb}.III. 20.—tab^v.3.
35. *By drawing a heavy load.*—— mu-xⁿ.
41. *By studying.*——c-ar^{ll}.; ^{aa}.
42. *By thinking about it.*——cic^{n·v}. 3-99.31.
43. *By reading.*——c-ar^x.βa^t.(8-31. 86).
51. *By noise.*—mt-n^v.
64. *When drinking.*——acoⁿ.35.86. —F.bry^w.V¹.
66. *After food.*——alo^{n·v}.V¹.VIII⁴. 8-31.—alm^q.29.(30).; ^{bb·2}.p. 29.(30).—mg-s^v.31.
72. *By vomiting.*—eug^x.II¹.ɗɛ.5.
74. *At stool.*—spi^v.V¹.3.16.28.
83. *During menses.*—mg-m^q.p.χ^{2·3}. 4.5.
86. *By speaking.*——acoⁿ.35.64.—— coc^v.26.31.——c-ar^x.βa^t.43. (8-31).—zin^p.
89. *By coughing.*——la-v^{u·v}.——F. mg-s^{v·bb·2}.29.
99. *On awaking.*—pho^v.V¹.30.
128. *By driving.*—P.cly^{n·w·ee}.II³.31.
x. **Numbness.**—C.ari.; O.—bap.ηx.; VI³.—bel.— bla.q.—O.bry.ii^d.κ⁵. —P^c.ca-c.——cch.—P.con.b.; F. —dig.V¹.—dio.—grp.——F.ham. V¹.ʑff.ʑ².—hur.ɗx.θx.; P^d.—F.itu.

q.σ^2.—jat.a^1b^s.; q.; p.$\kappa^5.\omega^9$.——P^d.
lah.g^b.5.——F.mg-m.——mrl.VI^3.
VII^5.; O V^1.βa^2.—O.mr-f.σ^2ff.——
mez.——F.mu-x^b.——F.na-a.5.——
ni-x^a.g^b.—pho.V^1.βa.30.35.(16).—
snt.——F.sil^c.——F.spr.; F.ϕ.—P^d.
str.—sum.$\beta a.\delta o$.—thu^c.; e$\mathfrak{v}$.

—— *as if scalp were contracted.*
  —C.pla.q.

—— *as if too tightly bound.*—
  pla.VI^3.w.; O.p.V^3.au.7.

—— *as if tied up in a hot cloth.*
  —ptv.III.

—— *as if of wood.*—pet.

—— *as if a board lay there.*—F.
  aco.

—— *as after electric shocks.*—
  fl-x.$\kappa^5.r^1$x.ω^2.

—— *as after a blow.*--F.pla.ff.ζxff.

x^a. **As if asleep.**—cb-a.σ^2.2.—C.cup.
  g^b.V$^{10\cdot u}$.$a^1\mathfrak{v}$.—ni-x.g^b.

x^b. **Torpid feeling.**—con.V^6.(63).—
  F.mu-x.

x^c. **Dead feeling.**—F.sil.—thu.

x^d. **Absence of feeling.**—lil.

ANATOMICAL SEAT.

F. FOREHEAD.—aco.—con.—ham.
  V^1.ζff.ζ^2.—itu.q.σ^2.—mg-m.—
  mu-x^b.—na-a.5.—pla.ff.ζxff.—
  sil^c.—spr.; ϕ.

C. CROWN.—ari.—cup^a.g^b.V$^{10\cdot u}$.$a^1\mathfrak{v}$.
  —pla.

P. PARIETES.——ca-c.r.——con.b.—
  hur.l.—lah.l.g^b.5.—str.l.

O. OCCIPUT.—ari.—bry.ii^d.—mrl.
  V^1.βa^2.—mr-f.σ^2ff.—pla.p.V^3.
  au.7.

CONCOMITANTS.

au. *Ill-humour.*—O.pla.p.V^3.7.
a^1b^s. *Incapable of thought.*—jat.
$a^1\mathfrak{v}$. *Stupefaction.*—C.cup^a.g^b.V$^{10\cdot u}$.
βa. *Vertigo.*——pho.V^1.30.35.(16).
  —sum.δo.
βa^2. *Whirling.*—O.mrl.V^1.
δx. *Numbness in muscles of eye.*——
  hur.θx.
δo. *Dimness of vision.*—sum.βa.

e$\mathfrak{v}$. *Noise in left ear.*—thu.
ζx. *Numbness of nose.*—F.pla.ff.
  ζff.
ζff. *Tightness in bridge of nose.*——
  F.ham.V^1.ζ^2.—F.pla.ζx.
ζ^2. *Epistaxis.*—F.ham.V^1.ζff.
ηx. *Numbness of face.*—bap.
θx. *Numbness in upper gums.*—hur.
  δx.
κ^5. *Nausea.*— O.bry.ii^d.——fl-x.r^1x.
  ω^2.—jat.p.ϕ.
σ^2ff. *Stiffness of nape.*—O.mr-f.
σ^2. *Pain in nape.*—F.itu.q.
σ^2. *Neck as if asleep and dislocated.*
  —cb-a^a.2.
τ^1x. *Numbness of hands.*—fl-x.κ^5.ω^2.
ϕ. *Sleepiness.*—F.spr.
ω^2. *Weakness.*—fl-x.κ^5.r^1x.
ω^9. *Yawning.*—jat.p.κ^5.

CONDITIONS.

2. *At night.*—cb-a^a.σ^2.
5. *In the evening.*—P^d.lah.g^b.—F.
  na-a.
7. *In a warm room.*——O.pla.p.V^3.
  au.
16. *By lying.*—pho.V^1.βa.30.35.
30. *By rising.*—pho.V^1.βa.35.(16).
35. *By moving.*—pho.V^1.βa.30.(16).
63. *By eating.*—con^b.V^6.

hh. **Perspiration.**——F.aga.p.VIII^4.
  —amp.——F.aml.——F.an-a.p.δ.——
  ber.29.30.p.4.66.——buf.——chi.;
  8-31.——cle.σ^1hh.4.6.8-31.—F.glo.
  q.—grp.p.w.—F.lau.p.ab,u.v^1b.(8).
  ——mez.p.VII^1.χ^1.3.——O.msc.p.;
  ηc^b.hh.; F.—na-m.3-30.; 2-99.—
  ni-x.; F.—ol-a.p.r^1p.; F.p.r^1hh.—
  pet.5-16.—phl.p.I.r^1hh.—pul.ηhh.
  —rap.30.—C.rut.—O.snt.—F.sar.
  p.63.—F.sec.—F.snc.——str.—F.
  sul.V^1.; O.——val.ρ.σ^1ff.——wis.;
  31.; v.

—— *cold.*—F.ars.—buf.—F.ver.
—— *after an apoplectic attack.*—
  lah.p.
—— *after heat of head.*—plc.
—— *followed by icy coldness of*
  forehead.—FC.phl.I.

ANATOMICAL SEAT.

F. FOREHEAD.—aga.p.VIII⁴.—aml.
—an-a.p.δ.—lau.p.ab,u.v¹b.(8).
—msc.—ni-x.—ol-a.p.r¹p.—C.
phl.I.6.—sec.—snc.—str.p.—
sul.V¹.
—— cold sweat.—ars.—ver.
C. CROWN.—rut.
O. OCCIPUT.—msc.p.—snt.—sul.

CONCOMITANTS.

ab. Laziness.—F.lau.p.au.v¹b.(8).
au. Ill-humour.——F.lau.p.ab.v¹b.
(8).
δ. Pain in eyes.—F.an-a.p.
ηcᵇ. Pale face.—msc.ηhh.
ηhh. Perspiration on face.—msc.ηcᵇ.
—pul.
ρ. Quick pulse.—val.σ¹ff.
σ¹ff. Stiffness of loins.—val.ρ.
σ¹hh. Sweat on loins.—cle.4.6.8-31.
r¹p. Heat of hands.—ol-a.p.
r¹hh. Sweat on hands.—F.ol-a.p.—
phl.p.I.
v¹b. Cold feet.—F.lau.p.ab,u.(8).

CONDITIONS.

2-99. On awaking at night.—na-m.
3-30. On rising in morning.—na-m.
4. In afternoon.—cle.σ¹hh.6.8-31.
6. In a room. —cle.σ¹hh.4.8-31.
5-16. In evening when lying.—pet.
8. In open air.—F.lau.p.ab,u.v¹b.
8-31. On walking in open air.—chi.
—cle.σ¹hh.4.6.
29. On stooping. —ber.30.p.4.66.
80. On rising.——ber.29.p.4.66.—
rap.
31. When walking.—wis.
63. When eating.—F.sar.p.

ii. Swelling.—aps.—ars.; ηii.; δii.
ηii.πii.σ²ii.—bel.; ψaa.—crt.ηii.—
cup.ηaa.—dig.—eub.—glo.a¹ɒª.ηii.
v¹.ω⁵.—lah.δɒ.—mr-c.ηii.—ph-x,
ddʰ.[Ha.].——r-vn.ηr¹ii.χ.—rhs. ;
ηii. ; πii.σ²ii. ; δɒ,Lii.ηii.—thr.—
til.βε.—ton.I.
—— like phlegmonous erysipelas.
—rhs.ηii.

—— as if had a strange head or
something else upon it.——
thr.
—— in forehead.——rs-v.q.33.—
sep.
—— on frontal protuberances,
hard, like a nut.—ars.5.
—— in left temple.—cha.ddʰ.
—— above temple.—sep.
—— in left side of head.—cau.I.

CONCOMITANTS.

a¹ɒª. Loss of consciousness.—glo.ηii.
v¹.ω⁵.
βε. Confusion of head.—til.
δii. Swelling of eyes.——ars.ηii.πii.
σ²ii.—rhs.δɒ.ηii.
δɒ. Eyes closed.——lah.—rhs.δLii.
ηii.
δLii. Swelling of lids.—rhs.δɒ.ηii.
ηaa. Red face.—cup.
ηii. Swollen face.—ars.; δii.πii.σ²ii.
—crt.—glo.aɒª.v¹.ω⁵.—mr-c.
—rhs. ; δɒ,Lii.—r-vn.r⁴ii.χ.
v¹. Copious urination.——glo.a¹ɒª.
ηii.ω⁵.
πii. Swelling of chest.——ars.δii.ηii.
σ²ii.—rhs.σ²ii.
σ²ii. Swelling of neck.——ars.δii.ηii.
πii.—rhs.πii.
r¹ii. Swelling of hands.—r-vn.ηii.χ.
χ. Fever.—r-vn.ηii.r¹ii.
ψaa. Redness of skin.—bel.
ω⁵. Convulsions.—glo.a¹ɒª.ηii.v¹.

CONDITION.

33. On going up-stairs.—F.rs-v.q.

Pains in the head generally.

I. Pain, undefined.—abi.—abs.—
am-m.—amy.——ar-i.—as-s.—asi.
—au-m.—bel.; x.—bro.—buf.—
cac.d.—cai.—cam.—can.—ca-x.—
cr-h.; q.—cr-s.—clf.—cmf.—
cin.—cnb.—col.—cvl.—con.—
cot.—cro.——crt.—cub.—cun.
—cup.—c-ar.—dig.——elc.p.—
eth.—glv.—glo.d.—gua.—hed.—
hur.—hy-x.q.—hfb.—hyo.; q.—
iod.—jab.—jal.—lah.d.—lam.—

U

led.—lep.p.—lo-i.—-mgt.—mnc.
—mel.S.I.—mrl.—mer.p.—mr-c.;
d.—mor.—-mo-m.—msc.—mu-x.
——nar.—nit.q.—-opi.— ox-x.—
ped.—ph-x.—phy.—plb.—pl-n.—
rho.—rs-r.p.—san.— src.—sec.—
sng.—so-a.—so-n.—spr.—str.—
sty.—tab.—tar.— tri.—val.—ver.
—vin.—vp-t.—wis. &c.
—— *furious.*—cu-a.—dgn.—k-hy.
—led.
—— *frightful.*—ars.
—— *maddening.*—mel.
—— *vague.*—ani.
—— *flying.*—arn.—elc.—k-bi.
—— *periodical.*—-ars.—-cmf.—
klm.— mrr.—ped.—-rs-r.
—san.
—— *intermittent.*—trf.
—— *congestive.*—fag.4.66.—lin.
—— *nervous.*—idm.κ^5.χ.66.—tan.
κ^5.38.
—— *nervous, gastric.*—hdr.
—— *here and there.*—aln.—am-c.
—chi.—coh.—-cch.— hur.
—phy.—plg.
—— *wandering.*—lyc.q.2.
—— *from front to back.*—-fag.σ^2.
(8.12.31.).
—— *from back to front.*—glo.
—— *from below upward.*—glo.
—— *deep in brain.*— bov.—glo.—
lah.
—— *as if from a chill when per-
spiring.*—aco.e$\mathfrak{v}$.ζ^3.λ.3.
—— *as from a draught of air.*—-
col.(8).
—— *as from a cold in head.*—æsc.
—amb.—ar-i.—aur.—cb-v.
—ep-p.--glo.ζ.—ign.ζ.--lah.
δt^m.—mgt.—ni-x.—-pul.5.
—rho.—sin.ω^2.
—— *as after intoxication.*— cb-a.
3-99.—chd.—hel.4.— lam.
—ni-x.δ.29.—-nit.3.—pul.
βt.—tep.
—— *as from eating too much.*—-
glo.—pul.
—— *as from deranged stomach.*—
ctn.—eub.—rhs.
——, *from fat meat.*—pul.

—— *as from displacement of flatulence.*—sul.
—— *as from want of sleep.*—grp.
3.—mg-m.ω^2.3.—nx-v.3.
—— *as from sitting up all night.*
—cle.5.—pul.
—— *as after sleeping too long.*—-
bov.3-99.
—— *as in fever.*—bap.
—— *as if from a wrong position.*
—lyc.2.
—— *as from lifting a heavy weight.*
—ph-x.q.
—— *as if plunged in cold water.*
—trn.(12).
—— *that depresses eyebrows.*—-
cb-a.
—— *with inclination to bend head
to one side.*—pul.
—— *stirring up brain.*—aga.
—— *alternating with diarrhœa.*—-
pod.
—— *alternating with pain in abdomen.*—cin.
—— *alternating with pain in loins.*
—alo^d.
—— *followed by dim vision.*—sil.
—— *followed by itching.*—sep.

II^1. **Burning.**—ail.i^a.—ard.—-ars.
—aru.—-bel.—ctn.— eug.δ.δt.
2.5.72.——hel.p.βt^a.——hel.30.—
k-bi.βa.δt^x.—lch.ηc^d.κ^3.$\chi^{1.3}$.—mer.
—-pla.—-pso.——tab.g^b.e.κ^1.χ^1.—
tax.

—— *burning points or sparks.*—-
ni-x.
—— *as if a hot iron were stretched
round head.*—aco.
—— *as if in contact with hot water.*
—aco.
—— *as if brain was on fire.*—-
hy-x.ω^2.

II^3. **Raw.**—mgt.*au*.36.—pho.
II^5. **Smarting, like a sore.**—bap.29.
—cam.—cth.—ca-x.; 26.—-chi.11.
41.86.—eup.6.8.(86).--glo.26.30.;
κ^5.—ham.—mr-s.3.35.66.; q.—
na-a.
—— *deep seated.*—msc.—phy.

—— *feels as if head would drop to pieces.*—glo.26.
—— *as if laced together.*—glo.26.

II⁶. **Stinging.**—nx-m.

II⁷. **Ulcerative.**—am-c.12.35.—cau. 2.—epn.——k-ca.66.(16).—mag.5. 12.

III. **Compressive.**——ac-l.—aps.$\beta\epsilon^{a}$. —buf.σ^{2}.—cn-i.ω^{2}.7.—cb-v.—cau. —cmf.—coc.——cu-a.—dph.p.—— hpm.κ^{5}.(19.20.31.35.).——hyp.5.— lcp.——msc.$a^{1}\mathbf{b}$.——na-m.—pet.—— ph-x.—sil.—tab.—trn.

—— *as if compressed by two boards.*—ipc.
—— *as if in a vice.*—aga.δl.—— alm.——ba-c.VI⁴.——bry.$\beta\epsilon$. --cad.ff --chd.q.—opi.(35).
—— *as if brain were bound up.*— æth.$\beta\epsilon$.—am-b.—bry.VI³. q.3.9.46.--cb-v.q.12.—coc. ——cch.—cyc.$a^{1}\mathbf{b}$.——mg-s. $\beta\epsilon^{a}$.$\chi^{2\cdot3}$.3-10.26.——mer.— oln.$\beta\epsilon^{a}$.—pim.— pla.—pul. —sar.—spi.—tar.$\beta\epsilon^{a}$.
—— *like a skin stretched over brain.*—ang.$\beta\epsilon$.—asa.
—— *as if by a pitch cap.*——aco. (8-31).
—— *as if compressed by a hot cloth.*—ptv.x.
—— *as if in armour.*—crt.π.
—— *as if a hoop were round it.*— bro.$\beta a,\epsilon$.——cer.— cle.$\beta\epsilon$. gua.—sul.q.
—— *as if bound round with a string.*—mer.q.ii^{d}.——na-m. —pso.V$^{10\cdot s}$.—spr.
—— *from both sides.*—aco^{d}.δO.— arg.$\beta a.\kappa^{4\cdot5}.\chi^{2\cdot3}$.18.43.—bel. —bov.4.--bry.—cam.(42). —chi.8-31.— cic.—com.— gam.5.——hel.— lam.—lyp. --mg-m.p.VIII⁴.12.--mg-s. p.ηaa.——men.VI³.— na-m. q.—pru.—sbd.—so-l.
—— *from behind and before.*—— nx-m.100.—spo.5.

III¹. **Contractive, constrictive.**—— aga.$a^{1}b^{n}$.——agn.43.——ang.$\beta\epsilon$.31.—

asa.—bov.$\beta\epsilon^{a}$.(66).— cam.——cn-i. $a^{1}\mathbf{b}$.—cb-v.35.——ca-x.p.ii.3.(12).— chd.—cl-h.i^{a}.3.—coc.—gn-c.aq.19. —gur.—hep.82.——hur.$\epsilon.\theta^{4}$.—kis. 43.— lau.——lep.——mur.——nat.— na-m.3.—pho.—tar.—ver.ι.

—— *as if integuments were con- tracted.*—cb-v.5.66.
—— *as if head were tightly bound.* —aco.—ca-x.—ni-x.—pet. —ziz.
—— *as if brain were compressed by its membranes.*—opi.
—— *as if from a tight hat.*—phs. d.
—— *as from an iron skull-cap.*— cn-i.—cle.**5.**
—— *like a band.*—gel.θ^{4}.—glo.i^{a}. χ^{2}.—iod.—ipc.i^{a}.— mer.5. —opi.—osm.—stn.
—— *as from a hoop.*--lam.$\beta\epsilon$.3-16. (30).
—— *as if a cord were drawn tightly over head.*—msc.
—— *like a tight ligature from nape to ears.*--ana.
—— *as if head became smaller.*— grt.af.
—— *brain feels too small for skull.* —glo.
—— *as if skull were too narrow.* —mer.q.
—— *on all sides.*—trx.

III². **Pinching.**—pet.—sil.31.
—— *here and there.*—cch.

III³. **Squeezing.**—dio.66.—hur.θ^{4}x. —lyc.—nx-v.—str.
—— *like an iron helmet.*—crt.
—— *from both sides.*—tax.

IV¹. **Cramp-like.**—am-c.—ang.

IV². **Griping, raking.**—pul.d.βa.

IV³. **Spasmodic.**—er-m.89.

V¹. **Aching.**—aco.— am-g.—ank.— ars.--asa.--bov.—bro.--cam. —cn-h.——chd.—chi.—cn-s.— ccs.——cu-a.q.--dig.d.q.; x.— dro.——eup.p.—gel.q.—gur.— ign.— ind.--iod.—ipc.--k-ca.— lah.d.--led.q.—mrl.—mo-a.—

na-m.—nx-v.—oln.—ol-a.q.—opi.
—phy.—plb.d.—rs-r.—sbd.q.—
spo.—sul. ; p.—trx.v.—ter.—vi-t.
&c.

—— *violent.*—ars.
—— *deep.*—cau.q.—ind.—nx-v.
47.
—— *sharp.*—crd.q.
—— *heavy.*—aml.—cn-i.
—— *stupefying.*—cep.
——, *as from a boisterous
wind.*—aur.
——, *as if he had not slept
enough.*—ca-a.3-30.
—— *here and there.*—bel.—clf.
—grp.—hy-x.q.—pho.
thu.
——→ *going and returning.*—ter.κ⁵.
—— *as from a chill.*—lah.κ⁵.29.
31.—mu-x.
—— *as from deranged stomach.*—
ccs.χ¹.

V². **Beaten, bruised.**—aco.*rν.*—alm.
ηaa.—aur.α¹b.3.41.43.44.86.—bov.
q.βeᵃ.5.—cam.—cha.q.—cob.iᵃ.βe.
3.—cup.48.—c-ar.—eup.βe.ζ³.5.
16.—gel.—grp.ω⁴.5.—hel.βeᵃ.29.
—ign.—idm.3-99.—ipc.θ².κ⁵.—
mt-n.βe.100.(18.**30ᶜ**.).—mnc.112.
—nat.—nic.
—— *as if crushed.*—æth.—cof.8.
(6).—mu-x.—pho.5.(98).
—sep.5.—sto.VI³.q.—su-x.
φ.3-99.
—— *as if shattered.*—ast.—ign.
3-99.41.(30).—ver.
——, *as in typhus fever.*—
alm.—mu-x.

V³. **Boring, digging.**—ac-l.—ac-s.
—aga.—cau.—hep.κ⁵.3-**10**.(12).—
mt-s.gᵇ.q.—mez.—nx-v.3-**10**.(30).
—oln.—pet.
—— *stupefying.*—stp.
—— *penetrating through bones.*—
spg.
—— *from within outwards.*—dul.
2.—pul.VI³.

V⁶. **Drawing.**—aco.—aga.—amb.—
aps.—ag-n.—bel.—bry.—ca-c.—

cth.—dul.—fer.—grp.—hyd.—ipc.
—lah.—lup.—mag.—ni-x.—nx-v.
—pet.—pul.—rhs.—sab.—sul.—
su-x.—thu., &c.
—— *as from exhaustion.*—cca.δtᵏ.
—— *hither and thither.*—amb.—
mt-n.33.
—— *here and there.*—ipc.—msc.
υ².6.(8).—nx-v.—ton.
—— *thread-like, as if in membranes and sinuses.*—car.
—— *as if in periosteum.*—mr-c.
—— *in stripes or lines.*—ag-n.
—— *round the head.*—bov.βe.3.—
cb-v.
—— *from behind forwards.*—cb-v.
—— *as if head were drawn backwards.*—chd.
—— *preceded by drawing in right
arm.*—pet.

V⁷. **Dull.**—abi.—ac-c.— æsc.βeᵃ.—
ail.—aml.—a-sc.q. ; iˣ.q.—aru.—
asr.—bov.—chd.—ch-s.—cmf.—
c-ar.—dig.—dio.—dor.q.—eri.—
gui.—hed.q.—hpm.p.—ign.—irs.
q.—jac.—lam.—lep.—mr-i.q.—
mit.—na-m.—ni-x.q.—ox-x.—
rs-r.—san.—sec.—spi.—str.—
su-x.iᵃ.—ve-v.q.—vi-t. &c.
—— *stupefying.*—aga.ηp.κ³.—ant.
κ⁵.65.—arn.—chi.3-99.—
gel.—irs.—r-vn.—snc.—
thu.—zin.
——, *as from charcoal
vapour.*—zin.3.
—— *as after intoxication.*—pho.
—sam.
—— *as if coryza were coming on.*
—pho.—sam.

V⁸. **Gnawing.**—pæo.

V¹⁰. **Pressing.**—hpm.5.—hfb.—
lil.—mr-i.1.— opi.—pet.ω³.—pso.
—sng.
—— *superficially.*—ph-x.2-99.16.
—— *outwards.*—aco.—ar-i.q.3-99.
29.35.41.— ast.iᵃ.—bry.q.
—ca-a.18.—cam.—erd.5.
—fag.3.—fl-x.—kre.eυᵘ·ᵖ.

29.83.—mns.—men.83.—mer.—-par.ꞵ0.31.43.49.—-pso.III.—sab.—sam.—sep.—trx.

—, *as if contents would be forced through every aperture.*—lil.i[a].

—— *inwards.*—ana.—asr.—hel.8-31.—mt-n.—spi.8-31.

—— *forwards.*—bry.q.— ni-x.—sil.δ.—sul.5.

—— *downwards.*—coc.31.—-hur.—mgt.ω.—mt-n.a[1]b.δ.ω[3].—man.2-99.5.— men.(12).—mer.VII[1].ζ.——mr-f.q.—mu-x.δ.16.(90).—ni-x.ζ[3].—sul.5.

—— *upwards.*—fl-x.—gui.2.—hln.49.—mep.i[a].

—— *from all sides.*—cau.e.θ[1].

—— *as if brain were pressed against skull.*—mez.—rho.

—— *as if from a tight hat.*—sul.

—— *like a crown.*—lep.3-99.

—— *as from a board.*—ca-c.b.χ[1].

—— *as from a stone.*—bel.au.—vi-t.w.ꞵe.31.

—— *as from something hard.*—ign.—mt-n.

—— *as if skull were pressed outwards with a sharp instrument.*—pru.

—— *as if parts of brain were pressed against sharp corners.*—sbd.43.

—— *as if lead were poured over it.*—rho.

—— *like a weight.*—glo.—squ.—thu.q.

—— *like a great weight, causing head to sink forwards.*—sar.

—— *like a bar of iron forcing head forwards.*—pau.

—— *as if eyes would be forced out.*—trn.

—— *stupefying.*—bry.5.

—— *as after exposure to sun.*—pru.

V[11]. Rheumatic.—cle.28.—glo.

V[12]. Screwing.—alm.q.4.29.—am-m.au.—atr.8-31.—bov.q.3.(8).—cau.q.(8).—cin.x.— eub.η.θ[1].—grp.i[a].—nic.F[a].VI[2].3.— pet.—pim.—rn-s.—rat.—sar.—sul.ηp.—til.i[a].

—— *from below upwards, as if chin and vertex were in a vice.*—dph.p.

—— *from both sides.*—æth.—bel.—cas.—ind.ꞵ0.(29).—k-hy.3.(8).—mag.-—sar.66.—zin.5.

—— *as if in a vice.*—cle.99.

V[14]. Tingling.—arg.g[b].

—— *bubbling.*—par.af.φ[1].2.

—— *as when a steel spring is bent and suddenly released.*—grt.δo.ea[a].

V[15]. Twisting.—k-ca.—na-m.5.28.—rhe.αꞵ.ꞵe[a].29.35.

V[16]. Wedge, peg, or other body pressed in.—ac-1.26.

—— *as if needles and nails were driven in.*—der.5.63.

—— *like fingers pressed in.*—mep.V[7].q.

—— *like a stick pressed in.*—pso.ω[2].(105).

—— *like a nail.*—mgt.au.36.—-pau.

—— *like a button.*—thu.

—— *as from a peg, on small spots.*—dul.

—— *from a sharp point.*—mgt.40.

VI[1]. Cutting.—k-cl.η.—na-m.V[6].δl.θ[4].4.8.—ni-x.—pul.

—— *as with knives.*—k-bi.V[3]—VI[3].

—— *as if half the brain were cut through.*—msc.(8).

VI[2]. Pricking, prickling.—at-a.g.—cba.δ.—ph-x.3-30.—thu.g[b].3.

—— *like thorns round head.*—lcp.

—— *as with nails.*—as-t.

—— *as from needles.*—con.—eug.—rhs.—thu.

VI[3]. Shooting.—alm.—am-c.—ast.—ba-c.g[b].p.—bel.—ca-c.—cap.—cau.p.—cha.—ccb.—cly.—crn.—dgn.— epn.—grn.—hep.—

hur.—hyo.— ign.—-iod.—iof.—
ipc.; q.—k-ca.—lah.—lau.g^b.—
mnc.—mer.—mu-x.—na-m.—
ni-x.—nit.w.—nx-v.—pet.p.—
pul.—rs-r.—sep.—stp.—sul.—
tar.—teu.—thu.—val. &c.

—— *flying.*—asa.βℯ.ρ.—ca-c.—
sto.

—— *by fits.*—rs-r.

—— *outwards.*—alm.4.—rhs.

—— *from without inwards.*—cnb.

—— *upwards.*—gui.—sil.

—— *from before backwards.*—
c-cs.

—— *from behind forwards.*—
na-m.6.

—— *obtuse.*—k-ca.

—— *jerking.*—thu.

—— *like a shock.*—nic.

—— *as from knives.*—alm.—bel.
—lah.δ.ζ.ηii.5.—-mag.VI⁴.
a¹c^a.2.—mg-s.4.—na-m^{zz}.6.

—— *like a sword thrust in and
out.*—ca-x.δℬ.51.111.(12).

—— *here and there.*—am-c.(31).
—bap.x.—ca-c.—hy-x.—
mag.—mg-s.—nic.5.29.—
plm.—-plb.ℯr.4.5.—rat.5.
—su-x.8-31.

—— *in different parts.*—lil.

—— *as if all round brain.*—alm.

—— *making her cry out.*—mrl.

—— *declining and increasing.*—
ba-c.

VI⁴. Tearing.—aga.—alm.— amb.
—am-c.—ars.—bel.—ber.—bov.
—ca-c.—cth.— cap.—cau.—cha.
—chi.—fer.—ign.—ipc.—klm.—
lah.—lam.—lyc.—mag.—man.—
mez.—msc.—nic.—pho.—pso.—
rhs.—su-x.—ter.—til.—zin. &c.

—— *flying.*—amb.—sel^q.

—— *intermitting.*—rhe.q.31.

—— *here and there.*—ant.—ber.
—rhs.5.29.

—— *deep.*—sel^b.

—— *upwards.*—am-c.VII¹.

—— *as if lacerated.*—nic.i^a.q.βℯ^a.
29.—nx-v.ζ.θ⁴.31.—opi.au.
βa.—pla.--stp.3-99.(96).—
zin.

—— *as if torn, as in typhus.*—
pul.βℯ.3-99.

—— *as with a saw.*—sul.

—— *as if brain were torn out.*—
ars.

—— *ceasing on the cheek swelling.*
—lyc.

VII¹. Bursting, splitting.—am-c.
VI^{4.v}.—ba-a.—bel.19.— bov.3-99.
(105).—bry.i^a.19.—cap.26.31.—
cha.3-99.—cn-s.p.q.δ.ℯʋ.—cle.5.—
con.i^a.3-99.—fag.ω².; 4.41.—gn-c.
i^a.ξ⁸.φ¹.35.83. (20).—glo.a¹ℬ⁸,ʋ.ω².
—gym.—ham.; βa.29.; 3-99.29.
—hdr.29.33.89.—hfb.28.29.35.—
ign.86.(43.44.).—la-x.4.—lyc.w.
30.31.33.—mt-n.4.—mns.σ.—mer.
—mil.—mo-a.q.—na-m.; ξ.29.83.
89.90.—nit.ℯl.r.—nx-m.—nx-v.
16.41.; 3-10.—pho.al.5.— phy.—
pru.a¹ℬ.—-ptl.κ⁵.—rat.—sbd.—
sep.; 89.—sil.—spi.86.89.—stn.
—sul.2.—su-x.

—— *outwards.*—fag.4.

—— *upwards from middle of head.*
—glo.

—— *as if brain split.*—glo.—
nx-v.—ol-m.89.—pau.

—— *as if split open with a wedge
from without inwards.*—
lch.βf.

—— *as if head opened.*—gua.,

—— *as if a lever forced open head.*
—bel.

—— *as if all would come out at
F. and O.*—cb-v.29.

—— *with pressure on top.*—hfb.

VII². Expanding.—bel.ii^a.—-ca-x.
δt^n.—dul.5.8-31.—eub.—so-n.p.q.
—sto.5.16.

—— *feeling of distension.*—hy-x.
—ind.

—— *here and there.*—trx.

—— *as if brain would fall out in
front.*—spi.29.

—— *like a circle round head.*—
mer.

—— *as if the brain would be forced
through ears.*—chd.ℯʋ.

—— *as if brain were too full.*——
cap.

—— *as if pressed asunder from
middle to each side and
front.*—amm.

VII³. **Stretching.**—ars.—ca-c.

—— *as if cerebral membranes were
on the stretch.*——par.
S.VII³.

VII⁴. **Swollen, as if.**—bel.—lap.3.
—ton.

VII⁵. **Tensive.**—amb.βe^a.—ag-n.41.
—ars.—asa.βe^a.—ber.—cb-a.—
cb-v.βe.—ce-s.— cof.3-99.w.29.—
—gel.—glo.d.σ^2.—grp.σ^2.3-99.—
ipc.—kre.29.—lah.μ^1.(8).—lo-i.
ηp.5.—mt-s.8.(6).—mrl.; p.q.;
i^a.—mor.—na-m.36.—ni-x.δL.—
nx-v.2.—opi.—pet.; βe.—pul.—
rhe.βa.—sbd.(41.49).—sul.

—— *cramp-like.*—cb-v.
—— *deep in.*—nit.66.
—— *tightness round head.*—ziz.
—— *tightness of brain.*—gel.
—— *as if from a tight skin.*—hel.
q.a^{1}b.
—— *as if dura mater tightened.*—
pet.
—— *as if the skull were too small.*
—glo.ρ.—mo-a.—scu.i^a.
—— *as from a bandage.*—chd.—
gym.
—— *in a rim round head.*—ch-s.
3.
—— *as if a thread were stretched
from nape to eyes.*—lah.o^1.
—— *like water in it.*—sam.βa.
3-26.
—— *as if caused by a ligature
round neck.*—bel.

VIII¹. **Blows, shocks.**—am-c.35.—
ba-c.βa.5.90.—bel.w.33.—bz-x.—
ca-c.—cn-i.—car.z.ηaa.29.33.—
cau³.—crt.βb.—fer.βa.—hy-x.; βe.
—bfb.βe.—led.—lo-i.—lyc.22.;
κ^7.; p.—mgt.r.χ^1.—mg-s.89.—
mer.29.35.—mil.—nx-v.—ph-x.
31.—pho.74.—pso.—rs-r.—sep.
100.—sul.—trn.aκ.ι.o^1.π.σ^2.$\omega^{2\cdot8}$.
3-30.

—— *here and there.*—zin.
—— *synchronous with pulse.*——
glo.
—— *like a concussion.*—hy-x.
—— *as with an axe.*—ph-x.
—— *as if head were covered by a
leaden cap on which some
one knocked.*—pau.
—— *from elbow to head.*—aga.θ^3.
ω^{10}.8-10.

VIII². **Hammering.**——cle.5.16.—
cu-a.—ele.—fer.κ^1.—hep.—ind.—
lep.w.—mnc.σ^2.29.—nic.35.—ni-x.
—ph-x.—pso.—rhe.—sul.; 86.—
trn.30.

—— *as if a carpenter were at
work in head with hammer
and chisel.*—ars.π^1.ρ.
—— *like a clock.*—mg-s.4.5.

VIII³. **Jerking.**—amb.—bel.31.33.
—bry.ηp.—ca-c.—cb-v.—cau^1.—
ctn.—epn.83.—glo.33.—ign.33.;
46.—k-ca.1.—lyc.ϕ^1.2.—mt-s.—
mag.q.4.40.(5.10.)—mil.— nat.—
na-m.31.—ni-x.5.—nx-v.—ph-x.—
sil.ll.—sul.

—— *blows.*—ni-x.16.29.
—— *here and there.*—chd.—sto.
—— *deep.*—rat.
—— *from one side to another.*——
sam.
—— *from behind forwards.*—ph-x.

VIII⁴. **Throbbing, pulsating.**—ac-l.
—æth.6.—cam.—cap.—cau.z.—
cha.—chd.—csn.—cup.—cu-s.βb^a.
—elc.—fag.—glo.; i^a.—ham.—hdr.
—ign.—na-p.i^a.—pet.— pgn.i^a.—
rhe.—rho.—rs-r.; p.
—— *by fits.*—f-mg.
—— *intermitting.*—ver.
—— *here and there.*—aco.—æth.
6.—ind.5.19.
—— *from within outwards.*—glo.
—lep.
—— *like throbbing of arteries.*—
pul.
—— *as if inflamed.*—dph.
—— *as if brain would suppurate.*
—man.6.(8).

—— as if it would burst the head. —ars.χ^3.2.

—— in the middle of the brain.— ca-c.3.

—— alternating between head and chest.—bel.

—— after epistaxis.—bor.

VIII⁵. **Undulating.**—fag.p.—fer.— glo.; 28.—hfb.—pet.d.kk.ꬲ.

—— like waves.—fer.—dig.18.28. (16.22.)——ind.đo.5.19.— lyc-ηp.—mr-f.

IX. **Peculiar.**

—— disagreeable feeling.——aga. (42).

—— tired feeling.—pi-m.3-99.— sil.

—— curious.—glo.—nx-m.—osm. —thr.

——, preceding convulsions. —sty.

—— hot pain.—lil.5.(90).

—— electric thrill.—ail.rv.

—— electric shocks.——-ast.d.a¹b. βɛᵇ.ρ.2-99.—cep.— hpm.— mor.

—— like crawling of a worm.— alm.V⁸-VI¹.

—— as if something were alive and tickling.—hyp.2-10.

—— as if blood trickled down from front to back of head.— la-x.

—— like humming.—stp.

—— trembling.—cop.

—— bubbling.—pul.2.

—— as if water in head.——am-c. —bel.—pla.au.¡.χ^3.2.

—— stirred up.—aga.

—— as if numb and stuffed.—grp.

—— head feels brittle.——na-m.

—— stupefying.——aga.—dul.— hel.4.—hy-x.w.29.—itu.29. —lam.w.29.

—— as if brain were raised up.— mgt.3-30.(96).

—— as if part of the brain were raised up here and there.— aco.35.64.86.

—— as if drawn up by hair.—aco.

—— sinking feeling in head and chest, as from working in a very hot room.—glo.

—— as if the brain lay hard against skull.—k-ca.i².

—— as if head were fastened to shoulders by a long peg.— cu-a.VI³.28.

—— as though it would crack off from temple to temple as low as the bottom of ears.— idm.

—— as if something were drawn out of head.—aco.đa.

—— as if brain would fall out.— msc.—stp.35.III.16.

—— as if eyes would fall out.— aco.—sep.—trn.V¹⁰.

—— as if wind blew through brain. —cor.26.35.—mil.—pul.— sab.V¹⁰·ˢ.

—— as if the brain were attached to skull.—cac.2.

—— as if the feet were in the brain.—amp.

Complex pains.

II¹–III¹–V³–VI⁴. **Burning,** constrictive, digging, tearing.—coc.

II¹–V¹–VII³. **Burning,** aching, outstretching.—arn.

II¹–V⁶–VI⁴. **Burning,** drawing, tearing.—nx-v.3.

II¹–V¹⁰·ᵛ. **Burning,** upward pressure.—trx.

II¹–VI³. **Burning,** shooting.—arg. —nat.p.5.—ol-a.—rho.

II¹–VIII⁴. **Burning,** throbbing.— aps.χ^3.29.35.(12).—cof.—rhs.

II⁵–V¹–VI³. **Sore,** aching, shooting. —cth.đ.

II⁵–V². **Sore,** bruised.——cbi.31. 106.

II⁵–VI³. **Sore,** shooting.—cb-v.

II⁵–VII⁵. **Sore,** tensive.—glo.

II⁵–VIII⁴. **Sore,** throbbing.—cob.3.

II⁷–VI³·⁴. **Ulcerative,** shooting, tearing.—sto.q.3-30.

II⁷–VIII⁴. **Ulcerative,** throbbing.— bov.3.6.8.—epn.

III–V⁷. **Compressive,** dull.—phl.

III–V$^{2\cdot6}$. **As if bound, digging, drawing.**—tar.ζ.

III–VI^3–VIII^1. **Compressive, shooting, blows.**—thu.29.(12.22.).

III–VI^4. **Compressive, tearing.**—alm.χ^1.5.

III–VII^2. **Compressive, forcing outwards.**—ca-c.

III–VIII^3. **Compressive, jerking.**—bry.

III^1–IV^1. **Contractive, cramp-like.**—pso.

III^1–V^1. **Contractive, aching.**—aco.(102).

III^1–V^6. **Constrictive, drawing.**—pet.

III^1–V^7. **Contractive, stupefying.** —— *as from a blow on vertex.*—val.

III^1–VI^3. **Contractive, shooting.**—na-m.—trn.ξ^2.

III^2–V^1. **Pinching, aching.**—pho.

III^2–VIII^3. **Pinching, jerking.**—cau.—sep.3-30.

III^3–IV^1–V^6. **Squeezing, cramp-like drawing.**—ni-x.βι.

III^3–V^1–VI^4. **Squeezing, aching, tearing.**—ph-x.

III^3–V^7. **Squeezing, dull.**—teu.

III^3–V^{10}. **Squeezing, pressing.**—col.—epn.

IV^1–V^6. **Cramp-like drawing.**—msc.—sto.δ.

IV^1–VII^5.**Cramp-like tension.**—glv.

V$^{1\cdot2}$. **Aching, bruised.**—cn-i.—nx-v.—trn.π.—ver.

V$^{1\cdot2}$–VI^4. **Aching, bruised, tearing.**—aur.3.

V$^{1\cdot3}$. **Aching, boring.**—bel.—msc.—sab.—thu.

V$^{1\cdot3}$–VI^4. **Aching, boring, tearing.**—con.

V$^{1\cdot3\cdot6}$–VI^4–VIII^4. **Aching, boring, drawing, tearing, throbbing.**—cth.

V$^{1\cdot3}$. **Aching, drawing.**—bel.—cb-v.—hel.βa,ε^a.—jun^z.—zng.δr.

V$^{1\cdot6\cdot7}$. **Aching, dull, drawing.**—bis.35.

V$^{1\cdot6}$–VII^5. **Aching, drawing, tensive.**—sto.5.

V$^{1\cdot7}$–VI^3. **Aching, dull, shooting.**—ber.

V$^{1\cdot10}$. **Aching, pressing.**—pet.

V^1–VI^2–VIII^4. **Aching, cutting, throbbing.**—bel.

V^1–VI^3. **Aching, shooting.**—amb.—bel.—cth.5.5.(31).—k-bi.—lyc.—men.q.(22).—nat.34.—na-m.(31).—pet.κ^5.—ph-x.—sab.—val.

VI^1–VI^4. **Aching, tearing.**—amb.—ar-h.βε^a.φ^1.2.—aur.βa.—bel.—cam.—cin.η.—fer.—rhe.—rhs.—squ.—vi-t.ηp.κ^8.

V^1–VI$^{3\cdot4}$. **Aching, shooting, tearing.**—ton.au.η.5.6.

V^1–VI$^{3\cdot4}$–VIII^4. **Aching, shooting, tearing, throbbing.**—tep.

V^1–VI^3–VIII^4. **Aching, shooting, throbbing.**—k-bi.

V^1–VI^4–VIII^3. **Aching, tearing, jerking.**—pho.βι.3–99.35.

V^1–VII^3. **Aching, outstretching.**—arn.8-31.—chi.8.

V^1–VII^5. **Aching, tensive.**—crn.—mrl.; i^a.29.—msc.w. —— *as if a cap were drawn down.*—ber.

V^1–VIII^2. **Aching, hammering.**—ang.

V^1–VIII^3. **Aching, jerking.**—dig.

V^1–VIII^4. **Aching, throbbing.**—k-ca.κ$^{5\cdot6}$.σ^2.11.—mez.ζ.θ^1.26.—opi.4.—pul.(12).

V^1–VIII^4. **Aching, pulsating.**—lyc.19.43.—ni-x.βa.5.—ver.

V^2–VI^3. **Bruised, shooting.**—mag.18.—nup.31.

V^2–VI^4. **Bruised, tearing.**—bov.q.—mer.

V^2–VII^1. **Bruised, splitting.**—con.

V$^{3\cdot6}$–VI^4. **Boring, drawing, tearing.**—cb-a.102.

V^3–VI^3. **Boring, shooting.**—pul.—sng.

V$^{3\cdot6}$. **Digging, drawing.**—ag-n.

V$^{3\cdot6}$–VI^3. **Digging, drawing, shooting.**—hpm.δ.2-**10**.

V$^{3\cdot7}$. **Digging, stupefying.**—mgt.3-99.

V$^{3\cdot10}$. **Digging, pressive.**—ca-c.ap.δ.ζ.η.θ^1.ω^2.—sep.v.σ^2.

x

V³–VI¹·³. **Digging, cutting, shooting.**—k-bi.

V³–VIII³. **Digging, jerking.**—lyc.

V⁶·⁷. **Drawing, dull.**—nat.βε.66.

V⁶–VI¹. **Drawing, cutting.**—na-m. δ.θ⁴.4.8.

V⁶–V³. **Drawing, shooting.**—fer.εᴅ.

V⁶–VI⁴. **Drawing, tearing.**—am-c. 3-30.—cld.—cth.35.—lah.rυ.—nx-v.—ol-a.βε.3.(4).—rhs.66.

V⁶–VII¹. **Drawing, bursting.**—sul. θ⁴.

V⁶–VII³. **Drawing, outstretching.**—bel.w.

V⁶–VII⁵. **Drawing, tensive.**—grp.—man.—su-x.

V⁶–VIII³. **Drawing, jerking.**—bry. η.θ⁴.3-30.—nx-v.3.

V⁶–VIII⁴. **Drawing, throbbing.**—ars.

V⁷·¹⁰·ᵛ–VIII⁴. **Dull, upward pressing, throbbing.**—gn-l.iᵃ.

V⁷–VI³. **Dull, shooting.**—sti.η.θ⁴.

V⁷–VII⁵. **Dull, tensive.**—sum.iᵃ.

V⁷–VIII⁵. **Dull, undulating.**—glo.

V⁷–VIII⁴. **Stupefying, throbbing.**—com.

V¹⁰–VI³. **Pressing, shooting.**—tep.

V¹⁰–VII¹. **Pressing, bursting.**—ind.ε.3.

V¹⁰–VIII⁴. **Pressing, throbbing.**—bov.5.7.—can.—glo.16.

V¹⁰·ᵗ·VIII³. **Pressing inwards, jerking.**—spi.8-31.

V¹⁰·ᵛ–VIII⁴. **Pressing upwards, throbbing.**—ph-x.

V¹¹–VI⁴. **Rheumatic tearing.**—lyc.

V¹²·¹⁵. **Screwing, twisting.**—sbd.6.

V¹²–VI³. **Screwing, shooting.**—k-ca.βε.

V¹²–VIII³. **Screwing, jerking.**—stn.

V¹²–VIII⁴. **Screwing, throbbing.**—ton.6.(66).

VI¹·³. **Cutting, shooting.**—cth.2.

VI¹·⁴. **Cutting, tearing.**—bel.

VI³·⁴. **Shooting, tearing.**—arg.—ber.ξ³.ω².83.—cau.—chd.—chi.26.—hyo.—hyp.—pho.—sil.— sil.4.—sul.ε.η.θ⁴.—vp-t.110.— zin.λ.ω⁹.63.66.

VI³–VII¹. **Shooting, bursting.**—hep.βε.2. ; δb.29.

VI³–VII¹–VIII⁴. **Shooting, bursting, throbbing.**—cle.υ¹.16.43.44. (8).

VI³–VII⁵. **Shooting, tensive.**—mrl.x.

VI³–VIII³. **Shooting, jerking.**—arn.κ⁴.ρ.29.—ctn.

VI³–VIII⁴. **Shooting, throbbing.**—æth.—bel.—fer.—lam.2.—nx-v. 3.29.

—— *as if from an internal abscess.*—aco.o².

VI³–VIII⁵. **Shooting, undulating.**—lyc.35.

VI⁴–VII². **Tearing, out-pressing.**—col.

VI⁴–VIII³. **Tearing, jerking.**—aga.—arn.29.89.—k-ca.—mgt.

VI⁴–VIII³·⁴. **Tearing, jerking, throbbing.**—spo.η.o².

VI⁴–VIII⁴. **Tearing, throbbing.**—cb-a.δ.ε.η⁴.66.(12).—mg-m.6.(19).—nat.83.—sil.χ¹.(12). ; κ⁷.—-zin. 3.5.

VII¹–VIII⁴. **Bursting, throbbing.**—chi.—mor.

VIII⁴·⁵. **Throbbing, undulating.**—par.33.

PAIN IN FOREHEAD.

Pains, undefined.——aps.——ard. ; p.—bs-n.—bro.——cn-i.—cn-h.—cas.q.——chi.—cnb.—cvl.——cro.—der.——dig.—dgn.—elp.—elc.—fag.p.—glo.iᵃ.—grn.r.—-hur.—k-cl.—mu-x.—nar.——nit.q.—opi.—plm.—pso.—-san.—sng.—spi.—spr.q.—tar. &c.

—— *severe.*—bap.—ca-x.iᵃ.—cnb.—dio.

—— *violent.*—cth.— cu-a.—-cyc.—dig.—eth.—glo.—-k-hy.—mo-å.—trn.p.

—— *intolerable.*—crt.—glo.

—— *deep-seated.*—cnt.

—— *wandering.*—au-m.

—— *across.*—ce-b.—gel.—gloᵉ.—-rs-r.4.

—— *diagonally.*—rhs.

—— *from before backwards.*—— ce-b.—glo.
—— *radiating into brain.*—thu.
—— *congestive.*—lin.q.
—— *as if full of blood.*—rn-b.4.
—— *neuralgic.*—ca-s.5.66.—ca-x. —cha\u1da0.—ch-s\u1d49.**50**\u1d48.—lcp\u1da0. —urt\u1d43.ηr.
—— *heavy.*—cac.—cn-i.—cth.— gur.
—— *as if cold coming on.*—dgn.ζ. —nx-j.δ.ζ.—sep.3.
—— *as after intoxication.*—ctn. —k-bi.29.—lau\u1d43.
—— *as from reading too much.*— lyc.
—— *as from much talking.*—dro. βε.31.
—— *alternating with pains in uterus like labour.*—gel.
II\u00b9. **Burning.**—au-m.—cb-v.δ.θp.— ca-x.—cau.—ce-b\u1d43.—chd\u1d49.—crt. —hfb.—hyo.q.—ipc.11.—k-hy.δ. ζ.θ.ι.—lil.—men\u1d4d.—mr-i.δs.5.— mur.3.29.—pho.; κ\u2075.—pso.—rs-r\u1d4d. 5.117.—rhs.; g.—sbd\u1d49.g\u1d47.—spi\u1d43. δ.48.—sto.—thr\u1d49.3-99.
—— *like a scald.*—naj\u1d4d.
—— *like fire.*—stn.p.κ\u2075.
—— *as if brain were inflamed.*— cau.6.
—— *as if a red hot iron were passed over it.*—grt.
II\u00b3. **Raw, as if.**—lyc.29.
II\u2075. **Smarting, sore.**—bap.—cth.— cb-a.29.—gel.b.δii\u1d48.—hdr.—lah\u2071.
—— *as if had been beaten.*—lil.δ.
II\u2076. **Stinging.**—cot\u1d4d.υb.—gel.b.δii\u1d48. —gos.
—— *like the sting of a bee.*— rs-r\u1d4d.
III. **Compressive.**—ail.βε.—bry\u1d49.— can.—fl-x\u207f.5.—gur.—ni-x.4.—ptv. 31.—sil.4.—stp.ε\u0280.—sul.
—— *by fits.*—pla.
—— *across.*—lep.5.
—— *from both sides.*—aga.μ\u00b2.— alm\u1d49.—chi.8-31.—cin\u1d48.— lyc.—spi.V\u2077.
—— *from front to back.*—spo.
—— *from behind and above.*—æth.

—— *dull.*—coc\u00b3.—oln.
—— *as from a band.*—ced\u1d49.—ind.
—— *as from a cord.*—cbd\u1d49.
—— *as if by an iron ring.*—fuc.
—— *as if too narrow.*—gel.δb. 3-99.(12).
III\u00b9. **Contractive, constrictive.**— aco.—ars\u1d49.—as-s.—bry.q.4.— cam\u1d47.p.r\u00b9υ\u00b9b.φ.12.16.29.—can.— ca-x.p.3-99.(12).—cof.—cch\u1d49.— elt.—hæm\u1d47.ε.—ipc\u1d4d.—lep.5.—nit. δ.ζ.—phl.—phs.d.βε.δ.δLq.; 43.— pso.—pul\u1d49.49.—sep.—su-x.
—— *intermittent.*—hyo\u1d48.af.βε\u1d43.
—— *first increasing, then suddenly going off.*—su-x.
—— *across.*—ham.5.—naj.δq.— phy.
—— *from both sides.*—alm\u1d49.5.χ\u00b3·\u00b3. 2.
—— *as if integuments were convulsively drawn together.*— arn\u1d49.
—— *as from a tight band.*—ca-x. V\u2077.q.8-31.; 2.— -cca.—ind. —irs.88.
—— *as if a band were stretched across.*—hln.—lil.VI\u00b2.5.7.
—— *alternating with expanding.* —trx\u1d47.βa.
III\u00b2. **Pinching.**—pso\u1d48.q.θ\u00b9.3.—rs-r\u1d47. p.
III\u00b3. **Squeezing.**—aco\u1d47.a\u00b9c\u1d43.8-31.— ars\u1d49.—cad\u1d47.—ca-c.—ign\u1d47.—lau.φ. —mez.δ.θ\u2074.
IV\u00b9. **Cramp-like.**—bel\u1d49.—ca-c.
IV\u00b2. **Griping, clawing.**—ag-n.— con.q.51.86.—la-v\u1d49.—na-s.(117).
V\u00b9. **Aching.**—æsc.—alo.—amb.— am-g.—ang.—ag-n.—arn.—assa. —asr.—au-n.q.—bs-n.—bov.— cai.q.—ca-c.—c-cs.—cnc.—cnu. —ca-x.—cs-e.—cas.—cnt.i\u1d43.— chd.—cnb.i\u1d43.—cle.—cca.—coc.— cch.—col.—con.—cvl.—cop.— cro.—cyc.; p.—dgn.q.—eub.— fl-x.—gn-l.—glo.—gui.—hur.— hy-x.—hfb.p.—jat.—jun.—lab.— led.—mag.—mg-m.—mrl.—msc. —na-m.—oln.—ol-a.—plc.—rhe. —rho.—sbd.v.—sng.—sep.p.—

spi.—spo.—-stn.—sul.—trx.—
vi-t.q.—zin. &c.
—— *as after intoxication.*—ph-x.
—— *as from want of sleep.*—nx-v.
—— *violent.*—gas.—nit.d.—sul.
—vrb.
—— *stunning.*—car.
—— *intermittent.*—cb-v.—chd.q.
—rut.
—— *across.*—thu.
—— *diagonally across.*—gui.
—— *obliquely.*—mez.
—— *deep.*—grp.
—— *very acute.*—aco.
—— *alternately slight and severe.*
—con.
—— *gradually increasing.*—la-v.
—— *going off gradually.*—opi.p.
—— *increasing and decreasing.*—
bel.
—— *as from a weight.*—sil^e.
—— *as if brain were too hard.*—
mez.a^{1}b^o.3.
—— *as if something hard were
held there.*—phs.βa.31.
—— *as from a blow.*—su-x^a.
—— *like a hoop.*—thr.
—— *as if brain were rolled into a
ball.*—arn.101.
—— *as if brain were concussed.*—
ana.3-99.31.
—— *making him wrinkle skin.*—
hyo.
V^2. **Beaten, bruised.**—ang.29.(8).
—ars.—am-i.—bap.—-cb-a^h.—
gel$^{e \cdot p}$.—glo^{a1}.—hep.λ.3-99.48.—
ind.—iod.κ^7.ω^3.—mg-s.5.—pla^n.
pul.βℓ^a.—so-n.
—— *as if brain were shattered.*—
glo.—stn.
—— *as on surface of brain.*—
ph-x.5.41.
—— *as after a violent blow.*—
arn^b.90.—chd.—so-n.—
su-x^o.
V^3. **Boring, digging.**—aga.—am-m.
3-30.—bel^n.3-99.—chi.19.—ch-s.
—cch^e.—elp^f.—hel^m.—ipc.—
lau^e.—lyp.[S^f.ff^a].—mez^b.—ol-a^o.
—ptv^d.—phl^b.—sab^n.—san^d.—
sep.5.35.—sil.—spi.—squ.

—— *violent.*—ign$^{a \cdot n}$.
—— *transient.*—lyc^h.—nup^b.5.
—— *intermittent.*—arg^b.5.16.
—— *deep.*—dul.ii^d.βℓ.3-30.——
na-m^g.
—— *outwards.*—ant.—bis^m.——
dro.29.44.—dul.q.
—— *backwards.*—ce-b^a.
—— *gradually diminishing.*—pla^d.
—— *dull.*—ccs.
—— *as with a blunt instrument.*
—tar^n.
—— *stretching skin of forehead.*
—so-1.
—— *alternate contraction and ex-
pansion.*—bis.δ.ζ.
V^4. **Broken, as if.**—na-s.φ.66.
V^6. **Drawing.**—aga.—ana.—asr.—
au-m.—bad.—bel.—bry.—cap.
chi.—epn.—grp.—k-cl.—mag.
men.—msc.—sng.—sep.—thu.—
val. &c.
—— *as in coryza.*—pso^i.
—— *flying.*—chd.
—— *deep.*—b-la.
—— *outwards.*—pot^h.
—— *upwards.*—kis^h.
—— *downwards.*—sin.
—— *as if a worm crept through.*—
sul.
V^7. **Dull, stupefying.**—æsc.—aga.
O.VIII^4.—alo.—ars.—asa.
bap.—bor.—bov.—cac.—ca-x.
—ch-s.—cnb.q.—cly.—crn.—cun.
—dig.—euc.—fgs.—f-io.—for.q.
—ham.i^a.—hdr.—hfb.q.—hyo.—
iof.—irs.q.—jug.—lah.—lau.—
lcp.—mn-o.—mr-s.—msc.—nat.
—ox-x.—phl.—ph-x.g^b.hh.—phy.
—pod.q.—pgn.—pul.—rs-r.—
sab.—sul.—sum.x. &c.
—— *as after intoxication.*—glo.q.
—eu-a.3-99.(66).—lup.
trx.
—— *as from waking too soon.*—
asr.
—— *intermitting.*—arn^g.
—— *externally.*—arn.
—— *deep-seated.*—cmf.—equ.[S.
VI^2.15].—lpt.
—— *from without inwards.*—chd^f.

—— *from above downwards.*—ana. |

—— *as if in meninges.*—hyo.

—— *as from a hard blow.*—oln.— sbd.rvq.—tar.

—— *as if an india-rubber band were stretched over it.*— ca-x.

—— *as if a board lay there.*— dul^b.

—— *wrinkling skin.*—hel.V^6.

V^8. **Gnawing.**

—— *as from worms.*—zin.

V^9. **Pecking.**—ari^n.——cb-a^b.3-30. (8).—ign^f.

V^{10}. **Pressing.**—bry.—ca-x.i^a.—col. cup.—gn-l.δ.—jat.q.—lil.p.—sar. &c.

—— *spasmodic.*—cis^f.

—— *outwards.*——aco. ; i^a.q.—— alo.—alm.66.—ana^a. ; ^{n}.— ang^e.20.35.——ag-n^a.—asa. ; ^{a}.—ba-a.δ.24.(29).——ba-c. —bel^o. ; ^{b}. ; (22).—ber.— bro$^{e\cdot h}$.—bry^g.δ. ; 31.66. ; δl. 29.——ca-a^g.q.18.29.—ca-c. βa.(8.12).——cn-i^e.4.—cas^a. —chd.1.8.29.53.89.(63).— chi.q.12.—cic^o.—cin^a.3-99. —col.——con^e.——cor.aq.χ^2. (130).—cup.βe.29.—dro.η. —dul^o.5.—epn. ; ^{a}.—gn-l. βe.—grp.66.—hel^a.——hfb. —ipc^b.26.——k-ca.44.——lil. —lyc.$\eta r.r$.—lcp.—mg-m.— men. ; q.33.——mer.$^\Delta$—mor. —mu-x. ; ^{b}.—na-m.—nx-m. ii^d.βa.—oln^d. ; ^{o}.(12).—opi. (12).—ph-x^n.—pru. ; ^{a}. ; ^{b}. ; ^{n}. ; a^1v^a.——pso.3-30.(66.117). ; 5.—ptl.1. ; q.2.29.—rn-b. rho^a.——snc.4.——spi.βe. ; ^{n}. ; ^{b}. ; 29.—spo^n. ; ^{b}.19.(30).— stn. ; ϕ.(12).—sul.—trx.— vrb^h. ; (29).—vi-t.

—— *inwards.*——aga.δ.——alm.—— bap.—bel^e.δb. ; 14.—bro.p. VIII^4.θ^4.—fer^m.3-30.33.(8. 12).—lau.—pla^b.—rn-s.κ^3. χ^1.5.—spi^o.—stn.

—— *upwards.*—glo.—val.δ.

—— *downwards.*—amb.p.δ.ηc^b.4.— asr.δ.δe.—bel^e.δb.3.—bry.δl. 29.—cin q.—coc.31.—glo.q. mu-x.—q.βe.δ.(12).—tar.δ.δb.

—— *as from a stone.*— asr.

—— *intermitting.*—asr.

—— *every other day.*— amb.p.δ.ηc^b.4.

—— *like a weight.*— rhs$^{f\cdot g}$.βe.

—— *forwards.*——lau.p.hh.ii^d,r^1. —mg^{i}s.d.q.3-30.——nx-m^g. 3.—rhs^r.

—— *against frontal bone.*—hdr.3.66.

—— *backwards.*——dio.w.—spo^e. σ^2.—tab.

—— *feels pressed flat.*—cor.

—— *as from a hard ball.*—mg-s^e. V^{12}.δ.

—— *as from a stone.*—bel.au.δP^2. (29).—con^d.

—— *as from a hard weight.*— dig^d.41.—grn.31.

—— *as with a finger.*—ol-a.—sto^f.

—— *as if too narrow.*—gel.δii^d.

—— *as if all would fall out.*— aco.i^a.29.—bel.29.——bro^d. 5.—bry. ; 29.—cth.28.29.— cb-v.I^a.29.—cau.29.—cep. —chd.29.—coh.V^3.—cch. —col.—epn.—k-ca^g.—kre. δ.29.—lyp.5.(14).—mg-m. 5.29.—mg-s.p.q.30.—mez.— pho^a.——pla.q.δb,e.ηp,aa.κ^3. σ^2,ρ.5.26.29.——pul.βe.5.48. —rat^c.74.—rho. ; VIII^4. (20).—sbd^e.—sep.V^9.VIII^5. p.δ.—so-l.5.(14).—spi.(12). —spo.—stn.29.—stp.29. sto.——tab.22.—tep.q.5. vrb.βe^a.

—— *as if eyes would be pressed out.*—fag.d.——gym.—ign^a. δr.4.—lch.

—— *as if brain receded from before backwards.*—bry.31.

—— *followed by ulcerative pain in left leg and gluteal muscles.* —osm.

V¹². Screwing.—chd.ζ.—grt.—sul.
—— *from both sides.*—chd.

V¹⁴. Tingling.—ail.βa.

V¹⁶. Wedge, peg, or the like pressed in.
  —— *nail.*—aco.7.—hel⁸.(12).—lyc^c.—pl-n⁸.—ptl^b.
  —— *blunt arrow.*—cro^o.
  —— *blunt instrument.*—hel^e.p.—msc^e.—rhs.27.
  —— *peg.*—jac^a.
  —— *wedge.*—k-hy^h.δɩ,Ca².ii.
  —— *like a wedge forcing brain asunder.*—aco^f.6.(8).
  —— *plug.*—su-x⁸.

VI¹. Cutting.—crd^c.
  —— *backwards and inwards.*—fag^b.5.
  —— *sharp.*—dio^a.ɛ.12.—snc^c.
  —— *thrusts.*—cam.16.
  —— *obtuse.*—bis^f.
  —— *as if something sharp were pressed in.*—ca-c.12.31.
  —— *as if cut open.*—ir-f^a.4.
  —— *as with a sharp knife.*—na-m^b.

VI². Pricking, prickling.—ard.—aur.—fer^m.3.(8).—lil.III¹.5.7.—thu.—vrb^i.—vi-o.d.
  —— *like needles.*—aga^b.VI³-VIII³.—am-c^f.—asa^o.—cph.—cep.—hep.; IX.2.29.89.—k-ca.—man^b.—na-m.—sep.κ⁵.31.
  —— *intermittent.*—ca-a^b.20.35.—vrb^a.

VI³. Shooting.—arn.—bel.—chi.—cnb.q.—con.—cyc.—dig.—eub.—k-bi.—k-ca.—lo c.k^r.—mer.—msc.—ped.—plb.q.—rho.—rs-r.—sbd.—sil.—tar.—til. &c.
  —— *violent.*—cam.—zng.
  —— *transient.*—dgn.
  —— *flying.*—asa.—jat^a1.
  —— *here and there.*—sep.
  —— *diagonally.*—chd.
  —— *outwards.*—ba-a^n.—bel^m.—con.3-30.; 4.(16); 5.—fer.—glo^c.—grn.—lyc.—ph-x^c.—pul.5.—snc.; δ.—sep⁸.δb.

3-30.(8).; δ.1.—sul.5.86.89.—vrb^o.
  —— *as if all would come out there.*—bry.ζ³.29.
  —— *inwards.*—cth^a.—gel^c.4.
  —— *upwards.*—ph-x⁸.—scu^a.1.
  —— *obtuse.*—pla.
  —— *slow.*—san.
  —— *fine.*—tax.
  —— *as with a knife.*—itu^a.—la-v.V¹.—man^b.—sab^n.II³.—tep.29.; βa.κ⁶.—ter.
  —— *as with a bodkin.*—kre^a.a¹b^a.4.
  —— *as with an awl.*—mg-s⁸.
  —— *like blows.*—su-x^o.
  —— *like electric sparks.*—acn.—ol-a^o.—san.2.
  —— *stunning.*—ptl.
  —— *and aching alternately.*—val^e.

VI⁴. Tearing.—aga.—agn.—alm.—amb.—aur.—bel.—ber.—bov.—cth.—chd.—cch.—grt.—ign.—ind.—ipc.—mag.—mrl.—mu-x.—phl.—pho.—plb.p.aa.—rho.—sep.—stn.—sul.—zin. &c.
  —— *violent.*—zin.
  —— *transient.*—rat.
  —— *flying.*—sng^b.
  —— *periodical.*—cha.—plb^c.
  —— *hither and thither.*—plb.
  —— *radiating.*—lyc^o.
  —— *upwards.*—ber⁸.
  —— *across.*—bry.σ².r.—klm.
  —— *fine.*—cam.
  —— *paralytic.*—cin^n.o.βɩ^a.
  —— *as if torn.*—grp.3-30.—rhs^p.3-99.46.48.
  —— *tearing out.*—hep.χ².2.

VII¹. Bursting, splitting.—aga.p.hh.—am-c.σ².29.—aml.—ant.ab^c.βv.; ^f.—ba-a^e^m.—cap.—cau.i^a.—cn-s^c.p.ɩv.—cca^b.74.89.—crt.q.2.—fer.—glo.31.—grp.66.—ham.κ⁴.—bel.—hdr.3.99.(12.35.41).—ind.—jun.29.—k-ca.—lil.(12).—lyc^c.κ⁵.rvkk.—mer.—mez^h.p.hh.χ¹.3.—nat.3.35.—oln.—rat.5.29.—rhs.p.q.θ.κ³.6.100.(16.10).—sab^n.—san.κ⁴.χ¹.—so-n.35.—stp^b.
  —— *as if split in two.*—pul.βɩ.
  —— *as if split open.*—cit.κ⁵.

VII³. **Expanding.**—er-a°.δ¹o.29.
—— *alternating with contraction.*
—trxᵇ.βε.

VII⁴. **Swollen, as if.**—aga.—an-sᵉ.
—— *feels broad and high.*—cun.

VII⁵. **Tensive.**—aco.——ang.14.—
asa.q.βε.—can.—ca-x¹.—chp.35.
—col.74.—crt.σ².—dig.48.—gloᵉ·ᵇ.
σ².—hepᵇ.—hy-x.——hyo.p.—hyp.
q.—k-cl.—mt-nᵇ.—mrl.—nat¹.—
nx-v.—sbd.(41.49).—sil.δ.ω².—
sul.; δ.3-99.50.—valᵐ.x.
—— *across.*—irs.—naj.ġj
—— *sharp.*—ca-c.
—— *as after a blow.*—pla.x.ζ.
—— *like a board.*—pla.βε.
—— *of skin of forehead.*—opi.
(15).
—— *as if a piece of bladder were
stretched across.*—mnc.41.
—— *as from a cord.*—chd.3.
—— *as from an india-rubber
band.*—cca.
—— *as if skull were too tight.*—
naj.3-99.31.

VIII¹. **Blows, shocks.**—acoᵃ·ᵇ.VIII⁴.
—ac-l.—ang.iᵃ.—hpm.V⁶·⁷.δ.(5).
—lau.—na-m.a¹bᵃ.βa.—pla.—rs-r.
—— *penetrating.*—squᵒ.
—— *deep.*—croᵒ.βε.(12).
—— *outwards.*—cle.
—— *as if all would come out
there.*—am-c.
—— *as if struck with an axe.*—
nx-v.3-10.(30).
—— *as with a finger.*—na-mᵉ.41.
86.
—— *as if struck by hail.*—ampᵃ.
—— *as if something were knocked
in.*—msc.
—— *from occiput to F.*—sbd.

VIII². **Hammering.**—am-mᶠ.—cic.
4.—kre.V¹⁰·ˢ.29.—oln.—pauᵍ.
—— *slow.*—vrbᵒ.
—— *as with a small sharp hammer.*
—nicᵃ.

VIII³. **Jerking.**—alnᵇ.3.—arn.—
bor.δ.κ⁵.4.—cn-iᵃ.—cauᵃ.—cha.66.
—chi.4.(5).—opi.v¹.ω.—sep.—sil.
2.—spr.—sulᶠ.—su-xᵒ.—thu.ηaa.3.
—— *across.*—sbd.

—— *backwards.*—pru.
—— *as if lumps of lead were
shaken there.*—pho.
—— *alternating with dull aching.*
—stn.

VIII⁴. **Throbbing.**—bor.—ca-c.—
cap.—con.—glo. ; d.q.—grp.—
iod.—k-ca.—k-cl.—klm.—lah.—
mag.—mr-f.—mo-a.—na-m. &c.
—— *violent.*—lau.—so-n.
—— *periodical.*—cn-sᵃ.
—— *outwards.*—asaⁿ.—canᵒ.—
lycᵉ.—natᵉ.
—— *as if everything would be
crowded out at forehead.*—
glo.
—— *upwards and backwards.*—
gloᵇ.
—— *synchronous with pulse.*—
glo.
—— *gradually diminishing.*—
sbdᵃ.
—— *slow.*—oln.
—— *as with a blunt point.*—cau.
V¹.
—— *making head fall forwards.*—
lep.

VIII⁵. **Undulating.**—ard.
—— *from right to left.*—glo.
—— *like a heavy body swaying
backwards and forwards.*—
opi.VI³–VIII⁴.q.26.

IX. **Peculiar.**
—— *as if brain were an ant-hill.*
—aga.iᵃ.ζ.
—— *pressive crawling pain spreading out from centre, as if
something alive.*—trx.8-31.
—— *formication.*—ard.—chdᵐ.—
cocⁿ.—cch.—lau.q.βεᵃ.29.
—pho.—pul.
—— *as if brain rose and sunk.*—
bel.31.(12).
—— *painful quivering.*—bovⁿ.au.
—— *like a board before forehead.*
—cb-a.q.—coc.βa,ɒ,εᵃ.—
hln.—lyc.βε.—opi.a¹ɒ.βa.
ω⁸.—sul.
—— *like something pushed in between forehead and brain.*
—cau.βεᵇ.

—— *as if lifted up.*—dio.
—— *like electric shocks.*—cep.V[1].
—— *hot pain.*—lil.ω^2.5.
—— *hollow pain.*—chd[h].
—— *as if a net were drawn through.*—cn-s.
—— *as if full of lead.*—cle.p.
—— *as if solid with pain.*—pi-m.
—— *like an abscess.*—hep.VI[2].2. 29.89.
—— *as if a cyst would form.*—epn[b].
—— *like a ball rolling round.*–hur.
—— *like toothache.*—au-m[o].
—— *like the stroke of a rusty saw.*—pan[e].
—— *like a thread drawn through temples to occiput.*—sbd[c].
—— *like bubbles of water.*—sed.
—— *like a bubble bursting.*—for.
—— *paralysed feeling.*—sep.
—— *like a leaden bullet that would not come loose.*—stp[e].26.
—— *like a rolled up lump and heavy weight.*—stp[h].—tar[b]. 2-99.; ª.5.
—— *as if cold water fell there.*—trn.eυ.
—— *as if cold air penetrated painfully.*—zin[i].
—— *left half of forehead feels higher than right; left dull, right clear.*—cun.

Complex pains.

II[1.6]–III[1]. **Burning, stinging, contractive.**—lil.
II[1]–III[1]. **Burning, contractive.**—bis.δ.—glo.a[1]b[s].$\beta\varepsilon.\delta.\eta$.
II[1]–IV[1]–VI[3]. **Burning, cramping, lancinating.**—bel.
II[1]–V[1]. **Burning, aching.**—aga.$\delta\varepsilon$.—alm.p.18.19.66.(8).—grt[a].—la-v.p.—lil[s].5.; $\delta\varepsilon$.—su-x.δ.
II[1]–V[1]–VII[5]. **Burning, aching, tensive.**—sep.δ.
II[1]–V[7]. **Burning, stupefying.**—bro[g].q.
II[1]–VI[5]. **Burning, shooting.**—chi[d].—cup[b].—men.ηp.—na-m.

II[1]–VI[3]–VII[1]. **Burning, shooting, bursting.**—pho.3.19.66.(15).
II[1]–VI[4]. **Burning, tearing.**—bel[o].
II[1]–VIII[5]. **Burning, undulating.**—hfb.
II[3]–V[1]. **Raw, aching.**—na-m.—pru.(42).
II[3]–V[2]. **Raw, beaten.**—ars.(15).
II[3]–V[2]. **Raw, bruised.**—mt-n.
II[3]–VI[3]. **Raw, shooting.**—sab[n].
II[3]–VIII[3]. **Raw, jerking.**—su-x[o].
II[5]–III[1]. **Sore, contractive.**—alm.
II[5]–V[2]. **Sore, bruised.**—glo.
II[7]–V[6]–VI[3.4]. **Ulcerative, drawing, shooting, tearing.**—sul.26.(8-12).
III–IV[1]. **Compressive, cramp-like.**—bel.
III–V[7]. **Compressive, dull.**—ana[o].—msc[h].—spi.
III–V[10.s]. **Compressed from both sides, out-pressing.**—chi.8-31.
III–VIII[5]. **Compressive, undulating.**—coc[b].
III[1]–IV[1]. **Contractive, cramp-like.**—mt-s[h].
III[1]–V[1]. **Contractive, aching.**—aco[d].a[1]$\mathfrak{c}$[a].ηc[b],ii.51.111.(98.114).—cau.8-31.(29).—dig.41.—ign.—par.—val[b].
III[1]–V[6]. **Contractive, drawing.**—ve-v[g].
III[1]–V[12]. **Contractive, screwed in.**—mer.$\delta\varepsilon$.
III[1]–V[12]–VI[3]. **Contractive, screwing, shooting.**—bov[g.h.o].$\delta\varepsilon$.
III[1]–VI[3]. **Contractive, shooting.**—man.8.
III[1]–VI[4]. **Contractive, tearing.**—plb.
III[1]–IV[1]–V[6]. **Constrictive, cramp-like, drawing.**—pla.
III[1]–V[1]. **Constrictive, aching.**—chi.31.
III[1]–V[3]. **Constrictive, digging.**—ana.au.4.(12).—pla.x.au[ff].eυ[k].χ^2.7.
III[1]–V[10.t]. **Constrictive, inward-pressure.**—bry.
III[1]–V[6.w]. **Constrictive, drawing across.**—val.
III[1]–VII[5]. **Constrictive, tensive.**—ber.q.29.(8).

III$^{2\cdot3}$. Pinching, squeezing.—aco. $\alpha^1\varsigma^a$.—mez.ζ.

III^2–V^1. Pinching, aching.—hæm$^{g.\ to\ f.}$.

III^2–VIII^3. Pinching, jerking.—gur^h.

III^3–V^1. Squeezing, aching.—eug.—til.2.

III^3–V^1–VI^4. Squeezing, aching, tearing.—ana.

III^3–V^6. Squeezing, drawing.—asa^e.—bry^f.—cro^o.ζ.

III^3–VII^5. Squeezing, tensive.—aco^p.

IV^1–V^{12}. Cramping, screwed in.—pla.

IV^1–VI^4. Cramp-like, tearing.—nat.$\delta.\zeta$.

IV^3–VIII^4. Spasmodic throbbing.—ca-s^a.3.

V$^{1\cdot2}$. Aching, bruised.—nx-v^g.$\delta\flat$.

V$^{1\cdot2}$–VI^4. Aching, bruised, torn.—thu.3-99.

V$^{1\cdot3}$. Aching, boring.—bov^g.4.7.—bry.29.31.—cb-v.—cle^a.η.5.—dul.—mg-m^i.(34.**105**.).—mez^c.—msc.—opi.$\delta\flat.\delta$Lq.—pla^b.6.8-31.66.

V$^{1\cdot3\cdot16}$. Aching, boring, like a plug.—mez^b.

V$^{1\cdot3}$–VI^3. Aching, boring, shooting.—stp^b.3-99.

V$^{1\cdot6}$. Aching, drawing.—aga$^{b.\ to\ a.}$; $^o.\delta$.—ars^a.—asr.72.—au-n^e.q.—bor$^{e\cdot h}.\lambda.\sigma^2$.29.43.44.—ca-a^g.—cth.$\beta\varepsilon$.—cau.; ^{h}.—cin^b.—cof^d.41.—col.—con.—cyc$^{a.\ to\ b}$.(11).—dul^o.—ign$^{t\cdot h}$.29.—k-ca.5.—men^h.—rut^a.—san.—squ.—stn.; ^{g}.—stp.—trx.18.—thu.q.—zng.34.

V$^{1\cdot6\cdot v}$. Aching, drawing upwards.—ni-x.—stp^f.

V$^{1\cdot6\cdot7}$. Aching, drawing, stupefying.—stn.

V$^{1\cdot6\cdot10}$. Aching, drawing, pressing.—hlt.(8-31).

V$^{1\cdot6}$–VI^3. Aching, drawing, shooting.—chd.—sil^e.—stp^b.

V$^{1\cdot6}$–VI^4. Aching, drawing, tearing.—k-ca^h.δ.—zin.

V$^{1\cdot6}$–VII^5. Aching, drawing, tensive.—tar.

V$^{1\cdot6}$–VIII^5. Aching, drawing, undulating.—asa^b.

V$^{1\cdot7}$. Aching, stupefying.—aco.5.—eub.—evo^f.—gel.—hel.

V$^{1\cdot7}$–VI^2. Aching, stupefying, pricking.—hyo^b.

V$^{1\cdot7}$–VI^4. Aching, stupefying, tearing.—hyo.

V$^{1\cdot7}$–VIII^5. Aching, stupefying, undulating.—pla^f.

V$^{1\cdot7}$–VIII^5. Aching, dull, undulating.—tar^n.

V$^{1\cdot8}$. Aching, gnawing.—rut.

V$^{1\cdot9}$. Aching, pecking.—vrb^o.

V$^{1\cdot10}$. Aching, pressing.—car.$\beta\varepsilon$.—idm^d.i^a.5.29.—k-ca.κ^6.—lil^g.

V^1–VI^1. Aching, cutting.—cam.—ptl.

V^1–VI^3. Aching, shooting.—aco^e.$\theta^4.\kappa^5$.—aga^e.—am-c^e.—ant^g.—bov.—bry^f.3.; ^{e}.—ca-a^b.31.—epn.—gui^n.—gym.i^a.δ.—lyc.3.— mag.—mr-c^g.29.—msc.—ni-x^m.—nit.; ^{a}.5.—opi^f.—pet^e.—pso^b.—rut.89.—sar^n.; ^{o}.—sep^g.6.35.(8-31).—trx.

V^1–VI$^{3\cdot4}$. Aching, shooting, tearing.—cam.

V^1–VI^3–VII^5. Aching, shooting, tensive.—ctn.

V^1–VI^3–VIII^3. Aching, shooting, jerking.—arn.χ^1.—val.

V^1–VI^4. Aching, tearing.—agn^o.—amb^h.$\beta\varepsilon$.—arg^o.; δ.—aur.βa.—bel.—bov$^{e\cdot h}$.—chd^h.$\delta\flat$.(66).—grn.—grt^b.—hel^o.δl.—iod^a.—lyc^a.δ.3.—mez.—ol-a^a.δ.3.; ^{b}.5.—phl^a.18.—sab^n.—sam^d.δ.—spi^o.—stn.; ^{a}.29.—stp^b.—sul.; θ^1.116.—vrb^g.—zin^o.66.

V^1–VI$^{4\cdot z}$. Aching, tearing backwards.—nit^q.31.**70**.(8-128).

V^1–VII^1. Aching, bursting.—amm.—bel^n.14.

V^1–VIII^4. Aching, swollen feeling.—ca-c.

V^1–VII^5. Aching, tensive.—bel^a.—bry.—cle.q.31.; 66.; $\beta\varepsilon$.—cof.$\delta\flat$.3-99.29.—col.—dig.5.—dul^f.—eub.σ^2.—gn-l.q.$\beta\varepsilon$.44.—hæm^h.x.ζ^3.—mrl.—mer.(12).—rho.—

sbd.—sil^e.82.——sul.(12).——tar. 3-99.(116).—zn-o.

V^1–VII^5–VIII^4. **Aching, tensive, throbbing.**—alo.

V^1–VIII^3. **Aching, jerking.**——sil^c. (28.29.86).——stn^b.al^g.——thu^o.; ^{n}. δ.

V^1–VIII$^{3.5}$. **Aching, jerking, undulating.**—sep.

V^1–VIII^4. **Aching, throbbing.**—bel^e.——cn-i.——cau.——col.3-99.—dgn^f.; ^{b}.——dul^b.βa.——mez.; ζ.θ^1. 26.—na-m^b.—nx-m^g.3.—spg.5.—sum^o.

V^1–VIII^5. **Aching, undulating.**——cin.—hyo.d.29.—vi-t.

V^2–VI^4. **Bruised, torn.**—cof.43.

V$^{3.7}$. **Boring, dull.**—cmf.3.

V$^{3.7}$–VI^3. **Boring, stupefying, shooting.**—man.

V$^{3.10.s}$. **Boring, pressing out.**—coh.—ipc^e.(12.47).—sul.η.

V$^{3.10.t}$. **Boring, pressing in.**—k-ca^g.

V$^{3.12}$. **Boring, screwing.**—nic.

V^3–VI^2. **Boring, pricking.**——coc^a.—spo^b.8-31.

V^3–VI^3. **Boring, shooting.**—am-c^n. 63.—ca-a^b.19.(11.18.31).; ^{c}.——ch-s^c.5.—jac^b.ζ^g.—mer^b.19.—rut^a. 19.—zin^n.

V^3–VI$^{3.x}$. **Boring, shooting diagonally across.**—hel.

V^3–VII^1. **Boring, bursting.**—na-s.

V$^{3.6}$. **Digging, drawing.**——ag-n^o.r. —cad.g^b.—mer.—mez^b.

V$^{3.10.t}$. **Digging, pressing inwards.** —ana^a-5.(12.16.63).

V^3–VI^3. **Digging, shooting.**—ag-n°. 4.; ^{b}.η.—sul^a.

V^3–VI^3–VIII^3. **Digging, shooting, jerking.**—ber^g.g^b.

V^3–VI^4. **Digging, tearing.**——spi^a. 35.51.86.(16).

V^3–VIII^4. **Digging, throbbing.**——hpm^i.g^b.ζ.

V$^{6.7}$. **Drawing, dull.**—hel.—hpm.δ. (5).

V$^{6.7}$–VIII^4. **Drawing, dull, throbbing.**—sul^b.

V$^{6.7}$. **Drawing, stupefying.**——vrb^o. 107.

V$^{6.9}$. **Drawing, pecking.**——na-m. 3-30.

V$^{6.10}$. **Drawing, pressing.**—bry^f.θ^1. —fer.

V$^{6.10.t}$. **Drawing, pressing inwards.** —ant^b.

V$^{6.10.u}$. **Drawing, pressing downwards.**—cro^c.

V^6–VI^1. **Drawing, cutting.**——aga. 18.V^7.19.

V^6–VI$^{1.4}$. **Drawing, cutting, tearing.**—stp.

V^6–VI^3. **Drawing, shooting.**—alo. aæ^t.βε.δb.—atr.—gui^o.—man.χ^1.8. (6).—pet^e.—tab.

V^6–VI$^{3.4}$. **Drawing, shooting, tearing.**—sep.

V^6–VI^4. **Drawing, tearing.**—aga. —cth.35.—cb-v^d.——cas.5.—ch-s. —f-io^e.——gui.—man^f.—rho.δ.6. 35.

V^6–VII^1. **Drawing, bursting.**--sul^f. θ^{4}r.

V^6–VII^2. **Drawing, expansive.**——bry^b.6.31.

V^6–VII^4. **Drawing, swelling.**—bel.

V^6–VII^5. **Drawing, tensive.**—bry^n. 4.—cau^b.—pul^e.50.

—— *as if a bud were expanding.* —bry^g.

V^6–VII^5–VIII^3. **Drawing, tensive, jerking.**—tar^g.

V^6–VIII^3. **Drawing, jerking.**——alo^f.δ.

V^6–VIII^4. **Drawing, throbbing.**—epn.—hyo^n.29.35.—zin.

V$^{7.8}$–VI^4. **Dull, gnawing, tearing.** —mr-i.2.

V$^{7.10}$. **Dull, pressing.**—mr-i^a.ρ.5.

V^7–VI^3. **Dull, shooting.**——æsc.——c-cs^o.—naj.φ^1.2.—tar.89.

V^7–VII^5. **Dull, tensive.**—zn-o.

V^7–VIII^4. **Dull, pulsating.**—for.i^a. p.—myr.

V^7–VII^5. **Stupefying, tensive.**—tar^h.

V^7–VIII^4. **Stupefying, throbbing.** —par^b.

V$^{9.10.s}$. **Pecking, forcing out.**—nx-v. 3.29.

V$^{9.10.s}$–VIII^3. **Pecking, pressing out, jerking.**—sep.p.δ.

V^9–VI^4. **Pecking, tearing.**—opi.$\kappa^{6.7}$.χ^3.

V^{10}–VI^3. **Pressing, stitching.**—mr-i.$\delta l.\eta l.\iota$.

V^{10}–VI^4. **Pressing, tearing.**—mu-x^f.

V^{10}–VII^1. **Pressing, bursting.**—fag.4.

V^{10}–VIII^5. **Pressing, undulating.**—col^b.

$V^{10.s}$–VI^1. **Pressing outwards, cutting.**—cap.

$V^{10.s}$–VI^3. **Pressing out, shooting.**—bry.29.—stp.35.(20).

$V^{10.s}$–VI^4. **Pressing out, tearing.**—cam^b.

$V^{10.s}$–VII^5. **Forcing out, tensive.**—mrl^e.29.—spi.

$V^{10.s}$–VIII^1. **Pressing out, knocking.**—na-m.33.

$V^{10.s}$–VIII^2. **Pressing out, hammering.**—kre.29.

$V^{10.s}$–VIII^3. **Pressing out, jerking.**—dul.35.

$V^{10.s}$–VIII^4. **Pressing out, throbbing.**—rho.(20).

$V^{10.t}$–VII^5. **Pressing inwards, tension.**—hel.q.χ.(8).

$V^{10.u}$–VI^4. **Downward pressing, torn.**—am-m^b.3-30.

$V^{10.v}$–VIII^4. **Upward pressure, beating.**—gn-l.i^a.q.

V^{14}–VIII^3. **Vibrating jerk.**—mag^s.31.35.

$VI^{1.2}$. **Cutting, pricking.**—dro^a.

$VI^{1.3}$. **Cutting, shooting.**—bel.—fer.

$VI^{3.4}$. **Shooting, tearing.**—alm^o.5.—ana^f.—bel^f.—bov^n.er.—cha.x.chd^o.—ccn.—con.—ctn.—dig^f.—grt.—k-hy^a.5.(12).—lab^e.—lyc^f.2.—mg-m^b.; 5.35.—mer^b.8.; ^{b}.p.ηp.r^1b.χ.19.—mez^o.—nat^o.—sil.q.w.—su-x^a.5.(12).—trx^b.—tar.4.—zin.e^3.5.; ^{g}.λ.

$VI^{1.4.v}$. **Shooting, tearing upwards.**—dig^f.

$VI^{3.4}$–VIII^3. **Shooting, tearing, jerking.**—k-hy^i.—mez.

VI^3–VII^1. **Shooting, bursting.**—am-m^b.29.—nit^b.29.

VI^3–VII^5. **Shooting, tension.**—mrl^e.x.

VI^3–VIII^3. **Shooting, jerking.**—aco.—arn.; $\kappa^5.\rho$.29.—bry.; θ^1.—con.1.—cyc^a.η.35.—mg-m.—pru^a.—spr^d.—spo.31.—squ.—val^c.

VI^3–VIII^4. **Shooting, throbbing.**—alm.4.—ar-c^a.—ber.29.—cam.χ^2.2.—cth.—grt.—lyc^n.4.—opi.q.w.26.—pet^e.—sil.3.—spi.$e v^b$.2.

$VI^{3.s}$–VIII^3. **Out-shooting, jerking.**—lyc.

VI^4.4–VI^3.5. **Tearing, shooting.**—alm.

VI^4–VII^5. **Tearing, tensive.**—agn.—cch^b.—dro.29.—spi^o.

VI^4–VIII^1. **Tearing, blows.**—mt-s^a.

VI^4–VIII^3. **Tearing, jerking.**—æth$^{g.i}$.19.—cac.ru.—chi^m.—mg-s.4.—spi^n.$\delta \iota^d$.18.19.

VI^4–VIII^4. **Tearing, throbbing.**—asr.—coc.5.—grt.—inu.66.—lyc$^{g.n}$.—mag.—zin.66.; ^{a}.1.

VII^1–VIII^4. **Bursting, throbbing.**—am-c.—aml.i^a.$\beta \varepsilon$.—k-bi^e.q.29.35.66.(8.14.16).

VII^1–$VIII^{4.5}$. **Bursting, throbbing, undulating.**—pet.(35).

$VIII^{3.4}$. **Hammering, throbbing.**—mg-s.4.5.

$VIII^{3.4}$. **Jerking, throbbing.**—dgn.—pho^h.δ.ζ.κ^6.3.

$VIII^{4.5}$. **Throbbing, undulating.**—ag-n.—mer.

ANATOMICAL SEAT.

F$^{a.1}$. **In both sides of forehead.**—aru.$V^{10.a}$.δq.—cb-v.$VI^{4.a}$.—glo.V^2.—jat.VI^3.—k-bi.δo.VIII^4.δo.—la-x.$V^{7.a}$.1.5.—rut.V^7.η.—seu.$VI^{3.v}$.—su-x.$VI^{3.q}$.—val.V^1.—vrb.V^7.

F^a. **In right side of forehead.**—ac-x.V^7.—aco.; VIII^1.$^b VIII^4$.—aga.$V^{1.q}$.—alo.V^6–VI^3.$a x^t$.$\beta \varepsilon$.δb.—amp.VIII^1.—ana.$V^{10.a}$.; IV^1.; V^3–$V^{10.t}$.5.(12.16.63).—ag-n.$V^{10.a}$.—arn.V^1.ε.o^3.—ars.$V^{1.6}$.—ar-c.VI^3.–VIII^4.—aru.; V^{10}.—asa^a.$V^{10.s}$.—ba-c.V^1.q.—bel.V^1–VII^5.—ber.$VI^{3.a}$.—bov^n.$VI^{3.q}$.—bro.V^1.ζ.—buf.V^1.ca-a.V^7.29.—cas.IV^3–VIII^4.3.—cth.$VI^{3.t}$.—cas.$V^{10.a}$.—ce-b.; II^1.; $V^{3.x}$.; V^{10}.—chd.$V^{1.b}$.—chi.V^1.—

cim.V⁶.—cn-s.; VIII⁴·ᵉ.—cnb.V⁷.
5.—coc.III.; V³–VI²·ᵉ.—cch.Iᵃ.
3-99.(35).——cot.V⁷.26.——crt.—
c-ar.—cyc.VI³–VIII³.η.35.; V⁷.—
dig.V⁷.5.——dio.VI¹.ₑ.12.——dro.
VI¹·².—eub.V⁷.; V¹.——epn.V¹⁰·ᵃ.
——fer.ζr.; V⁷.——f-io.V⁷.q.43.44.
130.(8.107).—fl-x.Iᵇ.5.; δr.3.16.—
glo.V⁷·ʷ.; VI³.88.—grt.II¹–V¹.—
hel.V¹⁰·ˢ.——hfb.V⁷.——ign.V¹.aᵏᵇ.
βɒ,ₑ.; V⁷.δ.δ𝔰.; V¹·q.; ⁿ.V³·ᵃ.—ind.
—iod.V¹.x.κ².; V¹–VI⁴.—ir-f.VI¹.
4.—itu.VI³.——jac.V¹⁶.; ᵈ.V¹.δ —
k-bi.——klm.V¹⁰.——kre.VI³.aᵏbˢ.4.
—lah.VI⁴.ζ.——lau.——lo-s.——mt-s.
VI⁴–VIII¹.—men.V¹.(12).; V⁶.—
mer.V¹.——mo-a.Iᵃ.δP².θ³.κ.σbh,b.
ω³.;V⁷.aᵏɒ.--msc.V¹.βₑ.--na-m.VI³.
4.—na-s.V¹·ᵉ.——nic.VIII².—ol-a.
V¹.(**15**).—opi.VI³·ᵃ.aᵏbˢ.; V⁷.; V¹.
p.43.—osm.; VI⁴·q.ᵥ.5.——phl.V¹–
VI⁴.18.; VI³.——phoᵉ.V¹.——pru.
V¹⁰·ᵃ.—pso.δ.—rat.VI³.; V⁶.31.—
rho.V¹⁰ ˢ.—rs-r.——rum.—rut.V⁷.
ηp.κ⁵.; V¹·⁶.; V³–VI³·ᵉ.19.——sbd.
VIII⁴.——sab.V¹.--san.V¹⁰.ₑ.18.
(31).; ₑ.θ¹.3-99.—sar.VIII⁴.8-31.
—sng.V¹.—sep.VI⁴.—spi.II¹.δ.
48.—squ.VI³.—stn.V¹–VI⁴.29.—
stp.V¹.—sul.V³–VI³.; V¹·⁶.; ᵃ.VI³.
—su-x.V¹.; VI³·⁴.5.(12).—trn.δ.
4.29.—tar.VIII⁴.; IX.5.—teu.V¹.
—thu.VI⁴.δ.ζ.η.3.5.—urt.V⁷.ηr.—
val.V¹.5.—vrb.VI²·ᵉ.——xip.V¹.βₑ.
r.—zin.VI⁴–VIII⁴.1.

—— *from right to left.*—cyc.V¹·⁶.
(11).—ign.V¹.—irs.

Fᵇ. In left side of forehead.—ac-x.
V⁷.——aco.VIII⁴.ᵃVIII¹.——æth.
VIII⁴.—aln.VIII³.3.—ant.V⁶·¹⁰·ᵗ.
—arg.V³·ᵉ.5.16.—ag-n.VIII⁴.—
arn.V².90.—asa.V¹·⁶–VIII⁵.—asr.
βa.3-30.—aur.V¹.; VI⁴.35.—au-m.
V⁶.;VIII⁴.—bel.V¹⁰·ᵃ·ˢ.;V⁷.—bov.
V¹·q.q.δ.δɒ.3.35.; V³·ˢ.5.—bry.VI³.
βa.;V⁶.--cac.V¹⁰.5.—ca-a.VI²·ᵉ.20.
35.; V¹–VI³.31.; V³–VI³.19.(11.
18.31).—cam.V¹⁰·ˢ.VI⁴.—cb-a.V⁹.
3-30.(8).—ca-x.V¹.——car.—cau.
V⁶.—cnt.--chd.VI³.5.—chi.VI³ d.
(11).; V³.—ch-s.VII¹.d.aᵏιᵗᵇ,ɒᵇ.βa,

ₑ.δtᶜ.ₑa,ɒ.ηp.κ²·³·⁵·⁷.λ².ρ.φ².χ³.ω².; Iᵃ.
βa.ₑɒ.3.—cin.V¹·⁶.—cle.V⁶.; Iᵃ.δO.
5.102.(12).——cca.VII¹.74.89.—
coc.III–VIII⁵.—cch.VI⁴–VII⁵.—
col.λ.μ³.; Iᵇ.; V¹⁰–VIII⁶.; 2-99.—
cun.V⁷.iiᵈ.—cup II¹–VI³.—dgn.
VI³.δLll.5.31.—dul.V¹–VIII⁴.βa.
—eub.VI⁴.βa.26.; VI³.—epn.IX.
—evo.V⁶.η.—fag.VIII⁴.35.;VI¹·ᵗ·ᶻ
5.—fl-x.5.; VI³.—glo.VIII⁴.; V¹.
—grt.V¹–VI⁴.——hæm.η.θ¹.—ham.
VI³.—hpm.V⁷.—hfb.V⁷.βₑᵃ.—hyo.
V¹·⁷.; VI³·ᵉ.δo.—iod.--ipc.V¹⁰·ˢ.26.
—jac.V³–VI³.ζ³.——k-bi.Iᵃ.—klm.
VI⁴.——la-x.——lau.29.——lep.—lil.
V⁷.δₑ.4.——lth.V¹⁰.κ⁵.——lyc.VI³·ᵃ.;
V¹.;VIII⁴.5.—mt-n.V¹.;VI³.3-30.
—mt-s.VI³·ᵇ.—mag.V⁷.δ.—mg-m.
VI³·⁴.—men.V⁶.——mer.V³–VI³·ᵉ.
19.—-VI³·⁴.18.; VI³·⁴.p.ηp.rᵏb.χ¹.
19.—mez.V³.; VI³·ʷ.3-**10**.—mu-x.
V¹⁰·ˢ.——nat.V¹.3-30.——na-m.VI³.
w.; V¹–VIII⁴.--na-s.δb.--nit.VI³–
VII¹.29.—nup.V³·ᵇ.5.; V⁷.; VI³.
—ol-a.V¹.(**15**).; VI⁴.; V¹–VI⁴.5.;
VI³.—opi.VI³·q.——par.V⁷–VIII⁴.
—phl.p.βa.rᵏp.; V¹.p.; V³.——ph-x.
V¹.—plg.Iᵃ.q.——pla.V¹⁰·ᵗ.; V¹·³.6.
8-31.66.—pru.V¹⁰·ˢ.--pso.V¹–VI³.
ptl.V¹⁶.—rho.V¹.; VIII⁴.——rs-r.—
sab.V¹⁰.—sar.V¹.—sng.V¹.δo.66.
(8).; VI⁴·ᵇ.——sil.VIII⁴.—spi.V¹⁰·ˢ.
—spr.——spo.V³–VI²·ˢ.8-31.; V¹.;
V¹⁰·ˢ.19.(30).—stn.V¹–VIII³.aᵏˢ.;
VI³.ζ³.—stp.VII¹.; V¹–VI⁴.; V¹·⁶–
VI³.—sul.; Iᵃ.3-99.; V⁶·⁷–VIII⁴·q.;
rᵥ.; V⁶·q.; V³.βa.δo,𝔰.—su-xᶜ.V⁶.
sum.βₑ.——tab.V⁶.δ.—trx.VI³·⁴.—
tar.IX.2-99.; V¹.δ.——tep.V¹.βa.—
ton.V¹.; V⁶·q.16.——val.III¹–V¹.—
vrb.V¹⁰·ᵃ.βₑᵃ.—zin.VI⁴.

—— *from left to right.*—aga.V¹·⁶.
——hæm.III²–V¹.——rs-r.—
squ.VI³.

Fᶜ. In middle of forehead.—ail.—
alo.V¹⁰·ᵗ·ᵘ.——ana.V⁷.2.—as-s.Iᵃ.—
atr.--bov.VI⁴·ᴾ.3.5.--ca-a.V³–VI³.
—cam.V¹.—ca-x.V⁷.—cau.VI⁴.σ².
φ¹.1-7.2.65.—chd.VI³.—chi.V¹.4.
—ch-s.V³–VI³.5.——cch.—col.V¹.
—con.V⁶.--cro.V⁶·¹⁰·ᵘ.--crt.—gel.

VI$^{3·t}$.4.——gen.V^{10}.3.——gn-l.V^1.——glo.VI$^{3·s}$.; VI^4.——kre.VIII^4.——lau. V^1.; VI$^{4·q}$.p.; VI^3.8-31.; V^6.——lyc. V^{16}.; VIII^4.1.——mt-s.VI^3.g^b.5.——mez.V$^{1·3·p}$.——mu-x^m.VI^3.——ph-x. VI$^{3·s}$.——pla.V$^{3·a}$.——plb.VI$^{4·e}$.——pso. ——rat.VI^3.29.; V$^{10·s}$.74.——sar.VI^3. ——sil.V^1–VIII^3.(28.29.86).——so-n. V^{10}.——stn.V$^{1·q}$.——stp.IX.26.——sto. VI^4.——su-x^b.V^6.——trx.IX.8-31.—— val.VI^3–VIII$^{3·q}$.——zin.V$^{1·d}$.

F^d. In upper part of forehead.——aco. V^1–III^1.a^1c^a.ηc^b.ii.51.111.(98.114). ——ber.V^1.——bro.V^{10}.5.——bry.V$^{1·10}$. 3-99.——cb-v.V^6–VI^4.——chi.II^1– VI$^{3·a}$.——cin.III.——cca.8-31.——cof. V$^{1·6}$.41.——cch.VI$^{3·b}$.; V^7.; V^1.(20. 101).——con.V^{10}.——dig.V^{10}.41.—— dib.——glo.i^a.——hyo.III$^{1·e}$.$af.\beta c^a$.—— idm.V$^{1·10}$.i^a.5.29.——jac^a.V^1.δ.——led. βc.130.——man.V^7.——mez.V^1.——naj.i^a. ——na-m.VI^3.——oln.V$^{10·s}$.——ptv.V^3. ——pl-n.V^7.——pso.III^2.q.θ^1.3.——sam. V^1–VI^4.δ.——san.V^3.——sep.V^1.——spr. VI^3–VIII^3.——sul.VI^3.——zin.VI^4.

F^e. Above eyes.——aco.V^1–VI^3.θ^4.κ^5. ——ac-l.VI^3.——aga.V^1–VI^3.; VI^3.—— ail.q.(12).——aln.πl.3.; V^{10}.3-99. (68).; V^{10}.βa.5.(16).——alo.V^7.; VI^3.; ^{m}.VI^3.——alm.VI^1.; III^1.5. $\chi^{2·3}$.2.; III.; VI^3.κ^5.ν^3.ω^2.3-99.—— am-g.——am-c.V^1–VI^3.——amy.V^1. ——ang.V$^{10·s}$.20.35.; VI^3.——an-s. VII^4.——arg.V^1.——arn.III^1.——ars. III^3.——asa.III^3–V^6.; V^1.q.x.ϕ.—— asp.——ast.V^1.q.——atr.VI^3.29.35.—— au-m.VI^4.βa.29.35.(8).——au-n.V$^{1·6}$. q.; V^3.——bap.——ba-a^m.VII^1.——bel. q.δ.3-99.; V$^{10·u}$.δb.3.; V$^{10·t}$.δb.—— V$^{10·s}$.δb,P^1,$_0\sigma^2$.; VI^4.; V^1–VIII^4. ——ber.VI^3.——bor.V^1.(8-31).; V^7. 3.; ^{h}.V$^{1·6}$.λ.σ^2.29.43.44.; V^6.—— bov^h.V^1–VI^4.——bro.V^1.——bry.III.; V$^{10·s}$.31.66.; V$^{1·10}$.3-30.; V^1.43.; V^1–VI^3.——cad.V^1.——c-cs.VI^4.—— cn-i^h.V^1.i^a.q.; V^6.; V$^{10·s}$.4.——cap. VI^3.e^h.V^1.——cb-v.V^1.δ.——ca-x.II^1. ——crd.VI^1.——cau.VIII^4.——ced.I^w.; III.——chd.II^1.——chi.5.31.(66).; V^1.i^a.——ch-s.V^1.; I.3.50^d.; V^1.28. 48.——cl-h.35.; δ.——cmf.——cin.

VI$^{3·q}$.——cnb.V^7.5.35.——cis.V^1.—— cca.I^a.ϵv.; 24.50.——ccs.V^{10}.; V^1. d.——cch.I^b.; V^3.; III^1.; I^a.ζ.; V^1. 4.——con.V$^{10·s}$.——cro.δ.2.115.—— crt.V^1.βa.κ^5.; 3.——ctn.V^7.hh.δLq. ——cun.V^7.1.——dig.V$^{1·h}$.——dio.—— dro.29.(31).——er-a.VII^2.δo.29.—— er-m.5.——fer.——f-io.V^6–VI^4.; q. ——gel^p.V^2.——glo.V^7.q.; I^w.; V^7. (98).; ^{h}.VII^5.σ^2.; V^1.i^a.——gur. V^{10}.——ham^h.V^7.——hel.V^1.——hpm. V^1.4.——hdr.3.——hur.δ.——hfb.8.31. ——ign.VI^3.——idm.V^{10}.θj.κ^3.$r^1 p$.—— iod.V^1.5.; VI^3.ii^d.29.——k-bi.; VII^1–VIII^4.q.29.35.66.(8.14.16). ——k-ca.V^1.——klm.; σ^2.rl.5.——lah^h. 1.; VI$^{3·4}$.——la-x.d.ηd.——la-v.IV^2. ——lau.V^3.——lil.V^7.——lo-i.V$^{7·w}$.q.—— lo-s.V^7.43.44.——lyc.66.; V^1–VI^4. δ.3.; VI^3.; VIII$^{4·s}$.——lcp.VI^3.—— mt-n.V^1.31.——mag.V^1.3-30.——mep. ——mrl.VI^3–VII^5.x.; V$^{10·s}$–VII^5. 29.——mr-i.VI^3.5.——mez.V^1.——mit. I^a.——msc.V^{16}.——naj.V^1.ak.; VIII^4. ——nat.VIII$^{4·s}$.——na-a.V^1.——na-m. V^1.q.; V^1.1.; VI^3.——ni-x.VI^3.3.; 66.——nx-j.βa.; V^1.35.——ol-a.VI^3. ——opi.VI^3.βc.; V^1.βa,ε.——osm.ϵ.δc. η.——pan.IX.——pau.I^q.——pet.V^6-VI^2.; V^1–VI^3.; VI^3–VIII^4.——ph-x.δb. ——pho.3-99.(30).; ^{a}.V^1.; V$^{10·s}$. I^a.ii.——phy.κ^5.——pim.VI^3.——plm. ——ptl.——pul.V^1.; V^6–VII^5.50.; III^1.49.——rap.I^a.δo.(72).; V^7. rhe.V^1.βc.δii.δP^2.——rs-r.; I^e.$a b^s$,k. ω^2.5.5.(4).——rhs.VI$^{3·s}$.$\kappa^{4·5}$.χ^2.63.—— sbd.II^1.g^b.; V$^{10·zz}$.——scr.31.——snc. VI^1.——sep.VI^4.——sil.V^1.q.; V^1–VII^5. 82.——sin.V^7.——so-n.3-99.35.——so-t. V^1.——spi.V^1.——stn.V^7.——sul.ζ.o^8.; ^{a}.VI^3.; V^1.——tab.V^1.p.——tax.δt^u. κ^4.(63).——teu.V^1.——thr.II^1.3-99.—— val.V$^{10·s}$.δ.4.48.66.; V^1.; V^6.29. ——xip.VI^3.βc.ζ^3.

—— *on a narrow line.*——bry.
—— *as if something lay there.*—— cb-a.δ.

F^f. Above right eye.——aco.V^1.128.; V^{16}.6.(8).—— æsc.——aga.II^1–V^1.δc. —alo.V^6–VIII^3.δ.——am-c.VI^2.—— am-m.VIII^2.; VI^4.(12).——ana.

VI$^{3\cdot4}$.—ant.VII^1.— ag-n. V^1.3-99.
—ars. V^7.II^3.$\mathbf{53}$.—au-m. V^3.--ba-a.
V^1.—bap. V^1.—bel. VI$^{3\cdot4}$.— bis^q.
VI^4.—bov. V^7.—bry. V^6.4.; V$^{6\cdot10}$.
θ^1.; VI^3.; III^3–V^6.; V^1–VI^3.3.
V^1.—cb-v. VI^3.—ca-x.i^a.—cau.
V^1.—chd.; V$^{7\cdot t}$.; VI^4.; V^1.; VI^3.
d.—cmf.5.—cnb. VI^3.λ.—cis. V^{10}.
—cca.δ.—coc. VI$^{3\cdot a}$.—cch. V^1.—
com.I^q.—crn.—ctn. VI^3.—dgn. V^1.
VIII^4.—dig. VI$^{3\cdot4\cdot a\cdot l\cdot v}$.—dio.$\mathbf{3}$.
dul. V^1–VII^5.; V$^{3\cdot s}$.— evo. V$^{1\cdot7}$.—
fl-x.v^1r.—gin^n. VI^3.p.δLq.ϕ.—glo.;
V^7.—ham.3.; V^{10}.16.19.(8-31).—
hyo. VI^3.89.—ign^h. V$^{1\cdot6}$.29.; V^9.
idm. VIII^4.δ.—irs. VI^3.—jac. V^7.
(8).—kis. V^1.—lah.; VIII^4.af.κ.κ^9.
—lyc^n. VI$^{4\cdot a}$.p.δp.4.—lcp.—man.
V^6–VI^4.; VI^3.31.—m-pu.$\delta\epsilon$.—
mr-f^h. VI^3.—mez. VI^3.—mu-x.
V^{10}–VI^4.—nab^q.I^q.5.—na-m. VI$^{3\cdot b}$.
—nit. V^1.3-30.—nx-v. V^1.3-$\mathbf{10}$.—
ol-m.—opi. V^1–VI^3.; VI^3.—pho.
VI^4.—phs.—phy.—pla. V$^{1\cdot7}$–VIII^5.
—rn-b.ak.5.; ηp.r^1b.16.(18.31).—
rs-r.; $\mathbf{5}$.41.—rhs^q. V$^{10\cdot n}$.$\beta\epsilon$.—rum.
—scu.(8-31).—spi. V^1.—stp. V^1.q.
8.; V$^{1\cdot6\cdot v}$.; V^1.—sto. V^{10}.—sul.
VIII^3.; V^6–VII^1.θ^4r.; V^1.; V^{10}.
$\mathbf{5}$.—tab. V^1.4.; VI^3.δO.—trn.
VIII^4.—ton. VI$^{4\cdot a}$.—vi-t. V^1.(11).
—zin. V^1.δL.—ziz. VI^3.

—— *first right, then left.*—oni.
V^1.ζ.—ptl. VIII^4.—sin.

F^g. Above left eye.—aco.—æsc.—
æth^1. VI^4–VIII^3.19.—amb. V^1.—
am-c. VI^3.δb.66.—an-s.—ant.
V^1–VI^3.—arn. V$^{7\cdot e}$.—ars.2.5.—
aru. VI^3.5.—asa.II^1.; V^7.—ast. V^3.
δ.δo.—ba-c. V^6.5.—ber. VI$^{4\cdot v}$.; ^{n}.
VI^3.; V^3–VI^3–VIII^3.g^b.—bov.
VI^3.ηaa.66.; $^{h\cdot o}$.III^1–V^{12}–VI^3.$\delta\epsilon$.
-bro. V^7.; II^1–V^7.q.-bry. V^6–VII^5.;
V^6.3.; V^{10}.; V^1.z.31.; V^6.—ca-a.
V$^{10\cdot s}$.q.18.29.; V^1.8-31.; V$^{1\cdot6}$.—
cam. V^1.5.—cn-i.—cph.—cau. VI^3.
—ced. VI^3.—cep.I^q.—chd. VI^3.;
V^1.—cl-h. V^7.q.63.—cmf. V$^{3\cdot7}$.—
cch.I^a.4.51.; 26.; 6.66.(8).—cot.
VIII^4.; II^6.vb.; VI^3.3.—er-a. V^7.
3-30.; VI^3.σ^2.r.19.—eub. V^1.—

glo.; (12).—ham.VIII^4.—hdr.(8).
—hel. V$^{16\cdot1}$.(12).—hfb.—ign. V$^{1\cdot a}$.
—idm.βa.θ^1.κ^5.λ^1.— k-bi^h. VI$^{3\cdot a}$.δo.
3.(5).; VI^3.κ^4.3-30.35.—k-ca.
V$^{3\cdot10\cdot t}$.; V$^{10\cdot s}$.—kis.δr^h.; V^1.—lab.
V^1.$\mathbf{5}$.; VIII$^{4\cdot a}$.—lil. V^{10}.δO.3-30.;
II^1–V^1.5.—lyc^b.VIII^4.5.—mag. V^{14}.
VIII^3.31.35.—mg-s. VI^3.; V^3.$\beta\epsilon^a$.
5-10.—men.II^1.—mr-c. V^1–VI^3.29.
—mr-i. V^{10}.—msc. V^7.—naj.II^1.—
na-m. V^1.; V$^{3\cdot q}$.; VI^3.4.—ni-x. VI^3.
—nx-j.—nx-m. V$^{10\cdot zz}$.3.; V^1–VIII^4.
3.—nx-v. V$^{1\cdot2}$.δb.— ph-x. VI$^{3\cdot v}$.—
pho.δt^q.—pla.I^b.—pl-n. V$^{16\cdot z}$.—ptl.
VI$^{3\cdot q}$.—rs-r.; II^1.5.117.; ak.$\delta\epsilon$.
ω^9.; I$^{a\cdot b}$.5.41.—sep. V^1–VI^3.6.35.
(8-31).; VI$^{3\cdot a}$.δb.3-30.(8).—stn.
V$^{1\cdot6}$.—sul.βa.—su-x. V^{16}.—tar.
V^6–VII^5–VIII^3.—ter. V^1.q.19.41.
—ur-n.ι.κ^7.v^1.—ver. VIII^4.—ve-v.
III^1–V^6.—vrb. V^1–VI^4.—zin. VI$^{3\cdot4}$.
λ.

—— *back towards occiput.*—plg.
I$^{a\cdot b}$.

F^h. Above root of nose.—aco.III^3.
$a^1\iota^a$.8-31.—aga. VI^4.; V^6.—amb.
V^1–VI^4.$\beta\epsilon$.—am-m. V$^{10\cdot u}$–VI^4.3-30.
—ana. V^7.$\beta\epsilon$.—an-s.—ars. VIII^4.
—asr. V^1.—ba-a–V^7.—bel. V^1.29.—
bor^e. V^6.λ.σ^2.29.43.44.—bov. VIII^4.
q.au.a^1b.ζo.16.100.; ^{e}. V^1–VI^4.; $^{g\cdot o}$.
III^1–V^{12}–VI^3.$\delta\epsilon$.—bry. V$^{1\cdot a}$.35.—
cad.III^3.—ca-c.—cn-i^e. V^1.i^a.q.
cth. V^1.—cap. V^1–VI^3.ϵ.—cb-a. V^2.—
cb-v. V^6.—cn-h.I^a.—cau. V^6–VII^5.;
V$^{1\cdot6}$.—chd. V^1–VI^4.δb.(66).; IX.;
VI^4.δ.δL.—cin^o. V^6.$\beta\epsilon$.—cis. V^1.—
ces. V^1.δCa^2.—col. V^1.ζ^3.; VI^3.$\beta\epsilon$.
—dul. V^7.—evo. V$^{1\cdot a}$.— fag.I^a.—
fer. V^7.5.—gam. VIII^4.5.—glo^e.
VII^5.σ^3.; VIII$^{4\cdot v\cdot z}$.—gur.III^2.
VIII^3.—gym. V^7.q.—ham. V^1–VII^5.
x.ζ^3.; V^7.—hel.—hln. V^1.—hdr.
V^1.—hep. VII^5.—ign. V^1.κ^5.; III^3.;
^{f}. V$^{1\cdot6}$.29.—ind. VI^3.—iod. V^1.—
k-bi^s. VI$^{3\cdot a}$.δo.3.(5).; hh.—k-ca.
V$^{1\cdot6}$–VI^4.δ.—klm. V^1.—kis. V$^{6\cdot v}$.—
lah^e.1.—la-v. V$^{1\cdot a}$.—lep. V^6.—lo-s.
V^7.4.—lyc.; V$^{3\cdot b}$.—mt-n. VII^5.—
mt-s.III^1–IV^1.—men. V$^{1\cdot6}$.— mrl.
V^1.—mr-f.^{f}. VI^3.—mez. VII^1.p.hh.

χ^1.3.—msc.III–V^7.; V^1.ζ.η.—na-a. V^1.q.—na-m. V$^{6 \cdot v}$.q.—nit.[S.ff^a.] —nx-v.V^6.——oni.V^1.—opi.V^1.; V^1.ζ.—ptv.V^7.5.—pho.a^{1}v.5.(66).; V^{10}.; VIII$^{3 \cdot 4}$.δ.ζ.κ^6.3.——phy.V^1. 66.; V^6.—rap.V^1.—rs-r.III^2.p.— rut.V^1.—sil.V^1.3.—stp.IX.q.—sti. V^7.q.—tab.V^7.; VI^3.—trx.III^1– VII^2.βa.—tar.V^1.;V^7-VII$^{5 \cdot x}$.; •V^7. —vrb.V$^{10 \cdot s}$.—vi-t.I^q.(8).—xip.V^1. 5.53^a.

F^l. **In frontal sinus.**——æth^g.VI^4– VIII^3.19.—aga.V^1.—ars.s.—c-cs. VIII^4.(**53**).—ca-x.VII^5.—col.V^{10}. —cor.V^{10}.ζ^3.(8).— gel.VI^3.δ.θ^4.— hpm.V^3–VIII^4.g^b.ζ.—hdr.VIII^4. —k-hy.VI$^{3 \cdot 4}$–VIII^3.; q.—kre.V^6. θ^4r.4.——lah.II^5.; V^6.ζ.—mg-m. V$^{1 \cdot 3}$.(34-**105**).—nat.VII^5.—nit.ζo. —ped.3.——pso.V^6.——rn-b.βa^t.ζ. n.VIII^4.1.—vrb.VI^2.—zin.IX.

—— *as if lobes of brain were drawn towards.*—dir.

F^m. **In frontal protuberances.**—æsc. —aga.V^7.—alo^e.VI^3.—ba-a^e.VII^1. —bel.V^1.3-30.; VI$^{3 \cdot s}$.—bis.V$^{3 \cdot s}$. —chi.VI^4–VIII^3.—cle.V^1.—cch. V^1.—dul.V^6.βe^a.; V^6.ζ.—elt.V^7.— fer.V^1.3.(4).; VI^2.3.(8).——grt. VI$^{3 \cdot b}$.—hel.V^3.—hfb.—hyo.VIII^4. —kis.ζ.—la-v.VI^3.q.βe.4.——lau. VI^3.4.—lcp.(12).——mu-x^c.VI^3.— my-s.5.—ni-x.V^1–VI^3.—opi.V^1.βe. ζ.ω^2.—phy.—rn-b.V^1.6.——rap.V^1. 2.——rhe.V$^{6 \cdot q}$.——rs-r.V^6.i^a.au^x.— stn.V$^{10 \cdot s}$.—sul.V^1.—val.VII^5.x.

—— *passing from one to other alternately.*—aga.VI^3.; V^7. —bis.V$^{3 \cdot s}$.—lep.

F^n. **In right frontal protuberance.** —aco.V^1.—æsc.VIII^4.—aga.51.— am-c.VIII^1.; V^3–VI^3.63.——ana^n. V$^{10 \cdot s}$.—an-s.VI^3.ϕ.5.—arg.3-99.— ari.V^9.—asa.VIII$^{4 \cdot e \cdot s}$.—ba-a.VI$^{3 \cdot s}$. —bel.V^1.; V^3.3-99.; VI^3.29.(11). ——ber^g.VI^3.——bov.VI$^{3 \cdot 4}$.er.; ^{a}. VI$^{3 \cdot q}$.; IX.au.—ca-a.V^1.δr.δb.— cas.VI^3.**5**.—cau.V^1.—cin.VI^4.βe^a. —fl-x.III.5.; 5.—gin^f.VI^3.p.δLq. ϕ.—gui.VI^3.; V^1–VI^3.——hel.V^1. 8-31.—hyo.V^6–VIII^4.29.——ign^a.

V$^{3 \cdot a}$.—ir-f.VIII$^{4 \cdot b}$.5.—k-bi.V^7.— k-br.66.—kre.V^1.—led.VI^3.—lcp. V$^{10 \cdot s}$.—lyc.VI^3–VIII^{14}.4.; f.VI$^{4 \cdot a}$. p.δp.4.; g.VI^4–VIII^4.5.—mr-c.V^7. —mez.; V^1.—my-s.V$^{10 \cdot s}$.(8).— nup.VI$^{3 \cdot q}$.—oln.V^1.—opi.V^1.— par.V$^{1 \cdot q}$.—ph-x.V$^{10 \cdot s}$.—pla.V$^{1 \cdot d}$.; V^2.—plc.VI^3.βe.—plb.VI^3.—pru. V$^{10 \cdot s}$.—rn-b.VIII^4.βa^t.ζ.1.—sab. V^3.; V^1–VI^4.; II^3–VI$^{3 \cdot q}$.——sar. V^1–VI^3.; VI^3.5.—spi.$^{10 \cdot s}$.; VI^4– VIII^3.δc^d.18.19.; VI^3.—spo.V$^{10 \cdot s}$. —squ.VI$^{3 \cdot u}$.ζ.——tar.V^7–VIII^5.; V^3.—teu.V^{10}–V^1.—thu.V^1-VIII^3. δ.—ton.V^6.—vrb.V$^{7 \cdot 10 \cdot s \cdot q}$.7.—zin. V^1.; VI^4.$\delta$LO.; V^3–VI^3.

F^o. **In left frontal protuberance.**— aga.V^3.; V^1.; V$^{1 \cdot 6}$.δ.—agn.V^1-VI^4. —alm.VI$^{3 \cdot 4}$.——amb.V^1.——ana. III–V^7.—arg.V^1–VI^4.; V^1–VI^4. δ.; V^6.—ag-n.V$^{3 \cdot 6}$.r.; V^3–VI^3.4. —arn.VI^3.d.—asa.V^7.; VI^2. au-m.IX^u.——ba-c.VI^3.29.——bel. V$^{10 \cdot a \cdot s}$.; II^{1}VI^4.——bov$^{g \cdot h}$.III^1–V^{12}. VI^3.δe.——can.VIII$^{4 \cdot s}$.; V^7.——cth. VI^3.18.—chd.VI$^{3 \cdot 4 \cdot a}$.—cim.V$^{10 \cdot s}$. —cin^h.V^6.βe.; VI^4.βe^a.—coc.VI^3– VIII^4.g^b.——cro.VIII$^{1 \cdot q}$.βe.(12).; III^3–V^6.ζ.; V^{16}.—dul.V^7.; V$^{10 \cdot s}$.5.; V^6.29.; V$^{1 \cdot 6}$.——evo.VI$^{3 \cdot q}$.——grn. V^1.; VI^3.——hel.V^1–VI^4.δl.; V^{16}.p. —hyo.VIII^4.—ign.V$^{7 \cdot e}$.——k-ca. VI^4.—k-hy.VI^3.—lah.I^q.ϵ.—la-v. VI^3.βe.29.——lyc.VI^4.; VI^3.—lcp. III.θ^1.: VI^3.—men.VI$^{3 \cdot a}$.q.(17^a). —mez.VI$^{3 \cdot 4}$.—mil.VI$^{4 \cdot a}$.——naj. na-n.V^1.—ni-x.VI^3–VIII^4.δb^b.5.— nx-m.V^1.—oln.V$^{10 \cdot s}$.(12).——ol-a. VI^3.; V^3.—ph-x.V$^{1 \cdot a}$.q.—plb.VI^3. —sab.V^1.; V^1.δ.—sar.V^1–VI^3.— sep.VI^4.—spi.V$^{10 \cdot t}$.; q.; VI^4–VII^5. —squ.V^1.; VIII^1.—su-x.VIII^3.; VI$^{3 \cdot q}$.; V^2.; II^3–VIII^3.—sum.V^1. V^1–VIII^4.—teu.V^1.29.(18).—thu. V^1–VIII^3.——vrb.V$^{1 \cdot 9 \cdot e}$.; VIII^2.; VI$^{3 \cdot e \cdot q}$.; V$^{6 \cdot 7}$.107.—vi-o.V^6.—zin. 66.; VI^4.; V^1–VI^4.66.

F^p. **Behind orbits.**—aco.III^3–VII^5. —cn-i.ϵ.——dig.VI^3.; VIII^4.—fag. V^{10}.; V^1.4.—gel^e.V^2.—nit.VI$^{3 \cdot d}$.4. 5.20.31.—thr.—ziz.

F^q. **Behind right orbit.**—bis^f.VI^4.—nab^f.I^q.5.—nit.V^1–VI$^{4.z}$.31.70.(8.128).—rhs^f.V$^{10.u}$.βε.

F^r. **Behind left orbit.**—nit.V$^{1.q}$.—rhs.V$^{10.zz}$.

Forehead and other parts.

F. and all through head.—lil.V^7.—mr-f.VI^3.

F. and temples.—aga.V^6.δ.; V^1.δL.5.; e.VI^3.—agn.V^1–VI^4.35.—ant.V^{3-s}.—ara.V^1.βε.ω^2.5.66.(12).—arn.VI^3.—ars.I^a.—aru.VI^3.δ.—atr.V^6–VI^3.—aur.VI$^{4.q}$.(8).—ba-a.V^3.—bel.V^{10-s-a}.14.; V^1–VI^4.; III–IV^1.—ber.V^{10-s}.; VI^4.η.; VI^3.—bov.VI^{4-a-e}.—bry.V^7.χ^1.117.; V^1.βε.; V^7.—cam.VI^1.16.; VI^4.; V^7–VI^3.ab°.βε.5.(8).—cnc.V^1.3.—cth.; VI^3–VIII^4.—ca-x.—car.d.—ced.VIII^4.—cnt.—chd.III.; V^1.σ^2.—chi.V^1.31.; V^1–VI^3.—ch-s.d.p.ε℧.5.; V^6–VI^4.—cle.βε.; V^1–VII^5.66.—cod.V^1.—csn.V^7.—col.III.δ.29.(8).—cor.V^{10}.—ctn.V^1.a^{1}b^y.βε.; V^1.(8).—c-ar.I^a.—cyc.I^a.—dig.III^1–V^1.—dio.V^7.—dir.4.—dul.V^{3-s}.q.; V^{3-s}.—elt.III^1.—equ.V^7.q.3.; III^1.—fag.V^{10}–VII^1.4.—fer.—fl-x.—gel.V$^{1-7}$.—glo.V^{7-w}.; VIII^4.—grn.V^1–VI^4.—hel.V^{10-t}.VII^5.q.χ.(8).—hlm.V^7.—hpm.V$^{6-7}$.δ.(5).—hur.I^a.—hy-x.V^7.—idm.V^7.κ^5.φ.—irs.V^7.q.—k-bi.VI^{3-w}.31.(20).—klm.I^a.—lch.V^7.—lil.VII^1.(12).—lol.VI^3.—lyc.VI^3.εl.—lcp.V^{10-s}.—mt-n.II^3–V^2.—mg-m.VI$^{3-4}$.p.—mg-s.σ^2.2.(3).—man.III^1–VI^3.8.—mns.—mr-f.V^7.q.η.—mez.III^3.δ.θ^4.; III$^{2-3}$.ζ.—mu-x.V^{10-s}.; VI^3.12.29.—myr.V^7.q.3-99.29.30.; V^7.σ^2.—naj.V^1.δLq.—na-a.; aa.a^{1}b.4.—na-m.V^1.8-31.; V^{10-s}.ε.—nup.V^1.(8).—opi.VII^1.βε.pan.—ph-x.aα^w.—phs.III^1.43.—phy.I^a.—pi-m.V^7.q.41.43.—pso.V^1.—rho.V^6–VI^4.δ.6.35.—sbd.V^1.βa.σ.—sab.V^6.—sel.VI^3.δ.5.5.7.—sng.V^1.5.—spi.III–V^7.—stn.V^{1-6-7}.—sul.V^6.; V^1–VI^4.; III.—tab.V^1.

βa.—tan.V^7.φ.—tar.V^7–VI^3.89.—ver.V^7.29.30.(22).—zin.V^1.3-99.

F., temples, and vertex.—equ.VI^3.3.—for.—mrl.VII^6.—stn.(12).—tep.V^3–VI^3.

F., temples, vertex, and sides of head.—pho.II^1–VI^3–VII^1.3.19.66.(15).

F., temples, vertex, and occiput.—cu-a.VI^3.12.

F., temples, and occiput.—aco.VI^3.—æsc.V^7–VI^3.—bov.VI^4.—ca-a.V$^{1-6}$–VI^4.(12.41).—can.VII^3.—nx-v.V^6.—rs-r.V^7.3.; V^7.ak.κ^4.φ^1.—spi.VI^{4-a}.

F. and right temple.—con.V$^{1-6}$.—ctn.VI$^{3-4}$.—c-ar.V^7.—dgn.V^{6-a}.—hyo.V^1.βa.δL.(8-31).—irs.VI^3.—lpt.—mur.V^1.—na-a.VI^3.—sab.V^6.—squ.VI^3–VIII^3.—tan.V^7.—trn.VI^3.

F., right temple, and vertex.—elc.VI^3.

F., temple, and right side of head.—am-m.VI^4.η.19.83.

F., right temple, and left occiput.—aco.VI^3.

F. and left temple.—cyc.V$^{1-6}$.(11).; VI^3.βa.3.—dig.V^1–VII^5.5.—irs.—lah.III.—mag.VI$^{4.q}$.—ph-x.VI^4.—rs-r.; VIII^1.—spi.II^1.—stn.V^{10-t}.

F., left temple, and vertex.—tab.V^6–VI^3.

F. and vertex.—ac-x.V^7.—aco.V^1.i^a.q.35.—alo.q.—amb.V^{10-u}.p.δ.ηc^b.4.—ant.V^7.33.—ag-n.IV^2.—ba-a.V^3.ω.3-30.(4).—bel.V^1–VII^5.—ber.V^1.; VI^3–VIII^4.29.—bor.5.—bry.VI^3–VIII^3.—buf.4.—ca-c.IV^1.—cn-i.V^1.o^2.—cb-a.II^5.29.—cas.V^1.σ^1.ω^2.83.—cau.VI^3.—cep.V^7.—cnb.V^7.3-99.12.16.(30.117).; V^1.3-99.16.(12).—crn.V^7.—cot.V^7.q.a^{1}b^s.δv,o.ρ^1.vb.(8).—ctn.V^7.—dig.V^1.—dio.V^7.—equ.III^1.—gel.V^{10}.q.ii^a.βε.δo.ε℧.; V^7.5.99.—glo.; II^1–III^1.a^{1}b^s.βε.δ.η.; V^{10-v}.aɡ.ηaa.χ^3.; VIII^4.—gos.II^6.—grp.V^7.3-10.(99).—hln.V^7.—hur.V^1.—hfb.I^a.4.; V^1.26.29.—ign.V^1.x.δl.; III^1–V^1.—ind.VI^4.—inu.VII^4–VIII^4.

lau.VI⁴.4.— lcp.V¹⁰·ˢ.——mag.VI⁴.
q.66.—men.VI³.—mer.VI⁴.—mez.
VI³.—mu-x.VI³.4.—myr.V⁷–VIII⁴.
—nab.αυᵇ.δL.ι.ψ.——naj.—nat.V¹.
p.—na-m.VIII¹.α¹ᵛᵃ.βa.; V¹.—
nup.V⁷.—nx-v.VI⁴.δ.κ⁵.o².π.—ol-a.
VI⁴.—ol-m.V⁷.—ox-x.V⁷.;VI³.χ²·³.
3.—phl.III¹.—rs-g.V⁷.—rs-r.Iᵃ·ʷ.
—sep.αg.ζ².ω⁸.——sil.VIII⁴.d.q.—
so-n.V¹.—stn.V¹·⁶.—tar.V¹·⁶.VII⁵.
—val.V¹⁰·ᵛ.δ.—zin.V¹·⁶–VI⁴·ᵈ.

F. and saggital suture.—aga.V⁷.—
la-v.V⁶·ᵇ.—lau. ; V⁷.—lpt.

F. and left side of head.—mr-i.V⁷·¹⁰.
5. ; V⁶–VI³.5.

F. vertex and parietal regions.—
trn.IX.єᴅ.

F. vertex and occiput.—amb.VI⁴.
—ana.V⁶.—dig.V¹.—glo.V⁷.q.—
grt.V¹².—hfb.VIII⁴.σ².—hy-x.V¹.
βє.δO¹.σ².—k-bi.V¹.3-99.——man.
V¹⁰·ᶻᶻ.4.——msc.V¹·³.——sep.V⁶–
VI³·⁴.

F. and parietal region.—ard.I�q.—
con.VI³.βa.σ².—eu-a.V⁷.3-99.(66).
—fag.V¹⁰·ˢ.—ind.V¹.—k-ca.VIII⁴.
18.31.66.—pgn δO.—sbd.q.35.—
sil.VI⁴.1.5.35.—sul.II⁷–V⁶–VI³·⁴.
26.(8.12).; V⁶.

F. and left parietal.—ptl.VI³.

F., parietes, and occiput.—fer.
VIII⁴.σ².29.35.

F. and right side of head.—alm.
VI³–VIII⁴.4.—cot.26.—pla.VIII¹.
—sul.VI⁴.p.θ¹.116.—tru.

F. and left parietal region.—ca-s.
I.5.66.— con.VI³·⁴.—dio.V⁷.5.—
hfb.VI⁴.— k-ca.VI³·ᵃ.rᴠb.1.—stn.
VI⁴.

F., left parietal, and occiput.—
mer.III¹–V¹².δє.

F. and occiput.—æth.V⁷.—aga.w.;
V³.ι.—alm.VI³.5.66.—ana.VI⁴.—
arn.VI³.3-99.—asa.VI³.βє.ρ.—aur.
VI⁴.35.—bel.VI³.— bra.κ⁵.φ.8-31.
(12).—bry.VIII⁴.; V¹.35.—ca-c.
V⁷·ᵃ.; VI¹.12.31.—c-cs.V⁷.; VI⁴.
—cam.V¹–VI¹.;VIII⁴.—cth.VI³·q.
—cap.V¹⁰·ˢ–VI¹.—cb-v.Iᵃ.V¹⁰·ˢ.29.
—ca-x.V⁷.—chd.V¹·⁶–VI³.—chp.
VII⁵.35.—ch-s.αυ α¹bº.βa.φ.ω².; 5.

—cl-h.—cmf.βє. ; q.—cin.V⁷.8-31.
—cch.5.—crn.VIII⁴.—dgn.VI³.
—dio.5. ; V³.—ept.—fer.V¹.5.—
gel.—glo.V⁷.26.—grp.V⁶.5.—
gui.V⁶–VI⁴.—hyo.V¹.—irs.—jun.
3.30.—k-bi.V¹.99.—k-ca.VI⁴.—
lch.V⁷.—lau.V¹.βa.δ.δP¹·².—lo-c.
VIII⁴.hh. ; V⁷.βєᶜ.—lyc.V⁷.35. ;
VIII⁴·ᵃ.σ².5.—lcp.4.—mag.V⁶.q.1.
83.— mg-m.VI³–VIII³.—mer.VI⁴.
—msc.VIII¹·ᶻᶻ.—mu-x.30.; V¹–
VII⁵.—na-m.VI³.κ¹.—nit.V¹.5.—
ol-m.κ⁵.—opi.V¹.βє.b.θ².κ.κ¹·⁵·⁹.4.
66.(5).—pet.VI³.3-99.—ptl.—
rap.lᵃ.—rhs.II¹.—sbd.VIII¹.—
sab.V⁶.—sar.V¹.—sng.V¹.δ.κ⁵.ρ.3.
7.19.(8.14).—ser.VI³.—spo.IIIᵃ.
—squ.V¹.βє.—sul.V¹.29.; V⁷.rᴠ.—
su-x.VI³.—tab.VI³·ᶻ.18.(8.16).—
thu.V¹·²–VI⁴.3-99.

F. and right occiput.—glo.V¹·ᵃ.—
ign.VI³.—iod.V⁷.—mez.V¹–VIII⁴.
ζ.θ¹.26.—ph-x.V¹.12.28.

F. and left occiput.—ign.VI⁴.ηp,aa.
r¹p.24.(17).

F. and base of brain.—glo.Iᵃ.—
pi-m.(35).

Fᵃ. and right temple.—aru.VI⁴.є.—
cle.V¹·³.η.5.—c-ar.V⁷–VIII⁴.—
cyc.VI³.—dgn.V⁶·ᵃ.5.—nat.VI⁴·ᵃ.
83.(12).—rs-r.5.—san.VI³.4.—
tri.

Fᵃ., right temple and crown.—cau.
II¹.

Fᵃ. and left temple.—crt.V¹.δr.ηr.θ¹.
ᴠl.5.—k-hy.VI³·⁴·ᵃ.5.(12).—lth.Iᵇ.
128.

Fᵃ. and vertex.—cas.VI⁴.19.—fl-x.
—nit.V⁷.66.—opi.V¹.βє.

Fᵃ., vertex, right side, and occiput.
—bel.VI¹·³.

Fᵃ., vertex and occiput.—msc.V⁷.
—spi.V³–VI⁴.35.51.86.(16).

Fᵃ. and right parietal region.—
cau.VIII³.—cin.V¹⁰·ˢ.3-99.—pho.
V⁷·q.αυ.—san.δ.ξ³.83.

Fᵃ., right side and occiput.—cle.
V¹.βa.χ¹.4.(5).

Fᵃ., left parietal and left occiput.
—con.V¹.

Fᵃ. and occiput.—cn-i.VIII³.—chi.

z

III^1–V$^{1·q}$.31.—hy-x.V^1.—opi.VI^3.
φ.—pru.VI^3–VIII$^{3·z}$.; V$^{1·z}$.

F^a. and right occiput.—lch.16.—
nup.V^7.q.δO.1.—ser.V^1.βɛ.(5).

F^a. and left occiput.—glo.

F^b. and temples.—mez.V$^{3·6}$.

F^b. and right temple.—bor.VI^3.

F^b. and left temple.—dgn.V^1–VIII^4.
—klm.VI^4.—pla.V^6.—rho.V^1.70.
—rs-r.—stn.V^1–VIII^3.αl^g.

F^b., left temple, vertex and left
side of head.—am-m.VI^3–VII^1.29.

F^b. and vertex.—hy·x.V^1.

F^b. and right vertex.—mez.V$^{1·3·16}$.

F^b., crown and occiput.—ctn.V^1.

F^b. and parietal region.—ag-n.η.—
cth.

F^b. and occiput.—arg.V^6.—bry.V^6–
VII^2.6.31.—cam.VI^4.—hæm.III^1.
ɛ.—na-m.VI^1.—nx-m.—sul.VI^3.
(12).

F^b. and right occiput.—gel.V$^{1·a}$.
2-99.

F^c. and temples.—cas.VI^4.χ^1.(8.12).
—ch-s.V^7.; V^6.—teu.V$^{10·q·s}$.

F^c., temples and occiput.—sbd.IX.

F^c. and left temple.—k-ca.V^{13}.

F^c., vertex and occiput.—cn-s.VII^1.
p.ɛʋ.

F^c. and occiput.—chd.VI^4.66.(12).

F^d. and temples.—k-ca.V^{13}.60.

F^d. and vertex.—msc.V^1.

F^d. and left side of head.—ptv.
VI$^{3·a}$.5.

F^d. and occiput.—pl-n.

F^e. and temples.—ars.III^1.—bor.
VI^3.σ.χ$^{1·2}$.; VI^3.rb,p.χ$^{1·2}$.—crt.βa.
κ$^{5·6}$.μ^1.(8-31).—glo.VIII^4.35.(12.
16.19).—hfb.VI$^{3·a}$.π.5.; I^a.αl^g.3.—
ipc.V$^{3·10}$ ⁶.(12.47).—k-bi.V^7.q.8.
35.—lep.11.50.—mnc.VI^3.—mez.
—na-a.V^7.5.—na-m.V^1.βɛ.—phy.
V^1.—rs-r.VI^3.

F^e. and vertex.—gym.V^1–VI^3.i^a.δ.;
VI$^{3·a}$.—lyc.VII^1.κ^5.rʋkk.—msc.βa.
δL.—na-a.V^7.—sil.V$^{1·6}$–VI^3.

F^e. and parietal region.—arn.V^7.

F^e. and right side.—bel.II^1–IV^1–
VI^{13}.

F^e. and occiput.—erd.V^7.q.4.—la-x.
2-99.—lil.—man.V^6.29.(12).—

mrl.V^1.—mo-a.V^1.—spo.V$^{10·z}$.σ^3.
—urt.V^7.

F$^{e·h}$. and vertex.—bro.V$^{10·s}$.

F$^{e·h}$. and behind ears.

F^f. and temple.—bel.V^6.—ca-x.δ.—
cyc.VI^3.—sil.V^1.χ^1.

F^f., temples and vertex.—cmf.VIII^4.
i^a.p.33.

F^f. and right temple.—dio.VI^3.—
hfb.VIII^4.—pi-m.V^1.ζ.

F^f., right temple and occiput.—
lyc.VI$^{3·4}$.2.

F^f. and vertex.—ch-s 2.43.(30).—
elp.V^3.

F^f. and left parietal.—ni-x.V^6.

F^f. and occiput.—bis.VI^1.—ca-a.V^6.
41.—cep.—ce-b.—glo.VII^5.—
hy-x.V^1.βɛ.(8).—kre.V^1.

F^f. and right occiput.—rs-r.

F^f. and occipital protuberance.—
ur-n.VI^3.5.

F$^{f·q}$. and right temple.—rhs.V$^{10·u}$.
βɛ.

F^g. and temple.—iod.VI^4.—lep.VI^3.
—ox-x.VI^3.βɛ^c.—pau.VIII^2.—sbd.
V^1.

F^g. and left temple.—au-m.VI$^{4·a}$.
βa.—ipc.III^1.

F^g., left temple and occiput.—lil.
V$^{1·10}$.

F^g. and left parietal region.—dio.4.

F^g. and occiput.—bov.V$^{1·3}$.4.7.—
cmf.—rs-r.VI^3.

F^g. and right occiput.—idm.κ^5.ω^2.2.

F^g. and left occiput.—cot.V^6.

F^h. and temples.—bis.V^1.q.19.—
cau.VI^4.ii.5.—cep.47.—glo.VIII^4.

F^h. and parietal regions.—pot.V$^{6·s}$.
—thr.V^1.

F^h. and occiput.—cam.III^1.p.r^{1}ʋ^{1}b.
φ.12.16.29.—glo.VIII^4.

F^h. and base of skull.—k-hy.V$^{16·a}$.
δɛ,Ca^2.ii.

F^i. and temples.—c-cs.VI^3.

F^m. and vertex.—fer.V$^{10·t}$.3-30.33.
(8.12).

F^m. and occiput.—ba-c.VIII^4.5.—
can.V$^{1·q}$.

F^n. and temples.—teu.V^1.

F^n., temple, vertex and left occiput.—amb.VI^4.

F^{n}. and right temple.—arg.VI^{4}.(20).—bel.V^{1}–VII^{1}.14.—mg-m.VI$^{3\cdot s}$.—plc.V^{6}.8.12.—sab.VII^{1}.

F^{n}. and parietal region.—bry.V^{6}–VII^{5}.4.

F^{n}. and occiput.—chi.VI^{4}.

F^{n}. and right occipital protuberance.—ccb.V^{7}.(12.102).—pgn.I^{b}.

F^{o}. and temple.—c-cs.V^{7}–VI^{3}.—man.VI^{4}.86.

F^{o}. and right temple.—lcp.VI^{3}.

F^{o}. and right parietal region.—alm.VI$^{3\cdot 4}$.4.5.

F^{o}. and left parietal region.—gui.V^{6}–VI^{3}.—sto.VI$^{3\cdot a}$.

F^{o}. and left parietal protuberance.—vrb.VI$^{3\cdot e\cdot q}$.

F^{o}. and left occiput.—nat.VI$^{3\cdot 4}$.—spi.V^{1}–VI^{4}.

F^{p}. and occiput.—ced.I^{q}.δb.—com.δ.δε.

VARIOUS PAINS IN VARIOUS PARTS.

Pulsation in F^{b}., strong blows in F^{a}.—aco.

Slight frontal headache, with sharp pain in r. T.—dio.

Congestive headache in F., dartings inward in both T.—dir.

Burning F^{e}., drawing in T. and C.—chd.

Pinching in F., shooting in T.—stp.18.19.(31).

Dull pain in head, aching in F.—vi-t.

Aching in F., shoots through head.—ser.

Aching in F., jerking through brain.—sam.

Aching in F., contractive in C.—k-bi.66.

Aching in F., drawing aching in O.—arg.βε^{a}.

Aching in F., drawing tension in O.—car.βa.ε^{a}.

Aching in F., tearing in temples.—con.66.

Shooting in middle of head and T., followed by aching in F., on stooping.—par.

Aching in F., changing into glowing tearing in r. P. and teeth, aggravated by contact with cold water.—sul.

Aching in F., beating in O. and T.—nit.

Stupefying aching in F., shootings in l. T.—ars.18.31.(19).

Dull aching in F. and O., shooting in T.—k-bi.

Aching, dull in F^{e}., shooting in O.—ph-x.4.

Aching in F^{e}., digging in C.—pho.1.

Drawing in F. and O., throbbing in temples.—chi.III^{1}.18.19 (12.31).

Aching in r. T., drawing shoots from O. to F.—sar.

Jerking in l. T., drawing in F.—pho.66.

Drawing in F., aching in O.—bry.

Drawing and shooting in F., pain in C. as if split.—zin.

Dull aching in O., drawing in F.—nat.βa.δo.κ$^{5\cdot 7}$.

Dull pain in F., shooting in r. T.—for.4.

Dull pain in F., contraction of skin of F.—cph.

Stinging sharp pain in T., dull in F. and F^{e}.—hdr.

Dull pain in F., sharp pricking in l. T., with throbbing and pinching.—hfb.

Dull in F., neuralgic in r. T.—ve-v.

Dull pain across F. and throbbing in T.—glo.

Drawing in O., gnawing as from worms in F.—zin.

Sudden violent drawing upwards in B^{pa}., then pressing in F^{b}. and r. wrist.—ag-n.5.19.

Shooting l. T., forcing out in F.—lau.βε^{a}.

As if a needle were driven in at C., as if F. would fall out.—thu.η.χ^{1}.3.(8-31).

Dull ache in T., pressing outwards in T.—glo.

Aching in T., screwing together in F.—chd.ζ.

Screwing in head, needle pricks in F^a.—nic.3.

Aching, fine shooting in F. and O., with burning hot feeling behind ear extending over O.—spo.σ^2.

Heaviness and shooting in F., whole head feels crushed.—sto.

Aching in r. T., shootings in F.—ber.δ.

Pressure inwards in r. T., shooting in F^o.—sab.

Aching in O., shooting in F.—sil. σb.

Tearing in l. P., shooting in F.—mu-x.$elv.\epsilon$C.

Sharp pain in F., throbbing in T.—nx-j.6.(8).

Tearing in F., sometimes in C.—cau.83.

Tearing in F. and T., sensitiveness in C.—cau.χ^1.(8.12).

F^p. as if lacerated, bruised in O., pressing out in T.—rhs.8-99.46.48.

Screwing together in T., bursting in F.—lyc.83.

Shooting in C., bursting pain in F.—nic.au.

Swollen feeling in F., aching in T.—aga.$j.\iota$.61.

Tightness in F. and headache in T. all day.—pol.

Hammering, forcing out in F., shooting in T.—kre.29.

Pulsating in F., aching in O.—cb-v. p.κ^7.66.

Throbbing in F., tearing in vertex.—grt.

Compression in P., throbbing in F.—mg-m.p.12.

Shooting, aching in O., throbbing in F.—pho.

Temples.

Pain undefined.—ars.—aru.—asi.—bz-x.—ced.—chi.—cvl.—dor.p.—elt.—eup.p.—k-bi.—lah.—plm.—ser.—sum. &c.
—— annoying.—ars.
—— violent.—cyc.—dor.
—— in fits.—sul.

—— directed inwards.—dir.(12).
—— from side to side across.—equ.
—— neuralgic.—b-la.—chd^a.—iof.—k-bi.—lcp.5.—ptl.—trn.
—— as after a debauch.—lau^a.

II^1. Burning.—alm^a.15.VI^4.—cn-i.—ca-x^a.—cau^a.—ctn^b.—mer^b.—phy^b.—spi^b.
—— as from a blow or bruise.—su-x.

II^3. Raw.—alm^a.VI^3.—dph.11.VIII^4.θ^1.—lam.

II^4. Scraping.—buf^b.31.

II^5. Smarting, like a sore.—dph.d^a.12.—dir.βa.—gym^b.
—— as from a wound.—hed^b.

III. Compressive.—ana.—asr^b.26.31.(19).—bov.—bry.d.—cth.—ced.—chi.—cmf.—hpm.—k-bi.—lab.5.31.—lep.5.—stn.—thr.
—— as with screws.—aco.
—— as if crushed together.—cph.
——from both sides.—men.(12).—mez.a^1b^b.35.—na-m.--ptl.—rn-s.$\beta\epsilon$.—rhs.—sar.q.$\beta\epsilon^a$.—sum.p.q.—tab.5.—tar.

III^1. Contractive, constrictive.—agn.—cyc.$\beta\epsilon^b$.—elp.δ.—equ.—hel.—ph-x.5-10.—pul.—squ.—sul.3.
—— as from intoxication.—ars.
—— like a vice.—dio.—pan.

III^2. Pinching.—sul.
—— as with forceps.—ph-x.—vrb.

III^3. Squeezing.—ca-a^a.; ^{b}.—dio.θj.κ^5.χ^1.3.; ^{a}.5.—ind^b.—oln^a.—opi^a.—zin^b.
—— from both sides.—mez.a^1b^a.35.

IV^1. Cramp-like.—na-m^a.θ^1.—pet^b.—pla^a.4.

V^1. Aching.—aco.—aga.—ang.—arn.—ast.—aur.—bla.—ca-c.—can.d.p.—cn-i.—cap.—cb-a.—ca-x.—crd.q.—cau.—chd.—col.—cly.—con.—fl-x.—gin.—grn.x.—hpm.—iod.—lyc.—mrl.—na-m.—ptv.—phy.—pot.d.—rhs.—sbd.—spi.—tab.—vin.—zin. &c.
—— paralytic.—lyc.

V^2. **Beaten, bruised.**—cop^b.2.5.12.—$hæm^b$.—ph-x.5.41.

V^3. **Boring, digging.**—$aco.\delta P^2.\eta.\eta c^h$, $p,aa.\rho^1$.chhb.$rv.\omega^{3\cdot8}.\phi$.66.—ang.—au-n.—$cb\text{-}v^b$.—cle^b.—$cyc^a.\theta^1.r^1$.—dul^a.—equ^b.5.—$for^a.\beta a$.——mez.tri^b.; ^{a}.2.

—— *violent.*—au-n.

—— *outwards.*—dul.q.

—— *inwards.*——alm^a.5.——na-a.p. κ^5.4.12.65.101.—$pæo^a$.

—— *upwards.*—hep^a.

—— *dull.*—aga^b.

—— *burrowing.*—inu^b.5.

—— *as with a borer.*—ind^b.

—— *as with a wedge.*—$au\text{-}n^b$.

V^6. **Drawing.**——bry.——chd.——msc. &c.

—— *inwards.*—dul.

—— *downwards.*—bel.δOr.

—— *dull.*—csc^a.

—— *gradually increasing and suddenly going off.*—cau.

—— *as if a worm crept through.*—sul.

—— *preceded by tickling in cheek.*—ind.

V^7. **Dull, stupefying.**——bap.——chd.—ch-s.—c-ar.—for. &c.

V^8. **Gnawing.**—$so\text{-}n^a.\delta b$.

V^{10}. **Pressing.**—clf.—com. &c.

—— *violent.*—ign.

—— *outwards.*—$aco.i^a.\delta L$.5.—alo. $\delta o^d.\eta p$.——asa^b.—ath.—bis.—bry.; ^{b}.4.—$ca\text{-}a^b$.—$cth^a.\theta^1$.—$cb\text{-}v^b$.—cs-e.—$cau.\kappa^{5\cdot6}$.—dro^a.——fag.—fl-x.; r.; ^{b}.—glo.—ign.; 3.17^a.(17).—ind.; ^{b}.—$k\text{-}ca^a$.—kre^b.5.—la-v.—lil.e.12.—lo-i.r.r^1.—mu-x.—nat^a.—na-m.—nx-m.p.—$ph\text{-}x^a$.—phy.—pru^a.; ^{a}.12.——rn-s.—rho^a.—sbd^a.—sab^a.; ^{b}.—snc.—spo^a.—stn^a.—sto.βa.—vi-t.

—— *inwards.*—alm^a.66.—ana^b.—asa^b.——$ca\text{-}a^b$.—coc^b.—fl-x.—jat.; 1.6.—k-ca.—lth.r.——mez^b.19.43.(85).——nat. βa.41.—$na\text{-}n^b$.—$ol\text{-}a^a$.——rn-s.—rho^b.——spi.—stn.1.

—— su-x.—tar^b.—tep^b.—thu.—val^a.—zin^a.

—— *increasing and declining gradually.*—stn^b.

—— *downwards.*—rhs.q.—sbd^b.

—— *upwards.*—rhs^a.5-10.(30).

—— *backwards.*—plg^a.

—— *forwards.*—vrb^b.

—— *as if something heavy pressed on them.*—iof.

—— *as with a finger.*—ptv^a.5.11.

—— *after pain in right jaw.*—iof.

V^{13}. **Screwing.**—coc.—col.—sul.

—— *as if a bolt were screwed from temple to temple.*—$ham.ax^9$.

V^{14}. **Tingling, vibration.**—sto.5.

V^{15}. **Twisting.**—dio^a.; ^{b}.

V^{16}. **Wedge, peg, &c., pressed in.**

—— *wedge.*—$au\text{-}n^b$.

—— *nail.*—$am\text{-}b^a$.——$arn.\chi^3.\omega^2$.2.—cca^a.—spr^a.

—— *peg.*—asa^b.—dul.—hel.

—— *sharp instrument.*

—— *from one temple to the other.*—$as\text{-}s.\rho.\chi^1$.

—— *blunt instrument.*—coc^a.—tar.

VI^1. **Cutting.**—chi.δO.29.35.—dio^a.—glo.e.—hdr.δo.; a^1n.—pl-n.

VI. **Pricking, prickling.**——ard^b.—cup.—coc^b.—eup^a.——$rs\text{-}r^b$.—trn^b.2.—trx^b.19.(18).—thu.

—— *as with a needle.*—nic.—zin^b.

—— *itching.*—$man.\theta^4$.88.

VI^3. **Shooting.**—ac-x.——ac-s.—aln.—bap.—bla.—ca-c.—cnc.—cap.—cap.—cb-v.—cau.—chp.—coc.—$ccs.i^a$.—crt.—ctn.—$dph.ii^d$.—dig.—ept.d.—frz.—ham.—hur.—iof.—irs.—k-bi.—k-ca.—mg-s.—ni-x.—pul.—rhe.—rs-r.—sep.—sil.—sti.—sul.—tar. &c.

—— *transient.*—trn.

—— *by fits.*—irs.

—— *outwards.*—bel^b.—dul.q.—for^a.—gen^a.5.31.—$rhs^b.i^a$. q.eb.

—— *outwards and inwards.*—stp^a.11.

—— *inwards.*—arn.—ber^a.—cth^b.—dir.—rhs^a.

—— *upwards.*—ch-s^b.14.
—— *upwards and downwards like electric shock.*—ang.
—— *forwards.*—na-m^a.
—— *in all directions.*—sto^a.
—— *from one t. to the other.*—bel.—ptl.κ^b.
—— *into head.*—aco.—alo^b.
—— *spreading out in a circle.*—cau^b.
—— *as if something were run through.*—glo.—mr-f.
—— *as with a knife.*—cyc.—fer. χ.2.—-lah.ζ³.σ²ff.—-ptv^a.4.—str^a.
—— *like an arrow.*—ph-x^a.
—— *as from splinters.*—aga^a.
—— *as with a blunt instrument.*—am-c^b.
—— *as with a large coarse instrument, leaving behind transient soreness.*—alm^a.II³.
—— *like electric shocks.*—irs. ; ^a.—spi^b.

VI⁴. Tearing.—agn.—am-c.—arn.—aur.—bel.—ca-c.—c-cs.—cth.—cha.—cch.—iod.—k-bi.—k-ca.—la-v.—ol-a.—plc.—rho.—spi.—teu.—zin. &c.
—— *flying.*—zin.
—— *deep.*—tep.
—— *outwards.*—cb-v^a.
—— *downwards.*—klm^a.
—— *upwards.*—alm^b.VI³.—mag^b. θ¹.
—— *upwards and downwards.*—lau^a.
—— *as if a blood-vessel were torn out.*—æth^b.

VII¹. Bursting, splitting.—cs-e.—ch-s.—ipc^b.—klm.—lil.i^a.(12).—so-n.
—— *pressed asunder.*—mt-n.—opi.

VII⁴. Swollen, as if.—ccn.

VII⁵. Tensive.—amb.—aml.—ber^b.q.—cau^a.δ.—glo^a.δ.—hyp.—lth.q.5.—mu-x^a.—na-m^b.i^a.5.
—— *as if squeezed in.*—tar.a¹ʋ.
—— *like an indiarubber band from t. to t.*—ca-x.

VIII¹. Blows.—agn.δ.35.—lah.82.—mt-s.—oln^b.—spr^b.
—— *sharp.*—ph-x^a.
—— *broad deep blow.*—cro.
—— *as if a peg there were struck in deeper.*—su-x^a.
—— *synchronous with pulse.*—chd^a.d.

VIII². Hammering.—ac-l.—bz-x.(16).—chi.—ele.—pau.—pso.
—— *like blows of a hammer.*—ars.ω².2.5.

VIII³. Jerking.—ca-a.q.29.(30).—cas^b.θ¹.83.—chi.p.q.48.; θ⁴.—glo.—k-ca^b.—la-v.—ox-x^b.—plb^a.—sul^a.ε.
—— *flying.*—val^a.
—— *momentary.*—lil^b.
—— *deep.*—ba-a^b.δOl.εl.
—— *downwards.*—ana^b.
—— *upwards.*—am-m^b.—spo.27.31.

VIII⁴. Throbbing.—all.—au-n.—bel.—bor.—ca-c.i^a.—ced.—fer.—glo. ; d.; i^a.—idm.p.—k-cl.—ni-x.—pho.—so-t.—stn.—tab. &c.
—— *violent.*—sep.

IX. Peculiar.
—— *formication.*—æsc.—ard.—gur.—sul.βa. (see also Scalp).
—— *twitching.*—chd^b.—ch-s^b.4.
—— *as if the blood suddenly stopped there.*—chd^b.VI³.
—— *like a foreign body.*—elp^a.
—— *as if lifted up.*—dio.3.
—— *like something running through*—glo.
—— *as if the bone would be smashed in.*—lyc^a.εa,ʋ.

COMPLEX PAINS.

II¹–V¹–VI³. **Burning, aching, shooting.**—pim.
II¹–VI². **Burning, pricking.**—pla^b.(15).—stp^b.
II¹–VI³. **Burning, shooting.**—am-m^b.60.90.—ba-c^a.—cup^b.—phl.
II¹–VIII⁴. **Burning, throbbing.**—cnb.

II¹–VIII⁵. **Burning, undulating.—**
su-x.

II³–VI³. **Raw, shooting.**—tab.

II⁵–V². **Sore, bruised.**—fag^b.4.

II⁵–VI⁴. **Smarting, rending.**—ana.

III–IV¹. **Compressive, cramp-like.**
—bel.

III¹–IV³–VI³. **Contractive, spasmodic, shooting.**—pla^a. to b.w.x.

III¹–V¹. **Contractive, aching.**—dig.
41.—tab.

III¹–VI³. **Contractive, shooting.—**
man.8.

III²·³. **Pinching, squeezing.——**mez.
ζ.

III²–V⁶. **Pinching, drawing.**—pet^b.

III²–V⁶–VIII³. **Pinching, drawing,
jerking.**—mer^a.σ².

III³–V¹. **Squeezing, aching.——**
ph-x^b.; ^a.35.

III³–V¹–VI³·t. **Squeezing, aching,
dartings inwards.**—arg^a.

III³–V⁶. **Squeezing, drawing.**—ca-c.
ηp.—crt^a.

III³–VI³. **Squeezing, shooting.—**
cap.

III³–VI⁴. **Squeezing, tearing.——**
k-ca^b.—zin.

III³–VIII⁴. **Squeezing, throbbing.**
—rhe.

IV¹–V¹. **Cramp-like aching.**—pla^b.

IV¹–V¹·⁶. **Cramping, aching, drawing.**—pet^b.

IV¹–V⁶. **Cramp-like drawing.**—cin.
12.—pet.

IV¹–V¹⁰·t. **Cramp-like pressing inwards.**—pla.—zin.

IV¹–VII⁵. **Cramp-like tension.**—pla.

IV²–V³. **Clawing, digging.——**buf^b.
31.

IV²–VIII⁴. **Clawing, banging.——**
mg-m.βa.5.16.(12).

IV³–VI³. **Spasmodic shootings.——**
an-a δ.

IV³–VIII³. **Spasmodic jerking.—**
ca-c^a.

V¹·³. **Aching, boring.**—alo^b.δl.4.5.—
ang.βa.24.(29).—cle^a.η.5.—col^c.—
man.δ.19.22.(29).—-ph-x^b.—stn^b.
1.—sul.ε.

V¹·⁶. **Aching, drawing.——**ang.——

chd^b.—dul^b.4.—-hep.1.—-msc^a.—
pet^a.98.—-ph-x^b.εaT.35.—-pho.—
rn-b.ag.σ¹.5.31.—-rho^b.—spi^b.—-
tox.—tar^a.—thu^b.—zng.8-31.**130.**
(6.18.130).

V¹·⁶·⁷. **Aching, drawing, stupefying.**—stn^c.

V¹·⁶–VI⁴. **Aching, drawing, tearing.**—ca-a.(12.41).

V¹·⁶–VII¹. **Aching, drawing, bursting.**—bel^a.

V¹·⁷. **Aching, stupefying.——**cld^a.
3-99.

V¹·⁸. **Aching, gnawing.**—rn-s^a.

V¹·¹⁰. **Aching, pressing.**—ca-a.—-
gn-c.—sto.—zin.

V¹·¹⁰–VIII¹·³. **Aching, pressing,
blow outwards.**—ba-a^b.

V¹·¹⁰·³. **Aching, pressing out.**—glo^b.
κ⁵.μ².σ¹.5-**10.**(66).—mez^b.

V¹·¹⁰·³. **Aching, forcing out.**—na-m.
e.

V¹·¹⁰·t. **Aching, pressing in.**—til.

V¹–VII¹. **Aching, cutting.**—col.

V¹–VI³. **Aching, shooting.**—ars^b.—
bor^a.—chd^a.—chi^c.—cch^a.—fer.—
k-bi.—k-ca^b.—lcp^b.—men^b.—
mrl^b.—nx-m^b.—tab.

V¹–VI³·t. **Aching, shooting inwards.**—ca-a.

V¹–VI⁴. **Aching, tearing.——**agn^a
35.—ana^a.; ^b.—arg^b.—asr^b.—
bel^a.—bis^a.12.—cam.— cin^b.(26).
—dul.—sul^b.δ.

V¹–VI⁴·v. **Aching, tearing upwards.**—mrl.

V¹–VI⁴–VII². **Aching, tearing, outstretching.**—arn^b.8-31.

V¹–VII¹. **Aching, bursting.——**bel^a.
14.

V¹–VII³. **Aching, stretching.——**
au-n.

V¹–VII⁵. **Aching, tensive.**—cle.66.;
σ².3.—dig^b.5.—glo.e.—ol-a.5-**10.**
—sul.41.——ver.βε.δP¹.18.19.(17.
29).

V¹–VIII³. **Aching, jerking.——**dig.
—ox-x^a.vl.—stn^b.al^s.

V¹–VIII⁴. **Aching, throbbing.——**
alm^a.q.4.——arn.——bov^a.au.σ².—
cam.—ccs.p.—col^b.—glo.

V$^{3\cdot6}$. Boring, drawing.—alm^b.5.—mt-n^a.η.

V^3–VI^3. Boring, shooting.——cld^b. (12).——ca-a^b.δB.60.—cam^a.3-99.—pso^b.

V$^{3\cdot a}$–VI^3. Boring out, shooting.—ca-a^b.(11.19).

V^3–VI^4. Boring, tearing.—alm.5.—grt.2.4.101.102.—rho^b.

V^3–VI^4–VIII^4. Boring, tearing, banging.—bov^b.4.

V^3–VIII^4. Boring, beating.—alm^a. VI$^{4\cdot p}$.

V^3–VI^1. Digging, cutting.—dio^b.5.

V$^{6\cdot7\cdot10\cdot t}$. Drawing, stupefying, inward pressure.—aco^b.

V$^{6\cdot10}$. Drawing, pressing.—cup^b.11.

V^6–VI^2. Drawing, pricking.—lam^b.

V^6–VI^3. Drawing, shooting.—æth^b.—alo^a.—kre.βa.θ^4.—nit.—equ^a.—tab^b.

V^6–VI^4. Drawing, tearing.—k-ca^b.—kre^b.—rho.δ.6.35.—sng.η.

V$^{6\cdot10\cdot s}$. Drawing, pressing outwards.—rho^a.

V$^{6\cdot10\cdot u\cdot v}$. Upward and downward drawing pressure.—oln^b.(8).

V^6–VIII^3. Drawing, jerking.——cyc^b.$\beta\iota$.σ^2ff.

V^6–VIII^4. Drawing, throbbing.—cth.

V^7–VIII^4. Dull, throbbing.—ptv^b.

V^7–VI^3. Stupefying, shooting.——vrb^a.θ^1.12.63.

V^7–VII^5. Stupefying tension.——alm^a.(12).

V^9–VI^3. Pecking, shooting.—ni-x^b. 4.

V^{10}–VI$^{1\cdot s}$. Pressing, cutting outwards.—bel.

V^{10}–VI$^{3\cdot s}$. Pressing, shooting outwards.—bel.

V^{10}–VI$^{4\cdot s}$. Pressing, tearing outwards.—chi.

V^{10}–VIII^3. Pressing, hammering.—glo.ηp,aa.18.28.29.31.

V$^{10\cdot s}$–VII^4. Pressing out, as if swollen.—ber^a.q.11.

V$^{10\cdot s}$–VII^5. Pressing out, tensive.—hel.d.q.1.(8).

V$^{10\cdot s}$–VIII^4. Pressing outwards, throbbing.—bry.10.

V$^{10\cdot t}$–VIII^4. Pressing in, throbbing.—jat.6.(8).

V$^{10\cdot t}$–VIII^5. Pressing inwards, undulating.—pla^b.

V$^{12\cdot15}$. Screwing, twisting.—sbd.6.

VI$^{1\cdot3}$. Cutting, shooting.—arg^b.

VI$^{3\cdot4}$. Shooting, tearing.——agn.35.—alm^a.89.—arn^b.—ars^b.——c-cs.—glo.η.—ind^b.5.—k-bi.—k-ca.αl^s. 2.; ^{b}.η.—k-hy^b.5.(12).—kre^x.θ^1.—lyc.2.—mrl^b.p.; ^{a}.—mez^b.—ol-a^b.—plb^a.—pul.—zin.—zn-o^a.2.

VI$^{3\cdot4\cdot s}$. Shooting, tearing outwards.—cha.

VI$^{3\cdot4}$–VIII^3. Shooting, tearing, jerking.—ana^b.

VI^3–VII^1. Shooting, bursting.——am-m^b.29.

VI^3–VIII^3. Shooting, jerking.——aco^b.—arn^b.—bov^b.——chd^b.—cyc. squ^a.

VI$^{3\cdot s}$–VIII^3. Outward shooting, jerking.—nx-m^b.

VI^3–VIII^4. Shooting, throbbing.—aco.—æth^b.5.(12).—cn-i^a.—cth.; ^{a}.(15).—hel^b.—stn.p.α^1b^s.ϕ.χ^1.

VI^4–VII^3. Tearing, stretching.——cin^a.

VI^4–VIII^1. Tearing blows.—mt-s.—spi^a.

VI^4–VIII^3. Tearing, jerking.—ana. 22.—chi^a.——cch.—lyc.—pul.—sul^b.31.—zin^b.

VI^4–VIII^4. Tearing, throbbing.—tep.

VII^1–VIII^4. Bursting, pulsating.—cac.

VIII$^{3\cdot4}$. Jerking, throbbing.—su-x^a.

ANATOMICAL SEAT.

T^a. Right temple.—æsc.V^{10}.—æth. VI^4.—aga.V^7.; V$^{1\cdot a}$.; VI^3.; VI^4.—alo.V^1.; ^{a}.V^6–VI^3.—alm.V$^{10\cdot t}$.66.; V^7–VII^5 5.(12).;VI^4.II^1.15.;VI$^{4\cdot p}$. V^3–VIII$^{4\cdot q}$.; VI^3.II^3.; V$^{3\cdot t}$.5.—am-b.V^{16}.——ana.V$^{1\cdot a}$.; V^1–VI^4.; VI^3.92.—ang.VIII^4.—an-s.VI^3. i^a.; I^b.er.—arg.III^3–V^1–VI$^{3\cdot t}$.—

ag-n.VI⁴.η.—ars.V¹.—ar-i.—aru.
VI³.θ³.—asa.V¹.; V⁷·ᵇ.—ast.VI³.
—au-m.VI⁴·ᵃ.—au-n.V³·ᵃ.—bap.
V¹.—ba-c.VI³.3.96.; II¹–VI³.—
bel.VI³·ᵃ.—ber.V¹⁰·ˢ–VII⁴.q.11. ;
VI³·ᵗ.; VI³.δ.; V¹·⁶–VII¹.—bis.V¹–
VI⁴.—bor.V¹–VI³.; VIII⁴.—bov.
V¹–VIII⁴.au.σ².—cai.VI³.—cld.
V¹·⁷.3-99.; VI³.δr.—ca-a.V¹.; III³.
—ca-c.IV³-VIII³.—cam.VI⁴. ; V³–
VI³.8-99.—can.VIII⁴·ᶻᶻ.p.ηp,aa.κ⁵.
—cn-i.VI³. ; VI³–VIII⁴. ; VI³.-
cth.VI⁴. ; VI⁴.66. ; VI³–VIII⁴.
(15).; VI³.4.; V¹⁰·ˢ.θ¹.—cb-v.VI⁴·ˢ.
—csc.V⁶·⁷.—cas.VI⁴.5.31.; VIII⁴.
18.66.—cau.V¹.; VII⁵.δ. ; V¹⁴. ;
VIII⁴.35.—chd.VIII¹.d.; V¹.ζo.;
V¹–VI³.;VI⁴.11.—chi.VI⁴–VIII³.;
VI³.—cin.VI⁴–VII³.; VI³·q.aᴠ.—
cnb.VIII⁴.iᵃ.q.35.; V¹⁰. ; Iᶻ.—cit.
βᴠ.—cca.V¹⁶.—coc.V¹⁶.—ccs.V¹.
—cod.VIII⁴.4.—cch.VI⁴.; 5.(16).;
V¹–VI³.-csn.—col.V⁷.au.31.; VII⁵.
—com.Iᵃ.; V¹⁰.—con.V⁶.31.; V⁶.er.
—cop.V².2.5.12.—cro.VIII¹·q.—
crt.VI³. ; III³–V⁶.—c-ar.VIII⁴.
—cyc.VI³. ; V³.θ¹.r¹r.—dig.V¹. ;
VI⁴.—dgn.VIII⁴.—dio.VI¹.; III³.
5.; V¹⁵.—dir.VI³.35.; VI³.r.3.—
dor.V⁷.—dro.V¹⁰·ˢ.; V¹.—dul.V³.
—elp.IX.—equ.—eup.VI².—evo.
V¹.;VI³·q.—fag.VI³.5.—fl-x.VIII⁴.
5.29.—for.V³.βa.; VI³·ˢ.—gel.V¹.
βa.δo.κ⁵.—gen.VI³·ˢ.5.31.—glo.
VI³.; VI³.δr.; VII⁵; δ.—grn.VI⁴.δ.
—gui.V¹.—hel.V¹.31.41.—bep.
V³·ᵛ.; VIII⁴.—hur.VIII⁴.—hfb.
VIII⁴.; V³.—hyo.V¹.βa.δL.(8-31).
—hyp.VI⁴·ᵇ.χ¹.5. ; VIII⁴.—ign.
V¹·ᵃ.; VI³·q.—ind.βa.κ⁶.66.; VI⁸.5.
VI⁴.θ⁴.r¹.—idm.V¹⁰.57.; V¹·ᵇ.; δre.
ζ³.θ³.—irs.VI³·ᶻ.; V⁷.—itu.VIII⁴.
—jac.VI³.; V⁷.3.—jug.V¹.5.—k-bi.
q.κ⁴.4.66.; VI³·ᵇ.—k-ca.V¹·¹⁰.; V¹.
5. ; V¹⁰·ˢ.—k-cl.VI³.—klm.V¹.;
VI⁴·ᵘ.—kre.VI³·⁴.θ¹.—lah.VIII⁴.
δOr.—lch.V¹⁰.—lam.V¹.—lau.
VI⁴·ᵘ·ᵛ.;VIII⁴.—led.V¹.—lin.VI³.
—lyc.IX.ea,ᴠ.—mt-n.V³·⁶.η.; V¹.
8-31.—mag.VI⁴.δb.;VI³.66.—mrl.
V¹⁰.; VI⁴.; V¹–VI⁴·ᵛ.; VI³·⁴.—mer.

V⁶·ᵃ.—mr-f.V⁷.; VI³.2-10.—mim.
V¹.σ².—msc.V¹·⁶.;V¹.—mu-x.VII⁵.
—nat.V¹⁰·ˢ.—na-a.29.; V⁶.—na-m.
IV¹.θ¹. ; VI³·ᶻᶻ.—nic.VI⁴.19.—
ni-x.V¹·ᵃ.κ⁷.λ.χ¹.3-30.; V⁶.; VI³·ᵃ.;
VIII⁴.κ⁵.3-99.—nit.V¹. ; VI⁴.1.
(12).;V⁶.5.—nx-m.VI³.—oln.III³.
—ol-a.V¹.ω⁹.66.(15). V¹⁰·ᵗ.—opi.
III³. ; V¹·ᵇ.δ.—ox-x.V¹–VIII³.vl.
—pæo.V³·ᵗ.—par.V¹.(12).—pau.;
q.—ped.VIII⁴.βe.3-30.—ptv.VI³.
4.; V¹⁰.5.11.—pet.V¹·⁶.98.—phl.
V¹.—ph-x.V¹⁰·ᵃ·ˢ. ; III³–V¹.35. ;
VI³·ᵉ·q.;VI³·ᵃ.δ.;VIII¹.—pho.VI³.
5.—phy.; V⁶.—pla.IV¹.4.—plb.
VI⁴.; VI³.; VIII³.—pru.VI³.12.;
V¹⁰·ˢ. ; III³.e.—pl-n.V⁷.q.—ptl.
V¹·¹.—rn-b.VI⁴·ᵃ.βa.31.—rn-s.V¹·⁸.
—rat.VI⁴·ᵃ.—rho.V¹⁰·ˢ. ; V⁶·¹⁰·ˢ.—
rs-r.3.5.; Iᵉ.26.; VI³.5.—rhs.V¹⁰·ᵛ.
5-10.(30). ; VI⁴.; VI³·ᵗ.; VI³·ˢ.iᵃ.q.
eᴠ.—sbd.V¹⁰·ˢ. ; V¹.VI³.—sab.V¹·ˢ. ;
V¹⁰·ˢ.—snt.V⁷.—sar.VI³.θ¹.; VI³·q.
—sil.V¹.4.—so-n.V².δb.—spi.V¹·ᵃ.;
VI⁴–VIII¹.—spr.; V¹⁶.—spo.V¹⁰·ˢ.
—squ VI³–VIII³.; V⁶–VI³·ᵃ.—
stn.V¹⁰·ˢ.;V¹.17ᵃ.(30).—stp.VI³·ˢ·ᵗ.
11.—str.VIII⁴.μ².; VI³.5.—sto.V⁶.;
VI³. ; VI³.4.—sul.VIII³.e.—su-x.
VI⁴.5.;VIII¹.;VIII³·⁴.—trn.; VI³.
—trx.V¹.—tar.V¹·⁶.;V⁶.η.θ⁴.—thu.
V¹·q.—til.VI⁴.; VI⁴.r.—ur-n.V⁷.
—val.V¹⁰·ᵗ.; VIII³.—vrb.V¹.; V⁷–
VI³.θ¹.12.63. ; V⁷–VI³.—zin.V¹.;
VI⁴.; VI³.; V¹·ᵃ.δr.—zn-o.VI³·⁴.2.
—ziz.Iᵃ.κ⁵.

—— *betwixt forehead and r.
temple.*—jac.V⁷.5.(12).
—— *from r. to l. T.*—glo.; VI³.βa.
ω².—jac.σ².5.8.—lil.VI³.—
pla.III¹–IV³–VI³.w.x.—
ptl.V¹⁰.
—— *over a large surface externally, concentrated to a point
internally.*—dio.V⁷.
—— *from r. to l., then back again
to r.*—hdr.

Tᵇ. **Left temple.**—aco.V⁶·⁷·¹⁰·ˢ.;VI⁴.;
VI³–VIII⁵.; VI⁴.eᴠᵖ.—æsc.V⁷.;
VI³.—æth.VI³–VIII⁴.(12). ; V⁶–

VI^{3}.; VI^{4}.—aga.V^{3}.—-agn.VI^{4}.—
alo.VI^{3}.31.; V^{1}.—alm.V$^{3.6}$.5.; VI^{4}.
$^{v.u}$.VI^{3}.—amb.VI^{3}.—am-b.VI^{3}.—
am-c.VI^{3}.60.;VI^{3}.--am-m.VIII$^{3.v}$.;
II^{1}–VI^{3}.60.90.--aml.VIII^{4}.—ana.
V^{1}–VI^{4}.; V$^{3.4}$.–VIII^{3}.; VIII$^{3.u}$.;
V$^{10.t}$.—-ant.V$^{6.b}$.(12).—arg.V^{1}–
VI^{4}.; VI^{4}.; VI$^{1.3.zz}$.; V^{6}.20.; V^{6}.19.
—ag-m.VI^{4}.—arn.VI^{3}–VIII^{3}.;
VI$^{3.4}$.; V^{1}–VI^{4}–VII$^{3.s}$.8-31.; VI^{4}.
—ars.VI^{3}.18.31.(19).; V^{1}–VI^{3}.;
VI$^{3.4}$.; VI^{3}.(11).—aru.V^{1}.; VI^{3}.;
VI^{3}.2.—ard.VI^{3}.;VI^{2}.—asa.V$^{10.s}$.;
V$^{10.t}$.;V^{16}.; VI$^{3.q}$.; VI$^{3.d}$.—asr.V^{1}.;
V^{1}–VI^{4}.—asp.V^{1}.βa.—au-m.VI^{4}.;
VIII^{4}.3-30.(116).—au-n.V$^{3.a}$.—
ba-a.V^{1}.;V$^{1.10}$–VIII$^{1.s}$.;VIII^{3}.δOl.
εl.—bel.V$^{10.a.t}$.22.; VI$^{3.s}$.; 4.—ber.
VII^{5}.q.; VI^{3}.—-bov.βε.29.; VI^{4}.ε.;
V^{3}–VI^{4}–VIII$^{4.q}$.4.; VI^{3}–VIII^{3}.
—bro.V^{1}.βa.—bry.V$^{10.s}$.4.; V$^{1.a}$.βε.
—bu-s.VI^{3}.—-buf.IV^{2}–V^{3}.31.; 2-
99.—cld.V^{3}-VI^{3}.(12).—ca-a.V$^{10.t}$.;
III^{3}.; V^{3}–VI^{3}.δB.60.; V$^{3.s}$.–VI$^{3.d}$.
(11.19).—ca-c.III^{3}–V^{6}.ηp.;VI^{3}.—
cth.VI$^{3.t}$.—-cb-v.V$^{10.s}$.; V^{3}.—ca-x.
V^{1}.;V^{7}.q.—cs-e.—cas.VIII^{3}.θ^{1}.83.
—cau.VI$^{4.a}$.4.;VI^{3}.—chd.VI^{3}-IX.;
VI^{3}–VIII^{3}.; VI^{4}.; IX.; V$^{1.6}$.; V$^{7.a}$.
$a^{1}b^{3}$.—-chi.V^{1}.; VI^{4}.; VI^{3}.—-ch-s.
IX.4.; I^{a}.δ.(16.102).; VI$^{3.v}$.14.—
crm.--cmf.V^{7}.q.--cin.V^{1}-VI^{4}.(26).
—-cit.—cle.V^{3}.; VIII^{4}.16.43.—
cob.κ^{5}.μ^{3}.ω^{2}.3.—cca.V^{7}.; V^{10}.βε.—
coc.V$^{10.t}$.; VI^{2}.—ccs.V^{1}.δl.—cch.
V^{6}.—-col.V^{1}–VIII^{4}.—-com.VI$^{3.e}$.
(8.35).; VI^{3}.—cvl.δl.; I^{a}.3.—cop.
VI^{4}.(12).—cot.VIII^{4}.--crt.V^{1}.βε^{c}.
θ^{1}n.; VI^{3}.—ctn.II^{1}.—cup.V$^{1.6}$.11.
—c-ar.I^{a}.—cyc.V^{6}–VI^{3}.(11).;V^{1}p.
βε.; βε.q.—-dph.I^{a}.—-dig.VI^{3}.5.2.
98.—-dio.; V^{10}.; V^{3}–VI^{1}.5.—-dul.
V$^{1.6}$.4.; VI$^{4.e}$.—dir.V$^{7.t}$.—equ.V^{3}.
—epn.VI^{3}.—fag.II^{5}–V^{2}.—-fl-x.
V$^{10.s}$.; V^{1}.—-gam.VI^{4}.4.—-gas.V^{6}.
—-gen.VI^{3}.—glo.VIII^{4}.; V^{6}.βε.
ζ.; V$^{1.10.s}$.κ^{5}.μ^{2}.σ^{1}.5-10.(66).—grp.
V^{1}.; VI^{3}.—-gui.V^{1}.—-gym.II^{5}.—
hæm.V^{2}.—hed.II^{5}.—hel.VI^{3}–
VIII^{4}.—hur.VIII^{4}.; V$^{1.a}$.—hdr.ζ.
—-hfb.V^{3}.3.—hyp.VIII^{4}.—-ind.
III^{3}.; VI$^{3.4.q}$.5.; V$^{3.e}$.; V^{6}.; IV^{1}.;
V$^{10.s}$.—inu.V^{3}.5.—ipc.VII^{1}.—
k-bi.VI^{3}.—k-ca.V^{1}.; V^{1}–VI^{3}; III^{3}–
VI^{4}.; VI^{4}.θ^{4}.5.; VIII^{3}.; VI$^{3.4}$.η.—
k-cl.—-k-hy.VI$^{3.4}$.5.(12).—VIII^{4}.
5.—klm.33.—kre.V$^{10.s}$.5.;V^{6}–VI^{4}.;
V^{6}–VI^{4}η.θ^{1}.—-lah.V^{1}.5.—lch.VI^{4}.
θ^{1}.—la-v.V^{7}.26.—lam.V^{6}–VI^{2}.—
lau.V^{1}.4.6.—lep.VI^{3}.—lil.V^{7}.βa.5.
31.; VIII$^{3.b}$.—lth.I^{b}.; δOl.κ^{4}.(63).;
ε.—lo-s.VI^{3}.—lcp.V^{1}–VI^{3}.—mt-s.
VI^{4}.—-mag.VI^{4}.(12.16).; VI$^{4.a.v}$.
θ^{1}.; VI^{3}.-mg-m.VI$^{4.a}$.-mg-s.VI^{4}.4.
—mnc.VI^{3}.—man.V^{1}.30.31.(19).;
VI^{4}.8-31.—m-pi.44.—men.V^{1}–
VI^{3}.—mrl.VI^{4}.; VI$^{3.4}$.p.; V^{1}–VI^{3}.;
VI$^{3.q}$.θ^{4}.; VI^{3}.—-mer.II^{1}.; V^{1}.—
mez.V$^{1.10.s}$.; VI$^{3.4}$.--mur.—mu-x.
V^{1}.; VI^{3}.—myr.V^{7}.q.--na-m.VII^{5}.
5.—na-n.V$^{10.t}$.—-ni-x.VI^{3}.5.; V^{9}–
VI^{3}.4.—-nit.VI^{4}.; VI^{3}.66.; V^{6}.δl.
—nx-m.VI$^{3.s}$–VIII^{3}.; VI^{4}.5.19.;
V^{1}–VI^{3}.--nx-v.VI$^{3.a}$.$\kappa^{5.6}$.5.(16).—
oln.V$^{6.10.u.v}$.(8).; V^{6}.;VIII^{1}.—ol-a.
V$^{1.b}$.4.; VI$^{3.4.b}$.; V^{6}.b.—-opi.θ^{4}.—
ox-x.VIII^{3}.—-par.V^{1}.; VI^{3}.—ped.
VI^{3}.—-ptv.V^{7}–VIII^{4}.—-pet.IV^{1}.;
IV^{1}–V$^{1.6}$.; III^{2}–V^{6}.—-phl.VI^{3}.—
ph-x.III^{3}–V$^{1.e}$.; V$^{1.6}$.εaT.35.; VI^{4}.
35.; V$^{1.3}$.—-phy.II^{1}.—-pla.V$^{10.t}$–
VIII^{5}.; IV^{1}–V^{1}.; II^{1}–VI^{2}.(15).—
plb.VI$^{3.4}$.—-pso.V^{1}.5.; V^{3}–VI^{3}.—
rn-s.VI^{3}.—rat.VI^{4}.—rho.V^{1}.βε.
(8-31.14).; V$^{10.t}$.; V$^{1.6}$.; V^{3}–VI^{4}.;
V^{1}.; VI^{3}.—-rs-r.; VI^{2}.—rum.—
sbd.VIII^{4}.; V$^{10.u}$.; V^{1}.—-sab.V^{6}.
δL.47.; V$^{10.s}$.—san.VI$^{3.e}$.—sar.V^{1}.
—snc.VI^{3}.δl.θ^{4}l.—-sep.VI^{3}.—ser.
VI^{3}.βε.—so-t.VIII^{4}.—spi.V$^{1.6}$.;
VI^{3}.—spr.VIII^{1}.—spo.VIII^{4}.;
VI$^{4.a}$.δl.—stn.V$^{10.t}$.;V^{1}–VIII^{3}.al^{8}.;
V$^{1.3}$.1.—stp.VI^{3}.; V$^{10.s.t}$.; II^{1}–VI^{2}.
—so-n.VIII$^{4.a}$.29.32.—sto.VI^{3}.4.
—-sul.V^{1}–VI^{4}.δ.; VI^{4}–VIII^{3}.31.;
VIII^{4}.31.;VI^{3}.δ.4.; V^{6}.—su-x.VI^{4}.
19.63.—tab.VI^{3}.;VI^{2}.2.—trn.VI^{3}.
5.; 2.—trx.V^{6}.19.(18.31).; VI^{2}.
19.(18).;VI^{3}.8-31.(18).—tar.V$^{10.t}$.
—tax.V^{1}.—tep.V$^{10.t}$.; V^{1}.117.;
VIII^{4}.; VI$^{3.q}$.—thu.V$^{1.6}$.—til.V^{6}.
η.—tri.V^{3}.—ur-n.—vrb.V$^{10.zz}$.—

vin.VI³.η.——vi-t.V¹.——zin.V¹⁰·ᵗ.;
III³.; VI⁴–VIII³.; V¹².

—— *from l. to r. T.*—au-m.VI⁴.—
ca-c.VI³.—hpm.V¹.5.35.—
lcp.VI³.—mr-f.VI³.—ol-m.
V¹.—ptl.VIII⁴.

Tᶜ. **One temple.**—cap.VIII⁴.—chi.
V¹–VI³.—col.V¹·³.—k-bi.VI³.—
na-m.V¹.βε.χ².—rs-r.

—— *from T. to T.*—aln.VI³.—
con.—glo.VIII⁴.—ham.
VI³.—hfb.Iª.1.; VIII⁴.—
mez.VI⁴.—naj.VI³.κ⁴.5(8).
—na-a.3-99.

—— *alternately in r. and l. T.*—
hdr.3.—lil.V⁷.3-30.

Temples and other parts.

T. and vertex.—ang.VI⁴·ᴾ.—ca-c.
V¹.; V⁶·ᶻᶻ.—cb-v.V¹.; VI⁴·ᵈ.—ccs.
V¹.(117).—crn.V¹.—equ.V⁷.q.—
glo.VIII⁴.—hdr.—jat.V¹⁰·ᵗ.6.(8).
—klm.VII¹.—lah.III.5.31.; VI³.
ζ³.σ²ff.—lth.Iª.3-99.—mt-s.V¹.19.
26.41.(22.29.31).—mez.35.86.—
ni-x.V¹.δ.—pau.VIII².—pho.V¹.iª.
—phs.V¹⁰·ˢ.—rhe.III³-VIII⁴.; V¹.;
VII⁵.βa.—sed.V¹.—spo.VIII³·ᵛ.
27.31.—tab.V¹.3-99.—ver.V¹–
VII⁵.βε.δP¹.18.19.(17.29).

T., crown, and parietes.—pim.II¹–
V¹–VI³.

T., crown, and occiput.—glo.VIII⁴.
—sbd.V¹.

T. and parietes.—cth.V⁶–VIII⁴.—
crn.VIII⁴.—glo.VIII⁴.σ².; III.

T., parietes, and occiput.—car.VI⁴.
(35).—grt.VI⁴.; VI³.

T. and r. side of head.—cau.V¹.—
gam.VI³.—hy-x.V¹.—sbd.V¹²·¹⁵.6.

T. and left side of head.—bel.—
k-ca.VI⁴.

T., l. side of head, and l. occiput.—
am-c.VIII⁴.ω⁹.

T. and occiput.—ail.VI³.α¹b.—ana.
VI⁴–VIII³.22.—ast.VI³·ᵇ.—cn-i.
—chi.VI¹.δO.29.35.—cca.V⁶.4.43.
—ccn.VII⁴.—cof.V¹.8-31.(6.19).
—cop.VI³.—dio.V⁷.3.—fag.29.30.
(22).—gel.V¹.—glo.V¹⁰–VII⁵.ε.;

V¹⁰·ᵗ.—iof.VI³.—klm.VI³·ᶻ.; V⁷.—
la-x.ω².3-30.[S.II¹·⁵].—lyc.VI³.—
mns.—msc.—pim.V¹⁰.σ¹.—rs-r.;
II¹·ᵇ.2.—rhs.V⁶.δ.3.(30).—sng.—
spi.VIII³.8-31.—stn.III.—sul.V⁶.
—zin.V¹.

T. and l. occiput.—irs.VI³.
T. and scalp.—sbd.VI³.
Tª. and vertex.—almª.VI³·⁴.89.—ard.
φ.—bel.V¹–VI⁴.—ber.VI³.δ.—
ca-x.II¹.—chd.V⁶·ª.(16).; V¹.—
cca.VI³·ᵛ.3-30.89.—glo.III.—lch.
VI⁴.η.—stp.V¹.

Tª. and r. side of head.—ced.—lyc.
VI⁴–VIII³.—trn.VI³.

Tª. and l. side of head.—bel.
Tª. and occiput.—cnc.εr.—mer.III³–
V⁶–VIII³.σ².

Tᵇ. and crown.—au-m.V⁶.—chd.V⁷·ª.
αb.—cup.II¹-VI³.—cyc.V⁶-VIII³.
βε.σ²ff.—lau.VI⁴.η.θ¹.

Tᵇ., vertex, and r. parietal.—cun.
3.—gym.VI³.ε.

Tᵇ., parietes and occiput.—asr.βε.
Tᵇ. and r. side of head.—mag.VI³.
Tᵇ. and l. side of head.—k-ca.V⁶–
VI⁴.—lah.VI³.—lil.η.19.(35).—
sep.VI⁴.

Tᵇ., l. side of head, and r. occiput.—
ca-a.V¹⁰·ˢ.

Tᵇ. and occiput.—asr.III.26.31.(19).
—atr.VI³.δb.3-99.(8).—lil.V¹·¹⁰.—
na-m.VIII⁴.—nx-m.—ph-x.V¹.αbᵇ.

Tᵇ. and r. occiput.—lyc.VI³.

VARIOUS PAINS IN VARIOUS PARTS.

**Sharp pressing pain in Tª., dull
pain in Tᵇ.**—æsc.
**Stinging sharp pain in T., hot dull
in C. and Fª.**—hdr.
Compression in T., aching in C.—
na-m.43.44.
Tension in head, compression in T.
—con.66.(14).
**Compression in T., drawing in oc-
cipital protuberance.**—bry.
Aching in T., pinching in l. P.—
na-m.βε.
Constriction in P., aching below T.
—lah.

Aching pain in T., screwing in F.—chd.ζo.

Aching in T., moving towards middle of brain, causing a dull undulating pain, at same time a bursting upward, with fine piercing pain on outer skull over l. temple.—glo.

Aching in C. and T., shooting in T.—cth.

Numbing and deep pressure in T., dull pain in C.—ptv.

Throbbing and aching in r. T., pressure as from a weight in C.—alm.4.

Aching in T., followed by jerkings in O., contractive pain in head.—aco.βe.

Screwing together in T., bursting in F.—lyc.83.

Aching in C., drawing, tearing in T.—ol-a.

Dull pain in Tᵇ., throbbing in Tᵃ.—mr-f.

Dull, heavy pain in T., with tight band across F.—ca-x.ζ.

Heavy weight in C., and pressing in T.—lth.af.δb.κ⁵.3.16.(8.19).

Aching in O.,pressing out in T.—glo.

Pressing out in T., and some pain Fᵖ.—fag.4.

Constriction in C., inward pressing in T.—ana.5.

Shooting in T., burning in C.—ptv.

Shooting through T., bruised pain in O.—mr-f.

Spasmodic drawing in C., shooting in T.—pho.

Compression in head, pulsative blows and shoots in T.—thu.29.(12.22).

Shooting in T., throbbing in head.—gui.18.19.(12.31).

Cramp-like drawing in C., shootings in temples.—ca-c.ep.

Pressive out-stretching in C., drawing in O., rends in T.—arn.

Tearing in T., throbbing and shooting in C.—pho.βa.

Tearing upwards in Tᵇ., followed by shooting in Fᵃ.—alm.

Dull pain in O., tension in T.—bov.

Pulsating pain in T., and twisting in r. O.—ced.

Pain in r. P., aching in Tᵃ.—pho.6.29.31.35.(8).

Aching in r. T., drawing shoots from O. to F.—sar.

Dull pain in Tᵃ. and O., followed by dull stitches in F. and Tᵇ.—æsc.

Cramping, tensive pains in r. mastoid process, shooting in Tᵃ.—sul.

Shooting in Tᵇ., pressure outwards in F.—lau.βe.

Tension and shooting in C., tearing in Tᵇ.—k-hy.σ².

Darting through Tᵇ., tensive jerking in C.—gn-c.41.49.

Crown.

I. Pain undefined.—aco.—æsc.—col.—crt.[S.ddʰ.]—dph.—gur.—hfb.—la-v.—lap.—ox-x.—san.—so-t.—spr.—trn.p.—tep.
—— in a small spot.—so-n.
—— like a weight.—alo.—ars.
—— neuralgic.—ch-sᵃ.
—— febrile.—sul.1.
—— as after intoxication.—lap.
—— increasing and diminishing alternately.—glo.a¹b.

II¹. Burning.—aga.a¹ʊ.—arn.σ².—ars.—bry.—ca-x.—cau.—ch-s.—glo.—grp.—mrl.—ph-x.—rn-s.—sul.3-99.—ur-nᵃ.q.d.iᵃ.65.
—— transient.—nat.
—— chilly.—cau.

II⁵. Smarting, like a sore.——chd.11.—cnb.11.—ferᵃ.
—— as if it had been bruised.——glo.26.

II⁶. Stinging.—aln.4.29.
II⁷. Ulcerative.—cas.12.
III. Compressive.—aco.——ccb.—sep.π.1.
—— from above downwards, and from both sides.——nx-m.a¹bˢ.φ.
—— from both sides.—men.q.33.

—— *as with a pitch cap.*——aco. (8-31).

—— *as by an elastic body.*—bz-x. aĝ.σ.

III¹. **Contractive, constrictive.**—crt.—fl-x².*or.*5.—k-bi.; 66.—lau. p.—nit.; q.2.4.—phl.

—— *as if bound with a cord.*—klm.

—— *as if brain were bound with a cloth.*—cyc.a¹ɒ.

—— *like a band drawn tight over C. from ear to ear.*—ipc.35.

III². **Pinching.**—con.31.(19).

III³. **Squeezing.**—ag-n.—bel².—k-ca^b.

IV¹. **Cramp-like.**—ca-c.

V¹. **Aching.**—aco.—ac-l.—ac-s.—aga.—alo.—am-c.—asa.—bov.—chd.; p.—coc.—cof.—cch.—frz.—hep.p.—iod.—pho.i².—rho.—spo.—stn.[H.m.]—sum.—val.—vrb.—ziz. &c.

—— *sharp.*—stp.

—— *slowly increasing and declining.*—sar.

—— *violent.*—spi.—tab.

—— *here and there.*—pho.

—— *as from catarrh.*—lyc.—mt-s.19.26.41.(22.29.31).

—— *as if brain were tied up in a cloth.*—cyc.a¹b.

—— *as if a sharp stone fell on it.*—cau^c.

—— *as if a cap pressed tightly.*—aco.

—— *as from a board.*—æsc.—tab.

—— *as if a weight lay there.*—cac.—can.—cb-v.—k-bi.—lau.—msc.—nit.—ptv.δq,ɒ.—sul.—tep.

V². **Beaten, bruised.**—bov.11.VI⁴·ᵃ. ₑCr.3.—gam.5.(8).—glo.26.—idm.(8).—lab.12.—phy.31.

V³. **Boring, digging.**—au-n².—bor.—cch^d.—lep^b.ₑ.—mg-s.βe².5.—mez².—mu-x.—oln.—pul.—sam.—sul.[S.dd^h.].

—— *deep.*—aga.

—— *forwards.*—elp.

—— *as if head were drawn backwards.*—spi.

—— *as if holes were bored through skull.*—ph-x.

V⁴. **Broken, as if.**—ast.

V⁶. **Drawing.**—bov.—ca-c.—spo.

—— *or raising up.*—dgn.

—— *deep.*—ol-a.5.

—— *diagonally across.*—au-n.

V⁷. **Dull.**—æth.—aru.b.—c-cs.—cn-i.—chd.a¹b.—iof.q.—ox-x.—ptv.x.—pho.

—— *deep.*—crn.

—— *across.*—chd.

—— *as after turning round rapidly.*—ca-c.

—— *distracting.*—glo.

—— *as from a blow.*—ptv^b.5.28.31.

—— *following pain in heart.*—mr-f.βa.κ^b.

V¹⁰. **Pressing.**—aln.—k-ca.5.—kre.—ziz.

—— *deep.*—con.

—— *outwards.*—c-ph.i². 29.35.(16).—fag.—opi.δOr.—ph-x.—phs.

—— *inwards.*—fer.33.(8.12).—glo.d.—hel.—ox-x.—pla.—sul.δb.5.2-**10**.

—— *downwards.*—amb.p.δ.ηc^b.3.4.—cin.q.12.—ctn.βe.ε.—cup.—cu-s.; g^b.x.a¹ɒ.—hdr.ε.—nx-m.p.

—— *upwards.*—hln.49.—lch.ii^d.

—— *upwards and outwards, as if no room for brain.*—cmf.—glo.35.(8.20).

—— *forwards.*—nx-m.29.

—— *as with a finger.*—lch^b.—ni-x.δ.

—— *as with a hand.*—nic.

—— *like a bar of iron.*—bel.ₑa.

—— *as from a weight.*—aln.κ^5. χ^{1·2}.—ind.

—— *like a close fitting form.*—hfb.

V¹². **Screwing.**

—— *screwed together.*—grt.

V¹⁵. **Twisting.**—mrl.

V¹⁶. **Wedge, peg, &c., pressed in.**

—— *peg.*—ana^b.—dul^b.

—— *nail.*—evo[a].——hur.η.θ[1].4.31.
—mgt.[S.dd[h].]—nic.
—— *something pointed.*——hel.——
pru[a].
—— *blunt instrument.*—rn-s.
—— *like claws.*—hel.—la-v.

VI[1]. Cutting.—ver.
—— *sharp.*—snc[c].

VI[2]. Pricking.—ard.—spg[a].
—— *as with a pin.*—mel.—thu.η.
θ[4].χ[1].3.(8-31).
—— *as with needles.*—pho.

VI[3]. Shooting.——aco.——æth.—aga.
—alm.——am-m.——ba-c.——bel. —
ber.—bov.—bry.——ca-c.—cap.—
cb-a.—cau.—chd.—chi.——cup.—
dig.— hur.—iod.—lah.—lau.—
lyc.—mag.—mez.——mil.——na-m.
—ni-x.—phl.—ph-x.—pho.—phy.
—spi.—sul.—tab.—val.—zin. &c.
—— *violent.*—cb-v.——ipc.—k-bi.
11.—ol-a.
—— *transient.*—ind.—mil.
—— *deep.*—cap.——ind.——lyc.—.
rat.—stp.[S.dd[h].]——tab.—
ton.
—— *inwards.*—alo.—ir-f[a].dd.2.—.
lyc.
—— *spreading all over head.*——.
bov.
—— *across.*—la-x.dd[h].4.
—— *sharp.*—mez.—rap.
—— *quivering.*—ana[b].
—— *as with knives and forks.*—
lah.ζ[3].σ[2]ff.
—— *boring through.*—sil.
—— *drawing head backwards.*—
phl.

VI[4]. Tearing.—aga.—amb.—am-c.
—ang.—ba-c.—bel.—bz-x.—bor.
—bov.—cth.—cb-v.——cas.——ctn.
—dul.—hyp.——ind.—klm.—lau.
—mg-s.—mer.—mu-x.—nx-v.—
ph-x.—rn-b.—rat.—thu.—zin. &c.
—— *deep.*—ind.
—— *diagonally over.*—au-n.
—— *as if a handful of hair were
pulled out.*—cth.—mu-x.βa.
—— *as if torn or smashed.*—ca⌐ι.
3-99.

VII[1]. Bursting, splitting.—am-m.
—cn-s[c].p.εʊ.—k-hy.p.χ[1].(101).—
la-x.3.——rn-b.δ.5.6.——sto.p.αg,ḅ.
ηp,aa.φ.5.—zin.
—— *as if skull were burst open.*—
cb-a.2.110.
—— *as if top of head would fly
off.*—cmf.i[a].p.33.
—— *a sensation of dull roaring.*
—byp.4.

VII[3]. Stretching.—dgn.—msc.βe.
VII[5]. Tensive.—aga.——cac.——ca-c.
—men.—mrl.δ.——rhe.βa.—sto.θ[4].
5.—ton.

VIII[1]. Blows.——ua-m.a[1]ʊ.βa.26.——
spr.
—— *violent.*—lyc.19.66.

VIII[2]. Hammering.—hyp.3.— pau.
VIII[3]. Jerking.—ana[b].—men.29.—
mu-x.5.—rn-s.
—— *here and there.*—k-hy.
—— *upwards.*—spo.27.31.

VIII[4]. Throbbing.——cn-i.—crn.[S.
II[5].]—glo. ; i[a]. ; ll.5.—hfb.—lyc.
—nat.3.—na-a.i[a].4.—sil.d.q.
—— *intermittent.*—plg.
—— *forwards.*—kre.
—— *ascending from base of skull.*
—glo.
—— *as if all would come out there.*
—cau.3-30.
—— *like the beating of waves.*——
zin.p.5.
—— *as of a vein too full.*——fer.ι.
κ[4].84.

VIII[5]. Undulating.——for.δo.5.——
mr-f.

IX. Peculiar.
—— *creeping.*—msc.
—— *as if skull-cap were too thin.*
—bel.V[3.15].VI[4].12.
—— *like an electric shock.*—na-s.
—— *as if top of head would come
off.*—cob.32.—irs.3.8.35.
—la-x.
—— *as if crown were raised up.*—
rs-r.
—— *as if crown would open and
brain jump out.*—rs-r.

—— *as if brain were loose.*—elp. κ[5].

—— *pressure and a crazy feeling.* —lil.

—— *like foam rising in anything fermenting.*—myr.

COMPLEX PAINS.

II[1.3]–III[3]. **Burning, raw, squeezing.**—sep.

II[1.3]–V[1]–VI[4]. **Burning, raw, aching, tearing.**—sul.4.8.(5).

II[1]–III[1]. **Burning, contractive.**— phl.

II[1]–V[1]. **Burning, aching.**——cb-v. 5-**10**.—ccs.—sul.5.—vi-t[a].19.

II[1]–V[1]–VI[3]. **Burning, aching, shooting.**—pim.

II[1]–V[6]. **Burning, drawing.**—sul.

II[1]–V[10]–VIII[4]. **Burning, pressing, throbbing.**—ars.βε.(15).

II[1]–VI[3]. **Burning, shooting.**——chi. —cup.—na-m.—ptv.—zin.

II[1]–VI[4]. **Burning, tearing.**—rat.2. 83.(8).

II[4]–VI[4]. **Scraping, tearing.**—sul.

III–VI[4]. **Compressive, tearing.**— dul.

III[1]–V[1]. **Contractive, aching.**—ign. —pla.q.x.—sep.—stp.βε.3.

III[1]–V[7]. **Contractive, stupefying.** —val.

III[1]–V[10.t]. **Contractive, pressing in.**—nx-m.p.

III[1]–VIII[5]. **Contractive, undulating.**—sep.5.

III[1]–V[10]. **Constrictive, pressing.**

—— *gradually increasing and declining.*—stn.

III[2]–VI[3]. **Pinching, shooting.**—— pim.41.

III[3]–V[1]. **Squeezing, aching.**—eug.

III[3]–V[1.6]. **Squeezing, aching, drawing.**—rn-s.

III[3]–V[10]. **Squeezing, pressing.**— con.θ[4].π.π[1].

III[3]–VIII[4]. **Squeezing, pulsative.** —rhe.

IV[1]–V[6]. **Cramp-like drawing.**—— ca-c.ερ.

IV[1]–VII[5]. **Cramp-like, tensive.**— ast.2.41.

IV[3]–V[6]. **Spasmodic, drawing.**—— pho.

V[1.3]. **Aching, boring.**—-msc.—opi. σ[2].—phl[b].

V[1.3]. **Aching, digging.**—cch.

V[1.6]. **Aching, drawing.**—chd[b].—- cle.—iod[b].—ph-x[a].35.—spi.

V[1.6]–VI[3]. **Aching, drawing, shooting.**—sil.

V[1.6]–VI[4]. **Aching, drawing, tearing.**—zin.

V[1.6]–VII[5]. **Aching, drawing, tensive.**—tar.

V[1.8]. **Aching, gnawing.**—bel[a].ε.θ[1]. —rn-s[b].

V[1.10]. **Aching, pressing.**—sul.τυ.ω[2]. 3-99.

V[1.10]–VI[3]–VIII[3]. **Aching, pressing, shooting, jerking.**—car.

V[1]–VI[3]. **Aching, shooting.**—aco.— ba-c.112.—chd.31.—cyc[c].βε.—lyc. 2.—ph-x[b].—sar[a].—tab.

V[1]–VI[4]. **Aching, tearing.**—aur[b].35. —stn[b].—zin[a].

V[1]–VII[1]. **Aching, bursting.**—-spi. q.**53**.

V[1]–VII[1]–VIII[4]. **Aching, splitting, throbbing.**—chd.16.

V[1]–VII[5]. **Aching, tensive.**—bel[b].— ver.βε.◊P[1].18.19.(17.29).—vrb[b].θ[4].

V[1]–VII[5]–VIII[3]. **Aching, tensive, jerking.**—gn-c.5.41.49.

V[1]–VIII[3]. **Aching, jerking.**——pet. 5.—sil.

V[1]–VIII[4]. **Aching, throbbing.**— bel.—cth.5.35.— glo[a].—-sul.3-99. —ton.—ver.35.

V[2.10.u]. **Bruised, pressing downwards.**—ph-x.

V[2]–VI[3]. **Bruised, shooting.**—nic.αu. **5**.

V[2]–VIII[4]. **Bruised, throbbing.**—— cau.**15**.

V[3.10]. **Boring, pressing.**—ir-f[a].4.

V[3.7]. **Boring, stupefying.**—ard.

V[3]–VI[3]. **Boring, shooting.**—lah.— ni-x.5.—opi[d].—tep.σ[2].

V[3]–VI[3.5]. **Boring, shooting outwards.**—stp.

$V^{3·15}$–VI^4. **Digging, twisting, tearing.**—bel.12.

V^3–VI^4. **Digging, tearing.**—cch[a.b].—spi[b].35.51.56.86.(16).

$V^{6·10·u}$. **Drawing, downwards pressing.**—nx-v.

$V^{6·11}$. **Drawing, rheumatic.**—ir-f[a].2.29.

V^6–VI^3. **Drawing, shooting.**—lip[a].—ph-x.(12).—tab.

V^6–$VI^{3·4}$. **Drawing, shooting, tearing.**—sep.

V^6–VI^4. **Drawing, tearing.**—k-ca.—thu.

V^6–VIII^4. **Drawing, throbbing.**—grt.

V^{10}–VIII^4. **Pressing, throbbing.**—nx-v.41.

$V^{10·s}$–VI^3. **Pressing out, shooting.**—ca-c.29.

$V^{10·s}$–VIII^4. **Forcing out, throbbing.**—sep.26.35.48.

$V^{10·v}$–VIII^4. **Pressing upwards, throbbing.**—aml.

$VI^{1·4}$. **Cutting, tearing.**—aur[a].

VI^1–$VIII^{1·s}$–VIII^4. **Cutting, blows outwards, throbbing.**—ca-a.

$VI^{3·4}$. **Shooting, tearing.**—aga.ϵl.—alm.89.—cau[b].—ol-a[a].ϵr.—phl[a].66.—rat.—sar[b].

VI^3–VII^1. **Shooting, bursting.**—am-m.29.—grp.3.4.(105).—ni-x.ϕ^1.4.

VI^3–VII^1–VIII^4. **Shooting, bursting, throbbing.**—cb-a.31.

VI^3–VIII^2. **Shooting, hammering.**—pho.

VI^3–VIII^3. **Shooting, jerking.**—bry.—chd.σ^2.11.—spi.[SII[7].]—sto.

VI^3–VIII^4. **Shooting, throbbing.**—æth.—ber.29.—cau.—cop.—phl.4.

VI^4–$VIII^{2·s}$. **Tearing, hammering outwards.**—vin.

VI^4–VIII^3. **Tearing, jerking.**—mag.rv.—rat.σ^2.

VI^4–VIII^4. **Tearing, throbbing.**—inu.66.

ANATOMICAL SEAT.

a. **Right side of crown.**—alm.VIII^4.3-99.—asa.$VI^{3·p}$.—aur.$VI^{1·4}$.—

au-n.V^s.—bel[b].V^1.; $V^{1·8}$.ϵ.θ^1.; VI^4.35.; $III^{3·b}$.—bov.VI^3.—chd.VI^3.—cch.I[a]; V^s–VI^4.—evo.V^{16}.—fer.II^5.—fl-x.III^1.σr.5.—glo.V^1–VIII^4.—ir-f.$V^{3·10}$.4.; $V^{6·11}$.2.29–$VI^{3·t}$.dd.2.—kre.$VIII^{3·d}$.—lth.VI^3.dd.; 5.—mg-m.$VI^{3·a}$.—mg-s.V^3.βϵ[a].5.—nit.p.(11).—oln.$VI^{3·q}$.; VI^4.—ol-a.$VI^{3·4}$.ϵr.—opi.V^1.βϵ.—phl.$VI^{3·4}$.66.—pru.V^{16}.—sbd.—sar.V^1–VI^3.—spg.VI^2.—til.V^6.ηl.—ur-n.II^1.q.d.i[a].**65**.—vi-t.II^1–V^1.19.—zin.V^1–VI^4.

——— r., then l.—cch.V^3–$VI^{4·b}$.g[a].lth.

——— r., then l., then back to r.—bel.V^{10}.

b. **Left side of crown.**—ana.VI^3.; V^{16}.; V^6.; VIII^3.—aur.V^1–VI^4.35.; VI^4.—au-n.$VI^{3·a}$.—bel[a].V^1.; V^1–VII^5.—bor.$VI^{3·b}$.ξ.—bov.$VI^{3·a}$.dd[h].—cau.V^6.; $VI^{3·4}$.—cep.—chd.VI^3.; $V^{1·6}$.—cin.VI^3.—cch.V^3–VI^4.; V^6.ζ.—dul.V^7.; $V^{16·t}$.—iod.$V^{1·6}$.—k-ca.III^3.—lch.V^{10}.—lau.V^1.; VI^4.—led.V^1.—lep.V^3.ϵ.—lth.VI^3.—nit.VI^3.—ol-a.VI^4.; $VI^{3·a}$.r[1]v[1]nn.ϕ^1.2.83.—opi.V^1.π.σ.—par.VI^3.—ptv.V^7.**5**.28.31.—phl.$V^{1·3}$.—ph-x.V^1–$VI^{3·q}$.—rn-s.$V^{1·8}$.—sar.$VI^{3·4}$.—stn.V^1–VI^4.—vrb.V^1–VII^5.θ^4.

c. **Coronal suture.**—ars.V^6.4.—cau.V^1.—cn-s.VII^1.p.ϵv.—cch.VI^3.; V^7.—cyc.V^1–VI^3.βϵ.; VI^3.5.—er-a.VI^3.ηr.—mr-s.$V^{7·q}$.3.34.(4).—rs-r.5.103.; VI^3.—src.V^7.—snc.VI^1.

d. **Sagittal suture.**—asr.q.βϵ.—au-m.V^1.—cch.V^3.—col.V^1.26.29.; $V^{1·p}$.—opi.V^3–VI^3.—sul.V^1.

Crown and other parts.

C. **and parietes.**—hur.VIII^4.π[2].—lyc.VI^4.5.; VI^3.43.—mag.VI^4.σ^2.83.(2).—na-a.VI^3.q.; V^7.—sin.q.

C., **parietes, and occiput.**—trn.p.

C. **and r. parietal.**—æth.VI^3–VIII^4.—cch.$V^{1·3}$.—hf b.V^{10}.q.

C. **and l. parietal.**—clo.(16).—glo.—ol-a.VI^3.2.84.(8-30).—zin.

C., l. parietal, and occiput.—pho. VIII⁴.

C. and occiput.—-ag-m.VI⁴.—ba-c. V¹.σ²ff.3-99.—-c-ph.σ².—cb-a.V¹. q.83.(8).—-cmf.V¹·ᵉ.3-30.—con.q. —cvl.—ctn.V¹.—dig.V¹.βε.; VI³·ᵃ. —dgn.V⁶.—gel.; V⁶.44.(19).; βa. —glo.V⁷.—ham.VIII⁴.—-hln. V¹⁰·ˢ.iᵃ.43.(41).—-hur.VIII⁴.—- hy-x.V¹.βε.δO.σ².—-ind.VI⁴·q.—- la.x.ι.—-mag.VI⁴–VIII³.rv.—- mg-s.III³–VI¹.; VI⁴.; VI⁴- VIII⁴.—man.V¹⁰·ᶻᶻ.4.; III¹.—- nat.—-nx-m.V¹.—-ol-a.V¹.—-opi. V¹·³.σ².—osm.V¹.iᵃ.4.22.—-ox-x. V¹⁰·ᵗ.—-phl.II¹–III¹.—-ph-x.VI⁴. —rat.VI⁴.—-sep.II¹·³–III³.—spi. V³.—stn.V¹⁰.5-10.—sto.VI³.VIII³. —-sul.V¹·ᵃ.δ.δb.χ¹·³.2.—-zin.VIII⁴. p.5.

C. and r. occiput.—mag.VI³·q.

C. and l. occiput.—am-c.VI⁴·ᵛ.VII¹.

Cᵃ. and l. parietal.—ch-s.I.

Cᵃ. and occiput.—-gel.V⁶.—ph-x.V¹·⁶. 35.—spi.V¹·⁶.

VARIOUS PAINS IN VARIOUS PARTS.

Undulation in head, compressive pain in C.—grp.4.

Constriction in C., inward pressure in T.—ana.(5).

Cramp-like in C., bruised in P.— chi.35.

Aching in C., soreness of H.—cb-v.

Aching in C., drawing round head. —cb-v.

Aching in C., drawing in O.—sul. 66.

Aching and outstretching in C., tearing in T., drawing in O.—arn.

Like a tight band across C., with throbbing behind ears.—ipc.35.

Brain as if tightly bound, boring in C.—pul.

Sharp shoots in C., cutting contraction in O.—ton.

Tearing in r. O., shooting in C.—zin.

Tearing and pain to touch in C., drawing in head.—rhs.66.

Tension and shooting in C., tearing in l. T.—k-hy.σ².

Blow on C., tearing in l. P., shooting in brain.—ton.αlˢ.

Pain in O., with pulsative pain in C.—hln.βa.29.

Parietes.

I. **Pain undefined.**—ch-x.q.3.—gloᵈ. —mim.

II¹. **Burning.**—ca-cᵇ.17.

II³. **Raw.**—rhsᵈ.θ¹.

II⁴. **Scraping.**

—— *forwards.*—indᶜ.5.19.

II⁵. **Smarting, sore.**—phyᶜ.103.

II⁶. **Stinging.**—cotᶜ.

III. **Compressive.**—-acoᵈ.—bryᵉ.— rs-rᵈ.

III¹. **Contractive, constrictive.**- aml.—ath.βa.—lahᵉ.

—— *like a band tied round head.* —dio.b.3.

III². **Pinching.**

—— *in fits.*—sepᵇ.

III³. **Squeezing.**—ca-cᵈ.—hurᶜ.θ⁴x. squᵃ.

IV¹. **Cramp-like.**—sarᵇ.a¹bº.δoᵃ,tᵐ. 86.—thuᵈ.p.

V¹. **Aching.**—alo.—-bov.—-chd.—- cca. &c.

V². **Beaten, bruised.**—arsᵇ.3-30.— bz-x.—bovᶜ.δr.—mt-nᵇ.—mag.18. —plaᵈ.

V³. **Boring, digging.**—ag-nᶜ.—aruᶜ. 3-99.—au-nᶜ.—cn-iʰ.—chiᵈ.19.— copᵈ.αl.—cycᵈ.—hepᵇ.—irsʰ.(29). —k-hyᵈ.—lauᵈ.βεᵃ.—magᵈ.— mg-mᵈ·5.—mg-sᵈ.p.4.—na-m. phoᶜ.βεᵃ.20.35.(8).—ratᶜ.(8).— zinᵈ.

V⁶. **Drawing.**

—— *from behind forwards.*—croᶜ. —su-xᶜ.

—— *from side to side across.*— ath.βa.

—— *upwards.*—gamᶠ.—lahᶠ.66.— menᵉ.

V⁹. **Pecking.**—mg-sᶜ.8-31.(6).

V¹⁰. **Pressing.**

—— *outwards.*—-asaᵈ.—-asrᵃ.—-

B B

bel^d.—ca-a^d.—cin^c.3-99.—
fag^d.δl.—kre^d.—mer.—
pau^c.—spo^c.16.—stn^c.—
vrb^c.—vi-t^c.
—— *inwards*.—k-ca^c.30.
—— *upwards*.—na-m^c.
—— *as with a blunt instrument*.
—dul^g.—vln^c.
—— *like a heavy board*.—eug^c.
—— *like a hoop*.—thr^e.ζ.
—— *the head over to left side*.—
lil^c.βe^a.

V^{11}. Rheumatic.—arn^b.

V^{12}. Screwing.—alm^c.q.3.—k-hy^c.
—mil^c.—sul^d.—su-x^g.

V^{16}. Wedge, peg, &c., pressed in.
—— *nail*.—aga^c.—cof^b.—hep^b.—
ign^b.—kis^c.—nx-v^b.—thu^c.
(11).
—— *blunt instrument*.—asa^d.
—— *peg*.—asa^c.—pla^c.

VI^1. Cutting.—bel^c.
—— *hither and thither*.—na-m^c.4.

VI^2. Pricking.
—— *as with needles*.—ca-c^d.βa.
χ^1.3-30.18.31.—lau^d.

VI^3. Shooting.—aco^c.—æth^d.—aga.
—alm^c.—am-c^c.—am-m^d.—ana.—
ag-n^d.—ba-a^d.—ba-c^d.—ca-a^c.—
ca-c^c.—cam^c.—cau^d.—cha^c. &c.
—— *outwards*.—mag^c.2.17.—
mg-m^d.
—— *inwards*.—plb^c.
—— *downwards*.—fl-x^c.
—— *upwards*.—alo^c.3.5.—men^d.
—— *backwards*.—tab.31.
—— *forwards*.—k-ca^c.—lep^c.
—— *as after a chill*.—cha^b.
—— *like a nail*.—na-m^d.2.
—— *as with a punch*.—ind.
—— *like a knife thrust across to
other side*.—arn.b.
—— *as with knives*.—ind^c.κ^4.4.19.
29.(30).

VI^4. Tearing.—aco^c.—æth^d.—aga^d.
— alm^c.—arg^c.—aur^c.—bry^d.—
cap^d.—chi^c.—grp^c.—lau^d.—lyc.—
mag^c.—man^d.—vrb^c.—zin. &c.
—— *downwards*.—nx-v^e.—phl^c.

—— *upwards*.—cch^d.—lah^e.—
pho^c.5.19.
—— *as if a nerve were torn*.—
arg^d.V^6.5.31.
—— *as if a handful of hair were
torn out*.—cth.

VII^1. Bursting, splitting.—bro^d.—
cor.29.—nic.—ptv^c.—pul^b.δ.

VII^2. Expanding.—spi^c.

VII^5. Tensive.—asr^e.βe.—cau^d.—
fl-x^c.—m-pi^f.—trx^d.a$\mathfrak{v}$.

VIII^1. Blows.—chd^d.—grp^c.—mt-n^b.
3-10.—pla^c.—sul^c.5.19.

VIII^3. Jerking.—æth^c.πl.—alm^c.
—cau^c.—chi^a.σ^2.—na-m^d.βe.(66).
—nic^c.$\epsilon \mathfrak{v}$.2.
—— *from before backwards*.—
ni-x^d.
—— *from behind forwards*.—
ni-x^d.

VIII^4. Throbbing.—æth^c.—am-c^d.
—arg^c.—ag-n^o.—bro^d.—bry^c.—
ccs^c.—glo^d.—rho^c. &c.
—— *felt with the hand*.—bry^c.
—— *like an abscess*.—bov^c.
—— *like beating of water against
skull*.—dig^a.βe.

VIII^5. Undulating.—mr-c.βe^a.
—— *like beating of waves*.—dig^a.
18.22.(16.29).

IX. Peculiar.
—— *electric shock*.—aga^d.—ail^d.
—mit^c.—na-s^d.
—— *cracking*.—ars^e.31.
—— *congestive*.—lin^d.
—— *neuralgic*.—ars^d.ω^2.—ca-s^d.5.
66.—ca-x^d.—ch-s^c.5.8-31.;
^{c}.5.19. ; ^{1}.4.29.
—— *as if a piece of lead were
nailed there*.—cf-t.26.
—— *as if a foreign body*.—con^c.
—— *as if something lay there*.—
fl-x^d.5.6.8.
—— *uneasiness*.—lep^d.q.
—— *as after a blow*.—mgt^b.
—— *like megrim*.—dgn.5.—nx-j^d.
5.86.
—— *grumbling*.—lil^c.θ^1.
—— *as if something lay in head
from ear to ear*.—plg.
—— *as if flames came out*.—mil^c.

COMPLEX PAINS.

II^1–V^1. **Burning, aching,**––man^c. (8-31).

II^1–V^6–VI$^{3.4}$. **Burning, drawing, shooting, tearing.**––mt-ʙ^d.

II^1–V$^{10.t}$. **Burning, in-pressing.**–– stp^g.

II^1–VI^3. **Burning, shooting.**––pho. 19.66.**(15).**––stp^d.

II^1–VI$^{3.v}$. **Burning, shooting upwards.**––lth^d.

II^1–VI^4. **Burning, tearing.**––ol-a^d. 4.––sul^c.θ^1.116.

II^2–VI^3. **Eroding, shooting.**––pla^d.

II^3–V^1. **Raw, aching.**––rho^c.19. ; ^{d}. 16.(30).

II^3–VI^4. **Raw, torn.**––sul^b.46.100.

II^5–V^1. **Smarting, aching.**––cb-v^c. 16.(24.30).––car^c.––2-**10.**

II^7–V^6–VI$^{3.4}$. **Ulcerative, drawing, shooting, tearing.**––sul.26.(8.12).

III–VII^5. **Compressive, tensive.**–– car.

III^1–V^1. **Constrictive, pressive.**–– com^a.

III^1–V^1–VII^1. **Contractive, aching, splitting.**––ber^c.ω^3.83.

III^3–VI^1. **Squeezing, aching.**–– ph-x.35.

III^3–V$^{1.2.6}$–VII^5. **Squeezing, aching, bruised, drawing, tensive.** ––crt^d.δO.θ^1.

III^3–VI^1. **Squeezing, cutting.**–– cb-v^g.

V$^{1.3.6}$. **Aching, boring, drawing.**–– zin^d.66.

V$^{1.3.7}$. **Aching, boring, stupefying.** ––stn^d.

V$^{1.3.10}$. **Aching, boring, pressing.**–– zin^c.

V$^{1.3}$–VI$^{3.t}$. **Aching, boring, shooting inwards.**––hfb^b.δ.5.

V$^{1.3}$. **Aching, digging.**––bry^c.θ^4.–– cle^c.31.

V$^{1.6}$. **Aching, drawing.**––ang^c.V^1. θ^4.––ag-n^c.q.35.(20).––pho^a.βε.

V$^{1.6.7}$. **Aching, drawing, stupefying.**––bel^a.

V$^{1.6}$–VI$^{3.4.22}$. **Aching, drawing, shooting, tearing forwards.**–– gui^c.

V$^{1.6.u}$. **Aching, down-drawing.**–– spo^c.σ^2.

V$^{1.6.v}$. **Aching, drawing upwards.** ––arn^g.

V$^{1.6.z}$. **Aching, drawing backwards.** ––arg^t.

V$^{1.6.zz}$. **Aching, drawing forwards.** ––hel^d.––stn^c.

V$^{1.10}$. **Aching, pressing.**––chi.

V$^{1.10.t}$. **Aching, pressing inwards.** ––fl-x^d.ηp.θ^1.5.86.

V^1–III^2–VIII^4. **Aching, pinching, pulsative.**––zin^c.

V^1–VI^3. **Aching, shooting.**––am-m^c. 6.––ana^c.––cap^b.a^{1}b^o.κ^5.24.29.**50.** ––eub^c.––k-bı^b. ; ^{c}.––lah^c.––rum^d. ––sab^d.q.––sar^d.3.

V^1–VI$^{3.4}$. **Aching, shooting, tearing.**––sar^c.ω^8.

V^1–VI^4. **Aching, tearing.**––aga^a.βε. η.––agn^d.11.35.––aur^c.––sar^d.–– stn^c.––stp^d.––vrb^c.

V^1–VII^5. **Aching, stretching.**––dig.

V^1–VII^5. **Aching, tensive.**––cle^e.

V^1–VIII^3. **Aching, jerking.**––dig^c. ––vrb^d.

V^1–VIII^4. **Aching, throbbing.**–– bel.

V^1–VIII^5. **Aching, undulating.**–– hpm.3.

V$^{2.10.u}$. **Bruised, downward pressure.**––con^b.48.

V^2–VI^3. **Bruised, shooting,**––rat^c.

V^2–VIII^1. **Bruised blow.**––lau^d.

V^3–VI^1–VIII$^{3.zz}$. **Digging, cutting, jerking forwards.**––ag-n^d.

V^3–VII^1. **Boring, bursting.**––zin^c. 5.18.

V^3–VI^3. **Digging, shooting.**––ag-n^d.; ^{d}.η.––bov^c.βε^a.––mag^c.3.––ol-a^a.

V^3–VI^4. **Digging, tearing.**––spi^d.5. 31.32.35.

V^3–VIII^4. **Digging, throbbing.**–– ag-n^c.a^{1}b^a.βa.σ^2.31.––aur^b.3-99.22. 89.––bel^c.η 35.

V$^{6.10}$. **Drawing, pressing.**––chd^d.–– sin.q.

V^6–VI^3. **Drawing, shooting.**––asa^f. ––gui^d.––lah^c.54.

V^6–VI$^{3.4}$–VIII^3. **Drawing, shooting, tearing, jerking.**––aco^c.

V^6–VI^4. **Drawing, tearing.**—arg^d. 5.31.; ^{c}.5-10.—cap^d.—cin^d.—man^d.—trx^d.—zin^d.

V^6–VII^5. **Drawing, tensive.**—bry$^{c \cdot d}$. 4.

V^6–VIII^3. **Drawing, jerking.**—hpm^d.—pla^a.

V^6–VIII^4. **Drawing, throbbing.**—arg^c.20.—bry^h.(11).

V^7–VIII^{12}. **Dull hammering.**—ir$_3^h$. 35.

V^7–VII^5. **Stupefying tension.**—asa^d.

V^7–VIII^4. **Stupefying throbbing.**—su-x^c.30.

V^{10}–VI^3. **Pressing, stretching.**—mr-i^c.4.

V^{10}–VII^5–$VIII^{3 \cdot u}$. **Pressing, tensive, jerking downwards.**—ca-c^c.

$V^{10 \cdot s}$–VI^3. **Pressing outward, shooting.**—mt-s^d.

$V^{10 \cdot s}$–VI^3–VIII^3. **Pressing out, deep shooting, jerking.**—ca-a^c.

$V^{10 \cdot t}$–VII^5. **In-pressing, tensive.**—tar^d.

$V^{12 \cdot 15}$. **Screwing, twisting.**—sbd^c.6.

V^{12}–VIII^4. **Screwing, throbbing.**—ton^a.6.(66).

V^{16}–$VI^{3 \cdot 4 \cdot q}$. **Like a nail driven in, deep shooting, tearing.**—cb-v^b.

$VI^{1 \cdot 3}$. **Cutting stitches.**—bel^c.

VI^1–VIII^3. **Cutting, jerking.**—cup^d.

$VI^{3 \cdot 4}$. **Shooting, tearing.**—æth^d.—alm^e.5.—cth^c.—con^d.—mag^c.19.66.—mg-m^a.1.—mil^c.—nic^c.4.—ol-a.^{e}.; ^{c}.—plb^c.—sar.—spi^d.—sto^c.—thu^c.—zin^c.66.

$VI^{3 \cdot 4 \cdot v}$. **Shooting, tearing upwards.**—man^d.3.18.

VI^3–VII^5. **Shooting, tensive.**—dig^b. θ^1.29.(30).

VI^3–VIII^3. **Shooting, jerking.**—nx-v^d.66.—pru^d.

VI^3–VIII^4. **Shooting, throbbing.**—æth^c.—alm^c.4.—ba-c^d.—ca-a^d.—cth^b.5.18.19.—cas^c.w.—lau^c.29.—mag^c.66.—plb^c.5.18.31.—ton^c. 14.

VI^3–VIII^5. **Shooting, undulating.**—fl-x^d.a$^{b a}$.

VI^4–VIII^3. **Tearing, jerking.**—grn^c.—lyc^c.—teu^c.

VI^4–VIII^4. **Tearing, throbbing.**—æth^c.—alm^c.4.—nat^d.83.

$VIII^{1 \cdot 3}$. **Blow, jerking.**—pru^c.35.—pul^c.—spi^d.

$VIII^{2 \cdot 4}$. **Hammering, beating.**—glo^a.35.50.—ol-a^a.

ANATOMICAL SEAT.

P^a. **Both sides simultaneously.**—asr. $V^{10 \cdot s}$—c-ph.V^1.(66).; VIII^4.35.—cb-a.V^7.5.55.(8).—cep.$I^{t \cdot u}$.—chi. VIII^3.σ^2.—com.III^1–V^1.—cyc. VI^3.—dig.VIII^5.18.22.(16.29).; VIII^4.$\beta\varepsilon$.—dio.V^7.—eu-a.w.4.—eup.VI^3.(102).—glo.$VIII^{2 \cdot 4}$.35. 50.—lyc.VI^4.5.—mag.VI^3.—mg-m. $VI^{3 \cdot 4}$.1.—mr-c.VIII^5.$\beta\varepsilon^a$.—mr-f. V^7.—ol-a.V^3–VI^3.; $VIII^{2 \cdot 4}$.—pbo. $V^{1 \cdot 6}$.$\beta\varepsilon$.—pla.V^6–VIII^3.—squ.III^3. —til.VI^3.χ^2.—ton.V^{12}–VIII^4.6. (66).

—— *from one side to the other.*—ca-x.VI^3.δ.δb.—glo.

—— *both sides alternately.*—bel. V^7.—cup.V^1.—evo.VI^3.—hel.$V^{6 \cdot 7}$.βa.—inu.—val.V^1.

P^b. **Semilateral.**—aco.V^6.—am-g.V^1.; VI^4.—arn.V^{11}.—ars.; V^2.3-30.; VIII^4.—aur.V^3–VIII^4.3-99.22. 89.; VIII^4.—bel.V^1.—bry.V^1.δ.4. —ca-c.κ^7.; II^1.17.—can.V^1.14.—cap.V^1–VI^3.a^1b^o.κ^5.24.29.50.—cb-v. V^{16}–$VI^{3 \cdot 4 \cdot q}$.—cha.V^6.; $VI^{3 \cdot a}$.; $VIII^{4 \cdot b}$.—cic.V^1.—cof.V^{16}.—col. —con.$V^{2 \cdot 10 \cdot u}$.48.—cot.VI^3.q.29.—dig.VI^3–VII^5.θ^1.29.(30).; v.—grp. κ^6.3.(30).; 2.17.—hel.V^{14}.χ^1.—hfb. $V^{1 \cdot 3}$–$VI^{3 \cdot t}$.δ.5.—hep.V^{16}.; V^3.—ign. V^1.8-31.41.86.;V^{16}.—k-bi.V^1–VI^3.; l^h.—k-ca.κ^5.ω^2.5.—mgt.IX.—mt-n. V^6.βa.; V^2.; VIII^1.3-10.—man. nx-v.$V^{16 \cdot u}$.; ω^2.5.—pho.V^1.(8).— phy.—pul.VII^1.δ.; VI^3.—sar.IV^1. a^1b^o.$\delta\sigma^a$,t^m.86.—sep.$V^{1 \cdot q}$.θ^1.; q.5. 16.; $III^{2 \cdot d}$.—spg.—sul.II^3–VI^4. 46.100.—ver.V^1.κ^4.

P^c. **Right side.**—aco.V^6–$VI^{3 \cdot 4}$.VIII^3. —æth.VI^3–VIII^4.q.; VIII^3.πl.— aga.V^{16}.; VI^3.βa.—alo.$VI^{3 \cdot v}$.3.5.;

V¹.—alm.V¹².q.3. ; VIII³. ; VI³·⁴. 5. ; VI³.29. ; VI³–VIII⁴.4. ; VI³. δL¹r.—am-c.VI³·q.(8).——ana.V¹– VI³. ; VI⁴.eυ.η.σ². ——ang.V¹·⁶.θ⁴.— arg.V⁶–VI⁴.5-10.;V⁶–VIII⁴.20.— ag-n.V¹·⁶.q.35.(20).;V¹.ıᵃ.q.;VIII⁴. af. ; V³–VIII⁴.aˡb.βa.σ².31. ; V³.— aru.V³.3-99.——asa.V¹.; V¹⁶.—ast. —aur.V¹–VI⁴.——au-n.V³.——ba-a. V¹.—bel.V³–VIII⁴.η.35. ; VI¹·³. V⁶.r.20.66. ; V¹.3.31.——ber.III¹ –V¹–VII¹.ω³.83.—— bor.VI³·q.eℓv. eυbʲ.—bov.V¹.q.; VI⁴·ᵃ.; VI³.; V³– VI³·q.βeᵃ.;VIII⁴.3.6.;VIII⁴.;V².δr. —bro.VI³.—bry.V¹·³.θ⁴.; VIII⁴·ᵈ.; V⁶–VII⁵.4.—buf.(55).—cac.VIII⁴. q.aˡᵍ.1.2.; Iᵃ.24.; Iᵃ.51.111.; V¹.— ca-a.29.;V¹⁰·ˢ–VI³–VIII³·ᵃ.—ca-c. V¹–VII⁵–VIII³·ᵘ.; V⁶.η.θ⁴.; VI³.δ. —cam.VI³. ; V⁶.—cn-i.VI³·ᵉ.iᵃ.— cth.VI³·⁴.; VI³.4.; VI³–VIII⁴.5. 18.19.;VIII⁴·q.——cb-aVI⁴.——cb-v. η.θ¹.χ¹.; 26.——car.II⁵–V¹.2-10.— ca-x.V¹.; VIII⁴.—cas.VI³.5.; VI³– VIII⁴.w.—cau.V¹.δ.; VI³.; VIII³. —cha.V¹³.—chd. ; VI⁴.—ch-s.V⁷. 44. ; V⁷.4. ; IX.5.8-31.—cim.VI³. θ⁴.r.89.—cin.V¹⁰·ˢ.3-99.—cnb.VI³. —cis.δ.—cit.VI³.—cle.V¹–VII⁵. ; V¹·³.31.—coc.VI³.——com.——con. VIII⁴.5-10. ; IX.—cot.V⁷.26. ; 3- 99.; II⁶·ᶻ.V⁷.—cro.V⁶·ᵇ·ᶻᶻ.—crt.— dig.V¹–VIII³.——elp.VI³.q.σ².— eug.V¹⁰·q.——eub.V¹–VI³.——eup. VI³.29.——epn.VI³.—fer.δB.ζv.— f-mg.3.——fl-x.VII⁵.; VI³·ᵘ.; V⁶. gel.V⁷.; V⁷.3.63.—gin.—grn.VI⁴.; VI⁴–VIII³.—grp VIII³.; VI⁴·ᵃ.5.; VIII⁴.5. ; VIII¹.—grt. ; VI⁴.e.— gui.V¹·⁶–VI³·⁴·ᶻᶻ.—hep.V¹.—hpm. V¹.βa.δ.θ².κ¹.29.35.——hdr.V⁷.—— hy-x.V¹.——hyp.VI³.41.——ibe.— ind.VI³.e.; II⁴.5.19.; V⁶.4.; VI³.κ⁴. 4.19.29.(30).—idm.μ².——inu.VI³. ——iof.——jug.V⁷.3.——k-bi.VI³·ᵈ.; VI³.e.η.—k-ca.V¹⁰·ᵗ.30. ; VI³·ᶻᶻ.— k-hy.V¹².——klm.Iᵃ.5.—kis.V¹⁶.— lah.σ².r. ; V⁶–VI³.54. ; V¹–VI³.— lau.V¹.11. ; VI³–VIII⁴·ᵃ.29.—lep. VI³·ᶻᶻ.—lil.V¹⁰.βe.; IX.θ¹.; VI³.— lyc.VI⁴–VIII³.; V¹.; VIII⁴.4.——

mt-s.VIII⁴.2-10.——mag.VI³·⁴.19. 66.;VI³·ˢ.2.17.;VI³.5.;VI³–VIII⁴. 66.;VI³·ᵗ.18.—mg-m.VI⁴.δ.; VI³·ᵃ. aˡᵍ.83.; VI³·⁴.δ.δb.; VI³.au.; VI³·ᵃ. aˡᵍ.—mg-s.VI³.3-30.28.—mnc.51. ——man.VI⁴.er.30.——men.V¹.— mr-f.V⁷.eℓ.σ²ff.——mr-i.d.2.——mez. V¹⁰.——mil.VI³·⁴.; VI³.; V¹².—mit. IX. ; VIII⁴.——mor.Iᵃ.——mo-a.Iᵃ. δP².; Iᵃ.ᴖq.ηæᶜ,hh,aa.ψv.--msc.VI⁴. —mu-x.VI⁴.eℓv.eCII¹.; VI³.er.— naj.V¹.—na-m.V¹⁰·ᵛ.; VI¹.4.—nic. VI⁴·ᵃ.5.19. ; VI³·⁴.4. ; VI³·ᵃ.3-10. ; VIII³.eᴅ.2.——nit.107.——nx-v.VI⁴. 3-10.17.——oln.V¹⁰.——ol-a.VI⁴. ; VI³·⁴.——par.VI³.——pau.V¹⁰·ˢ.; Iᵃ. —ped.VI³.——ptv.VII¹.——pet.δb. (16).——phl.VI⁴.26.; VI⁴·ᵘ.——pho. V⁶.5.;VI⁴·ᵛ.5.19.;V³.βeᵃ.20.35.(8).; VI³. ; VIII⁴·q.5. ; VI³.ζ.r¹r.—phy. II⁵.103.; Iᵇ.——plg.VI³.——pla.V¹⁶.; VIII¹.——plb.VI³·⁴. ; VI³·ᵗ. ; VI³– VIII⁴·ᵃ.5.18.31.——pru.VIII¹·³.35. —pul.VIII³·⁴.——rat.V².–VI³.; V³. (8).——rho.VI⁴. ; VIII⁴.——rhs. VIII⁴.—sbd.V¹²·¹⁵.6.; V¹.θ¹.—sar. V¹·q.v.3. ; V¹–VI³·⁴·ᵃ.ω⁸.; VIII⁴·q. 5.—spi.VII².;V¹.δr.3-30.28.31.74. —spo.V⁷.; V¹⁰·ˢ.16.; V¹·⁶·ᵘ.σ².— stn.V¹⁰·ˢ. ; V¹·⁶·ᶻᶻ.; V¹–VI⁴.—sto. VI³·⁴.—sul.II¹–VI⁴.θ¹.116.; VIII¹. 5.19. ; V⁷.——su-x.V⁷–VIII⁴.30. ; V⁶·ᶻᶻ.——tab.V¹.63.—trn.; V¹.ag.ηr. κ⁴.—trx.VI⁴·ᵈ.——ter.VI⁴.——teu. VI⁴–VIII³.——thu.V¹⁶.(11).—ton. VI⁴.29.(30).; VI⁴·ᵃ.; VI³.er.5. ; VI³·q.88.; VI³.aˡᵍ.; VI³–VIII⁴·ᶻᶻ. 14.—tri.σ.——val.V⁶.4.107.——vrb. V¹⁰·ˢ.; V¹–VI⁴.——vi-t.V¹⁰·ˢ.——zin. V¹–VI²–VIII⁴·ᵃ.; VI⁴.; VI⁴.θ¹.4.; V³–VII¹.5.18. ; V¹·³·¹⁰.; VIII⁴.5. —ziz.θ.σ.σ².

——— *first r. then l.*—bry.V⁶-VII⁵. 4.—inu.

——— *from O. to F.*—aur.V¹–VI⁴. ba-a.V¹.——chi.VI⁴.——mez. V⁷.——thu.VI³·⁴.

——— *from F. to O.*——bel.VI¹.—— ch-s.IX.5.19.—cnb.

Pᵈ. **Left side.**—aco.III.—æth.VI³·⁴. ——aga.V¹–V⁴.βe.η.; VI³.; IX.—

agn.V^1–VI^4.11.35.——ail.IX.——
alm.—ana.VI$^{3\cdot q}$.—ang.V^1.29.(24).
—ap-a.$_\tau$.—arg.V^6–VI^4.5.31.—
ag-n.V^3–VI^3; V^3–VI^3.η.; V^3–
VI^1–VIII$^{3\cdot zz}$.—ari.VI^3.5.—arn.
VI$^{3\cdot w}$.b.—ars.I^a.η.17.(19).; IX.
ω^2.; V^7.; VI^4.—asa.V^7–VII^5.;
V^{16}.; V$^{10\cdot s}$.—asr.βe.—au-n.VI^4.;
VI^1.19.——ba-c.VI^3.5.66.; VI^3–
VIII.^{4}——bel.V$^{10\cdot s}$.; VI^3.——bov.
V^7.; VIII^4.——bro.; VIII^4.70.
(17).; VII^1.; V^6.; δl.—bry.VI^4.
—cac.V^1.3-30.—ca-a.V$^{10\cdot s}$.; VI^3–
VIII^4.——ca-c.VI^2.βa.χ^1.3-30.
18.31.; III^3.——cn-i.I^e.——cth.
V^6.; VI^3.; V^7.—cap.V^6–VI^4.——
cb-v.VI$^{4\cdot a}$.; VI^4.$_\tau l$.—ca-x.; IX.
—cas.VI^3.4.—cau.VII^5.; VI^3.5.
—c-ph.VI^3.—chd.; VIII^1.; V$^{6\cdot 10}$.
—chi.V^3.19.; VIII^4.—ch-s.V^7.5.;
V^7.44.; VI^3.ζl.29.; VI^3.30.—clo.
—cmf.—cin.V^6–VI^4.—cn-s.VIII^4.
τvkk.ω^2.—cod.V^7.3-99.—cch.VI$^{4\cdot v}$.;
I^a.λ.4.(66).—cvl.— cop.V^3.b.al.—
cro.V^7.; V^{7}.$\epsilon.\iota$.; VIII^4.η.—crt.
III^3–V$^{2\cdot6}$–VII^5.δO.θ^1.— cup.VI^1–
VIII^3.—cu-a.V^6.$\epsilon.\eta.\sigma^2$.—cyc.V$^{3\cdot a}$.
—dph.VI$^{3\cdot b}$.σl.—der.VI^3.$\iota.\kappa^6$.—
dir.VIII^4.11.35.89.—dig.VI^4.—
dro.V^6.——elp.V^7.5.—epn.VI^3.—
eub.V^1.—eup.e𝔳.$\kappa^1$3.; VI^3.p.λ.—
fag.V$^{10\cdot s}$.δl.; V^7.19.41.(8).; δl.σ^2.
—fer.VI$^{3\cdot a}$.4.— fl-x.V$^{1\cdot 10\cdot t}$.ηp.θ^1.5.
86.; VI^3–VIII^5.a𝔥^a.; IX.i^a.5.6.8.
—for.66.; V^6.(66).—glo.VIII^4.
ii^d.29.; I^e.—grt.VI^3.(8).; V^6.3-31.
—gui.VI^4.; V^6–VI$^{3\cdot zz}$.—gym.πr.
$r.v$.—ham.3.5.(66).; V^7.q.—hel.
V$^{1\cdot 6\cdot zz}$.—hpm.V^6–VIII^3.—hur.I^a.;
VI^3.$\delta.\theta^4$.—hdr.V^7.q.1.—idm.; V^1.;
I^a.5.—iod.V$^{1\cdot zz}$.; V^6.θ^1.—jab.V^7.
ι.—k-hy.V$^{3\cdot a}$.—kre.V$^{10\cdot s}$.—lah.5.
—la-x.I^a.—lau.V^7.; V^3.βe^a.; VI^4.
4.; VI^2.; VIII^4.29.; V^2–VIII^1.
βe^a.—lep.IX.q.—lin.I.(8).—lth.
II^1–VI$^{3\cdot v}$.—lyc.VI^4.ϵ.; VI^4.q.—
mt-n.V^6.—— mt-s.II^1–V^6–VI$^{3\cdot 4}$.;
V$^{10\cdot s}$–VI^3.—mag.VI^3.5.; V^3.——
mg-m.VI^4.; VI$^{3\cdot a}$.; VI$^{\cdot 3\cdot s}$.; V^3.
5.; VIII^4.p.q.—mg-s.V^3.p.4.——
man.V^6–V^4.; VI$^{3\cdot 4\cdot v}$.3.18.—men.

VI$^{3\cdot v}$.—mrl.VI^4.θ^1.; VI^4.—mr-f.
I^a.—mr-i.V^{10}.βe^a.(8-31).; V^{10}.4.;
V^7.μ.——mez.V^7.(12).; V^1.; VI^3.
—mil.VI^3.—mu-x.V^1.—naj.I^1.128.
—nat.VI^3.; VI^4–VIII^4.83.—na-m.
VI^3.2.; VIII^3.βe.(66).; VI$^{3\cdot q}$.ϵ.5.
31.—na-s.IX.—nic.VI^4.ζl.—ni-x.
VIII$^{3\cdot z}$.; VIII$^{3\cdot zz}$.——nit.ι.5.——
nx-j.IX.5.86.—ol-a.VI^4.; VI^3.λ.
ξ^2.σ.2.84.(30).—pæo.V^{10}.66.—pau.
—pho.V^7.; VI^3.—plg.VI^3.—pla.
V^2.; VI^3.5-10.; II^2–VI$^{3\cdot d}$.—plb.
—pru.VI^2–VIII^3.—ptl.σ^1r.—rat.
VI^4.; VI^3.19.—rho.VI^3.; II^3–V^1.
16.(30).—rs-r.III.—rum.V^1–VI^3.
—sab.V^1–VI^3.q.; V^1–VI$^{3\cdot t}$.—san.
I^a.δl.v^1l.—sar.V^1–VI^3.3.; V^1–VI^4.;
VI^3.σ^2.—sec.—spi.V^1.; VIII$^{1\cdot 3}$.;
V^3–VI^4.5.31.32.35.; VI$^{3\cdot 4}$.—spg.
VI^3.26.—stn.V$^{1\cdot 3\cdot 7}$.—stp.V^1–VI$^{4\cdot a}$.;
II^1–VI^3.—sto.V^1.βa.5.— sul.V^7.5.
66.; V^{12}.—tab.VI^3.—trn.VI^3.ϵr.;
VI^3.2.; δl.— trx.VI^3.——tar.VII^5.
a𝔳.; V^6–VI$^{4\cdot zz}$.; V$^{10\cdot t}$–VII^5.—tep.
V^1.βa.—thu.IV^1.p.; V^7.—til.VI^4.
ϵ.—ton.VI^3.; VIII^4.6.—vrb.V^1–
VIII^3.; V^7.ηl.—zin.V^7.; V^6–VI^4.;
V^3.; V$^{1\cdot 3\cdot 6}$.66.—ziz.V^1.51.111.

—— *from O. to F.*—ba-c.VI^3.—
cyc.V^6.—sab.VI^4.

—— *from F. to O.*—ept.—lcp.σ^2.
—nx-v.VI^3–VIII^3.66.

P^e. **Above ears.**—ars.IX.31.——asr.
VII^5.βe.—bry.III.—hur.III^3.θ^4x.
—lah.III^1.; VI$^{4\cdot v}$.—mr-i.V^{10}–VI^3.
—nx-v.VI$^{4\cdot u}$.—pi-m.V^1.q.—sep.
VI^3.—spo.VIII^4.17.—thr.V^{10}.ζ.

—— *from one ear to the other.*—
m-pi.3-30.(16).; VI^3.28.
29.

P^b. **Above right ear.**—arg.V$^{1\cdot 6\cdot z}$.—
asa.V^6–VI^3.—gam.V^6 v.—lah.V$^{6\cdot v}$.
66.——mag.VI^3.——m-pi.VII^5.——
mu-x.VI^3.3-99.—nx-v.I^v.—plın.
I^b.—trn.2.

P^g. **Above left ear.**— aga.V$^{1\cdot q}$.a𝔥^q.11.
12.; VI^4.——arn.V$^{1\cdot 6\cdot v}$.—dul.V^{10}.
—ni-x.V^6.—^{4}stp.II^1–V$^{10\cdot t}$.—su-x.
V^{12}.

P^{ha}. **Parietal protuberances.**——lyc.
VI$^{3\cdot b}$.—lcp.V^{10}.q.

P^h. **Right parietal protuberance.**—
ber.VI^4.SI.11.——bry.V^6–VIII^4.
(11).——cn-i.V^3.——cch.—hdr.; 3.
33.—irs.V^7–VIII^2.35.; V$^{3·a}$.(29).
—mr-s.VI^3.—pho.VI^3.r.

P^i. **Left parietal protuberance.**——
agn.V^1.—ch-s.IX.4.29.—gel.I^d.—
hdr.V^{10}.5.——lo-i.—lo-s.——vrb.
VI$^{3·a·d·q}$.

P^j. **Right coronal suture.**—ccs.VI$^{3·a}$.
66.—hel.VI^3.

P^k. **Left coronal suture.**——fl-x.V$^{1·a}$.
3.—glo.—lo-s.

Parietes and other parts.

P. and occiput.——aml.VIII^4.—crn.
VIII$^{4·q}$.—hyo.——man.II^1–V^1.(8-
31).——na-m.V^3.——ol-a.VI$^{3·4}$.e.—
pi-m.V^1.66.—tab.VI^3.31.

P^c. and occiput.——cb-v.II^5–V^1.16.
(24.30).—con.V^1.—dro.V^6.—ign.
V^1.—k-bi.V^1–VI^3.—mag.V^3–VI^3.
3.—men.V$^{6·v}$.—ni-x.VI$^{3·a}$.11.

P^c. and r. occiput.——æth.VI^4.4.—
rho.II^3–V^1.19.—ton.VI^3.

P^d. and occiput.—mg-m.VI^3.—pho.
VIII^4.—rhs.II^3.$θ^1$.—sep.VI^3.4.5.

P^d. and r. occiput.—klm.VIII^4.$εl$.

P^d. and l. occiput.—asr.V^1.—ba-a.
VI$^{3·4}$.$σ^2$.

P^d. and occipital protuberance.—
ol-a.II^1–VI^4.4.

P^f. and r. occiput.—nx-m.V$^{10·b}$.

P^g. and l. occiput.—cb-v.III^3–VI^1.

VARIOUS PAINS IN VARIOUS PARTS.

**Tearing and throbbing in P^c., shoot-
ing in P^d.**—æth.

**Compression as from a vice in P^a.,
tearing in P^d. and l. O.**—ba-c.

Shooting in P^c., bruised in r. T.—
nic.

Dull pain in O., shooting in P^c.—
klm.

Shooting in P^c., tearing in r. O.—
mag.26.

**Tearing, throbbing in P^c., shooting
in P^d.**—æth.

Dull pain in O., throbbing in P^c.—
gel.3-30.

**Shooting in P^d., blow, afterwards
shooting in P^c.**—mil.

Occiput.

I. **Pain, undefined.**—ars.——ard.-—
crd.—cnt.—ce-b.——chd.—cch.—
elp.—ham.—lo-i.——sng.—spr.—
sum.—tri.q.
—— *transient.*—iod.
—— *violent.*—mur.—opi.—pl-c.
—— *inwards.*—dir.4.
—— *forwards and upwards.*—glo.
—— *as if head would be drawn
backwards.*—cas.

II. **Burning.**—erd.4.—rhs.
—— *violent.*—mo-a.$κ^4$.λv.rv.v.

II^3. **Raw.**—ana^d.—bry.q.r.3-99.17.

II^5. **Smarting, sore.**——ca-x.—cl-h.
q.16.35.(8).——c-ar^b.12.——glo.—
hyo.(12).—pi-m.d.dd^h.—sep^c.
—— *as if a wound were pressed.*
—sbd^c.

II^6. **Stinging.**—cf-t^c.

II^7. **Ulcerative.**—ton^b.

III. **Compressive.**—asr^d.26.31.(19).
—la-v.—nit.ff.a$\mathfrak{g}$.η.$ι$.$π^1$.$σ^2$.r.4.—sab^d.
3.—stn^g.—su-x^k.—tab.—ton.3-30.
—— *violent.*—sto.
—— *upwards.*—cep^d.
—— *within and without.*—stp.
—— *from front to back.*—pi-m.$κ^4$.
$π$.
—— *as with bands.*—tep.

III^1. **Contractive, constrictive.**——
cam.p.$ζ$.r^1v^1b.$φ$.12.16.29.——cch.ff.
grp^h.V^2.30.$π$.$σ$.——hur.—-man.—
na-m^d.—stn^b.
—— *a hot constrictive band.*—ccs.

III^2. **Pinching.**——cb-v.——chd^b.—
hpm^c.2.—lyc^d.—pet.

III^3. **Squeezing.**—am-m.——fl-x^c.3-
99.—k-ca^e.—lau.——mg-m.—mur.
(22).; ^{d}.

IV^1. **Cramp-like.**—dio^b.5.

IV^2. **Griping.**—epn^c.

IV^3. **Spasmodic.**—cro^e.

V^1. **Aching.**—aco.——ac-l.——aga.—
amb.—amm.—cai.q.—ca-a.—ca-c.
q.—cam.—cn-i.b.p.—cb-a.—cb-v.
—ca-x.—chd.—chi.—ch-s.—cot.

—elc.—glo.—grp.—lcp.—mg-m.
—mer.—msc.—na-m.; q.—nit.q.
—par.—pet.—pho.w.—sul.p.—
tab.—teu. &c.
——— *transient.*—squ.
——— *intermitting.*—phl.
——— *here and there.*—mt-s.
——— *deep.*—kis.
——— *forwards.*—arn^b.
——— *obtuse.*—sep.
——— *broad.*—til.
——— *as if lying on something hard.*
—ph-x.

V^2. **Beaten, bruised.**—æsc.—aga.—
alm.(16).—cic^e.—cof.i^a.100.—crt.
—elc.—grt^c.90.—hel.—nic.
phy.—zin.
——— *crushed.*—grp^h.30.III^1.π.σ.

V^3. **Boring, digging.**—au-n^c.; ^{f}.—
dgn^c.—equ.—gel.σ^2.τ.(14).—lyp^e.
—mer.—na-m.—na-s.—ol-a.—
oni^e.d.—phl^i.—ph-x^b.—rn-s^e.5.—
so-l^c.—sty.—zin^b.5.
——— *violent.*—sto^b.2.
——— *as if head would be drawn
backwards.*—spi.

V^5. **Dislocated.**—pso^b.5.

V^6. **Drawing.**—aga.—ana.—arg.—
arn.—au-n. —ba-a.—bry.—ca-c.
—cac.—cld.—can.—cau.—ce-b.
—chd.—cch.—glo.—grp.—mag.
—mer.—msc.—mu-x.—nat.—nit.
—nx-v.—rn-b.—rhs.—sep.—squ.
—stp.—sul.—val.—zin. &c.
——— *upwards.*—fl-x^e.
——— *across.*—lch.
——— *dull.*—er-a.—equ.σ^2.
——— *or raising up.*—dgn.
——— *as if freezing.*—nx-v.

V^7. **Dull.**—æsc.—aln.—bry.—eac.
—cln.—cb-v.—ca-x.—cop.—crn.
—c-ar.q.—cyc.—dgn.—gel.q.—
gna.—hfb.—la-v.q.—mil.—mit. ;
q.—nat.—oln.—rn-s.8.II^5.—rho.
—rs-r.—sec.—str.—thu.
——— *transient.*—alm.
——— *deep.*—rho.
——— *forwards.*—dio.
——— *preceded by pain in nose.*—
amb.

V^8. **Gnawing.**—ca-c.—dro^d.—glo.
—k-hy^f.ϵ.—ol-a.5.

V^{10}. **Pressing.**—bel^f.σ^3.—ccs.ii^d.—
na-a^h.—vrb.
——— *outwards.*—bry.σ^3.—ca-a^b.—
cb-v.29.—chi.—erd.5.—
fag.4.—mt-n^h.24.— mez^c.5.
—ph-x^b.—pru. ; ^{c}.—stn^c. ;
5.—stp.d.5.16.—til^d.
——— *as if brain would be forced
out.*—bov^k.4.5.
——— *inwards.*—ce-b.31.33.—ign.
—mep.—ox-x^g.—spi^b.29.
(12).
——— *downwards.*—crd.—ce-b.κ^5.
—mrl.
——— *upwards.*—erd.5.—rs-r.
——— *forwards.*—chd.—man.4.—
nx-v.—ol-a.—ph-x.q.29.
(22).—plb.q.δb.(18).—sbd.
βa.
——— *as with thumb.*—aco^f.
——— *gradually increasing and declining.*—sab^b.

V^{11}. **Rheumatic.**—ba-c.σ^2.—c-cs.

V^{12}. **Screwing.**—am-m.au.—grt.—
lil^i.σ^2.—mag.—mer.$\delta\epsilon$.—ox-x^d.

V^{15}. **Twisting.**—dio^c.15.

V^{16}. **Wedge, peg, &c.**
——— *wedge.*—bov.—rho^b.
——— *peg.*—can^e.
——— *plug.*—con^b.
——— *as if something were driven
in from O. to F.*—msc.
——— *nail.*—trn.

VI^1. **Cutting.**—bel^i.—chi.δO.29.35.
——— *as with a sharp knife.*—na-m.

VI^2. **Pricking.**
——— *as from a needle.*—dul.

VI^3. **Shooting.**—aco.—æth.—aga.
—ail.—alm.—ari.—asa.—au-s.—
bel.—bov.—ced.—glo.—grt.—
hep.—ind.—iod.—k-ca.—lau.—
lyc.—mag.—men.—mu-x.—na-m.
—ni-x.—nit.—ol-a.—pho.—sil.;
d.—teu.—zin. &c.
——— *violent.*—ari.—cau.
——— *diagonally across.*—aga.
——— *upwards.*—amb.5.—sep.
——— *backwards.*—crn.

—— *forwards.*—chd.
—— *as with a knife.*—con.
—— *as with knives.*—na-m.
VI[4]. **Tearing.**—aco.—æth.—aga.—
amb.—ana.—ag-m.—ars.—bov.
—ca-c.—cth.—cb-v.—for.—hyo.
—hyp.—ign.—ind.—lau.—lyc.—
mag.—mer.—mu-x.—nit.—ol-a.
—phl.—ph-x.—rat.—rhe.— sep.
—spi.—squ.—tar. &c.
—— *upwards.*—ol-a[e].(15).—sar[f].
4.
—— *upwards and forwards.*—
amb.—mg-m.—rat.
—— *forwards.*— ana[b].—aur[b].35.
—chi[b].—mer.
—— *as if brain were torn.*—con.
3-99.
VII[1]. **Bursting, splitting.**—alo.—
ca-a.—spo[c].—stp.8-31.—zin[b].
VII[4]. **Swollen.**—ccn.
VII[5]. **Tensive.**—am-c[e].—ba-a.—
cau[d].—chd.—ccs[f].ϵ𝔳.—glo.(8).—
hyo.—lah[b].δO.ζ.—lo-i.5.—lyc.σ[2].
5.—lyc.σ[2].5.—nit[e].2.—tea[h].σ[2]ff.
—— *upwards and downwards.*—
glo.ϵ.
—— *passing from l. to r. on raising hand to part.*—mur.
VIII[1]. **Blows.**—cn-i.q.σ[2].
—— *slight, soft.*—rn-b[c].
—— *forwards.*—sbd[s].
VIII[2]. **Hammering.**—ac-s.—trn.
VIII[3]. **Jerking.**—aco.—ced.—fl-x[f].
—glo.—k-ca[d].—rhs.4.
—— *painless.*—mu-x[i].δl.δLll[b].
—— *violent.*—spi.8-31.
—— *intermitting.*—cth[b].v.(15).
—— *downwards.*—bel.q.31.33.
—— *backwards.*—pru.
—— *forwards.*—ag-n.
VIII[4]. **Throbbing.**—æth.q.—aga.—
alo.2.16.—alm[b].—am-c[c].—aml.
ba-c.5.— bor.χ[1].—bry.—cam. —
cau[b].—ept.σ[2].(30).—glo.—hur.—
lau[c].—lo-c.σ[2].— mg-m.q 3-30.83.;
30.—mit.—msc.—ni-x.—pet.1.—
pho[c].—pul.—sep.
—— *violent.*—aga.
—— *deep.*—crn.
—— *from behind forwards.*—glo.

—— *dull.*—aml.
—— *as if suppurating.*—bor.χ[1].2.
—cb-v.1.— cas.19.—man[b].
20.35.—nx-v.16.83.(18).
—— *like beating of waves.*—zin[b].
p.5.
—— *as from a large artery.*——
ang[d].
VIII[5]. **Undulating.**
—— *forwards to temples.*—hdr[b].4.
IX. **Peculiar.**
—— *as if a vapour ascended.*—
ath.βϵ.31.
—— *as if a board bound to it.*—
ce-b[c].
—— *as if O. were detached from
F.*—ce-s.
—— *as if fastened to pillow and
broken off from rest of
head.*—chd.30.
—— *ebullition like boiling water.*
—ind.p.
—— *bubbling.*—jun[b].ϵ.V[7].—spi.
16.31.35.(19.22).
—— *like a thread drawn from F.
to O., leaving burning pain.*
—sbd.
—— *as if a sharp wind penetrated.*
—sab[c].V[1.3].
—— *as if gathering.*—sep.βϵ[b].2.
16.(12).
—— *as if scalp were inflamed.*—
lyc.3.
—— *as if arteries had to pulsate
over an obstacle.*—spi.
—— *like a stoppage of blood.*—
sul[c].99.
—— *like a cap on O.*—rs-r.βf.
—— *as if he were pulled back.*—
mer.

COMPLEX PAINS.

II[1.3]–III[3]. **Burning, raw, squeezing.**—sep[s].
II[1]–III[1]. **Burning, contraction.**—
phl.
II[1]–V[1]. **Burning, aching.**—k-ca.q.
—man.(8-31).—sul.—thu[e].
II[1]–VI[3]. **Burning, shooting.**—au-m.
—cb-v.—mg-m[b].—stp[b.c].

c c

II^1–VI$^{3·v}$. **Burning, shooting upwards.**—stp.

II^1–VI^4. **Burning, tearing.**—ol-a^i. 4.

II^1–VIII^4. **Burning, throbbing.**—nit^c.5-**10**.

II^3–V^1. **Raw, aching.**—mez.—pru^c. $\theta^1 l$.

II^5–V^1. **Sore, aching.**—alo^b.5.

II^5–V^2. **Sore, bruised.**—nic.$\beta \varepsilon^a$.

II^5–VI^3–VIII^4. **Sore, shooting, throbbing.**—alo.λ.2-**10**.29.

III–VIII^4. **Compressive throbbing.**—ped.δo^d.3-30.31.

III^1–VI^1. **Contractive cutting.**—ton.

III^1–V^1. **Constrictive aching.**—chi.31.

III^1–V$^{10·s}$. **Constrictive out-pressing.**—pso.

III^1–VIII^2. **Constrictive hammering.**—gur.

III^2–VI^3. **Pinching, shooting.**—chd^c.

III^3–V^6. **Squeezing, drawing.**—men^a.—zin^f.θ^4.

III^3–VI^1. **Squeezing, cutting.**—cb-v^f.

III^3–VI^4. **Squeezing, tearing.**—ph-x.35.51.

IV^1–V^1. **Cramp-like aching.**—man^f. 8-31.(11).

IV^1–V^6. **Cramp-like drawing.**—pla^c.θ^4.

V$^{1·2}$. **Aching, bruised.**—ni-x.

V$^{1·2}$–VI^4. **Aching, bruised, torn.**—thu.99.(98).

V$^{1·3}$. **Aching, boring.**—msc^d.—opi. σ^2.—til.

V$^{1·3}$–VI^3. **Aching, boring, shooting.**—bov.4.7.—ccs^f.

V$^{1·6}$. **Aching, drawing.**—arg.$\beta \varepsilon^a$.; σ^2ff.—ca-a^c.σ^2ff.—cau^b.σ^2.8-31.—chd^c.—col^e.—ph-x.35.—spi^b.—sul.5.—val^a.

V$^{1·6}$–VI^3. **Aching, drawing, stitches.**—hyp.5.

V$^{1·6}$–VI$^{3·zz}$.**Aching, drawing, shooting forwards.**—chd^c.

V$^{1·6}$–VI^4. **Aching, drawing, tearing.**—ca-a.(12.41).

V$^{1·6}$–VIII^3. **Aching, drawing, jerking.**—rho^b.

V$^{1·9}$. **Aching, jerking.**—rut^a.

V$^{1·10}$. **Aching, pressing.**—bry^i.35.—cch^g.5.—ign^b.5.—so-n^e.$\beta \varepsilon^a$.δP^1. ρ.v.

V$^{1·10·t}$. **Aching, ramming.**—pim.σ^2.

V^1–VI^r. **Aching, cutting.**—gel^c.3. 63.

V^1–VI$^{1·zz}$. **Aching, cutting forwards.**—cam^c.

V^1–VI^3. **Aching, shooting.**—aco.—cth.5.16.—cop^i.3.—k-bi.—lyc.5.—nit.11.—pet.3.—pho.—spo.p. 35.—su-x^c.—zin.

V^1–VI^4. **Aching, tearing.**—aur^b.—bel^e.-iod^e.σ^2.-pul.3.-rhe.-spi.-stn^c.
—— *sudden.*—vrb^e.

V^1–VII^1–VIII^4. **Aching, splitting, throbbing.**—chd.16.

V^1–VII^5. **Aching, tensive.**—car^i.—chp 35.—col^i.—ipe.σ^2.r.—la-v. p.r^1b.—mez^c.—pim.σ^2.—sul^c.
—— *as if skull were too small.*—ber.

V^1–VIII^4. **Aching, throbbing.**—bel^c.—cas^c.—lyc.—mez^e.ζ.θ^1.26.—nit.5.—sul^b.

V^2–VIII^1. **Bruised, blow.**—gin.

V$^{3·8}$. **Boring, gnawing.**—nic^c.

V^3–VI^3. **Boring, shooting.**—cau^f.χ^3.—mag.3.

V^3–VIII^3.**Boring, jerking.**—am-m^d.

V^3–VIII^4. **Boring, throbbing.**—cau^f.

V^3–VIII$^{5·e}$. **Boring, undulating, intermittent.**—ccs^d.

V^3–VI^4. **Digging, tearing.**—spi.35. 51.56.86.(16).

V$^{6·11}$. **Drawing, rheumatic.**—cof^c.

V^6–VI^3. **Drawing, shooting.**—epn. π.σ^3.—mu-x.q.βa.δo.σ^2.; ^{d}.σ^2ff.—rn-b.—sar.—squ.19.—sul^c.

V^6–VI$^{3·4·v}$. **Drawing, shooting, tearing upwards.**—sep.

V^6–VI^4. **Drawing, tearing.**—cb-v^c.—ccs^f.εʋ.—gui.—nit.σ^2ff.—opi^g.σ.
—— *up and down.*—grt^d.12.

V^6–VII^2. **Drawing, expansive.**—bry^c.6.31.

V⁶–VII⁵. **Drawing, tensive.**—car. βa,ℓᵃ.—mag.18.61.(19).—natᵇ.

V⁶–VII⁵–VIII⁴. **Drawing, tensive throbbing.**—almᵇ.5.

V⁶–VIII³. **Drawing, jerking.**—mer.σ².

V⁷–VIII⁴. **Dull, throbbing.**—gelᵇ.30.

V⁷·¹⁴. **Stupefying vibration.**—sul.4.31.

V⁹–VIII⁴. **Pecking, throbbing.**—msc.

V¹⁰–VI⁴. **Pressing, tearing.**—cchᵇ.

V¹⁰·ˢ–VI¹. **Out-pressing, cutting.**—cap.

V¹⁰·ˢ–VII¹. **Pressing out, bursting.**—nx-vʲ.p.(12).

V¹⁰·ˢ–VIII³. **Pressing out, jerking.**—ca-aᶜ.σ².

V¹⁰·ᶻᶻ–VII⁵. **Pressing forwards, tensive.**—mu-x.

VI³·⁴. **Shooting, tearing.**—bovᶜ.—cthᵍ.—cb-aᵇ.5.—casᵃ.4.18.—lyc.2.—mu-x.—natᶠ.—ol-a.ε.—samᶜ.βε.—trxᵉ.

VI³·⁴–VIII¹. **Shooting, tearing, blows.**—casᵇ.

VI³·⁴·ᶻᶻ. **Shooting, tearing forwards.**—æth.4.—agaᵃ.3.

VI³·ᶻᶻ–VI⁴. **Shooting forwards, tearing.**—chdᵇ.

VI³–VII⁵. **Shooting, tensive.**—magᵉ.(12).—mu-x.5.—nitᵈ.—pim.σ².—tonᵇ.

VI³–VIII³. **Shooting, jerking.**—mg-mᵇ.—sto.

VI³–VIII⁴. **Shooting, throbbing.**—cb-a.—hepʰ.—ind.5.—phoᵈ.

VI⁴–VII⁵. **Tearing, tensive.**—mezᶠ.

VI⁴–VIII¹. **Tearing blow.**—mt-n.8-31.;ᶠ.19.

VI⁴–VIII³. **Tearing, jerking.**—aco.—agaᵉ.—ana.22.—ba-cᵉ.11—cb-aᶜ.5.—inu.ε.—mag.rv.—mg-mᵇ.—thuᵇ.

VI⁴–VIII⁴. **Tearing, throbbing.**—k-eaᵇ.—mg-m.6.(19).—mezʰ.

VI⁴–VIII⁴·ᵛ. **Tearing, throbbing upwards.**—mg-m.

VIII³·⁴. **Jerking, pulsative.**—kreᶠ. sulᶜ.

ANATOMICAL SEAT.

Oᵃ. **In one side.**—au-n.V⁶.—cas.VI³·⁴.4.18.—men.III³–V⁶.—rs-r.—rut.V¹·⁹.—val.V¹·⁶.

—— *from one side to other.*—aga.VI³·⁴.3.—hdr.V¹.—plg.

Oᵇ. **In right side.**—æth.V⁷.;VI⁴·ᶻᶻ.—alo.II⁵–V¹.5.—alm.V⁶–VII⁵–VIII⁴.5.—ana.V¹.;VI⁴·ᶻᶻ.—arn.V¹·ᶻᶻ.—aur.V¹–VI⁴.;VI⁴·ᶻᶻ.35.—ca-a.V¹⁰·ˢ.—ca-c.VI³.—cn-i.V⁷.iᵃ.26.—cth.VIII³·ᵈ.ᵥ.(15).—cb-a.VI³·⁴.5.—cb-v.V¹.δ.;VI⁴.—cas.VI³·⁴–VIII¹.—cau.V¹·⁶.σ².8-31.;VIII⁴.—ce-b.V¹.—chd.VI³·ᶻᶻ·⁴.;III².—chi.VI⁴·ᶻᶻ.—cch.V¹⁰–VI⁴.;V¹·ᵃ.;22.50.—con.V¹⁶.—cro.V⁶.—c-ar.II⁵.12.—epn.VI³.3-10.—evo.VI³·ᑫ.—fag.VI³.—fl-x.V⁷.—gel.V⁷–VIII⁴.30.—gui.VI⁴.—hdr.VIII⁵·ᶻᶻ.4.—ign.V¹.βa.1.;x.α¹bˢ.;V¹·¹⁰.5.;V¹.—ind.VI³·ᵃ.—idm.δl.5.—jun.IX.ε.V⁷.—k-ca.V⁶.σ².σ²ff.;VI⁴–VIII⁴.—lah.VII⁵.δO.ζ.—lau.VI³.;V⁶·ᑫ.—mag.VI⁴.26.;VI³·ᑫ.—mg-m.VI⁴–VIII³.;II¹–VI³.;VI³–VIII³·ᶻᶻ.—man.VIII⁴.20.35.—mez.V⁶.—myr.nat.V¹.;V⁶–VII⁵.—ni-x.VI³·ᵃ.5.(16).—nit.VI⁴.—ptv.V¹.—phl.VI³.—ph-x.V¹.1.12.28.;V¹⁰ˢ.;V³.—pso.V⁵.5.—rn-b.VIII⁴.ω².19.—rho.V¹·⁶–VIII³·ᑫ·ᵛ.;V¹⁶·ᵃ.—rs-r.;V¹.4.41.—rum.V¹⁰.—sab.V¹⁰.—sep.V¹.—ser.V¹.βε.(5).—spi.V¹⁰·ᵗ.29.(12).;V¹·⁶.—stn.III¹.—sto.VI⁴·ᵃ.;V³·ᵃ.2.—sul.V¹–VIII⁴.—thu.VI⁴–VIII³.—ton.V⁶·ᶻᶻ.θ¹.;VI³–VII⁵.;II⁷.—zin.V⁶·ᑫ.βa.19.;V¹.;VII¹.;VI⁴.88.;V³.5.;VIII⁴.p.5.

—— *from r. to l.*—dig.V¹.βa,ℓ.—stp.II¹–VI³.

Oᶜ. **In left side.**—aga.19.;VI⁴.;VI³·ᵇ.—alo.V⁶.—am-c.VIII⁴.ω⁹.—asa.V¹.—asr.V¹·ᶻᶻ.—au-n.V³.;V⁶.—ba-c.VI⁴.(22).—bel.V¹–VIII⁴.;VI³.—ber.VI⁴.σ².—bov.VI³·⁴·ᵃ.;VI³·ᵃ.—bry.V⁶–VII².6.31.;V¹.—ca-a.V¹⁰·ˢ–VIII³.σ².;

V$^{1.6}$.σ^2ff.—cam.V^1–VI$^{1.zz}$.—cn-i.—
cth.VI$^{4.zz}$.βa.; VI^3.66.—cb-a.V$^{1.d}$.;
VI^4–VIII^3.5.——cb-v.V^6–VI^4.—
cas.V^1–VIII^4.——ce-b.IX.——chd.
V$^{1.6}$–VI$^{3.zz}$.; III^2–VI^3.; VI$^{4.zz}$.;
V^6.; V$^{1.6}$.—chi.V^6.(22).—ch-s.V^7.
5.; V^7.4.—cnb.——cob.**5**.—cof.
V^6.^{11}.—cf-t.II^6.—cch.VI^4.; $\delta l.\eta$.3.
—con.VI^4.31.; V^1.—dgn.V$^{3.a}$.—
dig.V$^{1.a}$.—dio.V^7.3.; IV^1.5.; VI^3.
4.; V^6.βe.—equ.VI^3.—epn.IV^2.—
fag.VI^3.—fl-x.V$^{1.a}$.; III^3.3-99.—
gel.V^1–VI^1.3.63.—glo.V^1.——grt.
V^1.q.; VI^3.θ^4.—hpm.III^2.2.—hdr.
V^7.p.q.ηc^b.(8.12).——ind.VI^3.$\pi.\tau$.;
V^6.4.; VIII^4.τ.—jab.V^7.5.; ^{h}.V^7.
q.— kis.V$^{6.b}$.—lau.VIII^4.; V^1.βa.
δc^d.δP$^{1.2}$.—lyp.V^3.——mez.V$^{10.s}$.5.;
V^1–VII^5.—nic.V$^{3.8}$.—ni-x.VI$^{3.a}$.
π^1.3.63.—nit.VI$^{3.a}$.83.; II^1–VIII^4.
5-10.—oln.V^1.; V^1.26.66.(29).—
pet.VI^3.4.——pho.VIII^4.; V$^{1.b}$.p.
κ^5.ρ.—pla.IV^1–V^6.θ^4.——pru.I^a.a^1b.;
V$^{10.s}$.; II^3–V^1.$\theta^1 l$.—pul.V^1–VI^4.3.
—rn-b.VIII^1.; VI$^{4.a}$.$\theta^4 l$.σ^2.—rs-r.
V^1.—sbd.II^5.——sab.V$^{1.3}$.IX.——
sam.VI$^{3.4}$.βe.—sar.VI^3.—sep.II^5.
—so-l.V^3.—spo.VII^1.—stn.V$^{10.s}$.;
V^1–VI^4.——sul.VIII$^{3.4}$.; IX.99.;
V^1–VII^5.; V^6–VI^3.—su-x.V^1–VI^3.
—ton.VI^3.v.—vrb.VI^3.—vi-t.VI^3.
—zin.V^6.

—— *from l. to r.*—squ.V$^{6.b}$.

O^d. **Behind ears.**——æth.VI^3.—amb.
VI^4.eL.—am-m.V^3–VIII^3.—ana.
II^3.—ang.VIII^4.—aps.VII^5.—
arn.VI^3.—asr.III.26.31.(19).; V^1.
—bel.VI^3.5.—can.V^6.—cas.—cau.
VII^5.—cep.III^v.——chi.V^6.— ccs.
V^3–VIII$^{5.e}$.—cch.VI^4.e.—col.V$^{1.6}$.
—dig.VI^3.—dro.V^8.—er-a.V$^{7.w}$.—
grt.V^6–VI$^{4.u.v}$.(12).—hel.V^1.—hur.
I^a.—ign.e.ea.—k-ca.VI^4.; VIII^3.
—lyc.III^2.; IV^1–VII^5.σ^2.; VI^3.
—msc.V$^{1.3}$.—mu-x.V^6–VI^3.σ^2ff.—
mur.III^3.—na-m.III^1.; V^1.64.—
ox-x.V^{12}.—ph-x.VI^3.4.—pho.VI^3–
VIII^4.—sbd.V^3.$\theta^{2.4}$.—sab.III.3.;
VI^3.—trx.V^1.θ^4.eM.; VI^3.σ^2.—til.
V$^{10.s}$.—ver.VI^3.

O^e. **Behind right ear.**——aga.VI^4–

VIII^3.—am-c.VII^5.——ba-c.VI^4.—
VIII^3.11.— bel.V^1–VI^4.—bor.V^1.
—can.V^{16}.—cth.V^1.—cb-v.VI^4.—
cic.V^2.—cro.IV^3.—fl-x.V$^{6.v}$.—hur.
—iod.VI^4.σ^2.—k-ca.III^3.——mag.
VI^3–VII^5.(12).—mez.V^1–VIII^4.
ζ.θ^1.26.——nit.VII^5.2.; VI$^{3.q}$.—
ol-a.VI$^{4.a.v}$.**(15)**.—oni.V^3.d.—rn-s.
V^2.5.—sep.VI^4.—sil.VI^4.—so-n.
V$^{1.10}$.βe^a.δP^1.ρ.—trx.VI$^{3.4}$.——thu.
II^1–V^1.—vrb.V^1–VI$^{4.1}$.

O^f. **Behind left ear.**—aco.V^{10}.—amb.
VI^4.σ^2.—ana.V^6.— aps.V^6.—au-n.
V^3.—bell.V^{10}.σ^2.—cap.VI^4.—cb-v.
III^3–VI^1.——cau.V^3–VIII^4.; V^3–
VI^3.χ^3.—ccs.V$^{1.3}$–VI^3.; V^6–VI^4.ev.;
VII^5.ev.—fl-x.VIII^3.—grp.V^1.—hy-x.
V^1.— ign.VI^4.ηp,aa.r^{1}p.24.**(17)**.—
kre.VIII$^{3.4}$.—lyc.VI^4.—mt-n.VI^4.
VIII^1.19.—mt-s.VI^4.—man.IV^1–
V^1.8-31.**(11)**.——mez.VI^4–VII^5.—
nat.VI$^{3.4}$.—nit.VI^3–VII^5.; VI^4.—
opi.—ph-x.V^1.—phy.—rhs.VI^4.—
sar.VI$^{4.v}$.4.—spo.VI^3.—thu.V^1.—
vi-o.V^1.—zin.III^3–V^6.θ^4.

O^g. **Upper part.**—a-sc.V^7.q.—cln.V^7.
—cth.VI$^{3.4}$.—cep.III.—ce-b.—cch.
V$^{1.10}$.5.—equ.VI^3.—for.**70.117**.—
hfb.V^{10}.— irs.V^7.4.—opi.V^6–VI^4.
σ.——ox-x.V$^{10.t}$.—sbd.VIII$^{1.zz}$.——
sep.II$^{1.3}$–III^3.—stn.III.

O^h. **Lower part.**—cam.III^1.p.ζ.r^{1}v^{1}b.
ϕ.12.16.29.——cb-v.V$^{1.a}$.——cnt.—
chi.V^7.—ch-s.VI^3.5.24.—grp.III^1.
V^2.30.π.σ.—hep.VI^3.–VIII^4.—iod.
V$^{1.a}$.4.8.——irs.I^a.; VI$^{3.a}$.—jab.;
V^1.; V$^{.7.zz}$.π.ρ^1.ω^2.; ^{c}.V^7.q.—k-ca.
V^1.(8).——lo-c.VIII^4.hh.——mt-n.
V$^{10.s}$.24.——mer.VI^4.——mez.VI^4–
VIII^4.—nat.**5**.—na-a.V^{10}.— ox-x.
—pul.V^6.——sep.V^6.; VI$^{4.e}$.——ser.
VI^3.—stp.V$^{1.6.11.v}$.——sul.V$^{1.a}$.δ.δb.
$\chi^{1.3}$.2.——trx.V^1.q.—tea.VII^5.σ^2ff.
—zin.VII^1.

O^i. **Occipital protuberance.**—arg.V^6.
20.—bel.VI^1.—bry.V$^{1.10}$.35.—car.
V^1–VII^5.—cch.V^7.(12.102).—col.
V^1–VII^5.; V$^{1.a}$.—cop.V^1–VI^3.3.
—dio.VI^3.(12).—glo.28.—grn.
V^1.—lil.V^{12}.σ^2.—lcp.V^1.— mg-m.

VI³.——mu-x.31.106.; VIII³.*δl.*
δL¹ll^b.—ni-x.θ⁴.—ol-a.II¹–VI⁴.4.
—phl.V³.—pim.VI³.—ur-n.V¹.—
vrb.V$^{1·a}$.

O^j. **Both sides.**—bov.V$^{10·a}$.4.5.—bry.
V¹.—cep.*βι*.**5.**(5.70).—elt.V⁷.—
fl-x.V¹.—k-ca.VI⁴.—mg-s.V¹.; V¹.
(16).—mil.VI³.—nx-v.V$^{10·a}$–VII¹.
p.(12).—sab.V⁷.—sil.V¹.—su-x.
III.—zin.VI⁴.

O^k. **Lambdoidal suture.**—lo-i.VII⁵.
41.

Ba. Base of brain.

I. **Pain, undefined, extending up to
vertex.**—la-x.*ηaa.ω.*35.(12).
III¹. **Constrictive.**——cam.p.*r¹v¹*b.*φ.*
11.16.29.
V¹. **Aching.**—erd.3.—ind.—ptl.*κ*⁵.
V³. **Beaten, as if.**—mnc.q.
V⁷. **Dull.**—for.—hyo.—mr-f.q.*ζ.ι.*—
mr-i.q.*ζ.ι.*
VI³. **Shooting.**—æsc.i^a.
VIII⁴. **Pulsation.**—na-m.
IX. **Disagreeable sensation.**—glo.
—— *a deep pain extending across
from temporal bones.*—plg.

B. Cranial bones.

I. **Pain undefined.**—ac-s.—hfb.
II¹. **Burning.**—bel.ii^d.—k-hy^{fa}.—
man^{pa}.v.29.(15).—mit^c.—spi^{fb}.—
tep^{ta}.*ε.*Cr.*ηr.*
II³. **Raw.**—na-m^f.11.—ole^c.—stp^{pa}.
11.17.
II⁵. **Smarting.**—ag-n^c.5.98.—cnb.
11.—c-ar^{pb}.*η.*—ham^{ma}.—lyc.—tan.
—— *as from a blow.*—par^{pb}.2.11.
III¹. **Contractive.**——con^f.*αu.α¹*b.*βa.*
χ¹.(12.29).
—— *from both sides.*—thu^o.
V¹. **Aching.**—arg^t.; ^{tb}.; ^{P}.—bel^m.
can^{oa}.; ^{P}.—cau^m.—cep^o.x.5.11.—
cic^{tb}.—con^f.*αʊ.*—fl-x$^{f·P}$.**5.**(16).—
ind.; ^{fa}.—la-v^P.—m-pu$^{f·P}$.5.—rn-b^t.
65^a.—rho^{tb}.—sab^t.—stn^m.
—— *forwards.*—ber^{ta}.
—— *as if from a knock.*—nx-v^{fb}.
δb.
V². **Bruised.**—ail^{ca}.—na-m^P.11.—
rut^{pb}.—rut^m.

—— *as after a blow.*—grt^{tb}.11.—
vi-t^P.11.
V³. **Boring.**—au-m^{fa}.; ^{fb}.; ^{fb}.*δl.*; ^{fb}.*δb.*
—cb-a^t.*ηZ.*—hel^f.4.—ind^{pb}.
man^f.—mn-m^{pa}.—mez.; ^{f}.; ^{pa}.; ^{o}.
oni^{ma}.d.—spg.3.16.66.(8-31).—
stn^o.q.—zin^{pb}.
—— *in shock-like paroxysms.*—
mez^e.
V⁴. **Broken.**—aur.*αk*.16.
V⁴. **Dislocated.**—cau^o.19.
V⁶. **Drawing.**—arg$^{o·ta·f}$.—au-m^o.; ^{f}.
19.—bel^f.*σ*².20.35.—chi^o.; ^{oc}.11.—
con^t.—dig.—gui^f.*ζ.*—ind.θ⁴*l.*—
k-bi.—kre^{tb}.*βι.*—la-v^{pa}.4.11.—
man^t.—mez. ; ^{pa}.—ph-x^o.—pho^{fb}.
p.—rho^{fb}.*ηb.*
V⁷. **Dull.**—ba-a$^{oa·P}$.4.
V⁸. **Gnawing.**—na-m.
V⁹. **Pecking.**—fl-x^{fa}.—sul^t.
V¹⁰. **Pressing.**—cn-i.*rl.ʋl.*—dul^{ob}.—
ham^t.3-99.—hyd^o.
—— *outwards.*—k-bi^m.—mer^f.11.
—— *inwards.*—ca-a^{tb}.—nx-m$^{pa·oa}$.
—thu^c.
—— *as with thumb.*—rho^{fb}.
V¹⁶. **As if a peg were driven in.**—
oln^m.
VI¹. **Cutting.**—au-m^{pa}.—k-bi^{pa}.
VI². **Pricking.**
—— *like a needle.*—k-bi.
VI³. **Shooting.**——aco^o.——aga^m.——
bov^{pb}.—can^m.—cth^{pa}. ; ^{pb}.*ε.* ; ^{pb}.θ⁴.
66.86.; $^{oa·pb}$.VI⁴.—cau^{ma}.—chd^{fb}.;
^{pb}.—cic^f.—con^m.—evo$^{ta·ma}$.—glo^{tb}.
—gui^{pb}.—ham^{mb}.—k-hy^{pa}.—kre^{tb}.
—mg-m^{pb}.22.—man^P. ; ^{tb}. ; ^{pb}.29.
—na-m$^{f·P}$.; ^{P}.5.63.—plg^m.VI³.—
plb^{pa}.—rum^f.*λ.*8.—sar^{tb}. ; ^{na}.(11).
—stp^f.—sul^f.—ter^{ma}.
—— *spreading out in a circle.*—
cau^{tb}.
—— *as if the point of a knife
were sticking from within
outwards.*—cyc.
VI⁴. **Tearing.**—aga.—arg$^{tb·mb}$.—
ag-m^f.—au-n^{fa}.; ^{pb}.—ba-c^{pb}.; ^{pa}.—
cth^{pa}.; $^{pb·oa}$.VI³.—cb-v.—chd$^{ta·o}$.
ηr.—cyc^{fa}.—gui^{fb}.*η.*—hel^{pb}.4.—
ind^{pa}.; ^{fb}.—lah^f.3.—mg-s^{fa}.4.11.—

man^{fb}.53.——-mn-m^{pa}.—mrl^{o}.; ^{pa}.—
mer^{f}.—mez^{o}.—mil^{pa}.—rut^{pa}.; ^{t}.—
sam^{t}.—ton^{m}.—zin$^{c.pb}$.
—— *wandering.*—hel.

VII^{1}. **Bursting.**
—— *as if bones were separating.*
　　—k-bi^{f}.[S.II^{1}.v.]
VII^{5}. **Tensive.**—con^{m}.——mil^{pa}.—
　rho^{fb}.
VIII^{1}. **Blows.**—ind^{pb}.ϵCl.19.66.
—— *with a blunt point.*—ipc^{p}.
VIII^{3}. **Jerking.**—cth^{oa}.—ind^{pa}.3-30.
　(35).—k-cl^{f}.—lyc.—na-m^{tb}.δ.5.—
　nit^{o}.v.
VIII^{4}. **Throbbing.**—ep-p^{ob}.—gos^{pa}.
　—ind^{ob}.; 5.19.—k-bi^{pb}.—nat^{c}.
—— *like an abscess.*—kre$^{tb.c}$.δL.;
　^{ob}.
IX. **Peculiar.**
—— *as after a blow.*—grt^{tb}.11.
—— *skull-cap seemed quite thin*
　　that it might be pushed
　　through.—bel.βa.
—— *as if bones had become soft*
　　and fallen apart.—bel.II^{1}.
—— *as if skull were cracking.*—
　　mr-f.4.
—— *as if suppurating.*—mez^{pa}.31.
—— *as if bone were hacked to*
　　pieces.—ca-c^{fb}.χ^{1}.
—— *as if something overlapped*
　　something else.—kis^{o}.
—— *as if part of bone were cut*
　　off.—lah^{pa}.

COMPLEX PAINS.

II^{1}–V^{1}. **Burning, aching.**—rhs^{ta}.
II^{1}–VI^{3}. **Burning, shooting.**—sar^{tb}.
　—stp^{f}.—vi-t^{f}.
II^{1}–VII^{5}. **Burning, tension.**—ba-c^{pb}.
II$^{4.5}$. **Sore, scraping.**—par^{f}.δ.δLp,
　aa.5.
II^{7}–V^{1}–VI^{1}. **Ulcerative, aching,**
　cutting.—mu-x^{m}.11.]
II^{7}–VI^{5}. **Ulcerative, tensive.**—sulp^{h}.
III^{1}-IV^{3}. **Contracted spasmodically.**
　—nx-m^{c}.a^{l}b^{s}.ϕ.
III^{1}–VI$^{3.4.e}$. **Intermitting, contrac-**
　tive, shooting, tearing.—spi^{pb}.
III$^{2.3}$. **Pinching, squeezing.**—aco^{f}.
　a^{l}c^{a}.

III^{3}–V$^{1.6}$–VI^{3}. **Pinching, aching,**
　drawing, tearing.—rho^{f}.70.
V$^{1.6}$. **Aching, drawing.**——-ca-a^{tb}.-—
　mez^{c}.31.——ni-x^{pb}.ϵMl.θ^{1}.——rn-b^{f}.
　[Hb.]5.66.—sar^{ta}.ϵC.—thu^{pa}.p.
V$^{1.6.11.v}$. **Aching, drawing, rheu-**
　matic, upwards.—stp^{oc}.
V$^{1.10}$. **Aching, pressing.**—rn-s^{o}.(12).
V^{1}–VI^{1}. **Aching, cutting.**—cau^{f}.27.
　29.
V^{1}–VI^{3}. **Aching, shooting.**—sar^{t}.11.
V^{1}–VI^{4}. **Aching, tearing.**——mez.2-
　99.——sab$^{ob.tb.fb}$.11.—sam^{tb}.29.——
　spi^{f}.—stn^{ob}.
V^{1}–VI^{4}–VIII^{3}. **Aching, tearing,**
　jerking.—lyc^{fa}.
V^{1}–VII^{5}. **Aching, tensive.**—cle^{pa}.
V^{1}–VIII^{4}. **Aching, throbbing.**——
　k-bi$^{tb.c.pb}$.$\kappa^{5.6}$.
V^{1}–VIII^{5}. **Aching, undulating.**—
　cin^{f}.
V$^{3.6}$. **Boring, drawing.**——-au-n^{f}.-—
　mez^{f}.
V^{3}–VII^{1}. **Boring, bursting.**—zin^{pa}.
　5.18.
V^{3}–VIII^{4}. **Boring, pulsating.**——
　aga^{tc}.—k-ca^{fb}.
V^{6}–VI^{3}. **Drawing, shooting.**—aur^{f}.
　—rut$^{f.t}$.—sar$^{ma.fb}$.; $^{ta.pa}$.
V^{6}–VI$^{3.4}$–VIII^{4}. **Drawing, shoot-**
　ing, tearing, pulsating.—stp$^{t.fb}$.
V^{6}–VI^{4}. **Drawing, tearing.**——nga.
　12.—arg^{t}.11.—-ca-c^{ca}.——cap^{fa}.—
　nit$^{f.p}$.βe.
V^{6}–VIII^{3}. **Drawing, jerking.**—lab.η.
　θ^{4}.
V^{6}–VIII^{4}. **Drawing, throbbing.**——
　cth^{ta}.
V^{8}–VI^{3}. **Gnawing, shooting.**—par^{fb}.
　$\theta^{4}l$.
V^{8}–VIII^{4}. **Gnawing, throbbing.**—
　pho^{pa}.5.
VI^{1}–VIII$^{1.t}$. **Cutting blows inwards.**
　—bel^{m}.
VI^{1}–VIII^{3}. **Cutting, jerking.**—sil^{m}.
VI$^{3.4}$. **Shooting, tearing.**—cth^{m}.—
　hfb.—man^{m}.—plb^{pa}.
VI^{3}–VII^{5}. **Shooting, tension.**——
　k-hy^{o}.—ole^{o}.
VI^{4}–VIII^{3}. **Tearing, jerking.**——
　bis^{ob}.

ANATOMICAL SEAT.

B^f. **Frontal bone.**—aco.III$^{2\cdot3}$.$a^1\epsilon^a$.—argo$\cdot$ta.V^6.—ag-m.VI^4.—aur.V^6–VI^3.—au-n.V$^{3\cdot6}$.; V^6.19.—bel.V^6.σ^2.20.35.——cau.V^1–VI^1.27.29.—cha.—cic.VI^3.——cin.V^1–VIII^5.—con.III^1.$au.a^1b^p.\beta a.\chi^1$.(12.29).; V^1.ab.—fl-x^p.V^1.5.(16).--gos.^{t}.II^6.V^6.—gui.V^6.ζ.—ham.V^{10}.3-99.—hel.V$^{3\cdot a}$.4.--k-bi.VII^1.[S.II^1.v.]—k-cl.VIII^3.—lah.VI^4.3.——man.V^3.—m-pu^p.V^1.5.—mer.V$^{10\cdot a}$.11.; VI^4.—mr-f^p.—mez.V^3.; V$^{3\cdot6}$.—na-m^p.VI^3.; II^3.11.—nit^p.V^6–VI^4.$\beta \epsilon$.—par.II$^{4\cdot5}$.$\delta.\delta$Lp,aa.5.——rn-b.V$^{1\cdot6}$.[Hb.]5.66.—rho.III^2–V$^{1\cdot6}$–VI^4.70.--rum.VI^3.λ.8.--rut^t.V^6–VI^3.--sab.$^{tb\cdot ob}$.V^1–VI^4.11.--sed.--spi.V^1–VI^4.—stp.VI^3.; II^1–VI^3.—sul.VI^3.—vi-t.II^1–VI^3.

B^{ta}. **Right frontal.**–au-n.V$^{3\cdot a}$.; VI$^{4\cdot a}$.—cap.V^6–VI^4.—ce-b.—cyc.VI$^{4\cdot a}$.—fl-x.V$^{9\cdot a}$.—ind.V^1.—k-hy.II^1.—lyc.V^1–VI^4–VIII^3.——mg-s.VI^4.4.11.

—— *r. then l.*—ac-x.V^7.

B^{tb}. **Left frontal.**—au-n.V^3.; V^3.δl.—ca-c.IX.χ^1.—chd.VI^3.—cic.V^1.—gui.VI^4.η.—ind.V^1.; VI^4.—k-bi.$\theta^{2\cdot4}$.3.--k-ca.V^3–VIII^4.--man.VI^4.53.--nx-v.V^1.δb.--par.V^8–VI^3.$\theta^4 l$.——pho.V$^{6\cdot a}$.p.——rho.V^6.ηb.; V^{10}.; VII^5.—sar^{ma}.V^6–VI^3.; VI^3.—spi.II^1.—stp^t.V^6–VI$^{3\cdot4}$–VIII^4.

B^t. **Temporal bone.**--arg.V^6–VI^4.11.; V^1.——cb-a.V^3.ηZ.——cau^p.VI^3.v.η.—con.V^6.—cyc.VI^3.--gos^f.II^6–V^6.——k-bi.g^b.--——man.V^6.——rn-b.V^1.65^a.——rut^f.V^6–VI^3.; VI^4.—sab.V^1.—sam.VI^4.—sar.V^1–VI^3.11.--stp^{fb}.V^6–VI$^{3\cdot4}$–VIII^4.—sul.V^9.—ur-n.I^{u}4.

B^{ta}. **Right temporal.**—argo$\cdot$f.V^6.—ber.V$^{1\cdot zz}$.—cth.V^6–VIII^4.—chd^o.VI^4.ηr.—evo^{ma}.VI$^{\cdot3\cdot q}$.—kre.VI^3.—rn-b.5.—rhs.II^1–V^1.—sar.V$^{1\cdot6}$.ϵC.; ^{pa}.V^6–VI^3.—tep.II^1.ϵCr.ηr.

B^{tb}. **Left temporal.**--arg^{mb}.VI^4.; V^1.—ca-a.V$^{10\cdot t}$.; V$^{1\cdot6}$.—cau.VI^3.—evo.——glo.VI^3.——grt.V^2.11.——

k-bi$^{c\cdot pb}$.V^1–VIII$^{4\cdot d}$.$\kappa^{5\cdot6}$.—kre.V^6.$\beta \epsilon$.; ^{c}.VIII^4.δL.—man.VI^3.—na-m.VIII^3.δl.—rho.V^1.—sab$^{fb\cdot ob}$.V^1–VI^4.11.—sam.V^1–VI^4.29.—sar.II^1–VI^3.

B^{tc}. **Squamous portion.**——aga.V^3–VIII^4.

B^c. **Crown.**—agn.II$^{5\cdot zz}$.5.98.—k-bi^{tb}.pb.V^1–VIII$^{4\cdot d}$.$\kappa^{5\cdot6}$.—kre^{tb}.VIII^4.δL.—mez.V$^{3\cdot d}$.—mit.II^1.--nat.VIII^4.—nx-m.III^1–IV^3.$a^1 b^s$.ϕ.—ole.II^3.—thu.V$^{10\cdot t}$.—zin^{pb}.VI^4.

B^{ca}. **Coronal suture.**—ail.V^2.—ca-c.V^6–VI^4.

B^p. **Parietal bones.**--arg.V^1.--ba-a^{oa}.V^7.4.—can.V^1.—cau^t.VI^3.v.η.—fl-x^f.V^1.5.(16).—gel.VI^3.θ^4.—ind.VIII^4.5.19.—ipc.VIII^1.—la-v.V^1.—man.VI^3.—m-pu^f.V^1.5.—mr-f^f.—na-m^f.VI^3.; VI^3.5.63.; V^2.11.—nit^f.V^6–VI^4.$\beta \epsilon$.—vi-t.V^2.11.

B^{pa}. **Right parietal.**—au-n.VI^1.—ba-c.VI$^{4\cdot q}$.—cth.VI^4.; VI^3.—cin.x.—cle.V^1–VII^5.—gos.VIII^4.—ind.VIII$^{3\cdot a}$.3-30.(35).; VI^4.--k-bi.—VI$^{1\cdot a}$.—k-hy.VI^3.—lah.IX.—la-v.V$^{6\cdot a}$.4.11.—lau.V^1.11.—man.II^1.v.29.(15).—mn-m.V^3.—mrl.VI^4.—mr-f.11.15.—mez.IX.31.—mil.VII^5.; VI$^{4\cdot a}$.—nx-m^{oa}.V$^{10\cdot t}$.——pho.V^8–VIII^4.5.——plb.VI^3.; VI$^{3\cdot4}$.—rut.VI^4.—sar^{ta}.V^6–VI^3.—stp.II^3.11.17.—sul.ii.11.—tab.12.—thu.V$^{1\cdot6}$.p.—zin.V^3–VII^1.5.18.

B^{pb}. **Left parietal.**—ant.12.—au-n.VI^4.--ba-c.II^1–VII^5.; VI^4.—bov.VI^3.—cth.VI$^{3\cdot a}$.e.; VI^3.$\theta^4 l$.66.86.; VI^4.^{oa}VI^3.——ce-b^{ob}.——chd.VI$^{3\cdot d}$.—c-ar.II^5.η.—gui.VI^3.—hel.VI^4.4.—ind.VIII^1.ϵCl.19.66.; V^3.—iof.V^1.q.3-99.—k-bi.VIII^4.——lth.—mg-m.VI^3.22.—man.VI$^{3\cdot a}$.29.—mr-c.VI^3.—ni-x.V$^{1\cdot6}$.ϵMl.θ^1.—par.II^5.2.11.—rat.V^3.—spi.III^1–VI$^{3\cdot4\cdot d}$.—sul.II^7–VII^5.--zin^c.VI^4.; V^3.

B^o. **Occipital bone.**--aco.VI^3.–arg$^{ta\cdot f}$.V^6.–au-n.V^6.–bry.11.—cau.V^5.19.; x.–cep.V^1.x.5.11.—chd^{ta}.VI^4.ηr.—chi.V^6.——hyd.V^{10}.——k-hy.VI^3–VII^5.—kis.; IX.--mrl.VI^4.—mer.

—mez.V³. ; VI⁴.—nit.VIII³.v.— ole.VI³-VII⁵.—ph-x.V⁶.—rn-s. V¹·¹⁰.(12).—stn.V³.q.—thu.III¹.

B^oa. **Right occipital.**—ba-aᵖ.V⁷.4.— can.V¹.—cth.VIII³.; VI³·ᵖᵇ.VI⁴. —mn-m.VI⁴.—nx-mᵖᵃ.V¹⁰·ᵗ.

B^ob. **Left occipital.**—bis.VI⁴-VIII³. —bry.—ce-bᵖᵇ.—dul.V¹⁰.—ep-p. VIII⁴.—ind.VIII⁴.—kre.VIII⁴. —sabᵗᵇ·ᶠᵇ.V¹-VI⁴.11.—stn.V¹-VI⁴.

B^oc. **Occipital joint.**—aga.VI³.— chi.V⁶.11.(22).—stp.V¹·⁶·¹¹·ᵛ.

B^m. **Mastoid process.**-bel.V¹·ᵃ.; VI¹-

VIII¹·ᵗ.—can.VI⁸.—cth.VI³·⁴.— cau.V¹.—con.VI³.; VII⁵.—ham. VI³.31.106.—irs.VIII⁴.4.(101).— k-bi.V¹⁰·ˢ.—lo-s.—men.VI³·⁴.— mu-x.II⁷-V¹-VI¹.11.—oln.V¹⁶.— rut.V².—sil.VI¹-VIII³.—stn.V¹.

B^ma. **Right mastoid process.**—cau. VI³.—evoᵗᵃ.VI³·q.—ham.II⁵.— oni.V³.d.—sarᶠᵇ.V⁶-VI⁴.; VI³. (11).—ter.VI³·ᵇ.—ton.VI⁴.

—— *first r. then l.*—lo-s.4.

B^mb. **Left mastoid process.**-aga.VI³. —argᶠᵇ.VI⁴.—ham.VI³.

SECTION II.—CONCOMITANTS OF PAINS IN THE HEAD.

aa. *Indifference :*
GEN.—opi.V¹.abº.4.—trn.ak. λp.τ¹.
F.—na-a.a¹ᵇ.4.

aa. *Apathy :*
F.—bel.V¹.q.βε.χ¹·².ω².3-99.

ab. *Laziness :*
GEN.—c-ph.p.au.ηp.—dul.κ⁶.χ¹.
F.—la-v.V⁷.ω².

abᶜ. *Disinclination for speaking :*
F.—ant.VII¹.βπ.—rs-rᵉ.Iᵉ. ak.ω².5.5.(4).

abᶜ. *Disinclination for thinking :*
GEN.—equ.V⁷.q.4.—phy.V¹. q.βa.4.—tep.V⁷.20.35.
F.—ail.V¹⁰.q.
O.—rs-r.

abᵐ. *Disinclination for movement :*
T.—ph-xᵇ.V¹.
O.—ph-x.V¹.

abº. *Disinclination for work :*
GEN.—cof.—col.5.—dig.4.— opi.aa.4.—pho.V¹.x.βa.φ. 3-30.(16).—sep.VI³.
F.—cam.V⁷-VI³.βε.5.(8).
T.—cam.VI³.βε.δO.5.(8).
O.—sep.VI³.

af. *Discomfort :*
GEN.—cin.—grt.III¹.βg.——

hy-x.εῦ.—par.V¹⁴.φ¹.2.— rut.V¹.66.—ser.5.—trn.I�q. ag,q,Iᵍ.δs. ; a¹cᵃ.θ³j.κ³.
F.—cld.V⁷.δ.ηp.65.— cyc.Iᵃ. 2.—hyoᵈ.III¹·ᵉ.βεᵈ.—lahᶠ. VIII⁴.κ.κ⁹.
P.—ag-nᶜ.VIII⁴.

ag. *Anxiety :*
GEN.—cad.— ch-s.V⁷.εa.ρ.χ³. ω⁸.—jab.V⁷.π.π¹.ρ.ρ¹.—rn-b. ω².63.—rhe.V¹⁵.βεᵃ.29.35. —trn.Iᵠ.αf,Iᵍ,q.δs.
F.—glo.V¹⁰·ᵛ.ηaa.χ³.—nit.βa, b.χ³.—sep.ζ².ω⁸.
T.—chd.VIII⁴·ᵃ.—nit.βa,b. χ³.
C.—bz-x.III.σ.—sep.ζ².ω⁸.— sto.VII¹.p.aῦ.ηp.aa.φ.5.
P.—trnᶜ.V¹.ηr.κ⁴.
O.—nit.IIIᵃ.ff.η.ι.π¹.σ².τ.4.

ab. *Fear :*
GEN.—glo.δs.ω².
C.—sto.VII¹.p.aᵍ.ηp,aa.φ.5.

abᵃ. *Fear of impending danger :*
P.—fl-xᵈ.VI³-VIII⁵.

abᵐ. *Fear of apoplexy :*
GEN.—ter.V¹.iᵃ.aIᵠ.

abᵃᵇ. *Fear of going mad :*
F.—amb.V¹.

ab^q. *Pusillanimity :*
P.—aga^g.V$^{1\cdot q}$.11.12.

ak. *Depressed spirits :*
GEN.—ana.VI^4.aq.χ^1.— con.βa.
—crt.—irs.ω^2.—kre.VI^4.au.
ηp.θ^1.φ^1.χ^2.ω^2.3-99.--mag.VI^3.
5.—sep.V^1.βa.ζ^3.—sil.VI^3.
au.βε.—tan.—trn.π.ρ^1.χ$^{2\cdot3}$. ;
VIII^1.ι.o^1.π.σ^2.ω$^{2\cdot8}$.3-30. ; aa.
λp.r^1.—thr.5.31.
F.—naj^e.V^1.—ptl.V^7.κ^4.—
rn-b^f.5.—rs-r.V^7.κ^4.φ^1. ; ^{e}l^e.
ab^s.ω^2.5.5.(4). ; ^{g}.δϵ.ω^9.—src.
V^7.q.
T.—cac.VIII^4.ϵ.
O.—rs-r.V^7.κ^4.φ^1.
B.—aur.V^4.16.

ak^f. *Despair :*
GEN.—trn.κ^5.ρ.o^1.—vp-r.aq.δa^b.
ηc^d,aa.θ^3.κ^3.μ^1.ν^1.ρ.σ^1.φ.χ^2.ω^3.
C.—aga.VIII^4.

al. *Weeping :*
GEN.—pho.VII^1.5.
P.—cop^d.V^3.

al^d. *Groaning :*
GEN.—sil.al^g.a^{1}ʊ.

al^g. *Cries :*
GEN.—sil.al^d.a^{1}ʊ.—trn.I^a.af,ɡ,ꞇ,
δ$\mathbf{s}$.—ter.V^1.i^a.ab$^{æ\cdot2}$.—ton.VI^3.
F.—hfb^e.3.—stn^b.V^1–VIII^3.
T.—k-ca.VI$^{3\cdot4}$.2.—stn^b.V^1–
VIII^3.
C.—ton.VIII^1.
P.—cac^c.VIII^4.q.1.2.—cup.11.
—mg-m^c.VI$^{3\cdot a}$.83. ; ^{c}.VI$^{3\cdot a}$.—
ton^c.VI^3.; ^{d}.VI^4.

ap. *Sensitiveness to noise :*
GEN.—ca-c.V$^{3\cdot10}$.δ.ζ.η.θ^1.ω^3.

aq. *Restlessness :*
GEN.—ana.VI^4.ak.χ^1.—a-sc.—
cad.—chi.III.a$\mathbf{s}$.a^1$\mathfrak{c}$^{m}.—gn-c.
III^1.19.—idm.χ.2.—k-hy.—
mns.δii^d.2.—nit.—trn.I^q.af,ɡ,
l^g.δ$\mathbf{s}$.—vp-r.ak^i.δa^b.ηc^d,aa.θ^3.
κ^3.μ^1.ν^1.ρ.σ^1.φ.χ^2.ω^3.
F.—cor.V$^{10\cdot a\cdot s}$.χ^2.(130).—hfb.
V^{10}.4.41.43.
T.—rn-b.V$^{1\cdot6}$.π^1.5.31.
P.—mo-a^c.I^a.ηæ^c,bh,aa.ψv.

ar. *Hurry :*
F.—ptl.VI^4.p.ηp.

as. *Excitement :*
GEN.—bap.—chi.III.aq.a^1$\mathfrak{c}$^{m}.
—nr-a.—pho.V^6.aæ.βs.δt^n.ρ.3.
(66).

au. *Ill-humour :*
GEN.—am-c.κ^4.1.—am-m.V^{12}.—
bel.V^{10}.; V^7.ω^2.—bov.VIII^4.
a^{1}b.ζo.16.100.—c-ph.p.ab.ηp.
—dul.VI^3.5.(16).--hfb.θ^4.r^{1}x.
—idm.VIII^4.χ^2.(116).—kre.
VI^4.ak.ηp.θ^1.φ^1.χ^2.ω^3.3-99.—
mgt.II^3.36. ; V^{10}.36.—na-m.
aæ^{cc}.1.—opi.VI^4.βa.—pæo.—
pho.V^7.3-30-99.--pla.V^1.$\mathfrak{c}$j.χ^3.
2.—sil.V^1.rυ. ; VI^3.ak.βε.—
stn.κ$^{1\cdot5}$.3.—str.I^a.a^{1}b.—ton.
V^1–VI$^{3\cdot4}$.η.5.6.
F.—ana.III^1–V^3.4.(12).—bel.
V^{10}.δP^2.(29).—bov^h.VIII^4.
a^{1}b^s.ζo.16.100.; ^{n}.IX.—ch-s.
a^{1}b^o.βa.φ.ω^2.—kln.χ.—k-ca.
V^1.4.31.—mer.V^7.5.—nic.
VII^1.—pho.V^7.q.—pla.III^1–
V^3.x.au^{ff}.ϵʊ^k.χ^2.7.
T.—bov^a.V^1–VIII^4.σ^2.--col^a.V^7.
31.—idm.V^7.q.φ.3-99.
C.—mer.V^7.5.—nab.δL.ι.ψv.—
nic.V^2–VI^3.5.
P.—mg-m^c.VI^3.—nic.VI^3.—
pho.V$^{1\cdot q}$.
O.—am-m.V^{12}.—ch-s.a^{1}b^s.βa.φ.
ω$^{2\cdot9}$.
B.—con^f.III^1.a^{1}b.βa.χ^1.(12.29).

au^{ff}. *Impatience :*
F.—pla.III^1–V^3.x.au.ϵʊ^k.χ^2.7.
—rs-r.^{m}.V^7.i^a.—zin.V^7.

$aæ^g$. *Feeling of self-complacency :*
T.—ham.V^{12}.

$aæ^t$. *Inclination for work :*
F.—alo^a.V^6–VI^3.βε.δb.

$aæ^w$. *Cheerfulness :*
GEN.--pho.V^6.ao.β^a.δt^n.ρ.3.(66)
F.—cca.V^7.(113).—ph-x.V^7.
T.—ph-x.V^7.
O.—lyc.VI^3.

$aæ^{cc}$. *Inclination to sing :*
GEN.—na-m.au.1.

$aæ^{ii}$. *Inclination to laugh :*
GEN.—sbd.41.

a^1b. *Confusion of mind :*
GEN.—str.I^a.au^b.

D D

F.—na-a.αa.4.
C.—glo.I.

a¹bᵇ. *Inability to collect thoughts*:
T.—mez.III.35.

a¹bᵉ. *Forgetfulness*:
F.—ca-a.V⁷.βε.43.—-ch-s.au.βa.
φ.ω².—mez.V¹.3.
P.—capᵇ.V¹-VI³.κ⁵.24.29.**50**.—
sarᵇ.VI¹.δoª,tᵐ.86.

a¹bᵖ. *Loss of memory*:
B.—conᶠ.III¹.au.βa.χ¹.(12.29).

a¹bˢ. *Diminished intellectual powers*:
GEN.—ail.—-ast.d.βeᵇ.ρ.2-99.—
aur.V².3.41.43.44.86.—-bov.
VIII⁴.au.ζo.16.100.—c-cs.V¹.
64.65.—cn-i.III¹.—glo.VII¹.
a¹ɒ.ω².—hel.VII⁵.q.—kre.p.φ.
—lau.V¹.—-mt-n.V¹⁰·ᵘ.δ.ω³.—
pru.VII¹.—rhs.βa.44.
F.—bov.V¹.q.βeᵇ.; ʰ.VIII⁴.q.au.
ζo.16.100.—-glo.II¹-III¹.βe.δ.
η.—hyoª.V¹.βɒ,ε.—ignª.V¹.βɒ,
ε.—klm.—lauᵇ.V¹.—lcp.V⁷.—-
opiª.VI³·ª.—zin.V¹.βε.
T.—ail.VI³.—chdᵇ.V⁷·ª.—mez.
III³.35.—stn.VI³-VIII⁴.p.φ.
χ¹.
C.—chd.V⁷.—cyc.V¹.—-nx-m.
III^{u.w.}φ.
P.—ag-nᶜ.V³-VIII⁴.βa.σ².31.—
can.V¹.
O.—ail.VI³·ª.—ch-s.au.βa.φ.ω²·⁹.
—ignᵇ.x.—-man.V⁷.βeᵇ.(12).
—pruᶜ.Iª.; Iª.29.
B.—nx-mᶜ.III¹-IV³.φ.

a¹bˢ. *Loss of thoughts*:
F.—-asr.V⁶.41.—coc.V¹·ª.5.43.
—-cot.V⁷.q.δv,o.ρ¹.vb.(8).—
kreª.VI³.4.

a¹bⁿ. *Idiocy*:
GEN.—aga.III¹.

a¹bʸ. *Obtuseness of senses*:
F. T.—ctn.V¹.βε.

a¹cª. *As if would lose senses or go mad*:
GEN.—aga.V⁶.—trn.af.b³j.κ³.
F.—-aco.III²·³.; ʰ.III³.8-31.;
ᵈ.III¹-V¹.ηcª,ii.**51**.111.(98.
114).
B.—acoᶠ.III²·³.

a¹cᵇ. *Delirium*:
F.—ch-sᵇ.VII¹.d.a¹ɒᵇ.βa,ε.δtᶜ.εa,
ɒ.ηp.κ²·³·⁵·⁷.λ².ρ.φ².χ³.ω².

a¹cᵈ. *Mania*:
GEN.—coc.V¹.**5**.41.43.—iod.

a¹cᵐ. *Delusions of fancy*:
GEN.—amp.—chi.III.aq,ꜱ.

a¹ɒ. *Stupefaction*:
GEN.—æth.βa.κ⁶.χ².**5**.—arn.βa.
ea.—cb-v.—ch-s.βa.—cyc.
III.—glo.VII⁵.a¹bˢ.ω².—k-bi.
V¹.—mor.V⁷.—msc.III.—nar.
99.—sab.VIII⁴.q.—sil.aᵈ·ᵍ.
F.—lyc.V¹.p.βa.128.—mag.VI⁴.
q.—mo-aª.V⁷.—nx-m.V¹.δ.ω⁹.
—opi.IX.βa.ω⁸.—pb-x.V¹·ª.
δɓ.o².3-99.35.—phoᵇ.**5**.(66).
T.—cinª.VI³·q.—hdr.VI¹.—tar.
VII⁵.
C.—aga.II¹.—cu-s.V¹⁰·ᵘ.; gᵇ.x.
—cyc.III¹.—na-m.VIII¹.βa.26.
P.—trxᵈ.VII⁵.
B.—conᶠ.V¹.

a¹dª. *Loss of consciousness*:
F.—na-m.VIII¹.βa.—pru.V¹⁰·ˢ.
—trx.V⁷.κ⁵.19.43.(8).

a¹dᵇ. *Coma*:
F.—ch-sᵇ.VII¹.d.a¹cᵇ.βa,ε.δtᶜ.
εa,ɒ.ηp.κ²·³·⁵·⁷.λ².ρ.φ².χ³.ω².

βa. *Vertigo*:
GEN.—æth.a¹ɒ.κ⁶.χ².**5**.—aga.V¹.
—ail.κ⁵.—ana.V¹.βeª.—arg.
III.κ⁴·⁵.χ²·³.18.43.—arn.a¹ɒ.
ea.—ars.—aur.V¹-VI⁴.—ba-c.
VIII¹.5.90.—bel.VI³.δ.—bis.
—bro.III.βε.—ca-c.3-99.—cth.
V⁷.ηcᵇ.v¹.ρ.χ³.ω².—cn-s.—cau.
III.—ch-s.a¹ɒ.; VII¹.z.eɒ.ηp.—
con.aɬ.—cup.V¹.11.35.; V⁶.ω⁴.
(16).—cyc.4.—dig.—dio.8.—eth.
—epn.VIII⁴.—fl-x.κ⁵.—gel.
—gn-c.III.—gen.4.26.(66).
ham.VII¹.29.—hel.V¹·⁶.βeª.
—hln.δo.—hep.26.—hpm.p.
—hy-x.—hdr.ω².5.—hfb.
VIII¹.—ibe.VI³.—ign.VI³.—
idm.V⁷.q.—k-bi.(**55**).; II¹.
δrᶻ.—k-cl.5.—lah.V¹.; 5.
—lam.—lo-i.VI³.— lcp.5.
—mnc.3.66.—mer.; VII⁴.
—mez.I¹.δɓ.κ⁴.—msc.V¹.—

mu-x.V¹.q.δɔ.φ.3-30.49.——-
nat.V⁷.p.19.20.(8-31).—ni-x.
V¹-VIII⁴.5.—ol-a.3-99.—opi.
VI⁴.au.—ped.κ⁵.5.—pho.V⁷.
δɔ.η.θ².ω².28.(16).; κ⁵.16.; V¹.
x.abᵒ.φ.3-30.(16).; V⁶.aɔ,ᴋ.
δtᵐ.ρ.3.(66).——phy.V¹.q.abᶜ.
4.—pgn.V⁷.—ptl.VI³.κ⁴.; Iᵉ.
κ⁵.λ.—pul.IV².d.—rhe.VII⁵.
—rhs.a¹b.44.——sam.VII⁵.βa.
3.26.——san.ᴇ.—sep.V¹.aᴋ.ζ³.
—so-n.σ²d.—spi.26.; V¹.—
stn.V¹.—str.κ³.ω³.—sul.VI³.;
eɔ.κ⁴·⁵.rʋkk,nn.ω²·⁹.; (47).—
tab.—tar.ρ¹.—tep.V¹.ζ².—
ve-v.δ¹ɔ.δP².—zn-o.

F.—aga.V¹.19.— ail.V¹⁴.—alnᵉ.
V¹⁰.5.(16).——ars.Iᵃ.—asrᵇ.
3-30.—aur.V¹-VI⁴.——au-mˢ.
VI⁴ ᵃ·; ᵉ.VI⁴.29.35.(8).—ber.
V¹.ω³.34.——bis.κ⁴·⁷.ρ.χ².5.35.
—bryᵇ.VI³.—ca-c.V¹⁰·ˢ.(8.12).
—cth.VI⁴.σ².——car.V¹.βeᵃ.—
ch-sᵇ.VII¹.d.au.a¹bᵒ.φ.ω².; ᵇd.
a¹cᵇ,ɴᵇ.βe δtᶜ.eᴀ,ɴ.ηp.κ²·³·⁵·⁷.λ².
ρ.φ².χ³.ω².; ᵇ.Iᵃ.eɔ.ω².—cit.
cca.χ¹.ω².4.; ᵃ.V¹.χ¹.4.(5).—
coc.IX.βɴ,ᴇᵃ.—con.VI³.σ².—
crtᵉ.V¹.κ⁵.; ᵉ.κ⁵·⁶.μ¹.(8-31).—
cup.V¹.11.35.—cyc.VI³.3.—
dulᵇ.Vᴸ-VIII⁴.—eubᵇ.VI⁴.26.
—gn-c.V¹.—grt.V¹.—hyo.
V¹.δL.(8-31).—idmˢ.θ¹.κ⁵.λ¹.
—irs.5.—lau.V¹.δ.δP¹·².—
lyc.V¹.p.a¹ɴ.128.—mn-o.V¹.
—mrl.V¹.x.—mscᵉ.V¹.δL.;
V¹.βe.35.—nat.V⁶.δɔ.κ⁵·⁷.—
na-m.VIII¹.aɴᵃ.—nit.aɢ.βb.
χ³.—nx-jᵉ.—nx-m.V¹⁰·ˢ.iiᵈ.
opi.IX.a¹ɴ.ω⁸.; ᵉ.V¹.βe.—phlᵇ.
p.r¹p.—phs.V¹.31.—pod.VI³.
δb.—rn-b.V¹·ᵇ.; ⁱ·ⁿ.VIII⁴.ζ.1.
—sbd.V⁷.βb.; V¹.σ.—sto.VI³.
4.—sulˢ.—tab.V¹.—trxʰ.III¹-
VII².—tepᵇ.V¹.; VI³·ʷ.κ⁶.—
til.V¹.q.δɔ.

T.—ang.V¹·³.24.(29).—aspᵇ.V¹.
—broᵇ.V¹.—cly.—cup.V¹.11.
35.—dir.II⁵.—gelᵃ.V¹.δɔ.κ⁵.
—glo.VI³.κ⁵.; VI³.ω².—hln.
iᵃ.——hyoᵃ.V¹.δL.(8-31).——

indᵃ.κ⁶.66.—kre.V⁶-VI³.θ⁴.—
lilᵇ.V⁷.5.31.-lo-i.VI³.—mg-m.
IV²-VIII⁴.5.16.(12).——nat.
V¹⁰·ᵗ.41.—nit.aɢ.βb.χ³.—pho.
VI⁴.—rn-bᵃ.VI⁴·ᵃ.31.; V¹.σ².
5.6.—rhe.VII⁵.—sto.V¹⁰·ˢ.—
sul.IX.—tab.V¹.—tep.VI³.

C.—aga.111.—bel.V³-VI⁴.12.
—con.V¹.— cyc.V¹.—dig.—
hln.VIII⁴.29.—mr-f.V⁷.κ⁵.—
msc.δL.; V¹.—mu-x.VI⁴.—
na-m.VIII¹.a¹ɴ.26.—pan.V¹.
δl.3.—pet.V¹.—rhe.VII⁵.

P.—agaᶜ.VI³.—ag-nᶜ.V³-VIII⁴.
a¹bˢ.σ².31.—ath.V⁶·ʷ.; I[I]¹.
—ca-cᵈ.VI².χ¹.3-30.18.31.—
con.VI³.σ².31.(19).—dig.V⁶.
—hpmᶜ.V¹.δ.θ².κ¹.29.35.—
mt-nᵇ.V⁶.—sbdᵈ.q.35.—stoᵈ.
V¹.5.—tepᵈ.V¹.

O.—ail.ηii.—clt.V⁶.—cthᶜ.
VI⁴·ᶻᶻ.—car.V⁶-VII⁵.βeᵃ.—
ch-s.au.a¹bˢ.φ.ω²·⁹.—cle.hh.
κ⁴·⁵.4.—cca.χ¹.ω².4.; V¹⁰.χ¹.
4.(5).—cup.V¹.11.35.—dig.
V¹.βe.—hln.29.—ignᵇ.V¹.1.
—lauᶜ.V¹.δcᵈ.δP¹·².—msc.
VIII⁴.κ⁵.σ.—mu-x.V⁶-VI³.q.
δɔ.κ⁵·⁷.σ².—nat.V⁷.δɔ.κ⁵·⁷.σ².
—sbd.V¹⁰·ᶻᶻ.—zin.V⁶·ᑫ.19.

B.—bel.IX.—conᶠ.III¹.au.a¹bᵖ.
χ¹.(12.29).

βb. *Staggering :*
GEN.—crt.VIII¹.—ver.31.(19).
F.—nit.aɢ.βa.χ³.— opi.V¹.βe.θ².
κ.κ¹·⁵·⁹.4.66.(5).—sbd.V⁷.βa.
—so-t.βeᵃ.—tep.V⁷.
T.—nit.aɢ.βa.χ³.

βc. *Falling down :*
GEN.—hy-x.VIII¹.

βɴ. *Intoxication :*
GEN.——par.V¹⁰·ˢ.31.43.49.——
tab.
F.—ant.VII¹.abᶜ.—coc.IX.βa,
eᵃ.—ignᵃ.V¹.a¹bˢ.βe.

βe. *Confusion :*
GEN.—æth.III.—ang.IV¹.31.;
III.—ara.V¹.(14).—ars.—
asa.V¹·¹⁰.4.—asa.VI³.ρ.—asr.
VII⁵.—ath.V⁷.—bor.ᴇl.5.—
bov.V⁶.3.—bro.III.βa.—bry.

III.—cn-i.V^1.—cb-a.V^1.5.66.
——-cb-v.VII^5.——-cn-s.66.——
cas.VI^3.— cau.VIII^4.(66).—
cit.—cle.III.—cob.V^2.i^3.3.—
cot.—ctn.3.——dig.—eup.V^2.
ζ^3.5.16.—gna.——hed.V^1.q.—
hel.V^7.$\beta\ell^a$.4.—hep.VI^3–VII^1.
2.—k-ca.V^{12}–VI^3.——lah.III.
d.q.29.——lam.III^1.3-16.(30).
—lo-i.V^1.ηp.5.66.—lup.V^7.—
mt-n.V^2.100.(18.**30**^{c}).—mnc.
44.—nat.$V^{6·7}$.66.—ni-x.III^3–
IV^3–V^6.—ol-a.V^6–VI^3.3.(4).
—opi.VI^3.—pet.VII^5.—ph-x.
5.7.——pho.V^1–VI^4–VIII^2
3-99.35.—pot.I^s.—pul.; VI^4.
3-99.—rut.V^1.—sbd.p.—scu.
V^7.3.(66).—sec.VIII^4.—sil.
VI^3.aᶄ,u.—tar.III.—tep.VI^3.
ζ^2.—vi-o.—vi-t.V^{10}.w.31.

F.—ac-x.V^7.——ail.III.— alo^a. ;
V^6–VI^3.aᵣᵗ.δb.—amb^h.V^1–VI^4.
——aml.VII^1–VIII^4.——ana^h.
V^7.—ang.VIII^4.—ara.V^1.ω^2.
5.66.(12).—ar-i.σ^2.5.26.—asa.
VII^5.q.; VI^3.ρ.—asp.V^1.—
ber.V^1.q.aa.$\chi^{1·2}$.ω^2.3-99.—bry.
VI^3.; V^6.$\beta\ell^b$.; V^1.—ca-a.V^7.
a^1bº.43.——ca-c.V^7.θ^3.3-99.—
c-cs.VI^3.; V^7.—cam.V^7–VI^3.
abº.5.(8).; V^1.—cnc.V^1.**5**.—
can.V^1.q.δL.b.—cth.VIII^4.3.;
$V^{1·6}$.—cb-v.V^1.— car.$V^{1·10}$.—
ch-s^b. VII^1. d.a¹ℓ^b,ᴆ^b.βa.δt^c.εa,
ᴆ.ηp.$\kappa^{2·3·5·7}$.λ^2.ρ.ϕ^2.χ^3.ω^2. ;　^{b}
3-99.—cmf.—cin$^{h·o}$.V^6.—cle.;
V^1–VII^5.—ccs.V^7.—col^h.VI^3.
——croº.$VIII^{1·q}$.(12).—ctn.
V^1.ab^y.—cup.$V^{10·s}$.29.—dro.
31.—dul.$V^{3·q}$.ii^d.3-30.—eup.
V^1.3.31.(117).—gel.V^{10}.q.ii^d.
δᴆ.εᴆ.—gn-l.V^1–VII^5.q.44.—
glo.II^1–III^1.a¹b^s.δ.η.—hel.V^1.
—hy-x.V^1.δO.σ^2.; V^1.(8).—
ign^a.V^1.a¹b^s.βᴆ.; V^1.3-99.33.
35.48.—iod.35.—k-ca.V^1.—
la-v^m.VI^3.q.4.——lau.V^7.ρ.;
$V^{10·s}$.—led^d.V^1.**130**.—lil.δᴆ.σ^2.
ω^2.—lyc.IX.——mg-s.i^a.ii^d.—
mnc.σ^2.29.—mez.V^1.41.; $^\ell$.V^1.
——msc.V^1.βa.35.; ^{a}.V^1.; V^1

q.δ.ζ.——mu-x.$V^{10·u}$.δ.(12).—
na-m.V^{10}.; $^\ell$.V^1.—nit.VIII^4.
——opi^a.V^1.; $^\ell$.VI^3.; ^{m}.V^1.ζ.
ω^2.; $^\ell$.V^1.βa.; V^1.βb.θ^2.κ.$\kappa^{1·5·9}$.
4.66.(5).; VII^1.—phs.III^1.
d.δ.δLq.——pla.VII^5.——plc^n.
VI^3.——-pul.VII^1.; V^{10}.5.48.
——rap.V^7.3-30.; V^1.; V^7.
3-99.—rhe$^\ell$.V^1.δii.δP^2.—rho.
26.—rhs$^{f·q}$.$V^{10·u}$.—rut.VIII^4.
3-99.5.—ser^a.V^1.(5).——spi.
$V^{10·s}$.—squ.V^1.—sul.V^{10}.3.—
sum^b.—vi-t.V^1.q.w.31.; V^1.
—xip$^\ell$.VI^3.ζ^3.; ^{a}.V^1.$_r$¹.—zin.
V^1.a¹b.; V^1.**5.5**.; V^1.δ.ϕ.**5**.;
V^1.δ.66.—zn-o.V^1.

T.—aga.V^1.——amm.V^1.—ara.
V^1.ω^2.5.66.(12).—asa.V^1.—
asr^b.——bov^b.29.——bry.V^1.;
^{b}.$V^{1·a}$.——c-cs.$VI^{3·b}$.——cam.
VI^3.abº.δO.5.(8).——crd.VI^3.
—chi.V^1.—cle.—cob.V^7.3.35.
—cca^b.V^{10}.——ctn.V^1.a¹b^y.—
cyc^b.V^6–VIII^3.σ^2ff.; ^{b}.V^1.p.;
^{b}.q.—fer.V^1.(35).—glo^b.V^6.ζ.
—lau^b.VI^3.——mez.V^{10}.1.—
na-m^c.V^1.χ^2.; V^7.12.——ped^a.
VIII^4.3-30.—rn-s.III.—rho^b.
V^1.(8-31.14).—rhe^a.V^1.—ser^b.
VI^3.—tar.V^1.—ver.V^1–VII^5.
δP^1.18.19.(17.29).

C.—ars^d.II^1–V^{10}–VIII^4.(15).—
asr^d.V^1.q.—ccs.V^1.—ctn.$V^{10·u}$.
$^\ell$.—cyc^c.V^1–VI^3.— dig.V^1.—
hy-x.V^1.δO.σ^2.—kre.VIII^4.θ^1.
—msc.VII^3.——opi^a.V^1.; V^1.
—stp.III^1–V^1.3.——sti.VI^3.η.
θ^4.——ver.V^1–VII^5.δP^1.18.19.
(17.29).

P.—aga^d.V^1–VI^4.η.—asr$^\ell$.VII^5.;
^{d}.—dig^a.VIII^4.—pho^a.$V^{1·6}$.
O.—asa.$VI^{3·b}$.ρ.—ath.IX.31.—
bry.V^6.σ^2.—c-cs.V^7.—cep^k.**5**.
(5.**70**).—cle.q.—dig.V^1.; V^1.
βa.—hy-x.V^1.σ^2.; $V^{1·a}$.(8).—
iod.V^1.35.(20).—la-v.V^1.q.—
phl.V^1.—sam^c.$VI^{3·4}$.—ser^b.
V^1.(5).—squ.V^1.—trn.I^a.
B.—kre^{tb}.V^6.—nit$^{f·p}$.V^6–VI^4.

$\beta\ell^a$. *Stupid feeling* :
GEN.—æsc.V^7.——amb.VII^5.—

ana.V^1.βa.—aps.III.—arg.χ^1.
——ag-n.i^a.q.3-99.35.——ar-h.
V^1–VI^4.φ^1.2.——asa.VII^5.——
asr.κ^5.41.; V^6.ε.σ^2.—bov.III^1.
(66).; V^2.q.5.——con.3.8-31.
(66).; V^6.(66).—hel.II^1.p.;
V^7.βε.4.; V^2.29.; V$^{1.6}$.βa.—
led.——mg-s.III.χ$^{2.3}$.3-**10**.26.
——nic.VI^4.i^a.q.29.; V^1.3-30.
--nx-v.3-99.(30).--ph-x.VII^1.
εʋ.89.——pul.7.——rhe.V^{15}.aᵷ.
29.35.——rhs.εʋ.——sul.VI^3.q.
(31).—zin.V^1.
F.—alm.VI^3.q.—arg.V^1.——car.
V^1.βa.—chi.V^1.—cin$^{n.o}$.VI^4.
——coc.IX.βa,ʋ.——dul^m.V^6.——
hfb^b.V^1.——hyo^d.III$^{1.e}$.af.——
idm.—lau.g^b.q.29.—lil.V^7.——
mg.s^g.V^3.5-**10**.——pho.p.——pul.
V^2.——so-n.V^{10}.——so-t.βb.——
vrb.V$^{10.s}$.; ^{b}.V$^{10.a}$.
T.—sar.III.q.
C.—mg-s.V^3.**5**.—nic.V^1.3-30.
P.—bov^c.V^3–VI$^{3.q}$.—lau^d.V^3.—
lil^c.V^{10}.--mr-c^a.VIII^5.--mr-i^d.
V^{10}.(8-31).——pho^c.V^3.20.35.
(8).
O.—arg.V$^{1.6}$.—bap.I^a.——car.
V^6–VII^5.—dio^c.V^6.—nic.II^5-
V^2.—so-n^e.V$^{1.10}$.δP^1.ρ.υ.

βε^b. *Empty feeling* :
G ᴇɴ.—ast.d.a^{1}ʋ.ρ.2-99.—asa.--
ca-c.VI^3.—hpm.p.3-99.
F.—b-la.I^q.ω^3——bov.V^1.q.a^{1}b^s.
——bry.V^6.βε.——cau.IX.——
mg-m.V^1.3-99.—rho.V^1.
T.—cyc.III^1.
P.—m-pu^c.V^7.r.5.
O.—man.V^7.a^{1}b.(12).—sep.IX.
2-16.(12).

βε^c. *Lightness* :
F.—lo-c.V^7.—ox-x^g.VI^3.
T.—crt^b.V^1.θ^{1}ɴ.
C.—ox-x.VI^3.
O.—ast.ω^7.41.

βꜰ. *Noise in head* :
O.—rs-r.V^7.5.41.

δa^b. *Glistening eyes* :
Gᴇɴ.—vp-r.aꜱ^i,q.ηc^d,aa.θ^2.⅄^{3}.μ^1.
ν^1.ρ.σ^1.φ,χ^2.ω^3.

F.—ag-n.VI^4.δ.δaa,ε.η.

δc^d. *Yellow eyes* :
Gᴇɴ.—myr.V^7.δd.3-99.

δd. *Congestion of eyes* :
Gᴇɴ.—myr.V^7.δc^d.3-99.

δp. *Heat of eyes* :
Gᴇɴ.—gym.κ^1.λ.——trn.p.ηp.
F.—epn.V^3.
C.—bov.V^7.

δq. *Heaviness of eyes* :
Gᴇɴ.—ptv.
F.—alo.V^7.κ^5.——aru^{a1}.V$^{10.a}$.——
cca.V^7.3.(31).——ipc.——naj.
III$^{1.w}$.
T.—ham.—naj.V^1.
C.—ptv.V^1.q.δꜰ.

δs. *Inflammation of eyes* :
Gᴇɴ.—bad.—ca-s.—led.VI^4.p.
hh.δ.κ^3,λ^2.χ^1.——mo-a.ηaa.ρ.χ^2.
ψv.—ver.φ^1.
F.—mr-i.II^3.5.

δv. *Itching of eyes* :
F.—cot.V^7.q.a^{1}b^s.δʋ.ρ^1.υb.(8).

δaa. *Redness of eyes* :
Gᴇɴ.—arg.VI^3.3.—bel.ηaa.
F.——ag-n.VI^4.δ.δa^b,ε.η.——bel^e.
ηaa.

δff. *Stiffness of eyes* :
F.—ni-x.V^1.δ.

δff. *Difficulty of moving eyes to the side* :
F.—mg-s.V^{10}.

δii. *Swelling of eyes* :
F.—rhe^e.V^1.βε.δP^2.
T.—lah.VI^3.δ.ζ.θ^4.**5**.

δii^d. *Swollen feeling of eyes* :
Gᴇɴ.—mns.aq.2.
F.—com.δ.δε.—gel.V^{10}.; II^6.b.

δa. *Drawing upwards of lids* :
Gᴇɴ.—aco.

δb. *Closure of lids* :
Gᴇɴ.—-cb-v.83.——ca-x.VI^3.51.
111.(12).——coc.—hep.VI^3–
VII^1.29.—kre.V^6.—mez.1^b.
βa.κ^4.—msc.V^7.—nit.—sul.--
trn.
F.—aga.V^7.(26).——alo^a.V^6–VI^3.
aᵹ^t.βε.—am-c^g.VI^3.66.—bel^e.
V$^{10.u}$.3.; ^{e}.V$^{10.t}$.; ^{e}.V$^{10.s}$.δP^1.
σ^2.--ca-a^n.V^1.δ.--can.V^1.q.δL.
—cb-v.V^1.δε.σ^2.——ced^p.I^q.——

chd^h.V^1–VI^4.(66).—cof.V^1–
VII^5.3-99.29.--cor.V^1.(8-31).
--epn.V^3.$\delta\epsilon.\theta^4$.—gel.III.3-99.
(12).—glo.VIII^4.ζ.—la-x.V^7.
--na-s^b.V^3.--ni-x^o.VI^3-VIII^4.
5.—-nx-m.a^1ʊ.ω^9.—-opi.V$^{1\cdot3}$.
δLq.--pho.VI^3.83.--pla.V$^{10\cdot s}$.
q.$\delta b,\ell.\eta p$,aa.$\kappa^3.o^2.\rho$.5.26.29.—
pod.VI^3.βa.—sep^g.VI$^{3\cdot a}$.3-30.
(8).—tar.V$^{10\cdot u}$.δ.
T.—atr^b.VI^3.3-99.(8).--lth.V^{10}.
$\beta\ell.\kappa^5$.3.16.49.(8.19).—mag^a.
VI^4.—so-n^a.V^8.
C.—sul.V$^{10\cdot t}$.q.2-**10.5.** ; V$^{1\cdot a}$.δ.
$\chi^{1\cdot3}$.2.
P.—ca-x.VI$^{3\cdot w}$.δ.--mg-m^c.VI$^{3\cdot4}$.
δ.—pet^c.(16).
O.—-cb-v.V^1.$\delta\epsilon$.—-plb.V$^{10\cdot zz}$.q.
(18).—sul^h.V$^{1\cdot a}$.$\delta.\chi^{1\cdot3}$.2.
B.—au-n^{fb}.V$^{3\cdot a}$.—nx-v^{fb}.V^1.

$\delta\epsilon$. *Inability to raise eyes :*
GEN.—ped.δO.
F.—cb-a^e.

δc^d. *Eyes fixed and immovable :*
F.—lau.V^1.βa.δP$^{1\cdot2}$.—spi^n.VI^4–
VIII^3.18.19.
O.—lau^c.V^1.βa.δP$^{1\cdot2}$.

$\delta\epsilon$. *Lachrymation :*
GEN.—bel.δLii.ηp.—eug.II^1.δ.
2.5.72.—mac.—pul.V^6.—spo.
49.—str.θ^1.
F.—aga^f.II^1–V^1.—ag-n.VI^4.δ.
δa^b,aa.η.—asr.V$^{10\cdot u}$.δ.-bov$^{g\cdot h\cdot o}$.
III^1–V^{12}–VI^3.--cb-v.V^1.$\delta b.\sigma^2$.
—com.δ.—con.I^a.δ.—epn.V^3.
$\delta b.\theta^4$.— k-hy^h.V$^{16\cdot d}$.δCa^{2}ii.—
lil^b.V^7.4.; II^1–V^1.5.7.—m-pu^f.
—mer.III^1–V^{12}.—osm$^e.\epsilon.\eta$.—
pla.V$^{10\cdot s}$.q.$\delta b.\eta p$, aa. $\kappa^3. o^2.\rho$.5.
26.29.—rs-r^g.a$\ell.\omega^9$.—tax.$\delta.\eta$.
T.—idm^a.ζo.θ^3.
C.—chd.I^a.
P.—mer^d.V^1.
O.—cb-v.V^1.δb.—mer.V^{12}.

δb. *Difficulty of opening eyes :*
F.—na-m.V$^{1\cdot a}$.δ.—ph-x^e. ; V$^{1\cdot a}$.
a^1ʊ.o^2. 3-99.35.—plc.V^1.δL.
3-99.
C.—ptv.V^1.q.δq.

δo. *Dimness of vision :*
GEN.—bry.VIII^4.35.—cro.$\delta.\theta^1$.

—hln.βa.—ind.VIII$^{5\cdot zz}$.**5.**19.
—jug.—mg-m.VIII^4.p.—
mu-x.V^1.q.βa.ϕ.8-30.49.--pho.
V^7.$\theta^2.\omega^2$.28.(16).——ve-v.βa.
δP^2.

F.—ast^g.V^3.δ.——bov^b.V$^{1\cdot q}$.q.δ.
3-35.——cot.V^7.q.a^1b^s.δv.ρ^1.υb.
(8).——er-a^e.VII^2.29.——gel.
V^{10}.q.ii^d.$\beta\epsilon.\epsilon$ʊ.--hyo^b.—k-bi^a.
VIII^4. ; $^{g\cdot h}$.VI$^{3\cdot a}$.3.(5).—lil.
$\beta\epsilon.\sigma^2.\omega^2$.——nat.V^6.$\beta$a.$\kappa^{5\cdot7}$.——
rap^e.I^a.(72).—sul^b.V^3.δs.—
til.V^1.q.βa.
T.—gel^a.V^1.βa.κ^5.--glo.V^1.12.--
hdr.VI^1.
C.—for.VIII^5.5.
P.—sar^b.IV^1.ab^o.δt^m.86.
O.—mu-x.V^6–VI^3.βa.σ^2.— nat.
V^7.βa.$\kappa^{5\cdot7}.\sigma^2$.

δo. *Difficulty of fixing eyes :*
GEN.—trn.

δo^b. *Blindness :*
GEN.—eth.—grt.V^{14}.ϵa^a.

δo^d. *Dazzling :*
T.—alo.V$^{10\cdot s}$.ηp.
O.—ped.III–VIII^4.3-30.31.

δr^h. *Diplopia :*
GEN.—con.$\delta t^q.\phi.\omega^2$.
F.—kis^g.

δr^z. *Objects appear in a yellow veil :*
GEN.—k-bi.II^1.βa.

δs. *Photophobia :*
GEN.—glo.aʊ.ω^2.——trn.I^q.aℓ,g,
l^g,q.
F.—ign^a.V^7.δr.--k-ca.V^1.--sul^b.
V^3.δo.

δt^c. *Sparks before eyes :*
F.—-ch-s^b.VII^1.d.$a^1\ell^h$,ʊ^b.βa,$\ell.\epsilon$a,
ʊ.$\eta p.\kappa^{2\cdot3\cdot5\cdot7}.\lambda^2.\rho.\phi^2.\chi^3.\omega^2$.

δt^k. *Flashes before eyes :*
GEN.—cca.V^6.—vi-o.V^7.

δt^m. *Flickering before eyes :*
GEN.—ca-x.VII^2.—cyc.3-30.—
lah.V^1.d.—pho.V^6.ao,x.βa.ρ.
3.(66).
P.—sar^b.IV^1.ab^o.δo^a.86.

δt^q. *Muscæ volitantes :*
GEN.—con.$\delta r^h.\phi.\omega^2$.
F.—pho^g.

δt^u. *Vision of bright rings in motion :*
F.—tax^e.κ^4.(63).

δ. *Pain in eyes:*

GEN.—-aco.V^{1}.—-aga.V^{6}.3-99.; III.*l*.—-a-sc.—-ag-n.V^{1}.*o*^{3}.—ars.VI^{4}.*r*.—bad.4.—bel.; VI^{3}.βa.—ca-c.V$^{3\cdot10}$.*ap*.ζ.θ^{1}.ω^{3}.;VI^{3}.—-cnc.δP^{2}.ηp,aa,ii.χ^{3}.—-cth. II^{5}–V^{1}–VI^{3}.—-cha.VI^{2}.—-ch-x.—-cin.3.—-cn-s.VII^{1}.p.q.*eb*.—-cis.V^{1}.—-coc.—-col.5.29.—-cro.δ*o*.θ^{1}.—-equ.I^{a}.**5**.—eug.II^{1}.δε.2.5.72.—-fag.3-99.—f-mg.ζ.—-hpm.V$^{3\cdot6}$–VI^{3}.2-**10**.—hfb.—idm.48.—-k-bi.ε.—klm.V^{6}.5.8.—-kre.VI^{4}.η.—lah.VI^{3}.ζ.ηii.**5**.—-lch.—-led. VI^{4}.p.hh.δs.λ.κ^{3}.χ^{1}.—lyc.VI^{3}.ζ^{3}.—lcp.5.—mt-n.V$^{10\cdot u}$.ω^{3}.—mg-m.V^{7}.66.—mu-x.V$^{10\cdot u}$.16.(90).—na-m.V^{6}–VI^{1}.θ^{4}.4.8.—nic.VI^{4}.*l*.—-ni-x.29.; 48.—-nx-j.V^{7}.—-par.V^{7}.δLp,aa.—-pho.V^{7}.κ^{1}.λii.φ.19.—scu.V^{7}.i^{a}.—sng.VIII^{4}.κ^{1}.ω^{4}.—sil.V^{1}.κ^{5}.χ^{1}.ω^{2}.3.; V$^{10\cdot zz}$.—-str.—-sto. IV^{1}–V^{6}.—-sul.VI^{3}.—val.V^{10}.θ^{4}.5.—-zin.λ.5.16.; 70.—zng. V$^{1\cdot6}$.

F.—aga.V^{1}.; V^{6}.; V$^{10\cdot t}$.; ^{o}.V$^{1\cdot6}$.—alo^{f}.V^{6}–VIII^{3}.—amb.V$^{10\cdot u}$.p.ηc^{d}.4.; VI$^{4\cdot u}$.; ^{h}.V^{1}–VI^{4}.βε.—-arg^{o}.V^{1}–VI^{4}.—-ag-n.VI^{4}.δa^{b},aa,ε.η.—-aru.VI^{3}.—-asr. V$^{10\cdot u}$.δε.—-bel^{e}.q.3-99.—ber. VI^{3}.—-bis.II^{1}–III.; V^{2}.ζ.—bor.VIII^{3}.κ^{5}.4.—bov^{b}.V$^{1\cdot q}$.q.δ*o*.3.35.; VI$^{4\cdot a}$.q.29.—bro.V^{7}.3.—bry^{g}.V$^{10\cdot s}$.; V$^{10\cdot s}$.29.—cld. V^{7}.*a*ε.ηp.65.—-ca-a^{n}.V^{1}.δ*b*.—cb-v^{e}.V^{1}.; II^{1}.θp.—-ca-x^{f}.—chd^{h}.VI^{4}.δL.—-cl-h^{e}.; ^{e}.p.—cmf.ιj.—-cis.V^{1}.—cob.—cca^{f}.—cch.V^{1}.—col.III.29.(8).—com.δε.—con.δε.—cro^{e}.2.115.—crt^{a}.V^{1}.ηr.θ^{1}.ν*l*.5.—-eri.V^{7}.3-99.—-eup.V^{1}.3.8-31.—fl-x. V^{1}.29.; ^{a}.5.16.—gel^{t}.VI^{3}.θ^{4}.—gn-l.V^{10}.—-glo.II^{1}–III^{1}.*a*^{1}*b*^{s}.βε.η.—gym^{e}.V^{1}–VI^{3}.i^{a}.—hel^{o}. V^{1}–VI^{4}.—-hpm.V$^{6\cdot7}$.(5).—-hur^{e}.—ign.V^{1}.x.; 35.; ^{a}V^{7}.δ*s*.; ^{a}.V$^{10\cdot s}$.4.—idm^{f}.VIII^{4}.—ipc^{e}. δLq.—-ituV^{1}.—-jac^{ad}.V^{1}.—-k-bi.—k-ca.I^{a}.; ^{h}.V$^{1\cdot6}$.VI^{4}.—k-hy^{h}.V$^{16\cdot a}$.δε,Ca^{2}ii.; II^{1}.ζ.θ.ι.—kre.V$^{10\cdot s}$.29.—-la-x.V$^{7\cdot w}$.q.—-la-v.V^{10}.3-99.41.—-lil.V^{6}.; II^{5}.—-lyc^{e}.V^{1}–VI^{4}.3.—-mag. V^{1}.; ^{b}.V^{7}.—mrl.V^{1}.—-mr-f^{a}. 2-**10**.–mr-i.V^{10}-VI^{3}.η*l*.ι.–mez. III^{3}.θ^{4}.—msc.V^{1}.q.ζ.—mu-x. V$^{10\cdot u}$.q.βε.(12).—-nat.IV^{1}–VI^{4}.ζ.—-na-m.V^{7}.x.14.; V$^{10\cdot s}$.(12).; V$^{1\cdot a}$.δ*b*.—ni-x.V^{1}.δff.—nit.III^{1}.ζ.; V^{1}.—nx-j.IX.ζ.—nx-v.VI^{4}.κ^{5}.*o*^{2}.π.—-ol-a^{s}.V^{1}–VI^{4}.3.—-opi.V^{1}.ζ.—-ptv.p.4.—pho^{h}.VIII$^{3\cdot4}$.ζ.κ^{6}.3.—-phs. III^{1}.d.βε.δLq.—-phy.V^{1}.—-pso.VI^{3}.—rn-b.V^{10}.3-**10**.(30).—rho.V^{6}–VI^{4}.6.35.—sab^{o}.V^{1}.—sam^{d}.V^{1}–VI^{4}.—-sel.VI^{3}.**5**.5.7.—snc.VI$^{3\cdot s}$.—sng.V^{1}.κ^{5}.ρ.3.7.19.(8.14).—sep.V^{1}.θ^{2}.κ^{5}.; II^{1}–V^{1}–VII^{5}.; VI$^{3\cdot s}$.1.—-sil. V^{1}.; VII^{5}.ω^{2}.—spi^{a}.II^{1}.48.—sul.VII^{5}.3-99.**50**.—su-x.II^{1}–V^{1}.—tab^{b}.V^{6}.; V$^{7\cdot10\cdot q}$.—trn^{a}.4.29.—tar.V$^{10\cdot u}$.δ*b*.; ^{b}.V^{1}.—tax.δε.η.—thu^{a}.VI^{4}.ζ.η.3.5.; ^{n}.V^{1}-VIII^{3}.—til.V^{1}.—val.V$^{10\cdot v}$.—zin.V^{1}.βε.φ.**5**.; V^{1}.βε.66.

T.—agn.VIII^{1}.35.—alo^{b}.V$^{1\cdot3}$.4.5.—an-a.IV^{3}–VI^{3}.—-asi.VI^{3}.3-99.89.—bad.; 48.—ber^{a}.V^{1}.; VI^{3}.;V^{10}.ζ^{3}.—cld^{a}.VI^{3}.—cau^{a}. VII^{5}.—-ch-s^{b}.I^{a}.(16.102).—-ccs^{b}.V^{1}.—-col.III.29.(8).—-cvl^{b}.—elp.III^{1}.—fag^{a}.VI^{3}.**5**.—glo^{a}.VI^{3}.; ^{a}.VII^{5}.—grn^{a}.VI^{4}.—klm.VI^{3}.—lah.VI^{3}.δii.ζ.ηii.θ^{4}.**5**.—man.V$^{1\cdot3}$.19.22.(29).—m-pu^{a}.5.—mez.III^{3}.θ^{4}.—ni-x. V^{1}.—-nit^{b}.V^{6}.—-opi^{a}.V$^{1\cdot b}$.—ph-x^{a}.VI$^{3\cdot a}$.—-pod.V^{10}.**5**.—rho.V^{6}-VI$^{4\cdot a}$.6.35.—rhs.V^{6}.3.30.—snc^{b}.VI^{3}.θ^{4}*l*.—spo^{b}.VI$^{4\cdot a}$.—sul^{b}.V^{1}–VI^{4}.; VI^{3}.4.—trn^{a}. VI^{3}.—zin^{a}.V$^{1\cdot a}$.

C.—-amb.V$^{10\cdot u}$.p.ηc^{b}.3.4.—-ber. VI^{3}.—-col.V^{1}.—-crt.V^{6}.5.—ign.V^{1}.x.—-mrl.VII^{5}.—-ni-x. V^{10}.—nx-v.VI^{4}.κ^{5}.*o*^{2}.ω^{2}.—opi.

—pau.V^1.βa.3.—rn-b.VII^1.5.
6.—sil.V^1.5.—sul.V^1.3-30.;
$V^{1\cdot a}$.δb.$\chi^{1\cdot 3}$.2.
P.—bov^c.V^2.—bro.—bry^b.4.—
ca-c^c.VI^3.—ca-x.$VI^{3\cdot w}$.δb.—
cau^c.V^1.—cis^c.—fag^d.$V^{10\cdot s}$.;
V^7.σ^2.—hpm^c.V^1.βa.$\theta^2.\kappa^1$.29,
35.—hur^d.VI^3.θ^4.—hfb^b.$V^{1\cdot 3}$
$VI^{3\cdot t}$.5.—mg-m^c.VI^4.;^{c}.$VI^{3\cdot 4}$.
δb.—mr-f^c.σ^2.—pul^b.VII^1.—
san^d.$I^a.v^1l$.;^{c}.$V^{10\cdot 9}.\xi^3$.83.—spi.
V^1.3-30.28.31.74.—trn^d.
O.—cb-a^b.V^1.—cch$^c.\eta$.3.—er-a.
38.—glo.I^a.—idm^b.—mu-x^i.
VIII^3.δL^{1}ll^b.—rhs.V^6.3.—sng.
V^1.7.(8-31.14).—sul^h.$V^{1\cdot a}$.δb.
$\chi^{1\cdot 3}$.2.
B.—au-n^{fb}.$V^{3\cdot a}$.—mr-f$^{fa\cdot pa}$.er.—
na-m^{tb}.VIII^3.5.—par^f.$II^{4\cdot 5}$.
δLp,aa.5.

δ. *Burning in eyes:*
GEN.—ail.V^7.—arn.ηp.
F.—lyc.II^1.6.

δ. *As if eyes would fall out:*
F.—bro.29.83.—glo.I^a.—nit.
V^1.—pho.V^1.—rhs.$\chi^1.\psi^9$.—
san$^a.\xi^3$.83.—sep.$V^{10\cdot s\cdot q}$.VIII^3.
p.—val^e.$V^{10\cdot s}$.4.48.

δBe. *Contraction of eyebrows:*
F.—ast^g.V^3.δo.

δBv. *Itching in eyebrows:*
P.—fer$^c.\zeta$v.

δB. *Pain in eyebrow:*
T.—ca-a^b.V^3–VI^3.60.

δLp. *Heat in eyelids:*
GEN.—par.V^7.δL.aa.
B.—par^f.$II^{4\cdot 5}$.δ.δL.aa.5.

δLq. *Weight in lids:*
F.—ctn^e.V^1.hh.—gin$^{f\cdot n}$.VI^3.p.
φ.—ipc^e.δ.—naj.V^1.—opi.
$V^{1\cdot 3}$.δb.—phs.III^1.d.βe.δ.

δLaa. *Redness of lids:*
GEN.—par.V^7.δ.δLp.
B.—par^f.$II^{4\cdot 5}$.δ.δLp.5.

δLii. *Swelling of lids:*
GEN.—bel.I^a.δe.ηp.

δLll. *Twitching of lids:*
F.—dgn^b.VI^3.5.31.
T.—col.V^1.3.

δLll^b. *Quivering of lids:*
B.—kre$^{tb\cdot c}$.VIII^4.

δL^{1}ll^b. *Quivering of left upper eyelid:*
O.—mu-x^i.VIII^3.δl.

δL. *Pain in eyelids:*
GEN.—ni-x.VII^5.
F.—aga^h.V^1.5.—can.V^1.βe.δb.
—chd^h.VI^4.δ—hyo.V^1.βa.(8-
31).—msc^e.V^1.βa.—nab.αⁱⁱ$^{b\cdot i}$.
ψv.—plc.V^1.δb.3-99.—zin^n.
VI^4.δo^f.V^1.
T.—aco.$V^{10\cdot s}$.i^a.5.—hyo^a.V^1.βa.
(8-31).—sab^b.V^6.47.
C.—msc.βa.—nab.au.ι.ψv.
P.—alm^c.VI^3.

δO. *Pain in orbits:*
GEN.—aco.III.—cb-a.VI^4.
VIII^4.e.$\eta.\theta^4$.66.(12).—nit.VI^3.
φ.—ped.δ.
F.—alo.V^1.—bad.p.4.48.—ba-a.
$V^{10\cdot s}$.24.(29).—cle^b.I^a.5.102.
(12).—hy-x.V^1.βe.σ^2.—ign.
$V^{1\cdot a}$.—lil^g.V^{10}.3-30.—mr-f.
V^7.; $V^7.\zeta$.—na-a^e.V^1.—nup^a.
V^7.q.1.—pæo.$V^{1\cdot a}$.q.3.5.—
pgn.—sng^b.66.(8).—sto.V^1.
—sul.V^1.—tab^f.VI^3.—zin^n.
VI^4.δL.
T.—ba-a^b.$VIII^{3\cdot q}$.el.—bel.$V^{6\cdot u}$.
—ca-c.$VI^4.\eta.\eta$ii.1.—cam.VI^3.
abº.βe.5.(8).—chi.VI^1.29.35.
—lah^a.VIII^4.—lth$^b.\kappa^4$.(63).
C.—hy-x.V^1.βe.σ^2.—opi.$V^{10\cdot s}$.
P.—crt^d.III^3–$V^{1\cdot 2\cdot 6}$–$VII^5.\theta^1$.—
pgn.
O.—chi.VI^1.29.35.—con.$VI^4 \kappa^5$.
σ^2.—lah^b.$VII^5.\zeta$.—man.V^6.
29.(12).

δCa²ii. *Swelling of inner canthus:*
F.—k-hy^h.$V^{16\cdot a}$.δe,Ca²ii.

δCa². *Pain in inner canthus:*
F.—ccs^b.V^1.—k-hy^h.$V^{16\cdot a}$.δe,
Ca²ii.

δLa⁴. *Pain in lachrymal gland:*
P.—arn.V^7.

δP¹. *Contracted pupils:*
F.—bel^e.$V^{10\cdot s}$.δb.o².—lau.V^1.βa.
δ.δP².
TC.—ver.V^1–VII^5.βe.18.19.(17.
29).
O.—lau^c.V^1.βa.δe^d.δP².—so-n^e.
$V^{1\cdot 10}$.βe^a.ρ.v.

δP². *Dilated pupils :*
GEN.—-cnc.δ.ηp,aa,ii.χ³.—ve-v.
βa.δo.
F.—bel.V¹⁰.*au.*(29).—-lau.V¹.βa.
δ.δP¹.—mo-aᵃ.θ³.κ.σb,hh.ω³.—-
rheᵉ.V¹.βε.δii.
T.——aco.η.ηcᵇ,p,aa.ρ¹.σb,hh.τv.
ω³·⁸.φ.66.
P.—mo-aᶜ.Iᵃ.
O.—lauᶜ.V¹.βa.δcᵈ.δP¹.

εb.p. *Cold l. ear, hot r. ear :*
F.—ter.VI⁴.e.

εhʲ. *Discharge from ears :*
P.—borᶜ.VI³·q.εr.εlv.

εiᵃ. *Fulness in ears :*
T.—glo.V¹·ᵃ.

εp. *Hot ears :*
C.—ca-c.IV¹–V⁶.
O.—grn.V¹.

εp.b. *Hot r. ear, cold l. ear :*
F.—ter.VI⁴.e.

εv. *Tickling in ears :*
F.—mu-x.VI³.eC.
P.—borᶜ.VI³·q.εr.εrhʲ.— mu-xᶜ.
VI⁴.eC.

εa. *Deafness :*
GEN.—arn.a¹ᴅ.βa.——ch-s.V⁷.aᶃ.
ρ.χ³.ω⁸.—grt.V¹⁴.δᴅ⁶.
F.—ch-sᵇ.VII¹.d.a¹cᵇ,ᴅᵇ.βa,ε.δtᶜ.
εᴅ.ηp.κ²·³·⁵·⁷.λ².ρ.φ².χ³.ω².
T.—bel.V¹.q.—lycᵃ.IX.εᴅ.
C.—bel.V¹⁰.
O.—ignᵈ.e.

εb. *Improved hearing :*
F.—phy.

εᴅ. *Noises in ears :*
GEN.—aco.ζ³.λ.3.—bor.VIII⁴.
83.—-chd.VII².— ch-s.VII¹.
z.βa.ηp.——cn-s.VII¹.p.q.δ. —
cle.—cca.ιj. —ccsᶠ.V⁶–VI⁴.—
eri.V⁷.——-fer.V⁶–VI³. ; VI³.
82.—hy-x.af.—kre.V¹⁰·ˢ.29.
83.—lah.VII⁵.ζ³.μ¹.o³.(12).—
myr.——pet.VIII⁵.d.—ph-x.
VII¹.βeᵃ.89.——rhs.βeᵒ.—squ.
V⁷.3-30.—stp.VI³.5.29.31.—
sul.βa.κ⁴·⁵.τvkk,nn.ω²·⁹.—trn.
d.ε.2.—ver.V⁷.
F.—bry.—-ch-sᵇ.VII¹.d.a¹cᵇ,ᴅᵇ.
βa,ε.δtᶜ.εa.ηp.κ²·³·⁵·⁷.λ².ρ φ².χ³.
ω². ; d.p.5. ; ᵇ.Iᵃ.βa.ω².3.——

cn-sᶜ.VII¹.p.—-ccaᵉ.Iᵃ.—gel.
V¹⁰.q.iiᵈ.βε.δo.——-stp.III.—-
trn.IX.
T.—acoᵇ.—lycᵃ.IX.εᴅ.—rhsᵇ.
VI³·ˢ.iᵃ.q.
C.—bor.VI⁴.— cn-sᶜ.VII¹.p.—
hyp.3-99.
P.—anaᶜ.VI⁴.η.σ².——-eupᵈ.κ¹.3.
—nicᶜ.VIII³.2.
O.——-ccsᶠ.V⁶–VI⁴. ; ᶠ.VII⁵.—
cn-s.VII¹.p.—sel.V⁶.εε.

εᴅᵇ. *Hammering in ears :*
F.—spi.VI³–VIII⁴.2.

εᴅᵏ. *Gurgling in ears :*
F.—pla.III¹–V³.x.ᴔuᶠᶠ.χ².7.

εε. *Stoppage of ears :*
P.—mr-fᶜ.V⁷.σ²ff.
O.—sel.V⁶.εᴅ.

ε. *Pain in ears :*
GEN.—alm.VI⁴.5.(12).—-asr.V⁶.
βεᵃ.σ².—bor.βε.5.—cb-a.VI⁴–
VIII⁴.δO.ηl.θ⁴.66.(12).—cau.
V¹⁰.θ¹.—-cep.VI³.——ce-b.—-
glv.3-99.—ham.4.—hur.VI³.
θ¹. ; l.II¹.θ⁴.—-ind.V¹⁰–VII¹.
3.—k-bi.δ. ; V¹.θ².—mr-i.V¹.
—msc.r.—nit.VII¹.l.r.—plb.
r.VI³.4.5.—san.βa.—sar.VI³.
—sul.VI³·⁴.η.θ⁴.——-tab.II¹.gᵇ.
κ¹.χ¹.—trn.d.εᴅ.2.—til.VI⁴.η.
F.— arnᵃ.V¹.o³.——-ar-i.VI³.128.
——-aruᵃ.VI⁴.—-bor.l.θ¹l.5.—-
bovᵒ.VI³·⁴.—cn-iᵖ.—cth.VI⁴.
θ⁴.——capᵉ.VI³·ʰ.V¹.——-dioᵃ.
VI¹.12.—-hæmᵇ.III¹.—-iof.V⁷.
33.—k-bi.—-lahᵒ.Iq.3.—-lyc.
VI³.—na-m.V¹⁰·ˢ.—osmᶜ.δε.η.
—sanᵃ.V¹⁰.18.(31). ; ᵃ.θ¹.3-99.
—ter.VI⁴.εrp.εlb.
T.—an-sᵃ.Iᵇ.—-aruᵃ.VI⁴.—ba-aᵇ.
VIII³·q.δOl.—bovᵇ.VI⁴.—-
broᵇ.29.—cac.VIII⁴.—-cncᵃ.
—conᵃ.V⁶.—-glo.VI¹. ; V¹⁰–
VII⁵.—gymᵇ.VI³.—-lah.V¹.
—lil.VII¹.(12).—lthᵇ.—lyc.
VI³.—na-m.V¹·¹⁰·ˢ.——pruᵃ.
III³.—-so-n.VI³.— sul.V¹·³. ;
ᵃ.VIII³.—zin.VI⁴.66.
C.——aga.VI³·⁴·ᵃ.——bel.V¹·⁸.θ¹.
——-ca-a.V¹.—ctn.V¹⁰·ᵘ.βε —-

hdr.V$^{10·v}$.3.—-lep^b.V^3.—-lip.
VI^3.—ol-a^a.VI$^{3·4}$.
P.—bor^c.VI$^{3·q}$.ϵrh^j.ϵlv.—-cro^d.
V^7.ι.—-cu-a.V^6.η.σ^2.—-grt^c.
VI^4.—ind^c.VI^3.—k-bic.V^3.
η.—klm^d.VIII^4.—lyc^d.VI^4.
—man^c.VI^4.30.—mu-x^c.VI^3.
—-na-m^d.VI$^{3·q}$.5.31.—-ol-a.
VI$^{3·4}$.—sul.VI^4.—trn^d.VI^3.
—til^d.VI^4.—ton^c.VI^3.5.
O.—ba-a.V^6.θ^4.—-cch^d.VI^4.—
glo.VII$^{5·u·v}$.—hæm^c.—ign^d.
ϵa.—-inu.VI^4–VIII^3.—-jun^l.
IX.V^7.—k-hy^f.V^8.—-msc.V^6.
θ^1.—ol-a.VI$^{3·4}$.—pul.VI^3.
B.—cth^{pb}.VI$^{3·a}$.

ϵM. *Pain in meatus:*
O.—trx^d.V^1.θ^4.
B.—ni-x^{pb}.V$^{1·6}$.θ^1.

ϵC. *Pain in concha:*
C.—bov.VI$^{4·a}$.V^2.11.3.
B.—ind^{pb}.VIII^1.19.66.—-sar^{ta}.
V$^{1·6}$.—tep^{ta}.II^1.ηr.

ϵC. *Burning in concha:*
F.—mu-x.VI^3.ϵlv.
P.—mu-x^c.VI^4.ϵlv.

ϵaT. *Pain in antetragus:*
T.—ph-x^b.V$^{1·6}$.35.

ϵL. *Pain in lobule of ear:*
O.—amb^d.VI^4.

ζp. *Heat of nose:*
F.—cvl.

ζv. *Itching in nose:*
P.—fer.δBy.

ζh^a. *Fetid nasal discharge:*
F.—sep.V^1.83.

ζo. *Stuffed nose:*
Gen.——-bov.VIII^4.au.a^{1}b.16.
100.
F.-bov^h.VIII^4.q.au.a^{1}b^s.16.100.
—chd.V^{12}.—nit^i.—sul^e.o^3.3.
T.—chd^a.V^1.—chi.—idm^a.$\delta r\epsilon$.θ^3.

ζ. *Pain in nose:*
Gen.—aga.V^1.—ca-c.V$^{3·10}$.ap.δ.
η.θ^1.ω^3.—f-mg.δ.—glo.—-hel.
—ign.—lah.V^6.; VI^3.δ.ηii.5.—
mer.V$^{10·u}$.VII^1.—mr-f.V^7.η.5.
—-mez.V^1–VIII^4.θ^1.26.—-
nx-v.VI^4.θ^4.31.—tar.III–V$^{3·6}$.
—— *as if epistaxis were coming
on.*—trn.

F.—aga.V^6.; IX.i^a.—bis.V^3.δ.
—bro^a.V^1.—css.—cro^o.III^3–
V^6.—-cch.I^a.—-c-ar.—dul^m.
V^6.—— dgn.—fer^a.5.—-glo.
VIII^4.δb.—hpm^c.V^3–VIII^4.
g^b.—igu.V$^{1·7}$.—jan.—k-hy.
II^1.δ.θ.ι.—kis^m.—lah^i.V^6.; ^{a}.
VI^4.—lch.π.τ.χ^2.—-lyc.V^1.3.
—mr-f.V^7.; V^7.δO.—mez.V^{10}.;
III$^{2·3}$.; V^1–VIII^4.θ^1.26.—msc.
V^1.q.$\beta\epsilon$.δ.; ^{h}.V^1.η.—-nat.IV^1–
, VI^4.δ.—nit.III^1.δ.—nx-j.IX.
δ.—onif.V^1.—opi.V^1.δ.; ^{m}.V^1.
$\beta\epsilon$.ω^2.; ^{h}.V^1.—ph-x.V^1.—pho^h.
VIII$^{3·4}$.δ.κ^6.3.—pi-m^f.V^1.—
pla.VII^5.x.—rn-b$^{i·n}$.VIII^4.βa.
1.—squ^n.VI$^{3·u}$.—-sul.V^1.η.—
trn.—thu^a.VI^4.δ.η.3.5.
T.—ca-x.V^7.q.—glo^b.V^6.$\beta\epsilon$.—
lah.VI^3.δ.δii.ηii.θ^4.5.——mez.
III$^{2·3}$.—pi-m^a.V^1.
C.—cch^b.V^6.—dul.V^6.5.63.
P.—ch-s^d.V^7.29.—nic^d.VI^4.—
pho^c.VI^3.rr.—thr^e.V^{10}.
O.——cam.III^1.p.$\tau^1 v^1$b.φ.12.16.
29.—crn.V^6.—lah^b.VII^5.δO.
—mez^e.V^1–VIII^4.θ^1.26.
Ba.—mr-f.V^7.q.ι.—mr-i.V^7.q.ι.
B.—gui^t.V^6.

ζ. *Pain in l. nostril:*
T.—hdr^b.

ζ^2. *Epistaxis:*
Gen.—ant.—-cad.—crt.—tep.
V^1.βa.; VI^3.$\beta\epsilon$.
F.—ham^h.V^1–VII^5.x.——sep.a$\mathfrak{g}$.
ω^8.
T.—ber.V^{10}.δ.
C.—sep.a$\mathfrak{q}$.ω^8.

ζ^3. *Coryza:*
Gen.—aco.ϵv.λ.3.—bad.—cep.
5.6.—clo.—cro.VI^3.—eup.V^2.
$\beta\epsilon$.5.16.——lah.VII^5.μ^1.o^2.ϵv^n.
(12).; ρ.; χ.—lyc.VI^3.δ.—ni-x.
V$^{10·u}$.—phy.—sep.V^1.a$\mathfrak{k}$.βa.
F.—æsc.V^7.—bry.VI^3.29.—cor^i.
V^{10}.(8).—dio.V^7.κ^5.—fer.V^7.
—jac^b.V^3–VI^3.—so-t.I^a.1.—
stn^b.VI^3.—xip^e.VI^3.$\beta\epsilon$.
T.—-lah.VI^3.σ^2ff.—nym.σ^1.—
phy.I^a.

C.—lah.VI³.σ²ff.
O.—cic.V⁷.

ζ³. *As if coryza were coming on :*
F.—cvlʰ.V¹.

ηœᶜ. *Dejected expression :*
P.—mo-aᶜ.Iᵃ.aq.ηaa,hh.ψv.

ηb. *Coldness of face :*
B.—rhoᶠᵇ.V⁶.

ηcᵃ. *Livid complexion :*
GEN.—mo-a.

ηcᵇ. *Pale face :*
GEN.—cth.V⁷.βa.ν¹.ρ.χ³.ω².
F.—acoᵈ.III¹-V¹.a¹tᵃ.ηii.51.111.
(98.114).—amb.V¹⁰·ᵘ.p.δ.4.
T.—aco.V³.δP².η.ηp,aa.σhhb.rυ.
ρ¹.ω³·⁸.φ.66.
C.—amb.V¹⁰·ᵘ.δ.3.4.; VI⁴.r¹lb.
O.—hdrᶜ.V⁷.p.q.(8.12).

ηcᵈ. *Yellow complexion :*
GEN.—lch.II¹.κ³.χ¹ ³.—vp-r.aꬶⁱ,q.
δaᵇ.ηaa.θ³.κ³.μ¹.ν¹.ρ.σ¹.φ.χ².ω³.

ηp. *Hot face :*
GEN.—aga.V¹.κ³.—alm.ρ¹.φ².82.
ang.—ara.δ.—bel.Iᵃ.δɛ,Lii.—
bry.VIII³.—c-ph.p.aꬴ,u.—
cnc.δ.δP².ηaa,ii.χ³.—ch-s.VII¹.
z.βa.ɛꬴ.—cop.d.—ind.ηaa.—
kre.VI⁴.aꬶ,u.θ¹.φ¹.χ².ω².3-99.
—lo-i.V¹.βɛ.5.66.; VII⁵.5.—
lyc.VIII⁵.—na-m.VIII⁴.p.
κ⁵·⁶.—nx-v.VI⁴.χ¹.—ptv.ρ.—
sul.V¹².—trn.p.δp.—til.—
vi-t.V¹–VI⁴.κ³.
F.—ang.V¹.5.—arn.VI³.κ³.**50**.
—cld.V⁷.af.δ.65.—ch-sᵇ.VII¹.
d.a¹tᵇ,ꬴᵇ.βa,ɛ.δtᶜ.ɛa,ꬴ.κ²·³·⁵·⁷.λ².
ρ.φ².χ³.ω².—equ.V⁷.ηaa.—ign.
VI⁴.ηaa.rp.24.(17).——kre.
VIII⁴.κ.ω².3-99.—lyc.; ηaa.5.;
VIII⁴.ηaa.4.—men.II¹–VI³.
—merᵇ.VI³·⁴.p.r¹b.χ¹.19.—
pla.V¹⁰·ˢ.q.δꬴ,ɛ;ηaa.κ³.υ².ρ.5.26.
29.—ptl.VI⁴.aꭆ.—rn-bᶠ.r¹υ¹.
16.(18.31).—rutᵃ.V⁷.κ⁵.—til.
VI³.p.
T.—aco.V³.δP².η.ηcᵇ,aa.ρ¹.σhhb.
ω³·⁸.φ.66.—alo.V¹⁰·ˢ.δοᵈ.—
ca-cᵇ.III³-V⁶.—canᵃ.VIII⁴·ᶻᶻ.
p.ηaa.κ⁵.—equ.V¹⁰.3.; ᵇ.VI³.
ηaa.—glo.V¹⁰–VIII².ηaa.19.
28.29.31.—mez.VI³.

C.—epn.VI³.v.φ.ω².—sto.VII¹.
p.aꬶ,ꬶ.ηaa.φ.5.
P.—fl-xᵃ.V¹·¹⁰·ᵗ.θ¹.5.86.
O.—ignᵍ.VI⁴.ηaa.r¹p.24.(17).

ηaa. *Red face :*
GEN.—alm.V².—ast.VIII⁴.p.q.
—cac.VIII⁴.—cnc.δ.δP².ηp,ii.
χ³.—car.VIII¹.29.33.—hfb.
—ind.ηp.—idm.V⁷.κ⁵.φ.χ¹.66.;
VIII⁴.p.4.—klm.—mg-s.III.
p.—mo-a.VIII⁴.; δs.—nx-j.
χ².v.—so-n.Iᵃ.—vp-r.aꬶⁱ,q.
δaᵇ.ηcᵈ.θ³.κ³.μ¹.ν¹.ρ.σ¹.φ.χ².ω³.
F.—belᵉ.δaa.—bovᵍ.VI³.66.—
equ.V⁷.ηp.—glo.V¹⁰·ᵛ.aꬶ.χ³.—
ign.VI⁴.ηp.rp.24.(17).—lyc.
ηp.5.—pla.V¹⁰·ˢ.q.δꬴ,ɛ.ηp.κ³.υ².
ρ.5.26.29.—thu.VIII³.3.
T.—aco.V².δP².η.ηcᵇ.,p.ρ¹.σhhb.
ω³·⁸.φ.66.—canᵃ.VIII⁴·ᶻᶻ.p.ηp.
κ⁵.—equᵇ.VI³.ηp.—glo.VIII⁴.;
V¹⁰–VIII².ηp.19.28.29.31.
C.—sto.VII¹.p.aꬶ,ꬶ.ηp.φ.5.
P.—mo-aᶜ.Iᵃ.aq.ηœᶜ,hh.ψv.
O.—car.VIII⁴.29.33.—ignᵍ.VI⁴.
ηp.r¹p.24.(17).—pho.V⁷.χ.
Ba.—la-x.ω.35.(12).

ηhh. *Sweat of face :*
P.—mo-aᶜ.Iᵃ.aq.ηœᶜ,aa.ψv.

ηii. *Swelling of face :*
GEN.—cnc.δ.δP².ηp,aa.χ³.—lah.
VI³.δ.ζ.**5**.
F.—acoᵈ.III¹-V¹.a¹tᵃ.ηcᵇ.51.111.
(98.114).
T.—ca-c.VI⁴.δO.η.1.—lah.VI³.
δ.δii.θ⁴.**5**.
O.—ail.βa.—k-bi.V¹.θ¹.3-99.

η. *Pain in face :*
GEN.—acn.44.—ac-c.34.—bry.
V⁶-VIII³.θ⁴.3-30.—ca-c.V³·¹⁰.
ηp.δ.ζ.θ¹.ω³.—cb-a.VI⁴-VIII⁴.
δO.ɛ.θ⁴.66.(12).—cin.V¹-VI⁴.
1.—c-ar.5.—eub.V¹².θ¹.—
grp.σ².—irs.V⁷.ν¹.—k-cl.VI¹.
kre.VI⁴.δ.—mr-f.V⁷.; V⁷ζ.5.;
VI².—pet.V¹.θ¹.—pho.V⁷.
βa.θ².ω².28.(16).—spo.VI⁴-
VIII³·⁴.σ².—sti.V⁷-VI³.θ⁴.—
til.VI⁴.ɛ.—ton.V¹-VI³·⁴.au.5.
6.
F.—amb.VI⁴.—am-m.VI⁴.19.

83.—ag-n.VI⁴.δ.δaᵇ,aa,ε.;V³.–VI³.—ber.VI⁴.—cleᵃ.V¹·³.—crtᵃ.V¹.δr.θ¹.ʋl.5.—cycᵃ.VI³.–VIII³.35.—dro.V¹⁰ ˢ.—elc.VI⁴.θ¹.—evoᵇ.V⁶.—glo.II¹–III¹.aˡbˢ.βε.δ.—hæmᵇ.θ¹.—ign.V¹.—ipc.VI⁴·ᵃ.—klm.—lyc.V¹⁰·ˢ.ᵣ.—mr-i.V¹⁰–VI³.δl.ι.—mscʰ.V¹.ζ.—osmᵉ.δε.ε.—rutᵃ·¹.V⁷.—sul.V¹.ζ.; V³·¹⁰·ˢ.—tax.δ.δε.—thu.V¹⁰·ˢ.χ¹.3.(8-31).—thuᵃ.VI⁴.δ.ζ.3.5.—urtᵃ.V⁷.

T.—aco.V³.δP².ηcᵇ,p,aa.ρ¹.σhhb.τʋ.ω³·⁸.φ.66.—am-mᵃ.VI⁴.19.83.—ag-nᵃ.VI⁴.—berᵃ.VI⁴·ᵇ.—ca-c.VI⁴.δO.ηii.1.—cleᵃ.V¹·³.**5**.—crtᵇ.V¹.θ¹.ʋl.5.—k-caᵇ.VI³·⁴.—kreᵇ.V⁶–VI⁴.θ¹.—lchᵃ.VI⁴.—lauᵇ.VI⁴.θ¹.—lilᵇ.19.(35).—mt-nᵃ.V³·⁶.—sng.V⁶–VI⁴.—tarᵃ.V⁶.θ⁴.—tilᵇ.V⁶.—vinᵇ.VI³.

C.—er-aᶜ.VI³.—hur.V¹⁶.θ¹.4.31.—pho.VI⁴·ᵃ.4.19.—sti.VI³.βε.θ⁴.—thu.VI².θ⁴.χ¹.3.(8-31).—til.V⁶.

P.—agaᵈ.V¹–VI⁴.βε.—anaᶜ.VI⁴.εᴅ.σ².—ag-nᵈ.V³–VI³.—arsᵈ.Iᵃ.17.(19).—belᶜ.V³–VIII⁴.35.—ca-cᶜ.V⁶.θ¹.—cb-v.θ¹.χ¹.—croᵈ.VIII⁴.—cu-aᵈ.V⁶.ε.σ².—k-biᶜ.VI³.ε.—mn-o.VI⁴.—trnᶜ.V¹.aᶃ.κ⁴.—vrbᵈ.V⁷.

O.—cchᶜ.δl.3.—nit.IIIᵃ.ff.aᶃ.ι.π.σ².ᵣ.4.

B.—cauᵗ·ᴾ.VI³.ʋ.—chd.ᵗᵃ·ᵒ.VI⁴.—c-arᵖᵇ.II⁵.—guifᵇ.VI⁴.—lab.V⁶–VIII³.θ⁴.—tepᵗᵃ.II¹.εCr.

η. *Pain in masseter muscle* :
O.—glo.VI³·⁴.

η. *Pain in zygoma* :
B.—cb-aᵗ.V³.

θj. *Dry mouth* :
F.—naj.III¹·ʷ.ʋ¹b.; ᵉ.V¹.q.κ⁵.
T.—dio.III³.κ⁵.χ¹.3.

θj. *Dry lips* :
GEN.—cod.V⁷.—nx-v.χ¹·².ω³.83.
F.—idmᵉ.V¹⁰.κ³.r¹p.—rhs.VII¹.p.q.κ³.6.100.(**10.16**).

P.—zizᶜ.σ.σ².

θ. *Sticking lips* :
GEN.—mr-i.

θp. *Heat of mouth* :
F.—cb-v.II¹.δ.

θʋ. *Itching of lips* :
F.—r-vn.ʋʋ.

θ. *Burning in mouth* :
F.—k-hy.II¹.δ.ζ.1.

θ. *Pain in palate* :
C.—na-m.VI³.

θ¹n. *Grinding of teeth* :
T.—crtᵇ.V¹.βeᶜ.

θ¹nᵃ. *Clenching of teeth* :
GEN.—ag-n.3-99.

θ¹nᶜ. *Chattering of teeth* :
GEN.—cad.
P.—cb-vᶜ.η.χ¹.

θ¹. *Toothache* :
GEN.—ag-n.—ath.V¹.x.—ca-c.V³·¹⁰.aᴾ.δ.ζ.η.ω³.—cau.V¹.ε.—cro.δ.δo.—eub.V¹².η.—hur.VI³.ε.—kre.VI⁴.aᵏ,u.ηp.φ¹.χ².ω².3-99.—mez.V¹–VIII⁴.ζ.26.—pet.V⁷.η.—str.δε.—ton.(69).
F.—bor.l.el.5.—bro.VI³.θ⁴.—bryᶠ.V⁶·¹⁰.; VI³–VIII³.—crtᵃ.V¹.δr.ηr.ʋl.5.—elc.VI⁴.η.—hæmᵇ.η.—idmᵍ.βa.κ⁵.λ¹.—klm.V¹.—lcpᵒ.—mez.V¹–VIII⁴.ζ.26.—psoᵈ.III².q.3.—sanᵃ.ε.3-99.—sul.V¹–VI⁴.116.
T.—cthᵃ.V¹⁰·ˢ.—cb-v.VI⁴.—casᵇ.VIII³.83.—con.V⁶.68.—crtᵇ.V¹.ηr.ʋl.5.—cycᵃ.V³.r¹r.—kreᵇ.V⁶–VI⁴.ηl.; ᵃ.VI³·⁴.—lchᵇ.VI⁴.—lauᵇ.VI⁴.η.—lo-i.V¹⁰.—magᵇ.VI⁴·ᵃ·ᵛ.—na-mᵃ.IV¹.—sarᵃ.VI³.—vrbᵃ.V⁷–VI³·q.12.63.
C.—belᵃ.V¹·⁸.ε.—hur.V¹⁶.θ¹.η.4.31.—kre.VIII⁴.βε.
P.—crtᵈ.III³.V¹·²·⁶–VII⁵.δO.—digᵇ.VI³–VII⁵.29.(30).—fl-xᵈ.VI·¹⁰·ᵗ.ηp.5.86.—iodᵈ.V⁶.—lilᶜ.IX.—mrlᵈ.VI⁴.—rhsᵈ.II³.—sbdᶜ.V¹.—sepᵇ.V¹·q.—sulᶜ.II¹–VI⁴.116.—zinᶜ.VI⁴.4.
O.—k-bi.V¹.ηii.3-99.—lcp.—

mez^e.V^1–VIII^4.ζ.26.——msc.
V^6.e.—pru^c.II^3–V^1.—rhs.II^3.
—ton^b.V^6.zz.
B.—ni-x^{pb}.V$^{1.6}$.$ε$Ml.

$θ^1$ii. *Swelling of gums:*
C.—hur.V^{16}.η.$θ^1$.4.31.

$θ^1$. *Pain in gums:*
T.—dph.VIII^4.II^3.11.

$θ^2$. *Pain in parotid gland:*
GEN.—k-bi.V^1.e.
T.—bry.2.
O.—sbd^d.V^3.$θ^4$.

6^2. *Flow of saliva:*
GEN.--pho.V^7.βa.δθ.η.ω^2.28.(16).
F.—opi.V^1.βb,e.κ.κ$^{1.5.9}$.4.66.(5).
—sep.V^1.δ.κ^5.
T.—idm^a.δre.ζo.
P.—hpm^c.V^1.βa.δ.κ^1.29.35.
B.—k-bi^{fb}.$θ^4$.3.

$θ^3$j. *Dry tongue:*
GEN.—trn.af.a^{l}c^a.κ^3.

$θ^3$. *Dry, slimy tongue:*
F.—ca-c.V^7.βe.3-99.

$θ^3$. *Moist, white tongue, with red edges:*
GEN.——vp-r.ak^i,q.δa^b.ηc^d,aa.κ^3. μ^1.ν^1.ρ.σ^1.φ.χ^2.ω^3.

$θ^3$. *White tongue:*
F.—mo-a^a.δP^2.κ.σhhb.ω^3.

$θ^3$. *Furred tongue:*
GEN.—ail.V^7.κ.κ^1.rjj.3-99.--jug. 3-99.

$θ^3$. *Pain in tongue:*
GEN.—ipc.V^2.κ^5.

$θ^3$. *Biting the tongue:*
GEN.—aga.VIII^1.ω^{10}.3-10.

$θ^4$x. *Numbness of jaw:*
GEN.—hur.III^3.
F.—hur^e.III^3.

$θ^4$. *Pain in jaws:*
GEN.—ara.V^6.—bry.V^6–VIII^3. η.3-30.—cb-a.VI^4–VIII^4.δO. e.η.66.(12).—gel.III^1.—hur. III^1.e.—hfb.au.r^{1}x.—na-m. V^6–VI^1.δ.4.8.——nx-v.VI^4.ζ. 31.—sti.V^7–VI^3.η.—sul.VI$^{3.4}$. e.η.; VI^3.2.(12).; V^6–VII^1. —val.V^{10}.δ.5.—vp-t.λ.ω^5.
F.——bro.V$^{10.t}$.p.VIII^4.——epn. V^3.δ.δe.—gel^i.VI^3.δ.——mez. III^3.δ.

T.—lah.VI^3.δ.δii.ζ.ηii.5.—mr-i. —mez.III^3.δ.—snc^b.VI^3.δl.
C.—con.III^3–V^{10}.π.π^1.
P.—bry^c.V$^{1.3}$.——ca-c^c.V^6.η.— cim^c.VI^3.r.89.
O.—k-cl.5.—ni-x^i.VI^3.
B.—gel^p.VI^3.

$θ^4$. *Pain in upper jaw:*
F.—aco^e.V^1–VI^3.κ^5.—kre^i.V^6.4. —sul^f.V^6–VII^1.
T.——chi.VIII^3.——kre.V^6–VI^3. βa.—tar^a.V^6.η.
C.—sto.VII^5.5.—thu.VI^2.η.χ^1. 3.(8-31).
B.—k-bi^{fb}.$θ^2$.3.

$θ^4$. *Pain in lower jaw:*
F.—bro.VI^3.$θ^1$.—cth.VI^4.e.
T.—aru^a.—dio^b.4.—hur.I^a.— ind^a.VI^4.r^1.—man.VI^1.v.88. —ox-x^b.
C.—sti.VI^3.βe.η.--vrb.V^1–VII^5.
P.—ang^c.V$^{1.6}$.—hur^d.VI^3.δ.
O.——ba-a.V^6.er.—bov.VI^4.— pla^c.I V^1–V^6.—rn-b^c.VI$^{4.a}$.σ^2. —sbd^d.V^3.$θ^2$.—trx^d.V^1.$ε$M.— zin^f.III^3–V^6.
B.—cth^{pb}.VI^3.66.86.——ind.V^6. —lah.V^6–VIII^3.η.—par^{fb}.V^8– VI^3.

$θ^4$. *Pain in maxillary joint:*
T.—k-ca^b.VI^4.5.—mrl^b.VI$^{3.q}$.

$θ^4$. *Pain in chin:*
O.—grt^c.VI^3.

ιj. *Dry throat:*
GEN.—cca.eD.——pla.V^1.au.ι.χ^3. 2.—str.κ$^{5.6}$.
F.— aga.VII^4.ι.61.——cmf.δ.— naj.VII^5.

ιv. *Tickling in throat:*
GEN.—san.5.

ι. *Irritation of throat:*
FT.—nab.au^b.δL.ψv.

ιe. *Constriction of throat:*
GEN.—cad.
F.—ur-n^g.κ^7.ν^1.
O.—la-x.

ι. *Choking in throat:*
T.—fer.VIII^4.κ^4.84.

ι. *Dysphagia:*
O.—nit.III^a.ff.ag.η.π^1.σ^2.r.4.

Pain in throat:
GEN.—c-ph.3.—pla.V^{1}.αu.ιj.χ^{3}.2.—trn.VIII^{1}.αk.ο^{1}.π.σ^{2}.ω$^{2\cdot8}$.3-30.—ver.III^{1}.
F.—mr-i.V^{10}–VI^{8}.δl.ηl.
T.—la-x.
P.—cro^{d}.V^{7}.ε.—nit^{d}.5.—jab^{c}.V^{7}.
Ba.—mr-f.V^{7}.q.ζ.—mr-i.V^{7}.q.ζ.

ι. *Sore throat:*
F.—aga.VII^{4}.ιj.61.—pod.I^{1}.5.—trn.
T.—str^{a}.

ι. *Burning in throat:*
F.—ca-x.V^{7}.3-99.—k-hy.II^{1}.δ.ζ.θ.—lyc.II^{1}.δ.

ι. *Burning in œsophagus:*
P.—der^{d}.VI^{3}.κ^{6}.

κ. *Altered taste:*
F.—lah^{f}.VIII^{4}.αf.κ^{9}.—opi.V^{1}.βb,ε.θ^{2}.κ$^{1\cdot5\cdot9}$.4.66.(5).

κ. *Bad taste:*
GEN.—ail.V^{7}.θ^{3}.κ^{1}.τjj.3-99.—cyc.ω^{2}.

κ. *Bitter taste:*
GEN.—trn.κ^{3}.ρ.
F.—kre.VIII^{4}.ηp.ω^{2}.3-99.—mo-a^{a}.δP^{2}.θ^{2}.σhhb.ω^{3}.

κ^{1}. *Anorexia:*
GEN.—ail.θ^{3}.κ.τjj.3-99.—ant.ω^{2}.117.—bz-x.—c-ph.VIII^{4}.ξ^{4}.σ.υ.84.—con.—fer.VIII^{2}.—gym.δp.λ.—pho.V^{7}.δ.λii.φ.19.—sng.VIII^{4}.δ.ω^{4}.—stn.αu.κ^{5}.3.—str.—tab.II^{1}.g^{b}.ε.χ^{1}.
F.—ibe.κ^{5}.—na-m.VI^{3}.—pho.V^{7}.ω^{2}.
P.—eup^{d}.εd.3.—hpm^{c}.V^{1}.βa.δ.θ^{2}.29.35.
O.—na-m.V$^{3\cdot z}$.

κ^{1}. *Dislike to tobacco:*
F.—opi.V^{1}.βb,ε.θ^{2}.κ.κ$^{5\cdot9}$.4.66.(5).

κ^{2}. *Hunger:*
GEN.—lyc.χ^{3}.
F.—ch-s^{b}.VII^{1}.d.α^{1}c^{b},d^{b}.βa,ε.δt^{c}.ea,d.ηp.κ$^{3\cdot5\cdot7}$.λ^{2}.ρ.φ^{2}.χ^{3}.ω^{2}.—iod.V^{1}.x.

κ^{3}. *Thirst:*
GEN.—aga.V^{7}.ηp.—cad.—cu-a.λ.—lah.II^{1}.ηc^{d}.χ$^{1\cdot3}$.—led.VI^{4}.p.hh.δ.δs.λ^{2}.χ^{1}.—str.βa.ω^{2}.—trn.κ.ρ.; αf.α^{1}c^{a}.θ^{3}j.—vi-t.V^{1}–VI^{4}.ηp.—vp-r.αk^{1},q.δa^{b}.ηc^{d},aa.θ^{3}.μ^{1}.ν^{1}.ρ.σ^{1}.φ.χ^{2}.ω^{3}.
F.—arn.VI^{3}.ηp.50.—ch-s^{b}.VII^{1}.d.α^{1}c^{b},d^{b}.βa,ε.δt^{c}.ea,d.ηp.κ$^{2\cdot5\cdot7}$.λ^{2}.ρ.φ^{2}.χ^{3}.ω^{2}.—idm^{e}.V^{10}.θj.τ^{1}p.—lyc.VI^{4}.χ^{2}.4.—pla.V$^{10\cdot s}$.q.δb,ε.ηp,aa.ο^{2}.ρ.5.26.29.—rn-s.V$^{10\cdot t}$.χ^{1}.5.—rhs.VII^{1}.p.q.θ.6.100.(10.16).
T.—cyc.I^{a}.χ^{2}.—str.VI$^{3\cdot z}$.
O.—trn.I^{q}.

κ^{4}b. *Cold feeling in stomach:*
GEN.—pgn.4.

κ^{4}. *Weakness of stomach:*
GEN.—mim.

κ^{4}. *Craving in stomach:*
T.—k-bi^{a}.q.4.66.

κ^{4}. *Empty feeling in stomach:*
F.—ham.VII^{1}.3-30.—tax^{e}.δt^{u}.(63).

κ^{4}. *Distended stomach:*
F.—cob.—rhs^{e}.VI$^{3\cdot s}$.κ^{5}.χ^{2}.63.

κ^{4}. *Deranged stomach:*
GEN.—cep.
F.—cob.V^{7}.—k-bi^{g}.VI^{3}.3-30.35.—k-ca.V^{1}.κ^{5}.31.(20).—pl-n.I^{a}.2.—ptl.V^{7}.αk.—rs-r.V^{7}.αk.φ^{1}.

κ^{4}. *Indigestion:*
GEN.—k-hy.
O.—rs-r.V^{7}.αk.φ^{1}.

κ^{4}. *Oppression in stomach:*
GEN.—mez.I^{1}.βa.δb.
F.—trn^{c}.V^{1}.αg.ηr.

κ^{4}. *Pain in stomach:*
GEN.—am-c.αu.1.—aps.V^{1}.i^{a}.—arg.III.βa.κ^{5}.χ$^{2\cdot3}$.18.43.—ars.—bz-x.—cas.κ^{5}.40.66.—glo.κ^{5}.—ham.—k-cy.—man.V^{1}.w.26.—ptl.VI^{3}.βa.—rs-r.κ$^{5\cdot6}$.—sul.βa.εd.κ^{5}.τυkk,nn.ω$^{2\cdot9}$.
F.—bis.βa.κ^{7}.ρ.χ^{2}.5.35.—ham.—lyc.4.128.—san.VIII^{1}.χ^{1}.
T.—lth^{b}.δOl.(63).—naj^{e}.VI^{3}.κ^{5}.(8).—phy.V^{1}.
C.—cob.30.—fer.VIII^{4}.ι.84.
P.—ind^{c}.VI^{3}.4.19.29.(30).—ver^{b}.V^{1}.
O.—cle.hh.βa.κ^{5}.4.—mo-a.II$^{1\cdot a}$.λv.τv.υ.—pi-m.III.π.

κ^5. *Nausea* :

GEN.—ail.βa.—aln.2-99.—alm. VI^3.—am-c.3-**10**.—ant.V^7.65. —arg.III.βa.κ^4.$\chi^{2\cdot3}$.18.43.— arn.VI^3–VIII^3.ρ.29.——ars. VIII^4.30.—asr.$\beta\epsilon^a$.41.—bz-x. —bor.ω^8.3.—buf.vb.ω^2.—cad. —ca-c.—ca-x.—cas.κ^4.40.66. —cau.—cit.—cob.ω^2.**5**.—coc. —con.κ^6.—cun.ν^1.3.—cup.— cyc.—dig.—fer.VIII$^{2\cdot4}$.— fl-x.βa.—for.—gel.5.(26).— glo.; μ^2.; κ^4.; II^5.—grp.κ^7. 83.——grt.4.——hep.V^3.3-**10**. (12).——hpm.III.(19.20.31. 35).—idm.χ.66.; V^7.ηaa.φ. χ^1.66.—ipc.V^2.θ^2.—k-bi.(72). —k-ca.V^1–VIII^4.κ^6.σ^2.11.— klm.—lah.V^7.; V^1.; V^1.29. 31.—mr-i.4.—mo-a.69.—msc. κ^6.—na-m.3-5.; κ^6.ω^3.30.31.; VIII^4.p.ηp.κ^6.——nx-m.κ^6.— nx-v.VI^3.κ^6.66.(5-16).—ped. βa.**5**.; 31.—pet.V^1–VI^3.— pho.βa.16.; 2.; V^7.θ^2.κ^7.—phs. κ^7.28.29.—phy.; (66).—rs-r.; 4.; $\kappa^{4\cdot6}$.—ptl.VII^1.; I^e.βa.λ. —san.σ^2.$\tau\nu$.; $\chi^{1\cdot2}$.—sar.VIII^4. κ^6.2.—sep.3.—sil.V^1.δ.χ^1.ω^2. —sin.V^7.—stn.αu.κ^1.3.—str. ιj.κ^6.——sul.; βa.κ^4.$\tau\nu$kk,nn. $\omega^{2\cdot9}$.—tan.βa.; 38.—trn.$a\beta^t$. o^1.ρ.—ter.V^1.—ver.λ.σ.; VI^3. 3.83.(5).—ziz.κ^6.51.111.(16).

F.—aco^e.V^1–VI^3.θ^4.—alo.V^7. δq.—alm^e.VI^3.ν^3.ω^2.3-99.— ag-m.V^1.3-99.(8.89).——arn. VI^3-VIII^3.ρ.29.—ars.VIII$^{4\cdot a}$. 30.—bor.VIII^3.δ.4.——bra.φ. 8-31.(12).——cam.V^7.—ch-s^b. VII^1.d.$a^l c^b$,$\mathfrak{v}^b$.βa,ϵ.δt^c.ϵa,$\mathfrak{v}$.ηp. $\kappa^{2\cdot3\cdot7}$.λ^3.ρ.φ^2.χ^3.ω^2.— cit.VII^1. 51.—ccs.26.28.——cro.V^6.— crt.V^1.; ^{e}.V^1.βa.; ^{e}.βa.κ^6.μ^1.(8- 31).—cyc.V^7.κ^7.—dig.V^7.3- 99.—dio.V^7.ζ^3.——dul.VI$^{3\cdot a\cdot q}$. —fag.d.(75).——for.—gas.V^1. —glo.—hæm.29.——ibe.κ^1.— ign^h.V^1.—idm.V^7.φ.; ^{g}.βa.θ^1.λ^1. —irs.V^7.q.κ^6.ω^2.—k-ca.V^1.κ^4.31. (20).—la-x.VI$^{3\cdot w}$.—lth^b.V^{10}.

lyc^e.VII^1.$\tau\nu$kk.; I^1.ω^2.—mag. V^6.——mr-i.I^a.5.—naj^e.—nat. V^6.βa.δo.κ^7.—nx-v.VI^4.δ.o^2.π. —ol-m.—opi.V^1.$\beta\mathfrak{b}$,ϱ.θ^2.κ.$\kappa^{1\cdot9}$. 4.66.(5).—pho.II^1.—phy^e.— rhs^e.VI$^{3\cdot s}$.κ^4.χ^2.63.—rut^a.V^7. ηp.—sng.V^1.δ.ρ.3.7.19.(8.14). —sep.V^1.δ.θ^2.; VI^2.31.; VI^3. (16).—stn.II^1.p.—trx.V^7.$a\mathfrak{v}^a$. 19.43.(8).

T.—can^a.VIII$^{4\cdot zz}$.p.ηp,aa.—— cau.V$^{10\cdot s}$.κ^6.—cob^b.μ^3.ω^2.3.— dio.III^3.θj.χ^1.3.—gel^a.V^1.βa. δo.——glo^b.V$^{1\cdot10\cdot s}$.μ^2.σ^1.5-**10**. (66).; VI^3.βa.; VIII^4.33.— lth.V^{10}.βf.$\delta\mathfrak{b}$.3.16.49.(8.19).— mr-f^a.V^7.—naj^c.VI^3.κ^4.(8).— na-a.V$^{3\cdot t}$.p.12.65.101.—ni-x^a. VIII^4.3-99.——nx-v^b.VI$^{3\cdot a}$.κ^6. 5.(16).—ptl.VI^3.—ziz^c.I^a.

C.—aln.V^{10}.$\chi^{1\cdot2}$.—elp.IX.— mr-f.V^7.βa.——nx-m.—nx-v. VI^4.δ.o^2.ω^2.—trn.

P.——cap^b.V^1–VI^3.ab^o.24.29.**50**. —k-ca^b.ω^2.5.

O.—ce-b.V$^{10\cdot u}$.—cle.hh.βa.κ^4.4. con.VI^4.δO.σ^2.—msc.VIII^4.βa. σ.—nat.V^7.βa.δo.κ^5.σ^2.—ol-m. —pho^c.V$^{1\cdot b}$.p.ρ.

Ba.—ptl.V^1.

B.—k-bi$^{tb\cdot c\cdot pb}$.V^1–VIII$^{4\cdot d}$.κ^6.

κ^6. *Vomiting* :

GEN.—æth.$a^l\mathfrak{v}$.βa.χ^2.5.—cad.— con.κ^5.—dul.ab.χ^1.——grp.μ^3. χ^3.ω^3.3-99.——k-ca.V^1–VIII^4. κ^5.σ^2.11.—lah.——msc.κ^5.— na-m.κ^5.ω^3.30.31.; VIII^4.p.ηp. κ^5.—nx-m.κ^5.——ol-m.κ^7.**5**.— rs-r.$\kappa^{4\cdot5}$.——snt.—str.ιj.κ^5.— vp-t.ω^5.

F.——crt.I^a.—irs.V^7.q.$\iota\kappa^5$.ω^2.— pho^h.VIII$^{3\cdot4}$.δ.ζ.3.——tep. VI$^{3\cdot w}$.βa.—ve-v.I^a.

T.—cau.V$^{10\cdot s}$.κ^5.

P.—grp^b.3.(30).

O.—bra.φ.8-31.(12).

B.—k-bi$^{tb\cdot c\cdot pb}$.V^1–VIII$^{4\cdot d}$.κ^5.

—— *sour* :

GEN.—nx-v.VI^3.κ^5.66.(5-**16**).— sar.VIII^4.κ^5.2.

F.—opi.V^9–VI^4.κ^7.χ^3.

T.—nx-v^b.VI$^{3\cdot a}$.κ^5.5.(16).
—— bitter :
GEN.—san.VIII^4.
—— bilious :
GEN.—ziz.κ^5.51.111.(16).
F.—crt^e.βa.κ^5.μ^1.(8-31).
—— of mucus :
P.—der^d.VI^3.ι.
—— of green mucus :
GEN.—ver.
—— of yellow, bitter mucus :
GEN.—for.πl.3-99.—glo.
—— of mucus and acid :
F.—k-ca.V$^{1\cdot 10}$.
κ^7. Eructation :
GEN.——ag-n.χ^1.——grp.κ^5.83.—
lyc.VIII^1.—ol-m.κ^6.5.— pho.
V^7.κ^5.θ^2.—pso.V^7.——sil.VI^4–
VIII^4.
F.——bis.βε.κ^4.ρ.χ^2.5.35.——cb-v.
VIII^4.p.66.——ch-s^b.VII^1.d.
a^{1}ζ^b,ᴅ^b.βa,ε.δt^c.εa,ᴅ.ηp.κ$^{2\cdot 3\cdot 5}$.λ^2.
ρ.φ^2.χ^3.ω^2.——cyc.V^7.κ^5.——iod.
V^3.ω^2.—lyc.—nat.V^6.βa.δσ.κ^5.
—opi.V^9–VI^4.κ^6.χ^3.—ur-n^g.ι.
ν^1.
T.—ca-c.V^1.3-99.—ni-x^a.V$^{1\cdot a}$.λ.
χ^1.3-30.
P.—ca-c^b.
O.—cb-v.V^7.66.—nat.V^7.βa.δo.
κ^5.σ^2.
—— bitter :
GEN.—phs.κ^5.28.29.
κ^8. Hiccough :
GEN.—cch.
κ^9. Water-brash :
F.——lah^f.VIII^4.af.κ.——opi.V^1.
βᴅ,ε.θ^2.κ.κ$^{1\cdot 5}$.4.66.(5).
κ^{10}. Retching :
GEN.—bz-x.
T.—ind^a.βa.66.
λp. Heat of belly :
GEN.—trn.aa,ᴋ.r^1.
λs. Inflammation of bowels :
F.—csn.V^7.
λv. Itching in linea alba :
O.—mo-a.II$^{1\cdot a}$.κ^4.rv.ν.
λii. Swelling of abdomen :
GEN.—nit.μ^2.χ^1.3-99.—pho.V^7.
δ.κ^1.19.—str.

λ. Sinking in umbilicus :
T.—ni-x^a.V$^{1\cdot a}$.κ^7.λ.χ^1.3-30.
λ. Pain in abdomen :
GEN.——aco.εᴅ.ζ^3.3.——ail.75.—
bis.—cu-a.κ^3.; π.—dig.χ^2.ν.—
dio.V^7.—gym.κ^1. ; δp.κ^9.—irs.
—lah.—lyc.V^1.3-99.—mrl.ξ^3.
84.—mer.σ.——naj.V^7.—ni-x.
ξ^3.83.——pho.VI^4.19.—ptl.I^e.
βa.κ^5.——rs-r.——ter.V^7.——ver.
κ^5.σ.——vp-t.θ^4.ω^5.——zin.δ.5.16.;
VI$^{3\cdot 4}$.ω^9.63.66.
F.——col^b.μ^3.——hep^1.V^2.3-99.48.
—hdr.V^7.q.σ^1.—ind.—lpt.—
trn.VI^3.——ve-v.V^6.——zin^g.
VI$^{3\cdot 4}$.
T.—lah.VIII^4.82.——ni-x^a.V$^{1\cdot a}$.
κ^7.λ.χ^1.3-30.
P.—cch^d.I^a.4.(66).——eup^d.VI^3.
p.—ol-a^d.VI^3.ξ^2.σ.2 84.(30).
O.—alo.II^5-VI^3-VIII^4.2-10.29.
—ced.VI^3.ν.
λ. Pain in pelvis :
GEN.—str.
λ. Pain in spleen :
GEN.—urt.V^7.
F.—bor$^{e\cdot h}$.V^1-V^6.σ^2.29.43.44.—
cnb^f.VI^3.
λ^1. Pain in liver :
GEN.—trn.p.χ$^{1\cdot 2}$.3-99.
F.—idm^g.βa.θ^1.κ^5.
λ^2. Flatulence :
GEN.——c-ph.——cb-v.V^1.——led.
VI^4.p.hh.δ.δs.κ^3.χ^1.
F.—ch-s^b.VII^1.d.a^{1}ζ^d,ᴅ^h.βa,ε.δt^c.
εa,ᴅ.ηp.κ$^{2\cdot 3\cdot 5\cdot 7}$.ρ.φ^2.χ^3.ω^2.—fer.
V^1.2-99.—naj.VI^3.
B.—rum^f.VI^3.8.
—— fetid flatus :
GEN.—glo.χ^2.3.
μ^1. Constipation :
GEN.—lah.; VII^5.(8).; VII^5.εᴅ.
ζ^3.o^3.(12).——vp-r.aᴋ^i,q.δa^b.ηc^d,
aa.θ^3.κ^3.ν^1.ρ.σ^1.φ.χ^2.ω^3.
F.—crt^e.βa.κ$^{5\cdot 6}$.(8-31).
μ^2. Diarrhœa :
GEN.—con.3-99.——glo.κ^5.—grp.
κ^6.χ^3.ω^3.3-99.—nit.λii.χ^1.3-99.
F.—aga.III^n.
T.——glo^b.V$^{1\cdot 10\cdot s}$.κ^5.σ^1.5-10.(66).
—str^a.VIII^4.

P.—idm^c.

μ^3. *Urging to stool :*
GEN.—cca.ν^1b.4.
F.—col^b.λ.
T.—cob^b.κ^5.ω^2.3.

μ^6. *Pain in anus like piles :*
P.—mr-i^d.V^7.

ν. *Pressure in bladder :*
GEN.—dig.λ.χ^2.

ν^1. *Diuresis :*
GEN.—cth.V^7.βa.ηc^b.ρ.χ^3.ω^2.——
irs.V^7.η.——ver.——vp-r.ak^i,q.
δa^b.ηc^d,aa.θ^3.κ^3.μ^1.ρ.σ^1.ϕ.χ^2.ω^3..
F.—ur-n^g.ι.κ^7.

ν^1. *Scalding urine :*
GEN.—jug.

ν^1. *Thick urine :*
GEN.—cun.κ^5.3.

ν^3. *Pain in kidneys :*
F.—alm^e.VI^3.κ.ω^2.3-99.

ξ. *Lasciviousness :*
T.—ori.

ξ. *Pain in genitals :*
C.—bor^b.VI$^{3 \cdot b}$.

ξ^1. *Erections :*
O.—ox-x.V^1.3-99.

ξ^2. *Pain in womb :*
GEN.—mel.π.(**55**).—-trn.III^1-
VI^3.

ξ^3. *Menses too soon :*
GEN.—cb-a.82.—gn-c.VII^1.i^a.
ϕ^1.35.83.(20).
P.—ol-a^d.VI^3.λ.σ.2.84.(30).

ξ^3. *Menses too soon and scanty :*
GEN.—alm.82.83.—na-m.VII^1.
29.83.89.90.

ξ^3. *Menses too early, too profuse, and painful :*
C.—lau.VI^4.2.83.(3).

ξ^3. *Menses retarded and profuse :*
GEN.—ni-x.λ.83.

ξ^3. *Menses profuse :*
GEN.—mag.5.83.
F.—san^a.δ.83.
P.—san^c.V$^{10 \cdot s}$.δ.83.

ξ^3. *Menses scanty :*
GEN.—mrl.λ.84.

ξ^3. *Menses irregular and watery :*
GEN.—ber.VI$^{3 \cdot 4}$.ω^2.83.

ξ^4. *Leucorrhœa :*
GEN.—c-ph.VIII^4.κ^1.σ.ν.84.

o. *Pain in larynx :*
T.—osm.o^2.

o^1. *Cough :*
GEN.—alm.χ^2.4.—-lah.VII^5.—-
trn.ak^f.κ^5.ρ.;   VIII^1.ak.ι.π.σ^2.
$\omega^{2 \cdot 8}$.3-30.
—— *alternating with :*
GEN.—lah.

o^2. *Slow speech :*
F.—cn-i.V^1.

o^2. *Difficulty of speaking :*
GEN.—aco.VI^3-VIII^4.
F.—ph-x.V$^{1 \cdot a}$.a^{1}v.δb.3-99.35.—
pla.V$^{10 \cdot a}$.q.δb,ι.ηp,aa.κ^3.ρ.5.26.
29.

o^2. *Weakness of voice :*
F.C.—nx-v.VI^4.δ.κ^3.π.

o^2. *Low voice :*
F.—bel^e.V$^{10 \cdot s}$.δb,P^1.

o^2. *Hoarseness :*
T.—osm.o.

o^3. *Sneezing :*
GEN.—-ag-n.V^1.δ.—-glv.V^1.—-
lah.VII^5.ϵv.ζ^3.μ^1.(12).
F.—arn^a.V^1.ϵ.—-sul^e.ζ.3.

o^3. *Ineffectual efforts to sneeze :*
F.—zin.VI$^{3 \cdot 4}$.**5**.

π. *Oppression of chest :*
GEN.—ail.V^7.—-crt.III.—-mel.
ξ^2.(**55**).-trn.ak.ρ^1.$\chi^{2 \cdot 3}$.; VIII^1.
ak.ι.$o^1$$\sigma^2$.$\omega^{2 \cdot 8}$.3-30. ; π^1.ρ^1.ω^2.
F.—ca-x.

π. *Constriction of chest :*
C.—sep.III.1.

π. *Sinking of chest :*
F.—nx-v.VI^4.δ.κ^5.o^2.

π. *Pain in chest :*
GEN.—cu-a.λ.—fag.V^7.4.—for.
κ^6.3-99.—-jab.V^1.ag.π^1.ρ.ρ^1.—-
mr-i.V^1.—na-m.VI^3.σ^2.—-sto.
VII^5.σ^1.ν^1.—-trn.V$^{1 \cdot 2}$.—-tep.
V^1.π^1.
F.—aln^e.3.—-cha.VI$^{3 \cdot 4}$.—-ch-x.
VIII^4.i^a.νb.—hdr.I^a.3.—-hfb^e.
VI$^{3 \cdot a}$.5.—jab.VIII^4.ρ.—-k-ca.
VI$^{3 \cdot a}$.$\tau$$\nu$b.1.——lch.$\zeta$.$\tau$.$\chi^2$.—-
rn-b.V^{10}.δ.3-**10**.(30).
T.—lth.V$^{10 \cdot t}$.5.
C.—con.III^3-V$^{10 \cdot a}$.θ^4.π^1.--opi^b.
V^1.σ.

P.—æth.VIII³.—-gym^d.*r*.*v*.—-
  k-ca^d.VI³·ᵃ.*r*υb.
O.—epn.V⁶-VI³.σ².—-grp^h.III¹.
  V².30.σ.——ind^c.VI³.*r*.—-jab^h.
  V⁷·ᶻᶻ.ρ¹.ω².—-pi-m.III.κ⁴.

π¹. *Dyspnœa :*
  Gᴇɴ.——ars.VIII².ρ.——-cac.——
  cb-v.VIII⁴.5.— glo.—jab.V⁷.
  aᶢ.π.ρ.ρ¹.——-trn.π.ρ.ω².—-tep.
  V¹.π.
  T.—rn-b.V¹·⁶.aᶢ.5.31.
  C.— con.III³–V¹⁰·ᵃ.θ⁴.π.
  O.—ni-x^c.VI³·ᵃ.63.–-nit.III³.ff.
  aᶢ.η.ι.σ².*r*.4.

ρ. *Slow pulse :*
  Gᴇɴ.—cth.V⁷.βa.ηc^b.ν¹.χ³.ω².—
  ch-s.V⁷.aᶢ.ε.χ³.ω².—phs.iᵃ.*r*x.
  ω³.
  F.—lau.V¹.
  O.—so-n^e.V¹·¹⁰.βℓᵃ.δP¹.υ.—lyc.
  VI³.

ρ. *Quick pulse :*
  Gᴇɴ.—aˢ-ˢ.——asa.VI³.βℓ.—glo.
  —pho.V⁶.ᴀᴏ.ᴈ.βa.δtⁿ.3.(66).
  F.—asa.VI³.βℓ.——ch-s^b.VII¹.d.
  aⁱℓ^b,ᴅ^b.βa,ℓ.δt^c.ℓᴀ,ᴅ.ηp.κ²·³·⁵·⁷.
  λ².φ².χ³.ω².——-lau.V⁷.βℓ.——
  mo-a.Iᵃ.χ².ω².
  O.—asa.VI³·ᵇ.βℓ.——pho^c.V¹·ᵇ.p.
  κ⁵.

ρ. *Weak pulse :*
  Gᴇɴ.—ars.VIII².π¹.——ptv.ηp.
  —-vp-r.aᴋⁱ.q.δa^b.ηc^d,aa.θ³.κ³.μ¹.
  ɪ¹.σ¹.φ.χ².ω³.
  T.—aˢ-a.V¹⁶.χ¹.

ρ. *Hard pulse :*
  Gᴇɴ.—ast.d.aⁱ𝐛ˢ.βℓ^b.2-99.—-lab.
  ζ³.

ρ. *Contracted pulse :*
  F.—bis.βa.κ⁴·⁷.χ².5.35.

ρ. *Anxiety at heart :*
  F.—pla.V¹⁰·ˢ.q.δb,ℓ.ηp,aa.κ³.ᴏ².5.
  26.29.

ρ. *Sinking at heart :*
  Gᴇɴ.—arn.VI³–VIII³.ᴀ⁵.29.
  F.—arn.VI³–VIII³.κ⁵.29.

ρ. *Uneasiness at heart :*
  F.—dig.V⁷.

ρ. *Pain in heart :*
  Gᴇɴ.—hfb.—jab.V⁷.aᶢ.π.π¹.ρ¹.
  —mr-i.—trn.aᴋ^f.κ⁵.ᴏ¹. ; κ.κ³.

F.—jab.VIII⁴.π.—-lcp^m.V7.—
  mr-iᵃ.V⁷·¹⁰.5.—-sng.V¹.δ.κ⁵.3.
  7.19.(8.14).
T.—sul.VIII⁴.σ².ω⁸.

ρ. *Violent action of heart :*
  Gᴇɴ.—glo.VII⁵.
  F.—lcp.Iᵃ.
  O.—lcp.Iᵃ.

ρ. *Fluttering of heart :*
  Gᴇɴ.—for.4.

ρ¹. *Palpitation :*
  Gᴇɴ.—alm.ηp.φ².82.—-buf.—
  elc.χ.—jab.V⁷.aᶢ.π.π¹.ρ.—-trn.
  aᴋ.π.ω²·³. ; π.π¹.ω².—tar.βa.
  F.—cot.V⁷.q aⁱ𝐛ᵃ.δν,ᴏ.υb.(8).
  T.— aco.V³.δP².η.ηc^b,p,aa.ᴏhbb.
  *r*υ.ω³·⁸.φ.66.
  C.—hep.V¹.5.
  O.—cle.V¹.σ².2.——jab^h.V⁷·ᶻᶻ.π.
  ω².

σb. *Chilliness of back :*
  F.—sil.VI³.
  O.—sil.V¹.

σx. *Numbness in a band from under l.
  scapula to l. hip :*
  Gᴇɴ.—ail.σ².

σhhb. *Cold sweat on back :*
  F.—mo-aᵃ.δP².θ³.κ.ω².
  T.—-aco.V³.δP².η.ηc^b,p,aa.*r*υ.ω³·⁸.
  φ.66.

σ. *Weariness of back :*
  O.—fag.σ².

σ. *Pain in back :*
  Gᴇɴ.—ail.σ².—c-ph.VIII⁴.κ¹.ξ².
  υ.84. ; 31.—cob.——mns.VII¹.
  —mer.λ.—myr.3.—ver.κ⁵.λ. ;
  V⁶.
  F.—sbd.V¹.βa.
  C.—bz-x.III.aᶢ.——fl-xᵃ.III¹.5.
  —opi^b.V¹.π.
  P.—dph^d.VI³·ᵇ.—ol-a^d.VI³.λ.ξ².
  2.84.(30).—tri^c.—ziz^c.θ.σ².
  O.—grp^h.III¹.V².30.π.——msc.
  VIII⁴.βa.κ⁵.—opiᵍ.V⁶–VI⁴.

σ¹. *Weakness in loins :*
  T.—nym.ζ³.

σ¹. *Pain in loins :*
  Gᴇɴ.—sto.VII⁵.π.ν¹.——ver.——
  vp-r.aᴋⁱ,q.δa^b.ηc^d,aa.θ³.κ³.μ¹.ɪ¹.
  ρ.φ χ².ω³.

F.—bro.—-cas.V^1.ω^2.83.—-hdr.
   V^7.q.λ.
T.—glo^b.V$^{1.10}$ ·.κ^5.μ^2.5-10.(66).
C.—cas.V^1.υ.83.
σ^{2}d. *Pulsation of carotids :*
GEN.—cod.VIII^4.—hyo.VIII^4.
   2.(98).—so-n.βα.—tea.
F.—gn-c.V^1.
σ^{2}ff. *Stiffness of neck :*
GEN.—ap-a.—grp.VII^5.3-99.—
   mag.—nat.82.—ph-x.—san.
   κ^5.rυ.—sep.V$^{3.10}$.v.—trn.VIII^1.
   aš.ι.o^1.π.ω$^{2.8}$.3-30.
F.—am-c.VII^1.29.—ar-i.βε.5.
   26.—cau.VIII$^{4.a}$.4.—crt.VII^5.
   —grp.V^6.σ^2.
T.—-cyc^b.V^6–VIII^3.βε.—-lah.
   VI^3.ζ^3.
C.—ba-c.V^1.3-99.—lah.VI^3.ζ^3.
P.—mr-f^c.V^7.εε.
O.—ap-a.—-arg.V$^{1.6}$.—-ca-a^c.
   V$^{1.6}$.—glo.V^7.σ^2.26.28.—k-ra.
   V^6.σ^2.—-mu-x^d.V^6–VI^3.—-
   na-m.VIII^4.q.—-nit.V^6–VI^4.
   —spi.I^a.3.(30).—tea^h.VII$^{5.b}$.
σ^2. *Weariness of neck :*
   O.—fag.σ.
σ^2. *Pain in neck :*
GEN.—ail.σx.—alm.10.(3-30).
   —asr.V^6.βε^a.ε.—-buf.III.—
   can.26.—-cn-i.VIII^4.q.—fag.
   V^7.—-ga-x.—-glo.VII^5.d.—
   grp.η.—byo.—k-ca.V^1–VIII^4.
   κ$^{5.6}$.11.—klm.VI^4.—lep.3-99.
   —lip.—mnc.VIII^2.29.—msc.
   V^6.6.(8).—-na-m.VI^3.π.—-
   rs-r.—-ser.V^1.—-spo.VI^4–
   VIII$^{3.4}$.η.
F.—aln.—bor$^{e.h}$.V^1–V^6.λ.29.43.
   44.—brv.VI$^{4.w}$.r.—-cth.VI^4.
   βα.; VI^4.—-cb-v.V^1.δb,ε.—-
   cau^c.VI^4.φ^1.1.7.2.65.—chd.V^1.
   —con.VI^3.βα.—-er-a^8.V^3.r.
   19.—-eub.V^1–VII^5.—grp.V^6.
   σ^{2}ff.—hfb.VIII^4.—-hy-x.V^1.
   βε.δO.—-klm^e.rl.5.—lil.βε.δο.
   ω^2.—lyc.VIII$^{4.a}$.5.—-mg-κ.2.
   (3).—mnc.βε.29.—-myr.V^1.-
   ptv.I^q.—plb.V^7.—-spo^e.V$^{10.a}$.
   —tep.V^3–VI^3.
T.—bov^a.V^1–VIII^4.au.—cle.V^1-

VII$^{5.a}$.3.—jac$^{a.b}$.5.8.—k-hy^b.
   VI^4.—klm.V$^{10.a}$.—-mer^a.III^2–
   V^6–VIII^3.—-mim^a.V^1.—pim.
   V^{10}.—-rn-b.V^1.βз.5.6.—-sul.
   VIII^4.ρ.ω^8.
C.—-arn.II$^{1.b}$.—-ard.VIII^4.-—
   c-ph.—-chd.VI^3–VIII^3.11. ;
   V$^{6.a}$.—glo.VIII^4.—-hur.VIII^4.
   —hy-x.V^1.βε.δO.—-hyo.V^1.
   28.—-k-hy.VI^3–VII^5.—klm.
   —mag.VI^4.83.(2).—-opi.V$^{1.2}$.
   —tep.V^3–VI^3.
P.—ana^c.VI^4.εδ.η.—-ag-n^c.V^3–
   VIII^4.a^{1}b^s.βα.31.—-ba-a^d.VI$^{3.4}$.
   —chi^a.VIII^3.—-con.V^3.βα.
   31.(19).—cu-a^d.V^6.ε.η.—elp^c.
   VI^3.q.—-fag^d.V^7.δl.—-hur.
   VIII^4.—lah^c.r.—lep^d.—mag.
   VI^4.83.(2).—-mr-f^c.δr.—ptl^d.
   —-sar^d.VI^3.—-spo^c.V$^{1.6.u}$.—-
   ziz^c.θ.σ.
O.—aco.—bel^f.V^{10}.—-cn-i.VIII^1.
   q.—com.VI^3.—-epn.V^6–VI^3.
   π.—equ.V^6.—gel.V^3.r.(14).—-
   lau.VI^4.(15).—-rs-r.—-ziz.V^7.

σ^2. *Pain in nape :*
   O.—amb.V^1.; ^{c}.VI^4.—ber^c.VI^4.
   —bry.V$^{10.s}$.; V^{10}.; V^6.βε.—-
   ca-a^c.V$^{10.s}$–VIII^3.—cb-a.V^1.
   44.—cb-v.V^1.rb,ε.—-cau^b.V$^{1.6}$.
   8-31.—-chd.V^6.—-cnb.V^1.i^a.
   3-30.—cle.V^1.q.2.—-con.VI^4.
   δO.κ^5.—-crn.V^6.—-ctn.VI^3.—
   ept.VIII^4.(30).—-glo.V^7.σ^{2}ff.
   26.28.—-grp.V^1.—-hel.V^1.—-
   hy-x.V^1.βε.—-iod^e.V^1–VI^4.—-
   ipc.V^1–VII^5.r.—-k-ca^b.V^6.σ^{2}ff.
   —klm.—-lil^i.V^{12}.–lo-c.VIII$^{4.a}$.
   —lyc.VII^5.5.—-mer.V^6–VIII^3.
   —mez.V^1.26.—-mu-x.V^6–V1^3.
   q.βα.δο.σ^2.—-nat.V^7.βα.δο.κ$^{5.7}$.
   —na-m.V^1.—-nit III^{a}ff.aġ.η.
   ι.π^1.r.4.—-opi.V$^{1.3}$.—-pæo.V^1.
   —pim.; VI^3–VII^5.; V^1–VII^5.;
   V$^{1.10.t}$.—-plc.V^6.—-rn-b^c.VI$^{4.a}$.
   θ^{4}l.—-rs-r.V^7.29.—-ser.V^1.—-
   sil.V^1.3.—-sul.V^6.—-trx^d.VI^3.
   —trn.V^1.—-tri.υ^{1}b,ff.
   B.—bel^f.V^6.20.35.
σ^2. *Feeling of strangulation in neck :*
   F.—glo$^{e.h}$.VII^5.

T.—glo.VIII[4].

σ^2. *Pain in cervical glands :*
F.—bor[e].VI[3].χ[1·2].
T.—bor.VI[3].χ[1·2].

σ^2. *Glandular swellings in neck :*
O.—ba-c.VI[11].—mu-x.V[6]–VI[3].q.
βa.δo.σ^2.

r. *Pain in clavicles :*
GEN.—nit.VII[1].ϵl.

r. *Pain in shoulders :*
GEN.—ch-s.VIII[4].29.—cot.—
mgt.VIII[1].χ[1].
F.—er-a[g].VI[3].σ^2.19.—klm[e].σ^2.5.
—lch.ζ.π.χ^2.
O.—bry.II[3].q.3-99.17.—gel.V[3].
σ^2.(14).——ipc.V[1]–VII[5].σ^2.—
nit.III[a].ff.a$\mathfrak{g}$.η.ι.π^1.σ^2.4.

r. *Pain in scapula :*
P.—m-pu[c].V[7].$\beta\epsilon$[b].r.5.

rv. *Itching in arms :*
O.—mo-a.II[1·a].κ^4.λv.v.

rx. *Numbness in l. arm :*
GEN.—phs.i[a].ρ.ω^3.

rjj. *Tingling in l. arm :*
GEN.—ail.V[7].θ^3.κ.κ^1.3-99.

r. *Pain in deltoid muscle :*
T.—fl-x.V[10·s].

r. *Pain in arms :*
GEN.—eup.VI[3·4].—ver.VIII[1].r[1].
F.—ag-n.V[3·6].—bry.VI[3·w].σ^2.—
c-ph.—lyc.V[10·s].ηr.
T.—dio[b].3.—dir[a].VI[3].3.—til[a].
VI[4].
P.—-ap-a[d].—bel[c].V[6].20.66.—
cb-v[d].VI[4].—cim[c].VI[3].θ^4.89.—
gym[d].πr.v.—-lah[c].σ^2.——pho[h].
VI[3].
O.—ap-a.VIII[4].—ind[c].VI[3].π.—
mag.VI[4]–VIII[3].v.

rx. *Numb feeling in l. elbow :*
O.—cep.V[1].5.

r. *Pain in elbow :*
T.—lo-i.V[10·s].r[1]y.
O.—ind[b].VIII[4].

r[1]b. *Cold hands :*
GEN.——bz-x.κ[1·4·5·10].ω^2.3-99.20.
36.107.130.—idm.VIII[4].p.
F.——mer[b].VI[3·4].p.ηp.χ^1.19.——
rn-b[f].ηp.16.(18.31).
T.—bor.VI[3].
C.—amb.VI[4].ηc[b].

O.—la-v.V[1]–VII[5].p.

r[1]p. *Hot hands :*
GEN.—mt-s.5.
F.—ign.VI[4].ηp,aa.24.(17).–la-v.
V[10·zz] p.hh.ii[d].—phl[b].p.βa.
O.—ign[g].VI[4].ηp,aa.24.(17).

r[1]b.p. *Hands alternately hot and cold :*
T.—bor.VI[1].χ[1·2].

r[1]x. *Numbness of hands :*
GEN.—hfb.au.θ^4.

ry. *Paralysed feeling of hand :*
T.—lo-i.V[10·s].r.

r[1]. *Pain in hands :*
GEN.—trn.aa,$\mathfrak{k}$.λp.
F.—pho.VI[3].ζ.

r[1]. *Pain in l. wrist :*
B.—cn-i.V[10].vl.

r[1]c[b]. *Paleness of fingers :*
GEN.—ver.VIII[1].r.

r[1]. *Pain in fingers :*
T.—cyc[a].V[3].θ^1.

r[1]. *Pain in thumb :*
T.—ind[a].VI[4].θ^4.

vv. *Itching of legs :*
F.—r-vn.θ.

v. *Weakness of legs :*
F.—nx-v.V[1].8.(14).
C.—cas.V[1].σ^1.83.

v. *Pain in legs :*
GEN.——aga.V[3].ϕ.ω^2.19.——ca-c.
VI[3].5.—c-ph.VIII[4].κ^1.ξ^2.σ.84.
—k-ca.5.(35).
F.—crt[a].V[1].δr.ηr.θ^1.5.–klm.VI[4].
3-30.—osm[a].VI[4·q].5.
T.—crt[b].V[1].ηr.θ.5.
C.—epn.VI[3].ηp.ϕ.ω^2.
P.—gym[d] πr.r.
O.——cth[h].VIII[3·a].(15).——ced.
VI[3].λ.— mag.VI[4]–VIII[3].r.—
mo-a.II[1·a].κ^4.λv.rv.

v. *Pain in hip-joint :*
B.—nit[o].VIII[3].

v. *Weakness of thighs :*
C.—so-n[e].V[1·10].$\beta\epsilon$[a].δP[1].ρ.

v. *Pain in knee :*
T.—ox-x[a].V[1]–VIII[3].

v. *Cramp in calves :*
O.—cn-i.V[1].b.p.

v[1]b. *Cold feet :*
GEN.—buf.κ^5.ω^2.—cca.μ^3.4.
F.—ch-x.VIII[4].i[a].π.—cot.V[7].q.

$a^1b^s.\delta v,o.\rho^1.(8).; {}^gII^6.$--fer.$I^a.$;
$V^6.$p.—naj.$III^{1\cdot w}.\theta j.$
C.—naj.$V^1.$
O.—tri.$\sigma^2.\upsilon$ff.

υ^1q. *Heavy feet* :
GEN.—cle.VI^3-VII^1–$VIII^4.16.$
43.44.(8).

υ^1ff. *Stiffness of feet* :
O.—tri.$\sigma^2.\upsilon$b.

$\upsilon^1.$ *Pain in feet* :
GEN.—sto.$VII^5.\pi.\sigma^1.$
F.—san$^d.I^a.\delta l.$

$\upsilon^1.$ *Pain in toe* :
F.—fl-x$^f.$—opi.$VIII^3.$w.—xip$^a.$
$V^1.\beta e.$

$\upsilon^1.$ *Pain in l. ankle* :
B.—cn-i.$V^{10}.\tau l.$

$\tau \upsilon$b. *Coldness of limbs* :
F.—k-ca$^d.VI^{3\cdot a}.\pi.$

$\tau \upsilon$q. *Heaviness of limbs* :
GEN.—ni-x.$V^1.$—sil.$V^1.$au.
F.—sbd.$V^7.$

$\tau \upsilon$kk. *Trembling of limbs* :
GEN.—sul.$\beta a.\epsilon \mathfrak{v}.\kappa^{4\cdot 5}.\tau \upsilon$nn.$\omega^{2\cdot 9}.$
F.—lyc$^e.VII^1.\kappa^5.$—pgn.
P.—cn-s$^d.VIII^4.\omega^2.$

$\tau \upsilon$nn. *Weakness of limbs* :
GEN.--k-bi.--sul.$\beta a.\epsilon \mathfrak{v}.\kappa^{4\cdot 5}.\tau \upsilon$kk.
$\omega^{2\cdot 9}.$

$\tau \upsilon.$ *Pain in limbs* :
GEN.—aco.$V^2.$—ail.—eri.—gel.
$V^7.$—lah.V^6-$VI^4.$—san.$\kappa^5.\sigma^2.$
F.—csn.$V^7.\omega^2.$--cac.VI^4-$VIII^3.$
—sul.$V^7.$; ${}^bV^6.$
T.——aco.$V^3.\delta P^2.\eta.\eta c^b,$p,aa.$\rho^1.$
σhhb.$\omega^{3\cdot 8}.\varphi.66.$
C.—mag.VI^4-$VIII^3.$--sul.$V^{1\cdot 10}.$
$\omega^2.3$-99.

$\tau \upsilon.$ *Aching in joints* :
GEN.—eri.$V^7.3$-99.

$\tau^1\upsilon^1$b. *Cold hands and feet* :
F.——cam$^h.III^1.$p.$\varphi.12.16.29.$——
k-ca.$VI^{\cdot 3\cdot a}.\pi.1.$—sul.$V^1.$d.
Ba.—cam.$III^1.$p.$\zeta.\varphi.12.16.29.$

$\tau^1\upsilon^1$hhb. *Cold sweat on hands and feet* :
F.—hur.$V^1.$

$\tau^1\upsilon^1$nn. *Weakness of hands and feet* :
C.—ol-a$^b.VI^{3\cdot a}.\varphi^1.2.83.$

$\varphi.$ *Sleepiness* :
GEN.——aga.$V^3.\nu.\omega^2.19.$—-ars.

$VI^4.$q.$\omega^2.$——con.$\delta \tau^h.$t q.$\omega^2.$—
crn.$\bar{V}^7.26.29.31.$; $V^1.$q.——
equ.3.—hyd.—idm.$V^7.\eta$aa.$\kappa^5.$
$\chi^1.66.$—kre.p.$a^1b.$—lah.$V^1.$—
lo-i.—mr-i.4.5.—mu-x.$V^1.$q.
$\beta a.\delta^1$o.3-30.49.——myr.——nit.
$VI^3.\delta O.$ ——pho.$V^1.$x.a$b^o.\beta a.$
3-30.(16).—so-o.——su-x.$V^2.$
3-99.--vp-r.a$\mathfrak{k}^i,$q.$\delta a^b.\eta c^d,$aa.$\theta^3.$
$\kappa^3.\mu^1.\nu^1.\rho.\sigma^1.\chi^2.\omega^3.$
F.——ail.q.4.——an-s$^n.VI^3.5.$—
asa$^a.V^1.$q.x.—bra.$\kappa^5.8$-31.(12).
—ch-s.au.$b^1b^o.\beta a.\omega^2.$——gin$^{f\cdot n}.$
$VI^3.$p.δLq.——ind.$VI^4.\omega^2.5.$—
idm.$V^7.\kappa^5.$——lau.$III^3.$——na-s.
$V^4.66.$——nx-j.——opi$^a.VI^3.$——
stn.$V^{10\cdot s}.(12).$—tan.$V^7.$--zin.
$V^1.\beta e.\delta.5.$
T.-aco.$V^3.\delta P^2.\eta.\eta c^b,$p,aa.$\rho^1.\sigma$hhb.
$\tau \upsilon.\omega^{3\cdot 8}.$——ard$^a.$——ign.$V^1.$——
idm.$V^7.$q.au.3-99.— stn.VI^3–
$VIII^4.$p.$a^1b^s.\chi^1.$—tan.$V^7.$
C.——epn.$VI^3.\eta$p.$\upsilon.\omega^2.$——nx-m.
$III^{u\cdot w}.a^1b^s.$—sto.$VII^1.$p.$a\mathfrak{g},\mathfrak{h}.$
ηp,aa.5.
O.——bra.$\kappa^6.8$-31.(12).——cam.
$III^1.$p.$\zeta.\tau^1\upsilon^1$b.12.16.29.--ch-s.
au.a$^1b^s.\beta a.\omega^{2\cdot 9}.$—opi$^b.VI^{3\cdot z}.$
Ba.—cam.$III^1.$p.$\tau^1\upsilon^1$b.12.16.29.
B.—nx-m$^c.III^1$–$IV^3.a^1b^s.$

$\phi.$ *Waking slumber* :
F.—cam$^b.III^1.$p.$\tau^1\upsilon^1$b.12.16.29.

$\phi^1.$ *Sleeplessness* :
GEN.——am-c.$VI^3.$w.2.——ar-h.
V^1–$VI^4.\beta e^a.2.$——ar-i.—buf.2.
4.—crn.$V^1.i^a.$—c-ar.2.—elp.
$VI^3.2.$--gn-c.$VII^1.i^a.\xi^3.35.83.$
(20).——kre.VI^4 a$\mathfrak{k},$u.ηp.$\theta^1.\chi^2.$
$\omega^2.3$-99.—lyc.$VIII^3.2.$--mr-i.
.——nit.2.3.——par.$V^{14}.$af.2.—
ver.δs.
F.—cau$^c.VI^4.\sigma^2.$——naj.V^7–$VI^3.$
$\lambda^2.2.$—rs-r.$V^7.a\mathfrak{k}.\kappa^4.$
C.—aco.$V^{1\cdot a}.$——ni-x.VI^3–$VII^1.$
4.—ol-a$^b.VI^{3\cdot a}.\tau^1\upsilon^1$nn.2.83.
O.—cca.2.$\omega^3.4.$——rs-r.$V^7.a\mathfrak{k}.\kappa^4.$

$\phi^2.$ *Dreams* :
GEN.——alm.ηp.$\rho^1.82.$——au-m.
$VIII^4.$
F.—ch-s$^b.VII^1.$d.$a^1c^b,\mathfrak{v}^b.\beta a,e.\delta t^c.$
e$a,\mathfrak{v}.\eta$p.$\kappa^{2\cdot 3\cdot 5\cdot 7}.\lambda^2.\rho.\chi^3.\omega^3.$

χ. *Fever:*
GEN.—ars.κ^6.——ch-s.χ^3.(8-31).—
elc.ρ^1.—fer.4.—idm.aq.2. ; κ^5.
66.—lah.ζ^3.—rho.83.
    F.—ca-s.—hel.$V^{10 \cdot t}$-VII^5.q.(8).
—hln.V^1.au.—pol.V^7.
    C.—hfb.V^1.ω^2.
    O.—pho.V^7.ηaa.

χ^1. *Chilliness:*
GEN.——arg.$\beta\epsilon^a$.——ag-n.κ^7.——ca-c.
VI^3.—chi.ω^2.—ccs.V^1.—dul.
αb.κ^6.—evo.—ind.I^a.—idm.
V^7.ηaa.κ^5.ϕ.66.—lah.—lch.II^1.
p.hh.ηc^d.κ^3.χ^3.——mns.I^a.ωq.—
nit.λi^a.μ^2.3-99.—nx-v.VI^4.ηp.
—san. ; κ^5.χ^2.—sep.101.—sil.
VI^4-VIII^4.(12).——trn.p.λ^1.
χ^2.3-99.
    F.—ca-x.V^7.—cca.βa.ω^2.4.; $^aV^1$.
βa.4.(5).— mez^h.VII^1.p.hh.3.
—san.VII^1.κ^4.—sil^f.V^1.
    T.—as-s.V^{16}.ϕ.——cas.VI^4.5.II^3.
11.——dio.III^3.θj.κ^5.3.———fer.
VI^3.2.—hyp.^{a}.$VI^{4 \cdot b}$.5.
    C.—aln.V^{10}.κ^5.χ^2.—k-hy.VII^1.
p.(101).—sul.$V^{1 \cdot a}$.δ.δb.χ^3.2.
    P.—ca-c^d.VI^2.βa.3-30.18.31.—
hel^b.VI^4.
    O.—cca.βa.ω^2.4. ; V^{10}.βa.4.(5).
—sul^h.$V^{1 \cdot a}$.δ.δb.χ^3.2.
    B.--con^f.III^1.au.a^{1}b^p.κa.(12.29).

χ^1. *Rigor:*
GEN.—ail.χ^2.—alm.III–VI^4.—
ana.VI^4.αk,q.—ag-n.V^1.99.—
ca-c.V^{10}.b.——cca.4.—k-ca.V^1.
5.—led.VI^4.δ.δs.κ^3.λ^2.——mgt.
VIII^1.τr.— mez.V^1.—nx-v.θ.
χ^2.ω^3.83.——pet.V^7.5.—pul.
VI^3.ω^3.5.66.—sil.V^1.δ.κ^5.ω^2.3.
—tab.II^1.g^b.ϵ.κ^1.
    F.—arn.V^1–VI^3–VIII^3.——bry.
V^7.117.——cas.VI^4.(8.12).——
man.V^6–VI^3.8.(6).—— mer^b.
$VI^{3 \cdot 4}$.p.ηp.τ^1b.19.——pet.V^6.5.
—rn-s.$V^{10 \cdot t}$.κ^3.5.——rhs.$V^{10 \cdot s}$.
ωq.—thu.$V^{10 \cdot s}$.η.3.(8-31).
    T.—cas.VI^4.(8.12).—ni-x^a.$V^{1 \cdot a}$.
κ^7.λ.3-30.—stn.VI^3–VIII^4.p.
α^1b^s.ϕ.
    C.——ced.V^1.——thu.VI^2.η.ι.4.3.
(8-31).

P.—cb-v^c.η.θ^1.
O.—bor.VIII^4.2.
B.—ca-c^{fb}.IX.

χ^2. *Heat:*
GEN.—æth.a^{1}b.βa.κ^6.5.—agn.V^7.
(75).—ail.χ^1.—alm.o^1.4.——
ang.5.8.——arg.III.βa.$\kappa^{4 \cdot 5}$.χ^3.
18.43.—ag-n.—dig.λ.ν.—gam.
V^1.p—glo.III^1.i^a. ; λ^2.3.—
hyo.—idm.VIII^4.au.(116).—
kre.VI^4.ak,u.ηp.θ^1.ϕ^1.ω^2.3-99.
—lyc.4.——mg-s.III.$\beta\epsilon^a$.χ^3.3-
10.26.—mo-a.δs.ηaa.ψv.—na-s.
χ^3.43.(30.35).—nit.5.—nx-v.
θj.χ^1.ω^3.83.——san.κ^5.χ^1.—sul.
VI^4.ω^2.4.(14).——trn.ak.π.ρ^1.
χ^3.; p.λ^1.χ^1.3-99.——vp-r.ak^i,q.
δa^b.ηc^d,aa.θ^2.κ^3.μ^1,ν^1.ρ.σ^1.ϕ.ω^3.
    F.——bis.βa $\kappa^{4 \cdot 7}$.ρ.5.35.——cam.
VI^3–VIII^4.2.—cor.$V^{10 \cdot a \cdot s}$.aq.
(130).——hep.$VI^{4 \cdot s}$.2.—lch.ζ.
π.τ.—lyc.VI^4.κ^3.4.——mo-a.I^a.
ρ.ω^2.——ox-x.VI^3.χ^3.3.——pla.
III^1–V^3.x.au^{ff}.$\epsilon$$D^k$.7.——rhs^e.
$VI^{3 \cdot s}$.$\kappa^{4 \cdot 5}$.63.—trn.χ^3.1.S^{f}k^1.5.
    T.—cyc.I^a.κ^3.—na-m^c.V^1.$\beta\epsilon$.
    C.—aln.V^{10}.κ^5.χ^1.—ox-x.VI^3.χ^3.
    P.—til^a.VI^3.
    O.—pul.V^1.χ^3.

$\chi^{1 \cdot 2}$. *Alternate heat and cold:*
GEN.—cb-v.
    F.—bor^e.VI^3.σ^2.
    T.—bor.VI^3.σ^2.rb,p.

$\chi^{1 \cdot 2}$. *Rigor alternating with heat:*
    F.—ber.V^1.q.aa.$\beta\epsilon$.ω^2.3-99.

χ^3. *Sweat:*
GEN.-aps.II^1-VIII^4.29.35.(12).
——arg.III.βa.$\kappa^{4 \cdot 5}$.χ^2.18.43.—
ars.VIII^4.2.—cnc.δ.δP^2.ηp,aa,
ii.—cth.V^7.βa.η^1.ν^1.ρ.ω^2.—ch-s.
V^7.ag.ϵa.ρ.ω^8.; χ.(8-31).—hyo.
ω^2.83.—lch.II^1.ηc^a.κ^3.χ^1.—lyc.
κ^2.——mg-s.III.$\beta\epsilon^a$.χ^2.3-10.26.
——na-s.χ^2.43.(30.35).——pla.
V^1.au.ι.2.—trn.ak.π.ρ^1.χ^2.
    F.—ant.V^7.8-31.—cnt.—ch-s^b.
VII^1.d. a^1ϵ^b,D^b.βa,ϵ.δt^c.ϵa,D ηp.
$\kappa^{2 \cdot 3 \cdot 5 \cdot 7}$.$\lambda^2$.$\rho$.$\phi^2$.$\omega^2$.——glo.$V^{10 \cdot v}$.
ag.ηaa.—na-a.4.—nit.ag.βa.b.
—opi.V^9–VI^4.$\kappa^{6 \cdot 7}$.—ox-x.VI^3.
χ^2.3.—trn.χ^2.1.S^{f}k^1.5.

T.—arn.V^{16}.ω^2.2.—nit.ag.βa,b.
C.—ox-x.VI^3.χ^2.
O.—cau^f.V^3–VI^3.—pul.V^1.χ^2.

χ^8. *Cold sweat :*
GEN.—grp.κ^6.μ^3.ω^3.3-99.

χ^3. *Fetid sweat :*
C.—sul.V$^{1\cdot a}$.δ.δb.χ^1.2.
O.—sul^h.V$^{1\cdot a}$.δ.δb.χ^1.2.

ψk. *Burning miliary eruption :*
GEN.—bel.

ψv. *Itching of skin :*
GEN.—mo-a.I^a.δaa.ηaa.ρ.χ^2.
F.C.—nab.au.δL.ι.
P.—mo-a^c.I^a.αq.ηæ^c,aa,hh.

ωq. *Heaviness in side :*
F.—as-t.

ωff. *Stiffness :*
GEN.—ver.

ωll. *Twitchings :*
GEN.—aga.VIII^1.θ^3.3-10.

ω. *Soreness of body :*
GEN.—bad.5.

ω. *Pain all over body :*
F.—opi.V$^{10\cdot a}$.(12.15).

ω. *Pain in other parts of body :*
GEN.—lyc.VI^4.

ω. *Gouty pains :*
GEN.—sul.20.

ω. *Rheumatic pains in bones :*
Ba.—la-x.ηaa.35.(12).

ω. *As if body were pressed downwards :*
GEN.—mgt.V$^{10\cdot a}$.

ω^2. *Weakness :*
GEN.—-ant.κ^1.117.—as-t.3-30.—bor.VI$^{3\cdot 4}$.ξ^3.83.—bov.V^7.—çn-i.III.7.— cth.V^7.βa.ηc^b.ν^1.ρ.χ^3.—cu-a.—cyc.κ.; VI^3.(83).—glo.VII^1.a^{1}b^a.$\eth$.; a$\eth$.δs.—hdr.βa.—hy-x.II^1.—hyo.χ^3.83.—irs.aκ.—kre.VI^4.aκ,u.ηp.θ^1.ϕ^1.χ^2.3-99.—lah.81.—lau.V^1.7. (8). ——pso.V$^{10\cdot t}$.(105).——ptl.VIII^4.3-30.-—rn-b.ag 63.—sil.V^1.; V^1.δ.κ^5.χ^1.3.-—sul.βa.e$\eth$.$\kappa^{4\cdot 5}$.rvkk,nn.ω^9.; VI^4.χ^2.4.(14).-trn.VIII^1.aκ.ι.o^1.π.σ^2.ω^8.3-30.; π.π^1.ρ^1.
F.—alm^e.VI^3.κ^5.ν^3.3-99.-—-ara.V^1.βe.5.66.(12).— ch-s^b.I^a.βa.

$\epsilon\eth$.—iod.V^2.κ^7.—irs.V^7.q.$\kappa^{5\cdot 6}$.—lil.βe.δo.σ^2.—lyc.I^1.κ^5.; V^7.3-30.-pho.V^7.κ^1.(102).--rs-r^e.I^e.ab^c,ᵏ.5.5.(4).—sil.VII^5.δ.
T.—ara.V^1.βe.5.66.(12).—ars.VIII^2.2.5.——glo.VI^3.βa.—la-x.3-30.[SII$^{1\cdot 5}$].
C.—hfb.V^1.χ.—nx-v.VI^4.δ.κ^5.v^2.—sul.V$^{1\cdot 10}$.rv.3-99.
P.—cn-s^d.VIII^4.rvkk.——nx-v^b.5.
O.——jab^h.V$^{7\cdot zz}$.π.ρ^1.——rn-b^b.VIII^4.19.

ω^2. *Paralysed feeling :*
P.—ars^d.IX.

ω^2. *Weariness :*
GEN.—aga.V^3.v.ϕ.19.—ars.VI^4.q.ϕ.—bel.ηaa.—bz-x.—buf.$\kappa^5$$vb$.—cac.— chi.$\chi^1$.—cob.$\kappa^5$.5.—con.$\delta$r^h,t^q.$\phi$.——mg-m.3. —opi.— pho.V^7.βa.η.θ^2.28.(16).—rs-r.44.—sin.—str.
F.—anh.V^3.4.--asa.V^1.—ber.V^1.q.αa.$\chi^{1\cdot 2}$.3-99.—-cas.V^1.σ^1.83. --ch-s.au.a^{1}b^o.βa.ϕ.; ^{b}.VII^1.d.a^{1}ɩ^b,$\eth$^{b}.βa,e.δt^c.ea,$\eth$.ηp.$\kappa^{2\cdot 3\cdot 5\cdot 7}$.$\lambda^2$.$\rho$.$\phi^2$.$\chi^3$.—-cca.$\beta$a.$\chi^1$.4.—csn.V^7.rv.—-ind.VI^4.ϕ.5.—-idm^g.κ^5.2.—kre.VIII^4.ηp.κ.3-99.--la-v.V^7.ab.—lil.IX.5.—mo-a.I^a.ρ.χ^2 --naj.ω^9.--opi^m.V^1.βe.ζ.
T.—arn.V^{16}.χ^3.2.—cob^t.κ^5.μ^3.3.
C.—epn.VI^3.ηp.v.ϕ.--glo.V^7.βe.
P.—k-ca^b.κ^5.5.
O.——ch-s.au.a^{1}b^s.βa.ϕ.ω^9.——cca.βa.χ^1.4.; 4.ϕ.2.—na-m.V^1.q.66.

ω^3. *Faint feeling :*
GEN.—ca-c.V$^{3\cdot 10}$.ap.δ.ξ.η.θ^1.-grp.κ^6.μ^3.χ.^{3}.3-99.— mt-n.V$^{10\cdot u}$.δ.—mr-f.—-na-m.$\kappa^{5\cdot 6}$.30.31.—-nx-v.θ.$\chi^{1\cdot 2}$.83.——pet.V^{10}.—phs.i^a.ρ.r^1.—-pul.VI^3.χ^1.5.66.—-str.βa.κ^3.—-vp-r.aκⁱ,q.δa^b.ηc^d,aa.θ^3.ᵏ^3.μ^1.ν^1.ρ.σ^1.ϕ.χ^2.
F.—ber.V^1.βa.34.—b-la.I^q.βe^b.
T.-——-aco.V^3.δP^2.η.nc^b,p,aa.ρ^1.σhbb.rv.ω^8.ϕ.66.
P.—ber^c.III^1-V^{1}VII^1.83.

ω^3. *Syncope :*
F.—mo-a^a.δP^2.θ^3.κ.σhbb.

ω⁴. *Ill-feeling :*
　GEN.——cup.V⁶.βa.(16).——grp.
　　V².5.—sng.VIII⁴.δ.κ¹.
ω⁵. *Convulsions :*
　GEN.—vp-t.κ⁶.; θ⁴.λ.
ω⁷. *Cramps :*
　O.—ast.βℓᵇ.41.
ω⁸. *Trembling :*
　GEN.——aco.——bor.κ⁵.3.——ch-s.
　　V⁷.aℊ.ℓa.ρ.χ³.— trn.VIII¹.ak.
　　ι.o¹.π.σ².ω².3-30.
　F.—opi.IX.a¹ɒ.βa.—sep.aℊ.ζ².
　T.——aco.V³.δP². η.ηcᵇ,p,aa.ρ¹.

σbhb.rν.ω³.φ.66.— sul.VIII⁴.
ρ.σ².
C.—sep.oℊ.ζ².
P.—sarᶜ.V¹–VI³·⁴·ᵃ.
ω⁹. *Yawning :*
　GEN.—cyc.——mns.I⁴.χ¹.——sul.
　　βa.ℓɒ.κ⁴·⁵.rνkk,nn.ω².——zin.
　　VI³·⁴.λ.63.66.
　T.—am-c.VIII⁴.——ol-aᵃ.V¹.66.
　　(15).
　P.—am-cᵈ.
　O.—am-cᶜ.VIII⁴.——ch-s.aυ.a¹bˢ.
　　βa.φ.ψ².

SECTION III.—CONDITIONS OF PAINS IN HEAD.

---

1. *All day.*
　GEN.——aga.V⁶.——am-c.aυ.κ⁴.;
　　VI³.——ca-c.VIII⁴·ᵠ.——can.—
　　cau.VI³.—cl-h.V⁷.—cin.V¹–
　　VI⁴.η.—cn-s.—cis.——cob.V⁷.
　　6.31.35.—fl-x.26.—jac.V⁷.
　　k-ca.VIII³.-–lyc.VIII⁴.22.—
　　mr-i.V¹⁰.—na-m.aᴂᶜᶜ,u.—pau.
　　—stp.VI³.
　F.—cauᶜ.VI⁴.σ².φ¹.7.2.65.—chd.
　　V¹⁰·ˢ.8.29.53.89.(63).; V¹⁰·ˢ.;
　　V⁷.——con.V¹·ᵠ.;VI³–VIII³.6.
　　—cunℯ.V⁷.—k-ca.VI³ ᵃ.π.rνb.
　　—lahℯ·ʰ.—-lil.V⁷.—lycᶜ.VIII⁴.
　　—mag.V⁶.q.83.—na-mℯ.V¹.—
　　nupᵃ.V⁷.q.δO.—ped.26.—pet.
　　V⁶.χ¹.5.—phoℯ.V¹.—ptl.V¹⁰·ˢ.
　　——rn-bⁱ·ⁿ.VIII⁴.βa.ζ.——sep.
　　VI³·ˢ.δ.—sil.V¹.; VI⁴.5.35.—
　　so-t.Iᵃ.ζ³.——trn.χ²·³.Sᶠk¹.5.—
　　zinᵃ.VI⁴–VIII⁴·ᵃ.
　T.—ars.V¹.——ca-c.VI⁴.δO.η.ηii.
　　—hel.V¹⁰·ˢ.–VII⁵.d.q.(8).—-
　　hep.V¹·⁶.—hdr.VIII⁴.—hfb.
　　Iᵃ.—jat.V¹⁰·ᵗ.6.—mez.V¹⁰.βℓ.
　　—nitᵃ.VI⁴.(12).—-stn.V¹⁰·ᵗ.;
　　V¹·³.

C.—sep.III.π.—-sul.Iᵃ.—-tab.
　V¹.3-99.
P.—cacᶜ.VIII⁴.q.aᶦᵍ.2.—ferᵈ.—
　hdrᵈ.V⁷.q.—mg-mᵃ.VI³·⁴.
O.—cb-v.VIII⁴.—ignᵇ.V¹.βa.—
　mag.V⁶.83.——pet.VIII⁴.—
　ph-xᵇ.V¹.12.28.

2. *At night.*
　GEN.——ac-sᵈ.31.——am-g.1.——
　　am-c.VI³.ω.φ¹.—ars.VIII⁴.χ³.
　　——ar-h.V¹–VI⁴.βℯᵃ.φ¹.——aru.
　　—ast.VI³.53.—bov.30.(3).—
　　buf.φ¹.4.; *buf.*(16).—cac.IX.
　　—cth.VI¹·³.——cau.II⁷.—ced.
　　VII².——cha.VI⁴.——ch-s.—
　　cn-s.—cis.—cch.Iᵃ.— c-ar.φ¹.
　　—cyc.—dul.V³·ˢ.—elp.VI³·ᵃ.
　　φ¹.; V⁷.—eug.II¹.δ.δℓ.5.72.—
　　glo.—gui.V¹⁰·ᵛ.—ham.—hep.
　　VI³–VII¹.βℓ.—hy-x.—hyo.
　　VIII⁴.σ².(98).——ign.VI⁴.16.
　　(17).—idm.aᵠ.ⱳ.—lah.V¹.72.
　　—lam.VI⁴.; VI³–VIII⁴.—lin.
　　V⁷.—lo-i.—lyc.; q.; VIII³.φ¹.
　　--mag.98.99.(24).–mil.VIII⁴.
　　——mns.aᵠ.δiiᵃ.—-m-cy.VI⁴.—
　　nit.φ¹.3.—nx-v.; VII⁵.—par.

$V^{14}.\alpha f.\phi^1$.—pau.—pho.κ^5.—
pla.$V^1.\alpha u.\iota.\iota j.\chi^3$.—pul.$VIII^4$.;
IX.—rs-r.—sar.$VIII^4.\kappa^{5\cdot6}$.—
sil.—sul.VII^1.; $VI^3.\theta^4$.(12).
—trn.d.$\epsilon.\epsilon\flat$.—zin.

F.—ana^c.V^7.—ag·n.V^1.—ars^g.5.
—cam.VI^3–$VIII^4.\chi^2$.—ca-x.
III^1.—cau^c.$VI^4.\sigma^2.\phi^1$.1–7.65.
—ch-s^f.I.43.(30).—cro$^e.\delta$.
115.—crt.VII^1.q.—cyc.$I^a.\alpha f$.
—fag^b.VIII^4.35.—hep.VI^2–
IX.29.89.; $VI^{4\cdot a}.\chi^2$.—hur.
VIII^4.—k-ca.V^6.5.—lch.VI^4.
—la-x^e.VI^3.—lyc^f.$VI^{3\cdot4}$.—
mg-s.σ^2.(3)—mr-i.$V^{7\cdot8}$–VI^4.—
—naj.V^7–$VI^3.\phi^1$.—pl-n.$_\Lambda^4$.—
ptl.$V^{10\cdot s}$.q.29.—rap^m.—sil.
VIII^3.—spi.VI^3–$VIII^4.\epsilon\flat^b$.—
til.III^3–V^1.

T.—arn.$V^{16}.\chi^3.\omega^2$.—ars.VIII^2.
ω^2.5.—aru^b.VI^3.—bry.θ^2.—
cac.VIII^4.—cop^a.V^2.5.12.—
dig^b.VI^3.5.98.—fer.$VI^3.\chi^1$.—
grt.V^3–VI^4.4.101.102.—k-ca.
$VI^{3\cdot4}.\alpha l^g$.—lyc.$VI^{3\cdot4}$.—mg-s.
(3).—rs-r.$II^{1\cdot6}$.—trn^b.VI^2.;
^{a}.$VI^2.\delta$.; ^{b}.I.—tri^a.V^3.—zn-o^a.
$VI^{3\cdot4}$.

C.—aco.V^1.—ast.IV^1–VII^5.41.
—cb-a.VII^1.110.—fer.V^1.35.
—hpm.V^7.16.–ir-f^a.$V^{6\cdot11}$.29.; ^{a}.
$VI^{3\cdot t}$.S^c.dd.–lau.$VI^4.\xi^3$.83.(3).
–lyc.V^1–VI^3.—mag.$VI^4.\sigma^2$.83.
—nit.III^1.4.—ol-a^b.$VI^{3\cdot a}$.
$r^1\nu^1$nn.ϕ.83.; VI^3.84.(3-30).—
rat.II^1–VI^4.83.(8).—sul.$V^{\cdot1a}$.
$\delta.\delta\flat.\chi^{1\cdot3}$.

P.—cac^c.VIII^4.q.αl^g.1.—grp^b.
17.—mag.$VI^4.\sigma^2$.83.; mag^c.
$VI^{3\cdot a}$.17.—na-m^d.VI^3.—nic^c.
$VIII^3.\epsilon\flat$.—nit^d.I^a.(130).—
ol-a^d.$VI^3.\lambda.\xi^3.\sigma$.84.(30).—
trn^d.VI^3.; ^{h}.VI^3.

O.—bor.$VIII^4.\chi^1$.—bov.$V^{1\cdot a}$.q.
3.8-31.(6).—cle.$V^1.\rho^1.\sigma^2$.—
hpm^c.III^2.—lyc.$VI^{3\cdot4}$.—nit^e.
VII^5.—sep.$IX.\beta\epsilon^b$.16.(12).—
sto^b.$V^{3\cdot a}$.—sul^h.$V^{1\cdot a}.\delta.\delta\flat.\chi^{1\cdot3}$.

B.—par^{pb}.II^5.11.

2-10. *At night in bed.*
GEN.—fag.VII^1.—hpm.; $V^{3\cdot6}$–
$VI^3.\delta$.—hyp.IX.
F.—mr-f$^a.\delta r$.
T.—mr-f^a.VI^3.
C.—sul.$V^{10\cdot t}.\delta\flat$.5.
P.—car^c.II^5–V^1.—mt-s^c.VIII^4.
O.—alo.II^5–VI^3–$VIII^4.\lambda$.29.—
k-cy.V^7.

2-99. *At night on waking.*
GEN.—aln.κ^5.—ast.d.$a^1b^s.\beta\epsilon^b.\rho$.—
man.$V^{10\cdot u}$.5.—mr-f.V^7.—ph-x.
$V^{10\cdot P}$.16.
F.—cth.$V^{10\cdot s}$.(30).—cnb.q.—
col^b.—fer.$V^1.\lambda^2$.—gel^b.$V^{1\cdot a}$.
—la-x^e.—m-pi.—tar^b.IX.
T.—buf^b.—plc.VI^3.
C.—glo.
O.—rum.
B.—mez.V^1–VI^4.

3. *In the morning.*
GEN.—aco.$\epsilon\flat.\zeta^3.\lambda$.—arg.$VI^3.\delta$aa.
—ars.V^1.q.—as-t.—aur.V^2.
a^1b^s.41.43.44.86.; $V^{1\cdot2}$–VI^4.—
bor.$\kappa^5.\omega^8$.—bov.$V^6.\beta\epsilon$.; V^{12} q.
(8).; II^7–VIII^4.6.8.; bov.2.
30.—bry.46.48.; III–VI^3.q.
29.46.—buf.66.—ca-c.VIII^4.
—c-ph.ι.—ca-x.III^1.p.ii.(12).
—ch-s.VII^5.— cl-h.$III^1.i^a$.—
cin.δ.—cn-s.—cle.— cub.V^2.
$i^a.\beta\epsilon$.; II^5–VIII^4.—cca.(66).
—col.—con.$\beta\epsilon^a$.8-31.(66).—
cvl.4.— ctn.$\beta\epsilon$.—cun.$\kappa^5.\nu^1$.—
cyc.—dio.βa.; V^7.—equ.V^7.;
ϕ.3.—fag.$V^{10\cdot s}$.—gas.V^7.—
gen.(8-31)γ.—glo.$\lambda^2.\chi^2$.; VI^3.
29.—grp.—hep.26.—hpm.
V^1.—idm.—irs.$V^7.\eta.\nu^1$.—k-ca.
q.83.—k-hy.V^{12}.(8).—lah.
III.d.—lch.—lap.VII^4.—lep.
—lil.V^7.—lyc.—mg-m.ω^2.—
mnc.βa.66.—mr-s.II^6.38.66.
—myr.(117).; σ.—na-m.κ^5.
5.; III^1.—nit.; ϕ^1.2.—nx-j.
V^7.—nx-v.; II^1–V^6–VI^4.;
V^6–VIII^3.; VI^3–VIII^4.29.—
ol-a.V^6–$VI^4.\beta\epsilon$.(4).—pœo.14.
—pau.—ped.29.—pet.; (66).
—pho.31.35.; $V^6.\alpha$ū,$_\mathbb{R}^w.\beta$a.δt^n.
ρ.(66).—plm.5.—pod.p.—

rum.V⁷.— sam.VII⁵.βa.26.—
src.—sar.VIII⁴.—scu.V⁷.βeª.
(66).—sng.V⁷.— sep.κ⁵.—sil.
V¹.δ.κ⁵.χ¹.ω².—stn.au.κ¹·⁵.-sul.
V¹.; VIII⁴.—thu.VI².gᵇ.—
trf.—ver.VI⁴.83 (5).——zin.
V⁷.; VI⁴-VIII⁴.5.

F.—ac-s.V¹.—alnᵇ.VIII³.; ᵉπl.
—am-m.V¹.p.—belᵉ.V¹⁰·ᵘ.δᵇ.
—borᵉ.V⁷.—bovᵇ.V¹·�q.δ.δo.
35.; ᶜVI⁴·ᵖ.—bro.V⁷.δ.—brysᵍ.
V⁶.; f.V¹–VI³.—ca-sª.IV³–
VIII⁴.—cnc.V¹.—cth.VIII⁴.
βe.—chd.VII⁵.—ch-sᵉ.50ᵈ.;
ᵇIª.βa.εᴅ.——cmfᵍ.V³·⁷.—-cca.
V⁷.δq.(31).—cotᵍ.VI³.—crtᵉ.
—cyc.VI³.βa.—dioᶠ.; V⁷.—
equ.V⁷.; VI³.—ech.V⁷.—
—-eup.V¹.δ.8–31.; V¹.βe.31.
(117).—-ferᵐ.V⁷.(4).; ᵐVI².
(8).—-for.V⁷.—genᶜ.V¹⁰.—
gua.29.—hdr.Iq.π.; V¹⁹·ᶻᶻ.66.;
ᵍ.(8–31).; ᵉ.—-hfbᵉ.Iª.aᵇᵍ.—
jun.V³.30.——k-biᵍ·ʰ.VI³·ª.δo.
(5).—k-ca.VI³.—lahᵒ.Iª.ε.—
lil.V⁷.5.—lyc.V¹.ζ.; ᵉV¹–VI⁴.
δ.; V¹–VI³.—mag.V¹.; V⁶.
——mg-s.V¹⁰·ᶻᶻ.d.q.30.; mg-s.
σ².2.—mrl.V¹·ª.—mezʰ.VII¹.
p.hh.χ¹.; V¹.aᵇo.; VI⁴.19.—
mur.II¹.29.—naj.V¹.(5).—
nat.VII⁵.35.—nic.VI².—ni-x.
V¹.; ᵉVI³.——nx-mᵍ.V¹⁰·ᶻᶻ.;
ᵍV¹–VIII⁴.—nx-v.V⁹·¹⁰·ˢ.29.
—ol-aª.V¹–VI⁴.δ.—ox-x.VI³.
χ²·³.—pœo.V¹·ª.q.δO.5.—ped.
ⁱV¹.—phoᵇ.VIII³·⁴.δ.ζ.κ⁶.; II¹–
VI³–VII¹.19.66.(15).— psoᵈ.
III².q.θ¹.—rs-r.V⁷.; V⁷.βᵇ.5.
41.—scr.V¹.—-scu.V⁷.—sng.
V¹.δ.κ⁵.ρ.7.19.(8.14).— sep.—
silʰ.V¹.; VI³–VIII⁴.—-sul.
V¹⁰.βe.; ᵉζ.σ³.——trn.—thu.
V¹⁰ ˢ.η.χ¹.(8–31).; VIII³.ηaa.—
ªVI⁴.δ.ζ.η.5.—zin.V¹.
T.—am-c.VI⁴.5.—ba-cª.VI³.96.
—cam.V³.98.(99).—cs-e.V¹.
— cep.—cle.V¹–VII⁵·ª.σ².—
cob.V⁷.βe.35.; ᵇκ⁵.μ³.ω².—col.
V¹.δLllr.—con.VI⁴.—colᵇ.Iª.
—-cop.VI³.117.—cunᵇ.Iª. —

dio.IX.; ʰ.r.; V⁷.; ᵇ.V⁷.; III⁸.
θj.κ⁵.χ¹.; ᵇV³.—dirª.VI³.r.—
equ.V¹⁰.ηp.—-grp.V¹.16.—
ham.—hfbᵇ.V³.—ign.V¹⁰·ˢ.
17ª.(17).—jacª.V⁷.—lth.V¹⁰.f.
δᵇ.κ⁵.16.49.—mg-s.2.—na-aª.
V⁷.—nitᵇ.V¹.—pho.II¹–VI³.
19.66.(15).—rs-rª.5.—rhs.V⁶.
δ.(30).—sul.III¹.

C.—amb.V¹⁰·ᵘ.δ.ηcᵇ.4.—ast.V¹.
(8–31).— bov.VI⁴·ª.V².11.εC.
—cvl.Iª.—-grp.V⁷.98.(99).;
VI³–VII¹.4.(105).—hdr.V¹⁰·ᵛ.
ε.—hyp.VIII².—irs.IX.8.35.
—la-x.VII¹.—lau.VI⁴.ξ².2.83.
— mr-sᶜ.V⁷·q.34.(4).——nat.
VIII⁴.—-pan.V¹.βa.δl.—-stp.
III¹-V¹.βe.—-thu.VI².η.θ⁴.χ¹.
(8–31).

P.—alocᶜ.VI³·ᵛ.5.—almᶜ.V¹².—
belᶜ.V¹.31.—bovᶜ.VIII⁴.6.—
ch-s.VII⁵.38.—ch-x.q.—dio.
III¹.b.—eupᵈ.εᴅ.κ¹.—f-mgᶜ.—
fl-xᵏ.V¹·ª.—gelᶜ.V⁷.63.—grpᵇ.
κ⁶.(30).—hamᵈ.5.(66).—hpm.
V¹–VIII⁵.——hdrʰ.33.—jugᶜ.
V⁷.—-magᶜ.V³–VI³.—manᵈ.
VI³·⁴·ᵛ.18.—sarᶜ.V¹·q.ᵛ.

O.—agaª.VI³·⁴.——all.V⁷.17.—
aru.VI³.50.—ced.V¹.—ch-s.
V¹·ª.(30).—cob.; 8.—cchᶜ.δl.
η.—copⁱ.V¹–VI³.—dioᶜ.V⁷.;
V⁶.—gel.V⁷.66.; ᶜV¹–VI¹.63.
—jun.V³.30.—lo-i.V¹.8.—lyc.
IX.—mac.—mag.V³–VI³.—
mg-s.V¹.(8).— ni-xᶜ.VI³·ª.π¹.
63.—pet.V¹–VI³.—pulᶜ.V¹–
VI⁴.—rs-r.V⁷.; II¹·ᵇ.; V⁷.βᵇ.
5.41.—rhs.V⁶.δ.—sabᵈ.III.—
sil.V¹.σ².—spi.Iª.σ²ff.(3–30).

Ba.—erd.V¹.

B.—k-bifᵇ.θ²·⁴.—lahᶠ.VI⁴.—spg.
V³.16.66.(8–31).

3-10. *In the morning in bed.*
GEN.—aga.; VIII¹.θ³.ωll.—
am-c.κ⁵.—cha.(30).—dul.30.
—-hep.V⁷.(30).; V³.κ⁵.(12)
—ign.(30).—k-hy.(30).—lam.
III¹.βe.(30).——mag.—mg-s.
III.βeª.χ²·³.26.—mer.V²·⁶.—

na-m.(30).—nx-v.VII¹.; V³.
(30).— ptl.VI³.—rho.V¹.α¹ʊ.
(30).

F.—grp.V⁷.(99).—mezᵇ.VI³·ʷ.
—nx-vᶠ.V¹.17ª.(17).; VIII¹.
(30).—rn-b.V¹⁰.δ.π.(30).

C.—hel.V⁶.

P.—mt-nᵇ.VIII¹.—nicᶜ.VI³·ᵃ.—
nx-vᶜ.VI⁴.17.

O.—aga.V⁶.23.91.—epnᵇ.VI³.—
jug.V¹.(30).—jg-v.V¹.(30).

3-30. *In the morning on rising.*

GEN.—*alm*.σ².**10**.--am-c.V⁶-VI⁴.
—aps.V¹·⁷.—as-t.ω².—au-m.
—ba-c.VI³.p.—bry.V⁶-VIII³.
η.θ⁴.—ca-a.V¹.—*cha*.3-**10**.—
ch-s.29.35.—cob.—cod.V⁷.(5).
—cch.26.—cyc.; ¿tⁿ.—dig.
29.—dul.**10**.—fag.V⁷.—ham.
6.(31.41.43.86).—hdr.V⁷.—*ign*.
99.—idm.V⁷.(66).—ipc.VI⁴.(4).
—jug.—*k-hy*.3.**10**.—lyc.V¹⁰.—
mgt.3-99.—mag.VI³.—*mur*.99.
—mu-x.V¹. q.δo.βa.φ.49.—
na-m.3-**10**.—nic.V¹.βeᵃ.—*ni-x*.
3-99.—*nx-v*.βe.3-99.; V³.**10**.
—ped.—pet.—*ph-x*.99.; VI².
—pho.V⁷.au.3-99.; V¹.x.abᵒ.
βa.(16).—ptl.VIII⁴.ω².—*rho*.
V¹α¹ʊ.3-**10**.—rum.V¹.—rut.
V¹.—sep.V⁷.; III²-VIII³.—
squ.V⁷.εʊ.—sto.II⁷-VI³·⁴.q.—
sul.V¹. —trn.VIII¹.aⁱ.ι.οⁱ.π.
σ².ω²·⁸.—ton.VIII⁴.q.

F.—am-mᵇ.V¹⁰·ᵘ-VI⁴.; ᵇV³.—
asrᵇ.βa.; VIII⁴.—ba-a.V³.w.
(4).—bryᵉ.V¹·¹⁰.—cb-aʰ.V⁹.
(8).—cob.—con.VI³·ˢ.—dul.
V³·q.iiᵈ.—er-aᵍ.V⁷.—ferᵐ.
V¹⁰·ᵗ.33.(8.12). —grp.VI⁴.;
V⁷.35.—ham.VII¹.κ⁵.—ibe.—
k-biᵍ.VI³.ε⁴.35.—klm.; VI⁴.
ʋ.—lilᵍ.V¹⁰.δO.—lyc.V⁷.ω².—
mt-nᵇ.VI³.— mageᵉ.V¹.—natᵇ.
V¹.—na-m.V⁶·⁹.—nitᶠ.V¹.—
nx-v.VIII¹.3-**10**.—*pho*ᵉ.3-99.
—pso.V¹⁰·ˢ.(66.117).—*rn-b*.
V¹⁰.δ.π.3-**10**.—rap.V⁷.βe.—
sepᵍ.VI³·ˢ.δb.(8).—sil.V¹.

T.—au-mᵇ.VIII⁴.(116).—ccaᵃ.
VI³·ᵛ.89.—lilᵃ·ᵇ.V⁷.—ni-xᵃ.

V¹·ᵃ.κ⁷.λ.χ¹. —pedᵃ.VIII⁴.βe.
—sul.V¹.

C.—ba-a.V³.w.**5**.(4).—cau.VIII⁴.
—cmf.V¹·ᵉ.—nic.V¹.βeᵃ.—nit.
—*ol-a*.VI³.2.84.— pod.—sep.
VIII⁴.—sul.V¹.δ.

P.—arsᵇ.V².—cacᵈ.V¹.—ca-cᵈ.
VI².βa.χ¹.18.31.—gelᶜ.VIII⁴.
—m-piᵉ.(16).—*mr-ι*ᶜ.—mg-sᶜ.
VI³.28.—spiᶜ.V¹.δr 28.31.74.

O.—cmf.V¹·ᵈ.—cnb.V¹.iᵃ.—gel.
V⁷.—mg-m.VIII⁴.q.83.—mr-f.
—nx-v.V¹! —ped.III-VIII⁴.
δoᵈ.31.—*spi*.Iᵃ.σ²ff.3.—ton.
III.

B.—indᵖᵃ.VIII³·ᵃ.(35).

3-99. *In the morning on waking.*

GEN.—aga.V⁶.δ.—ail.V⁷.θ³.κ.κ¹.
rjj.—ag-n.θ¹.; iᵃ.q.βeᵃ.35.—
ar-i.V¹⁰·ˢ.q.29.35.41.—asi.—
bz-x.—bov.; VII¹.(**105**).—
ca-c.βa.—cn-i.—cb-a.—cau.
VI³.—cha.VII¹.—chi.V⁷.—
cl-h.V⁷.—cob.6.—cof.VII⁵.w.
29.—cch.4.—con.VII¹.iᵃ.; μ².
—cot.—c-ar.V⁷.—dig.V¹.—
elp.V⁷.—equ.V⁷.q.abᶜ.—eri.
V⁷.τʋ.—fag.δ.—for.κ⁶.πl.
fer.VI⁴.—glv.ε.—grp.; κ⁶.μ³.
χ³.ω³.; VII⁵.σ².—hel.V¹.q.
hep.V¹.; VI³.(8-31).—hpm.p.
βeᵇ.—ign.(30).; V² 41.(30).—
idm.V².—iof.—jug.θ³.—k-ca.
—klm.5.—kre.VI⁴.aⁱ.u.ηp.θ¹.
φ¹.χ².ω².—lam.8-31.—lep.
V¹⁰.; σ².—lil.V⁷.—lo-i.—lyc.
V¹.λ.—mgt.(3-30).; V³·⁷.—
mit.—mur.(30).—mu-x.VI³.
—myr.V⁷.δcᵈ.d.—mr-f.V⁷.—
na-m.V¹·⁷.—ni-x.(30).—nit.
λiᵃ.μ².—nx-v.βeᵃ.(3-30).; Iq.
47.—ol-a.βa.—opi.V¹.(8).—
ptv.—ph-x.(30).—pho.V⁷.au.
3-30.; V¹-VI⁴-VIII³.βe.35.;
VIII⁴.—pi-m.IX.—pgn.Iᵃ.
—pul.VI⁴.βe.—rs-r.V⁷.—
rum.—sep.—stn.p.—stp.VI⁴.
(96).—su-x.V².φ.—trn.p.λ¹.
χ¹·².

F.—alneᵉ.V¹⁰.(64).—almeᵉ.VI³.κ⁵.
ʋ³.ω³.—ana.V¹.31.—argⁿ.V⁶.

—ag-m.V^1.κ^5.(8.89).—ag-n^f. V^1.—arn.VI$^{3 \cdot a}$.—bel^e.q.δ. ; ^{n}. V^3.—ber.V^1.q $aa.\beta\epsilon.\chi^{1 \cdot 2}.\omega^2$.— bry^d.V$^{1 \cdot 10}$.——ca-c.V^7.$\beta\epsilon.\theta^3$.— ca-x.V^7.$\iota$.; III^1.p.(12).—ch-s. I^a.;^{b}.$\beta\epsilon$.—cin^a.V$^{10 \cdot s}$.—cnb.V^7. 12.16.(30.117).; V^1.16.(12).; VIII^4.(12).—cof.V^1–VII^5.δb. 29.—cch^a.I^a.35.; V^1.—col. V^1–VIII^4.—dig.V^7.κ^5.—eri. V^7.δr.——eup.V^1.—eu-a.V^7. (66).—fag.35.—fl-x.I^b.—gel. III.δb.(12).—glo.—grp.VI^4. —hep.V^2.λ.48.—hdr.VII^1. (12.35.41).—ign.V^1.$\beta\epsilon$.33.35. 48.—idm.V^7.(5).—k-bi.— klm.—kre.VIII^4.ηp $\kappa.\omega^2$.— la-x.—la-v.V^{10}.δ.41.—lyc.V^1. —mag.V^1.——mg-m.V^1.$\beta\epsilon^b$.— myr.V^7.q.——naj.VII^5.31.— na-a.V^7.—ol-a.V$^{10 \cdot a}$.41.—pet. VI^3.——ph-x.V$^{1 \cdot a}$.$a^1 \mho.\delta b.o^2$.35. —pho^e.(30).—plc.V^1.δb,L.— rap.V^1.$\beta\epsilon$.—rhs^p.VI^4.46.48.— rum.V^7.—rut.VIII^4.$\beta\epsilon$.5.— san^a.ϵ.θ^1.—so-n^e.35.——stp^b. V$^{1 \cdot 3}$–VI$^{3 \cdot s}$.—sul.VII^5.δ.50.; I^a.(63).;^{b}.I^b.—tar.V^1–VII^5. (116).—thr^e.II^1.—thu.V$^{1 \cdot 2}$– VI^4.

T.—ail.I^a.—asi.VI^3.δ.89.—atr^b. VI^3.δb.(8).—cld^a.V$^{1 \cdot 7}$.—ca-c. V^1.κ^7.——cam^{a}V^3–VI^3.——cs-e. V^1.—cof.V$^{10 \cdot zz}$.29.—idm.V^7. q.$au.\varphi$.——lah.VIII^4.—lth.I^a. —na-a.V^1.—ni-x^a.VIII^4.κ^5.— tab.V^1.—zin.V^1.

C.—alm^a.VIII^4.—ba-c.V$^{1 \cdot 2}$.σ^2ff. —bry.VIII^4.—buf.—ca-c.V^1. —ca-x.—cau.VI^4.—ced.V^7. cro.V^7.q.—byp.$\epsilon \mho$.—k-bi.V$^{1 \cdot a}$. —sul.V^1–VIII$^{4 \cdot a}$.; II^1.b.30.; V$^{1 \cdot 10}$.$r \upsilon.\omega^2$.—tab.V^1.1.—ver. V^1.

P.—aru^c.V^3.——aur^b.V^3–VIII^4. 22.89.—cin^c.V$^{10 \cdot s}$.—cod^d.V^7. —cot^c.—mr-i^d.(5).——mu-x^f. VI^3.—pho^c.6.29.35.(8).—tab. V^1.(30).

O.—arn.VI$^{3 \cdot a}$.——bry.II^3.q.r.17. —con.VI^4.—fl-x^c.III^3.—k-bi.

V^1.ηii.θ^1.—mil.—ox-x.V^1.ξ^1.— pet.VI^3.—rhs.V^2.—ur-n. B.—ham^f.V^{10}.—iof^{pb}.V^1.q.

4. *In the afternoon.*

GEN.——alm.o^1.χ^2.; V^{12}.q.29.; VI$^{3 \cdot s}$.; VIII^4.16.31.—am-c.q. —asa.V$^{1 \cdot 10}$.$\beta\epsilon$.—bad.; δ.— bov.III.——buf.φ^1.2.——cb-v. VIII^4.—ch-s.9-31.—cn-s.(5). —cob.V^7.—cca.χ^1.; μ^3.v^1b.— cch.3-99.——cvl.3.——cun.— cyc.βa.——dig.ab^o.——dgn.—— equ.V^7.—fag.VII^1.; VII^1.41.; d.66.——fer.χ.—for.ρ.29.—gam. V^1.q.—gel.I^a.κ^5.(26).—glo.— grt.κ^5.—ham.ϵ.—hel.; V^7.$\beta\epsilon$.— hfb.—ibe.V^7.—idm.VIII^4.p. ηaa.—*ipc*.VI^4.3-30.—la-x.VII^1. —lau.VI^3.—lep.—lin.V^7.— lyc.V^1.29.; VI^4.5.; χ^2.—lcp. I^a.—mt-n.VII^1.—mag.VIII^3. q.40.(5-**10**).—mg-s.V$^{1 \cdot 7}$.;VI^3.; VIII^2.5.——mr-i.φ.——mez.I^a. 11.40.—nat.VI^4.——na-m.V^6– VI^3.$\delta.\theta^4$.8.—nit.V^1.—*nx-j*.V^1. q.66.—ol-a.V^6.VI^4.$\beta\epsilon$.3.—opi. V^1.aa,b^o.; V^1–VIII$^{4 \cdot zz}$.—ped. —ph-x.—phy.V^1.q.$ab^i.\beta a$.— plb.VI^3.ϵr.5.——pgn.κ^4.b.—— rs-r.κ^5.; I^e.—sec.—sil.VI$^{3 \cdot 4}$. —sto.—sul.VI^4.$\chi^2.\omega^2$.(14).

F.—ail.q.φ.—alo.V^7.—alm.VI^3. q.18.V^{12}.; VI^3–VIII^4.—amb. V$^{10 \cdot u}$.p.$\delta.\eta$c^b.——ana.III^1–V^3. au.(12).—anh.V^3.ω^2.—ag-n^o. V^3–VI^3.——bad.p.δ.48.—*ba-a*. V^3.w.3-30.—bor.VIII^3.$\delta.\kappa^5$.— bov^g.V$^{1 \cdot 3}$.7.——bry^f.V^6.; ^{n}.V^6. VII^5.; III^1.q.—buf.——ca-s^a. —cn-i^e.V$^{10 \cdot s}$.—cas.VIII^4.q. —cau.VIII$^{4 \cdot a}$.σ^2.—chi^c.V^1.; VIII^3.(5).——ch-s.—cmf.V^7. —cic.VIII^2.—cca.$\beta a.\omega^2$.; ^{a}. V^1.$\beta a.\chi^1$.(5).—cch^g.I^a.51.; ^{e}. V^1.—con.VI$^{3 \cdot a}$.(16).——cyc. V^7.—dio.—dir.—fag.V^{10}– VII^1.; ^{p}.V^1.—*fer*^{m}.V^7.3.— for.V^7.—gel.VI$^{3 \cdot t}$.—grp.VI^4. p.—hpm^e.V^1.—hfb.I^a.—ign^a. V$^{10 \cdot s}$.δ.—idm.V^7.—ir-f^a.VI^1. —jab.VIII^4.—k-ca.V^1.au.31.

—k-cy.V^{10}.8.31.——kre^i.V^6.
$\theta^4 r$.; ^{a}.VI^3.a^{1}b^a.——la-v^m.VI^3.q.
$\beta \iota$.—lau.VI^4.; ^{m}.VI^3.—lil^b.
V^7.$\delta \iota$.—lo-s^b.V^7.—lyc.κ^4.128.;
V^1.; ^{n}.VI^3–VIII^4.; VI^4.κ^3.
χ^2.; VIII^4.ηp,aa.—mg-s.VI^4–
VIII^3.; VIII$^{2 \cdot 4}$.5.—man.V$^{10 \cdot zz}$.
—mr-i.——mu-x.VI^3.—na-a.
χ^3.——na-m^b.VI^3.; ^{a}.VI^3.——ni-x.
III ——nit^p.VI$^{3 \cdot d}$.5.20.31.——
opi.V^1.βb,ι.θ^2.κ.$\kappa^{1 \cdot 5 \cdot 9}$.66.(5).—
ped.I^a.——ptv.p.δ.——ph-x.V^7.
——pho^b.VI$^{3 \cdot d}$.5.——rn-b.d.—
rs-r.I$^{a \cdot w}$.; rs-r^c.I^e.$_a$b^s,k.ω^2.5.5.
—san^a.VI^3.; i^a.—snc.V$^{10 \cdot s}$.—
ser.V^1.—sil.III.; VI^4.; VIII^4.
—so-t.I^a.31.—sto.VI^3.βa.; V^1.
—sul.V^1.83.; ^{g}.V^1.; VI$^{3 \cdot s}$.—
tab^f.V^1.——trn^a.δ.29.——tar.
VI$^{3 \cdot 4}$.——val^e.V$^{10 \cdot s}$.δ.48.66.

T.——alo^b.V$^{1 \cdot 3}$.δ.5.——alm^a.V^1–
VIII^4.q.——bel^b.——bov^b.V^3–
VI^4.–VIII^4.q.——bry^b.V$^{10 \cdot s}$.——
cth^a.VI^3.—cau^b.VI$^{4 \cdot a}$.—ch-s.
(5).; V^7.; ^{b}.IX.——cca.V^6.43.
——cod^a.VIII^4.——col^b.V$^{1 \cdot a}$.18.
31.77.(19).——dio.θ^4.——dul^b.
V$^{1 \cdot 6}$.—fag.56.——gam^b.VI^4.—
grt.V^3–VI^4.2.101.102.—gua.
29.——hpm.V^1.—ibe.VIII^4.
——k-bi^a.q.κ^4.66.——lau^h.V^1.6.
—lyc^b.V^{10}.128.——mg-s^b.VI^4.
——na-a.V$^{3 \cdot t}$.p.κ^5.12.65.101.—
ni-x^b.V^9–VI^3.——ol-a^b.V$^{1 \cdot b}$.
ptv^a.VI^3.—pla^a.IV^1.—sil^a.V^1.
—sto^a.VI^3.—sul^b.V1^3.δ.

C.—aln.II^6.29.——alm.V^1.—amb.
V$^{10 \cdot u}$.δ.ηc^b.3.——ars^c.V^6.—ba-a.
V^3.w.3-30.5.——buf.——ca-s.
VI^3.66.—cb-v.V^1.—cmf.5.—
grp.VI^3–VII^1.3.(105).; III.
—hln.V^{10}.——hur.V^{16}.η.θ^1.31.
—hyp.VIII^4.p.; VII^1.—ind.
VI$^{3 \cdot b}$.——ir-f^a.V$^{3 \cdot 10}$.——la-x.
VI$^{3 \cdot w}$.dd^h.——man.V$^{10 \cdot zz}$.——
mr-i^a.VIII^4.ζ.——mr-s^c.V$^{7 \cdot q}$.3.
34.-mu-x.VI$^{3 \cdot a}$.—na-a.VIII^4.
i^a.—ni-x.VI^3–VII^1.ϕ^1.——nit.
III^1.2.—osm.i^a.22.—phl.VI^3–
VIII^4.——pho.VI$^{4 \cdot a}$.η.19.——
sul.II$^{1 \cdot 3}$–V^1–VI^4.8.(5).

P.—æth^c.VI^4.—alm^c.VI^3–VIII^4.;
^{c}.VI^4–VIII^4.——bry^b.δ.; ^{c}.V^6.
VII^5.—cth^c.VI^3.——cas^d.VI^3.
—ch-s^c.V^7.; ^{h}.IX.29.——cca^c.
V^1.βa.χ^1.(5).——cch^d.I^a.(66).—
fer^d.VI$^{3 \cdot a}$.——grp^c.VIII^4.——
ind^c.V^6.; ^{c}.VI^3.κ^4.19.29.(30).
—lau^d.VI^4.——mg-s^d.V^3.p.—
mr-i^a.V^{10}–VI^3.——na-m^c.VI^1.
—nic^c.VI$^{3 \cdot 4}$.—ni-x^d.VIII^4.—
ol-a^d.II^1–VI^4.——sep^d.VI^3.5.—
val^c.V^6.107.—zin^c.VI^4.θ^1.

O.——æth^b.VI$^{4 \cdot 7z}$.; VI$^{3 \cdot 4 \cdot zz}$.——aga.
V^6.—ang.V^1.——bov^k.V$^{10 \cdot s}$.5.;
V$^{1 \cdot 3}$–VI^3.7.——cth.VI$^{3 \cdot zz}$.——
cas^a.VI$^{3 \cdot 4}$.18.——ch-s^c.V^7.——
cmf.V^1.6.(8-31).; V^7.——cle.
hh.βa.$\kappa^{4 \cdot 5}$.——cca.ω^2.ϕ.2.; V^{10}.
βa.χ^1.(5).; V$^{6 \cdot zz}$.43.——dio^c.
VI^3.; V^7.q.—dir.I^t.—erd.V^{10}.;
II^1.; V$^{10 \cdot s}$.—fag.V$^{10 \cdot s}$.—hdr^b.
VIII$^{5 \cdot zz}$.——ind^c.V^6.——iod^h.
V$^{1 \cdot a}$.8.—irs^g.V^7.—man.V$^{10 \cdot zz}$.
——nit.III^a.ff.a$\mathfrak{g}$.η.ι.π^1.σ^2.τ.——
ol-a^i.II^1–VI^4.——osm.i^a.4.——
pet^c.VI^3.—ph-x^d.VI^3.—rs-r^b.
V^1.41.——rhs.VIII^3.——sar^f.
VI$^{4 \cdot v}$.—sul.V$^{7 \cdot 14}$.31.

B.—ba-a$^{oa \cdot p}$.V^7.—hel^{pb}.VI^4.; ^{f}.
V$^{3 \cdot a}$.——irs^m.VIII^4.(101).——
la-v^{pa}.V$^{6 \cdot a}$.11.——mg-s^{fa}.VI^4.
11.—mr-f.IX.—ur-n^t.I^a.

5. *In the evening.*

GEN.—aco.——alm.III–VI^4.χ^1.;
VI^4.ϵ.(12).——ang.; χ^2.8.—ari.
VI^3.—art.—bad.ω.—ba-c.51.
—bor.$\beta \iota$.ϵl.—bov.V^{10}–VIII^4.
7.; V^2.q.$\beta \iota^a$.—bry.V^{10}.—ca-c.
VI^3.v.—cth.V^1–VI^3.5.(31).—
cb-aV^1.$\beta \iota$.66.—cb-v.III^1.66.;
VIII^4.π^1.——cn-s.V^7.——ced.8.
——cep.ζ.6.——ch-s.——cmf.——
cin.VI.——cn-s.4.——cle.VIII^3.
16.; VII^1.——cob.II^5–VIII^4.
——cch.I^b.——col.ab^o.; δ.29.;
28.29.—cu-a.— c-ar.V^7.q.—
cyc.—der.V^{16}.63.—dgn.—dul.
V^7.; VII^2.8-31.; V^6.; VI^3.au.
(16).—erd.V$^{10 \cdot s}$.——eug.II^1.δ.
δa.2.72.——eup.V^2.$\beta \iota$.ζ^3.16.——
fer V^{10}.8-31.—f-io 7.26.29.81.

43.44.(8.107).—for.V^7.—glo.
—grp.83.; $V^2.\omega^4$.——hpm.V^{10}.
—hdr.βa.ω^2.—hfb.—hyp.III.
—ind.V^7.—jug.—k-ca.v.(35).
—k-cl.βa.—klm.3·99.; $V^6.\delta$.8.
——lah.βa.—lch.VI^2.(66).——
la-x.V^7.q.—lep.III.—lil.IX.
(90).—lo-i.$V^1.\beta\varepsilon.\eta$p.66.; VII^5.
ηp.—lyc.VI^4.4.; VI^3.—lcp.βa.;
δ.—mac.(71).——mt-s.r^1p.——
mag.ξ.83.; II^7.12.; VI^3.ak.—
mg-s.VIII^2.4.——man.$V^{10\cdot a}$.2-
99.—mer.43.(16.19).; III^1.—
mr-f.$\eta.\zeta$.—mr-i.ϕ.—msc.V^7.—
nat.II^1–VI^3.p.——na-m.κ^5.3.;
na-m.$\kappa^{5\cdot6}.\omega^3$.30.31.——ni-x.$V^1$-
VIII^4.; VIII^3.——nit.V^1.——
nx-v.$VI^3\kappa^{5\cdot6}$.66.(16).—par.V^7.
δp,aa.——pau.29.——pet.8-31.;
—ph-x.$\beta\varepsilon$.7.—pho.; 41.; V^2.
(98).; VII^1.ab.; VI^3.—plm.3.
—plb.$VI^3.\varepsilon r$.4.——pso.——pul.
$VI^3.\chi^1.\omega^3$.66.——rat.$VI^{3\cdot g}$.—
rho.V^7.; V^1.—rhs.$VI^{4\cdot g}$.29.—
san.ιv.——sep.26.; VIII^4.—
so-t.—spr.—stp.$VI^3.\varepsilon\mathfrak{d}$.29.31.
——sto.$V^{1\cdot6}$-VII^5.; VII^2.16.;
$VII^5.\pi.\sigma^1.v$.——sul.V^7.—su-x.
V^6.—ter.—thr.ak.31.—trf.
val.$V^{10}.\delta.\theta^4$.— ver.$VI^4.\kappa^5$.3.83.
—wis.—zin.$\delta.\lambda$.16.; V^{12}.; VI^3-
VIII^4.3.

F·—aco.$V^{1\cdot7}$.—aga.; ^{h}.$V^1.\delta$L.—
aln^e.$V^{10}.\beta$a.(16).——alm^e.III^1.
$\chi^{2\cdot3}$.2.; VI^4.(8).; ^{o}.$VI^{3\cdot4}$.; VI^3.
66.——ana^a.$V^{3\cdot10\cdot t}$.(12.16.63).
—ang.$V^1.\eta$p.——an-s.31.; ^{n}.VI^3.
ϕ.——ara.$V^1.\beta\varepsilon.\omega^2$.66.(12).——
arg^b.$V^{3\cdot e}$.16.——ag-m.V^1.p.q.
29.—ars^g.2.—aru^g.VI^3.—bad.
d.p.—ba-c^g.V^6.; ^{m}.VIII^4.—
bis.βa.$\kappa^{4\cdot7}.\rho.\chi^2$.35.—bor.$\varepsilon l.\theta^1$l.
—bov^c.$VI^{3\cdot p}$.; ^{b}.$V^{3\cdot5}$.——cac^b.
V^{10}.——ca-s.—cam^g.V^1.; V^7-
VI^3.ab$^o.\beta\varepsilon$.(8).—cas.V^1.; V^6-
VI^4.—cau^b.VI^4.ii.—chd^b.VI^3.
——chi.VIII^3.4.——ch-s.; d.p.
$\varepsilon\mathfrak{d}$.; ^{c}.V^3–VI^3.—cmf^f.——cin.
V^1.—cnb^e.V^7.35.; ^{a}.V^7.—cle.
—cca^a.$V^1.\beta$a.χ^1.4.——coc.VI^4-
VIII^4.—crt^a.$V^1.\delta r.\eta r.\theta^1.vl$.—

dig.V^1-VII^5.—dgn.$V^{6\cdot a}$.--dio.
V^7.--dul^o.$V^{10\cdot s}$.—ech.V^7.—eri.
V^7.--er-m.—fag^b.$VI^{1\cdot t\cdot z}$.--fer^h.
V^7.; $^a.\zeta r$.—fl-x^n.III.; $^a.\delta r$.16.;
^{n}.; ^{b}.—grp.V^6.—ham.III^1.—
hpm.$V^{6\cdot7}.\delta$.—bur.—bfb^e.; ^{e}.
$VI^3.\pi$.—ibe.V^7.--ind.$VI^4.\phi.\omega^2$.
--idm^d.$V^{1\cdot10}$.i^a.29.--iod^e.V^1.--
ir-f^n.$VIII^{4\cdot b}$.--irs.βa.--k-$bi^{g\cdot h}$.
$VI^{3\cdot a}.\delta$ᴅ 3.——k-ca.$V^{1\cdot6\cdot a}$.
k-hy^a.$VI^{3\cdot4\cdot a}$.(12).--klm.;V^{10}.;
$^e.\sigma^2.rl$.—lab.V^1.6.19.(8-35).—
la-x$^{a\cdot1}$.V^7.i^a.—lep.III.——lil.
IX.ω^2.; ^{g}.II^1–V^1.—lyp.$V^{10\cdot s}$.
(14).—lyc.$VIII^{4\cdot a}.\sigma^2$.; ηp,aa.;
^{b}.V^1.——mt-s^c.VI^3.g^b.——mag.
VI^3.——mg-m.$V^{10\cdot s}$.29.; VI^4.
q.; $VI^{3\cdot4}$.35.; ^{c}.VI^3.——mg-s.
$VIII^{2\cdot4}$.—mer.V^7.αu.—mr-i^a.
$V^{7\cdot10}.\rho$.; $V^{7\cdot10}$.; V^6–VI^3.; II^1.
δs.——nab$^{f\cdot q}$.Iq.——naj.V^1.3.—
na-m.V^1.——ni-x^o.VI^3–VIII^4.
δb^b.--nit^p.$VI^{3\cdot d}$.4.20.31.; ^{a}.V^1.-
VI^3.; V^6.——nup^b.$V^{3\cdot h}$.—nx-j.
—ol-a^b.V^1–VI^4.——opi.$V^1.\beta\mathfrak{b},\varepsilon$.
$\theta^2.\kappa.\kappa^{1\cdot5\cdot9}$.4.66.—osm^a.$VI^{4\cdot q}.v$.
—pæo.$V^{1\cdot a}$.q.δO.3.——ped.31.
66.——ptv^h.V^7.--ph-x.V^2.41.
--pho^h.$^{a1}\mathfrak{d}$.(66).; V^1.; ^{b}.$VI^{3\ d}$.
4.—pla.$V^{10\cdot s}$.q.δb,$\varepsilon.\eta$p,aa.$\kappa^3.o^2$.
ρ.26.29.——plb.$VI^{3\cdot a}$.——pod.I^1.
ι.—pso.$V^{10\cdot s}$.—pul.$V^{10}.\beta\varepsilon$.48.;
VIII^4.29.41.(31).; $VI^{3\cdot s}$.
rn-b^f.ak.——rn-s.$V^{10\cdot t}.\kappa^3.\chi^1$.——
rat.VII^1.29.—rs-r^f.; ^{e}.I^e.ab^c,
$k.\omega^2$.5.(4).; ^{g}.II^1.117.; ^{g}.$I^{a\cdot b}$.
41.; $V^7.\beta\mathfrak{y}$.3.41.——rum.VI^3.;
$VIII^4.\beta\varepsilon$.3-99.——sar^n.VI^3.
sel.$VI^3.\delta$.5.7.—sng.V^1–VIII^4.
—ser^a.$V^1.\beta\varepsilon$.—sil.VI^4.1.35.—
so-l.$V^{10\cdot s}$.(14).——so-t.VI^3.66.
--stp.VI^4.19.VI^3.29.(31).—
sul.VI^3.VI^3.86.89. ——su-x^a.
$VI^{3\cdot4}$.(12).—tar^a.IX.—thu^a.
$VI^4.\delta.\zeta.\eta$.3.——val^a.V^1.; V^1.—
xip^h.V^1.(53^a).——zin.$V^1.\beta\varepsilon$.5.;
V^1.; VI^4.g^a.63.
T.—aco.$^{10\cdot s}$.i$^a.\delta$L.—alo^b.$V^{1\cdot3}.\delta$.4.
—alm^b.$V^{3\cdot6}$.; ^{a}$V^{3\cdot t}$.—am-c.
VI^4.3.—ana.$V^{10\cdot t}$.--ara.$V^1.\beta$a.
ω^2.66.(12).——cam.VI^3.ab$^o.\beta\varepsilon$.

δO.(8).——cas.VI^4.χ^1.II^3.11.; ^{a}VI^4.31.——cau^b.VI^4.ii.——chi. V^1.—ch-s.4.; I^a.—cnb.VI^3.— cch^a.(16).——cop^a.V^2.2.12.—— crn.VIII$^{4 \cdot a}$.— crt^b.V^1.$\eta r.\theta^1.vl$. —dig^b.V^1–VII^5.—dio.; ^{a}V^7.; ^{a}III^3.—equ^b.VI^3.ηp,aa.—fl-x^a. VIII^3.29.——hdr.I^a.36.(8.12). —hyp.VI^3.; ^{a}VI$^{3 \cdot b}$.χ^1.—inu^b. V^3.—jac$^{a \cdot b}$.σ^2.8.; ^{a}V^7.(12).— —k-ca^b.VI^4.θ^4.—k-hy^b.VI$^{3 \cdot 4 \cdot a}$ (12).; ^{b}VIII^4.—kre^b.V$^{10 \cdot s}$.— lah.III.31.—la-x.VIII^4.—lep. III.—lin.V$^{1 \cdot a}$.——lth.VII^5.q.; V$^{10 \cdot t}$.π.—lcp.I.—mg-m.IV^2.— VIII^4.βa.16.(12).——m-pu^a.δ. —mez^b.19.——na-m^b.VII^5.— ni-x^b.VI^3.—nit^a.V^6.——nx-v^b. VI$^{3 \cdot a}$.$\kappa^{5 \cdot 6}$.(16).——ph-x.V^2.41.; ^{a}VI^3.; VI^3.—pso^b.V^1.—rn-b. V^1.βa.σ^2.6.; V$^{1 \cdot 6}$.$aq.\pi^1$.31.—— rs-r^a.3.—sep.VI^3.——str^a.VI^3. —sto^b.VI^3.; V^{14}.—sul.V^1.43. —su-x^a.VI^4.—tab.III.—trn^b. VI^3.

C.—amb.V^1.q.—ana.III^1.—cth. V^1–VIII^4.35.——cb-a.VI^3.—— cmf.4.—cvl.I^a.— crt.V^6.δr.— cyc^c.VI^3.—dul.V^6.ζ.63.—fag. ——for.VIII^5.δo.——gn-c.V^1– VII^5–VIII^3.41.49.— hep.V^1. ρ^1.—hyp.VI$^{3 \cdot a}$.; VI^4.—k-ca. V^{10}.—k-hy.VI^3.—lth^a.— lyc. VI^4. ——mer.V^7.au.——mu-x. VIII^3.—ni-x.V^3–VI^3.—ol-a. V$^{6 \cdot q}$.— pet.V^1–VIII^3.—rn-b. VII^1.δ.6.——rhs^c.103.——sep. III^1–VIII^5.—sil.V^1.δ.—sto. VII^5.θ^4.; VII^1.p.aq,b.ηp,aa.ϕ. —sul.V$^{10 \cdot t \cdot q}$.δb.2-10.; II^1-V^1. —zin.VIII^4.p.

P.—alo^c.VI$^{3 \cdot v}$.3.—arg^d.V^6–VI^4. 31.—ari^d.VI^3.—ba-c^d.VI^3.66. —ca-s^d.66.—cth^c.VI^3–VIII^4. 18.19.— cau^d.VI^3.—ch-s^d.V^7.; ^{c}IX.8-31.; ^{c}IX.19.—cca^c.V^1. βa.χ^1.4.—dgn.IX.——elp^d.V^7. —fl-x^d.V$^{1 \cdot 10 \cdot t}$.ηp.θ^1.86.—grp^c. VI$^{4 \cdot a}$.—ham^d.3.(66).——hfb^b. V$^{1 \cdot 3}$–VI$^{3 \cdot t}$.δ.—idm^d.I^a.-k-ca^b. κ^5.ω^2.—lyc^a.VI^4.—mag^c.VI^3.;

^{d}VI^3.18.--mg-m^d.V^8.--m-pu^c. V^7.βe^b.τ.—mr-i^d.V$^{7 \cdot 10}$.; d.V^6. VI^3.nic^c.VI$^{4 \cdot a}$.19.——nit^d.ι.— nx-v^b.ω^2.—pho^c.V^6.; ^{c}.VI$^{4 \cdot v}$. 19.; ^{c}.VIII$^{4 \cdot q}$.—pul.VI^4.17.-- sep^b.q.16.; ^{d}.VI^3.4.-sil.VI^4.35. —spi^d.V^3–VI^4.31.32.35.—sul^d. V^1.; ^{c}.VIII^1.19.——ton^c.VI^3. er.--zin.V^7–VII^1.18.; ^{c}.VIII^4.

O.—alm.VI^3.66.—amb.VI$^{3 \cdot v}$.-- ba-c.VIII^4.—bel^d.VI^3.—bov^k. V$^{10 \cdot s}$.4.——cth.V^1–VI^3.16.— cb-a^c.VI^4–VIII^3.—cep^k.βe.5. (70).——ch-s.; ^{c}.V^7.; ^{h}.VI^3. 24.——cca.V^{10}.βa.χ^1.4.—cch. V^6.; ^{g}.V$^{1 \cdot 10}$.—dio^c.IV^1.—erd. V$^{10 \cdot v}$.—for.VI^4.—gel.V^7.29. 35.—grp.V^6.—hyp.V$^{1 \cdot 6}$.VI^3.; VI^4.—ign^b.V$^{1 \cdot 10}$.——ind.VI^3– VIII^4.—jab^c.V^7.—k-br.I^a.— k-cl.θ^4.--lo-i.VII^5.; V^7.p.— —lyc.VII^5.σ^2.—mag.VI$^{3 \cdot a}$.— mez^c.V$^{10 \cdot s}$.—mu-x.VI^3–VII^5. —ni-x^b.VI$^{3 \cdot a}$.(16).—nit.V^1– VIII^4.--ol-a.V^8.--rn-b^c.VI$^{4 \cdot a}$. θ^4l.σ^2.—rn-s^e.V^3.--rs-r.V^7.βb. 41.—sng.V^7.—sep.V^1.; VI^3. —ser^b.V^1.βe.--stn.V$^{10 \cdot s}$.--stp. V$^{10 \cdot s}$.d.16.—sto.V^{10}.— sul.I^a. —zin.V^3.; ^{b}.VIII^4.p.

B.— agn^c.II$^{5 \cdot zz}$.98.— cep^o.V^1.x. 11.—m-pu$^{f \cdot p}$.V^1.--na-m^p.VI^2. 63.; ^{tb}.VIII^3.δl.—par^f.II$^{4 \cdot 5}$. δ.δLp,aa.——pho^{pa}.V^8–VIII^4. —rn-b^f.V$^{1 \cdot 6}$.H^{f}b.66.——zin^{pa}. V^3–VII^1.18.

5-10. *In the evening in bed.*
GEN.-cyc.-lau.VI^4.-lyc.VIII^4.
——*mag*.VIII^3.q.4.40.—pho.
F.—c-ar.V^7.—mg-s^g.V^3.βe^o.
T.—chd.VIII^4.—glo^b.V$^{1 \cdot 10 \cdot s}$.—
κ^5.μ^2.σ^1.(66).— ol-a.V^1–VII^5.
—ph-x.III^1.—rhs^a.V$^{10 \cdot v}$.(30).
C.—cb-v.II^1–V^1.—stn.V^{10}.
P.—arg^c.V^6–VI^4.—con^c.VIII^4.
—pla^d.VI^3.
O.—dul.—nit^c.II^1–VIII^4.

5. *In the forenoon.*
GEN.——æth.a^1b.βa.κ^6.χ^2.——alm.
VI^4.—ant.VI^4.—cth.V^1–VI^3.
5.(81).— cn-s.V^1.—cle.III^1.

—cob.; $\kappa^5.\omega^2$.—coc.$V^1.a^1\zeta^d$.41.
43.—ccs.V^7.26.—*cod.*V^7.3.—
cop.—equ.$I^a.\delta$.—gam.; III.
—gen.112.--hfb.--ind.VIII^4.
19.; $VIII^{5 \cdot zz}$.19.—jab.—k-ca.
$V^1.\chi^1$.—klm.—lah.$VI^3.\delta.\zeta.\eta$ii.
—la-v.—lcp.V^7.—mr-f.V^7.
na-m.V^{15}.28.—nic.VI^3.29.—
ol-m.$\kappa^{6 \cdot 7}$.—ped.$\beta a.\kappa^5$.—pet.V^7.
χ^1.—pgn.—rs-r.V^7.—sep.V^2.
—ser.af.—so-t.—spo.III.—
sul.$V^{10 \cdot u}$.——ton.V^1–$VI^{3 \cdot 4}$.au.
η.6.

F.—ar-i.$\beta e.\sigma^2$.26.——bro^d.V^{10}.—
bry.V^7.—ca-s.I^a.—cnc.$V^1.\beta e$.
—ca-s^n.VI^3.—chi^e.31.(66).—
cle^b.$I^a.\delta$O.102.(12).; ^{a}.$V^{1 \cdot 3}.\eta$.
—coc.$V^{1 \cdot a}.a^1b^s$.43.—col.31.--
con.$VI^{3 \cdot s}$.—dig^a.V^7.—eup.V^1.
—fl-x^a.I^b.—— gam^h.VIII^4.;
VIII^4.q.--*idm.*V^7.3.99.--k-ca.
V^6.2.—-k-cy^s.$VI^{3 \cdot v}$.31.128.—
lah^s.V^1.—*la-x*^{e}.V^7.—lep.III^1.
—lyc.V^1.p.; VIII^4.—mg-s.V^2.
—mr-i^e.VI^3.—my-s^m.—na-a^e.
V^7.—ptv^d.$VI^{3 \cdot a}$.—rs-r.V^7.; f.
41.; ^{e}.I^e.ab^o,$k.\omega^2$.5.(4).—sar.
V^1.q.66.—sel.$VI^3.\delta$.5.7.--sng.
V^1.——sep.V^3.35.—sul.V^1.;
f.V^{10}.—zin.$V^1.\beta e$.5.; $V^1.\beta e.\delta$.
ϕ.; $VI^{3 \cdot 4}.o^3$.

T.——alm^a.V^7–VII^5.(12).; V^3–
VI^4.— ars.$VIII^2.\omega^2$.—asr.V^6.
(8-16).——cle^a.$V^{1 \cdot 3}.\eta$.—dio.;
^{b}.V^3–VI^1.—fag^a.$VI^3.\delta$.—gen^a.
$VI^{3 \cdot s}$.31.——hpm$^{a \cdot b}$.V^1.35.—
hdr^b.—ind^a.VI^3.; ^{b}.$VI^{3 \cdot 4 \cdot p}$.—
jug^a.V^1.—k-ca^a.V^1.—lah^b.V^1.;
$VI^3.\delta.\delta$ii.$\zeta.\eta$ii.θ^4.——lil^b.$V^7.\beta a$.
31.—lcp^b.--mg-s.$VI^{3 \cdot e}$.--na-a.
V^7.—ptv^a.V^{10}.11.—pod.$V^{10}.\delta$.
—rs-r^a.VI^3.—sng.V^1.

C.—alm.VIII^4.— an-s.V^3.g^b.—
ba-a.V^3.w.3-30.(4).—bov.V^1.
—fl-x^a.$III^1.\sigma$r.—gam.V^2.(8).
—glo.VIII^4.ll.— k-cy.VI^4.—
mg-s.$V^3.\beta e^a$.—nic.V^2–VI^3.au.
—nx-m.V^{10}.--ptv.V^7.28.31.--
rs-r.VI^3.—sul.V^1.; *sul.*$II^{1 \cdot 3}$–
V^1–VI^4.4.8.

P.--alm^c.$VI^{3 \cdot 4}$.--cac^b.V^1.--cb-a^a.

V^7.55.(8).—cas^c.VI^3.— fl-x^d.
IX.i^a.6.8.—hdr^i.V^{10}.—-ind.
VIII^4.19.; ^{c}.$II^{4 \cdot zz}$.19.—klm.
^{c}.I^a.—lah^d.—-na-m^d.$VI^{3 \cdot q}.\epsilon$.
31.—nx-j^d.IX.86.—ptv.$VI^{3 \cdot a}$.
—plb^c.VI^3–$VIII^{4 \cdot a}$.18.31.—-
sar^c.$VIII^{4 \cdot q}$.—sto^d.$V^1.\beta a$.

O.—alm^b.V^6–VII^5–VIII^4.—
bov.$V^{1 \cdot zz}$.—-cs-e.$V^{10 \cdot q}$.—cep.
V^1.rx.; $^k.\beta e$.(5.**70**).—cob^c.—
dio.I^a.—gel.V^1.—la-v.—lyc.
V^1–VI^3.—nat^h.—-pso^b.V^5.—
spo.III.—sul.$V^{1 \cdot 6}$.

B.—fl-x$^{f \cdot p}$.V^1.(16).—ind.VIII^4.
19.—rn-b^{ta}.

6. *In a room.*

G$_{EN}$.—æth.VIII^4.—bov.II^7–
VIII^4.3.8.—cep.(8).; ζ^3.5.—
chd.—cob.3-99.; V^7.1.31.35.
—cof.66.(8).; *cof.*V^2.8.—
cch.V^1.(98).—eup.II^5.8.(86).
—ham.3-30.(31.41.43.86).—
*hep.*III.8-31.—hpm.8.—hyo.
(8).—iod.31.128.—*mt-s.*VII^5.
8.--mag.V^1.122.—mg-m.VI^4–
VIII^4.(19).—man.V^7.; (8).;
VIII^4.(8).—msc.$V^6.\sigma^2$.(8).—
na-m.$VI^{3 \cdot zz}$.--nic.8-31.--sbd.
$V^{12 \cdot 15}$.—*sul.*8.—ton.V^1–$VI^{3 \cdot 4}$.
au.η.**5**.; V^{12}–VIII^4.(66).--
zin.(8).

F.—-aco^f.V^{16}.(8).——*bel.*$V^{10 \cdot t}$.8.
(19).—-bry^b.V^6–VII^2.31.—
cac.V^1.—-cau.II^1.--cch^s.66.
(8).—con.VI^3–VIII^3.1.—
lah.V^1.5.19.(8.35).—*man.*V^6–
VI^3.8.—nx-j.VI^3.(8).—pla^b.
$V^{1 \cdot 3}$.8-31.66.—-rn-b^m.V^1.—
rho.V^6–$VI^{4 \cdot a}.\delta$.35.--rhs.VII^1.
p.q.$\theta.\kappa^3$.103.(10.16).--—sep^s.
V^1–VI^3.35.(8-31).--tep.$V^{10 \cdot s}$.
q.

T.—*cof.*$V^{1 \cdot z}$.8-31.(19).—*hyo.*8.
—jat.$V^{10 \cdot t}._\iota$.; $V^{10 \cdot t}$–VIII^4.
(8).—lau^b.V^1.4.—*ol-a.*VI^4.8.
—- pho^a.V^1.29.31.35.(8).—
rn-b.$V^1.\beta a.\sigma^3$.5.——rho.V^6–
$VI^{4 \cdot a}.\delta$.35.—sbd.$V^{12 \cdot 15}$.—*zng.*
$V^{1 \cdot 6}$.8-31.**130**.(18.130).

C.—*fer.*V^1.8.—rn-b.$VII^1.\delta$.5.
P.--am-m^d.V^1–VI^3.--bov^c.VIII^4.

3.—eup.VI$^{3.b}$.—fl-x^d.IX.i^a.**5**.
8.--mg-s^c.V^9.8-31.--pho^c.3-99.
29.35.(8).--sbd^c.V$^{12.15}$.--ton^d.
VIII^4.; ^{a}.V^{12}–VIII^4.(66).
O.--bov.V$^{1.a}$.q.3.8-31.(2).--bry^c.
V^6-VII^2.31.--cmf.V^1.4.(8-31).
——-mt-s.(8).——-mg-m.VI^4-
VIII^4.(19).; V^1.(8).—mez.
V^1.

7. *In a warm room.*
GEN.—aps.V$^{1.u}$.43.—-bov.V^{10}–
VIII^3.5.— cn-i.III.ω^2.—f-io.
26.29.31.43.44.(5.8.107).-—
lau.V^1.ω^2.(8).——-mr-f.βe^a. —-
nit.—ph-x.βe.5.— pho.(8-31.
66).—pul.βe^a.--sin.(8).--tan.
κ^5.
F.——-aco.V^{16}.——-bov^g.V$^{1.3}$.4.—-
ca-x.——-cau^c.VI^4.σ^2.ϕ^1.1.2.65.
—la-v.V^1.w.——-lil.III^1.VI^2.5.
-—pla.III^1–V^3.x.au^{ff}.ϵv^k.χ.—
sel.VI^3.5.5.——-sng.V^1.δ.κ^5.ρ.3.
19.(8.14).—vrb^n.V$^{7.10.a.q}$.
P.—spo^c.V^7.
O.—bov.V$^{1.3}$–VI^3.4.—-sng.V^1.δ.
(8-31.14).

8. *In the open air.*
GEN.—ang.χ^1.5.—-ag-n.—-bel.
VII^1.89.—ber.35.—bov.V^{12}.q.
3.; bov.II^7–VIII^4.3.6.—cad.
-—c-ph.29.; (15).—cau.V^{12}.
q.—ced.5.—cep.6 —-chd.29.
53.89.——-chi.V^1–VII^2.-—cmf.
— cle.VI^3–VII^1–VIII^4.v^1.16.
43.44.—cof.6.66.; cof.V^2.(6).
—col.— con.V^6.(47).—cot.—
eup.II^5.6.(86).-——fag.I^2.(12.
31).-f-io.7.26.29.31.43.44.(5.
107).—gas.—glo.V^1.; glo.—
grt.35.; grt.VIII^4.—ham.—
hpm.6.—hfb.— hyo.6.— k-hy.
V^{12}.3.——klm.V^6.δ.5.—–lah.
VII^5.μ^1.—lau.V^1.ω^2.7.—-lin.
—mt-s.VII^5.(6).——mg-s.VI^4.
—man.6.; VIII^4.6.—men.V^1.
—mez.—msc.V^6.σ^2.6.; VI^1.—
na-m.; V^6–VI^1.δ.θ^4.4.—opi.
V^1.3-99.-—$phl.$; V^7.(63).—-
pho.29.; pho.—sin.7.—spi.
sul.(6).—tab.—trn.—zin.6.
F.—aco^f.V^{16}.6.——alm.II^1–V^1.p.

18.19.66.; VI^4.5.-——ang.V^2.
29.—ag-m.V^1.κ^5.3-99.(89).—
aur.VI^4.-——au-m^e.VI^4.βa.29.
35.—-bel.V$^{10.t}$.(6.19).—–ber.
III^1–VII^5.q.29.-——ca-c.V^1.;
ca-c.V$^{10.s}$.(12).—cam.V^7–VI^3.
ab^o.βe.5.—cb-a^b.V^9.3-30.—–
ca-x.V^7.—-cas.VI^4.χ^1.—-chd.
V$^{10.s}$.1.29.53.89.(63).-—-cch^g.
6.66.—col.III.δ.29.--cor^i.V^{10}.
ζ^3.—cot.V^7.q.a^{1}b^s.δv,o.ρ^1.vb.—
ctn.V^1.—eup.V^1.δ.3.; eup.V^7.
—fer^m.V$^{10.t}$.3-30.33.(12).; ^{m}.
VI^3.3.—f-io^a.V^7.q.43.44.**130**.
(107).—ham.--hel.V$^{10.t}$–VII^5.
q.χ.—hy-x.V^1.βe.—jac^f.V^7.—
k-bi^e.VII^1–VIII^4.q.29.35.66.
(14.16).; k-bi^e.V^7.q.35.; VI$^{3.b}$.
-—lah.V^1.5.6.19.(35).——lch.
VI^4.—mg-s.VI^4.——man.V^6–
VI^3.(6).; III^1–VI^3.—my-s^n.
V$^{10.s}$.—nup.V^1.—nx-j.VI^3.G.
——nx-v.V^1.v.(14).——plc.V^6.
12.—sar.VI$^{3.a}$.—sng.V^1.δ.ρ.3.
7.19.(14).--sep^g.VI$^{3.s}$.δb.3-30.
--stp^f.V^1.q.—sul.II^7-V^6-VI$^{3.4}$.
26.(12).—tab.VI$^{3.z}$.18.(16).
—trx.V^7.av^a.κ^5.19.43.——vi-t.
^{h}.I^q.
T.—asr.V^6.**5**..(16).-—atr^b.VI^3.
δb.3-99.——aur.VI$^{4.q}$.——cam.
VI^3.ab^o.βe.δO.5.—cas.VI^4.χ^1.
(12).—col.V^1.; col.III.δ.29.
-—$comb^b$.VI$^{3.e}$.(35).—-ctn.V^1.
—equ^b.VI^3.3.—glo.V^{10}.—hel.
V$^{10.s}$–VII^5.d.q.1.——-hdr.I^a.5.
36.(12).—hyo.(6).—jac$^{a.b}$.σ^2.
5.—jat.V$^{10.t}$–VIII^4.6.—k-bi.
V^7.q.35. -——lth.V^{10}.βf.δb.κ^5.3.
16.49.(19).——man.III^1–VI^3.
—naj^c.VI$^{3.w}$.$\kappa^{4.5}$.—nup.V^1.—
oln^b.V$^{6.10.u.v}$.——ol-a.VI^4.(6).
—pho^a.V^1.6.29.31.35.
C.—cb-a.V^1.q 83.—fer.V^1.(6).;
fer.V$^{10.t}$.33.(12).—gam.V^2.**5**.
—glo.V$^{10.v}$.35.(20).—idm.V^2.
-—irs.IX.3.35.——nit.—-rat.
II^1-VI^4.2.83.—sul.V^1.; II$^{1.s}$-
V^1–VI^4.4.**(5)**.
P.—am-c^c.VI$^{3.q}$.—cb-a^a.V^7.**5**.55.
fag^d.V^7.19.41.—fl-x^d.IX.i^a.**5**.

6.—*grt*^{d}.VI^3.—*lin*^{d}.I.—*pho*^{b}.V^1.; ^{c}.V^3.$\beta\epsilon^a$.20.35.; ^{c}.3-99.6.29.35.—*rat*^{c}.V^3.—*sul*.II^7–V^6–VI$^{3\cdot4}$.26 (12).

O.—*cb-a*.V^1.q.83.—*cl-h*.II^5.16.35.—cob.3.—*glo*.VII^5.—*hdr*^{c}.V^7.p.q.(12).—*hy-x*.V$^{1\cdot a}$.$\beta\epsilon$.—iod^h.V$^{1\cdot a}$.4.—*k-ca*^{h}.V^1.—lo-i.V^1.3.—mt-s.6.—*mg-m*.V^1.6.—mg-s.V^1.3.

B.—rum^f.VI^3.λ.

8-31. *In open air when walking.*

GEN.—*aco*.III.—alm.—*ant*.VI^4.—*ara*.19.(65).—arn.V^1–VII^3.—atr.V^{12}.—bel.—chi.III.—ch-s.; *ch-s*.χ.χ^3.—con.$\beta\epsilon^a$.3.(66).; V^7.—dul.VII^2.5.—*fag*.—fer.V^{10}.5.—*gen*.3.—hel.V$^{10\cdot t}$.—hep.III.(6).; *hep*.VI^3.3-99.—hfb.—lam.3-99.—*lyc*.20.—mu-x.—*nat*.V^7.p.19.20.—*na-m*.—nic.6.—pet.5.—*pho*.7.(66).—pul.—rhs.g.—spi.V$^{10\cdot t}$–VIII^3.—su-x.VI^3.

F.—aco^h.III^3.a^1c^a.—ant.V^7.χ^3.—asi.—*bor*^{e}.V^1.—bra.κ^5.ϕ.(12).—ca-a^g.V^1.—ca-x.III^1–V^7.q.—cau.III–V^1.(29).—chi.III^n-V$^{10\cdot s}$.—cin.V^7.—cca^d.—*cor*.V^1.δb.—*crt*^{e}.βa.$\kappa^{5\cdot6}$.μ^1.—*ham*^{f}.V^{10}.18.19.—*hlt*.V$^{1\cdot6\cdot10}$.—hel^n.V^1.—*hdr*^{g}.(3).—hfb^e.—*hyo*.V^1.βa.δL.—k-cy.V^{10}.4.—*lyc*.V^1.—mer.VI^3.—na-m.V^1.—pla^b.V$^{1\cdot3}$.6.66.—sar^a.VIII^4.—*scu*^{f}.—*sep*^{g}.V^1–VI^3.6.35.—spo^b.V^3–VI$^{2\cdot s}$.—trx^c.IX.—*thu*.V$^{10\cdot s}$.η.χ^1.3.

T.—arn^b.V^1–VI^4–VII$^{3\cdot s}$.—bry.VI^3.—cof.V$^{1\cdot z}$.(6.19).—equ.VI^3.(66).—hyo^a.V^1.βa.δL.—mt-n^a.V^1.—man^b.VI^4.—na-m.V^1.—*pso*.V^{10}.41.—*rho*^{b}.V^1.$\beta\epsilon$.(14).—spi.VIII^3.—trx^b.VI^3.(18).—zng.V$^{1\cdot6}$.**130**.(6.18.130).

C.—*aco*.III.—*ast*.V^1.3.—*thu*.VI^2.η.θ^4.χ^1.3.

P.—ch-s^c.IX.5.—grt^d.V^6.—ign^b.V^1.41.86.—mg-s^c.V^9.(6).—*man*^{a}.II^1-V^1.—*mr-i*.V^{10}.$\beta\epsilon^a$.

O.—bov.V$^{1\cdot a}$.q.3.(2.6).—bra.κ^6.ϕ.(12).—cau^b.V$^{1\cdot6}$.σ^2.—ce-b.V$^{10\cdot t}$.33.—*cmf*.V^1.4.6.—cin.V^7.—mt-n.VI^4–VIII$^{1\cdot zz}$.—*man*.II^1–V^1.; man^f.IV^1–V^1.(11).—*sng*.V^1.δ.7.(14).—spi.VIII$^{3\cdot a}$.—stp.VII^1.—*tab*.VI^3.18.(16).—zin.V^1.

B.—*spg*.V^3.3.16.66.

9-31. *When walking in the sun.*

GEN.—au-s.VI^3.—ch-s.4.—hpm.(114).

10. *In bed.*

F.—*cch*.V^1.—*rhs*.VII^1.p.q.θ.κ^3.6.100.(16).

T.—bry.V$^{10\cdot s}$–VIII^4.

10. *On going to bed.*

GEN.—alm.σ^2.(3-30).

11. *When touched.*

GEN.—bel.—chi.II^5.41.86.—cup.V^1.βa.35.—hfb.—k-ca.V^1–VIII^4.$\kappa^{5\cdot6}$.σ^2.—mez.I^a.4.40.—sar.31.—trn.

F.—*bel*^{n}.VI^3.20.—*ca-a*^{b}.V^3-VI^3.10.(18.31).—*chi*^{b}.VI^3.d.; chi.V$^{6\cdot g}$.—cup.V^1.35.—*cyc*.V$^{1\cdot6}$.—ipc.VI^3.; VI$^{1\cdot4}$.; II^1.—lep^e.**50**.—*mu-x*.V^7.—na-m.II^3.**53**.; VIII^4.—*vi-t*^{f}.V^1.

T.—*ars*^{b}.VI^3.—ber^a.V$^{10\cdot s}$–VII^4.q.—*ca-a*^{b}.V$^{3\cdot s}$–VI^3.(19).—cas.II^3.VI^4.χ^1.5.—chd^a.VI^4.—*chi*^{b}.VI^3.—con.V^6.—cup.V^1.βa.35.; VI^4.; ^{b}.V$^{1\cdot6}$.—*cyc*^{b}.V$^{1\cdot6}$.; ^{b}.V^6–VI^3.—dph.II^3.VIII^4.θ^1.—lep.**50**.—nx-m.—ptv^a.V^{10}.**5**.—stp^a.VI$^{3\cdot s\cdot t}$.

C.—bov.V^2.VI$^{4\cdot a}$.ϵC.3.—chd.II^5.; VI^3–VIII^3.σ^2.—cnb.II^5.—k-bi.VI$^{3\cdot a}$.—ptv.V$^{7\cdot q}$.19.86.(31.35).—pho.VIII^4.60.

—— *by laying hand on it.*—*nit*^{a}.p.

P.—aga^g.V$^{1\cdot q}$.$a\mathfrak{h}^q$.12.—agn^d.V^1-VI^4.35.—bor.VI^3.θ^1.116.—*bry*^{h}.V^6–VIII^4.—cup.$a\mathfrak{l}^g$.—dir^d.VIII^4.35.89.—lau^c.V^1.—ni-x^c.VI$^{3\cdot a}$.—*thu*^{c}.V^{16}.

O.—ba-c^e.VI^4-VIII^3.—cup.V^1.35.—*man*^{f}.IV^1-V^1.8-31.—ni-x.VI^3.—nit.V^1–VI^3.

B.—arg^t.V^6-VI^4.—bry^o.—cep^o. V^1.x.5.—chi^{oc}.V^6.(22).—cnb. II^5.—grt^{tb}.V^2.—k-bi.—la-v^{pa}. V$^{6 \cdot a}$.4.——lau^{pa}.V^1.—mg-s^{fa}. VI^4.4.— mer^f.V$^{10 \cdot s}$.—mr-f^{pa}. 15.——mez.——mu-x^m.II^7-V^1. VI^1 --na-m^f.II^3.; P.V^2.--pa$_1$p^b. II^5.2.--sab$^{ob \cdot tb \cdot fb}$.V^1-VI^4.— sar^t.V^1-VI^3 ; sar^{ma}.VI^3.—— stp^{pa}.II^3.17.—sul^{pa}.ii.—vi-t^p. V^2.

12. *By pressure.*
GEN.—alm.VI^4.ε.5.—am-c.II^7. 35.—aps.V^1.; II^1-VIII^4.29. 35.—ag-n.—cam.VI^4.p.—cb·a. VI^4.VIII^4.δ.ε.η.θ^4.66. —ca-x. III^1.p.ii.3.; VI^3.δ.51.111.— cnb.; cnb.V^1.41.43.—fag.I^z. (8.31).—glo.—hep.V^3.κ^5.3-10. —idm.—lah.VII^5.p.εᵇ^u.ζ^3.σ^3. μ^1.—nag.II^7.5.—mg-m.III. VIII^4.p.—men.V$^{10 \cdot u}$.—mr-f. V^7.—na-m 89.90. —pul.V^1- VIII^4. —sab.V^1.—sil.VI^4- VIII^4.χ^1.--sul.VI^3.θ^4.2.--trn. b.——thu.III-VI^3-VIII^1.29. (22).

F.—ail^e.q. —am-m^f.VI^4.—ana. III^1-V^3.au.4. ; ^{a}.V$^{3 \cdot 10 \cdot t}$.5.(16. 63).—ara.V^1.βε.ω^2.5.66.--bel. IX.31.—bra.κ^5.φ.8-31.—ca-a. V^1.; ca-a.V$^{1 \cdot 6}$—VI^4.(41).—— ca-c.VI^1.31. ——cam^h.III^1.p. r^{1}v^{1}b.φ.16.29.——ca-x.III^1.p. 3-99.—cas.VI^4.χ^1.—chd^c.VI^4. 66.—chi.V$^{10 \cdot s}$.; III^1-V^6.18. 19.(31).—cle.l^a.δO.5.102.— cch^n.(102).—cro^o.VIII$^{1 \cdot q}$.βε. — cu-a.VI^3.—dio^a.VI^1.ε.— fer^m.V$^{10 \cdot t}$.3-30.33.(8).—gel. III δ̇b.3-99.——glo.VIII^4.35. (16.19).—ham.I^a.18.19.(15. 16).— hel^g.V$^{16 \cdot 1}$.—hdr.VII^1. 3-99.(35.41).——ipc^e.V$^{3 \cdot 10 \cdot s}$. (47).—k-hy^a.VI$^{3 \cdot 4 \cdot a}$.5.—lil. VII^1.i^a.—lcp^m.; V^7.—mg-m. VIII^4.p.—man^e.V^6.29.--men^a. V^1.—mer.V$^{10 \cdot s}$.16.; V^1-VII^5. ——mu-x.V$^{10 \cdot u}$.q.βε.δ.; mu-x. VI^3.29.——nat^a.VI$^{4 \cdot a}$.83.—— na-m.V$^{10 \cdot s}$.δ.--oln^o.V$^{10 \cdot s}$.—opi.

V$^{10 \cdot s}$.ω.; V$^{10 \cdot s}$.(15).—ph-x.V^1. 28.—plc.V^6.8.--sbd.V^7.—spi. V$^{10 \cdot s}$.—stn.V^1.; V^1.22.; V$^{10 \cdot s}$. φ.—sul II^7-V^6-VI$^{3 \cdot 4}$.26.(8).; V^1-VII^5.; ^{b}.V1^3.—su-x.VI$^{3 \cdot 4}$. 5.—teu.V^1.

—— *with cold hand.*—ca-c.V$^{10 \cdot s}$. (8).

—— *pressing head into pillow.*— cnb.V^7.3 99.16.(30.117).; cnb.V^1.3-99.16.; VIII^4. 3-99.

T.—æth^b.VI^3-VIII^4.—alm^a.V^7- VII^5.5.— ant^b.V$^{6 \cdot b}$.—ara.V^1. βε.ω^2.5.66.—asp.V^{10}.—bis^a. V^1-VI^4.--cac.q.--cld^b.V^3-VI^3. ——ca-a.V$^{1 \cdot 6}$—VI^4.(41).—cas. VI^4.χ^1.(8).—chi.VIII^4.18.19. (31). —cin.IV^1-V^6.—ccs.VI^3. --cop^b.VI^4.; cop^a.V^2.2.5.— dio^b.—dir.I^t.—dph.II^5.d^a.— glo.VIII^4. —— gui.VI^3.18.19. (31). —hdr.I^a.36.(8).——iod. V$^{10 \cdot s}$.(47).——k-hy^b.VI$^{3 \cdot 4}$ ^{a}.5. —lil.; lil.VII^1.i^a.—mag^b.VI^4. (16). —mg-m.IV^2-VIII^4.βa. 5.16.—men.III. —mu-x.VI^3. 29. —nat^a.VI$^{4 \cdot a}$.83.——na-a. V$^{3 \cdot t}$.p.κ^5.4.65.101.—na-m.V^7. βε.— nit^a.VI^4.1.—par^a.V^1.— pho.VI^4.--pod.V^7.--pru^a.VI^3.; ^{a}.V$^{10 \cdot s}$. —stn.V^1.—thu.VI^3- VIII^1.29.(22).——ver.V^7.29 30.(22).—— vrb^a.V^7-VI$^{3 \cdot q}$.θ^1. 63.

—— *by pressing on other side.*— jac^a.V^7.5.

C.—bel.V$^{3 \cdot 15}$-VI^4.—cac.q.--cas. II^7.—cin.V$^{10 \cdot u}$.—dir.66.— ept.p.--fer.V$^{10 \cdot t}$.33.(8).--k-ca. —lah.V^2.—nat.VIII^4.66.— nit.V^1.—ph-x.V^6-VI^3.——stn. V^1.

P.—aga^g.V$^{1 \cdot q}$.ab^q.11.—mez^d.V^7. —sul.II^7-V^6-VI$^{3 \cdot 4}$.26.(8).

O.— bra.κ^6.φ.8-31.—ca-a.V$^{1 \cdot 6}$- VI^4.(41).—ca-c.; VI^1.31.— cam.III^1.p.ζ.r^{1}v^{1}b.φ.16.29.— cch^i.V^7.(102).— c-ar^b.II^5.— dio^c.VI^3.—grt^d.V^6-VI$^{4 \cdot v}$.— hdr^c.V^7.p.q.η^{c}b^b.(8).—hyo.II^5.

------mag^e.VI^3–VII^5.------man.
V^7.a^{1}b^a.βe^b.; V^6.δO.29.--nx-v^j.
V$^{10.s}$-VII^1.p.--ph-x^b.V^1.1.28.
--sab.V^{10}.q.--sep.IX.βe^b.2.16.
--spi.V$^{10.t}$.29.--sul.V^1.--trn.
Ba.--cam.III^1.p.r^{1}v^{1}b.φ.16.29.
la-x.ηaa.ω.35.
B.--aga.V^6–VI^4.--ant^{pb}.--con^f.
III^1.au.a^{1}b^p.βa.χ^1.(29).--rn-s^o.
V$^{1.10}$.--tab^{pa}.

13. By pressure of hat.
GEN.--cb-a.--cb-v.III.q.--sul.
V^1.(130).

14. By leaning against anything.
GEN.--ara.V^1.βe.--gym.--sul.
VI^4.χ^2.ω^2.4.
F.--ang.VII^5.--bel.V$^{10.a.s}$.; n.
V^1.VII^1.--dro.VI^4.48.--k-bi^e.
VII^1 – VIII^4. q.29.35.66.(8.
16).--lyp.V$^{10.s}$.5.--na-m.V^7.
x.δ.
T.--bel^a.V^1–VII^1.--con.III.66.
--cyc^b.V^3.--rho^b.V^1.βe.(8-31).
O.--sng.V^1.δ.7.(8-31).

14. By leaning to r. side.
T.--ch-s^b.VI$^{3.v}$.

14. By leaning to l. side.
GEN.--pæo.3.

14. By leaning head on high pillow.
O.--gel.V^3.σ^2.τ.

14. By leaning head on table.
F.--nx-v.V^1.v.8.

14. By supporting head.
F.----sng.V^1.δ.κ^5.ρ.3.7.19.(8).
--so-l.V$^{10.s}$.5.
C.--na-m.VI^3.
P.--can^b.V^1.-ton^c.VI^3-VIII$^{4.zz}$.

15. By rubbing.
GEN.--c-ph.8.
F.--ars.II^3-V^2.--ham.1^a.18.19.
(12.16).--ol-a$^{a.b}$.V^1.----opi.
VII^5.; V$^{10.s}$.(12).--pho.II^1-
VI^3-VII^1.3.19.66.--phs.I^q.
T.--alm^a.II^1-VI^4.--cth^a.VI^3-
VIII^4.--ol-a^a.V^1.ω^9.66.--pho.
II^1-VI^3.3.19.66.--pla^b.II^1-
VI^2.
C.----ars.II^1-V^{10}-VIII^4.βe.----
cau.V^2-VIII^4.
P.--pho.II^1-VI^3.19.66.

O.--cth^b.VIII^3 d.v.--dio^c.V^{15}.
--lau.VI^4.σ^2.--ol-a.VI$^{4.a.v}$.

15. By scratching.
B.--man^{pa}.II^1.v.29.

15. By combing hair.
GEN.--for.--glo.
B.--mr-f^{pa}.11.

16. By lying.
GEN.--alm.VIII^4.4.31.; alm.--
amb.VI$^{1.3}$.31.--arn.30.--bov.
VIII^4.au.a^{1}b^s.ζo.100.-buf.(2).
--cad.--chi.VIII^3.31.35.--
cle.VIII^2.5.;VI^3-VII^1-VIII^4.
v^1.43.44.(8).----cch.(101).--
cup.V^6.βa.ω^4.--dig.VIII^5.18.
22.(29).----dio.V^7.--dul.VI^3.
au.5.--eup.V^2.βe.ζ^3.5.--glo.
V^{10}-VIII^4.--hel.(20).--hpm.
--ign.VI^4.2.(17).--k-ca.(19).;
k-ca.II^7.66.--lch.VIII^4.--
lyc.V^1.--mer.5.(19).--mu-x.
V$^{10.u}$.δ.(90).----ni-x.VIII$^{1.3}$.
29.--nx-v.VII^1.41.; nx-v.VI^3.
κ$^{5.6}$.66.(5).----pho.V^7.βa.δo.η.
θ^2.ω^2.28. ; V^{1}x.ab^o.βa.3-30. ;
pho.βa.κ^5. ; VIII^4.--rs-r.--
san.--sin.--spi.(31).--stp.
35.--zin.δ.λ.5.--ziz.κ$^{5.6}$.51.
111.
F.--aln^e.V^{10}.βa.5.--alm.VI^3.--
ana^a.V$^{3.10.t}$.5.(12.63).--arg^b.
V$^{3.e}$.5.----bel.V^1.35.(19).--
bov^h.VIII^4.q.au.a^{1}b^s.ζo.100.--
bry.VIII^4.--ca-c.VI^3.--cam^h.
III^1.p.r^{1}v^{1}b.φ.12.29.; VI^1.--
cnb.V^7.3-99.12.(30.117).;V^1.
3-99.(12).----con.VI$^{3.s}$.4.--
fl-x^a.δr.5.--glo.VIII^4.35.(12.
19).----ham.1^a.18.19.(12.15).
--k-bi^e.VII^1-VIII^4.q.29.35.
66.(8.14).----lch^a.--mel^h.35.
41.--mer.V$^{10.s}$.(12).--pi-m.
--rn-b^f.ηp.r^{1}b.(18.31).--rhs.
VII^1.p.q.θ.κ$^{3.6}$.100.(10).-sep.
VI^3.κ^5.----spi^a.V^3-VI^4.35.51.
86.--tab.VI$^{3.z}$.18.(8).--ton^b.
V$^{6.q}$.
T.--asr.V^6.5.(8).----bz-x.VIII^2.
--cam.VI$^{1.3}$.--chd^a.V$^{6.a}$.--
ch-s^b.I^a.(102).--cle^b.VIII^4.43.
--cch^a.5.--fer.V^1.--grp.V^1.3.

—lth.V^{10}.βℓ.δb.κ^5.3.49.(8.19).
——*mag*^{b}.VI^4.(12).——mg-m.
IV^2–VIII^4.βa.5.(12).—*nx-v*^{b}.
VI$^{3·a}$.κ$^{5·6}$.5.

C.——*c-ph*.V$^{10·a}$.i^a.29.35.——chd.
V^1–VII^1–VIII^4.—*clo*.—hpm.
V^7.2.—*spi*^{b}.V^3–VI^4.35.51.56.
86.

P.—cb-v^c.II^5–V^1.(24.30).—*dig*^{a}.
VIII^5.18.22.(29).——*m-pi*^{e}.3-
30.—pet^c.δb.—rho^d.II^3–V^1.
(30).—sep^b.q.5.—spo^c.V$^{10·a}$.

O.—*alm*.V^2.—cam.III^1.p.ζ.r^{1}v^{1}b.
φ.12.29.——cth.V^1–VI^3.5.——
chd.V^1–VII^1–VIII^4.——cl-h.
II^5.q.35.(8).—*iod*.VI^3.—lch^b.
—mg-s^j.V^1.—*ni-x*^{b}.VI$^{3·a}$.5.—
nx-v.VIII^4.83.(18).——pi-m.
—pul.VI^3.(30).—*spi*.V^3–VI^4.
35.51.56.86.; spi.IX.31.35.
(19.22).—stp.V$^{10·a}$.d.5.—*tab*.
VI^3.18.(8-31).

Ba—cam.III^1.p.r^{1}v^{1}b.φ.12.29.

B.—aur.V^4.ak.—*ſl-x*$^{f·p}$.V^1.5.—
spg.V^3.3.66.(8-31).

16. *By lying on it.*
O.—sep.IX.βℓ^b.2.(12).

16. *By lying with head low.*
GEN.—sto.VII^2.5.

16. *By lying in an improper position.*
GEN.—ana.V^7.

17. *By lying on back.*
GEN.—*ign*.VI^4.2.17^a.
F.—col.V^{10}.26.29.48.—*ign*.VI^4.
ηp,aa.r^{1}p.24.——*nx-v*^{f}.V^1.3-10.
17^a.
T.—*ign*.V$^{10·a}$.3.17^a.——*ver*.V^1–
VII^5.βℓ.δP^1.18.19.(29).
C.——*ver*.V^1–VII^5.βℓ.δP^1.18.19.
(29).
O.—all.V^7.3.—bry.II^3.q.r.3-99.
—cac.q.(17^a).——*ign*.VI^4.d.i^a.
30.(19.29).; ^{g}.VI^4.ηp,aa.r^{1}p.
24.—pet.VIII^4.—plc.V^1.

17^a. *By lying on side.*
GEN.—cld.(19).—*ign*.VI^4.2.17.
F.—nx-v^f.V^1.3-10.(17).
T.—ign.V$^{10·a}$.3.(17).
P.—grp^b.2.
O.—cac.q.17.

17^a. *By lying on r. side.*
P.—*bro*^{d}.VIII^4.70.——*nx-v*^{c}.VI^4.
3-10.17^a.
B.—stp^{pa}.II^3.11.

17^a. *By lying on l. side.*
P.—nx-v^c.VI^4.3-10.(17^a).

17^a. *By lying on affected side.*
GEN.—*arn*.VI$^{3·a}$.26.89.——ph-x.
V$^{10·P}$.2-99.
T.—stn^a.V^1.30.
P.—ars^d.I^a.η.(19).—cld.V^1.100.
(19).——ca-c^b.lI^1.——*hpm*.—
mag^c.VI$^{3·a}$.2.——pul.——sep.
VIII^4.—spo^c.VIII^4.

17^a. *By lying on opposite side.*
P.—pul.VI^4.5.

17^a. *By laying head on one side.*
F.—men^o.VI$^{3·a}$.q.

18. *By standing.*
GEN.—arg.III.βa.κ$^{4·5}$.χ$^{2·3}$.43.—
ca-a.V$^{10·a}$.—dig.VIII^5.22.(16.
29).—*mt-n*.V^2.βℓ.100.(30^c).—
mag.VI^3.V^2.
F.——*aga*.V^6–VI^1.V^7.19.——alm.
VI^3.q.V^{12}.4.; II^1–V^1.p.19.66.
(8).——ars.V^7.VI^3.31.(19).——
ca-a^g.V$^{10·a}$.q.29.——*ca-a*^{b}.V^2–
VI^3.19.(11.31).—cth^o.VI^3.—
chi.III^1–V^6.19.(12.31).—ham.
I^a.19.(12.15.16).-k-ca.VIII^4.
31.66.——mer^b.VI$^{3·4}$.——phl^a.
V^1–VI^4.—rn-b^f.ηp.r^{1}b.16.(31).
—rhe.VIII^4.—san^a.V^{10}.ε.(31).
——*spi*^{n}.VI^4–VIII^3.δℓ^d.19.—
stp.V^7.29.; III^2.19.(31).—
tab.VI$^{3·z}$.(8.16).—trx.V$^{1·6}$.—
teu^o.V^1.29.
T.——ars^b.VI^3.31.(19).——cas^a.
VIII^4.66.—chi.VIII^4.19.(12.
31).—col^b.V$^{1·a}$.31.77.(19).—
glo.V^{10}–VIII^3.ηp,aa.28.29.31.
—gui.VI^3.19.(12.31).——stp.
VI^3.19.(31).——*trx*^{b}.V^6.19.
(31).; VI^2.19.; ^{b}.VI^3.8-31.—
ver.V^1–VII^5.βℓ.δP^1.19.(17.
29).——*zng*.V$^{1·6}$.8-31.130.(6.
130).
C.-rn-b.VI^4.44.—su-x.V^1.—ver.
V^1–VII^5.βℓ.δP^1.19.(17.29).
P.—ca-c^d.VI^2.βa.χ^1.3-30.31.——
cth^c.VI^3–VIII^4.5.19.——dig^a.

VIII⁵. 22. (16. 29).——k-ca.
VIII⁴.31.66.——mag^c.VI³. ; ^d.
VI³.5. ; V².——man^d.VI³·⁴·ᵛ.3.
——plb^c.VI³–VIII⁴·ᵃ.5.31.——
zin^c.V³–VII¹.5.

O.——cas^a.VI³·⁴.4.——k-ca.V¹·ᵃ.d.
q.——mag.V⁶–VII⁵.61.(19).—
n.x-v.VIII⁴.16.83.——plb.V¹⁰·ᶻᶻ.
q.δb.——†ab.VI³.(8-31.16).——
trx.VI⁴.31.

B.—zin.V³–VII¹.5.

19. *By sitting.*
GEN.—aga.V³.υ.φ.ω².——an-s.—
ara.(8-31.65).——bry.VII¹.iᵃ.
——buf.**30**^c.——cld.17.——cha.
V¹·⁷.41.——c-ar.31.—fer.29.31.
—gel.—glo.—gn-c.III¹.aq.—
hpm.III.κ⁵.(20.31.35).——ind.
VIII⁴.**5.** ; VIII⁵·ᶻᶻ.**5.**——k-ca.
16.—lam.30.—lyc.V¹–VIII⁴.
43.——mg-m.VI⁴–VIII⁴.6.——
mer.5.(16).——mr-i.100.— nat.
V⁷.p.20.(8-31).—pho.V⁷.δ.κ¹.
λii.; VI⁴.λ.—ver.ab.31.

F.——aco.V¹.VI³.VIII⁴.31.——
æth.ᵍ·ⁱ.VI³–VIII³.——aga.V¹.
βa.—alm.II¹–V¹.p.18.66.(8).
——am-m.VI⁴.η.83.——ars.V⁷.
VI³.18.31.——bel.V¹⁰·ᵗ.8.(6). ;
V¹.35.(16).——bis^b.V¹.q.——
ca-a^b.V³–VI³.(11.18.31).——
cas^a.VI⁴.——cau.V⁷.43.——chi.
V¹.22.; ^b.V³.;VI³.——com.Iq.—
glo.VIII⁴.35.(12.16).——ham.
Iᵃ.18.(12.**15.16**).——lah.V¹.5.
6.(8.35).——mer^b.V³–VI³·ᵉ.; ^b.
VI³·⁴.p.ηp.r¹b.χ¹.——mez.VI⁴.
3.——pho.II¹–VI³–VII¹.3.66.
(**15**).—rut^a.V³-VI³·ᵉ.——sng.V¹.
δ.κ⁵.ρ.3.7.(8.14).——spiⁿ.VI⁴–
VIII³.δc^d.18.—spo^b.V¹⁰·ˢ.(30).
-stp.VI⁴.5.VI³.29.(31).; III².
18.(31).——trx.V⁷.aᴰᵃ.κ⁵.43.
(8).—terᵍ.V¹ q.41.—ver.VI³.
—— *in a bending posture.*—
er-aᵍ.VI³.σ².r.

T.—am-mᵃ.VI⁴.η.83.——argᵇ.V⁶.
—ars^b.VI³.18.31.——asr^b.III.
26.31.——ca-a^b.V³·ˢ–VI³.(11).
—chi.VIII⁴.18.(12.31).——cof.
V¹·ᶻ.8-31.(6).——col^b.V¹·ᵃ.18.

31.77.—lil^b.(35).——lth.V¹⁰.βf.
δb.κ⁵.3.16.49.(8).——mt-s.V¹.
26.41.(22.29.31).——man^b.V¹.
30.31.; man.V¹·³.22.(29).——
mez^b.V¹.43.(35). ; ^b.VI⁴.5.—
nic^a.VI⁴.——pho.II¹–VI³.3.66.
(**15**).——stp.VI³.18.(31).——
su-x^b.VI⁴.63.——trx^b.V⁶.(18-
31).;VI².(18).——ver.V¹–VII⁵.
βε.δP¹.18.(17.29).

C.——cas.VI⁴.——con.III².31.——
gel.V⁶.44.—lyc.VIII¹·ᵃ.66.—
mt-s.V¹.26 41.(22.29.31).——
ptv.V⁷·q.11.86.(31.35).——pho.
VI⁴·ᵃ.η.4.——ver.V¹–VII⁵.βε.
δP¹.18.(17.29).——vi-tᵃ.II¹–V¹.

P.——am-m^c.VI⁴.83.——ars^d.Iᵃ.η
17.—au-n^d.VI¹.——cld.V¹.17.
100.——cth^c.VI³–VIII⁴.5.18.
—chi^d.V³.——cb-s^c.IX.5.——con.
VI³.βa.σ².31.——fag^d.V.7.41.(8).
——ind.VIII⁴.**5.**; ^c.II⁴.**5.**; ^c.VI³.
κ⁴.4.29.(30).——mag^c.VI³·⁴.66.
——nic^c.VI⁴·ᵃ.5.——pho^c.VI⁴·ᵛ.
5.; II¹–VI³.66.(**15**).——rat^d.
VI³.——rho^c.II³–V¹.——sul^c.
VIII¹.5.

O.——aga^c.——asr^d.III.26.31.——
cas.VIII⁴.——chi.V⁶.——ign.VI⁴.
d.iᵃ.30.(17.29).——ind.VI³·ᵃ.——
mt-n^f.VI⁴–VIII¹.——mag.18.
61.——mg-m.VI⁴–VIII⁴.6.——
men.V⁶.——rn-b^b.VIII⁴.ω².——
spi.IX.16.31.35 (22).——squ.
V⁶–VI³.—zin^b.V⁶·q.βa.

B.—au-n^f.V⁶.——cau°.V⁵.—ind.
VIII⁴.**5.**; ^pb.VIII¹.εCl.66.

20. *When at rest.*
GEN.—bz-x.κ¹·⁴·⁵·¹⁰.r¹b.ω².3-99.
36.107.130.——cap.VI³.(35).
—c-ar.31.; 35.—gn-c.VII¹.iᵃ.
ξ.φ¹.35.83.——glo.—hel.(16).—
hpm.III.κ⁵.(19.31.35).——lyc.
(8-31).—nat.V⁷.p.19.(8-31).
—sul.ω.—tep.V⁷.ab^i.35.

F.—angᵉ.V¹⁰·ˢ.35.——argⁿ.VI⁴.
bro.V⁷.(128).——ca-a^b.VI²·ᵉ.
35.——ca-c.V⁷.35.——cch^d.V¹.
(101).——k-bi.VI³·ʷ.31.——k-ca.
V¹.κ⁴·⁵.31.——men.V⁷.35.——

nitᵖ.VI³·ᵈ.4.5.31.—*rho*.V¹⁰·ˢ_
VIII⁴.—*stp*.V¹⁰·ˢ–VI³.35.
T.—argᵇ.V⁶.—epn V⁶.—*k-bi*.
VI³·ᵃ.31.—*lyc*.31.
C.—*glo*.V¹⁰·ᵛ.35.(8).; II⁵.29.31.
P.—argᶜ.V⁶–VIII⁴.—*ag-n*ᶜ.V¹·⁶.
q.35.—belᶜ.V⁶.*rr*.66.—phoᶜ.
V³.βeᵃ.35.(8).—pi-m.V¹.(35).
O.—argⁱ.V⁶.—*iod*.V¹.βe.35.
—manᵇ.VIII⁴.35.—pi-mV¹.
(35).
B.—belᶠ.V⁶.σ².35.

22. By bending head backwards.
Gᴇɴ.—dig.VIII⁵.18.(16.29).—
elp.(29).—lyc.VIII⁴.1.—*thu*.
III–VI³–VIII¹.29.(12).
F.—*bel*.V¹⁰·ˢ.—chi.V¹.19.—lin.
V⁷.q.43.—stn.V¹.(12).—*ver*.
V¹.29.30.
T.—ana.VI⁴–VIII³.—thu.VI³-
VIII¹.29.(12).
C.—osm.iᵃ.4.
P.—aurᵇ.V³–VIII⁴.3-99.89.
O.—ana.VI⁴–VIII³.—*ba-a*ᶜ.
VI⁴.—*chi*ᶜ.V⁶.—cchᵇ.**50.**—
mur.III³.—osm.iᵃ.4.—*ph-x*.
V¹⁰·ᶻᶻ.29.—*rhs*.—*spi*.IX.16.
31.35.(I9).
B.—*chi*ᵒᶜ.V¹.11.

22. By bending head sideways.
Gᴇɴ.—men.V⁷.; *men*.V¹–VI³.q.

22. By bending head to left.
T.—belᵇ.V¹⁰·ᵃ·ᵗ.—*fag*.29.30.

22. By bending head to painful side.
F.—tab.V¹⁰·ˢ.
P.—mez.V¹⁰.

22. By bending backwards.
T.—chi.V¹.—*mt-s*.V¹.19.26.41.
(29.31).—man.V¹·³.19.(29).
—*ver*.V⁷.29.30.(12).
C.—*mt-s*.V¹.19.26.41.(29.31).
P.—digᵃ.VIII⁵.18.(16.29).

22. By bending to right.
B.—mg-mᵖᵇ.VI³.

23. By stretching.
O.—aga.V⁶.3-**10.91.**

24. By raising head.
Gᴇɴ.—lin.—*mag*.2.98.99.—ver.
(29).
F.—ba-a.V¹⁰·ˢ.(29).—ccaᵉ.**50.**—
ign.VI⁴.ηp,aa.r¹p.(17).

T.—ang.V¹·³.(29).
P.—*ang*ᵈ.V¹.29.—cacᶜ.Iᵃ.—
capᵇ.V¹–VI³.α¹bᵒ.κ⁵.29.(**50**).-
cb-vᶜ.II⁵–V¹.16.(30).
O.—ch-sʰ.VI³.5.—ignᵍ.VI⁴.ηp,
aa.r¹p.(17).—mt-nʰ.V¹⁰·ˢ.—
ver.Iᵃ.(29).

26. By moving head.
Gᴇɴ.—ac-l.V¹⁶.—am-c.VI³.w.
φ¹.2.—arn.VI³·ˢ.89.(16).—
ars.w.V¹.31.—can.σ².—cap.
VII¹.31.—ca-x.II⁵.—cau.—
chi.VI⁴.31.; VI³·⁴.—ch-s.—
cle.—ccs.V⁷.5.—cch.3-30.—
cor.IX.35.—crn.V⁷.φ.29.31.
-f-io.7.29.31.43.44.(5.8.107).
—fl-x.1.—*gel*.κ⁵.—gen.(66).
—gn-c.—glo.II⁵.30.; II⁵-
VII⁵.;V¹.35.—grp.—hep.βa.;
3.—lo-c.V⁷.iᵃ.35.—lyc.28.—
mg-s.III.βeᵃ.χ²·³.3.**10.**—man.
V¹.w.κ⁴.—mez.V¹–VIII⁴.ζ.θ¹.
—nx-j.V¹.—sam.VII⁵.βa.3.—
sep.5.—spi.βa.
F.—*aga*.V⁷.δb.—*ar-i*.βe.σ².5.—
ccs.κ⁵.28.—cchᵍ.—col.V¹⁰.17.
29.48.—cotᵃ.V⁷.—eubᵇ.VI⁴.
βa.—glo.VIII⁴.—hfb.V¹.29.
—ipcᵇ.V¹⁰·ˢ.—mez.V¹–VIII⁴.
ζ.θ¹.—naj.VI³.—nx-j.48.—
opi.VI³–VIII⁴·⁵.q.—ped.1.—
pla.V¹⁰·ˢ.q.δb,ε.ηp,aa.κ³.o².ρ.5.
29.—rho.βe.—stp.V⁷.18.; ᶜ.
IX.—sul.II⁷-V⁶-VI³·⁴.(8.12).
T.—asrᵇ.III.31.(19).—*cin*ᵇ.V¹_
VI⁴.—gloᵃ.—la-vᵇ.V⁷.—mt-s.
V¹.19.41.(22.29.31).—na-m.
VI³.w.—rs-rᵃ.Iᵉ.
C.—colᵈ.V¹.29.—glo.V²·ᵉ.; II⁵.
—mt-s.V¹.19.41.(22.29.31).
—na-m.VIII¹.α¹b.βa.—sep.
V¹⁰·ˢ.VIII⁴.35.48.
P.—cb-vᶜ.—cf-t.IX.—cotᶜ.V⁷.
—phlᶜ.VI⁴.—spgᵈ.VI³.—sul.
II⁷-V⁶-VI³·⁴.(8.12).
O.—asrᵈ.III.31.(19).—cac.V⁶.
—cn-iᵇ.V⁷.iᵃ.—glo.V¹.σ².ff.
28.—mez.V¹.σ³.; ᵉ.V¹–VIII⁴.
ζ.θ¹.—ol-aᶜ.V¹.66.(29).
—— *to one side*.—glo.Iᵛ.
—— *sideways*.—glo.Iᵛ.

—— to l. side.—mag[b].VI[4].
—— on the side to which head
moves.—ca-c.V[6].(90).

27. *By moving arms.*
GEN.—f-mg.29.33.
F.—ptl.51.—rhs.V[16].
T.C.—spo.VIII[3·v].31.
B.—cau[f].V[1]–VI[1].29.

28. *By turning head.*
GEN.—cth.V[10·zz].29.—cle.IX.
—col.5.29.—cu-a.VI[3].—gen.
—grp.—hfb.VII[1].29.35.—
lyc.26.—na-m.; V[15].5.—nit.
—pho.V[7].βa.δо.η.θ[2].ω[2].(16).—
phs.ʌ[5·7].29.
F.—cth.V[10·s].29.—ch-s[e].V[1].48.
—ccs.ʌ[5].26.—gel[c].VI[3·t].29.48.
—ph-x.31.; V[1].12.
—— *quickly.*—nat.
—— *to right.*—æth.VI[3].
C.—hyo.V[1].σ[2].—ptv[b].V[7].5.31.
P.—mg-s[c].VI[3].3-30.—m-pi[e].VI[3].
29.—spi[c].V[1].δr.3-30.31.74.
O.—glo[i].; V[1].σ[2]ff.26.—ph-x[b].
V[1].1.12.

28. *By turning body.*
F.—cha.Vl[4].w.30.—— *sil[c]*.V[1]–
VIII[3].(29.86).
T.—glo.V[10]–VIII[2].ηp,aa.18.29.
31.

29. *By stooping.*
GEN.—ac-c.—alo.35.—alm.V[12].
q.4.—— aps.II[1]–VIII[4].χ[3].35.
(12).—arn.VI[3]–VIII[3].κ[5].μ.;
VI[4]–VIII[3].89.—ar-i.V[10·s].q.
3-99.35.41.—bap.II[5].— bry.
III-Vl[3].q.3.46.—ca-a.VIII[3].
q.(30).—ca-c.VI[3].30.—c-cs.
—c-ph.8.—cth.V[10·zz].28.—
cb-v.VII[1].—ca-x.—car.VIII[1].
ηaa.33.—chd.8.53.89.—ch-s.;
3-30.35.; VIII[4].r.——*cin*.41.
43.—cn-s.—cnb.—cob.—cch.
35.41.—col.δ.5.; 5.28.—com.
101.—crn.V[7].φ.26.31.—cyc.
VI[3].—dig.3-30.; *dig*.VIII[5].
18.22.(16).—*elp*.22.—*fag*.
fer.31.(19).—f-io.7.26.31.43.
44.(5.8.107).—f-mg.27.33.—
for.4.—glo.; VI[3].3.; VIII[4].—
ham.VII[1].—hel.V[2].βe[a].—hep.

VI[3]–VII[1].δb.—hdr.VII[1].33.
89.—hy-x.w.—hfb.VII[1].28.
35.—ign.; (30).—*ind*.V[12].30.
—itu.——k-bi.VIII[4].—kre.
VII[5].; V[10·s].eⅮ[u·P].83.—lah.V[1].
κ[5].31.; III.d.q.βe.; VIII[4].—
lyc.V[1].4.—muc.VIII[2].n[2].—
mrl.V[1]–VII[5].q.—mer.VIII[1].
35.—*mez*.—mil.—nat.VIII[4].
d.**30**.(30).—na-m.VII[1].ξ[3].83.
89.90.—nic.VI[4].i[a].q.βe[a].; VI[3].
5.—ni-x.δ.; VIII[1·3].16.—nit.
—nx-v.VI[3]–VIII[4].3.—par.
VI[3·q].—pau.5.—ped.VI[3·d].;
3.—pet.V[1].—pho.8.—phs.ʌ[5·7].
28.—phy.**50**[a].—pul.V[1].—rhe.
V[15].ag.βe[a].35.—rs-r.35.—rhs.
VI[4·g].5.—san.VIII[4].35.—spi.
VII[2].; V[1].—stp.VI[3].◦Ⅾ.5.31.
—sul.—thu.III-VI[3]-VIII[1].
(12.22).—*ver*.(24).

F.—aco.V[10].i[a].—am-c.VII[1].σ[2].
—am-m[b].VI[3]–VII[1].—ang.V[2].
(8).—anh.d.66.—ag-m.; V[10].
κ[5].3-99.(8.89).; V[1].p.q.5.—
arn.VI[3].—VIII[3].κ[5].ρ.——asr.
VIII[4].—atr[e].VI[3].35.—au-m[e].
VI[4].βa.35.(8).—*ba-a*.V[10·s].24.
—ba-c[o].VI[3].; VIII[4·q].—*bel*.
V[10].au.δP[2].; bel[h].V[1]; V[10·s].;
ⁿ.VI[3].(11).——ber.III[1]-VII[5].
q.(8).; VI[3]-VIII[4].——bor[e·b].
V[1·6].λ.σ[2].43.44.—bov.VI[4·a].q.
δ.—bro.δ.83.—bry.V[1·3].31.;
V[1].; Vl[3].ζ[3].; V[10].; V[10·s]-VI[3].;
V[10·s].δl.—ca-a[a].V[7].; g.V[10·s].q.
18.—cam[h].III[1].p.r[1]v[1]b.φ.12.
16.—cth.V[10·s].28.—cb-a.II[5].
—cb-v.I[a].V[10·s].—crd.V[1].—
cau.III-V[1].8-31.; cau.V[10·s].—
——chd.V[10·s].1.8.53.89.(63).;
V[10·s].—cob.—cof.V[1]-VII[5].δb.
3-99.—col.V[10].17.26.48.; III.
δ.(8).—cup.V[10·s].βe.——cyc.
VI[3].—dro[e].(31).; V[3·s].44.;
VI[4].; VI[4]-VII[5].—dul[o].V[6].
er-a[e].VII[2].δо.; V[7].43.44.—
fag.V[1].41.—fl-x.V[1].δr.—gel[c].
Vl[3·t].—gua.3.—hæm.κ[5].—
hep.VI[2]-IX.2.89.——hyo.V[1].
VIII[5].d.—hfb.V[11].26.—hyo[n].

V⁶–VIII⁴.35.; V¹–VIII⁵.d.—
ignᶠ·ʰ.V¹·⁶.——idmᵈ.iᵃ.5.——iof.
VI³.——ipcᵉ.VI³·ᵃ.iiᵈ.——jun.
VII¹.——k-bi.; ᵉ.VII¹–VIII⁴.
q.35.66.(8.14.16).—k-hy.VI³.
—kre.V¹⁰·ˢ.δ.; V¹⁰·ˢ–VIII².
la-vᵒ.VI³.—lau.gᵇ.q.βeᵃ.; ᵇ.—
lyc.II³.—mg-m.V¹⁰·ˢ.5.; VI³·⁴.
—mnc.βe.σ².—manᵉ.V⁶.(12).
——mrlᵉ.V¹⁰·ˢ–VII⁵.——. mer.
V³.q.—mr-cᵍ.V¹–VI³.—mur.
II¹.3.—mu-x.VI³.12.—myr.
V⁷.q.3-99.——nitᵇ.VI³–VII¹.
—nx-v.V⁹·¹⁰·ˢ.3.—ped.—pla.
V¹⁰·ˢ.q.δ♭,e.ηp,aa.κ³.o².ρ.5.26.-
ptl.V¹⁰·ˢ.q.2.——pul.VIII⁴.5.
41.(31).—ratᶜ.VI³.; VII¹.5.—
rs-v.V⁷.q.31.—silᶜ.V¹–VIII³.
(28.86).—so-nᵉ.—spi.V¹⁰·ˢ.—
stnᵃ.V¹–VI⁴.; V¹⁰·ˢ–VI³.—
stp.VI³.5.(31).VI⁴.19.; V¹⁰·ˢ.
—sul.V¹.—tru.Iᵇ.; ᵃ.δ.4.—
tep.VI³·ᵃ.—teuᵒ.V¹.(18).—
valᵉ.V⁶.——ver.V¹.30.(22).—
vrb.V¹⁰·ˢ.

T.——am-mᵇ.VI³–VII¹.——ang.
V¹·³.24.—bovᵇ.βe.—broᵇ.el.—
ca-a.VIII³.q.(30).——chi.VI¹.
35.—cof.V¹⁰·ᶻᶻ.3-99.—col.III.
δ.(8).——cot.VI³.—dio.31.—
fag.30.(22).——fl-xᵃ.VIII⁴.5.
—glo.V¹⁰–VIII².ηp,aa.18.28.
31.—gua.4.——mt-s.V¹.19.26.
41.(22.31).——man.V¹·³.19.22.
—mu-x.VI³.12.——na-aᵃ.—
phoᵃ.V¹.6.31.85.(8).——so-nᵇ.
VIII⁴·ᵃ.32.—thu.VI³–VIII¹.
(12.22).—ver.V¹–VII⁵.βe.δP¹.
18.19.(17).; ver.V⁷.30.(12.
22).

C.—aco.V⁷.—aln.II⁶.4.—am-m.
VI³–VII¹.——ber.VI³–VIII⁴.
—ca-c.V¹⁰·ˢ–VI³.—c-ph.V¹⁰·ˢ.
iᵃ.35.(16).—colᵈ.V¹.26.—glo.
II⁵.——hln.VIII⁴.βa.——ir-fᵃ.
V⁶·¹¹.2.——lau.VI³.30.—mt-s.
V¹.19.26.41.(22.31).——men.
VIII³.—nx-m.V¹⁰·ᶻᶻ.——ver.
V¹–VII⁵.βe.δP¹.18.19.(17).

P.——almᶜ.VI³.——angᵈ.V¹.(24).
—ca-aᶜ.—capᵇ.V¹–VI³.a¹♭ᵒ.κ⁵.

24.50.—-ch-sᵈ.ζl.; ¹.IX.4.—
cor.VII¹.—cotᵇ.VI³.—digᵇ.
VI³-VII⁵.θ.(30).; digᵃ.VIII⁵.
18.22.(16).—eupᶜ.VI³.—gloᵈ.
VIII⁴.iiᵈ.——hpmᶜ.V¹.βa.δ.θ².
κ¹.35.—indᶜ.VI³.κ⁴.4.19.(30).
——irsʰ.V³·ᵃ.——lauᶜ.VI³–
VIII⁴·ᵃ.; ᵈ.VIII⁴.—m-piᵉ.VI³.
28.——phoᶜ.3-99.6.35.(8).—
tonᶜ.VI⁴.(30).

O.—alo.II⁵-VI³-VIII⁴.λ.2-10.
—cam.III¹.p.ζ.r¹ν¹b.φ.12.16.
—cb-v.V¹⁰ʲˢ.—car.VIII⁴.ηaa.
33.—chi.VI¹.δO.35.—cch.V¹.
q.35.—gel.V⁷.5.35.—hel.V².
—hln.βa.——ign.VI⁴.d.iᵃ.30.
(17.19).——k-ca.VI³.31.—
man.V⁶.δO.(12).——ol-aᶜ.V¹.
26.66.——ph-x.V¹⁰·ᶻᶻ.(22).—
pru.Iᵃ.a¹bᵃ.—rs-r.V⁷.σ².—spiᵇ.
V¹⁰·ᵗ.(12).—ver.Iᵃ.24.

Ba.—cam.III¹.p.r¹ν¹b.φ.12.16.

B.—caufᶠ.V¹-VI¹.27.—confᶠ.III¹.
au.a¹bᵖ.βa.χ¹.(12).——manᵖᵇ.
VI³·ᵃ.; ᵖᵃ.II¹v.(15).—samᵗᵇ.
V¹–VI⁴.

30. *By rising.*

Gᴇɴ.—arn.(16).——glo.II⁵.26.;
V¹.—*hep.*V⁷.8-10.—*ign.*3-99.
66.; V².3-99.41.—mt-n.48.—
*nat.*VIII⁴.d.**30.**29.——na-m.
κ⁵·⁶.ω³.31.(5).; κ⁵·⁶.ω³.31.——
na-s.χ²·³.43.(35).—*rs-r.*—trn.
VIII².

F.——*ch-sᶠ.*2.43.——cnb.V⁷.8-99.
12.16.(117).——glo.VIII⁴.—
*spo*ᵇ.V¹⁰·ˢ.19.—ver.V¹.29.(22).

T.——*ca-a.*VIII³.q.29.—fag.29.
(22).—lcp.—*rhs*ᵃ.V¹⁰ᵛ.5-10.;
V⁶.δ.3.——*stn*ᵃ.V¹.17ᵃ.—vér.
V⁷.29.(12.22).

C.—lau.VI³.(29).

P.——*cb-v*ᶜ.II⁵–V¹.16.(24).——
ch-sᵈ.VI³.—*dig*ᵇ.VI³-VII⁵.θ¹.
29.—grpᵇ.κ⁶.3.——*ind*ᶜ.VI³.κ⁴.
4.19.29.——*ol-a*ᵈ.VI³.λ.ξ².σ.2.
84.—*rho*ᵈ.II³–V¹.16.——*tab.*
V¹.3-99.—*ton*ᶜ.VI⁴.29.

O.—*ch-s.*V¹·ᵃ.3.——*ept.*VIII⁴.σ².
—*gel*ᵇ.V⁷–VIII⁴.—*jug.*V¹.3-
10.—*jg-v.*V¹.3-10.—*pul.*VI³.16.

I I

—— *from sitting.*
Gen.—-aps.V$^{1.7}$.——-grt.—-lam.
(19).
T.—man^{b}.V^1.31.(19).
C.—cob.κ^4.

—— *from stooping.*
Gen.—*ca-a.*VIII^3.q.29.——-hep.
VI^3.8-31.35.——*ign.*29.——*ind.*
V^{12}.(29).—-lam.I^q.—-lyc.VII^1.
w.81.33.———mg-m.VIII^4.——
mu-x.VI^3.66.
F.—asr.VI^4.——-mg-s.V$^{10.s}$.p.q. ;
V$^{10.zz}$.d.q.3.
P.—k-ca^c.V$^{10.t}$.———man^c.VI^4.*er.*
—-su-x^c.V^7–VIII^4.
O.—mg-m.VIII^4.

—— *from lying.*
Gen.—aps.V$^{1.7}$.——ars.VIII^4.κ^5.
—-bov.2.(3).—-ca-c.VI^3.29.—
ign.3-10.——*lam.*III^1.βe.3-16.

—— *in bed.*
F.—-ars.VIII$^{4.a}$.κ^5.——-*cth.*V$^{10.s}$.
2-99.——-cha.VI^4.w.28.——jun.
V^3.3.—-mu-x.
O.—chd.IX.—-mu-x.

30. *By sitting up.*
Gen.—cic.—hel.II^1.—-tri.
O.—ign.VI^4.d.i^a.(17.19.29).——
jun.V^3.3.

30. *By lifting.*
Gen.—nat.VIII^4.d.29.(30).

30. *By carrying a weight on shoulders.*
O.—mg-s.

30^a. *By spinning.*
F.—cb-a.V^7.(66).

30^c. *By working.*
Gen.—buf.19.——*mt-n.*V^2.βe.100.
(18).—-so-t.

31. *By walking.*
Gen.———ac-s^d.2.———alm.V$^{1.7}$.;
VIII^4.4.16.——-*am-c.*VI^3.——
ang.IV^1.βe.——ars.V^1.ω.26.—
ast.VIII^4.33.——-bel.; VIII^3.
33.——-cad.——-*cth.*V^1–VI^3.5.5.
—-cap.VII^1.26.——-chi.II^5–V^2.
106.; VI^4.26.; VIII^3.35.(16).
—-cob. ; V^7.1.35.——-coc.V$^{10.u}$.
———crn.V^7.q.ϕ.26.29.——-c-ar.
(20).; (19).—-dig.—*fag.*I^z.(8.
12).—-fer.29.(19).——-grn.V^1.
q.—*ham.*3-30.6.(41.43.86).——

bpm.q.w.—hur.——-iod.6.128.
—lah.V^1.κ^5.29.—lyc.VII^1.w.
30.33.—mr-f.—*na-m.*V^1-VI^3.
——-nx-v.VI^4.ζ.θ^4.——par.V$^{10.s}$.
βv.43.49.——-ped.κ^5.——-ph-x.
VIII^1.—-pho.3.35.——phy.——
plm.—-ptl.V^7.33.——rhe.VI$^{4.d}$.
q.—sar.11.—sil.III^2.—*spi.*16.
—stp.VI^3.$e v$.5.29.——*sul.*VI^3.
q.βe^a.——trn.——thr.a$\mathbf{k}$.5.—-vi-t.
V^{10}.w.βe.

F.—aco.V^1.VI^3.VIII^4.(19).——
ana.V^1.3-99.——-an-s.5.112.—
arn.V^{10}.33.41.43.———ars.V^7.
VI^3.18.(19).—-bry.V$^{10.s}$.66. ;
^{b}.V^6–VII^2.6. ; V$^{10.z}$.——-ca-a^b.
V^1-VI^3.; ca-a^b.V^3-VI^3.19.(11.
18).——-ca-c.VI^1.12.——cnt.——
chi^e.5.(66). ; V$^{1.a}$. ; III^1–V^1. ;
*chi.*III^1–V^6.18.19.(12).——cle.
V^1–VII^5.q.——-cca.V^7.8q.3.——
coc.V$^{10.a.u}$.——-col.5.——-dgn^b.
VI^3.δLll.5.——*dro^e.*29.; βe.——
eup.V^1.βe.3.(117).——-grn.V^{10}.
q.——idm.——-k-bi.VI$^{3.w}$.(20).
—-k-ca.V^1.au.4$_.$; V^1.$\kappa^{4.5}$.(20). ;
VIII^4.18.66. — k-cy^g.VI$^{3.v}$.5.
128.—-lpt.I^a.——lcp.V.——mt-n^e.
V^1.——-mag^g.V^{14}-VIII^3.35.——
naj.VII^5.3-99.——nit^q.V^1–VI^4.
70.(8.128).; ^{P}.VI$^{3.d}$.4.5.20.——
ped.5.66.——ptv.III.——phs.V^1.
βa.——*pul.*VIII^4.5.41. ; pul.V^1.
——*rn-b^f.*ηp.r^1b.16.(18).——rat^a.
V^6.——rs-v.V^7.q.29.——*san^a.*V^{10}.
e.18.——sar.VI$^{4.q}$.86.——scr^e.——
so-t.I^a.4.——spo.VI^3–VIII^3.——
*stp.*VI^3.5.29.VI^4.19.; III^2.18.
19.——sul.VI^3.——-vi-t.V^1.q.w.
βe.

T.—ars^b.VI^3.18.(19).——asr^b.III.
26.(19).——buf^h.IV^2–V^3.——cas^a.
VI^4.5.———chi.V^1. ; *chi.*VIII^4.
18.19.(12).——col^b.V$^{1.a}$.18.77.
(19).——con^a.V^6.——dio.29.——
gen^a.VI$^{3.s}$.5.——glo.VIII^4.;V^{10}-
VIII^2.ηp,aa.18.26.28.29.——
*gui.*VI^3.18.19.(12).——hel^a.V^1.
41.——k-bi.VI$^{3.a}$.(20).———lil^b.
V^7.βa.5.———*mt-s.*V^1.19.26.41.
(22.29).——man^b.V^1.30.(19).——

pho^a.V^1.6.29.35.(8).——rn-b^a.
VI$^{4·a}$.βa. ; V$^{1·6}$.aq.π^1.5.——*stp*.
VI^3.18.19.——sul^b.VI^4–VIII^3.;
^{b}.VIII^4.——*trx*^{b}.V^6.19.(18).
C.——cb-a.VI^3-VII^1-VIII^4.——
con.III^2.(19).——glo.II^5.(20).
——hur.V^{16}.η.$θ^1$.4.——*mt-s*.V^1.
19.26.41.(22.29).——*ptv*.V$^{7·q}$.
11.19.86.(35).; ptv^b.V^7.5.28.
——phy.V^2.——*san*.V^1.——spo.
VIII$^{3·v}$.27.——sul.V^1.
P.——arg^d.V^6–VI^4.5.——ag-n^c.V^3–
VIII^4.a^{1}b^s.βa.σ^2.——ars^e.IX.——
bel^c.V^1.3.—— ca-c^d.VI^2.βa.χ^1.
3-30.18.——cle^c.V$^{1·3}$.——con.
VI^3.βa.σ^2.(19).——k-ca.VIII^4.
18.66.——na-m^d.VI$^{3·q}$.e.5.——
plb^c.VI^3–VIII$^{4·a}$.5.18.——spi^d.
V^3–VI^4.5.32.35.; ^{c}.V^1.δr.3-30.
28.74.
O.——asr^d.III.26.(19).——ath.IX.
βe.——bel.VIII$^{3·u}$.q.33.——bry^c.
V^6–VII^2.6.——ca-c.VI^1.12.——
chi.III^1–V$^{1·a}$.——con^c.VI^4.——
k-ca.VI^3.29.——mu-x^i.106.——
ped.III-VIII^4.δ$σ^d$.3-30.——spi.
IX.16.35.(19.22).——sul.V$^{7·14}$.
4.——trx.VI^4.(18).
B.——ham^m.VI^3.106.——mez^{pa}.IX.
—— *slowly*.
GEN.–hpm.III.κ^5.(19.20.31.35).
—— *quickly*.
GEN.——ca-c.VIII^4.——f-io.7.26.
29.43.44.(5.8.107).
F.——bry.V$^{1·3}$.29.; ^{g}.V^1.z.——man^f.
VI^3.——sep.VI^2.κ^5.
C.——chd.V^1–VI$^{3·d}$.
PO.——tab.VI$^{3·z}$.
—— *at every step*.
GEN.——alm.VI^3.——amb.VI$^{1·3}$.
(16).——bry.V^1.; VI$^{3·z}$.——c-ph.
σ.——ccs.V^1.——con.——dro.
na-m.κ$^{5·6}$.ω^3.30.——ni-x.51.——
nup.V^2–VI^3.——sep.VI^3.——sul.
F.——bel.IX.(12).——ph-x.28.——
sul.V^1.hh.; VI$^{3·a}$.86.89.
T.——alo^b.VI^3.——col^a.V^7.au.——
glo.VIII^4.——hdr.V^7.i^a.66.——
lah.III.5.——lyc.(20).——spo.
VIII$^{3·v}$.27.
B.——mez^{pa}.V$^{1·6}$.

—— *treading roughly*.
GEN.——pho.VIII^4.88.
—— *running*.
GEN.——hpm.III.κ^5.(19.20.35).——
na-m.34.; VIII^3.
32. *By a false step*.
T.——so-n.I^a.; VIII$^{4·a}$.29.
C.——cob.IX.
P.——spi^d.V^3–VI^4.5.31.35.
33. *By going up-stairs*.
GEN.——alm.VIII^4.66.——ast.
VIII^4.31.——bel.VIII^3.31.——
cad.——cat.VIII^1.ηaa.29.——
c-ar.——f-mg.27.29.——gel.——
glo.VIII^4.35.; VIII^3.——hdr.
VII^1.29.89.——ign.VIII^3.——
lo-i.——lyc.VII^1.w.30.31.——
mt-n.V^6.——men.V$^{10·s}$.q.——msc.
——na-a.VIII^4.—— par.VIII$^{4·5}$.
——ph-x.V^1.——ptl.V^7.31.——rhs.
——sul.
F.——ant.V^7.——arn.V^{10}.31.41.43.
——cmf^f.VIII^4.i^a.p.——ign.V^1.
βe.3-99.35.48.——men.V$^{10·s}$.
VIII^1.——sul.V^1.
T.——glo.VIII^4.κ^5.——klm^b.——sul.
VIII^4.
C.——ant.V^7.——cmf.VII^1.i^a.p.——
fer.VIII^4.35.——lo-i.35.——men.
III.q.
P.——hdr^h.3.
O.——bel.VIII$^{3·u}$.q.31. ——car.
VIII^4.ηaa.29.
33. *By going down-stairs*.
GEN.——men.V$^{10·s}$.q.
F.——fer^m.V$^{10·t}$.3-30.(8.12).——iof.
V^7.e.——men.V$^{10·s}$.
T.——mr-f.VI^3.
C.——*fer*.V$^{10·t}$.(8.12).
O.——ce-b.V$^{10·t}$.8-31.
34. *By violent exertion*.
GEN.——ac-c.η.——ana.VI^4.——c-ph.
——glo.VIII^4.——*mr-f*.3-99.——
nat.V^1–VI^3.——na-m.31.——*rs-g*.
V^7.q.
F.——ber.V^1.βa.ω^3.——mg-m^i.V$^{1·3}$.
(105).——rs-r.——zng.V$^{1·6}$.
C.——mr-s^c.V$^{7·q}$.3.(4).
O.——*cac*.V^1.(41).
35. *By motion*.
GEN.aco.64.86.——alo.29.——am-c.

VIII^1. ; II^7.12.—ana.—aps. II^1–VIII^4.χ^3.29.(12).—ag-n. i^a.q.βe^a.3-99.——ar-i.$V^{10 \cdot s}$.q. 3-99.29.41.——bap.$V^{1 \cdot 7}$.—bel. —ber.(8).— bis.$V^{1 \cdot 6 \cdot 7}$.—bry. VIII^4.δ^1.—buf.—cth.V^6-VI^4.; V^1.q.--*cap.*VI^3.20.--cb-v.III^1. —chi.VIII^3.(16).--ch-s.3-30. 29.—cl-h.V^7.--cn-s.29.—cob. V^7.1.31.——cch.29.41.——cup. V^1.βa.11.—c-ar.(20).—fag.-- gn-c.VII^1.i^a.ξ^3.ϕ^1.35.83.(20). —glo.VIII^4.33.; V^1.26.--grn. VI^8.—grt.8.—*gur.*—hep.VI^3. 8-31.30.—*hpm.*III.$_4{}^5$.(19.20. 31).—hfb.VII^1.28.29.—idm. —iod.VIII^4.--k-ca.v.5.--lo-c. V^7.i^a.26.— lyc.VI^3–VIII^5.— mac.VIII^4.5.--mer.VIII^1.29. --mr-s.II^5.3.66.--*mor.*—na-a. ---*na-m.*$\chi^{2 \cdot 3}$.43.(30).——nic. VIII^2.—*opi.*III.—pho.3.31.; V^1-VI^4-VIII^3.βe.3-99.--phy. βa.—rat.VI^3.94.—rhe.V^{15}.ag. βe^a.29.—rs-r.29.--rum.--sbd. q.--san.VIII^4.29.--sep.VIII^4. —stp.III.16.--tar.VI^3.—tep. V^7.$_a b^i$.20.

F.—aco.i^a.q.——agn.V^1–VI^4.— ang^e.$V^{10 \cdot s}$.20.——ars.$VIII^{4 \cdot a}$. ---atr^e.VI^3.29.——aur^b.VI^4.; VI^4.—au-m^e.VI^4.βa.29.(8).-- bel.V^1.(16.19).$V^{10 \cdot t}$.8.—-bis. V^1.q.—b-la.V^7.—bov^b.$V^{1 \cdot q}$.q. δ.δo.3.——bry^h.$V^{1 \cdot a}$. ; V^1.— ca-a^b.$VI^{2 \cdot e}$.20.——ca-c.V^7.20. —cth.V^6–VI^4.—chp.VII^5.— cl-h^e.--cnb^e.V^7.5.——cup.V^1. 11.—cyc^a.VI^3–VIII^3.η.--dig. V^7.——dul.$V^{10 \cdot s}$–VIII^3.—fag. 3-99. ; ^{b}.I^4.d.83. ; ^{b}.VIII^4.2. --glo.VIII^4.26.--grp.V^7.3-30. ---*hdr.*VII^1.3-99.(12.41).— ign.V^1.βe.3-99.33.48.; δ.; $^n V^6$- VIII^4.35.—iod.βe.——k-bi^g. VI^3.κ^4.3-30. ; ^{e}.VII^1–VIII^4. q.29.66.(8.14.16). ; ^{e}.V^6.q.8. —*lah.*V^1.5.6.19.(8).—lyc.V^7. —mag^g.V^{14}–VIII^3.31.--mg-m. $VI^{3 \cdot 4}$.5.--mel^h.41.(16).--men. V^7.20.--msc.V^1.βa,e.——nat.

VII^1.3.--nx-j^e.V^1.--*pet.*VII^1- $VIII^{4 \cdot 5}$.--ph-x.$V^{1 \cdot a}$.$a^1 \mathfrak{d}$.$\delta \mathfrak{h}$.o^2. 3-99. ; VI^4.—*pi-m.*—rho.V^6- $VI^{4 \cdot a}$.δ.6.—rum).—sbd.q.— sep.V^3.5. ; ^{g}.V^1–VI^3.6.(8-31). —sil.VI^4.1.5.——so-n^e.3-99. ; VII^1.——spi^a.V^3–VI^4.51.86. (16).—stp.$V^{10 \cdot s}$–VI^3.(20).— sul.V^1.——tab.V^7.66.——tar. V^1.

T.——agn.$VI^{3 \cdot 4}$. ; ^{a}.V^1–$V I^4$. ; VIII^1.δ.——*car.*VI^4.——cau^a. VIII^4.—-chi.VI^1.29.—cnb^a. VIII^4.i^a.q.——cob.V^7.βe.3.—— com^b.$VI^{3 \cdot a}$.(8).——cup.V^1.βa. 11.— dir^a.VI^3.—*fer.*V^1.βe.— glo.VIII^4.——hpm$^{a \cdot b}$.V^1.5.— k-bi.V^7.q.8.——*lil*^{b}.19.—*mez*^{b}. V^1.19.43. ; mez.86. ; III^3. $a^1 b^8$.—ph-x^a.III^3–V^1. ; ^{b}.$V^{1 \cdot 6}$. $e a$T. ; ^{b}.VI^4.——pho^a.V^1.6.29. 31.(8).—rho.V^6–$VI^{4 \cdot a}$.δ.6.

C.—aur^b.V^1–VI^4.— bel^a.VI^4.— c-ph.$V^{10 \cdot s}$.i^a.29.(16).——cth. V^1–VIII^4.5.—chi.IV^1.—dor. —fer.V^1.2. ; VIII^4.33.—glo. $V^{10 \cdot v}$.(8.20).—ipc.III^1.—irs. IX.3.8.—lo-i.33.—mez.86.— *ptv.*$V^{7 \cdot q}$.11.19.86.(31).—— ph-x.$V^{1 \cdot 6}$.—sep.$V^{10 \cdot s}$–VIII^4. 26.48.——spi^b.V^3–VI^4.51.56. 86.(16).—ver.V^1–VIII^4.

P.——agn^d.V^1–VI^4.11.——ag-n^c. $V^{1 \cdot 6}$.q.(20).—bel^c.V^3–VIII^4. η.——c-ph^a.VIII^4.——chi.V^2. —dir^d.VIII^4.11.89.——glo^a. $VIII^{2 \cdot 4}$.**50.**—hpm^c.V^1.βa.δ.θ^2. κ^1.29.--irs^h.V^7–VIII^2.—ph-x. III^3–V^1.-pho^c.V^3.βe^a.20.(8). ; ^{c}.3-99.29.(8).--*pi-m.*V^1.20.— pru^c.$VIII^{1 \cdot 3}$.--sbd^d.q.βa.--sil. VI^4.5.—spi^d.V^3–VI^4.5.31.32.

O.—aur.$VI^{4 \cdot zz}$.——bis.V^1.q.— bry^i.$V^{1 \cdot 10}$.——*car.*VI^4.——chp. V^1–VII^5.— chi.VI^1.δO.29.— cl-h.II^5.q.16.(8).——cch.V^1.q. 29.——cup.V^1.11.——gel.V^7.5. 29.--hyp.V^1.—iod.V^1.βe.(20). —la-x^i.VI^3.—man^b.VIII^4.20. —ph-x.III^3–VI^4.51. ; $V^{1 \cdot 6}$.— *pi-m.*V^1.20.—spi.V^3–VI^4.51.

56.86.(16). ; IX.16.31. (19.
22).—spo.V¹–VI³.p.
Ba.—la-x.ηaa.ω.(12).
B.--belᶠ.V⁶.σ².20.-indᵖᵃ.VIII³·ᵃ.
3-30.
—— *quick.*
GEN.—cor.IX.26.—pet.VI³.d.
F.—bis.βa.κ⁴·⁷.ρ.χ².5.—na-m.
—— *violent.*
GEN.—ca-c.VI⁴.w.
T.—mez.III.a¹bᵇ.
—— *on commencing.*
GEN.—thr.
—— *on changing position in bed.*
F.—cchᵃ.Iᵃ.3-99.
36. *By mental emotion.*
GEN.— bz-x.—kre.—-mgt.II³.
au. ; V¹⁰.au.—na-m.VII⁵.
T.—hdr.Iᵃ.5.(8.12).
37. *By fright.*
GEN.—hpm.
38. *By excitement.*
GEN.—tan.κ⁵.
P.—ch-s.VII⁵.3.
O.—er-a.δ.
40. *By vexation.*
GEN.—cas.κ⁴·⁵.66.—mgt.V¹⁰.—
mag.VIII³.q.4.(5-10).—mez.
Iᵃ.4.11.—pho.
O.—rn-b.
41. *By mental exertion.*
GEN.--acn.η.—ag-n.VII⁵.—ar-i.
V¹⁰·ˢ.q.3-99.29.35.—am-i.V⁷.
105.--asr.βeᵃ.κ⁵.—aur.V²·a¹bˢ.
3.43.44.86.—cad.—cha.V¹·⁷.
19.—chi.II⁵.11.86.—-cin.V⁶.
43.66. ; 43.(29).—cnb.V¹.12.
43.—-coc.V¹.a¹ςᵈ.5.43.— cch.
29.35.—-dph.—fag.VII¹.4. ;
V¹.—-ham.3-30.6.(31.43.86).
—hpm.—ign.V².3-99.(30).—
lyc.—mag.V¹.—-mo-a.43.—
nx-v.VII¹.16.—-par.—pho. ;
5.—-pi-m.—-ptl.66.—sbd. ;
aₓᶜᶜ. ; sbd.VII⁵.(49).
F.—arn.V¹⁰.31.33.43.—asr.V⁶.
a¹bˢ.—-ca-aᶠ.V⁶. ; ca-a.V¹·⁶.
VI⁴.(12).—cofᵈ.V¹·⁶.—digᵈ.
V¹⁰. ; III¹-V¹.—fag.V¹.29.—
hdr.VII¹.3-99.(12.35).—hfb.
V¹⁰.aq.4.43.--klm.V⁷.q.--la-v.

V¹⁰.δ.3-99.—-mnc.VII⁵.—-
melᵇ.35.(16).—mez.V¹.βe.—
na-mᵉ.VIII⁵.86.—ol-a.V¹⁰·ᵃ.
3-99.—ph-x.V²·5.—pi-m.V⁷.
q.43.—pul.VIII⁴.5.29.(31).
—rs-rᶠ.5. ; ˢ.Iᵃ·ᵇ.5. ; V⁷.βɧ.3.
5.—sbd.VII⁵.(49).—sil.V¹.—
terᵍ.V¹.q.19.
T.—ca-a.V¹·⁶-VI⁴.(12).—-dig.
III¹-V¹.--gn-cᵇ.VI³.49.--helᵃ.
V¹.31.——mt-s.V¹.16.26.(22.
29.31).—nat.V¹⁰·ᵗ.βa.—nx-v.
—ph-x.V²·5.—-pi-m.V⁷.q.41.
—pso. ; V¹⁰.(8-31).—sul.V¹-
VII⁵.
C.—ast.IV¹-VII⁵.2.—gn-c.V¹-
VII⁵-VIII³.5.49.—*hln*.V¹⁰·ᵃ.
iᵃ.43.—mt-s.V¹.19.26.(22.29.
31).—nx-v.V¹⁰-VIII⁴.—pim.
III²-VI³.—sep.V¹.
P.—hypᶜ.VI³.—-ignᵇ.V¹.8-31.
86.
O.—ast.βɛᵇ.ω⁷.—*cac*.V¹.(34).—
ca-a.V⁶. ; *ca-a*.V¹·⁶-VI⁴.(12).
—cch.V¹·q.—-lo-i¹.VII⁵.—
ni-x.Iᵇ.—rs-r.V⁷.βɧ.5. ; ᵇ.V¹.
4.
42. *By thinking of the pain.*
GEN.—*aga*.—*cam*.III.
F.—*pru*.II³-V¹.
P.—sin.
43. *By reading.*
GEN.—agn.III¹.—aps.V¹·ᵘ.7.--
arg.III.βa.κ⁴·⁵.χ²·³.18.—-aur.
V².ab.3.41.44.86.--cn-s.—cin.
41.(29). ; V⁶.41.66.—cnb.V¹.
12.41.—cle.VI³-VII¹-VIII⁴.
v¹.16.44.(8).—-coc.V¹.a¹ςᵈ.5.
41.—fag.—f-io.7.26.29.31.44.
(5.8.107).—glo.—-*ham*.3-30.
6.(41.86).—ign.V¹.d.44.100. ;
ign.VII¹.86.(44).—kis.III¹.
—lyc.V¹-VIII⁴.19.—-mer.5.
(16.19).—mo-a.41.--na-s.χ²·³.
(30.35).—par.V¹⁰·ˢ.βɧ.31.49.
—ptl.—sbd.V¹⁰.
F.— arn.V¹⁰.31.33.41.—-borᵉ·ʰ.
V¹·⁶.λ.σ².29.44.—-bry.V¹. ; ᵉ.
V¹.—-ca-a.V⁷.a¹bᵒ.βe.—-cau.
V⁷.19.——ch-sᶠ.2.(30).—-coc.
V¹·ᵃ.a¹bˢ.5.—-cof.V²-VI⁴.—-

er-a.V^7.29.44.—f-io^a.V^7.q.44.
130.(8.107).——hfb.V^{10}.$_n$q.4.
41.—lin.V^7.q.22.—lo-s^e.V^7.
44.—opi^a.V^1.p.—phs.III^1.—
pi-m.V^7.q.41.—trx.V^7.$_a$ᴅ^a.κ^5.
19.(8).
T.—ca-x.V^{10}.x^a.—cle^b.VIII^4.16.
—cca.V^6.4.—mez^b.V^1.19.(35).
—na-m.III.44.—phs.III^1.—
pi-m.V^7.q.41.—sul.V^1.5.
C.—cb-v.VI^3.—hln.$V^{10 \cdot s}$.i^a.(41).
—lyc.VI^3.—na-m.V^1.44.
P.—lyc.VI^3.
O.—cca.$V^{6 \cdot zz}$.4.

44. *By writing.*
G$_{EN}$.—aur.V^2.$_a{}^1$b^s.3.41.43.86.—
cle.VI^3–VII^1–VIII^4.ν^1.16.43.
(8).—fer.—f-io.7.26.29.31.43.
(5.8.107).—glo.—ign.V^1.d.
43.100.; *ign.*VII^1.86.(43).—
k-ca.VIII^4.—mnc.$\beta\ell$.—rs-r.
ω^2.—rhs.$_a{}^1$b^s.βa.
F.—bor$^{e \cdot h}$.$V^{1 \cdot 6}$.λ.σ^2.29.43.—dro.
$V^{3 \cdot s}$.29.—er-a.V^7.29.43.—f-io^a.
V^7.q.43.**130**.(8.107).——gn-l.
V^1–VII^5.q. $\beta\ell$.—k-ca.$V^{10 \cdot s}$.—
lo-s^e.V^7.43.—lyc.V^1.——opi.
$V^{10 \cdot s}$.(12.15).
T.—m-pi^b.—na-m.III.43.
C.—gel.V^6.(19).—na-m.V^1.43.
—rn-b.VI^4.18.
P.—ch-s^c.V^7.; ^{d}.V^7.
O.—cb-a.V^1.σ^2.

46. *By opening eyes.*
G$_{EN}$.—bry.3.48.; III–VI^3.q.3.
29.—coh.V^1.—ign.3-99.(30).;
VIII^3.
F.—rhs^p.VI^4.3-99.48.
P.—sul^b.II^3–VI^4.100.

47. *By closing eyes.*
G$_{EN}$.——*con.*V^6.8.——nx-v.$V^{1 \cdot q}$.;
I^q.3-99.—*sul.*βa.
F.—cep^b.—ipc^e.$V^{3 \cdot 10 \cdot s}$.(12).
T.—cep.—*iod.*$V^{10 \cdot s}$.(12).—sab^b.
V^6.δL.

48. *By moving eyes.*
G$_{EN}$.—bel.—bry.3.46.—ch-s.—
cup.V^2.—idm.δ.—mt-n.30.—
nx-v.V^1.q.66.
F.—bad.p.δ.4.—chd.V^1.—ch-s^e.
V^1.28.—dig.VII^5.—dro.VI^4.

(14).—gel^c.VI$^{3 \cdot t}$.28.29.—hep.
V^2.3-99.—ign.V^1.$\beta\ell$.3-93.33.
35.—mu-x.V^1.—nx-j.26.—
pul.V^{10}.$\beta\ell$.5.—rhs^p.VI^4.3-99.
46.— spi^a.II^1.δ.—val^e.$V^{10 \cdot s}$.δ.
4.66.
—— *eyelids.*—col.V^{10}.17.26.29.
T.— bad.δ.—chi.VIII^3.p.q.—
sul.VI^3.49.
C.—sep.$V^{10 \cdot s}$–VIII^4.26.35.
P.—con^b.$V^{2 \cdot 10 \cdot u}$.
49. *By looking fixedly.*
G$_{EN}$.—cad.—hln.$V^{10 \cdot v}$.—mu-x.
V^1.q.βa.θa.ϕ.3-30.—par.$V^{10 \cdot s}$.
βᴅ.31.43.—*sbd.*VII^5.(41).—
spo.$\delta\ell$.
F.—glo.—pul^e.III^1.—*sbd.*VII^5.
(41).
T.—gn-c^b.VI^3.41.—lth.V^{10}.$\beta\ell$.δᴅ.
κ^5.3.16.(8.19).—sul.VI^3.48.
C.—gn-c.V^1–VII^5–VIII^3.5.41.
—hln.$V^{10 \cdot v}$.
50. *By looking up.*
G$_{EN}$.—aco.**50**^{b}.
F.—arn.VI^3.ηp.κ^3.—cca^e.24.—
grn.I^a.—lep^e.11.—pul^e.V^6–
VII^5.—sul.VII^5.δ.3-99.
T.—lep.11.
P.——cap^b.V^1–VI^3.$_a{}^1$b^o.κ^5.24.29.
—glo^a.VIII$^{2 \cdot 4}$.35.
O.—aru.VI^3.3.—cch^b.22.
50^a. *By looking down.*
G$_{EN}$.—phy.29.
50^b. *By looking sideways.*
G$_{EN}$.—aco.**50**.
50^d. *By raising eyebrows.*
F.—ch-s^e.3.
51. *By noise.*
G$_{EN}$.—ars.111.—bap.—ba-c.5.
—bel.—buf.111.—ca-x.VI^3.
δᴅ.111.(12).—con.86.—ph-x.
—ziz.$\kappa^{5 \cdot 6}$.111.(16).
—— *of falling water.*—ni-x.31.
F.—aco^d.III^1–V^1.$_a{}^1\ell^a$.ηc^b.ii.111.
(98.114).—aga^n.VI^3.—cac.q.
111.—cit.κ^5.—cch^g.I^a.4.—
con.IV^2.q.86.—iod.86.—ptl.
27^a.—spi^a.V^3–VI^4.35.86.(16).
C.—cac.V^7.q.—iod.—spi^b.V^3–
VI^4.35.56.86.(16).
P.—cac^c.I^a.111.—ziz^d.V^1.111.

—— of an hammer on an anvil.
—mnc^c.
O.—ph-x.III^3–VI^4.35.—spi.V^3–
VI^4.35.56.86.(16).

53. *By blowing nose.*
GEN.—ast.VI^3.2.—chd.8.29.89.
—mu-x.VI^3.
F.—chd.V$^{10.s}$.1.8.29.89.(63).
C.—sul.60.89.

53. *By frowning.*
F.—ars^a.II^3.V^7.—c-cs^i.VIII^4.—
na-m.II^3.11.

53. *By moving frontal muscles.*
B.—man^{fb}.VI^4.

53. *By moving facial muscles.*
C.—api.V^1–VII^1.q.

53^a. *By coryza.*
F.—xip^h.V^1.5.

54. *By smelling coffee.*
P.—lah^c.V^6–VI^3.

55. *By smell of alcohol.*
GEN.—so-t.(4).

55. *By smell of dirty clothes.*
P.—cb-a^a.V^7.5.(8).

55. *By epistaxis.*
GEN.—dig.—k-bi.βa.—mel.$\xi^2.\pi$.
F.—hyo.V^1.p.
P.—buf^c.

55^a. *On stopping nasal discharge.*
GEN.—k-bi.I^{zz}.

56. *By opening mouth.*
T.—fag^b.4.
C.—spi^b.V^3–VI^4.35.51.86.(16).
O.—spi.V^3–VI^4.35.51.86.(16).

57. *By clenching teeth.*
T.—idm^a.V^{10}.

60. *By chewing.*
F.—k-ca^d.VI^3.
T.—am-c^b.VI^3.—am-m^b.II^1–
VI^3.90.—ca-a^b.V^3–VI^3.δB.—
k-ca.VI^3.
C.—pho.VIII^4.11.—sul.53.89.
O.—sul.V^6.

61. *By swallowing.*
O.—mag.V^6–VII^5.18.(19).

63. *By eating.*
GEN.—chd.—der.V^{16}.5.—grp.
66.—lin.—mnc.VI^3.—phl.V^7.
(8).—rn-b.αg.ω^3.—sin.—zin.
VI$^{3.4}$.λ.ω^9.66.

F.—am-c^n.V^8–VI^3.—ana^a.V$^{3.10.t}$.
5.(12.16).—chd.V$^{10.s}$.1.8.29.
53.89.—cl-h^g.V^7.q.—rhs^e.
VI$^{3.s}$.$\kappa^{4.5}$.χ^2.—sul.I^a.3-99.—
tax^e.δt^u.κ^4.—zin.VI^4.g^a.5.
T.—con.VI^4.—lth^b.δOl.κ^4.—
su-x^b.VI^4.19.—vrb^a.V^7–VI$^{3.q}$.
θ^1.12.
C.—dul.V^6.ζ.5.—sab.V^1.
P.—gel^c.V^7.3.—tab^c.V^1.
O.—gel^c.V^1–VI$^{1.b}$.3.—ni-x^c.
VI$^{3.a}$.π^1.3.
B.—na-m^p.VI^3.5.

64. *By drinking.*
GEN.—aco.35.85.
—— *cold water.*
F.—aln^c.V^{10}.3-99.
—— *quickly.*
O.—na-m^d.V^1.

65. *By smoking.*
GEN.—ant.V^7.κ^5.—ara.19.(8-31).
—c-cs.V^1.a^{1}b^s.64.—ca-x.—
cle.—gel.—glo.—opi.—par.
F.—cld.V^7.af.δ.ηp.—cau^c.VI^4.
σ^2.ϕ^1.1-7.2.—f-io.V^7.q.
T.—na-a.V$^{3.t}$.p.κ^5.4.12.101.

65^a. *When fasting.*
GEN.—idm.V^7.(66).—nx-v.—
sil.
F.—cis.(66).
C.—ur-n^a.II^1.q.d.i^a.
B.—rn-b^t.V^1.

66. *After food.*
GEN.—alm.VIII^4.32.—am-c.
—a-sc.V^7.—aru.; V$^{1.7}$.—bel.
—bov.III^1.βe^a.—buf.3.—
c-ph.—cth.—cb-a.V^1.βa.5.;
VI^4–VIII^4.δ.ϵ.η.θ.(12).—cb-v.
III^1.5.—ca-x.—cn-s.βe.—cas.
$\kappa^{4.5}$.40.—cau.VIII^4.βe.—clo.
—cin.V^6.41.43.—cca.3.—cof.
6.(8).—con.βe^a.3.8-31.; V^6.—
ctn.—dio.III^3.—fag.d.4.—
gel.; gel.V^7.—gen.26.; gen.
V^7.q.—glo.—grp.63.—ign.
V^1.—idm.κ^5.χ.; V^7.ηaa.κ^5.ϕ.
χ^1.; idm.V^7.3-30.; V^7.65^a.—
jug.—k-ca.II^7.(16).—lch.
VI^3.5.—lo-i.V^1.βe.ηp.5.—lo-s.
—m-gm.V^7.δ.—mr-f.V^7.—
mr-s.II^5.3.35.—mor.—mu-x.

VI^{3}.30.—-nat.V$^{6.7}$.*βe*.—-nit.; VII$^{5.q}$.—-nx-j.V^{1}.q.(4).—- nx-v.V^{1}.q.48.; VI^{4}.ηp.χ^{1}.; VI^{3}. κ$^{5.6}$.(5.16).—*pet*.3.—-phl.hh. —-*pho*.V^{6}.ao,æ.βa.δt^{n}.ρ.3. ; 7. (8-31).—*phy*.κ^{5}.—pgn.—ptl. 41.—- pul.VI^{3}.χ^{1}.ω^{3}.5.—- rhs. V^{6}-VI^{4}.—rut.V^{1}.af.—sar.V^{12}. —-*scu*.V^{7}.βe^{a}.3.——*ton*.V^{12}-VIII^{4}.6.—zin.VI$^{3.4}$.λ.ω^{9}.63.

—— *bread*.—mnc.βa.3.

F.—alm.V$^{10.s}$.; II^{1}-V^{1}.p.18.19. (8).; VI^{3}.5.—am-c^{g}.VI^{3}.δb.— anh.d.29.-ara.V^{1}.βe.ω^{2}.5.(12). —bov^{g}.VI^{3}.ηaa.—-bro.—bry. V$^{10.s}$.31.—-ca-s.I^{a}.5.—-cln.p. —*cb-a*.V^{7}.**30**^{a}.—- cb-v.VIII^{4}. p.κ^{7}.—-cha.VIII^{3}.—-*chd*^{h}.V^{1}-VI^{4}.δb.; chd^{c}.VI^{4}.(12).—chi^{e}. 5.31.—-ch-s.—-*cis*.**65**^{a}.—cle. V^{1}-VII^{5}.—-cch^{g}.6.(8).—con. V^{1}.—*eu-a*.V^{7}.3-99.—-*gen*.— grp.V$^{10.s}$.; VII^{1}.—hdr.V$^{10.zz}$. 3.— inu.VI^{4}-VIII^{4}.—-k-bi^{e}. VII^{1}--VIII^{4}. q. 29. 35. (8. 14. 16).; V^{1}.--k-br^{n}.--k-ca.VIII^{4}. 18.31.—lyc^{e}.—-mag.VI^{4}.q.— na-s.V^{1}.; V^{4}.φ.—-nit^{a}.V^{7}.— opi.V^{1}.βb,e.θ^{2}.κ.κ$^{1.5.9}$.4.(5).— ped.5.31.—-pho^{h}.a^{1}b.5.; V^{6}.; II^{1}-VI^{3}-VII^{1}.3.19.(**15**).--phy. V^{1}.q.; ^{h}.V^{1}.—pla^{b}.V$^{1.3}$.6.8-31. —*pso*.V$^{10.s}$.3-30.(117).—-sar. V^{1}.q.**5**.—- so-t.VI^{3}.5.—-sul. V^{1}.—tab.V^{7}.35.—val^{e}.V$^{10.s}$.δ. 4.48.—zin^{o}.; V^{1}.βe.δ.; ^{o}.V^{1}-VI^{4}.; VI^{4}-VIII^{4}.

—— *veal*.—nit^{e}.

T.—alm^{a}.V$^{10.t}$.—ara.V^{1}.βe.ω^{2}.5. (12).—cth^{a}.VI^{4}.--cas^{a}.VIII^{4}. 18.—cle.V^{1}-VII^{5}.—-con.III. (**14**).; VI^{4} —-dio.V^{7}.—-*equ*. VI^{3}.8-31.—-*glo*^{b}.V$^{1.10.s}$.κ^{5}.μ^{2}. σ^{1}.5-10.--hdr.V^{7}.i^{a}.31.—ind^{a}. βa.κ^{6}.—- k-bi^{a}.q.κ^{4}.4.—-mag^{a}. VI^{3}.—nit^{b}.VI^{3}.—ol-a^{a}.V^{1}.ω^{9}. (**15**).—-pho^{b}.VIII^{3}.; II^{1}-VI^{3}. 3.19.(**15**).—zin.VI^{4}.*er*.

C.—bad.I^{a}.(98).—-ca-s.VI^{3}.4. —cas.VI^{4}.q.—dir.(12).—inu. VI^{4}-VIII^{4}.— k-bi.III^{1}.—lyc. VIII$^{1.a}$.19.—-mag.VI^{4}.q.— nat.VIII^{4}.12.—phl^{a}.VI$^{3.4}$.— rhs.VI^{4}.—sul.V^{1}.—tab.V$^{1.a}$.

P.—ba-c^{d}.VI^{3}.5.--bel^{c}.V^{6}.*rr*.20. —*c-ph*^{a}.V^{1}.—-ca-s^{d}.5.—-ccs^{j}. VI$^{3.a}$.—*cch*^{d}.I^{a}.4.--for^{d}.; *for*^{d}. V^{6}.—ham^{d}.3.5.—k-ca.VIII^{4}. 18.31.--lah^{f}.V$^{6.v}$.--mag^{c}.VI$^{3.4}$. 19. ; ^{c}.VI^{3}-VIII^{4}.——*na-m*^{d}. VIII^{3}.βe.— nx-v^{d}.VI^{3}-VIII^{3}. —pæo^{d}.V^{10}.--pho.II^{1}-VI^{3}.19. (**15**).—-pi-m.V^{1}.—-*ton*^{a}.V^{12}-VIII^{4}.6.—— zin^{c}.VI$^{3.4}$. ; ^{d}. V$^{1.3.6}$.

O.—-aga.V$^{1.a}$.—alm.VI^{3}.5.— cth^{c}.VI^{3}.—cb-v.V^{1}. ; V^{1}.p.ι^{8}. —dio.V^{7}.—-gel.V^{7}.3.—-mil. V$^{6.b}$.— na-m.V^{1}.q.ω^{2}.—-ol-a^{c}. V^{1}.26.(29).—pi-m.V^{1}.

B. —-cth^{pb}.VI^{3}.θ^{4}*l*.86.—-ind^{pb}. VIII^{1}.εC*l*. 19.——rn-b^{f}.V$^{1.6}$. H^{f}b.5.—spg.V^{3}.3.16.(8-31).

68. *By cold drinks.*
T.—con.V^{6}.θ^{1}.

69. *By acids.*
GEN.—mo-a.κ^{5}.—sel.—*ton*.θ^{1}.

70. *By wine.*
GEN.—sel.—so-t.—zin.δ.
F.—rho^{b}.V^{1}.
T.—rho.V^{1}.
B.—rho^{f}.III^{2}-V$^{1.6}$-VI^{4}.

70. *By drinking beer.*
GEN.—c-cs.V^{1}.a^{1}b^{s}.65.
O.—cep^{k}.βe.**5**.(5).

70. *By drinking coffee.*
GEN.—aru.V^{10}.—-*cn-i*.—*glo*. VIII^{4}.; glo.—*hyo*.
F.—nit^{q}.V^{1}-VI$^{4.z}$.31.(8-128).
O.—for^{g}.

70. *By drinking tea.*
GEN.—ca-x.—sel.

70. *By drinking milk.*
P.—bro^{d}.VIII^{4}.(17).

71. *By retching.*
GEN.—*mac*.5.
F.—asr.V$^{1.6}$.

72. *By vomiting.*
GEN.—ba-m.—ars.—eug.II^{1}.δ. δe.2.5.—k-bi.κ^{5}.—lab.V^{1}.2.
F.—phy.—rap^{e}.I^{e}.δo.

74. *When at stool.*
GEN.—con.—ham.i^a.—idm.—pho.VIII^1.
F.—cca^b.VII^1.89.—col.VII^5.—rat^c.V$^{10\cdot s}$.
P.—spi^c.V^1.δr.3-30.28.31.

75. *After stool.*
GEN.—*aga.*V^7.χ^2.—alo.λ.; *alo.*
F.—fag.d.κ^5.

75. *By discharge of flatus.*
GEN.—cic.

77. *While urinating.*
T.—col^b.V$^{1\cdot a}$.18.31.(19).

78. *After urinating.*
GEN.—gel.i^a.q.

81. *By pollutions.*
GEN.—lah.ω^2.
F.—pi-m.

82. *Before menses.*
GEN.—alm.d.ηp.ρ^1.φ^2.; ξ^3.83.—ca-c.—cb-a.ξ^3.—fer.VI^3.εʋ.—hep.III^1.—nat.σ^2.
F.—sil^e.V^1–VII^5.
T.—lah.VIII^1.; VIII^4.λ.

83. *During menses.*
GEN.—alm.ξ^3.82.—ber.VI$^{3\cdot4}$.ξ^3.ω^2.—bor.VIII^{1}εʋ.—bro.—cb-v.δ.—*cyc.*VI^3.ω^2.—epn.VIII^3.—gn-c.VII^1.i.ξ^3.φ^1.35.(20).—grp.κ$^{5\cdot7}$.; 5.—hyo.χ^3.ω^2.—k-ca.; q.3.—kre.V$^{10\cdot s}$.εʋ$^{n\cdot p}$.29.—lyc.V^7.—mag.ξ^3.5.; p.q.—nat.VI^4–VIII^4.—na-m.VII^1.ξ^3.29.89.90.—ni-x.λ.ξ^3.—nx-m.d.—nx-v.χ$^{1\cdot2}$.θ.ω^3.—rho.χ.—ver.VI^4.κ^5.3.(5).; *ver.*
F.—am-m.VI^4.η.19.—bro.δ.29.—cas.V^1.σ^1.ω^2.; VI^4.—fag^b.I^a.d.35.—lyc.VII^1.—mag.V^6.q.1.—nat^a.VI$^{4\cdot a}$.(12).—pho.VI^3.δb.—san^a.δ.ξ^3.—sep.V^1.ζh^a.—sul.V^1.4.
T.—am-m^a.VI^4.η.19.—cas^b.VIII^3.θ^1.—lyc.V^{12}.—nat^a.VI$^{4\cdot a}$.(12).
C.—ca-c.V^1.—cb-a.V^1.q.(8).—cas.V^1.σ^1.v.—lau.VI^{4}ξ^3.2.(3).—mag.VI^4.σ^3.(2).—ol-a^b.VI$^{3\cdot a}$.$_r{}^1v^1$nn.φ^1.2.—rat.II^1–VI^4.2.(8).
P.—am-m^c.VI^4.η.19.—ber^c.III^1–

V^1·VII^1.ω^8.—mag.VI^4.σ^2.(2).—mg-m^c.VI$^{3\cdot a}$.alg.—nat^d.VI^4–VIII^4.—san^c.V$^{10\cdot s}$.δ.ξ^3.
O.—cb-a.V^1.q.(8)—mag.V^6.q.1.—mg-m.VIII^4.q.3-30.—nit^c.VI$^{3\cdot a}$.—nx-v.VIII^4.16.(18).

84. *After menses.*
GEN.—c-ph.VIII^4.κ^1.ξ^4.σ.v.—fer.—lyc.VI^3.—mrl.λ.ξ^3.
C.—fer.VIII^4.ι.κ^4.—ol-a.VI^3.2.(3-30).
P.—ol-a^d.VI^3.λ.ξ^3.σ.2.(30).

86. *By speaking.*
GEN.—aco.; 35.64.—aur.V^2.ab.3.41.43.44.—chi.II^5.11.41.—con.51.—eup.II^5.6.8.—*ham.*3-30.6.(31.41.43).—ign.VII^1.(43.44).—sul.VIII^{12}.
F.—con.IV^2.q.51.—iod.51.—man^o.VI^4.—na-m^e.VIII^1.41.—sar.VI$^{4\cdot q}$.31.—*sil^c.*V^1–VIII^3.(28.29).—spi^a.V^3–VI^4.35.51.(16).—sul.VI$^{3\cdot s}$.5.89.; VI$^{3\cdot s}$.31.89.
T.—aga$^{a\cdot b}$.VI^3.—mez.35.
C.—mez.35.—ptv.V$^{7\cdot q}$.11.19.(31.35).—spi^b.V^3–VI^4.35.51.56.(16).
P.—fl-x^d.V$^{1\cdot10\cdot t}$.ηp.θ^1.5.—ign^b.V^1.8-31.41.—nx-j^d.IX.5.—sar^b.IV^1.a^{1}b^o.δσ^a.t^m.
O.—spi.V^3–VI^4.35.51.56.(16).
B.—cth^{pb}.VI^3.θ^{4}l.66.

86. *By loud speaking.*
GEN.—spi.VII^5.89.

87. *By singing.*
T.—alm.VI^3.

88. *By laughing.*
GEN.—pho.VIII^4.31.
F.—irs.III^1.
T.—man.VI^2.v.θ^4.
P.—ton^c.VI$^{3\cdot q}$.
O.—zin^b.VI^4.

89. *By coughing.*
GEN.—aps.—arn.VI^3.; VI$^{3\cdot s}$.26.(16).;VI^2–VIII^3.29.—bel.VII^1.—chd.8.29.53.—er-m.IV^3.—hdr.VII^1.29.33.—irs.—lyc.VIII^4.—mg-s.VIII^1.—na-m.90.(12).; VII^1.ξ^3.29.83.

90.—ol-m.VII^1.—ph-x.VII^1.
βc^a.eᴅ.—sep.VII^1.—spi.VII^5.
86.—sul.I^q.90.
F.—*ag-m*.V^1.κ^5.3-99.(8).—arn.
VI^3.——chd.V$^{10\text{-}a}$.1.8.29.53.
(63).——cca^b.VII^1.74.—hep.
VI^2-IX.2.29.—hyo^f.VI^3.—
rut.V^1-VI^3.—sul.VI$^{3\text{-}a}$.5.86.;
VI$^{3\text{-}a}$.31.86.—tar.V^7-VI^3.
T.—alm^a.VI$^{3\cdot4}$.—asi.VI^3.δ.3-99.
—cca^a.VI$^{3\cdot v}$.3-30.—trn.—
tar.VI^3.
C.—alm.VI$^{3\cdot4}$.—sul.53.60.
P.——aur^b.V^3-VIII^4.3-99.22.—
cim^c.VI^3.θ^4.r.—dir^d.VIII^4.11.
35.
O.—alm.V^1.

90. *By sneezing.*
Gᴇɴ.—ba-c.VIII^1.βa.—cnc.—
lil.IX.5.— *mu-x*.V$^{10\text{-}u}$.δ.16.—
na-m.89.(12).; VII^1.ξ^3.29.83.
89.—sul.I^a.89.
F.—arn^b.V^2.—na-m.
T.—am-m^b.II^1-VI^3.60.
O.—*ca-c*.V^6.26.—grt^c.V^2.

91. *By holding breath.*
O.—aga.V^6.3-10.23.

92. *During inspiration.*
T.—ana^a.VI^3.

94. *By breathing deep.*
Gᴇɴ.—rat.VI^3.35.

96. *By yawning.*
Gᴇɴ.— *mgt*.IX.3-30.—*stp*.VI^4.
3-99.
F.—*chd*.—phy.V^1.
T.—ba-c^a.VI^3.3.

97. *Before going to sleep.*
Gᴇɴ.—aga.V$^{1\cdot d}$.
P.—nx-m^d.V^7.

98. *During sleep.*
Gᴇɴ.——cha.—cch.V^1.6.——*glo*.
V^7.—*ham*.—hyo.VIII^1.σ^3.2.
—led.V^7.—mag.2-99.(24).—
pho.V^2.5.
F.——aco^d.III^1-V^1.a$^1\varsigma^a$.ηc^b.ii.51.
111.(114).—ars.—*glo*^{a}.V^7.
T.—cam.V^3.3.(99).—dig^b.VI^3.
2.5.—pet^a.V$^{1\cdot6}$.
C.—*bad*.I^a.66.—grp.V^7.3.(99).
O.—*thu*.V$^{1\cdot2}$-VI^4.99.
B.—agn^c.II$^{5\cdot sx}$.5.

99. *On awaking* (comp.8-99).
Gᴇɴ.—ag-n.V^1.χ^1.—cad.—cl-h.
—cle.V^{12}.——mag.2.98.(24).
—nar.a^{1}ᴅ.—na-a.I^a.
F.—gel.V^7.5.——*grp*.V^7.3-10.—
k-bi.V^1.
T.—*cam*.V^3.3.98.
C.—*grp*.V^7.3.98.
O.—rs-r.—sul^c.IX.—thu.V$^{1\cdot2}$-
VI^4.(98).

100. *After a siesta.*
Gᴇɴ.--bov.VIII^4.au.a^{1}b^a.ζo.16.-
cld.—ign.V^1.d.43.44.—mt-n.
V^2.βe.(18.30^c.)——mr-i.19.—
nx-m.III^a.—sep.VIII^1.
F.——bov^h.VIII^4.q.au.a^{1}b^a.ζo.16.
—ca-s.—*nit*^{a}.V^1.5.—rhs.VII^1.
p.q.θ.κ^3.6.(10.16).
T.—cb-v.VIII^4.i^a.
P.—cld.V^1.17.(19).——sul^b.II^3-
VI^4.46.
O.—cof.V^2.i^a.

101. *By heat.*
Gᴇɴ.—alo.(102).——am-c.V^1.—
ba-c.VI^3.——*cch*.(16).—com.
29.—dig.—sep.χ^1.—*sum*.
F.—arn.V^1.—*cch*^{d}.V^1.(20).
T.—grt.V^3-VI^4.2.4.102.—na-a.
V$^{3\cdot t}$.p.κ^5.4.12.65.
C.—*k-hy*.VII^1.p.χ^1.
O.—*sil*.V^1.
—— *of hand.*
F.—cnb.V^7.b.
B.—*irs*^{m}.VIII^4.4.

102. *By cold.*
Gᴇɴ.— *aco*.V^1-III^1.—*alo*.101.
—cad.—cb-a.V$^{3\cdot6}$-VI^4.—*sng*.
F.——cle^b.I^a.δO.5.(12).——*cch*^{n}.
(12).—*mr-c*.V$^{7\cdot1}$.a$\mathbf{k}$.28.29.—
pho.V^7.κ^1.ω^2.
T.—*ch-s*^{b}.I^a.(16).—grt.V^3-VI^4.
2.4.101.
P.—*eup*^{a}.VI^3.
O.——*cch*^{i}.V^7.(12).——*mr-c*.V$^{7\cdot1}$.
a$\mathbf{k}$.28.29.

102. *By sitting in a cool room.*
F.—gen.I^a.

103. *By damp.*
C.—rs-r^c.5.
P.—phy^c.II^5.
O.—am-i.V^7.

105. *In stormy weather.*
GEN.—am-i.V⁷.41.

105. *By perspiration.*
GEN.——bov.VII¹.3-99.——pso.
V¹⁰·ᵗ.
T.—mg-mᶜ.V¹·³.(34).
C.—grp.VI³–VII¹.3.4.

106. *By wind.*
GEN.—chi.II⁵–V².31.
O.—mu-xⁱ.31.
B.—hamᵐ.VI³.31.

107. *By a draft of air.*
GEN.—bz-x.——·cad.——f-io.7.26.
29.31.43.45.(5.8).
—— *entering mouth.*—nx-v.6¹.
F.—an-a.V¹.——f-ioᵃ.V⁷.q.43.44.
130.(8).—lcp.V⁷.—vrbᵒ.V⁶·⁷.
P.—nitᶜ.Iᵃ.—valᶜ.V⁶.4.

110. *By changes in the weather.*
GEN.—vp-t.VI³·⁴.

110. *By wet weather.*
C.—cb-a.VII¹.2.

111. *By light.*
GEN.——ars.51.——buf.51.——
ca-x.VI³.δb.51.(12).—ziz.κ⁵·⁶.
51.(16).
F.——acoᵈ.III¹–V¹.a¹ɩᵃ.ηcᵇ,ii.51.
(98.114).—cac.q.51.
C.—aga.V¹.βa.
P.—cacᶜ.Iᵃ.51.—zizᵈ.V¹.51.

111. *By daylight.*
GEN.—lo-s.

112. *By exposure to the sun.*
GEN.—alo.—bro.q.(114).--cad.
—gen.5.—mnc.V².
F. —an-s.5.31.—ign.V¹.
C.—ba-c.V¹–VI³.

113. *By twilight.*
F.—cca.V⁷.aɼ.

114. *In the dark.*
GEN.—bro.q.112.—hpm.9-31.
F.——acoᵈ.III¹–V¹.a¹ɩᵃ.ηcᵇ,ii.51.
111.(98).

115. *By candlelight.*
F.—croᵉ.δ.2.

116. *By applying cold water.*
GEN.—alo.——ars.——cyc.—idm.
VIII⁴.au.χ².—zin.
F.——sul.V¹–VI⁴.θ¹.——tar.V¹–
VII⁵.3-99.

T.—au-mᵇ.VIII⁴.3-30.
P.—-bor.VI³.θ¹.11.—sulᶜ.II¹–
VI⁴.θ¹.

117. *By cold bathing or washing.*
GEN.—ant.κ¹.ω².—-fer.V¹.5.——
myr.Iᵃ.3-99.(30).
F.—bry.V¹.χ¹.--cnb.V⁷.3-99.12.
16.(30).——eup.V¹.βɛ.3.31. —
na-s.IV².——pso.V¹⁰·ˢ.8-30.
(66).
T.—ccs.V¹·ᵛ.—cop.VI³.3.
C.—aco.V¹.
O.—for.70.

117. *By washing the hands.*
F.—rs-rᵍ.II¹.5.

117. *By the douche.*
T.—tepᵇ.V¹.

122. *When in society.*
GEN.—mag.V¹.6.

128. *By driving.*
GEN.—grp.—iod.6.31.—mep.
F.—aco.V¹.——glo.——lyc.κ⁴.4. ;
V¹.p.a¹ᴅ.βa.——nitq.V¹–VI⁴·ᶻ.
31.70.
T.—lthᵇ.Iᵇ.—lyc.V¹⁰.4.
C.—lyc.V¹⁰.4.
P.—najᵈ.I¹.

128. *By riding.*
F.—bro.V⁷.20.——-k-cyᵍ.VI³·ᵛ.5.
31.
—— *in cold wind.*—ar-i.VI³.e.
C.—phy.

130. *By uncovering head.*
GEN.—ctn.130.—sul.V¹.13.
T.—zng.V¹·⁶.8-31.130.(6.18).
P.—nitᵈ.2.
O.—lo-i.V¹.

130. *By undressing.*
GEN.—bz-x.
F.—cor.V¹⁰·ᵃ·ˢ.aq.χ².

130. *By covering head.*
GEN.——ctn.(130).——k-cy.——
mg-m.
F.—f-ioᵃ.V⁷.q.43.44.(8.107).—
ledᵈ.V¹.βɛ.
T.—zng.V¹·⁶.8.31.(6.11.130).

130. *By tying up hair.*
O.—nit.

SECTION IV.—COURSE, PROGRESS, DIRECTION, QUALITY, ETC., OF PAINS IN HEAD.

From F. all over head.—val.V^1.

Recurring 8 or 10 times in an hour, lasting half a minute.—sep.V^1.

First F^a. then F^b.—cch.V^1.—glo.—ign.V^1.—jat.$VI^{3 \cdot b}$.—ol-a.V^1.(15).—su-x.$VI^{3 \cdot q}$.—val.V^1.

First F^a. then F^b., afterwards T^b.—cyc.$V^{1 \cdot 6}$.(11).

First F^b. then F^a.—glo.

First F^a. and r. eye, then T^b.—lah.V^1.$\eta r.vl.5$.

First F^f. then F^g.—bap.VI^3.

First F^g. then F^e.—glo.V^2.

First F^g. then F^f.—hæm.III^2–V^1.—oni.V^1.

F^g. morning, F^f. afternoon.—bry.V^6.

F^n. and F^o. alternately.—bis.$V^{3 \cdot s}$.—lcp.

From F. to T.—ca-s.5.

First F. then T.—zin.V^1.

First F^g. then T.—sbd.V^1.

First F^n. and P^c. then F^o. and P^d. alternately.—bry.V^6–VII^5.4.

First F^f. then about l. ear.—ni-x.V^6.

First F^o. VI^3–$VIII^{4 \cdot a}$. then F^n. g^b.—coc.

First F^o. then F^n.—cin.VI^4.βe^a.—lau.VI^3.4.

From F. to T. and O^i.—lil.$V^{1 \cdot 7}$.q.

From F. to T^a. and O^c.—aco.VI^3.

From F^b. to T. and O.—mez.V^3–VI^4.

From F. to C.—val.V^1.

From F. to C., whirling in F.—sbd.

First in F. then extended to P., and on lying down in bed went round both P. to O. and medulla.—pi-m.

From F. to O.—bel.VI^3.—bis.VI^1.—bry.VI^3.—lcp.4.—mer.i^a.βa.

Alternately F. and O.—msc.

From F^a. to O^b.—bel.VI^1.—ch-s.IX.5.19.—cnb.

From F^b. to O^c.——ept.—lcp.σ^2.—nx-v.VI^3–VIII^3.66.

First from F. to O., afterwards in B^{pb}.—bel.VI^1.

From F^b. to O^c., concentrating in T^b.—lil.V^7.

From F^b., on talking goes to O.—mel.35.41.(16).

Pressure behind and above F^b., then higher up in F^a., followed by aching in O^b. at night in bed, going r. and l. deep in brain in morning.—xip.(53^a).

From F^a. to B^{mb}., then to T^b., then to T^a.—hy-x.V^1.

From F^g. to O^i.—mac.VI^3.

From T^a. extending into head.—pso.V^1.5.

From T. to F.——bry.$VI^{3 \cdot 1}$.——lyc.$VI^{3 \cdot b}$.5.—naj.V^7.—so-n.$V^{10 \cdot q}$.

From T^a. to F^o.—lcp.

First T^b. then F^c.—k-ca.$VI^{3 \cdot s}$.

First T^b. then F., followed by F.V^1.—cyc.VI^3.βa.

From T., over F., to nose.——col.$V^{10 \cdot a}$.

From T., meets in F^c., and passes down to nose.—c-ar.

From T^a. then T^b.—aps.V^7.8-99.—dig.VI^3.—dul.V^{16}.—hdr.I.—hyp.VI^3.5.—jac.i^a.——tax.I.q.δe.89.—zin.III^3–VI^4.

First stitch in T^a., then stitch followed by pressure in T^b.—aga.86.

First T^a., then T^b., then C., where there is burning.—ptv.VI^3.

From T^b. extending into T^a.—au-m.VI^4.1.

First T^b. then T^a.—cyc.VI^3–VIII^3.—iod.VI^4.

First T^b.$VI^{4 \cdot v}$. then T^a.VI^3.—alm.

First T^b., then T^a., then lower jaw. —aga.

From T^b. to F.—lyc.V^6.

First T^b. afterwards P^f.—mag.VI^3.

T^6.II^1.p. changing into $V^{10 \cdot t}$., followed by P^c.p.ϵp., then ηp. and F^o.V^1.—na-n.

First T^b. then T^a. and C.—rhe.III^3-VIII^4.

First T^b. then spreading over C. to P^d., as if upper part of skull were pulled up.—cun.I^a.

T^b.V^1. followed by P^d.$\beta\epsilon$.—cyc.p.

From T^a., over C. to O^c.—irs.V^7.

From T. to O.—str.VI^3.κ^3.

From T^b. to O.—pho.3.

From C. over whole head.—bov. VI^3.

From C. to F.—mr-f.—mez.VI^3.ηp.

From C. to T^b.—lyc.V^{10}.4.128.

Formicating digging in C., forenoon, headache afternoon.—an-s.

First C^a. then C^b.—cch.V^3-$VI^{4 \cdot h}$.g^a. —lth.

From C^a., then C^b., then back to C^a. —bel.V^{10}.

From P. downwards and inwards. —cep.I.

From P^a. all over head.—asa.I.

First P^c., later in whole head.— aga.$VI^{3 \cdot a}$.

First P^c. then F^a.—nx-m.V^{10}.

In P^c. forenoon, in F^o. evening.— alm.$VI^{3 \cdot 4}$.

Pain transversely through head between ears.—cch.4.

First P^c. then P^d.—ana.$\beta\epsilon$.—cup.V^1. —inu.I.—klm.I.q.—mr-i.I.(66).; I.d.—pho.$V^{1 \cdot 6}$.$\beta\epsilon$.

First P^d. then P^c.—evo.VI^3.

First P^c., then F., then P^d.—sbd.I. q.35.

First P^d. then C.—mez.VI^4.ϵ.

In P^c. when walking, afternoon, in T^b. when sitting, evening, then in T^a.—ag-n.V^3.35.

First P^d.V^7.; then T^a.III^1-V^6., then ear and throat.—cro.I.

From P. to B^m.—gel.I^d.

First O^b. then O^c.—hdr.V^1.

From O^b. to O^c.—dig.V^1.βa,ϵ.—stp. II^L-VI^3.

From O^b., then O^c., then F.—k-ca. VI^4.

From O^c. to O^b.—squ.$V^{6 \cdot b}$.

First O. then F.—glo.VIII^4.

From O. to F.—gel.V^7.—ol-m.I.κ^5.

From O^h. to P^a.—aur.V^1-VI^4.— ba-n.V^1.—chi.VI^4.—mez.V^7.— thu.$VI^{3 \cdot 4}$.

From O^c. to F^b.—ba-c.VI^3.—cyc.V^6. —sab.VI^4.

First in O., going to F. on lying down.—la-x.

From O. to F^o.—ag-n.V^3-VI^1.

First dull pain in O., becoming worse and burning when lying, when it goes into F., on rising a shoot in F., and the pain goes gradually into O. again.—aga.$\beta\epsilon$.

Something rises from O. and F. to C.—glo.

From O^c. through T^b. to F.—cyc. V^6.

From O. to T.—lcp.

First O^i. then F^e.—mr-i.V^7.

In O^c. in morning, C^a. in evening. —alo.I.15.

From O^f. to C.—am-c.$VI^{4 \cdot v}$-VII^1.

From O^b. to O^c., extending to C.— dig.V^1.βa,ϵ.

First in O. then in C.—glo.I.

From O. to C.—glo.V^1.—lyc.VIII^3. 5.

From O. to C. and F.—mac.V^7.(12).

From O^h., through P^d., to F.—jab. V^7.π.ρ.ω^2.

Awoke with pain O^h., aggravated by raising up or moving head, towards noon the pain increased and spread over C. to F., where there was congestive headache with throbbing of carotids till evening.—dir.

Pain from O. over P^c., leaving a bruised feeling at C.—idm.3.

Pain from O^d. diagonally upward and forward.—ce-b.ϵ.

From middle of brain backwards in straight lines to O^i.—la-x.VI^3. 35.

First B^{pa}. then B^{fb}.—ac-x.V^7.

First B^{pa}. then B^{pb}.—evo.$VI^{3 \cdot a}$.

B^{pb}. VI^3, at same time B^{pa}. VIII^1, followed by VI^3.—mil.

B^{pb}. extending to T^a.—bel.

B^{ma}. then B^{mb}.—lo-s.4.

From head into eye.—bad.I.—lah. VI^3.—pul.I.5.

From head to teeth.—stp.V^6–VI^4.

From F^f. to eye.—aps.$VI^{3 \cdot a}$.

From F. or T. to eyes, or from eyes to F.—ber.VI^3.

From F. to l. eye.—bad.

From F. to l. eye and l. side of face.—ag-n.VI^4.δa^b,aa,ϱ.

From F. to ear.—man.V^6–VI^3.5-31. (20).

Drawing and aching in F^e., alternating with drawing in a carious tooth.—bry.

Sudden throbbing pain in F. and C., then pain in chest and round heart.—jab.

From F^p. to back of neck.—fag.V^1. 4.

From F. to thigh.—opi.$VI^{3 \cdot 4 \cdot a}$.

From T. to l. eye.—bad.

From T. to zygoma.—bry.V^6–VI^4.

Acute darting pain from T^b. to malar bone, with sensation as if brain were compressed, followed by irritation of scalp over line of pain.—lcp.

From T. to jaw.—bry.V^6.

From T. to jaws and teeth.—rhs. VI^3–VIII^1.

From T. to upper jaw and teeth.— ag-n.V^6–VI^4.

From T. to lower jaw.—ox-x.

First in T^a., then in T^b., then going to l. side of nape and disappearing.—jac.5.8.

From T^a. to O. and nape.—fel.I^a.3. 12 (on T^a).—mr-f.I^a.

From C^a. to nose.—mr-i.VIII^4.q.4.

From C. to upper jaw.—mrl.V^1.

From C. to l. shoulder.—lyc.VI^4 4.

From P^d. to malar bone.—lcp.VI^3. [Sv].

From O^i. to l. eye.—mu-x.VIII^3. $\delta L^1 ll^b$.

From O^e. to lower jaw.—arg.V^6.

From O^e. to neck.—crt.V^6.

From O^f. to nape and frontal muscles.—bel.V^{10}.

From O^d. down to neck and shoulders.—ars.V^6–VI^4.

From O. to l. shoulder.—mil.5.

From Ba. to jaw.—osm.V^7.2.

From B^{mb}. obliquely across through O. to r. ear.—la-x.I.

From B^{ma}. to teeth.—mez.V^6.

First sudden, violent drawing upwards in B^{pa}., then pressing in F^b. and r. wrist.—ag-n.5.19.

From r. eye into brain.—cb-v.V^6. —ch-x.I.—lah.V^e–VI^3.

From eye to supraorbital region and brain.—aco.I.

As if a thread from eye to centre of brain were stretched.—par. V^7.δLp,aa.

From eye to F.—aga.$V^{6 \cdot 10}$.—ber. $VI^{3 \cdot a}$.

From l. eye to F.—ccs.VI^4.2-16.

From deep in eye through middle of supraorbital border upwards and outwards to F., first in r. eye then in l.—ber.V^3–VI^3.

From l. eye over T. to ear.—ba-c.I^a.

From eyes to T.—bad.I.48.

From eyes to-C. as if nerves were excited.—cmf.

From eyes to C.—lah.VI^3.

From l. eye to C., going and returning.—phy.VI^3.

From l. eye and T^b. to P^d. and F.— bad.I^a.

From l. eye to P^d. and O.—cch.V^6– VI^4.

From r. eye along squamous portion of temporal bone to O., as if a fluid were injected by jerks into a bloodvessel.—ccs.$VIII^{4 \cdot a}$.

From r. eye to O.—tab.V^1.

Pressure in eyes, tearing down from F. or ear to O.—amb.

From r. inner canthus to F.—san.I.

From inner canthus to P^c.—cn-i. VI^3.

From ear upwards and outwards through brain.—chi.VI^3.

From l. ear to T^b.—bro.I.29.—chd. I.

From ear to T. and C.—la-x.I.

From ear to T. and B^p.—ind.I.19.

From r. ear to C.—gam.V^6.5.

From r. ear to B^{pa}.—rn-b.I.

From meatus auditorius to O.—ast. VI^3.

From nose to F.—sil.VIII^4.

From nose to F^e.—cap.III^1–VIII^3.

From nose through back of eyes to F.—fag.I^a.

From nose to F^i. and T.—cor.VII^1. ζp,ii.

From l. side of nose to P^d.—cb-v. VI^4.

From nose and r. eye to O.—cic.VI^3.

From face to ear and head.—cch. VI^4.—col.VI^4–VII^5.

From l. side of face to T.—mil.VI^4. 5.

From l. cheek over l. ear to O.— sep.VI^4.

From malar bone to T.—am-g.V^6. —ber.$VI^{3.4}$.—k-cl.V^{10}–VII^5.

From r. malar bone to T^a.—bry. VI^4–VIII^3.11.

From l. malar bone to C.—glo.I.

From mouth up through head and down to nape.—hfb.I.

From palate to brain.—mer.$V^{2.6}$. 3-10.—stp.VI^3.

From gums to head.—aps.I.

From teeth to head.—ant.VIII^3.2. 11.—grt.—mer.$VIII^{3.4}$.5.(16).— ni-x.V^6.—nx-v.107.—ph-x.VI^4.

From teeth to eye and head.—cau.

From teeth through head to nape. —ton.VI^3.

From teeth to F.—sep.I^3.(5-10).; $V^{1.11}$.

From teeth to F^f.—k-hy.VI^4.

From teeth to T.—alm.—ars.$VIII^{3.e}$. 10.(30).—ca-c.V^6.68.—kre.V^6.— lyc.VI^4.—mag.2.—mez.VI^3.4.

From teeth to T. and C.—cle.

From teeth to ear and T.—ba-c.— cau.

From teeth to zygoma and T.—alm.

From teeth to face and T.—kre. 3-99.

From teeth to P.—bor.VI^8.11.116. —na-m.VI^3.—thu.

From teeth to ear and P.—alm.

From a hollow tooth to P^d.—bor. VI^4.

From parotid region to T.—bry.2. —ind.V^3–VI^4.(15).

From r. lower jaw up over T.— man.VI^2.v.88.

From upper jaw to C.—spi.V^6–VI^3.

From l. lower jaw into head.— mg-s.VI^4.

From lower jaw to P^c.—vi-t.V^6– VI^4.

From jaws to T.—hfb.I.

As if the flesh were torn from the bones from lower jaw over zigoma to T.—na-m.4.

From r. maxillary joint to C.—mil. $VI^{4.a}$.

From l. maxillary joint to T.—sil. IV^1.

From stomach to head.—cb-v.a^1v. —nx-m.—rhe.VIII^2.

Weight and drawing as from stomach, with sensitiveness of brain to noise and speaking.— con.

Something rising from r. hypochonder through chest to head, and then throbbing.—glo.

Like a ball rising from umbilicus and spreading a cool air in C. and O.—aco.

As if something ran from anus to head during the fever.—lab.

From back to head.—sep.VI^3.31.

From back to C.—lyc.$VIII^{1.a}$.19.66.

From scapula through O. to F.— c-cs.VI^4.

From nape to head.—ca-c.V^6–VI^3. ev.—fl-x.V^7.—ve-v.

From nape to F.—amb.$V^{1.6}$.—cth. V^{10}.28.29.—cau.ff.—dph.—mez.

From nape and O. to F. and T.— chd.VIII^4.

From nape through O. into F. and r. side of face.—elc.VI^4.

From l. nape to over C., obliquely, and terminating in a shock.— gin.V^1.

From nape to C.—hel.—sil.

From muscles of neck to P^c.—kre. V^1.

From nape to C.—rat.VI^4–VIII^3. 31.

From nape to O.—dul.V^7.—glo.— k-ca.VI^3.—klm.VIII^1.p.—mez.— val.V$^{1.6}$.22.

From nape to behind l. ear.—aps. V$^{6.a}$.

From nape and O. to F. and T.— chd.VIII$^{4.a}$.

Throbbing in O^c., which on walking goes into C., where it pains as if bruised.—cau.

From nape across O. to ears.—cch.

From nape to O., F., and r. side of face.—elc.VI^4.

From nape to behind l. ear and P^d. —aps.V$^{6.a}$.

From nape to behind r. ear and B^{pb}.—ba-a.V^7.4.

As if something ran from l. shoulder to head.—lah.

A sharp pain like electric shock from l. thigh to C.—dio.16.66.

From limbs to head.—cb-v.VI^4.

a. **Violent.**

GEN.—I.ars.—cu-a.—dgn.— k-hy.—led.—mr-c.—mr-f.— mr-i.κ^5.4.—mor.—str.$au^b.a^1$b. =V^1.ars.

F.—I.bap.—cth.—ca-x.i^a.— cnb.—crt.—cu-a.—cyc.— dig.—dio.—eth.--glo.—k-hy. —mer.—mr-i.κ^5.5.—mo-a.— trn.p.=V^1.gas.—nit.d.—sul. --vrb.=V^3.ign$^{a.n}$.=VI^3.cam. —k-bi$^{g.h}$.—zng.=VI^4.zin.— VIII^4.lau.—so-n.

T.—I.cyc.—dor.=V^3.au-n.= V^6.cau. = V^{10}.ign. = VIII^4. sep.

C.—V^1.spi.—tab.=VI^3.cb-v.— ipc.—k-bi.11.—ol-a.=VIII^1. lyc.19.66.

P.—I.mr-f^c.=V^1.aco.(116).

O.—I.mur.—opi.—pl-c.=II^1. mo-a.$\kappa^4.\lambda$v.rv.v. = III.sto.= V^1.fl-x^c. = V^3.sto^b.2. = VI^3.

ari.--cau.=VIII^3.spi.8-31.= VIII^4.aga.

B.—V^3.mez. &c.

b. **Transient.**

GEN.—I.arn.—elc.— k-bi.= V^1.mez.=VI^3.asa $\beta\ell.\rho$.--ca-c. —sto.=VI^4.amb.—sel.

F.—V^3.lyc^h.--nup^b.5.=V^6.chd. =VI^3.asa.—dgn.—jat^{a1}.— lyc.; ^{o}.=VI^4.—rat.—sng^b.

T.—VI^3.trn.=VI^4.zin.=VIII^3. bel^b.—val^a.

C.—II^1.nat.=VI^3.ind.—mil.

P.—VI^3.lyc^h.

O.—I.iod.=V^1.squ.=V^6.squ.= V^7.alm. &c.

d. **Paroxysmal.**

GEN.—VI^3.rs-r.=VIII^4.f-mg.

F.—III.pla.=VI$^{3.a}$.lyc.

T.—I.sul.=VI^3.irs.

P.—I.sep^b.

B.—V^3.mez^c.

e. **Intermittent.**

GEN.—I.pso.—trf.=VI^4.rhe.q. =VIII^4.ver.

F.—I.glo.=III^1.hyo^d.af.$\beta\ell^a$.= V^1.cb-v.—-chd.q.—rut.=V^3. arg^b.5.16. = V^7.arn^g. = VI^2. ca-a^b.20.35.—-vrb^a.=VIII^4. cn-s^a.

C.—VIII^4.plg.

O.—V^1.phl.=cth^b.v.(15).=V^3- VIII^5.ccs^d.

B.—III^1-VI$^{3.4}$.spi^{pb}. &c.

g. **Here and there.**

GEN.—I.aln.—am-c.—chi.— coh.—cch.—hur.--phy.—plg. =III^2.cch.=V^1.bel.—clf.— grp.—hy-x.q.—pho.—thu.= V^3.mez.=V^6.amb.—ipc.— mt-n.33.—msc.σ^2.6.(8).— nx-v.—ton.=VI^3.am-c.(31). —bap.x.--ca-c.—hy-x.—mag. —mg-s.—nic.5.29.—plm.— plb.er.45.—rat.5.--su-x.8-31. =VI^4.ant.—ber.—rhs.5.29. = VII^2.trx. = VIII^1.zin. = VIII^3.chd.—sto.=VIII^4.aco. —æth.6.—ind.5.19.

F.—VI^3.sep.=VI^4.plb.

C.—V^1.pho.=VIII^3.k-hy.

P.—VI¹.na-m^d.4.

O.—V¹.mt-s.

h. In a small spot.

F.T.—pso.V¹⁰.βʊ.ℓ^a.

C.—I.so-n.=V$^{7.10}$.pso.

P.—I.k-bi^b.

l. Sudden.

GEN.—I.lip.σ². —mez.βa.δb.κ⁴. —mor.

F.—I.lyc.κ⁵.ω². —V¹.sab°.=V⁷. mr-c.28.29.=V¹⁰.sab°.=VI³. mr-f^a. =VIII⁴.jab.π.ρ. =V¹– VIII³.stn^b.

T.—V¹–VIII³.stn^b.

C.——V¹.stn.=V⁷.mr-c.28.29. (102).=VIII⁴.jab.π.ρ.

p. Superficial.

F.—— V².ph-x.5.41.=V⁷.arn.= VI⁴.bov^c.

q. Deep-seated.

GEN.—I.bov.—glo.—lah.=II⁵. msc.—phy.=V¹.cau.q.—ind. –nx-v.47.=VI$^{4.b}$.sel.=VII⁵. nit.66. = VIII³.rat.=VIII⁴. ca-c.3.

F.——I.cnt.=V¹.grp.=V³.dul ii^d.βℓ.3-30.—na-m^g.=V⁶.b-la. =V⁷.cmf.—equ.[S.VI³.15]. -lpt.=VI³-su-x^a.=VI⁴.osm^a. v.5.=VIII¹.——cro°.βℓ.(12). squ°.

T.—VI⁴.tep.=VIII³.ba-a^b.δOl. el.

C.——V³.aga.=V⁶.ol-a.5.=V⁷. crn.——mr-s.3.34.(4).=V¹⁰. con.=VI³.cap.-ind.-rat.-stp. SI.11.—tab.—ton.=VI⁴.ind.

O.——V¹.kis.=V⁷.rho.=VIII⁴. crn. &c.

r. Wandering.

GEN.—I.ani.

F.—I.au-m.

B.—VI⁴.hel.

s. From within outwards.

GEN.——V³.dul.2.——pul.VI³.= V¹⁰.aco.——ar-i.q.3-99.29.35. 41.—ast.i^a.—bry.q.—ca-a.18. —cam.—erd.5.—fag.3.—fl-x. —lil.i^a.——kre.ℓʊ$^{u.P}$.29.83.—— mns.—men.33.——mer.—par. βʊ.21.43.49.—pso.III.—sab.

—sam.—sep.—trx.=VI³.rhs. =VII¹.fag.4.=VIII⁴.glo.— lep.

F.—V³.ant.—bis^m.—dro.29.44. —dul.q.=V⁶.pot^h.=V¹⁰.aco. ; i^a.q.—alo.——alm.66.—ana^a. ; ^{n}.—ang^e.20.35.—ag-n^a.—asa.; ^{a}.—ba-a.δ.24.(29).——ba-c. bel^b.; °.; (22).—ber.—bro$^{e.h}$. ——bry^e.δ.; 31.66.; δl.29.— ca-a^g.q.18.29.—ca-c.βa.(8.12). —cn-i^e.4.—cas^a.—chd.1.8.29. 53.89.(63)⟶chi.q.(12).—cic°. —cin^a.3-99.—col.—con^e.— cor.aq.χ².(130).——cup.βℓ.29. —dro.η.—dul°.5.—epn.; ^{a}.— gn-l.βℓ.——grp.66.—hel^a.— hfb.—ipc^b.26.—k-ca.44.—lil. —mg-m.—men.; q.33.; V⁷. —mer.—mu-x.; ^{b}.—na-m. nx-m.ii^d.βa.—oln^d.; °.(12). —opi.(12).—ph-x^n.— pru. ; ^{a}.; ^{b}.; ^{n}.; ^{a}l$^{b a}$.—pso.3-30.(66. 117).; 5.-ptl.1.; q.2.29.—rn-b. —rat^c.74.—rho^a.—snc.4.—spi. ; βℓ.; ^{n}.; ^{b}.; 29.—spo^n.; ^{b}.19. (30).—stn. ; φ.(12).—sul.— trx.—vrb^h.; (29).—vi-t.= VI³.ba-a^n.—bel^m.—bry.ζ³.29. ——con.3-30.; 4.(16).; 5.— fer.—glo^c.——grn.—ph-x^c.— pul.5.—snc.; δ.—sep^g.δb.3-30. (8).; δ.1.—sul.5.=VI⁴.hep. χ².2.=VIII¹.am-c.—— cle.= VIII⁴.asa^n.—can°.— glo.— lyc^e.——nat^e. = III–V¹⁰.chi. 8-31.=V$^{3.10}$.cob.——ipc^e.(12. 46).——sul.η.=V³-VI².spo^b. 8-31. = V$^{9.10}$.nx-v.3.29.· = V$^{9.10}$–VIII³. sep.p.δ. = V¹⁰– VI¹.cap.=V¹⁰–VI³.bry.29.— stp.35.(20). = V¹⁰–VI⁴.cam^b. = V¹⁰–VII⁵.mrl.29.—spi.= V¹⁰–VIII¹. na-m. 33. = V¹⁰– VIII².kre. 29. = V¹⁰–VIII³. dul.35.=V¹⁰-VIII⁴.rho.(20). VI³–VIII³.lyc.

T.——V³.dul.q.=V¹⁰.aco.i^a.δL.5. —alo.δo^d.ηp.—asa^b.—ath.— bis.—bry.; ^{b}.4.—ca-a^b.—cth^a. θ¹.—cb-v^b.—cs-e.—cau.κ$^{5.6}$.——

dro^a.—-fag.—-fl-x.; r.; ^{b}.—
glo.—ign.; 3-17^a.(17).—ind.;
^{b}.—k-ca^a.—kre^b.5.—la-v.—
lil.ϵ.(12).—lo-i.r.r^1.—mu-x.—
nat^a.--na-m.--nx-m.p.--ph-x^a.
—phy.—pru^a.; ^{a}.12.—rn-s.
--rho^a.--sbd^a.; ^{b}.—snc.--spo^a.
—stn^a.—sto.$\beta\epsilon$.—vi-t.$=$VI^3.
bel^a.— dul.q.—for^a.—gen^{a}5.
31.—rhs^b.i^a.q.ϵᴅ.$=$VI^4.cb-v^a.
$=$V$^{1·10}$–VIII^1.ba-a^b.$=$V$^{1·10}$.
glo^b.κ^5.μ^2.σ^1.5-**10**.(66).--mez^b.
—na-m.ϵ.$=$V^3-VI^3.ca-a^b.(11.
19).$=$V^{10}-VI^1.bel.$=$V^{10}-VI^3.
bel.$=$V^{10}-VI^4.chi.$=$V^{10}-VII^4.
ber^a.q.11.$=$V^{10}–VII^5.hel.d.q.
1.(8).$=$V^{10}–VIII^4.bry.**10**.

C.--V^{10}.c-ph.i^a.29.35.(16).--fag.
—-opi.δOr.—ph-x.—phs.$=$
V^{10}·VI^3.ca-c.29.$=$V^{10}-VIII^4.
sep.26.35.48.$=$VI^1–VIII$^{1·4}$.
ca-a.$=$VI^4–VIII^2.vin.

P.–V^{10}.asa^d.--asr^a.—bel^d.--ca-a^d.
—cin^c.3-99.—fag^d.δl.—kre^d.
—mer.—-pau^c.—-spo^c.16.—
stn^c.--vrb^c.--vi-t^c.$=$VI^3.mag^c.
2.17.——mg-m^d.$=$V^{10}–VI^3.
mt-s^d.$=$V^{10}-VI^3–VIII^3.ca-a^c.

O.—V^{10}.bov^k.4.5.——bry.σ^2.—-
ca-a^b.—cb-v.29.--chi.—erd.5.
—fag.4.—mt-n^h.24.—mez^c.5.
—ph-x^b.—pru.; ^{c}.—stn^c.; 5.
--stp.d.5.16.--til^d.$=$III^1-V^{10}.
pso.

B.—V^{10}.k-bi^m.--mer^f.11.$=$VI^3.
cyc.

—— *outwards and inwards.*
T.—VI^3.stp^a.11.

t. From without inwards.
GEN.—V^{10}.ana.—-asr.—-hel.8-
31.—mt-n.—spi.8-31.$=$VI^3.
cnb.$=$V^{10}–VIII^3.spi.8-31.

F.—V^7.chd^f.$=$V^{10}.aga.δ.–alo^c.-
alm.--bap.—bel.δb.; 14.--bro.
p.VIII^4.θ^4.—fer^m.3-30.33.(8.
12).—lau.—pla^b.—rn-s.κ^3.χ^1.
5.—spi^o.——stn.$=$VI^1.fag^b.5.
$=$VI^3.cth^a.——gel^c.4.$=$V$^{3·10}$.
k-ca^g.$=$V$^{3·10}$.ana^a.5.(12.16
63).$=$V$^{6·10}$.ant^b.--cro.$=$V^{10}.
VII^5.hel.q.χ.(8).

T.—I.dir.(12).$=$V^3.alm^a.5.—
pæo^a.$=$V^6.dul.$=$V^{10}.alm^a.66.
—ana^b.—asa^b.--ca-a^b.—coc^b.
--fl-x.—jat.; 1.6.—-k-ca.—
lth.π.——mez^b.19.48.(35).—
nat.βa.41.—na-n^b.—ol-a^a.—
rn-s.—rho^b.—spi.—stn.1.—
su-x.—tar^b.——thu.—val^a.—
zin^a.$=$VI^3.aco.—alo^b.—arn.
—ber^a.—cth^b.--dir.—rhs^a.$=$
III^3–V^1–VI^3.arg^a.$=$IV^1-V^{10}.
pla.—zin.$=$V$^{1·10}$.til.$=$V^1–VI^3.
ca-a.$=$V^{10}.VIII^4.jat.6.(8).$=$
V^{10}–VIII^5.pla^b.$=$VI$^{3·4}$.cha.
$=$VI^3–VIII^3.nx-m^b.

C.——V^{10}.fer.33.(8.12).——glo.d.
—hel.—ox-x.——pla.—sul.δb.
5.2-**10**.$=$V^{16}.dul^b.$=$VI^3.alo.-
ir-f^a.dd.2.$=$III^1–V^{10}.nx-m.p.

P.—V^{10}.k-ca^c.30.$=$VI^3.plb^c.$=$
II^1–V^{10}.stp^g.$=$V$^{1·3}$–VI^3.hfb^b.
δ.5.$=$V$^{1·10}$.fl-x.ηp.θ^1.5.86.$=$
V^{10}–VII^5.tar^d.

O.—I.dir.4.$=$V^{10}.ce-b.31.33.—
ign.—mep.—ox-x^g.—spi^b.29.
(12).

B.--V^{10}.ca-a^{tb}.--nx-m$^{pa·oa}$.--thu.

u. From above downwards.
GEN.—V^{10}.coc.31.--hur.—mgt.
ω.—mt-n.a^1b^s.δ.ω^3.--man.2-99.
5.—men.(12).——mer.VII^1.ζ.
—mu-x.δ.16.(90).—-ni-x.ζ^3.—
sul.**5**.

F.——III^{zz}.æth.$=$V^7.ana.$=$V^{10}.
—alo^c.—amb.p.δ.ηc^b.4.—asr.;
δ.$\delta\epsilon$.—bel^e.δb.3—cin.q.—coc.
31.--glo.q.--mu-x.q.$\beta\epsilon$.δ.(12).
—rhs$^{f·g}$.$\beta\epsilon$.$=$VI^3.squ^n.—tar.
δ.δb.$=$V$^{6·10}$.cro^c.$=$V^{10}–VI^4.
am-m^h.3-30.$=$IX.au-m^o.

T.—V^6.bel.δOr.$=$V^{10}.rhs.q.——
sbd^b.$=$VI^4.klm^a.——lau^a.$=$
VIII^3.ana^b.

C.—III.nx-m.a^1b^s.ϕ.$=$V^{10}.amb.
p.δ.ηc^b.3.4.—cin.q.12.——ctn.
$\beta\epsilon$.e.—cup.—cu-s.; g^b.x.a^1ᴅ.
——hdr.e.$=$V$^{2·10}$.ph-x.$=$V$^{6·10}$.
nx-v.

P.——VI^3.fl-x^c.$=$VI^4.nx-v^e.—-
phl^c.$=$V$^{1·6}$.spo^c.σ^2.$=$V^{10}–
VII^5–VIII^3.ca-c^c.

O.—V^{10}.crd.—ce-b.κ^5.—mrl.=
VIII^3.bel.q.31.33.

v. From below upwards.

GEN.—V^{10}.fl-x.——gui.2.—hln.
49.——mep.i^a.=V^{12}.dph.p.=
VI^3.gui.-sil.=VII^1.glo.=II^1
-V^{10}.trx.=V^{10}-VIII^4.ph-x.

F.—V^6.kis^b.—na-m.q.=V^{10}.glo.
—val.δ.=VI^3.ph-x^g.—scu^{a1}.
=VI^4.ber^g.=VIII^4.glo^h.=
$V^{1 \cdot 6}$.ni-x.—stp^f.=V^{10}-VIII^4.
gn-l.i^a.q.=$VI^{3 \cdot 4}$.dig^f.

T.——V^3.hep^a.=V^{10}.rhs^a.5-10.
(30).=VI^3.ch-s^b.14.=VI^4.
alm^b.VI^3.—lau^a.—mag^b.θ^1.
=VIII^3.am-m^b.—spo.27.31.
=V^1-VI^4.mrl.

C.——V^{10}.hln.49.——lch.ii^d.=
VIII^3.spo.27.31.=VIII^4.glo.
=V^{10}-VIII^4.aml.

P.—V^6.gam^f.—lah^f.66.—men^c.
=V^{10}.na-m^c.=VI^3.alo^c.3.5.—
men^d.=VI^4.cch^d.—lah^e.—
pho^c.5.19.=II^1-VI^3.lth^d.=
$V^{1 \cdot 6}$.arn^g.=$VI^{3 \cdot 4}$.man^d.3.18.

O.—III.cep^d.=V^6.fl-x^e.=V^{10}.
erd.5.—rs-r.=VI^3.amb.5.—
sep.=VI^4.ol-a^e.(15).—sar^f.4.
=II^1-VI^3.stp.=$V^{1 \cdot 6 \cdot 11}$.stp^j.
=V^6-$VI^{3 \cdot 4}$.sep.=VI^4-VIII^4.
mg-m.

Ba.—I.la-x.ηaa.ω.35.(12).

—— *upwards and downwards.*

T.--VI^3.ang.=VI^4.lau^a.=$V^{6 \cdot 10}$.
oln^b.(8).

O.—VII^5.glo.ϵ.

—— *upwards and outwards,*

C.—V^{10}.cmf.—glo.35.(8.20).

w. From side to side across.

GEN.—VIII^3.sam.

F.—I.ce-b.—gel.—glo^e.—rs-r.
4.=III.lep.5.=III^1.ham.5.
—naj.δq.—phy.=V^1.thu.=
V^7.glo^a.—phy.=VI^3.mez.=
VI^4.bry.σ^2.r.—klm.=VII^5.
irs.—naj.ij.=VIII^3.sbd.=
III^1-V^6.val.

T.—I.equ.=VI^3.bel.—ptl.κ^5.

C.—V^7.chd.=VI^3.la-x.dd^h.11.

P.—V^6.ath.βa.

O.—V^6.lch.=V^7.er-a^d.

Ba.—I.plg.

x. Diagonally.

F.—I.rhs.=V^1.gui.——mez.=
VI^3.chd.=V^3-VI^3.hel.

C.—V^6.au-n.=VI^4.au-n.

O.—VI^3.aga.

y. Periodical.

GEN.—I.ars.——cmf.—klm.—
mrr.—ped.—rs-r.—san.

F.—VI^4.cha.-plb^c.=VIII^4.cn-s^a.

z. From front to back.

GEN.--I.fag.σ^2.(8.12.31).=VI^3.
c-cs.

F.—I.ce-b.—glo.—phy.=III.
spo.=V^3.ce-b^a.=V^{10}.dio.w.
—spo^a.σ^2.-tab.=VI^1.fag^b.5.=
VIII^3.pru.=VIII^4.glo^h.=
V^1-VI^4.nit^q.31.70.(8-128).

T.—V^{10}.plg^a.=VI^3.irs^a.

P.——II^6.cot^c.=VI^3.tab.31.=
VIII^3.ni-x^d.=$V^{1 \cdot 6}$.arg^f.

O.—III.pi-m.κ^4.π.=VI^3.crn.=
VIII^3.pru.

zz. From back to front.

GEN.—I.glo.——V^6.cb-v.——V^{10}.
bry.q.—ni-x.——sil.δ.—sul.5.
—VI^3.na-m.6.=VIII^3.ph-x.

F.—III^u.æth.=V^{10}.hdr.3-66.—
lau.p.hh.ii^d.r^1.-mg-s.d.q.3-30.
——nx-m^g.3.—rhs^r.—sbd^e.=
VIII^1.sbd.

T.——V^6.ca-c.=V^{10}.vrb^b.=VI^3.
na-m^a.

C.—V^3.elp.=V^{10}.man.—nx-m.
29.=VIII^4.kre.

P.——II^4.ind.5.19.=V^6.cro^c.—
su-x^c.=VI^3.k-ca^c.——lep^c.=
VIII^3.ni-x^d.=$V^{1 \cdot 6}$-$VI^{3 \cdot 4}$.gui^c.
=$V^{1 \cdot 6}$.hel^d.—stn^c.=V^3-VI^1-
VIII^3.ag-n^d.=V^6-VI^4.tar^d.

O.—V^1.arn^b.—asr^c.=V^7.dio.—
jab^h.=V^{10}.chd.-man.4.—nx-v.
—ol-a.—ph-x.q.29.(22).--plb.
q.δb.(18).--sbd.βa.=VI^3.chd.
=VI^4.ana^b.—aur^b.35.—cth^c.
βa.—chd^c.——chi^b.——mer.=
VIII^1.sbd^g.=VIII^3.ag-n.=
VIII^4.glo.=$V^{1 \cdot 6}$-VI^3.chd^c.=
V^1-VI^1.cam^c.=$VI^{3 \cdot 4}$.æth.4.--
aga^a.3.——chd^b.=VI^3-VIII^3.
mg-m^b.

B.—V^1.ber^{ta}.

—— *forwards and upwards.*

O.—I.glo. =VI^4.amb.—mg-m.—rat.

Remitting.—amb.I.(as if catarrh would come on).—ag-m.F.V^{10}.κ^5.3.4.29.(89).—ag-n.B^{fb}.31.—asa.I.—ba-c.VI^3.—bel.F^n.V^1.—dio.F^a.VI^1.3.8.12.—glo.C.I.a^1b.—opi.F.I.

Gradually increasing.—aco.P.V$^{1\cdot a}$.(116).—bry.F^g.V^6.—ech.F.V^7.1.—la-v.V^1.—lo-i.I.—sar.F^n.V^1–VI^3.

Gradually going off.—opi.F.V^1.p.—pla.F^d.V^3.—sbd.F^a.VIII^4.—eth.

Gradually increasing and decreasing.—ba-c.VI^3.—crt.I.—jab.O^h.I.—k-bi.F^g.VI$^{3\cdot a}$.—opi.C.δl.—pla.T.^{b}.IV^1–V^1.—sar.C.V^1.—stn.T^b.V$^{10\cdot t}$.; C.III^1–V^{10}.—vrb.F^o.VI^3.

Rapidly increasing and decreasing.—ag-n.P^d.V^3–VI$^{1\cdot zz}$.

Gradually coming, suddenly going off.—arg.P^d.V^6–VI^4.5.(31).—cau.T.V$^{6\cdot a}$.—su-x.F.III^1.; F^a.V^1.; F^g.V^{16}.; F^o.(pain as from a blow).

Suddenly coming, gradually going off.—asa.P^d.V^{16}.—ca-a.O.V^1.—fl-x.O^c.V$^{1\cdot a}$.—rn-s.C.V^8.—sab.V$^{10\cdot s}$.

Suddenly coming, suddenly going off.—ast.F^g.V^3.—cca.T^b.I.—mr-c.F.C.V^7.ak.—su-x.F^o.VI$^{3\cdot q}$.

SECTION V.—SCALP.

CHARACTER.

b. **Coldness.**—aga.e.—grp.III^1–IV^1.—ind$^{ta\cdot pa}$.VI^3.—lyc.VI^1.107.—ph-x.—pho^{pb}.IV^3.—rho^t.g^b.

—— *as if ice lay there.*—c-ph.g^a.p.[H.II^5.].

107. *By a draft of air.*—lyc.VI^1.

b^a. **Feeling of coldness.**—am-c.g^b.6.—na-m^c.dd.δb.

δb. *With closure of eyes.*—na-m^c.dd.

6. *In a room.*—am-c.g^b.

d. **Congestion.**

—— *as if full of blood.*—ars^o.II^7.v.

—— *like rush of blood.*—opi.p.ηp.

e. **Contraction.**—æsc^f.—aga.b.—gel^f.—hur^f.—hyd$^{c\cdot o}$.—irs.—k-bi.g.—kis.—lyc.IX.—mer.r.kk.[H.b.].—mil^f.—na-m^c.—nit^c.3-30.—par^f.II^4.$\beta\epsilon$.δ.δLp,aa.—ped.—pla^c.x.q.—rn-s.—rhs.IX.—spi.ff^a.—ve-v^f.[F^g.V^6.].

—— *as in anger.*—cyc^f.

—— *wrinkling.*—grt^f.ff^a.—hel^f.V^6.—rhe^f.

—— *as if wrinkled.*—grp^f.

—— *as if skin were drawn together.*—tep^o.IX.—zin.

—— *and pinched up.*—hfb.

—— *spasmodic.*—lyc.

$\beta\epsilon$. *Confusion.*—par^f.II^4.δ.δLp,aa.

δ. *Pain in eyes.*—par^f.II^4.δLp,aa.

δLp,aa. *Heat and redness of lids.*—par^f.II^4.δ.

3-30. *On rising, morning.*—nit^c.

f. **Convulsions.**—evo^f.ff^a.

—— *cataleptic, of occipito-frontalis muscle.*—glo.$\beta\epsilon^a$.

—— *drawing up of skin of F., with opening of eyes, then drawing down of skin, with closing of eyes.*—lyc.

$\beta\epsilon^a$. *Stupid feeling.*—glo.

g. **Creeping.**—aco.(101).—alm$^{f\cdot t}$.; g^b.v.—c-ph.r.x.—cau^c.—fag.v.(15).—k-bi.e.—rhs.; ^{f}.ζg.19.(29).; ^{f}.II^1.—sbd.v.31.105.

—— *like a beetle.*—rn-b^f.5-10.—rn-r^f.5-10.(30).

—— *as from ants.*—aco^t.—cic^f.

—— *as from lice.*—ag-n.3.; v.

—— *as from a brush.*—aco^{pb}.

—— *as from fleas or flies.*—lau^f.(15).

—— *as if an ulcer were forming.*—rhs^o.4.

ζg. *Creeping in nose.*—rhs^f.19.(29).

4. *In the afternoon.*—rhs^o.

5-10. *In the evening in bed.*—rn-b^f.—rn-r^f.(30).

15. *By scratching.*—*fag*.v.—*lau*^{f}.

19. *When sitting.*—rhs^f.ζg.(29).
29. *By stooping.*—rhs^f.ζg.19.
30. *On rising up.*—rn-r^f.5-10.
31. *When walking.*—sbd.v.105.
105. *When perspiring.*—sbd.v.81.

g^a. **Crawling.**—ba-c.v.(15).——bry^P.
g^b.5.——c-ph^c.b.p.[H II^5.]—cn-i^c.
——chi^f.——cch^f.——cu-s.x^a.a^{1}ɒ [C.
V$^{10·u}$.]——nx-ᵥ^f.; $^{f·c}$.——spi^f.v.(15).——
——thu^o.II$^{2·6}$.
—— *as from lice.*—ham.—led^f.v.
a^{1}ɒ. *With stupefaction.*—-cu-s.x^a.
  [C.V$^{10·u}$.].
5. *In forenoon.*—bry^P.g^b.
15. *By scratching.*—-ba-c.v.—spi^f.v.

g^b. **Formication**—alm.g.v.——am-c.b.
6.—arn^f.; ^{c}.—ars.2.—ard^f.; ^{t}.—
bz-x^f.——bro^{pb}.v.ηl.——bry^P.g^a.5.—
ca-a.v.——ca-c.v.II^1.η.v.2.——can.—
car$^{c·o}$.III^1.——chd.; ^{fc}.; ^{P}.(15).——ccs.
——col^{pb}.v.——crt^o.——cup^c.; ^{c}.x^a.V$^{10·u}$
——dro.ff^a.q.1.——elc.——fer.dd.[H^c.].
——hyo^c.; ^{p}.——hyp^c.——k-ca^f.——lah^{ta}.;
^{pb}.x.5.——lau.q.29.——lyc.5.8-31.——
mt-s^{pb}.——ni-x^{pa}.——rhe^t.——rhot.b.——
sbd^f.II^1.; ^{e}.II^1.——spi^c.v.——sul$^{p·o}$.;
^{t}.; ff^a.——tab.II^1.ε.κ^1.χ^1.; ^{tb}.
—— *as from ants.*—ba-c.5.—pla^{ta}.
  θ^4.χ^1.
—— *as if roots of hair moved.*—
  ars.
—— *as if something ran about.*—
  mt-s^c.VI^4.
ε. *Pain in ear.*—tab.II^1.κ^1.χ^1.
ηv. *Itching of face.*—ca-c.v.II^1.2.
η. *Pain in face.*—bro^{pb}.v.
θ^4. *Pain in lower jaw.*—pla^{ta}.χ^1.
κ^1. *Anorexia.*—tab.II^1.ε.χ^1.
χ^1. *Chilliness.*—pla^{ta}.θ^4.
χ^1. *Rigor.*—tab.II^1.ε.κ^1.
1. *All day.*—dro.ff^a.q.
2. *At night.*—ars.—ca-c.v.II^1.ηv.
5. *In the evening.*—ca-c.—lah^{pb}.x.
5. *In the forenoon.*—bry^P.g^a.
15. *By scratching.*—chd^P.
29. *By stooping.*—lau.q.

h^i. **Watery discharge.**—ars.
i^a. **Fulness.**—cnu.ff^a.
j. **Dryness.**——bad.v.k^b.hh.——dir.ff^a.
——mt-s^f.——sin^f.p.

k. **Eruptions.**—ca-c.σ^{3}ψ^{2}ii.— hpm.v.
—lyc.σ^{2}ψ^{2}ii.——mer.v.—na-m$^{fe·t·o}$.v.
—pho.v.II^5.—plg^f.v.—rs-r.—su-x.
η.σ^2.
—— *fetid.*—na-m.
—— *great.*—cic.η.
—— *bad.*—ca-c.
ηk. *Eruption on face.*—cic.—su-x.
  σ^2.
σ^{2}k. *Eruption on nape.*—su-x.η.
σ^{3}ψ^{2}ii. *Glandular swellings in neck.*
  —ca-c.—lyc.
k^c. **Blotches.**
—— *red, serous.*--cnc.s.σ^2.π.(**105**).
πs. *Inflammation of chest.*—cnc.s.
  σ^2.(**105**).
σ^{2}s. *Inflammation of neck.*—cnc.s.
  π.(**105**).
105. *By perspiring.*—cnc.s.π.σ^2.
k^d. **Boils.**—ag-n.v.σ^2.—aur^{fb}.; ^{c}.V^3.
11.—ba-c^f.—belt.—ca-c^{ta}.3.(5).;
^{tb}.; ^{f}.—cau^e.—k-ca^{pa}.—led^f.k^l.—
lyc^o.—mu-x^{tb}.--na-m.θ^4.σ^2.—sul^{tb}.
—thu^e.
—— *painless.*—ca-c^{pa}.—nat^o.
—— *hard.*—bry^c.—cb-a^f.
—— *lentil-sized.*—ana.II^3.11.15.
—— *size of a walnut.*—lyc^o.—
  rut^{pa}.II^7.11.[B^{pa}.VI^4.].
—— *size of a hazel nut.*—nat^o.
—— *an old painless boil becomes
  painful and large.*—ba-c.II^7.11.
θ^{4}k^d. *Boils on chin.*—na-m.σ^2.
σ^{2}k^d. *Boils on nape.*—ag-n.v.—-
  na-m.θ^4.
3. *In the morning.*—ca-c^{ta}.(5).
5. *In the evening.*—cac^{ta}.3.
k^f. **Rhagades.**—pet^e.l^a.aa.—-vi-t.k^o.
  v.II^1.η.
η. *Eruption on face.*—vi-t.k^o.II^1.
k^g. **Elevations.**—cnb.—hep^f.
—— *steatoma.*—gur.
—— *soft.*—pet.dd^h.
—— *soft moveable tubercles size
  of pigeon's eggs.*—tep.
—— *small, painless swellings.*—-
  sul^c.
—— *shining, painless.*—pho^f.[F^e.
  I^a.].
—— *as if a pimple would come
  there.*—sel^{fd}.

—— *tubercles.*—sil.σ^2.
—— *small, hard tubercle.*—na-mᶠ. σ^2.II¹.11.
—— *red painful tubercles.*—thuᵗ.
—— *round sore, coming off in dry scabs.*—sumᵖᵇ.ddʰ.
—— *size of a hemp seed.*—sulᶜ.k¹.
—— *small tumours.*——helᶠ.V².—pul.II⁷.
—— *small painful tumours.*—nx-vᵗ.
—— *nodosoties resembling exostoses in several parts.*—bel.
—— *size of a penny.*—rut.ddʰ.VI³·⁴.
—— *round, the size of a penny, with red base.*—arsᵉᵃ.II¹–VI³–VIII³.
—— *large tumours.*—wis.
—— *a big lump.*—mg-mₗᵒ.ddʰ.VI⁴.
—— *a broad lump.*—lycᶠ.
—— *hard painful lumps at edge of hair.*—ca-s.
—— *red stripe.*—rutᶠᵈ·ᶠᶜ.
—— *like mosquito bites.*—-rs-r.v. II¹·⁵.**15**.
σ^2kᵍ. *Tubercles on nape.*—na-mᶠ. II¹.11.—sil.
kʰ. **Herpetic.**—badᶠ.ddʰ.βa.—ba-cᶠ. v.II¹.—bel.—ipcᶠ.η.—na-mᶠ.
—— *dry.*—tep.η.[Hc.].
βa. *Vertigo.*—badᵗ.ddʰ.
ηkʰ. *Herpes on cheeks.*—ipcᶠ.—tep. [Hc.].
kⁱ. **Mattery.**—ard.kᵐ·q.——ca-cᵉᵃ.— k-caᵉ.—lyc.
kj. **Dry.**—gur.—mer.ddʰ.
kʲ. **Miliary.**—na-mᵉ.v.—rheᶠ.v.r.— rhsᵗ.v.II³.η.θ.—spi.
η. *Miliary eruption on face.*—rhsᶠ. v.II².θ.
θ. *Miliary eruption round mouth.* —rhsᶠ.v.II².η.
r. *Miliary eruption on arm.*—rheᶠ. v.
kᵏ. **Moist.**—grpᵉ.ddʰ.; II⁷.11.—mer. V¹.[Hₕ.].—sulᶜ.kᵐ.—vin.v.pp.II¹. 15.—vi-tᵉ.kᶠ·ᵒ.v.II¹.ηkᵒ.—zinᵗ.v.
—— *thin.*—ca-c.
—— *scaly.*—na-m.v.
kˡ. **Pimples.**——acoᶠ.——aga.; ᶠ.v.— almᵉᵃ.VII⁵.; ᶠ.ₗ.—ambᶠ.—am-mᵒˢ.

v.5.(2).—argᵗᵇ.II7.11.—ars.II⁵.11. 15.—ba-cᵖ.—bu-sᶠ.—ca-cᶠ.—c-phᶠ·— ca-s.—can.ddʰ.σ^2.—cb-vᵗ.—crt.— cycᵒ.—droᶜᵇ.—helᶠᵇ.V².11.—hepᶠ. 6.(8).—hurᶠ.—k-bi.v.II¹.—k-ca. —ledᶠ.kᵈ.; πkᵇ.v.II⁵.—mgt.pp.— mt-n.ddʰ.——mu-xᶠ.kᵒ.; ᵉ.v.II⁵.— mrrᵒ.—nitᵒ.σ^2.—oln.v.—parᶠ.V¹. 11.—pet.—pho.v.II7.11.—psoᶠ.— sepᶠ.dd.—sil.v.—stpᶠ.v.VI².; ᶠ.η.θ. v.VI³.II7.11.; ᶠ.η.θ.r¹.v.V⁶.(15).— sul.v.; ᶠ.v.VI³.15.; r.; ᶠᵇ.; ᵐᵃ.; ᶜ. kᵍ.; ᶜ.σ^2.—trxᵗᵃ.II7.11.—zin.v.
—— *with red areola.*—anaᵗᵇ.
—— *inflamed.*—k-biᵒ.σ^2k¹.—sul.
—— *painful.*—cleᶠ.—cobᵒ.—f-mg. —sulᶜ·ᵒ.; ᶜ.
—— *painless.*—cycᵒ.
—— *small.*—ac-s.—ga-xᶜ.—pedᶠ. —na-mᵉᵇ.—sbdᶜᵃ.
—— *papulæ.*—almᶠ.ηl.—cyc.—— ledᶠ.—scpᶠ.dd.—sulᶠ.ddʰ.
—— *white papulæ.*—antᶠᵉ.ddʰ.— cb-vᶠ.
—— *irregular papulæ.*—-ag-nᵒ.v. ddʰ.s.kᵏ.15.
—— *lentil-sized flat papulæ.*—— ant.gᵇ.dd.12.
—— *like large pins' heads.*—tep. gᵇ.; ᶠ.gᵇ.
—— *large.*—cun.—najᶠ.—ph-xᵉᵃ. ddʰ.
—— *as big as a hazel nut.*—conᶠ. ddʰ.
—— *exuding bloody serum.*—arsᵗᵇ. II³.**15**.; ᶠᵈ.kᵐ.—-belᵗ.θr.θ⁴. **15**.
—— *fill with serous fluid, dry, and scab off.*—acoᶠ.η.σ^2.
—— *hard.*—rn-s.
—— *hard, painful.*—bel.—grpᵉᵃ.
—— *red.*—ars.—cb-vᶠ.ddʰ.—pedᵗ. r.v.—sepᶠ.
—— *red, hard.*—antᵉᵈ.II³.11.
—— *large, red.*—k-caᶠᶜᵇ.ddʰ.
—— *red, smooth, painless.*—cb-vᶠ.
—— *white.*—pedᶠ.
—— *large, with white head.*—stpᵉ.
—— *covered with a scab.*—arsᵖᵇ. II⁵.**15**.
ηkˡ. *Pimples on face.*—aco.σ^2.—

alm^f.—stp^f.θ.v.VI^3.II^7.11.; ^{f}.θ.r^1. v.V^6.(15).

ηk^o. Scabby face.--vi-t^e.k$^{f.k.o}$.v.II^1.

θk^l. Pimples on r. side of mouth. —bel.θ^4.

θk^l. Pimples round mouth.—stp^b. η.v.VI^3.II^7.11.

θ^{4}k^l. Pimples on chin.—bel.θr.

$ι$k^l. Pimples on throat.—alm^f.

πk^h. Herpes on chest.—led^f.v.II^5.

σ^{2}k. Eruption on nape.—k-bi^o.

σ^{2}k^l. Pimples on nape.—aco.η. nit^o.—sul^c.

rk^l. Pimples on shoulders.—ped^t. v.—sul^f.

r^1. Pimples on wrist.—stp^f.η.θ.v. V^6.(15).

vk^l. Pimples on legs.—ped^t.r.

2. At night.—a-m^{oa}.v.5.

5. In the evening.—am-m^{oa}.v.(2).

6. In the room.—hep^f.(8).

8. In the open air.—hep^f.6.

11. When touched.—stp^f.η.θ.v.VI^3. II^7.

k^m. Pustules.—arn^f.——ars.II^1.η.—- ca-a^{feb}.— c-ph^{cb}.II^3.11.—ca-x^c.—- cun^{fd}.(117).——gas.dd^h.—k-ca^{fcb}. dd^h.—mr-i.——mu-x$^{f.t}$.—nat^f.II$^{1.3}$. —pul^o.VI^4.—rho^f.

—— hard.—ars.

—— erysipelas pustulosum.—ars. η.σ^2.π.r.

—— with red areola.—ard.k$^{i.o}$.— irs^c.

—— copious.—irs.

—— exuding bloody serum.--eub^{fca}. 15.

—— painful.—nx-v.η.—rho^f.

—— growing to an ulcer.—sep^o.v.

—— drying up to scabs.—mr-i.— sul^c.k^k.

ηk^m. Pustules on face.—ars.II^1.— nx-v.

η.π.σ^2.rk^m. Erysipelas pustulosum on face, chest, neck, and shoulders. —ars.

117. By washing.—cun^{fd}.

k^n. Red spots.—msc^f.[F.V^1.].

—— pimple.—amb^f.II^3.11.

—— hard, elevated.—ant^f.v.

—— lentil-sized.—cyc^f.

k^o. Scabs.—ars.— ard.k$^{i.m}$.—bel.— cle.v.— grp.k^p.v.— mag^{pb}.—mu-x^f. k^l.—sil^e.——stp.v.; $^{e.ec}$.v.—sul^o.— trn^c.VI^2.—vi-t.k^f.v.II^1.η.

—— painful.—sul^{pb}.; ^{ta}.

—— dry.—mez.

—— as thick as the finger.—ars.

—— thick-leather like.—mez.

—— small.— elc^{pb}.—f-mg.—mer. —nit.v.—par.—sul^c.

—— moist below.—grp.

—— very fetid.—grp.

—— elevated, white.—mez.

—— exuding watery fluid.--stp.v.

ηk. Eruption on face.—vi-t.k^f.v.II^1.

k^b. Scales, scurf, desquamation.— bel.—-ca-c^c.—cle.; v.—crt.v.— grp.k^o.—gur.VI^4.— lah.η.—lyc.— mer.v.II^1.15.—naj.——na-m.—oln. —pho.v.——sep.—wis.v.; v.(15). [Ht.].; χ^3.3.

—— white.—mez.

—— dandriff.——bad.v.[Hj.].— ch-s.5.15.

—— scaly spot.—k-ca^f.

ηk^p. Desquamation of face.—lah.

χ^3. Perspiration.—wis.3.

3. In morning.—wis.χ^3.

5. In the evening.—ch-s.15.

15. By scratching.—ch-s.5.

k^q. Spots.—cvl^f.

k^r. Vesicles.—aco^t.— alm^f.ζr.θl.v.— chi.—gur.II^1.—lo-c^f.dd^h.[F.VI^3.]. —pho^e.—rs-v^{eb}.—sul^{fc}.

—— with black apices.—ped$^{f.t}$.η. θ^4.

—— painful.—sul^o.

—— miliary.—trn^f.[F.I.].

—— that dry to scabs.—til.v.II^1. 15.

ζk^r. Vesicles on nose.—alm^f.θl.v.

ηk^r. Vesicles on face.—ped$^{f.t}$.θ^4.

θk^r. Vesicles round mouth.—alm^f. ζr.v.

θ^{4}k^r. Vesicles on chin.—ped$^{f.t}$.η.

k^s. Wheals.—hep.dd^h.σ^2.

—— nettle-rash.—aps^f.

σ^2. Wheals on nape.—hep.dd^h.

k^s. Warts.

—— moist.—thu^e.

k^t. **Black points.**
—— *clusters of.*—sul^f.

l^s. **Rawness.**—ni-x^e.—pet^e.k^f.aa.

p. **Heat** (see also HEAD).—agn.r.ff^a.
— alo.x.ff^a.——cau^f.ff^a.δ.ζp.—chd^c.
dd^h.—fag.v.—hyo.g^b.—-mg-s^c.IX.
—mit.dd^c.—mez.—opi.d.ηp.—-pho.
II^1.κ^1.—sin^f.j.—spr.v.
—— *feverish.*—for.
—— *flush of.*—cle.V^{10}.

δ. *With pain in eyes.*—cau^f.ff^a.ζ.

ζp. *Heat of nose.*—cau^f.ff^a.δ.

ηp. *Heat of face.*—opi.d.

κ^1. *Anorexia.*—pho.II^1.

q. **Heaviness.**—bov^{fd}.ff^a.V^1.—mr-i.

r. **Horripilation, rigor.**——ac-s.——
agn.ff^a.p.— alm^o.III^2–IV^2.—arg^{pa}.
—c-ph.g.x.—cap.v.II^1.(**15**).—cch.
—crt.(Hb.).—-klm^c.σ^{2}ḣ.aḣ.εὖ.5-**10**.
—mer.e.kk.[Hb.].—myr^c.ff^a.—sng.
—til.—ver.(Hdd.).
—— *followed by burning itching.*
—cap.

σ^{2}ḣ. *Crackling noise in neck.*—-klm^c.
aḣ.εὖ.5-**10**.

aḣ. *Alarm.*—klm^c.εὖ.σ^{2}ḣ.5-**10**.

εὖ. *Sound of a horn in ears.*—klm^c.
aḣ.σ^{2}ḣ.5-**10**.

5-**10**. *In the evening in bed.*—klm^c.
aḣ.εὖ.σ^{2}ḣ.

15. *By scratching.*—cap.v.II^1.

s. **Inflammation.**—cad^e.II^3.—-cnc.k^c.
σ^2.π.(**105**).
—— *erysipelas.*—dor.η.—-rs-v.η.—-
rut^f.

ηs. *Erysipelas of face.*—dor.——
rs-v.

πs. *Inflammation of chest.*—cnc.
k^c.σ^2.(**105**).

σ^{2}s. *Inflammation of neck.*—cnc.
k^e.π.(**105**).

105. *By perspiring.*—cnc.k^c.π.σ^2.

v. **Itching.**—-aco.11.—aga.; 3-30.
(**15**).; °.ev.; ^{f}.k^1.—alm.g.g^b.; II^5.
15.; k^p.—am-g.VI^2.——am-c.dd^h.;
°.—am-m.— ani^{pb}.(11).—aps.4.—
ag-n.; °.2.; °.II^5.; q.—ars.1.—
at-a.—ard^f.—asr^{tb}.VI^2.—au-m^f.—
au-s.2.--bad.j.k^h.hh.—ba-c.g^a.(**15**).
—-bz-x.—bro^{fb}.; ^{pb}.g^b.ηl.; $^{fa.ob}$.;
(**15**).——bry.**15**.--ca-a.dd^h.; g^b.

—ca-c.; °.; °.βa.**15**.; 8-31.; II^1.;
eb.dd^h.ii.II^7.—c-ph.5.—cant.—cth^f.
(**15**).—cb-a.—cb-v^e.--ca-x.—cau.;
^{f}.—chd$^{f.fc.t.o}$.; ^{f}.(**15**).—ch-s.**5**.;
$^{f.c.mb}$.ην.; $^{c.ob}$.—clef^f.; k^p.—cob.2.;
ην.II$_s^1$.**15**.--cod.ηs.ψv.—cof.—col^{pb}.
g^b.—com^{pb}.—con.—cro^{fcb}.—crt.k^p.
—c-ar.; 2.—dph.—elp.—ep-p.—
fag.g.(**15**).; p.; °.ζv.; 4.——fer.;
v^{1}b.—f-mg.—fl-x.—grp.; °.—gur.
—hpm.3.—hur^f.—hfb^o.3.—idm.v^1.;
^{c}.3.--iof^o.—jug.—k-bi^f.II^1[B.VII^1].;
II^1.k^i.--k-ca.; °.; II^5.**15**.--kis.--lah.
ψv.—lau^{oa}.(**15**).; ^{p}.; ^{f}.(**15**).; ^{fca}.;
^{pb}.; ^{f}.4.—led^f.g^a.—lyc^{ta}.II^1–VI$^{3.4}$.
15.; ην.—mag^{fa}.VI$^{3.s}$.; 110.—m-pu^o.
4.(**15**).—mer^f.; II^1.; 2.—mr-s.—
mez.$^{c.o}$.; ψv.—mr-f.; ^{c}.—msc.(**15**).
—mu-x^c.—na-m.; σ^{2}v.; ην.. ^{f}.3.
--nx-v.II^5.σ^2.5.--par.II^1.**15**.--pau^o.
gg.—ped.5.; ^{f}.; ^{tb}.—pet.; II^3.**15**.
—phl^{eb}.v.VI^4.—ph-x.—pho.--plg.
k^f.—pso.—rn-s.—rut.; ^{ta}.; ^{ob}.ψ^{2}ii.
—rho.; II^1.**15**.5.; ^{eb}.σ^2.—rs-r.; 5.;
^{f}.8-31.—rut^{ob}.dd^h.(**15**).—sbd.; II^1.
βε.; g.31.**105**.—sam^f.(**15**).—sar^o.
——sng.——sep.; dd^h.V$^{3.10}$.σ^{2}ff.; ^{c}.
[Hc.].; °.5.—sil.; ^{ou}.; °.; ^{pb}.; II^5.
15.—spi^f.g^a.(**15**).; g^b.—-spr.p.—
stp.—sul.; au^{ff}.; ^{f}.; ^{f}.II^1.5.; °.—
su-x.——tab.—thr.σ^{2}v.5.—thu.—
til.; ^{e}.aa.——ton^{oa}.VI^3.(**15**).—ver^f.
—-vi-t^{eb}.VI^3.—wis.; k^p.; (**15**).k^p.
[Hc.].; **105**.—zin.II^3.

—— *as if something were healing.*
—aga.(**15**).
—— *as if an eruption were there.*
—hur$^{o.m}$.
—— *as from mosquitoes.*—jac^f.
—— *as from something from within.*—hfb^c.
—— *like lice.*—ped.—rut^{pb}.II^6.
—— *like vermin.*—rho.5.—sbd^c.
—— *as if a hair hung down.*—
grt^f.
—— *desire to scratch without itching.*—fl-x.5.[Hc.].

v-II^1. *Burning.*—ars.—ca-c.—-cap.
r.(**15**).—mer^f.——na-m^{ea}.—ol-a.
II^1.(**15**).

—— *as from caterpillar's hairs.*— glo.σ²v.

—— *as from nettles.*—ca-c.g^b.ηg^b.2.

v-II². *Corrosive.*—dro.—rhs.ηθv,k^j.

—— *as if an eruption would break out.*—squ^f.ηv. (15).

v-II³. *Raw.*—zin^c.

v-II⁴. *Scraping.*—bel^f.

v-II⁵. *Smarting.*—mt-n.— mer.σ²v. —pul.--vin^c.

—— *as from salt.*—wis.

v-II⁶. *Biting.*—oln.—ph-x^f.--sep. —stp°.15.; °.II³.5.; 15.--ver. VI³.—vin.

—— *as from lice.*—oln.1.; II⁵.15.; 2.—rut^pb.

v-II⁷. *Ulcerative.*—ars.d.dd.

v-V⁸. *Gnawing.*—arg^f.--ars.--ba-c. —cha^f.--dro^f.(15).

—— *as from vermin.*—cap.dd.15.

—— *here and there.*—agn.

v-VI¹. *Cutting.*—ter^tb.5-10.(15).

v-VI². *Prickling.*—bry^fa.—cu-a.— vi-t^eb.

—— *like needles.*-bry^fa.-stp.[Fk^j].

v-VI³. *Shooting.*--agn.(15).--ang^f.t. —arn.—chi.—mez.(15).

—— *here and there.*—cyc.(15).

CONCOMITANTS.

aꞩ. *Excitement.*—cod.ψv.

aꞙ^ff. *Impatience.*—sul.

βa. *Vertigo.*—ca-c°.15.

βε. *Confusion of head.*—sbd.II¹.

εv. *Itching in ears.*—aga°.

ζv. *Itching in nose.*—fag°.

ηg^b. *Formication in face.*--ca-c. II¹.g^b.2.

ηv. *Itching of face.*—ch-s^f.c.mb.19. —na-m.—lyc.—rhs.II².θv,k^j.

ηῦ. *Itching on chin.*--squ^f.II².(15).

η. *Pain in face.*—bro^pb.g^b.

θk^j. *Miliary eruption round mouth.* —rhs.II².ηv.θv.

θv. *Itching round mouth.*—rhs.II². ηv.θk^j.

σ³v. *Itching of nape.*—glo.Il¹.— mer.II⁵.--na-m.—thr.5.--rho^eb.

σ²ff. *Stiff neck.*—sep.dd^h.V³.10.

σ³. *Pain in nape.*—nx-v.II⁵.5.

vv. *Itching of toes.*—idm.

ψv. *Itching of skin.*—cod.aꞩ.—lah. —mez.

ψ²ii. *Swollen gland.*—rat^ob.

CONDITIONS.

1. *All day.*—ars.
2. *At night.*—ag-n°.—au-s.--ca-c. II¹.ηg^b.— cob.—mer.—mr-f^c.— oln.II⁶.
3. *In the morning.*—hpm.—hfb°. --idm^c.—na-m.
3-30. *In the morning on rising.*— aga.(15).
4. *In afternoon.*—aps.—fag.— lau^f.—m-pu°.(15).
5. *In the evening.*—c-ph.—ch-s.-- fag.—ped.—rho.; II¹.15.—rs-r. —sep°.—stp. ; °.II⁶.—thr.σ²v.
5-10. *In bed, evening.*—ter^tb.VI¹. (15).
5. *In the forenoon.*—nx-v.II⁵.σ².
8-31. *On walking in open air.*— ca-c.—rs-r^f.
11. *When touched.*—aco.—ani^pb.
15. *By scratching.*—aga. ; 3-30. —agn.VI³.—-ba-c.g^a.—bro^e.— bry.—ca-c°.βa.—cth^f.— cap.V⁸. dd. ; cap.II¹.r.—chd^f.—cyc.VI³. —dro^f.V⁸.—fag.g.—lau°^a.; ^f. m-pu°.4.--mez.VI³.--msc.--rut^ob. dd^h.--sam^f.--spi^f.g^a.--squ^f.II².ηv. —-stp°.II⁶.—ter^tb.VI¹.5-10.— ton°^a.VI³.—wis. ; k^p.[Hc.].
19. *When sitting.*—ch-s^f.c.mb.ηv.
31. *When walking.*—sbd.g.105.
105. *When perspiring.*—sbd.g.31. —wis.
110. *In rainy weather.*—mag.

w. **Movements.**—pl-c°.σvrw.

—— *towards forehead.*—cau.

—— *from behind forwards.*—nat. —na-m.—sul.

—— *backward and forward.*— sep.θ¹.

CONCOMITANTS.

θ¹. *Clenching of teeth.*—sep.

σvw. *Movements in muscles of back and limbs.*—pl-c°.

x. **Numbness.**—aco.ii^a.—alo.p.ff^a.— ber.ff^a.ii^d.ηx.--c-ph.g.r.— glo.——

hfb^{pb}.; ^{pa}.ff.—lah^{pb}.g^b.5.—mrl.dd.
ff^a.q.—mr-f.—pla^c.e.q.

CONCOMITANT.

ηx. *Numbness in face.*—ber.ff^a.ii^d.

CONDITION.

5. *In the evening.*—lah^{pb}.g^b.

x^a. **As if asleep.**—alm.—cs-e^o.99.—
cup^c.g^b.V$^{10\cdot u}$.——cu-s^c.g^a a^{1}ᴅ.[C.
V$^{10\cdot u}$.].

—— *as if lying on ice.*—cs-e^o.98.

CONCOMITANT.

a^{1}ᴅ. *With stupefaction.*—cu-s^c.g^a.
[C.V$^{10\cdot u}$.].

CONDITIONS.

98. *During sleep.*—cs-e^o.
99. *On awaking.*—cs-e^o.

z. **Pulsation.**—glo^p.33.

CONDITION.

33. *On running up stairs.*—glo^p.

aa. **Redness.**—ni-x^{eb}.v.ii.—pet^c.kf.l^a.
—tab^{eb}.ii^a.VI^3.—thu^e.v.

cc. **Roughness.**—alm^f.ηcc.—na-m^t.—
sep^f.

CONCOMITANT.

ηcc. *Roughness of face.*—alm^f.

dd. **Sensitiveness.**—aga.II^7.—ast.
—bry.5.; ff^a.—ca-a.21.—cap.v.V^8.
15.—cb-a^e.—car.; **15.**—cas^c.83.
[F.VI^4.].; ^{c}.χ^1.12.[T.VI^4.].—cau.
15.—cle^f.4.—cly.; $^{f\cdot t}$.βa.—con^{fca}.
II^1.—cop.—ep-p.—fer.g^b.[Hc.]—
frz.41.70.**70.**—gn-c.26.—gin.—
hur.η.—hfb.—hyp^t.βa.κ^5.3-99.4.—
iod.κ^7.ω^2.35.[F.V^2.].—ipc^o.σ^2.26.
—irs^m.θ^4.60.86.—kre$^{f\cdot c}$.11.**15.**—
lah.; ^{c}.—lep.—lil$^{f\cdot t\cdot pb}$.—lyc.—
mag.q.—mg-m^c.IX.—mg-s^o.[F.
VIII^1.16.89].—man.**15.**q.3.5.—
mel.—mrl.x.ff^a.q.; i^a.ff^a.V^1.βe.
naj.—na-m^c.b^a.δb.—na-s.**15.**—nic^c.
V^2–VI^3.au.[F.VII^1.].—nit^c.V^2.
12.—pet^c.V^2.—pho^c.ll^a.IX.—plb^{ta}.
[T^a.VI^3.].—rs-r.**15.**—rhs.**15.**—
sab^c.12.—sar.**15.**[Hc.].—so-t.—
spo.21.—squ^c.; ^{c}.βe^a.3.—sul^c.; ^{t}.;
3.—teu^f.12.——thu^{oc}.2.11.16.[H
dd^h.].—ton^o.[O.III.].3-3Q.; [V^1–

VI$^{3\cdot4}$.].au.ηl.5.; [P.V^{12}–VIII^4.].
6.(66).

—— *as if had a blow.*—pho^c.12.
ω^2.vx.19.(35).

—— *as after severe headache.*——
sil.

—— *as if lay on something hard.*
—lam^o.17.—pla.2.(30).

CONCOMITANTS.

au. *Ill-humour.*—nic^c.V^2–VI^3.[F.
VII^1.].—ton.ηl.5.6.[V^1–VI$^{3\cdot4}$.].

βa. *Vertigo.*—cly$^{f\cdot t}$.—hyp^t.κ^5.3-99.
4.

βe. *Confusion.*—mrl.i^a.ff^a.V^1.

βe^a. *Stupid feeling.*—squ^c.3.

δb. *Closing of eyes.*—na-m^c.b^a.

η. *Pain in face.*—hur.— ton.au.5.
6.[V^1–VI$^{3\cdot4}$.].

θ^4. *Sensitiveness of lower jaw.*——
irs^m.60.86.

κ^5. *Nausea.*—hyp^t.βa.3-99.4.

κ^7. *Eructation.*—iod.w^2.35.[F.V^3.].

σ^2. *Pain in nape.*—ipc^o.26.

vx. *Numbness of legs.*——pho^c.12.
ω^2.19.(35).

χ^1. *Rigor.*—cas^c.12.[T.VI^4.].

ω^2. *Weakness.*—iod.κ^7.35.[F.V^1.].
—pho^c.12.vx.19.(35).

CONDITIONS.

2. *At night.*—pla.(30).—thu^{oc}.11.
16.[Hdd^h.].

3. *In morning.*—man.q.5.15.—squ^c.
βe^a.—sul.

3-30. *On rising, morning.*——ton^o.
[O.III.].

3-99. *On waking in morning.*——
hyp^t.βa.κ^5.4.

4. *In afternoon.*—cle^f.——hyp^t.βa.
κ^5.3-99.

5. *In evening.*—bry.—man.q.**3.**15.

5. *In forenoon.*—ton.au.ηl.6.[V^1–
VI$^{3\cdot4}$.].

6. *In the room.*——ton.[P.V^{12}–
VIII^4.]. (66).; au. ηl. 5. [V^1–
VI$^{3\cdot4}$.].

11. *By touching.*——kre$^{f\cdot c}$.**15.**——
thu^{oc}.2.16.

12. *By pressure.*—cas^c.χ^1.[T.VI^4.].
—nit.—pho^c.12.vx.ω^2.19.(35).—
sab^c.—teu^f.

15. *By stroking head.*—rhs.
15. *By scratching.*——cap.v.V⁸.—cau.
15. *By combing hair.*—car.—kre^{f·c}.11.—man.q.3.5.—na-s.—rs-r.—sar.[Ht.].
16. *When lying on it.*—thu^{oc}.2.11.[H.dd^h.].
17. *By lying on side.*—lam°.
19. *When sitting.*—pho^c.12.vx.ω².(35).
21. *By moving scalp.*—ca-a.—spo.
26. *By moving head.*—gn-c.—ipc°.σ².
30. *By rising.*—pla.2.
35. *By motion.*—iod.κ⁷.ω².[F.V¹.].—pho^c.12.vx.ω².19.
41. *By mental exertion.*—frz.70.**70.**
60. *Ry chewing.*—irs^m.θ⁴.86.
66. *After eating.*——ton.[P.V¹²–VIII⁴.].6.
70. *By drinking beer.*—frz.41.**70.**
70. *By drinking coffee.*—frz.41.**70.**
83. *During menses.*—cas^c.
86. *By speaking.*—irs^m.θ⁴.60.

dd^b. **Sensitiveness to cold.**—am-c.—bor.

dd^c. **Sensitiveness to draught of air.**—aco.dd^h.—mit.p.

dd^h. **Sensitiveness to touch.**—aco.dd^c.—aga.—alo°.**15.**—alm^c.q.βe.4.; ^f.—amb.V¹³.σ².1.—am-c.v.; **15.**—aps^{f·c}.—ari^t.1.—ars^c.—aru^c.—asr.ff^a.—bad^f.k^h.βa.5.—ba-a.; ^{mb.}V⁶–VI³.28.—bel.—bov^c.V1³.; **15.**—bry^f.—buf^{f·tb·c}.——ca-a.v.—ca-c.; ^{eb.}v.ii.II⁷.—cn-i.—cap^m.ii.—cau^c.—cha^{tb}.ii.—chd^c.p.—chi.—ch-s.—cnb.—crt^c.I.—der.—hur^{pa}.—hyd°.—hfb.—ign.—k-hy^{fb·c}.q.2.3-30.—lah^{tb·pb}.60.88.; ^f.—lch.—la-v^c.—mgt^c.[C.V¹⁶.].—mt-s.V².—mag^c.V².5.83.84.——mg-m.V⁷.δ.66.——man°.VI⁴–VIII³.4.——mrl^{f·t}.η.mer.; ^{eb.}III²–VIII³.φ¹.—mez^t.p.hh.χ¹.3.[F.I.].; ^c.—msc.—nat^{oc}.—na-m.—ni-x.; aᶢ.5.—nit^c.—nx-m^t.—nx-v.—par.—pho^p.V⁶–VI⁴.2.—rho.—rhs^c.[C.VI⁴.].66.—rut.ii.VI³·⁴.; ^{ob.}v.(**15**).——sep.v.

V³·¹⁰.σ²ff.—sil.—spi.; ^f.βe.ℓ^b.[Hb.].;
21.—stp^c.[C.VI³.].—sul^c.; ^c.[C.V³.].—sum^{pb}.k^g.—ton.; ^{oa}.II⁷.; ^c.

CONCOMITANTS.

^aᶢ *Anxiety.*—ni-x.5.
βa. *Vertigo.*—bad^f.k^h.**6.**
βe. *Confusion.*—alm^c.q.4.—spi^f.βe^b.[Hb.].
βe^b. *Emptiness of head.*——spi^f.βe.[Hb.].
δ. *Pain in eyes.*—mg-m.V⁷.66.
η. *Pain in face.*—mrl^{f·t}.
σ²ff. *Stiff-neck.*—sep.v.V³·¹⁰.
σ². *Pain in neck.*—amb.V¹².1.
φ¹. *Sleeplessness.*—— mer^{eb}. III²–VIII³.
χ¹. *Rigor.*—mez^t.p.hh.3.[F.I.].

CONDITIONS.

1. *All day.*—amb.V¹².σ².—ari^t.
2. *At night.*—k-hy^{fb·c}.q.3-30.—pho^p.V⁶–VI⁴.
3. *In morning.*— mez^t.p.hh.χ¹.[F.I.].
3-30. *On rising, morning.*—k-hy^{fb·c}.q.2.
4. *In afternoon.*—alm^c.q.βe.—man°, VI⁴–VIII³.
5. *In evening.*— mag^c.V².83.84.—ni-x.aᶢ.
5. *In forenoon.*—bad^f.k^h.βa.
15. *By stroking head.*—am-c.
15. *By scratching.*—rut^{ob}.v.
15. *By combing hair.*—alo°.—bov.
21. *By moving scalp.*—spi.
28. *By turning head.*—ba-c^{mb}.V⁶–VI³.
60. *By chewing.*—lah^{tb·pb}.88.
66. *After food.*——mg-m.V⁷.δ.—rhs^c.[C.VI⁴.].
83. *During menses.*——mag^c.V².5.84.
84. *After menses.*—mag^c.V².5.83.
88. *By laughing.*—lah^{tb·pb}.60.

dd^i. **Sensitiveness to pressure of hat.**—crt.—hep^f.

ff. **Stiffness.**—hfb^{pa}.x.—jat^f.σ².—sum°.

CONCOMITANT.

σ². *Pain in nape.*—jat^f.

ff^a. **Rigidity, tension.**—agn.p.r.—alo.x.p.—aps^c.a$\flat$.—ar-c.**15.**—asr.dd^h.—bap.δr.—ba-a^t.ηb.—ba-c^f.66.—ber.x.ii^d.η.—bry^f.48.; dd.; f. IV^3–V^6.—c-ph^f.—cnu.i^a.—cn-i.—cb-a$^{f.c}$.—cb-v$^{f.t}$.δb.—cau^f.; p.$\delta.\zeta$.—dir.j.—dul.g^b.q.1.—equ^f.; ϕ^2.2. 46.—evo^f.f.—grt^f.c.—hur^f.—irs.—k-bi^t.—kis^{pb}.η.—lam^c.—lau^{oa}. IX.—lyp^f.V^3.—mrl.x.dd.q.; dd. V^1.i^a.$\beta\epsilon$.—mu-x^{pb}.—myr^c.r.—nat^o.—ni-x.—nx-m.—opi^f.(15).—pho^f. a$\mathfrak{g}$.—sbd.η.—so-l^f.V^3.—spi.e.—sul.g^b.—vi-o$^{f.o}$.; $^{f.t.o}$.$\epsilon.\zeta.\sigma^2$.; ^{o}.26.

—— *as if drawn up.*—hyp.

—— *as if closely attached to skull.*—arn.—mt-n.$\beta\epsilon$.—par$^{f.o}$.—sab^f.21.—sin.—trx^f.

—— *as if skin were too scanty.*—bov^f.q.V^1.

—— *as if cerebral membranes were stretched.*—par.δBii^d.

—— *with desire to wrinkle forehead.*—equ.

CONCOMITANTS.

a$\mathfrak{g}$. *Anxiety.*—pho^f.

a$\flat$. *Fear.*—aps^c.

$\beta\epsilon$. *Confusion.*—mt-n.——mrl.dd. V^1.i^a.

δb. *Closure of eyes.*—cb-v$^{f.t}$.

δ. *Pain in eyes.*—bap.—cau^t.p $\wr$.

δBii^d. *As if skin round eyebrows were thickened.*—par.

e. *Pain in ears.*—vi-o$^{f.t.o}$.$\zeta.\eta.\sigma^2$.

ζ. *Pain in nose.*—cau^f.p.δ.—vi-o$^{f.t.o}$.$\epsilon.\eta.\sigma^2$.

ηb. *Coldness of face.*—ba-a^t.

ηii^d. *Face feels swollen.*—ber.x.ii^d.

η. *Pain in face.*—kis^{pb}.—sbd.—.vi-o$^{f.t.o}$.$\epsilon.\zeta.\sigma^2$.

σ^2. *Pain in nape.*—vi-o$^{f.t.o}$.$\epsilon.\zeta.\eta$.

ϕ^2. *Confused dreams.*—equ.2.46.

CONDITIONS.

1. *All day.*—dul.g^b.q.
2. *At night.*—equ.ϕ^2.46.
15. *By stroking with hand.*—ar-c.—opi^f.
21. *On moving scalp.*—sab^f.
26. *On moving head back and forward.*—vi-o^o.

46. *By opening eyes.*—equ.ϕ^2.2.
48. *By moving eyes.*—bry.
66. *After food.*—ba-c^f.

gg. **Suppuration.**—pau^o.v.

hh. **Moisture.**—sep.

hh. **Sweat.**—bad.j.v.k^h.

ii. **Swelling.**—ca-c^{eb}.v.dd^h.II^7.—cap^m. dd^h.—cha^{tb}.dd^h.—gur.p.—k-ca^{fd} —ph-x.V^2.11.IX.—rut.dd^b.VI$^{3.4}$.

—— *in periosteum.*—bz-x^e.—cb-a^{ea}. VI^3.5.

—— *of glands.*—dig^e.—ni-x^e. VI$^{3.4}$.5.

CONDITIONS.

5. *In evening.*—cb-a^{ea}.VI^3.—ni-x^e. VI$^{3.4}$.
11. *When touched.*—ph-x.V^2.IX.

ii^a. **Hard swelling.**—tab^{eb}.aa.VI^3.

ii^d. **Sensation of swelling.**—aco.x.—ber.x.ff^a.ηii^d.—cch^{eb}.5.—lah^m.12.—nx-m^{pb}.VI^2.q.$\beta\epsilon.\eta$ii^d.—rap.I.

—— *thick-skin feeling.*—am-g^o.

CONCOMITANTS.

$\beta\epsilon$. *Confusion.*—nx-m^{pb}.VI^3.q.ηii^d.

ηii^d. *Swollen feeling of face.*—ber.x.ff^a.ii^d.—nx-m^{pb}.VI^3.q.$\beta\epsilon$.

CONDITIONS.

5. *In evening.*—cch^{eb}.
12. *By pressure.*—lah^m.

kk. **Trembling.**—mer.e.r.[Hb].

ll. **Twitching.**—aga^{fa}.; ^{ta}.; ll^a.—chd^{fa}.—crt^{tm}.—k-ca^{tma}.—lyc.—sar^{oa}.

—— *in muscles.*—arg$^{f.ta.o}$.σ^2ll.

CONCOMITANT.

σ^2ll. *Twitching of neck muscles.*—arg$^{f.ta.o}$.

ll^a. **Jerking.**—aga.ll.—ang^{pb}.V^2.12.—opi^{tm}.—pho^c.dd.IX.—rat^{ta}.

CONDITION.

12. *On pressure.*—ang^{pb}.V^2.

ll^b. **Quivering.**—cas^o.—cau^{ta}.—opi$^{f.c}$.V^6.

mm. **Ulcers.**—bel.—grp^e.

—— *small.*—rut$^{pb.o}$.v.II^6.

—— *eroding.*—ars.

pp. **Lice.**—mgt.k^l.

qq. **Peculiar sensations.**

—— *as if eyebrow were depressed.*—can.

—— *skin wrinkled.*—cha^f.
—— *action of occipito-frontalis heard and felt, like a cap on O.*—rs-r.
—— *as if scalp were loose.*—san^{pa}.; ^{P}.V^6.**50**.
—— *as if hollow.*—sep^o.II^7.2.(12).
—— *as if a drop of water ran down.*—ver^t.

CONDITIONS.

2. *At night.*—sep^o.II^7.(12).
12. *By pressure.*—sep^o.II^7.2.
50. *On looking up.*—san^P.V^6.

PAINS.

I. **Pain undefined.**—cas^e.—for.$\sigma.\sigma^2$. r.**110**.—lah.—nit$^{fa\cdot t\cdot c\cdot o}$.20.26.28. 31.89.(12).
—— *making him bend double.*— lyc^e.

II^1. **Burning.**—alm^{ta}.**15**.VI^4.—ars.; ^{c}.—cob.**15**.v.ηv.—con^{fca}.dd.—grt^e. —k-bi^f.v.[B.VII^1].—lah.**15**.d.— lyc^{oc}.—men^{fa}.—mer^{fb}.(11).; v.; ^{fb}. —mu-x^t.—ol-a.v-II^1.(**15**).—par. **15**.v.—ph-x^{pa}.; ^{fb}.—pho.p.κ^1. phy^{tb}.[T.I].—rho.**15**.v.5.—rhs^f.g. —sbd.; v.βe.; ^{f}.g^b.—spi^{tb}.; ^{ta}.— spo^{pa}.—sul^o.**15**.16.; ^{f}.; ^{f}.v.5.; ^{t}.**5**.— tab.g^b.e.$\kappa^1.\chi^1$.—vi-t^{ta}.; ^{f}.

II^3. **Raw.**—ana^e.—arg.12.—ars.11. —bry^o.11.—cad^e.s.—dph^t.θ^1.11. —dro^{fa}.; ^{fcb}.; ^{tb}.—elp^o.—grp^f.11.— men^{tb}.11.—msc.11.—nx-v.106.— pet.**15**.v.—ph-x.IX.11.—rn-b^f.4.— zin.; ^{pa}.
—— *as if hair were drawn up-wards.*—col^c.
—— *as if burnt.*—bel.

II^4. **Scraping.**—par^f.e.$\beta e.\delta.\delta$Lp,aa.
II^5. **Smarting.**—alm.**15**.v.—ag-n^o.v. —at-a^{pb}.—bor.$\kappa^5.\omega^8$.3.—c-ph.— cr-s^c.**15**.—cep.—crn^c.VIII^4.— c-ar^{ta}.12.—er-a.12.—ep-p.—fer. [F.V^{10}].—glo^f.—grp.—gym^{tb}.— iod^{oa}.—k-bi^c.[H]—k-ca.**15**.v.— la-x^f.11.—lyc^f.11.—mg-m^c.11.; 11. 29.—mit^c.11.—msc.11.—myr. oln.**15**.v.II^6.—pod^f.[F.q.V^7].— rn-s.; [O.V^7].—san.11.—sep.11.

—— *sil*.v.**15**.—so-n.**15**.—spi^{fb}.—sul. 11.; ^{c}.11.
—— *transient.*—lau^c.
—— *like touching a pustule.*—as-t^{ob}.
—— *like an ulcer healing.*—nx-v. v.σ^2.**5**.
—— *as from a sinapism.*—trn^o.σ^2.
—— *like a wound.*—tep^o.βa.
—— *as from a blow.*—cic^{eb}.

II^6. **Stinging, biting.**—ph-x^b.v.— rs-r^{fb}.—sec.
—— *as from lice.*—mez.5.(**15**).— oln.v.1.; II^5.**15**.; v.2.—rho. —rut^{pb}.v.; ob.v.(**15**).
—— *as from vermin.*—wis.[Hϵ.].

II^7. **Ulcerative.**—aga.dd.—alo^c.5. 11. ; ^{o}.—am-c^o.12.35.—ca-c^{eb}.v. dd^b.ii.—cb-a^{pb}.—k-hy.**15**.—kre^{fa}. —mag^{ob}.[F.q].; 5.12.—mer.11.— mu-x$^{f\cdot t}$.—spi^c.11.VIII^3.—su-x.11. —ton^{oa}.dd^b.—zin^c.5.11.
—— *as if gathering.*—epn.—iod^f. —ni-x.11.—pet.p.11.; ^{pb}. —rho^c.11.—rhs.11.—sep^o. 11.[O.V^6].; ^{o}.qq.2.(12).— stn.—sul^{pb}.11.—zin^P.

III. **Compressive.**—na-m^t.—stp^o.
III^1. **Contractive.**—ars^t.—bel^f.δ.— cb-v.; ^{c}.; 5.66.—car$^{c\cdot o}$.g^b.—cph^f. —chi^{ob}.; ^{c}.—frz^f.
—— *as if skin were drawn to-gether.*—chi^{ob}.
—— *like a band drawn across.*-mil.

III^3. **Squeezing.**—bel^{fc}.η.θ^4.
IV^1. **Cramp-like.**—aga^{tb}.—bel.[Ha]. —coc^{tb}.—pso^{ta}.
IV^2. **Griping.**
—— *as if skin were grasped.*—chi^c.
IV^3. **Spasmodic.**—pho^{pb}.b.
V^1. **Aching.**—ana^{fb}.—arn^c.—aur^f.; ^{tb}.11.—bov^f.q.ff^a.—cam^{fa}.—chd. con^f.—eub^{fb}.δe,$\flat$.—eup^c.βe. ; ^{f}. grt^f.—hep^{oa}.σ^2.r.—jat^f.—led^t.11. —mt-n^{tb}.; ^{fa}.—mrl.i^a.dd.ff^a.βe.— opi.—ph-x^{ta}.—pho.η.σ^2.—plb^f. spo^{fa}.—sul^c.—zng.(11).
—— *violent.*—ph-x.2.12.16.99.
—— *sharp.*—k-ca^t.—oln^{ob}.—spo^t.
—— *on a small spot.*—con.
—— *as from lying on something hard.*—ph-x^o.(**15**).

—— *as from a tight hat.*—alm^{f.o}.
—— *as if pimples were beneath skin.*—pho.

V². **Bruised.**—alo^c.(12).—ang^{pb}.12. ll^a.—ars.11.—bov^c.11.eCr.3.; ^c.11. —cb-a^f.—cauc.11.—dig^{oc}.—eub^{ob}. 12.—gym^{pb}.—hel^{c.o}.χ¹.VIII³.29. 33.35.(12).—ign^{f.t}.11.V⁶.—mt-s. dd^h.—mag^c.12.VI⁴–VIII³.; ^c.dd^h. 5.83.84.—nat.—nic^c.dd.VI³.au. [F.VII¹].—ni-x^{pa}.—nit^c.dd.; ^t.— nx-v.[Hdd^h].; ^c.11.—pet.; ^c.dd. ph-x^o.; 11.ii.IX.—rat^{pa}.[P^c.VI³]. —rho^{oa.ε}.—sil^c.—tab^P.
—— *here and there.*—rat.
—— *as from a fall.*—rut^{t.o}.
—— *as from a blow.*—spi^o.

V³. **Boring.**—so-l^f.ff^a.
—— *obtuse.*—dro.
—— *as with a bodkin.*—alm^{pb}.

V⁶. **Drawing.**—ac-l.21.—alo.—am-c^f. 3-99.(30).—cac^o.(22).—cb-a^f.— cb-v.; ^{oa}.—chi^{oa}.—col.—con^f.— grt^{fd}.—hel^f.c.—ign^{f.t}.V².11.—ind. —k-bi^{tb}.—lyc^{pa}.σ².—na-m.η.θ¹.— ni-x^{tm}.—nx-v.—opi^{f.c}.ll^b.—pul.15. —san^P.qq.50.—sep^{f.o}.—so-t.15.— stp^{oc}.26.—su-x^{tb}.—thu^{tm}.60.—zin^c.
—— *transient.*—car.—lah^t.
—— *intermittent.*—par^{oa}.
—— *here and there.*—mg-m.βε.e. η.θ¹.(90).—pla.—stp.11.
—— *downwards.*—hel^o.
—— *upwards.*—sbd^f.w.[C.V¹].
—— *from behind forwards.*—cch.

V⁷. **Dull.**—cic^f.20.—cin^{f.t}.19.—ptv. [O^b.V¹].—ph-x.
—— *as from a debauch over night.* —led^f.

V⁸. **Gnawing.**—bel^{fc}.—cth^{ta}.—cap. v.dd.15.—lyc.—men^c.—rn-s^c.— spo^c.
—— *here and there.*—agn,
—— *like a mouse.*—zin^{oc}.

V¹⁰. **Pressing.**—cle.p.
—— *sharp.*—con.
—— *inwards.*—spi^{fcb}.
—— *as with finger.*—stp^{tb}.

V¹¹. **Rheumatic.**—ac-l.11.—bz-x.
V¹³. **Sprained.**—amb.dd^h.σ².1.

VI¹. **Cutting.**—lyc^c.; b.107.—ter^{tb} v.5-10.(15).
—— *as if it would cut through skin.*—mag^{fb}.

VI². **Prickling.**—aga^o.σ.—am-g.v.— aps^f.—ard^f.—asr^{tb}.v.—ch-s^f.βε.— crt^c.—cyc.βε^b.η.—eup^{tb}.—lep^t.v.1. —mag.66.—vrn^f.
—— *across.*—spo^{fb}.
—— *as from electricity.*—nx-m^{pb}. q.ii^d.βε.ηii^d.
—— *as with needles.*—ang^{ta}.— ar-c^{fa}.—aur^f.—cld^f.—ir-f^{tma}. 4.—man^{oa}.σ².3-10.28.— na-m^f.—pru^o.
—— *rather agreeable.*—ep-p.

VI³. **Shooting.**—aco.; ^{tma}.—ant.— ard.—aur^f.—bov^c.dd^h.—ca-a^c.— cep^{fb}.e.θ^{1.4}.5.—chi^{pb}.—cyc.v.(15). —dig^{fb}.; ^o.—eup^{fa}.—gui^{ob}.—hel^f. 3.—ind^c.; ^{ta.pa}.b.—k-ca.; ηii.θ¹.σ². —nab^o.σ²ff.5.28.—na-m^{oc.ma}.— nic.ε.—ph-x^c.11.—rn-b^{tb}.εl.[O^b. VI⁴].—sbd^{fcb}.; ^t.; ^{tb}.—spo^{f.tb}.— stn^{fcb}.; ^f.; ^c.—trx^{fb}.—thu^{tb}.— ton^{oa}.v.(15).
—— *transient.*—lah^{pa}.
—— *outwards.*—mag^{fa}.v.
—— *here and there.*—ba-a.
—— *as with a knife.*—am-g.

VI⁴. **Tearing.**—aga^o.—alm^{ta}.; ^{ta}. II¹.15.—ang^{t.c}.—ag-m^{tb}.—bel^f.— cb-a.—cb-v^{tb}.—gui^{tb}.—k-bi^{oa}.rl.— lah.—lyc^{fa}.—mt-s^c.g^b.—mrl^{tb}.— mer.; ^f.—pho^{pa}.IX.19.—rhs.— sep^f.δ.4.5.—so-t^c.12.—stp.θ¹.— trx^o.31.—ton^{fa}.; ^{c.pa}.
—— *transient.*—lyc.8-31.
—— *fine.*—cch.
—— *like catarrh.*—grp.3.

VII⁵. **Tensive.**—crt^f.σ².—kis.43.— stp^{ob}.σ².φ¹.2.
—— *dull.*—cro^{fcb}.
—— *as if skin were drawn to vertex.*—sto.

VIII³. **Jerking** ——hel^{c.o}.29.33.35. (12).V².χ¹.—spi^c.II⁷.11.
VIII³. **Throbbing.**—gui.[T.VI³.].— 18.19.(12.31).—hel^{f.t}.ηp.—k-ca^{pb}. 12.—sul.

IX. Peculiar.
—— *electric shocks.*—arn°.
—— *as if hairs were drawn out.* —arn°.—ind.—kre^f.—lau^ea. ff^a.—lyc.e.—sul^c.5.[Hb.]. —tep°.e.
—— *as if hair had been pulled.*— bel.—cap.v.V^8.dd.15.
—— *as if a hair was pulled.*—lyc^pb. —pho^pa.VI^4.19.
—— *as if hair was pulled.*—ind^c. — mag^c.4.—mg-m^c.dd.— mg-s^c.p.—nit^c.—ph-x.II^3. 11.; ii.V^2.11.—pho^c.dd.ll^a. —rhs.e.
—— *as if skin were loose.*—ca-c. σ^2.
—— *bed feels too hard.*—sul.
—— *as from ecchymosis.*——fer. [Hdd.].—pho^c.
—— *neuralgic.*—hyd^f.
—— *sharp, thread-like pains.*— fag.
—— *as if a foreign body were sticking there.*—tep°.

COMPLEX PAINS.

II^{1·2}. **Burning, corrosive.**—sbd^c.
II^{1·3}. **Burning, raw.**—dro^pa.(11).
II^{1·5}. **Burning, smarting.**—au-s.— col.—dro^c.—la-x^c.ω^2.3-30.
—— *as from nettles.*—pæo.π.πυ.
II^1–III–V^7. **Burning, compressive, stupefying.**—rut.
II^1–III^1. **Burning, contractive.**— oln°.
II^1–V^1. **Burning, aching.**—mu-x^fb. —teu^f.—thu^ea.
II^1–V^1–VII^5. **Burning, aching, tensive.**—teu^fc.
II^1–V^3. **Burning, digging.**—mrl.
II^1–VI^1. **Burning, cutting.**—clo^fb. 23.
II^1–VI^2. **Burning, pricking.**—stp^c. —vrb^tb.
II^1–VI^3. **Burning, shooting.**—aps. —asa^fc.(11).—bel^fcb.—men^f.ηp.— ph-x.—stn^c.
II^1–VI^3. **Burning, stitches.**
—— *as if a hair was drawn out.* —ind.

II^1–VI^{3·4}. **Burning, shooting, tearing.**—lyc^ta.v.15.
II^1–VI^4. **Burning, tearing.**—cau^c. —cup° 29.
II^1–VII^5. **Burning, tensive.**—stn^fa.
II^1–VIII^3. **Burning, jerking.**—— mn-o^f.p.
II^1–VIII^4. **Burning, throbbing.**— nit^ob.5-10.
II^{2·5·6}. **Corrosive, smarting, biting.** —thu^pa.5.
II^{2·5}–VI^3. **Corrosive, smarting, shooting.**—aga.
II^{2·6}. **Corrosive, biting.**—thu°.g^a.
II^{3·6}. **Raw, biting.**—stp°.v.5.
II^{3·7}. **Raw, ulcerative.**—ca-a°.11.
II^3–VI^4. **Raw, tearing.**—cas^t.χ^1.5. 11.
II^{5·6}. **Smarting, stinging.**—lyc^ea.
II^5–V^1. **Smarting, aching.**—alo°.
II^5–V^8. **Smarting, gnawing.**–bry.2.
II^6–VI^3. **Biting, shooting.**—ver.v.
II^7–V^6–VI^4. **Ulcerative, drawing, tearing.**—aga^c.2.12.
II^7–VI^2. **Ulcerative, pricking.**— hep^f.3.11.
III–V^1. **Compressive aching.**—— thu^fcb.δb.
III^1–IV^1. **Contractive, cramp-like.** —grp.b.
III^1–IV^3. **Contractive, spasmodic.** —pho^c.4.5.
III^2–IV^2. **Pinching, clawing.**—— alm°.r.29.
III^2–VI^3. **Pinching, stitch.**—chd^ob.
III^2–VIII^3. **Pinching, jerking.**—— mer.dd^h.φ^1.
IV^1–VIII^3. **Cramp-like, jerking.**— hep^f.4.16.(30).
IV^3–V^6. **Spasmodic drawing.**–bry°. ff^a.
V^{1·6}. **Aching, drawing.**——ca-a^ta.θ^1. 5.(12).
V^{1·6·v}. **Aching, drawing upwards.** —rhs^pb.
V^{1·7}. **Aching, stupefying.**—vrb^f.
V^{1·8}. **Aching, gnawing.**——dro^c.; ^f. —hyo.11.35.—ph-x^f.
V^{1·10}. **Aching, pressing.**—sul^f.3-99. (30).
V^1–VI^1. **Aching, cutting.**—sar.

V¹–VI³. **Aching, shooting.**—chi^fcb.
βa.κ⁵.; ^fca.11.—dig^fb.—eub^t.—spi^ob.
—— *as from sharp instrument.*—
par^fca.

V¹–VI⁴. **Aching, tearing.**—bis^ta.12.
—cyc.—lyc^oa.—sar.31.35.

V¹–VIII⁴. **Aching, throbbing.**——
cas^ob.

V³·⁶. **Boring, drawing.**—sep.e.θ¹.2.
(30).

V³–VIII⁴. **Boring, throbbing.**——
pho^pa.19.

V³·¹⁰. **Digging, pressing.**——sep.v.
dd^h.σ²ff.

V⁶·¹¹. **Drawing, rheumatic.**—sep^pb.

V⁶–VI³. **Drawing stitches.**—ba-a^mb.
dd^h.23.—cic^f.—ni-x.—rn-s^c.—rut^c.

V⁶–VI⁴. **Drawing, tearing.**—k-bi^ta.
—pho^p.dd^h.2.—sul.

V⁶–VI⁴–VIII³. **Drawing, tearing,
jerking.**—stn^fb.

V⁶–VII⁵. **Drawing, tension.**—aps^f.
—lah^pa.2.

—— *as from a blow.*—rut^p.

V⁶–VIII⁴. **Drawing, throbbing.**—
cth^ta.

V⁷–VI³. **Stupefying, stitch.**—par^fb.

V¹⁰·ˢ–VI³. **Pressing outwards, shooting.**—stp^ta.11.

VI²·³. **Prickling, shooting.**—sbd^f.
33.101.

VI³·⁴. **Shooting, tearing.**—chp.——
dig^tb.— eup^ob.4.—lyc.—men^fa.—
mu-x^ta.(11.96).—rut.dd^h.ii.—sbd^fb.
—vi-t^tb.—zin^f.; ^fb.

VI³–VIII³. **Shooting jerks.**—cch.η.
φ¹.2.—vrb^t.

VI³–VIII⁴. **Shooting, pulsation.**—
ant^tb·f.—sar^f.

VI⁴–VIII³. **Tearing, jerking.**——
mag^c.V².12.—man^o.dαʰ.4.

VII³–VIII³. **Stretching, jerking.**—
bry^ta.

VARIOUS PAINS IN VARIOUS PARTS.

**Shooting in Sᶠ., boring stitch in Sᵗ.,
tearing shoots in Sᶠ. and Sᵗ.**—col.
(11).

**Shooting in Sᵖᵃ. and bruised feeling
in Sᶦᵃ.**—nic.

ANATOMICAL REGIONS.

Sᶠ. **Forehead.**—aco.k¹.; k¹.v.η.σ².—
ac-s.k¹.v.—æsc.e.——aga.v.k¹.——
alm^t.g.; dd^h.; °.V¹.; k¹.ι.; cc.η.; k^r.v.
ζr.θl.; k¹.ηl.—amb.k¹.; kⁿ.II³.11.—
am-c.V⁶.3-99.(30).——angᵗ.v-VI³.
—ant^tb.VI³–VIII⁴.; kⁿ.v.—aps.
V⁶–VII⁵.; ^c.dd^h.; VI².; kˢ.—arg.v-
V⁸.—arn.g^b.; k^m.—ard.v.; VI².; g^b.
—aur.V¹.; VI³.—au-m.v.—bad.k^h.
dd^h.βa.5.—ba-c.ff^a.66.; k^d.—bel.
VI⁴.; III¹.δ.; v-II⁴.—bz-x.g^b.—
bov.q.ff^a.V¹.—bry.dd^h.; ff^a.48.; ff^a.
IV³–V⁶.—buf^tb·c.dd^h.——bu-s.k¹.—
cld.VI².—ca-c.k¹.; k^d.—c-ph.ff^a.;
k¹.—cn-i.ff^a.——cth.v.(15).——cb-a.
V².; ^c.ff^a.; V⁶.; k^d.—cb-v^t.ff^a.δb.;
k¹.; k¹.dd^h.——cph.III¹.——cau.v.
—cha.v-V⁸.; qq.—chd.v.; V¹.—
chi.g^a.——ch-s.VI².βe.; ^f.c.mb.v.ηv.
19.——cic.V⁷.20.; g.; V⁶–VI³.—
cinᵗ.V⁷.19.—cle.v.; dd.4.; k¹.—cch.
g^a.—cly^t.dd.βa.—con.V¹.; V⁶.; k¹.
dd^h.—cvl.k^q.——crt.VII⁵.σ².—cyc.
e.; kⁿ.—dro.v-V⁸.(15).; V¹·⁸.—equ.
ff^a.; ff^a.φ².2.46.——eup.V¹.—evo.f.
ff^a.—fer.II⁵.——frz.III¹.—gel.e.—
glo.II⁵.—grp.e.; II³.11.—grt.V¹.;
e.ff^a.; v.—hel.e.V⁶.; VI³.3.; e.; ^t.
VIII⁴.ηp.; kˢ.V².—hep.II⁷–VI².3.
11.; IV¹–VIII³.4.16.(30).; dd^c.;
k¹.6.(8).; kˢ.—hur.e.; v.; ff^a.; k¹.
hyd.IX.—ignᵗ.V⁶.V².11.—iod.II⁷.
—ipc.k^h.η.—jac.v.—jat.ff.σ².; V¹.;
I.ηr.—k-bi.v.II¹.—k-ca.g^b.; k^p.—
kre.IX.; ^c.dd.11.15.——lah.dd^h.—
la-x.II⁵.11.——lau.ff^a.ηl.v.(15).; v.
4.; g.(15).—led.V⁷.; g^a.v.; k^d·ᶦ.; k¹.
π.k^h·ⁿ.v.II⁵.; k^b.—lil^t·pb.dd.—lo-c.
k^r.dd^h.[F.VI³].—lyc.II⁵.11.; ^c.I.e.
η.θ⁴.5.(4).; kˢ.——mt-s.j.——mn-o.
II¹–VIII³.p.—men.II¹–VI³.ηp.—
mrl^t.dd^h.η.—mer.v-II¹.; VI⁴.—msc.
kⁿ.[F.V¹].—mu-x^t.II⁷.; ^t.k^m.k¹·o.—
naj.k¹.—nat.k^m.II¹·³.—na-m.VI².;
v.3.; kˢ.σ².II¹.11.—nx-v.g^a.; ^c.g^a.;
kˢ.—opi.ff^a.(12).—par^o.ff^a.; e.II⁴.
βe.δ.δLp.aa.—ped.v.; ^t.k^r.η.θ.; k¹.
ph-x.V¹·⁸.; v-II⁶.—pho.αg.; kˢ.[Fᵉ.
Iᵃ].—plb.V¹.—pod.II⁵.[F.q.V⁷].—

pso.k^l.—rn-b.II^3.4.—rn-r.g^a.5-**10**.
(30).—rhe.e. ; k^j.v.r.—rho.k^m.—
rs-r.v.8-31.—rhs.g.ζ.19.(29).; g.
II^1.; v.II^2.$\eta.\theta$.k^j.—rut.s.—sbd.
V$^{6 \cdot v}$.w.[C.V^1].; g^b.II^1.; VI$^{2 \cdot 3}$.33.
101.; ff^a.21.—sam.v.(**15**).—sar.
VI^3–VIII^4.—sep^o.V^6.; VI^4.δ.4.5.;
k^l.cc.—so-l.ff^a.V^3.—spi.g^a.v.(**15**).;
dd^h.$\beta e, e^b$.[Hb].—spot.VI^3.—squ-v-
II^2.(**15**).—stn.VI^3.—stp.k^l.v.VI^2.;
k^l.$\eta.\theta$.v.VI^3.II^7.11.; k^l.$\eta.\theta.r^l$.v.V^6.
(**15**).—sul.v.; II^1.; v.II^1.5.; V$^{1 \cdot 10}$.
3-99.(30).; k^l.v.VI^3.**15**.; k^l.r.; k^t.
—trn.k^r.[F.I].—trx.ff^a.—tep.k^l.
g^b.—teu.II^1–V^1.; dd.12.—ver.v.—
ve-v.e.[F^g.V^6].—vrn.VI^2.—vrb.
V$^{1 \cdot 7}$.—vi-o^o.ff^a.; $^{t \cdot o}$.ff^a.e.$\zeta.\eta.\sigma^2$.—
vi-t.II^1.—zin.VI$^{3 \cdot 4}$.

S^{fa}. **Right side of forehead.**—aga.ll.
—ar-c.VI^2.—bro^{ob}.v.—bry.v-VI^2.
—cam.V^1.—chd.ll.—dro.II^3.—
eup.VI^3.—kre.II^7.—lah.g^b.[B.
VII^1].—lyc.VI^4.—mt-n.V^1.—
mag.v.VI$^{3 \cdot 8}$.—men.VI$^{3 \cdot 4}$.; II^1.—
nit$^{t \cdot c \cdot o}$.20.26.28.31.89.(12).—spo.
V^1.—stn.II^1–VII^5.—ton.VI^4.

S^{fb}. **Left side of forehead.**—ana.V^1.
—aur.k^d.—bro.v.—cep.VI^3.$e.\theta^{1 \cdot 4}$.
5.—cle.II^1–VI^1.23.—dig.V^1–VI^3.;
VI^3.—eub.V^1.$\delta e, b$.—hel.k^l.V^2.11.
—jat^t.V^1.—k-hy^c.dd^h.q.2.3-30.—
lil$^{tb \cdot pb}$.dd.—mag.VI^1.—mer.II^1.
(11).: II^1.—mu-x.II^1–V^1.—par.
V^7–VI^3.—ph-x.II^1.—rs-r.II^6.—
sbd.VI$^{3 \cdot 4}$.—spi.II^5.—spo.VI$^{2 \cdot w}$.—
stn.V^6–VI^4–VIII^3.—sul.k^l.—trx.
VI^3.—zin.VI$^{3 \cdot 4}$.

S^{fc}. **Frontal eminences.**—asa.II^1-VI^3.
(11).—bel.V^8.; III^3.$\eta.\theta^4$.—chd.g^b.
(**15**).; v.—mor.I.[P^c.I].—rut^{fd}.k^g.
—sul.k^r.—teu.II^1–V^1–VII^5.

S^{fca}. **Right frontal eminence.**—chi.
V^1–VI^3.11.—con.dd.II^1.—lau.v.
—par.V^1–VI^3.

S^{fcb}. **Left frontal eminence.**—bel.
II^1–VI^3.—chi.V^1.VI^3.$\beta a.\kappa^5$.—cro.
VII^5.; v.—dro.II^3.—grt.V^6.—
k-ca.k^m.dd^h.—sbd.VI^3.—spi.V$^{10 \cdot t}$.
—stn.VI^3.—thu.III–V^1.δb.

S^{fd}. **Glabella.**—ars.k$^{l \cdot k \cdot m}$.—cun.k^m.
(117).—k-ca.ii.—rut^{fc}.k^g.—sel.ii.

S^{fe}. **Above eyebrows.**—ant.k^l.dd^h.—
na-m$^{t \cdot o}$.k.v.

S^{fea}. **Above r. eyebrow.**—eub.k^m.v.

S^{feb}. **Above l. eyebrow.**—ca-a.k^m.

S^t. **Temples.**—aco.g.; k^r.—alm^f.g.—
ang^c.VI^4.; ^{f}.v–VI^3.—ari.dd^h.1.-ba-a.
ff^a.ηb.—bel.k^d.—can.v.—cb-v.k^l.—
cas.II^8-VI^4.χ^1.5.11.—chd.v.—col.
V^3-VI^3.(11).—cly^f.dd.βa.—dph.II^3.
θ^1.11.-eub.V^1–VI^3.—hel^f.VIII^4.ηp.
—hyp.dd.$\beta a.\kappa^5$.8-99.4.—ign^f.V^6.
V^2.11.—k-bi.ff^a.—k-ca.V^1.—led.
II^5.11.—lep.v.VI^2.1.—mrl^f.dd^h.η.
—mez.dd^h.p.hh.χ^1.3.[F.I].—
mu-x^f.II^7.; II^1.; ^{f}.k^m.—na-m.III.;
$^{fc \cdot o}$.k.v.; cc.—nit$^{fa \cdot c \cdot o}$.20.26.28.31.
89.(12).—nx-m.dd^h.—rn-s.k^l.—
rhe.g^b.—rho.b.g^b.—rut^o.V^2.—sbd.
VI^3.—spo.V^1.—sul.dd.; g^b.; II^1.5.
—thu.k^g.—ver.qq.—vrb.VI^3–
VIII^3.—zin.k^k.v.

Sta. **Right temple.**—aga.ll.-alm.VI^4.;
VI^4.II^1.15.—ang.VI$^{2 \cdot d}$.—bis.V^1-
VI^4.12.—bry.VII^3–VIII^3.—ca-a.
V$^{1 \cdot 6}$.θ^1.5.(12).—ca-c.k^d.3.(5).—
cth.V^8.; V^6–VIII^4.—cau.ll^b.—
c-ar.II^5.12.—ind^{pa}.b.VI^3.—k-bi.
V^6–VI^4.—k-ca.ll.—lyc.II^1–VI$^{3 \cdot 4}$.
v.15.— man.VI^3.βb.—mu-x.VI$^{3 \cdot 4}$.
(11.96).—ph-x.V^1.—pla.g^b.$\theta^4.\chi^1$.
—plb.dd.[T^a.VI^3].—pso.IV^3.—
rat.ll^a.; v.—spi.II^1.—stp.V$^{10 \cdot s}$.
VI^3.11.—sul.k^o.— -trx.; k^l.II^7.11.
—vi-t.II^1.

— *from r. to l. temple.*—lah.
V$^{6 \cdot b}$.

S^{tb}. **Left temple.**—aga.IV^1.—ana.k^l.
—ant^f.VI^3–VIII^4.—arg.k^l.II^7.11.
—ag-m.VI^4.—ars.k$^{k \cdot l}$.II^3.15.—
asr.v.VI^2.—aur.V^1.11.—buf$^{f \cdot c}$.
dd^h.—ca-c.k^d.—cb-v.VI^4.—cha.
dd^h.ii.—dig.VI$^{3 \cdot 4}$.—dro.II^3.—
equ^f.ff^a.3.—eup.VI^2.—gui.VI^4.—
gym.II^5.— k-bi.V^6.—lah^{pb}.dd^h.60.
88.—lil$^{fb \cdot pb}$.dd.—mt-n.V^1.—men.
II^3.11.—mrl.VI^4.—mu-x.k^d.—
ped.v.—phy.II^1.[T.I].—rn-b.VI^3.
el.[O^b.VI^4].—sbd.VI^3.—spi.II^1.
—spo^f.VI^3.—stp.V^{10}.—sul.k^d.—
su-x.V^6.—tab.g^b.—ter-v-VI^1.5-**10**.

(15).—thu.VI³.—vrb.II¹–VI³.—
vi-t.VI³·⁴.

Sᵗᵐ. **Temporal muscles.**—crt.ll.—
opi.llᵃ.—ni-x.V⁶.—thu.V⁶.60.

Sᵗᵐˢ. **Right temporal muscle.**—aco.
VI³.—ir-f.VI³.4.—k-ca.ll.

Sᶜ. **Crown.**—aco.v.11.—aga.II⁷–V⁶-
VI⁴.2.12.—alo.II⁷.5.11.; V².(12).
—alm.ddʰ.p.βε.4.—angᵗ.VI⁴.—
aps.ffᵃ.αꜰ.; ꜰ.ddʰ.—arn.gᵇ.; V¹.—
ars.II¹ ʰ.; ddʰ.—aru.ddʰ.—aur.kᵈ.
V³.11.-bov.V².11.εCr.3.; ddʰ.VI³.;
V².11.—buff·ᵗᵇ.ddʰ.—ca-a.VI³.—
ca-c.kᵖ.—c-pb.b.gᵃ.p.[H.II⁵].—
cn-i.gᵃ.—cb-a.dd.; ꜰ.ffᵃ.—cb-v.III¹.
—ca-x.kᵐ.—cr-s.II⁵.15.—carᵒ.gᵇ.
III¹.—cas.dd.83.; dd.χ¹.—cau.V².
11.; ddʰ.; II¹–VI⁴.g.—chd.ddʰ.p.
—chi.IV².; III¹.—ch-s.ꜰ·ᵐᵇ·v.ηv.
19.; ᵒᵇ.v.—col.II³.—crn.II⁵-VIII⁴.
—crt.VI².—cup.gᵇ.; gᵇ.xᵃ.V¹⁰·ᵘ.—
cu-s.gᵃ.xᵃ.a¹ᴅ.—dro.II¹·⁵.; V¹·⁵.—
eup.V¹.βε.—ga-x.k¹.—grp.kᵏ.ddʰ.
—helᵒ.V².χ.VIII³.29.33.35.(12).
—hfb.v.—hydᵒ.e.—hyo.gᵇ.—hyp.gᵇ.
—ind.VI³.; V⁶.; II–IV³.5.19.—k-bi.
II⁵.[Hᵇ.].—k-hyᶠᵇ.ddʰ.q.2.3-30.
— klm.r.αꜰ.εᴅ.σ²ᵇ.5-10.—kreꜰ.dd.
11.15.—lah.dd.—la-v.ddʰ.—lam.
ffᵃ. —lau.II⁵·ᵇ.—lycꜰ.I.ε.η.θ⁴.5.(4).;
VI¹.—mgt.ddʰ.[C.V¹⁶].—mt-s.gᵇ.
VI⁴.—mag.VI⁴-VIII³.V².12.; ddʰ.
V².5.83.84.; IX.4.—mg-m.dd.IX.
II⁵.11.—mg-s.p.IX.—men.V⁸.—
mez.ddʰ.; ᵒ.v.—mit.II⁵.11.—mu-x.
v.—myr.v.ffᵃ.—na-m.e.; b.dd.δᵇ.—
nic.dd.V².VI³.αu.[F.VII¹].—nit.
dd.V².; IX.; e.3-30.; ddʰ.—nx-v.
V².11.; ꜰ.gᵃ.—oln.II¹–III¹.—pet.
dd.V².—ph-x.VI³.11.—pho.dd.llᵃ.
IX.; IX.; III–IV³.4.5.; dd.12.ω².
vx.19.(35).—pla.e.x.q.—rn-s.V⁶-
VI³.; V⁸.—rho.II⁷.11.—rhs.ddʰ.
[C.VI⁴].66.—rut.I.; V⁶-VI³.—
sbd.v.; II¹·².—sab.dd.12.—sep.v.
[Hε.].—sil.V².—so-t.VI⁴.12.—spi.
II⁷.11.VIII³.; gᵇ.v.—spo.V⁸.—
squ.dd.; dd.βεᵃ.3.—stn.VI³.; II¹-
VI³.—stp.ddʰ.[C.VI³].; II¹–VI².
—sul.II⁵.11.; ddʰ.; IX.5.[Hᵇ.].;V¹.
ddʰ.[C.V³].; dd.; I.3-99.; k¹.; ᵒ.k¹.;

kᵍ·¹.; kᵍ.; kᵏ·ᵐ.; kᵒ.—trn.kᵒ.VI².—
tonᵖᵃ.VI⁴.; ddʰ.—vin.v-II⁵.—zin.
II⁷.5.11.; V⁶.; v-II³.

Sᵖ. **Parietal.**—ba-c.k¹.—bry.gᵃ·ᵇ.5.—
chd.gᵇ.(15).—glo.z.33.—lau.v.—
nat.Iᵇ.ε.—pet.II¹.11.—pho.ddʰ.
V⁶–VI⁴.2.—rut.V⁶–VII⁵.—san.
qq.V⁶.50.—sulᵒ.gᵇ.—tab.V².—zin.II⁷.

Sᵖᵃ. **Right parietal.**—ca-c.kᵈ.—dro.
II¹·³.(11).—hur.ddʰ.—hfb.ff.x.—
indᵗᵃ.b.VI³.—k-ca.kᵈ.—lah.VI³·ᵇ.;
V⁶–VII⁵.2.—lyc.V⁶.σ².—ni-x.V².;
gᵇ.—ph-x.II¹.—pho.VI⁴.IX.19.;
V³-VIII⁴.19.—rn-b.II¹–VI².d.a¹ᵇ.
βε.—rut.kᵈ.II⁷.11.[Bᵖᵃ.VI⁴].—
san.qq.—spo.II¹.—thu.II²·⁵·⁶.5.—
tonᶜ.VI⁴.—zin.II³.

Sᵖᵇ. **Left parietal.**—acoᵍ.—alm.V³·ʰ.
—ang.llᵃ.V²·ʰ.12.—ani.v.(11).—
ars.k¹·ᵒ.II⁵.15.—at-a.II⁵.—bro.gᵇ.
v.ηl.—cb-a.II⁷.—chi.VI³.—col.gᵇ.
v.—com.V.—elc.kᵒ.—gym.V².—
hfb.x.—k-ca.VIII⁴.12.—kis.ffᵃ.η.
—lahᵗᵇ.ddʰ.60.88.; gᵇ.x.5.—la-x.
II¹·⁵.ω².3-30.—lau.v.—lilᶠᵇ·ᵗᵇ.dd.
—lyc.I.ε.θ¹.5.12.43.44.; IX.
mt-s.gᵇ.—mag.kᵒ.—mu-x.ffᵃ.—
nx-m.iiᵈ.V².q.βε.ηiiᵈ.—pet.II⁷.
phoᵇ.IV³.—rhs.V¹·⁶·ᵛ.—rutᵒ.mm.
v-II⁶.—sep.V⁶·¹¹.—sil.v.—sul.II⁷.
11.; kᵒ.—sum.kᵍ.ddʰ.—vi-oꜰ·ᵒ.ffᵃ.ε.
ζ.η.σ².

Sᵒ. **Occiput.**—aga.v.εv.; VI⁴.; VI².
σ.—alo.II⁵–V¹.; ddʰ.15.—almꜰ.V¹.;
III²–IV².r.29.—amb.dd.— am-g.
iiᵈ.—am-c.v.; II⁷.12.35.—ag-n.v.
2.; v.II⁵.; k¹·ᵏ.s.v.15.—arn.IX.
—ars.gᵇ.—bry.II³.11.; IV³–V⁶.
ꜰ.ffᵃ.—cac.V⁶.(22).—ca-a.II³·⁷.11.
—ca-c.v.; v.βa.15.—carᵒ.gᵇ.III¹.
—cs-e.xᵃ.99.; xᵃ.98.—cas.llᵇ.—
chd.v.—cob.k¹.—crt.gᵇ.—cup.II¹-
VI⁴.29.— cyc.k¹.—dig.VI³.—elp.
II³.—fag.v.; v.ζv.—helᶜ.V³.χ¹.
VIII³.29.33.35.(12).; V⁶·ᵘ.—
hurᵐ.v.—hfb.v.3.—hydᶜ.e.; ddʰ.—
hy-x.I.q.—iof.v.—ipc.dd.σ³.26.—
k-bi.k¹.σ².—k-ca.v.—lam.dd.17.—
lyc.kᵈ.—mg-m.kᵍ.ddʰ.VI⁴.—mg-s.
dd.[F.VIII¹.16.89].—man.VI⁴-
VIII³.ddʰ.4.— mezᶜ.v.—mrr.k¹.—

nab.VI³.σ²ff.5.28.—nat.I.; kᵈ.—na-mᶠᵉ·ᵗ.k.v.—nitᶠᵃ·ᵗ·ᶜ.20.26.28.31. 89.(12).; k¹ᴗ².—parᶠ.ffᵃ.—pau.v. gg.—ph-x.V¹.(15).; V².—pl-c.w. στυw.—pru.VI².—pul.kᵐ.VI⁴.— rs-r.I.26.—rhs.g.4.—rutᵗ.V³.—sar. v.—sep.II⁷.11.[O.V⁶.].; ᶠ.V⁶.; qq. II⁷.2.(12).; v.5.; kᵐ.v.—sil.v.— spi.V².; I.16.—stp.III.; v-II⁶.15.; v-II³·⁶.5.—sul.II¹.15.16.; ᴘ.gᵇ.; v.; ᶜ.k¹.—sum.ff.—trn.II⁵.σ².—trx. VI⁴.31.—tep.II⁵.βa.; e.IX.; IX. —thu.gᵃ.II³·⁶.—ton.dd.[O.III.]. 3-30.—vi-oᵇ.ffᵃ.; ᶠ·ᵗ.ffᵃ.ε.ζ.η.σ².; ffᵃ. 26.

Sᵒᵃ. **Right occiput.**—am-m.k¹.v.5. (2).—ar-c.ffᵃ.**15**.—cb-v.V⁶.—chi.V⁶. —hep.V¹.σ².r.—iod.II⁵.—k-bi.VI⁴. rl.—lau.ffᵃ.IX.; v.(15).—lyc.V¹– VI⁴.—man.VI².σ².3-10.28.—par. V⁶·ᵉ.—rho.V²·ʰ.ᵉ.—sar.ll.—sil.v.— sul.kʳ.—ton.v.(15).VI³.; ddʰ.II⁷.

Sᵒᵇ. **Left occiput.**—as-t.II⁵.—broᶠᵃ. v.—cas.V¹-VIII⁴·ʰ.—chd.III²-VI³. —chi.III¹.—ch-sᶜ.v.— eub.V².12. —eup.VI³·⁴.4.—gui.VI³.—mag.II⁷. [F.q.]—nit.II¹-VIII⁴.5-10.—oln. V¹.—rat.v.ψ²ii.—rut.v.ddʰ.(15).; v.II⁶.(15).—spi.V¹–VI³.—stp.VI¹⁵. σ².φ¹.2.

Sᵒᶜ. **Occipital protuberance.**—dig.V². —lyc.II¹.—nat.ddʰ.—na-mᵐᵃ.VI³. —sil.I.12.—stp.V⁶.26.—thu.dd.2. 11.16.[Hddʰ.].—zin.V⁸.

Sᵉ. **Behind ears.**—ana.II³.—bz-x.ii. —bro.v.(15).—bry.kᵈ.—cad.s.II³. —can.k¹.ddʰ.σ².—cb-v.v.—cau.kᵈ. —chi.kʳ.—grp.v.— k-ca.k¹.—mez. k¹.—mu-x.k¹.v.II⁵.—na-m.kʲ.—ni-x. lᵃ.—pet.kᶠ.lᵃ.aa.—pho.kʳ.—rap.iiᵈ. I.—sbd.gᵇ.II¹.—stpᵉᶜ.kᵒ.v.; k¹. thu.kᵈ.; kˢ.; v.aa.—til.v.aa.—vi-t. kᶠ·ᵒ.v.II¹.ηkᵒ.

Sᵉᵃ. **Behind right ear.**—alm.VII⁵.— ars.kᵍ.II¹-VI³-VIII³.—ca-c.k¹.— cb-a.ii.VI³.5.—grp.k¹.—lyc.II⁵·⁶. —mag.l .5.12.—na-m.v-II¹.—sbd. k¹.—thu.II¹-V¹.

Sᵉᵇ. **Behind left ear.**—ca-c.v.ddʰ.ii. II⁷.—c-ph.kᵐ.II².11.—cic.II⁵.— cch.iiᵈ.5.—mer.ddʰ.III²-VIII³.φ¹.

—na-m.k¹.—ni-x.v.aa.ii.—rho.v. σ²v.—tab.aa.ii.VI³.—vi-t.v.VI².

Sᵉᶜ. **Above ear.**—stpᵉ.kᵒ.v.

Sᵉᵈ. **Before ear.**—ant.k¹.II³.11.

Sᵐ. **Mastoid process.**—cap.aa.ii.— hurᵒ.v.—fag.v.—lah.ddʰ.— irs.dd. θ⁴.

Sᵐᵃ. **Right mastoid process.**— na-mᵒᶜ.V1³.—rs-r.I.3-**10**.—sul.k¹.

Sᵐᵇ. **Left mastoid process.**—ba-a. V⁶-VI³·ʰ.ddʰ.28.—ch-sᶠᶜ.v.ηv.19. —rs-r.I.4.

SUB-SECTION II.
CONCOMITANTS OF PAINS.

au. *Ill-humour.*—nicᶜ.ddʰ.VI³.[F. VII¹.].

a¹bˢ. *Loss of thought.*—rn-bᵖᵃ.II¹- VI².d.βε.

βa. *Vertigo.*—chiᶠᶜᵇ.V¹-VI³.κ⁵.—tepᵒ. II⁵.

βε. *Confusion.*—ch-sᶠ.VI².—eupᶜ.V¹. —mg-m.V⁶·ᵍ.ε.η.θ¹.(90).—mrl.iᵃ. dd.ffᵃ.V¹.—nx-mᵖᵇ.iiᵈ.VI².q.ηiiᵈ.— parᶠ.e.II⁴.δ.δLp,aa.—rn-bᵖᵃ.II¹- VI².d.a¹b.—sbd.v.II¹.

βεᵃ. *Stupid feeling.*—glo.e.—squᶜ.dd.3.

βεᵇ. *Emptiness of head.*—cyc.VI².η.

δ. *Pain in eyes.*—belᶠ.III¹.— mg-m. ddʰ.V⁷.66.—parᶠ.e.II⁴.βε.δLp.aa.— sepᶠ.VI⁴.4.5.

δb. *Closure of lids.*—thuᶠᶜᵇ.III–V¹.

δε. *Lachrymation.*—eubᶠᵇ.V¹.δ♭.

δ♭. *Difficulty of opening eyes.*—eubᶠᵇ. V¹.δε.

δLp. *Heat of lids.*—parᶠ.e.II⁴.βε.δ. δLaa.

δLaa. *Redness of margins of lids.*— parᶠ.e.II⁴.βε.δ.δLp.

ε. *Pain in ear.*—cepᶠᵇ.VI³.θ¹·⁴.5.— lycᵖ·ᵇ.I.θ¹.5.12.43.44.; ᶠ·ᶜ.I.η.θ⁴.5. (4).— mg-m.V⁶·ᵍ.βε.η.θ¹.(90),— natᵖ.Iᵇ.—nic.VI³.—rn-bᵗᵇ.VI³.[Oᵇ. VI⁴.].—rhoᵒˢ.V².—sep.V³·⁶.θ¹.2. (30).—tab.gᵇ.II¹.κ¹.χ¹.

εC. *Pain of concha.*—bovᶜ.V².11.3.

η. *Pain in face.*—belᶠᶜ.III³.θ⁴.—cyc. VI².βεᵇ.—jat.I.—k-ca.V1³.ηii.θ¹.σ². —lycᶠ·ᵉ.I.ε.θ⁴.5.(4).—mg-m.V⁶·ᵍ.βε. ε.θ¹.(90).—na-m.V⁶.θ¹.—ᶜhe.V¹. σ².—rhs.v-II².θkʲ.

ηk^o. *Scabs on face.*—vi-t^e.k$^{t.o}$.v-II^1.

ηp. *Hot face.*—hel$^{f.t}$.VIII^4.—men^f. II^1–VI^3.

ηv. *Itching of face.*—ca-c.v-II^1.g^b.2. —cob.v.II^1.15.

ηv-II^2. *Corrosive itching on chin.*— squ^f.v-II^2.(15).

ηaa. *Red face.*—ca-c.VI^4.4.

ηii. *Swelled face.*—k-ca.VI^3.η.θ^1.σ^2.

ηii^d. *Swollen feeling of face.*—nx-m^{ph}. ii^d.VI^2.q.$\beta \epsilon$.

θk^j. *Miliary pimples round mouth.*— rhs.v-II^2.η.

θ^1. *Toothache.*—ca-a^{ta}.V$^{1.6}$.5.(12).— cep^{pb}.VI^3.ϵ.θ^4.5.—k-ca.VI^3.ηii.σ^2. —lyc^{pb}.I.ϵ.5.12.43.44.—mg-m.V$^{6.g}$. $\beta \epsilon$.ϵ.η.(90).—na-m.V^6.η.—sep.V$^{3.6}$. ϵ.2.(30).—stp.VI^4.

θ^1. *Pain in gums.*—dph^t.II^3.11.

θ^4. *Pain in jaws.*—lyc$^{f.c}$.I.ϵ.η.5.(4).

θ^4. *Pain in upper jaw.*—cep^{pb}.VI^3.ϵ. θ^1.5.

θ^4. *Pain in lower jaw.*—bel^{fc}.III^3.η.

κ^1. *Anorexia.*—pho.p.II^1.—tab.g^b.II^1. ϵ.χ^1.

κ^5. *Nausea.*—bor.II^5.ω^8.3.—chi^{fcb}.V^1. VI^3.βa.

π. *Pain in chest.*—pæo.II$^{1.5}$.τv.

σ. *Pain in back.*—aga^o.VI^2.

σ^2. *Pain in neck.*—amb.dd^h.V^{13}.1.— crt^f.VII^5.—hep^{oa}.V^1.τ.—man^{oa}. VI^2.3-10.28.—nab^o.VI^3.σ^2ff.5.28. —pho.V^1.η.

σ^2. *Pain in nape.*—ca-c.IX.—k-ca. VI^3.ηii.θ^1.—lyc^{pa}.V^6.— mer.v-II^5. —nx-v.v.II^5.5.—stp^{ob}.VII^5.ϕ^1.2.

σ^2v. *Itching on neck.*—glo.v-II^1.

σ^2ff. *Stiffness of neck.*—nab^o.VI^3.σ^2. 5.28.—sep.v.dd^h.V$^{3.10}$.

τ. *Pain in arms.*—k-bi^{oa}.VI^4.

τ. *Pain in scapulæ.*—hep^{oa}.V^1.σ^2.

τv. *Pain in limbs.*—pæo.II$^{1.5}$.π.

ϕ^1. *Sleeplessness.*—cch.VI^3–VIII^3.2. —mer^{eb}.dd^h.III^2–VIII^3.—stp^{ob}. VII^5.σ^2.2.

χ^1. *Chilliness.*—cas^t.II^3–VI^4.5.11.

χ^1. *Rigor.*—hel$^{c.o}$.V^2.VIII^3.29.33.35. (12).—tab.g^b.II^1.ϵ.κ^1.

ω^2. *Weakness.*—la-x^{pb}.I1$^{1.5}$.3-30.

ω^8. *Trembling.*—bor.II^5.κ^5.3.

SUB-SECTION III.

CONDITIONS OF PAINS.

1. *All day.*—amb.dd^h.V^{13}.σ^2.—lep^t. v.VI^2.—oln.v-II^6.

2. *At night.*—aga^c.II^7-V^6-VI^4.12.— bry.II^5–V^8.—ca-c.v-II^1.g^b.ηv.— cch.VI^3-VIII^3.ϕ^1.—lah^{pa}.V^6-VII^5. —ph-x.V$^{1.a}$.12.16.99.—pho^p.dd^h. V^6–VI^4.—sep.V$^{3.6}$.ϵ.θ^1.(30).; ^{o}.qq. II^7.(12).—stp^{ob}.VII^5.σ^2.ϕ^1.

3. *In the morning.*—bor.II^5.κ^5.ω^8.— bov^c.V^2.11.ϵCr.— grp.VI^4.—hel^f. VI^3.—hep^f.II^7–VI^2.11.

3-10. *In the morning in bed.*—man^{oa}. VI^2.σ^2.28.—rs-r^{ma}.I.

3-30. *In the morning on rising.*— am-c^f.V^6.3-99.—la-x^{pb}.II$^{1.5}$.ω^2.

3-99. *In the morning on waking.*— am-c^f.V^6.(30).—sul^c.I.; ^{f}.V$^{1.10}$. (30).

4. *In the afternoon.*—ca-c.VI^4.ηaa. —eup^{ob}.VI$^{3.4}$.—hep^f.IV^1–VIII^3. 16.(30).—ir-f^{tma}.VI^2.—lyc$^{f.c}$.I.ϵ.η. θ^4.5.—mag^c.IX.—man^o.dd^h.VI^4– VIII^3.—pho^c.III^1–IV^3.5.—rn-b^f. II^3.—rs-r^{mb}.I.—sep^f.VI^4.δ.5.

5. *In the evening.*—ca-a^{ta}.V$^{1.6}$.θ^1.(12). —cb-v.III^1.66.—cas^t.II^3–VI^4.χ^1. 11.—cep^{pb}.VI^4.ϵ.$\theta^{1.4}$.—lyc^{pb}.I.ϵ.θ^1. 12.43.44.; $^{f.c}$.I.ϵ.η.θ^4.(4).—mag. II^7.12.; ^{c}.dd^h.V^2.83.84.—mez.II^6. (15).—nab^o.VI^2.σ^2ff.28.—pho^c. III^1–IV^3.4.—rho.v.II^1.(15).—sep^f. VI^4.δ.4.—stp^o.v.II$^{3.4}$.—sul^c.IX. [Hb.].; ^{f}.v.II^1.—thu^{pa}.II$^{2.5.6}$.—zin^c. II^7.11.

5-10. *In the evening in bed.*—nit^{ob}. II^1–VIII^4.—ter^{tb}.v-VI^1.(15).

5. *In the forenoon.*—alo^c.II^7.11.—ind^c. IX.19 —nx-v.v.II^5.σ^2.—sul^t.II^1.

8-31. *By walking in open air.*—lyc. VI$^{4.b}$.

11. *By touching.*—ac-l.V^{11}.—alo^c. II^7.5.—ars.II^3.; V^2.—asa^{fc}.II^1– VI^3.—aur^{tb}.V^1.—bov.V^2.ϵCr.3.; V^2. —bry^o.II^3.—ca-a^o.II$^{3.7}$.—cas^t.II^3– VI^4.χ^1.5.—cau^c.V^2.—chi^{fca}.V^1-VI^3. —col^t.V^3-VI^3.—dph^t.II^3.θ^1.—dro^{pa}. II$^{1.3}$.—grp^f.II^3.—hep^f.II^7–VI^2.3. —hyo.V$^{1.8}$.35.—ign$^{f.t}$.V$^{2.6}$.—la-x^f.

II^5.—led^t.II^5.—lyc^f.II^5.—mg-m^c.
II^5.; II^5.29.—men^{tb}.II^3.—mer^{fb}.
II^1.; II^7.—mit^c.II^5.—msc.II^3.; II^5.
—mu-x^{ta}.VI$^{3.4}$.(96).—ni-x.II^7.—
nx-v^c.V^2.—pet^p.II^7.—ph-x.II^3.IX.;
^{c}.VI^3.; V^2.ii.IX.—rho^c.II^7.—rhs.
II^7.—san.II^7.—san.II^3.—sar.I.31.
—sep^o.II^7.[O.V^6.].; II^5.—spi^c.II^7.
VIII^3.—stp^{ta}.V$^{10.s}$–VI^3.; V^6.—
sul^{pb}.II^7.; ^{c}.FI^5.; II^5.—su-x.II^7.
—zin^c.II^7.5.—εng.V^1.

12. *By pressure.*—aga^c.II^7–V^6–VI^4.
2.—alo^c.V^2.—am-c^o.II^7.35.—ang^{pb}.
V^2.ll^a.—arg.II^3.—bis^{ta}.V^1–VI^4.—
ca-a^{ta}.V$^{1.6}$.θ^1.5.—c-ar^{ta}.II^5.—er-a.
II^5.—eub^{ob}.V^2.—*gui.*VIII^4.[T.
VI^3.].18.19.(31).–hel$^{c.o}$.VIII^3.29.
33.35.V^2.χ^1.—k-ca^{pb}.VIII^4.—lyc^{pb}.
I.ε.θ^1.5.43.44.—mag.^{ea}.II^5.; II^7.5.;
^{c}.V^3.VI^4–VIII^3.—nit$^{fa.t.c.o}$.20.26.
28.31.89.—sep^o.qq.II^7.2.12.—so-t^c.
VI^4.

12. *By pressure of hat.*—sil^{oc}.I.

12. *By pressure of head on pillow.*—
ph-x.V$^{1.a}$.2.16.99.—sep^o.qq.II^7.2.
(12).

15. *By friction or scratching.*—alm.
II^5.v.; ^{ta}.II^1.VI^4.—cap.dd.v-V^8.
[Hdd.].; *cap.*v-II^1.r.—cob.II^1.v.
ηv.—dro^f.v-V^8.—k-ca.II^5.v.—k-hy.
II^7.—lah.II$^{1.a}$.d.—lyc^{ta}.II^1–VI$^{3.4}$.
v.—*mez.*II^6.5.—oln.II^5.v–II^6.—ol-a.
v-II^1.—par.II^1.v.—pet.II^3.v.—
ph-x^o.V^1.—rho.II^1.v.—*rut^{ob}.*v.II^6.
—sil.II^5.v —*squ^f.*v-II^2.η.—stp.
v-II^6.; ^{o}.v-II^6.—sul^o.II^1.16.—*ter^{tb}.*
v-VI^1.5-10.—ton^{oa}.v.VI^3.

15. *By combing hair.*—cr-s^c.II^5.—
cr-a.I.—so-t.V^6.—spr.I.

15. *By stroking head.*—pul.V^6.—
so-n.II^5.

16. *When lying.*—hep^f.IV^1–VIII^3.
4.(30).—ph-x.V$^{1.a}$.2.12.99.
—— *by lying on it.*—spi^o.I.—sul^o.
II^1.15.

18. *When standing.*—gui.VIII^4.[T.
VI^3.].19.(12.31).

19. *When sitting.*—cin$^{f.t}$.V^7.—gui.
VIII^4.[T.VI^3.].18.(12.31).—ind^c.
IX.5.——pho^{pa}.VI^4.IX.; ^{pa}.V^3–
VIII^4.

20. *By rest.*—cic^f.V^7.—nit$^{fa.t.c.o}$.26.
28.31.89.(12).

21. *By moving scalp.*—ac-l.V^6.

22. *By bending head backwards.*—
cac^o.V^6.

23. *By drawing skin smooth.*—cle^{fb}.
II^1–VI^1.

26. *By moving head.*—nit$^{fa.t.c.o}$.20.
28.31.89.(12).—rs-r^o.I.—stp^{oc}.V^6.

28. *By turning head.*—ba-a^{mb}.V^6–
VI^3.dd^h.—man^{oa}.VI^2.σ^2.3-10.—
nab^o.VI^3.σ^2ff.5.—nit$^{fa.t.c.o}$.20.26.
31.89.(12).

29. *By stooping.*—alm^o.r.III^2–IV^2.
—cup^o.II^1–VI^4.—hel$^{c.o}$.VIII^3.33.
35.(12).V^2.χ^1.—mg-m.II^5.11.

30. *By rising.*—hep^f.IV^1–VIII^3.4.
16.—sep.V$^{3.6}$.ε.θ^1.9.—sul^f.V$^{1.10}$.
3-99.

31. *By walking.*—gui.VIII^4.[T.VI^3].
18.19.(12).——nit$^{fa.t.c.o}$.20.26.28.
89.(12).——sar.V^1–VI^4.35.; I.11.
—trx^o.VI^4.

33. *By going up stairs.*—hel$^{c.o}$.VIII^3.
29.35.(12).V^2.χ^1.—sbd^f.VI$^{2.3}$.101.

35. *On moving.*——am-c^o.II^7.12.——
hel$^{c.o}$.VIII^3.29.33.(12).V^2.χ^1.—
hyo.V$^{1.8}$.11.—sar.V^1–VI^4.31.

43. *By reading.*—kis.VII^5.—lyc^{pb}.
I.ε.θ^1.5.12.44.

44. *By writing.*——lyc^{pb}.I.ε.θ^1.5.12.
43.

50. *By raising eyes.*—san^p.qq.V^6.

60. *By chewing.*—thu^{tm}.V^6.

66. *After food.*—cb-v.III^1.5.—mag.
VI^2.—mg-m.dd^b.V^7.δ.

83. *During menses.*—mag^c.dd^b.V^2.5.
84.

84. *After menses.*——mag^c.dd^h.V^2.5.
83.

89. *By coughing.*——nit$^{fa.t.c.o}$.20.26.
28.31.(12).

90. *By sneezing.*—mg-m.V$^{6.g}$.βt.ε.η.
θ^1.

96. *By yawning.*—mu-x^{ta}.VI$^{3.4}$.(11).

99. *On awaking.*—ph-x.V$^{1.a}$.2.12.16.

101. *By heat.*—sbd^f.VI$^{2.3}$.33.

106. *By wind.*—nx-v.II^3.

110. *Before a snow-storm.*—for.I.σ.r.

SECTION VI.—H. HAIR.

CHARACTER.

c. **Discoloured.**—bel.c.ᴅ.
cᵉ. **Darker.**
—— *red hair becomes chestnut.*—
iod.
cᶠ. **Grey.**—aps.—ars.ᴅ.—grp.—hpm.
—hyo.—kre.—lyc.—spg.—su-x.c.
cᵍ. **Green.**—cup.
gᵃ. **Crawling.**
—— *like insects.*—cs-e.
j. **Dryness.**—alo.—alm.—bad.[S.v.
kᵖ.]—hpm.—k-ca.
—— *woolly.*—cl-h.
—— *as if dead.*—hpm.
—— *of roots.*—pho.c.
o. **Hardness.**—wis.ᴅ.
dd. **Sensitiveness.**—aco.b.—asr.[S.
ffᵃ.].—cop.[S.dd.].—na-mᶜ.—na-s.
15.—ni-x.—nx-vᵒ.—parᶜ.c.—sul.
15.—ver.b.p.
—— *of roots of hair.*—aco.—ard.
—bel.—c-ph.[C.gᵇ.O.b.].
—cap.15.[S.v-V⁸.].—col.
—elpᵒ.—so-t.[S.dd.].—
spr.
—— *as if ulcerated be-
neath.*—chd.15.
15. *On combing.*—chd.—na-s.
15. *On scratching.*—cap.[S.v-V⁸].
—sul.
ddʰ. **Sensitiveness to touch.**—alm.
—ambᵖᵃ.—am-c.;[S.r.].15.—arˢ.
—cb-v.[C.V¹.].;3-10.(30).[C.I.].
—cnb.[S.ddʰ.].—cu-a.—fer.[S.
IX.].—mez.—na-m.—na-sᵒ.—nx-v.
b.[S.V².].—par.—pho.2.[P.V⁶–
V¹⁴.]—spi.[S.ddʰ.].—thuᵒᶜ.[Sᵒᶜ.
ddʰ.].2.17.—zinᶜ.
—— *of roots of hair.*—ca-a.[S.v.].
—chi.[S.ddʰ.].—ni-xᶜ.—
sep.—sul.
2. *At night.*—pho.[P.V⁶–VI⁴.].
2-17. *On lying on l. side, night.*—
thuᵒᶜ.[Sᵒᶜ.ddʰ.].

3-10. *In bed, morning.*—cb-v.(30).
[C.I.].
15. *On stroking.*—am-c.[S.r.].
30. *On rising.*—cb-v.3-10 [C.I.].
a. **As if pulled.**—belᶜ.—bryᵗ.—epnᶜ.
[T.I.p.].δε.σ².—lpt.—nitᶜ.—ph-x.
[S.II³.11.].;[S.ii.V².11.].—phoᶜ.
[Sᶜ.dd.VIII³.].;[γ.VII¹.].3.19.
66.(15).—rhs.[S.c.].—sec.
—— *upwards.*—aco.—almᶜ.—
ba-cᵖᵃ.—c-csᶠ.—cch.[Sᶜ.II³].
—indᶜ.—lauᵒᵃ.—lyc.gᵇ.5.
8-31.—mu-x.βa.[C.VI⁴.].
—— *pulled out.*—arnᵒ.—cap.15.—
cthᵗ·ᶜ·ᵖ.[Sᵗ·ᶜ·ᵖ.VI⁴.].—sulᶜ.
b.5.—tepᵒ.[S.e.O.Iᵃ.].
—— *by one hair.*—phoᵖᵃ.19.[Pᶜ.
VI³.].
—— *as if raised from ground suspended by hair.*—ped.
—— *as if every single hair were
pulled out.*—tep.
βa. *Vertigo.*—mu-x.[C.VI⁴.].
δε. *Lachrymation.*—epnᶜ.σ².[T.I.
p.].
σ². *Pain in neck.*—epnᶜ.δε.[T.I.
p.].
3. *In morning.*—pho.[γ.VII¹.].19.
66.(15).
4. *In afternoon.*—lyc.gᵇ.8-31.
5. *In evening.*—sulᶜ b.
8-31. *When walking in open air.*
—lyc.gᵇ.4.
15. *By rubbing.*—pho.[γ.VII¹.].3.
19.66.
19. *When sitting.*—pho.[γ.VII¹.].
3.66.(15).;ᵖᵃ.[Pᶜ.VI³.].
66. *After dinner.*—pho.[γ.VII¹.].
3.19.(15).
b. **Standing on end.**—aco.;dd.—
aloᵒ.[Sᵒ.dd.].—am-c.[S.b.gᵇ.].6.—
arn.[P.VI³.].b.—ba-a.—cocᵒᵇ.r.
—crt.r.—hypᶜ.—k-biᶜ.[C.II⁵.].—
lchᵒ.—lo-i.b.—man.[C.b.].—mer.

r.—-mez.—-mu-x.37.—-nx-v.dd^h.
[S.V².].——ped^{pb}.r.3.—-rn-b^f.[B^f.
V¹·⁶.].5.66.—-sil.—spi.β*t*.[S.dd^h.].
—spo^c.m.35.—-sul^c.a.5.—-ver.n.[S.
g.r.].—zin^{eb}.

—— *during the convulsions.*—-cth.

β*t*. *Muddled feeling.*—spi.[S.dd^h.].

3. *In morning.*—ped^{pb}.r.

5. *In evening.*——rn-b^f.[B^f.V¹·⁶.].
66.—sul^c.a.

6. *On coming into room from air.*
—am-c.[Sb.g^b.].

35. *By moving.*—spo^c.m.

37. *By a fright.*—mu-x.

66. *After supper.*——rn-b^f.[B^f.
V¹·⁶.].

c. **Falling out.**—alm.—amb.—aps.
—ars.; ^{pb}—ard.—as-t.—au-s.—
ba-c.15.—bel.—bov.—buf.—ca-c.
15.—cth.15.——cb-a.—cb-v.—car.
—cau.——ce-b.15.—-chd.; °.15.—
cn-s.—cch.—con.—cop.—elp.—
fer.[S.g^b.II⁵.].—f-mg.—fl-x.3.—
glo.—grp.—hep.—hyp.—ign.—
iod.—k-bi.—k-ca.—k-hy.—kre.—
lyc.; 15.—mag.——mer.—nat.—
na-m.—ni-x.—nit.—osm.—par^c.
dd.—ped.—pet.—ph-x.—pho.; j.
—sar.[S.dd.15.].—sel.15.—sep.;
[S^c.v.].—sil.15.—spg.—spr.—stp.
—sul.—su-x.c^f.—tab.15.—tep.[S.
k^b.η.].—wis.; [S.v.(15).k^p.].; [S.
II⁶.].; 26.29.; g.—zin.

—— *and whiskers.*—na-m.

—— *of eyebrows and moustaches.*
—plb.

—— *hairs loosely attached.*—ars.
—stp.

3. *In morning.*—fl-x.

15. *By combing.*—ba-c.—ca-c.—
cth.—ce-b.—chd°.—lyc.—sel.
—sil.—tab.

26. *By shaking head.*—wis.29.

29. *By stooping.*—wis.26.

v. **Brittle.**—ars.c^f.—bel.c.*t*.—wis.o.

t. **Increased softness.**—iod.—mez.

f. **Greasiness.**—bra.—bry.[S.b.].3.
—hfb.—plb.

—— *greasy dirt.*—ard.

3. *In morning.*—bry.[S.b.].

g. **Increased growth.**—elc.—lah.—
wis.; *t.*

—— *ceases to fall out.*—fl-x.—
for.—m-pi.

þ. **Bald spots.**—grp.—pho^e.

í. **Curling.**—bra.

ȷ. **Entanglement.**—chd^{ea}.—fl-x.——
for.—mil.—na-m.l.

—— *as in plica polonica.*—bor.—
vin.

k. **Corrosion.**—mer.[S.k^k.].

l. **Mouldy smell.**—na-m.ȷ.

m. **As if moving.**—ars°.[S°.g^b].—
cb-v°.g.—spo^c.b.35.—stn^c.[C.V¹].

35. *By moving.*—spo^c.b.

n. **As if electrified.**—ver^{pa}.b.[S.g.r.].

o. **Loss of electricity.**—bel.

ANATOMICAL SEAT.

H^f. **Front of head.**—c-cs.a.——chd°.b.
—rn-b.b.[B^f.V¹·⁶].5.66.

H^t. **Temples.**—bry.a.—eth^{c·p}.a.[S^{t·c·p}.
VI⁴].

H^c. **Crown.**—alm.a.—bel.a.—cth^{t·p}.a.
[S^{t·c·p}.VI⁴].—hyp.b.—ind.a.—k-bi.
b.[C.II⁵].—na-m.dd.—ni-x.dd^b.—
nit.a.——par.dd.*c.*——pho.a.[S^c.dd.
VIII³].—spo.b.m.35.——stn.m.[C.
V¹].—sul.a.b.5.—zin.dd^h.

H^p. **Parietals.**—cth^{t·c}.a.[S^{t·c·p}.VI⁴].

H^{pa}. **Right side.**—amb.dd^h.—ba-c.a.
—ver.b.n.[S.g.r.].

H^{pb}. **Left side.**—ars.*c.*—ped.b.r.3.

H^e. **Above ear.**—pho.þ.

H^{ea}. **Above right ear.**—chd.ȷ.

H^{eb}. **Above left ear.**—zin.b.

H°. **Occiput.**—alo.b.[S°.dd].—arn.a.
—ars.m.[S°.g^b].—cb-v.m.g.—chd^f.
b.; °.c.15.—elp.dd.—lch.b.—na-s.
dd^h.—nx-v.dd.

H^{ea}. **Right occiput.**—lau.a.

H^{eb}. **Left occiput.**—coc.b.r.

H^{ec}. **Occipital protuberance.**—thu.
dd^h.[S^{oc}.dd^h].2.17.

A REPERTORY;

OR,

SYSTEMATIC ARRANGEMENT AND ANALYSIS

OF THE

Homœopathic Materia Medica.

CONTENTS.

HAHNEMANN PUBLISHING SOCIETY.

LIVERPOOL:

THE HON. SECRETARY, 117, GROVE STREET, E.

LONDON:

H. TURNER, 170, FLEET STREET, E.C.

NEW YORK:

BOERICKE AND TAFEL, 145, GRAND STREET.

1878.

Price 12s. 6d.   To Members, 7s. 6d.

The Works already—1878—published by the Hahnemann Publishing Society are:

I.—The HAHNEMANN MATERIA MEDICA, containing: *Kali Bichromicum*, by Dr. Drysdale; *Aconitum*, by Dr. Dudgeon; *Arsenicum*, by Dr. Black; *Uranium Nitricum*, by Dr. E. T. Blake; and *Belladonna*, by Dr. R. Hughes.

II.—The "REPERTORY OF THE MATERIA MEDICA PURA," containing: chaps. i. "Disposition," ii. "Mind," iii. "Head" (published under the title of "Pathogenetic Cyclopædia, vol. i), iv. "Eyes," v. "Ears," by Dr. Dudgeon; vi. "Nose and Smell," vii. "Face and Neck," viii. "Teeth and Gums," ix. "Mouth and Tongue," x. "Throat," xi. "Appetite, Taste, and Digestion," xii. "Acidity, Nausea, and Vomiting," xiii. "Stomach," by Drs. Drysdale and Stokes; xiv. "Abdomen," by Drs. Drysdale, Stokes, and Hayward; xv. "Stools, Rectum and Anus," by Dr. H. Nankivell.

III. The "THERAPEUTIC PART," specimen chapters: "Bronchitis," by Dr. R. Hughes; "Jaundice," by Dr. J. Gibbs Blake; "Acute Rheumatism," by Drs. Drysdale and Blake; "Obesity," by Dr. Ker; and "Morbid Growths," by Dr. Black.

The work now in hand is—MATERIA MEDICA: *Natrum Muriaticum*, by Dr. Galloway; *Naja Tripudians*, by Dr. Pyburn; *Crotalus*, by Dr. Hayward; *Phosphorus*, by Dr. Burnett; *Iodine*, by Dr. R. Hughes; *Rhus*, by Dr. Hawkes; *Conium*, by Dr. D. Dyce Brown; *Nux Vomica*, by Dr. Charles Jones, of Albany, U.S.A.; *Actæa* and *Aesculus*, by Dr. H. M. Paine, of Albany; *Pulsatilla*, by Dr. Woodward, of Chicago; *Colocynth*, by Dr. Nichol, of Montreal, Canada; and *Sepia*, by Dr. Gale, of Quebec; *Argentum*, by Dr. Klauber, of Mentone. REPERTORY. —Chaps., Female Genitals, by Drs. Drysdale and Stokes; Urinary Organs and Male Genitals, by Dr. Simpson; and Skin, by Dr. J. G. Blackley; Larynx, Trachea, and Chest, by Dr. Hawkes; Neck and Back, by Dr. A. B. Brown; Upper Extremities, by Mr. Cyrus Clifton.

PRINTED BY J. E. ADLARD, BARTHOLOMEW CLOSE.

www.ingramcontent.com/pod-product-compliance
Lightning Source LLC
Chambersburg PA
CBHW080550090426
42735CB00016B/3198